How to Get Into the TOP COLLEGES

RICHARD MONTAUK
Author of *How to Get Into the Top MBA Programs*
AND
KRISTA KLEIN

Prentice
Hall Press

To my mother, who still believes that education can change the world
—Richard Montauk

To Mom and Dad, who made sure
I received the best education possible and supported me every step of the way
—Krista Klein

A member of Penguin Putnam Inc.
375 Hudson Street
New York, New York 10014

www.penguinputnam.com

Library of Congress Cataloging-in-Publication Data
Montauk, Richard.
  How to get into the top colleges / Richard Montauk, Krista Klein.
    p. cm.
  Includes index.
  ISBN-0-7352-0100-5 (alk. paper)
   1. Universities and colleges—United States—Admission—Handbooks, manuals, etc.
  2. College applications—United States—Handbooks, manuals, etc.   I. Klein, Krista. II. Title.

LB2351.2 .M66 2000
378.1'1—dc21   99.-51497

This publication is designed to provide accurate and authoritative information in regard to the subject matter covered. It is sold with the understanding that the publisher is not engaged in rendering legal, accounting, or other professional service. If legal advice or other expert assistance is required, the services of a competent professional person should be sought.

—From a Declaration of Principles jointly adopted by a Committee of the American Bar Association and a Committee of Publishers and Associations.

Printed in the United States of America

10 9 8 7 6

ISBN 0-4352-01005

ATTENTION: CORPORATIONS AND SCHOOLS

Prentice Hall books are available at quantity discounts with bulk purchase for educational, business, or sales promotional use. For information, please write to: Penguin Putnam Inc., 375 Hudson Street, New York, New York 10014.

ACKNOWLEDGMENTS

We wish to thank those people who have been so helpful to the development and writing of *How to Get Into the Top Colleges.*

First, we thank the admissions and financial aid directors at top colleges in the United States and Great Britain, who have been so generous with their time and knowledge in discussing how admissions and financial aid decisions are made at their schools. In particular, we would like to thank those we interviewed for this book and who have allowed themselves to be quoted at length throughout the text: Joe Paul Case (Amherst College), Katie Fretwell (Amherst College), Leigh Campbell (Bates College), Meg Woolmington (Bennington College), Bernard Pekala (Boston College), Walter Moulton (Bowdoin College), Richard Steele (Bowdoin College), Michael Bartini (Brown University), Michael Goldberger (Brown University), Nancy Monnich (Bryn Mawr College), David Levy (California Institute of Technology), Richard Black (University of California, Berkeley), Simon Goldhill (King's College, University of Cambridge), Ray Jobling (St. John's College, University of Cambridge), Leonard Wenc (Carleton College), Alicia Reyes (University of Chicago), Lucia Whittelsey (Colby College), Eric J. Furda (Columbia University), Tom Keane (Cornell University), Nancy Hargrave Meislahn (Cornell University), Karl Furstenberg (Dartmouth College), Virginia Hazen (Dartmouth College), Kathleen Stevenson-McNeely (Davidson College), James Belvin (Duke University), Christoph Guttentag (Duke University), Julia Perreault (Emory University), Dan Walls (Emory University), Barbara Bergman (Georgetown University), Patricia McWade (Georgetown University), Marlyn McGrath Lewis (Harvard University), James Miller (Harvard University), David Hoy (Haverford College), Delsie Phillips (Haverford College), Robert Massa (Johns Hopkins University), Louise Burton (London School of Economics and Political Science), Marilee Jones (Massachusetts Institute of Technology), Pam Fowler (University of Michigan, Ann Arbor), John Hanson (Middlebury College), Jane B. Brown (Mount Holyoke College), Richard Avitabile (New York University), Rebecca Dixon (Northwestern University), Sheppard Shanley (Northwestern University), Joseph A. Russo (University of Notre Dame), Howard Thomas (Oberlin College), Michael Allingham (Magdalen College, University of Oxford), Anne Daniel (Christ Church College, University of Oxford), Eric Kaplan (University of Pennsylvania), Lee Stetson (University of Pennsylvania), Patricia Coy (Pomona College), Don Betterton (Princeton University), Heather McDonnell (Sarah Lawrence College), Myra Smith (Smith College), Nanci Tessier (Smith College), Catherine Thomas (University of Southern California), Cynthia Hartley (Stanford University), Jonathan Reider (Stanford University), James Bock (Swarthmore College), Larry Burt (University of Texas, Austin), Elaine Rivera (Tulane University), David Mohning (Vanderbilt University), David Borus (Vassar College), John Blackburn (University of Virginia), Yvone Hubbard (University of Virginia), Janet Lavin Rapelye (Wellesley College), Barbara-Jan Wilson (Wesleyan University), Philip Smith (Williams College), Philip Wick (Williams College), Steve Van Ess (University of Wisconsin, Madison), Donald Routh (Yale University), and Richard Shaw (Yale University).

Second, we thank two others who were critical aides in the writing of this book: our Degree of Difference colleague Carmel Murphy, formerly of Stanford University's admissions office, who helped us conduct invaluable research for the development of this book; and Michael Denning, the college counselor at Noble and Greenough School, for his help in editing our final product.

Third, we thank our clients, from whom we have learned a great deal.

Fourth, we thank the recent top college applicants who allowed us to reproduce their essays in the back of this book.

Fifth, we thank those editors who have been indispensable to the production of this book. We thank Christa Weil for her timely and extremely insightful advice and Tom Power, of Prentice Hall, for his patience and encouragement.

Sixth, we thank the family and friends who supported us through our efforts. Krista especially thanks Bill and her brother Eric for their unwavering encouragement and good spirits.

Richard Montauk and Krista Klein

How to Benefit Most from This Book: For College Applicants

WHY READ THIS BOOK?

The most difficult part of graduating from a top college is getting admitted. After all, making it through a top college program will be demanding, but most of the top schools have very small attrition rates, with 90 to 95% of their classes graduating within five years. Compare this figure to the percentage of applicants accepted at the top schools—in recent years, admit rates at the most selective schools have hovered below 20%—and it is clear that getting in is the hardest part of the process.

In applying to the nation's top colleges, you will be competing for limited spots against others who are likely to have academic credentials similar to yours (or perhaps even better). Most students who apply to the top schools have good grades and scores—those alone are not adequate to ensure you a place at a top school anymore. In fact, the leading colleges generally turn down more top-ranked students (often even valedictorians) than they admit. Credentials get you in the running at these colleges, but they are only one of several important factors by which you will be judged.

The leading colleges admit students on the basis of their academic records as well as their extracurricular pursuits, personal backgrounds, and other distinguishing features, as evidenced through the written application, the recommendations, and the interview. The bottom line is that no matter who you are or how good your high school record is, you need to do everything you can to distinguish yourself. You cannot afford to submit anything less than a stellar application.

This does not mean that you should throw in the towel now and decide to settle for something less than a top college! *How to Get Into the Top Colleges* provides the strategic understanding and detailed advice that is necessary for positive outcomes in applying to the most competitive colleges. It is the result of our direct work with thousands of applicants to the top schools, as well as in-depth research and interviews with admissions officers at the most competitive colleges. It is our hope that with this book we at Degree of Difference will make our advice and expertise available to even greater numbers of students (and their families) who dream of attending the top schools.

WHO SHOULD READ THIS BOOK?

How to Get Into the Top Colleges is written with two audiences in mind. It is first and foremost a reference for college applicants themselves. It is also written for the benefit of parents and others who are providing assistance and support in the college application process. Although the text is oriented toward high-performance students applying to the most competitive schools, anyone who wants to improve his or her candidacy to any school, whether it is a top-tier institution or not, would benefit from an understanding of the application strategies presented here. Our advice is aimed at standard American college applicants but also pays attention to applicants with special profiles or concerns. The whole of Chapter 7, in fact, offers advice to nine varieties of "special case" applicants, such as those applying from overseas or those who have been home schooled.

WHAT IS THE MOST IMPORTANT WAY IN WHICH THIS BOOK WILL HELP?

The main purpose of this book is to help applicants get into the best college possible. Schools assess a great deal of information when looking for their future students. Some of this is objective and quantifiable, such as a candidate's standardized test scores and high school GPA, whereas much of it—a student's personal background or expression of her career goals, for example—is not. The objective elements of a candidate's application—the academic credentials—are obviously important. The subjective elements, however, ultimately become even more important. Broadly speaking, the more competitive the college, the more its admissions committee cares about crafting a class and ensuring that you can contribute to others' experience at the college, something about which it learns from your essays, recommendations, and interview.

Objective credentials are thus only part of the total picture. Colleges use all of the information given to them, including the essays, recommendations submitted on the candidate's behalf, and interview results, to determine whether or not a candidate should be admitted. This means that you have an opportunity to become more than just a pawn in a game of numbers. You in fact have a real chance to help yourself in the college admissions process by presenting your materials—and thus yourself—in the most effective way possible.

In addition to doing many other things, *How to Get Into the Top Colleges* shows you how to maximize the value of your credentials, and utilize the subjective elements of your candidacy, to get into the best schools that are appropriate for you, given your desires, goals, and needs.

WHAT IS INCLUDED IN THIS BOOK?

This book analyzes and discusses each step of the college application process in a thorough, detailed fashion, with supporting comments from the admissions and financial aid directors at the top colleges. (We conducted in-depth interviews with seventy of the most senior officers in admissions and financial aid, all cited by name and school in the Acknowledgments, at top colleges in the U.S. and Great Britain.)

The book contains these parts:

Part I, "The Context: What You Need to Know Before You Apply," provides the context for the decisions you will have to make during the college application process. It is crucial that you understand this context before diving into the application process. The information in Part I will teach you how to decide where to apply. It will also give you a general introduction to the admissions process, showing you how it works at various schools.

Part II, "Applying to College," shows you how to plan and put together the various components of the application to achieve your best possible outcome. It introduces the idea of "positioning" and discusses in detail the three main vehicles for presenting and marketing yourself: the essays, the recommendations, and the interview.

In Part III, "On the Road to College," contains information and advice to prepare you for the steps you must take after colleges notify you of their decisions.

Part IV, "Financing College," offers guidance to students and their families about college finances. Growing concerns over the burden of college education expenses, as well as the extensive research and interviews that went into this portion of our book, necessitated that we dedicate an entire section to college financial aid and financing alternatives. This section of the book is likely to be of greater interest to your parents and others helping you to finance college than to you, but we strongly encourage you to become familiar with how financial aid works, even if your family is not requesting that you take a substantial role in the process.

Part V, "Application Essay Examples," offers fifty recent essays from twenty-three candidates to the top colleges. The essays are accompanied by our own critiques, explaining what worked and why.

WHAT ARE THE UNIQUE FEATURES OF THIS BOOK?

We felt compelled to write this book because we wanted to offer students and their families a single source of reliable information and advice on applying to the top colleges.

Some of this book's unique features include

- ■ Advice and information from seventy admissions and financial aid directors at the top schools, gleaned from extensive interviews with each of them.

- ■ Fifty actual application essays, from twenty-three successful applicants to the top colleges. These essays were written by students of a variety of socioeconomic, ethnic, racial, geographic, and personal backgrounds.

- ■ A thorough discussion of alternatives to entering college immediately after high school.

- ■ A first-of-its-kind chapter dedicated to exploring the alternative of attending a British university for American college students.

- ■ Suggestions for how to use college rankings without becoming overly influenced by them.

- ■ A college application organizer to help you organize and keep track of the process of applying to various schools.

- ■ Personal profile worksheets to help you think about how best to market yourself.

- ■ The most thorough discussion of teacher recommendations and interviews available, with a full chapter devoted to each of these often-overlooked topics.

- ■ Advice and exercises to help spark the creativity and thought necessary to write successful and persuasive college application essays.

- ■ A sophisticated discussion of college financial aid and alternative funding sources.

- ■ Advice aimed specifically at transfer applicants, international applicants, older applicants, minority applicants, home-schooled applicants, learning disabled applicants, physically challenged applicants, legacy applicants, and recruited athlete applicants.

HOW BEST TO BENEFIT FROM THIS BOOK

This book is designed to be used efficiently by people with radically different needs. Some will want to read it cover to cover, but many will want to dip into it for help on specific problems they face. Here are some suggestions for how to get the most out of the book, depending on your own situation.

If you are a high school senior in the midst of applying to college right now, and if you have applications due in just a few weeks, you should read several core chapters of the book immediately to avoid making terrible mistakes. Chapter 5 is a good place to start, to get a feel for how schools will evaluate your application. After that, concentrate on the chapters in Part II to help you get through each step of the application process. You can worry about reading Parts III and IV after you are finished with the urgent tasks ahead of you!

If you are a high school junior, preparing to apply to college next year, you might want to start by looking over Appendix III, "College Preparation and Application Timetable." You should also do an early read of Chapter 8, "Acquiring Strong Academic Credentials," to learn more about how you can shape your objective data throughout the rest of this year and during your senior year as well. Then start from the beginning, with Parts I and II, to get a good feel for the context of the decisions you will be making in the year ahead and to learn about the details of the application process. When reading Part II, remember that you will want to review these chapters over the summer or as you begin the actual application process next year. Part III can be read at a later point if you wish. Part IV should be read by you or your parents as soon as possible. The finance section of this book contains a lot of complex information. You will be less frustrated and anxious trying to digest it if you do so at your leisure, rather than trying to deal with the details of the application process itself.

If you are a high school freshman or sophomore, just starting to think about the college application process, you have chosen the best time possible to pick up this book! You still have time to shape your high school career in a way most favorable for college admissions and to digest how the college application process works before placing yourself in its hands. Our advice to you is similar to that for high school juniors. You will probably first want to review Appendix III, "College Preparation and Application Timetable." After that, you should read Chapter 8, "Acquiring Strong Academic Credentials," to learn more about how you can shape your objective data throughout your entire high school career. Then start from the beginning, with Parts I and II, to get a good feel for the context of the decisions you will eventually be making and to learn about the details of the application process. When reading Part II, remember that you will want to review these chapters when you begin the actual application process. Part III can be read at a later point in time if you wish. Part IV should be read by you or your parents as soon as possible.

A FINAL NOTE

Many applicants look upon the task of producing hundreds of details about their lives, writing dozens of essays about intimate or obscure topics, securing recommendations from teachers they would rather avoid than befriend, and enduring interviews as a modern form of "death by a thousand cuts." They feel that it is trial enough simply to research the schools and figure out what they are looking for, let alone manage the intensive application process.

If that is your view, keep in mind that the application process, however imperfect it may be, forces applicants to think about where they want to go in their lives and careers—often for the first time ever. Many high school students, after all, have never had to make decisions about what school to attend, and have never had to apply to become part of something in their lives. Too few people take the time on their own, when not forced by such processes as applications to colleges, to take stock of their past, present, and future circumstances. College applicants are at a point where sensible decisions about these matters can yield a lifetime of benefits, and failure to consider their options carefully can result in missed opportunities. Confronting such important education and career decisions might open doors you never even realized exist. Believe it or not, the application process may actually prove to be more than just a painful experience—it may actually be a helpful one.

How to Benefit Most from This Book: For Parents of College Applicants

WHY READ THIS BOOK?

It is sometimes very difficult for the parents of excellent students to believe that their kids do not have a sure or easy shot at getting into the best colleges. Gaining admission to the top colleges is now much more difficult than it was in previous generations, or even just a decade ago. Competition is very stiff and the application process is complex. You and your child cannot afford to treat the matter lightly.

WHO SHOULD READ THIS BOOK?

How to Get Into the Top Colleges is written for college applicants, but it is also written for *parents* of future college applicants. Although the text is written as if to a college applicant, we realize that it may well be you, not your child, who first picks up this book. We indeed encourage parents to familiarize themselves with the college application process and, when appropriate, assist their children in preparing applications and making decisions.

You may in fact discover that you have to take a leading role in the college search and application process in order to get your son or daughter going. We urge you to trust your instincts as far as your involvement in your child's college applications is concerned. If your child genuinely needs your motivational encouragement (or motivational nagging), is used to your involvement in decisions and activities, or seems to encourage your input, by all means play a significant role. On the other hand, if your child is motivated to dive into the college research and application process on his or her own, is used to being independent and making his or her own decisions, or strongly discourages your input, try to let him or her have as much freedom as possible.

It will be difficult at times, as a loving and concerned parent, to balance the right amount of involvement with the right amount of distance. It may also be as tough for you as it is for you child to retain the proper perspective during the upcoming project. You will want to help and support your child through this difficult phase, but you should also think about giving him or her some independence. Your child is about to embark upon his or her first adult experience, to begin to live and work away from your embrace and in the company of other young adults. This is a good time to practice your new parenting role—one in which you care for your child from a distance, one in which you may become more friend and advisor than disciplinarian and protector.

As a special note for parents, it is likely to be you rather than your child who will take the dominant role in financial aid applications and college finance decision making. We urge you to read Part IV (Chapters 18 and 19) as soon as possible, so that you can prepare to tackle the complexities of college financial aid early on. Another reason to read this chapter as soon as possible is that your child's need-based financial aid package will be based upon financial information submitted to colleges for the calendar year prior to his or her application submission (usually the calendar year beginning during the middle of the junior year and ending in the middle of the senior year). Your finances should thus be aligned in a way that will best benefit you in the college financial aid award procedures well before the middle of your child's junior year of high school.

Please turn now to page iv and read the "How to Benefit from This Book: For College Applicants" to learn more about this book's purpose, content, and unique features. This section also advises readers how best to utilize the book, depending upon what stage of the college application process you and your child are in.

SOME GUIDELINES FOR PARENTS IN THE COLLEGE ADMISSIONS PROCESS

➤ Do not start discussing college in serious terms when your child is in the eighth or ninth grade. Early discussions about college—even through sophomore year in high school—should be loose and exploratory, not serious or intimidating.

➤ Pay attention to what your child finds attractive about certain schools so that you can remain attuned to his or her desires and make helpful suggestions. Be on the alert, however, that there may be instances in which your child is merely mouthing the reigning attitudes of friends or others, rather than forming his or her own opinions. Try to help your child sort out his or her own needs when this is the case.

➤ Focus on finding the best colleges that will bring your child success and satisfaction rather than emphasizing "winning" or beating out friends to get into the most selective schools.

➤ View the college selection and application process as a matter of helping your child to reach an outcome he or she will value, not an outcome that you will be able to brag about to your friends.

➤ Give help and guidance, but try to resist imposing your desires on your child.

➤ Do not let the college application process take over family life. Make sure you set aside time for activities in which college and applications are not discussed.

➤ Assist your child, but do not take complete control of the college application process. Help to keep your child on schedule, but do not do things for him or her. Do not, for example, write essays, type applications, or make admissions phone calls (except those concerning financial aid) for your child.

➤ When visiting colleges or attending college fairs, do not be pushy in order to monopolize the time of school representatives. It is fine for you to be interested and ask questions, but your child should be the principal actor.

➤ Remain realistic about your child's chances of getting into chosen schools. Help your child retain perspective, too.

➤ Interact with your child's college counselor (or counselors) on a regular basis. Make the application process a partnership among the three parties.

ABOUT DEGREE OF DIFFERENCE

Founded by Richard Montauk in 1991, Degree of Difference (formerly Education USA) is a premier educational consulting firm that provides quality one-on-one service to individuals submitting applications for college and graduate study in a variety of fields. We help hundreds of individuals each year plan their college and graduate careers and complete successful applications to the top programs worldwide.

Our advice for you—a college-bound student set on attending one of the top schools—is informed not only by the years of service we have provided to successful college applicants, but also by our work with college graduates working on later steps in their educations and careers. Because our collective expertise extends beyond the realm of college, into the areas of graduate study and career advising, our perspective is like that of a wide-angle lens. (For more information on some of our advisory services to those preparing for post-graduate study, see *How to Get Into the Top MBA Programs* and *How to Get Into the Top Law Schools,* both by Richard Montauk and also published by Prentice Hall.)

Degree of Difference provides a full menu of services for college applicants and their families:

- **Matching students with colleges:** We begin the consulting process with each client by inquiring into past experiences and ambitions for the future. After learning more about you, your background, your education, and your goals, we help you to research colleges and discover what programs and options are available to you. We help you to select colleges that are most appropriate for your needs and desires, and also ensure that your final list of target colleges includes an adequate number of "stretches," "possibles," and "safeties."

- **Strategizing:** We help you develop a coherent strategy to follow during the college application process, as follows:
  - We advise you on when to apply to school. We evaluate whether or not you would benefit from a year off before college (i.e., to what extent your value to colleges will increase or decrease with time off) as well as whether or not you should consider applying Early Decision or Early Action to a particular college.
  - We help you develop a comprehensive self-promotional positioning strategy. We teach you how to market your strengths, account for or overcome your weaknesses, and best position yourself to enhance your candidacy.
  - We teach you how to tailor your applications to each particular school.
  - We help you make decisions regarding applications to special programs for early entry into professional school or joint degrees.

- **Interviewing:** Interviews for undergraduate admissions are often daunting for high schoolers who have never experienced the interview process. We teach you how to approach your interviews with confidence and make a positive impression:
  - We coach you on successful interviewing techniques, providing assistance not only regarding what to say but also regarding how to say it, what to wear, and how to act in a variety of formal and informal interview settings.
  - We provide mock interview sessions, either face-to-face in our offices or over the phone.
- **Soliciting recommendations:** Getting the most from recommenders is often one of the most difficult—and one of the most overlooked—tasks in the college application process.
  - We teach you how to look at your application in its entirety in order to determine what is most needed from your recommenders to fill in the gaps, enhance your strengths, and compensate for your weaknesses.
  - We provide advice on how to approach recommenders tactfully, and how to best provide them with the information you would like conveyed in your letters of recommendation.
  - We assist your recommenders (if desired) to develop high-impact letters of endorsement through our creative and editorial services.
- **Completing applications:** A sloppy application will do you no good. We are happy to review any and all of your written materials to ensure that all the necessary information is neat, well communicated, and correct.
  - We review all of the written product, including application data forms; listings of extracurricular activities, work experience, and community service; and responses to short answer and essay questions.
  - We can help you write a successful general or special talent resume.
- **Essay writing:** For most of our clients, essay writing is the area of greatest concern.
  - We help you craft themes in order to make your entire body of essays convey a set of consistent and solid messages.
  - We provide advice on appropriate material for use in each essay. We help you to fashion each set of essays so that it contains neither redundancies nor inconsistencies and makes the most out of your experiences and strengths.
  - We edit essays and provide advice on essay structure and form, yet strive to do so in a way that retains a client's own voice, style, and personality.

  Please note that we do not write essays for our clients under any circumstances.

HOW TO INITIATE A RELATIONSHIP WITH DEGREE OF DIFFERENCE

If you are interested in our services, you initiate a relationship with us by conversing with a Degree of Difference associate about your current situation and goals. Some of our most successful clients sign up for our services a year or two in advance of actually applying for college, in order to discuss long-term strategy and goals that need to be accomplished before applications are under way. This way, you will be best prepared to market yourself to schools when the time comes.

On the other hand, plenty of clients come to us at a later stage in the game—at the beginning of their senior year or even well into the college application process. We realize that many high school students have not given much thought to the college application process before it is suddenly upon them and they feel in over their heads. We are prepared to help you at any point in your college application work and encourage panicked students who find themselves behind schedule to contact us for immediate assistance.

With headquarters in San Francisco and London, Degree of Difference also maintains satellite offices in the Boston and New York vicinities. If you would like to contact us, please do so at one of our primary locations:

Degree of Difference, Inc.
2443 Fillmore Street #330
San Francisco, CA 94115
Tel. (415) 263-0567
Fax (415) 567-1616
www.degreeofdifference.com
or
Degree of Difference, Inc.
126 Aldersgate Street
Barbican, London EC1A 4JQ
United Kingdom
Tel. (44) 171-608-1811
Fax (44) 171-250-3109

CONTENTS

Part I

THE CONTEXT: WHAT YOU NEED TO KNOW BEFORE YOU APPLY

1

GETTING IN IS THE
HARDEST PART

— KEY POINTS —

The rewards of attending a top college are immense:
—*Living and learning amongst the best and the brightest provides a highly stimulating and enjoyable college experience*
—*Graduate school prospects, career choice and flexibility, earnings, networking opportunities, and recognition are all maximized*

■

Once upon a time, good students did little more than submit an application in order to ensure their admission to a top college;
now the competition to get into these schools is extremely intense

■

Admissions rates are now at all time lows
—*Furthermore, the difficulty of being admitted to the top schools will continue to rise*

■

The college search and application process are more complex than ever before
—*You must command a thorough understanding of the best application tactics in order to compete in a game where students and college counselors use sophisticated timing, marketing, and information relaying strategies*
—*Be sure you have a competent and knowledgeable college counselor at your disposal*

INTRODUCTION

Unlike in previous generations or even just a decade ago, getting into a top undergraduate institution now really requires a sophisticated, strenuous effort. Once upon a time, good high school students got into the best colleges without having to try very hard. These days, getting into the leading schools is *much* more difficult. Many students with impressive academic records and pursuits find themselves out in the cold, unable to get into the schools they most wanted to attend.

We assume that readers of this book have already decided that they want to go to college, and want to go to the best college possible. What you might not have already decided, however, is that you intend to spare no effort in the application process. The fact is that if you want to be successful in getting into the best colleges, then you must realize here and now that the competition is stiff and you need to devote your all to the project.

GETTING INTO A TOP COLLEGE IS INCREASINGLY DIFFICULT

Over the past several years, the top colleges have consistently reported increases in their numbers of applicants, thus forcing them to become more discerning than ever when selecting students for their upcoming classes. The rise in applications at the top colleges is due to a number of factors:

- A growing college-aged population
- An increasingly mobile and flexible population
- A more sophisticated education industry full of savvy consumers and private consultants
- The greater ease with which students can apply to multiple schools (because of the Common Application and the use of online application methods)
- More need- and merit-based financial aid for students at the top schools
- Growing awareness that a college education is no longer sufficient to guarantee success—now the emphasis is upon getting the *best* college education possible

Not only are the colleges receiving greater numbers of applications, but also, more important, they are receiving greater numbers of applications from superbly talented students. For admission in 1999, for example, Brown received

applications from 3000 students who achieved a 750 or above on the verbal portion of their SAT I tests, and from 3500 who ranked among the top five students
in their classes. Brown could have filled its entire incoming class of 1350 more
than two times just by choosing students of such high academic standing. The top
schools are now so competitive that they have to turn away many students they
would once have accepted without a second thought.

What all this means is that recent rates of admission at the top schools are
daunting. The 1998–1999 application season was the most competitive in the
nation's history, with the best colleges reporting extremely low admit rates. Just
to name a few, Harvard and Princeton admitted 11% of their applicants;
Columbia, 14%; Stanford, 15%; Amherst, 19%; and Swarthmore, 21%. Those
excluded from these small percentages of admitted students include many highly qualified applicants who believed they were likely or certain to do well in the
college application process because their numbers and scores looked just like
those of the fortunate few who got in.

STIFF COMPETITION FOR COLLEGE ADMISSION WILL INCREASE

Fierce competition for admission to the best colleges will only continue. The
trend will, in fact, become more pronounced over the next decade, with more
people reaching college age in each of the next years to come. In addition, the
education industry and college applicants themselves will grow more sophisticated, with students spending even greater efforts on college admissions; multiple
applications will become easier to generate with new technology and encouragement from admissions offices; and the evidence that a premier college education
is extraordinarily valuable is sure to become that much more compelling.

THE ADMISSIONS OFFICERS DISCUSS INCREASING NUMBERS OF APPLICATIONS AND THE DIFFICULTY OF ADMISSION IN RECENT YEARS

"The competition certainly has been increasing. This year [1999] we had an
admit rate of 11.3%, the lowest yet."

—*Marlyn McGrath Lewis, Director of Admissions, Harvard University*

"The pool is so strong. It just keeps getting better and better with
each passing year."

—*Karl Furstenberg, Dean of Admissions and Financial Aid, Dartmouth College*

"For a while we had been in a buyer's market, but now there are more candidates appearing everywhere. Through the first decade of the next century, there will be an even greater increase in competition to attend the top schools."
—*Richard Avitabile, Director of Admissions, New York University*

"You wouldn't believe the quality of the kids we see these days! It's difficult to turn down so many highly qualified applicants."
—*Jonathan Reider, Senior Associate Director of Admissions, Stanford University*

"There has really been a rise in competition to get into the best schools over the past few years."
—*Lee Stetson, Dean of Admissions, University of Pennsylvania*

COLLEGE ADMISSION IS MORE COMPLEX THAN EVER BEFORE

As competition grows tougher at all of the top colleges, the game of getting into these schools has become more and more complex. No matter who you are or how good your grades and test scores are, there is no guarantee that you will be admitted to your desired schools. You must commit yourself to putting in a valiant effort if you want to compete in this game where students and college counselors are increasingly using sophisticated timing, marketing, and information relaying strategies in order to get ahead.

In order to be confident that you will do your best in the process, you must research your college and program options, finding those that best fit your needs and desires; understand college admissions, recognizing application options such as Early Decision and identifying the goals or philosophies of the admissions officers at your target schools; and then, based on information gained during these first two tasks, launch a sophisticated application and marketing strategy.

THE IMPORTANCE OF MARKETING YOURSELF

Marketing yourself—by sophisticated positioning (see Chapter 6)—is of the utmost priority for everyone. In applying to the nation's top schools, you will be up against others who are likely to be equally (or better) qualified. Most students who apply to the top schools have excellent grades and scores. Those alone no longer give you a place in the freshman class at a leading college. The top colleges admit students on the basis of their academic records as well as their extracurricular pursuits, personal backgrounds, and other distinguishing features, as evidenced through the written application, the recommendations, and the interview. You must be prepared to marshal all the right evidence on your behalf so that you market yourself in the best way possible.

Schools want candidates who will be successful college students and, by extension, prominent scholars, civic leaders, entrepreneurs, artists, scientists, inventors, athletes, doctors, business executives, teachers, politicians, and humanitarians. To find these future success stories, colleges assess a great deal of information. Some of this is objective and quantifiable, such as a candidate's standardized test scores and high school grade point average (GPA), whereas much of it—an applicant's family background or display of leadership, for example—is not. The objective elements of a candidate's application, or the academic credentials, are still extremely important to the top schools. They are, in fact, generally responsible for putting you in the running for consideration at the top schools. (Note, however, that this is not the case with recruited athletes or applicants who are particularly compelling for another nonacademic reason but may not have the best academic record.) The subjective elements, however, ultimately become much more important than the objective ones in terms of what you can do to ensure the best treatment in the college application process.

As mentioned earlier, the top schools could fill their classes with candidates who have excellent objective credentials. They could, for example, fill their classes with students in the top 10% of their classes at the country's top preparatory high schools who scored 1400 or better on their SATs. Of course, the top schools *do* accept people who fit this profile, but they actually reject more of them than they accept. The point is that schools are looking for more from their candidates than just a good high school transcript and exceptional standardized test scores. They are even looking for more from their candidates than a good high school transcript, exceptional standardized test scores, and a nice athletic or artistic talent or two.

Colleges admit people rather than numbers. Stanford says it succinctly: "In essence, we are looking for high-energy students who will pursue our academic program with vigor and still have the time and interest to contribute actively to Stanford's residential community." This is a lot different from saying that it wants students with good transcripts and SAT scores. Schools look for *leaders*—students who take initiative and work well in teams. Schools look for *visionaries*—students who are determined to make an impact on the community around them, who have ideas about what they want to do with their lives. Schools look for *humanitarians*—students who show empathy and compassion for others and contribute their own energy toward furthering the lives of other people. Schools look for persistent *go-getters*—students who have overcome substantial odds in reaching their accomplishments.

In other words, given a certain baseline of academic achievement, colleges look far beyond the numbers and objective credentials to find other bases upon which to admit students into their classes. This is because numbers alone do not account for the many personal characteristics and nonacademic talents the top colleges are looking for in their students.

In addition to looking for particular characteristics and traits, colleges are looking for diversity on all levels. In order to create challenging learning environments that are reflective of the world's various walks of life, the top colleges want to put together classes whose members represent a wide range of socioeconomic, racial, ethnic, religious, geographic, and educational backgrounds. They also look to include students who bring with them a variety of special talents and skills. As Dartmouth puts it, "A large and well-qualified applicant pool offers Dartmouth the opportunity to enroll a first-year class that is not only very capable but also broad in the variety of backgrounds, talents, and interests represented. Indeed, the main objective of the admissions process is to develop a class that will constitute an educational resource for the College." Generally speaking, the better the school, the more likely its admissions committee is to care about crafting a class and ensuring that you can contribute to others' experience at the college.

The basic message that all of the top colleges communicate is that their admissions committees *do* consider objective credentials, but only as part of the total picture. They use all of the information given to them, including the written application, recommendations, and interview results, to determine whether or not a candidate has the potential to become successful in whatever role he or she chooses to pursue.

Thus, you must use the written application, recommendations, and interviews in ways that will influence the admissions committees to interpret the objective data in the best light possible. For example, a GPA of 3.3 on a 4.0 scale means different things in different contexts. If a student has to work thirty hours per week to help support his or her family, which a college should learn from a written application or during the interview, that performance is much more impressive than it is for a well-off student whose time and energy are not constrained by financial responsibilities to his or her family. Similarly, if an applicant with a good high school record reveals that he or she has an enormous aptitude for playing the viola, is a minority student, or has grown up on a twelve-person island in Puget Sound, then a college might be that much more interested in him or her than it would be in a good student who did not reveal any of those things. In other words, you must utilize the essays, recommendations, and interviews not only to present new information but also to help "frame" your objective data, thus showing what talent or characteristic you can bring to a college or how you can add to the campus's diversity.

WHY A TOP COLLEGE?

There have always been good returns on an investment in education. This is even more true today for those who attend the top colleges, given the "winner-take-all" nature of the society and economy in which we live. This world is characterized by increasing income inequality (often referred to as the "income gap") and intense competition for a limited supply of not only wealth, but also status, success, and happiness. Those at or near the very top receive a disproportionate share of such rewards.

Education plays a very important role in the winner-take-all society. Each new move in education has the power to launch an individual that much closer toward the top (or to disqualify him or her from the race). Just as education's role as the gatekeeper grows, the quality and prestige of the institution you attend becomes more important. Although you can succeed in life after attending an average college, just as you can fail in life after graduating from Princeton, the deck is stacked for you (rather than against you) if you attend the best college possible.

The specific benefits of going to a top-tier institution are numerous. They include: greater learning from fellow students; a greater chance of acceptance to the top graduate programs; greater career choice; greater career flexibility; higher salaries; greater networking options; and the ability to open doors nationally and internationally.

GREATER LEARNING FROM OTHER STUDENTS

Much of what you learn in college is gained from your exposure to and work with other undergraduate students. Going to a top college nearly ensures that you will gain more from your fellow students than you would at an average school.

Many schools contain a handful of extremely bright and interesting young people. But clearly the more competitive and selective schools—the ones whose incoming students have the best high school records, highest standardized test scores, and most accomplished backgrounds—feature a far greater number of highly intelligent students. The brilliant, accomplished student from whom you are sure to learn a great deal—both inside and outside of the classroom—is the norm on the campus of a top college, but one of only a few similar students at a less competitive school. When you are surrounded by interesting and diverse people of such high academic quality, you cannot help but benefit from their knowledge and stimulation. Furthermore, you will be pushed harder because you will want to keep up with those around you.

GREATER CHANCE OF ACCEPTANCE TO THE TOP GRADUATE PROGRAMS

Whereas competition for college is stiff, competition for spots at the leading graduate schools—professional schools as well as other master's and doctoral programs—can be even greater. Having attended a top undergraduate institution can help you stand above the crowd of other applicants to the world's finest higher education programs. Graduate admissions committees favor graduates from the top colleges because they know that these individuals have already jumped through several academic hoops to get where they are. They know that students who attended the leading colleges have already competed successfully against other impressive students, have been intellectually challenged, are prepared for the tough and grueling work ahead of them, and will not be overwhelmed by the demands of the graduate program.

GREATER CAREER CHOICE

Some professions are virtually off-limits to graduates of lesser colleges. The top investment banks and management consulting firms, for example, simply do not recruit at "good" schools, let alone run-of-the-mill schools, thus barring all but students from the strongest colleges from entering their ranks. Having the name of a top school on your resume can put and keep you in the running for positions at companies that will not even glance at the credentials of candidates who went to lesser colleges.

GREATER CAREER FLEXIBILITY

The career benefits of going to a top college are not limited to your initial job upon graduation. If you decide to change careers in the future, the quality of your education will be one of the determining factors in your ability to make the switch successfully. The quality of the college you attended can determine how potential employers in new fields rate your chances of success and whether they will risk hiring you.

HIGHER SALARIES

The better the reputation and caliber of the school, the more its graduates earn. The pay gap between graduates of the top schools and graduates of average colleges begins upon graduation but increases dramatically in later years. One reason that graduates of the best colleges earn more is that they are accepted at much greater rates at the leading graduate schools of business, medicine, law, engineering, and other fields. Similarly, those who have attended top colleges move up in their fields faster and to a higher level than do graduates of average schools.

GREATER NETWORKING OPTIONS

Graduating from a top college means that you automatically become part of an exclusive "club" of other graduates from that school. Your friends and acquaintances from college will be able to help you in your career and personal endeavors for the rest of your life, but college networking involves more than just the people you meet while in school. You will have the opportunity to benefit from the combined experiences and connections of all the alumni of your school as well. Alums from the top colleges come in all shapes and sizes. They are Hollywood executives, philosophy professors, choreographers, bankers, and writers. They are American, Kenyan, Korean, Pakistani, and French. They are involved in numerous social and political endeavors. Furthermore, if you attend a top college, chances are that you will be able to find an alum wherever you choose to live, be it Atlanta or Jerusalem.

THE ABILITY TO OPEN DOORS NATIONALLY AND INTERNATIONALLY

When you graduate from a top school, you have little reason to worry about what your degree will mean to people in a different region of the country or world. A degree from a noncompetitive college, on the other hand, will open doors for you locally but may not mean much to companies or graduate schools outside of the immediate area. A degree from a top college will carry clout no matter where you take it. The most competitive and selective schools—even the smallest ones—are nationally recognized as fine institutions. Indeed, most of the top colleges are internationally renowned as well. A degree from MIT will carry as much weight in Beijing or Frankfurt as it does in the United States.

USING YOUR COLLEGE COUNSELOR

The complexity of today's college application game requires a thorough understanding of college and program options, how the admissions process works, and how best to position or market yourself. Applicants will want to ensure that they have a knowledgeable and savvy college counselor at their disposal to help them with each stage of the college admissions project. Although it is up to you to decide how much you want your college counselor (also sometimes called a "guidance counselor") to help you (or interfere) with your applications, you should do everything possible to cultivate a good relationship with him.

Even if you have reason to believe that your high school's guidance counselor is not very good, you need his or her support and good wishes, so do not do anything that might harm your relationship with that person. He or she will be writing and compiling the guidance counselor recommendation required for application to all colleges and will also be responsible for getting your high school profile to your target colleges. Even if you do not expect to use the counselor's services in any other significant way (e.g., in helping you to decide where to apply, writing your essays, or keeping in touch with schools during the spring in the event that you are waitlisted), you will definitely need to be on good terms to ensure that the guidance counselor's recommendation writing is done with the greatest of care.

You can expect varying degrees of attention and assistance from your counselor, depending upon what type of school you attend and how experienced the guidance counselor is.

GUIDANCE COUNSELORS IN SCHOOLS THAT SEND FEW STUDENTS TO COLLEGE

If you attend a public school that is not at all geared toward preparing its students for college, the school may not even have a full-time counselor. Most high schools at the very least have part-time assistance available for those who have decided to apply to college, but if your school is not accustomed to sending many students off to good four-year colleges, this part-time worker may be unfamiliar with applications to the top colleges. A part-time counselor may or may not be able to give you the assistance you need, depending upon his or her experience, how much time he or she has, and how many seniors are applying to college. In this case, you should consider asking your school administration if you can use the assistance of a counselor at another school in the district, especially if the counselor you are working with cannot give you enough time or does not have the proper resources to help you. If you can show the school administration officials that you are serious about applying to college (in which case you are doing them a favor, since your matriculation at a good college would benefit the reputation of the school), they might consider allowing you to seek the help of someone else in the district. (But good luck trying to win attention from the other school's counselor, who probably already has a large caseload!)

GUIDANCE COUNSELORS IN LARGE PUBLIC HIGH SCHOOLS

If you attend a large public high school that sends many or nearly all of its seniors to college, you can expect that your school will have more than one guidance counselor. Each counselor likely has a caseload of anywhere from 50 to 500 students (usually 100 to 250), however, and though he or she may be very experienced, he or she will probably not have a lot of time to devote to your college applications. You will have to take special care to cultivate a relationship with this person to make sure everything goes smoothly. Do not, however, do anything to jeopardize the time that others spend with this person by shoving your way into the office or interrupting appointments with other students. You cannot risk making this person dislike you—which is what will happen if you appear overly greedy and selfish, with no concern for the welfare of others—because your personal attributes and character are a large part of what this person is asked to comment on in the recommendations he or she will send to your target colleges.

GUIDANCE COUNSELORS IN PRIVATE HIGH SCHOOLS

If you attend a private school—large or small—you are likely to receive the best assistance possible from a high school guidance counselor. If your school is an elite college preparatory school that sends almost every graduate on to a four-year institution, then you can expect that you have at your disposal a fairly experienced counselor (or counselors, if your class is large). It is also likely that there are enough of them to go around for all the seniors in the class, so you may not have too much trouble getting attention from your advisor. Many counselors at private schools have been working in the college counseling field for many years and have in-depth knowledge of the various colleges and their application processes; many are also in touch with admissions officers at some colleges and go on college visits themselves to keep up to date.

HIRING A PRIVATE OR INDEPENDENT COUNSELOR

There are many reasons to seek a private or independent college counselor. If you find yourself in one of the following situations, you might want to consider seeking college application help outside of high school:

- Your counselor at school is responsible for too many students. If your guidance counselor is assigned to conduct college admissions assistance for 100 or more students, you have every right to feel panicked about the kind of attention you will receive.

- You are not getting adequate attention from your high school counselor for reasons other than his or her large caseload.

- The assistance your high school counselor is providing does not meet the level of expertise you expect or need.

- You do not get along personally with your high school counselor.

- Your high school counselor seems more concerned with how your admissions success will impact his or her job performance ratings than with how it will affect *you*.

- Your high school counselor is not listening to your needs and is pushing unacceptable or unsuitable options onto you.

■ You and your parents are having difficulty seeing eye to eye and working with one another (i.e., you need a good counselor to pull you together).

You will have to decide with your family whether hiring an independent counselor is something in which you are willing to invest resources. Hiring a good one—one who is right for you—may prove highly worthwhile since there are essentially unlimited advantages to getting into the best college possible.

Follow these rules if you plan to hire a private or independent college counselor:

■ Investigate the credentials of the counselor. Be sure he attended a top college (and/or graduate program) and is experienced in educational consulting.

■ Do not hire anyone who makes promises about your acceptance at certain colleges or tells you he or she has connections that will get you into a particular college.

■ Do not hire anyone who says he will do the college application work for you. Counselors are consultants. They should *help* with each stage of the process by making suggestions, keeping you on the right track, and providing you with ideas and expertise. They should not, however, perform the work for you. Doing so compromises the integrity of the college application process and the honorable foundations upon which the top institutions of higher learning stand.

■ Look for counselors who encourage a collaborative partnership among themselves, college applicants, and their parents.

■ Look for counselors who seek to retain the applicant's personality and voice in the application materials, with the aim of avoiding an overprocessed presentation.

■ Although it is convenient and comfortable to use a counselor in your own area, do not accept mediocrity for the sake of proximity. Excellence at a distance will be more valuable than mediocrity in your own backyard. (Only one-third of our clients at Degree of Difference are located within 100 miles of our offices.)

■ Make sure you feel comfortable with the counselor's personality and approach.

WHAT THE ADMISSIONS OFFICERS SAY ABOUT USING AN INDEPENDENT COLLEGE COUNSELOR OR CONSULTANT

"I know of cases where a good independent counselor has been very helpful and of great service to an applicant without packaging or 'fixing' the application. I also know of very bad college counselors who have no right to be doing what they are doing. The level of competence is very uneven."

—*Jonathan Reider, Senior Associate Director of Admissions, Stanford University*

"I have made it a policy in my office not to go either way on the independent counselor issue. If your guidance counselor at school isn't very good, why shouldn't you hire someone else if you can? I serve as an independent counselor all the time for my friends and their kids—free of charge, of course. It's natural to want to get as much input and expertise as possible."

—*Barbara-Jan Wilson, Dean of Admissions and Financial Aid, Wesleyan University*

"Wouldn't you prepare the best you could? I really get frazzled when people talk about how evil test prep courses and independent counselors are. Why shouldn't kids do everything in their power to do better in the admissions process?"

—*Marilee Jones, Dean of Admissions, Massachusetts Institute of Technology*

What Does a Good Independent Counselor Do?

"My advice for independent counselors and students using them is this: Don't leave fingerprints. Don't have outside counselors write us a letter or contact us in any way. Don't predict results for students. Don't write a student's essays for him. Do give students cautionary advice and help them to develop realistic expectations."

—*Jonathan Reider, Senior Associate Director of Admissions, Stanford University*

How Does One Choose an Independent Counselor?

"My advice to those hiring independent consultants is to avoid people who make promises or claim connections with certain schools that can help get you in. That's not the way it works."

—*Barbara-Jan Wilson, Dean of Admissions and Financial Aid, Wesleyan University*

"There are good ones and there are bad ones. Good ones put the student first and don't advertise 'I'll get your kid into school X.'"

—*Delsie Phillips, Director of Admissions, Haverford College*

CONCLUSION

You probably recognized long before reading this chapter that the rewards of attending the best college possible are immense. What you might not have realized is that the process is increasingly complex, and that students are scrambling more and more to get into the top colleges. This means that you, too, must devote more than just the ordinary amount of diligence, attention, and time to your college applications. Thus, you need to work hard, but you also need to work *smart*.

2

TAKING TIME OFF
BEFORE COLLEGE

— KEY POINTS —

Some students benefit substantially from taking a year (or two) off
before college:
*—The "late bloomers" who need lengthier track records of success before applying
to the top colleges*
—Those who are uncertain as to what they are looking for in a college
—Those who are uncertain as to what kinds of possible career options lie ahead
—Those who are "burnt out" from high school, unable to face a rigorous academic schedule
—Those with "wanderlust" who need time for adventure before focusing on college

■

You can apply to college before *or* after the year off.
*—Top colleges encourage successful applicants to defer entry for a year or two in pursuit
of personal interests*
*—Taking time off before applying to college can make all the difference in turning dull or
otherwise underpowered candidates into desirable admits*

■

Time off can be spent:
—Studying, working, volunteering, traveling, or some combination of these activities
—These can be done at home, elsewhere in the U.S., or abroad

■

Potential benefits to taking time off include:
—Becoming a stronger college applicant
*—More knowledge of yourself and the world, enabling you to make better choices
regarding which college to attend, course to pursue, and career to enter*
—Increased maturity, confidence, focus, and skills

INTRODUCTION

Most people who attend top colleges start right after graduating from high school. That does not mean, however, that it is always a good idea to plunge into college without taking time off first. There are plenty of people who would be much better off spending a year (perhaps even two years) pursuing other interests and gaining some additional maturity before heading off to college.

People with a variety of interests and needs may find it beneficial to spend a year (or even two) doing something other than full-time, formal education. They include those who:

■ Are not yet ready to get the most out of their (expensive) college education

■ Can substantially improve their chances of getting into a top college by waiting a year to apply

■ Are considering British universities, which place a premium upon maturity, course and career focus, and necessitate living far from home in a different culture (see Chapter 4)

■ Are fed up with school

■ Want to acquire specific skills or experience

■ Want the opportunity to sort out career and/or study options

■ Are filled with wanderlust

■ Can benefit in study or career terms by improving language skills or cultural knowledge abroad

Anyone who can see how a year off will benefit her should consider the opportunities available, and weigh the advantages and disadvantages of pursuing one or more of them before going to college.

TIMING ISSUES: DEFERRING COLLEGE OR WAITING A YEAR TO APPLY

If you intend to take time off before college you have a choice between applying to college during your senior year—and, upon acceptance, seeking a year's deferment—or waiting until a year later and applying during your year off. (The two approaches are not mutually exclusive, of course, insofar as you can try to get into your chosen college(s) during your senior year and, if you succeed, defer at your chosen school. If you fail to get in, you can try again during your year off.)

DEFERRING COLLEGE

There are substantial advantages to applying while a senior and simply deferring after being admitted. One is that you will have the peace of mind of knowing that you are indeed guaranteed a seat at a prestigious college whatever you manage to do or not do during your year off. Another advantage is that it is generally much easier to apply when in high school than when you are out of school. High schools are set up to deal with seniors applying for college. More than that, you are in a milieu in which you can get things done: you are probably in the same town as those who will recommend you, for example. If you are working in Paris, doing a succession of scientific projects in Latin America, or just traveling a thousand miles from home in the U.S., it can be very difficult to get documents (such as transcripts or old recommendations), sign up for and take SAT or AP exams, discuss your preferred positioning strategy with recommenders who are still back in your home town, and so on.

WAITING TO APPLY

If you apply during your year off, on the other hand, you have the possibility of improving your chances via each of the following:

- You can take your standardized exams when you are better prepared to score well on them. You may do better on the SAT I because you will have had more opportunity to study and take practice tests. Similarly, you can expect to do better on the SAT II exams with the proper coursework under your belt. [If you are spending your year off abroad and/or taking language classes, you can certainly expect to do better on the relevant SAT II language exam (and AP test) too.]

- You may be able to present a much more impressive array of AP results.

- Your recommendations can be more impressive. First, you will be able to offer recommendations from your senior year teachers based upon a full year rather than a half-year of work. Second, you may be able to offer a supplemental recommendation from someone who has supervised you in the work world after high school.

- You can look more interesting as a result of having done something unusual during your time off.

- You can reinforce your positioning effort (see Chapter 6 for an in-depth discussion of this critical concept) by what you do after high school.

■ You can look more mature and focused than you did a year earlier. This is especially significant for those whose freshman and sophomore academics look weak or who encountered disciplinary difficulties early in high school. The passage of time, coupled with good academic results and a showing of seriousness, can relegate the earlier problems to the dustbin.

■ You can reduce or eliminate most weaknesses by devoting yourself to the right activities after high school, whether they are personal, academic, or extracurricular in nature.

The key is to choose activities that will be most helpful to your chances of admission, something that depends entirely upon your own starting point. For example, if you suffer from the perception of being rather frivolous and not particularly interested in academics, you might be helped by a year spent working in an analytically demanding job and taking some courses at night; this particular problem is unlikely, however, to be overcome by a stint as a cruise ship entertainer. On the other hand, if you are trying to position yourself as an environmentally-driven scientist, you may be able to help this positioning by working for a time in an organization that does interesting conservation work, or taking time off to pursue several Earthwatch projects around the world, but you would not be helped to the same degree by a stint as a chambermaid in a local hotel.

The question of when to apply is likely to be a matter of trading off the potential improvement in your value to top colleges with the increased difficulty of applying when out of school.

YOUR OPTIONS

The activities you might choose to pursue during a year off include those in the following categories:

Working in the U.S. You can work part-time or full-time, in your hometown or elsewhere. You can use your year off to make money (or in an unpaid internship), to develop skills for college or future jobs, to investigate careers that interest you, or simply for the fun of the job—or the fun of being where the work is (e.g., a ski resort).

Working abroad. The primary differences between working in the U.S. and working abroad are that in the latter case you will face even greater difficulty getting an appropriate job, but the potential rewards (such as improving a language, learning another culture, and so on) are all the greater.

Volunteering in the U.S. The range of organizations (local, national, or international) and the focus of their efforts (at-risk kids, the homeless, conservation, the environment, crime prevention, culture, and so on) are virtually limitless.

Volunteering abroad. As with volunteer organizations in the U.S., the possibilities are endless. The difficulty is to find something that fits you, and a responsible organization that will meet your needs (not just those of its intended beneficiaries).

Traveling (in the U.S. or abroad). Only your imagination, wallet, and sense of adventure limit the possible destinations.

Pursuing short courses. You can study academic or non-academic subjects, including: cooking, a language, furniture repair, office skills, culture (art history, decorative arts, sculpture, et al.), sports, acting, or anything else that you believe would prepare you to make money during your year off (or at college or later on), allow you to explore a subject (before choosing a major for college) or career, or further your personal interest in a field.

Pursuing a post-graduate year of study. (See the box below.)

POST-GRADUATE YEARS

Spending an extra, thirteenth ("postgraduate" or "PG') year in high school is another way to improve credentials and thereby impress college admissions officers. Traditionally, however, only two categories of students have taken advantage of this opportunity. Recruited athletes whose academics are not up to snuff have often been urged by their prospective college coaches to put in an extra year of high school in order to be able to survive college classes—and to demonstrate to skeptical admissions officers that they can do so. A handful of relatively well-to-do kids have also taken the opportunity to demonstrate that they are newly serious about academics or have put discipline problems behind them.

One reason for this not being a popular choice is that it requires money: essentially only private high schools offer a PG year and the price can be equal to a year at a private college. A second reason is that it delays the ultimate graduation date from college by a year, something that has prevented most students (and their parents) from considering a break of any sort between high school and college.

On top of all this, it can be very difficult to perform well in the PG environment. Going to a new school requires adapting to a new environment and, in most cases, a new system. It is not easy to adjust quickly enough to get top grades in the first term (the only one that colleges will see when making admissions decisions), without which the effort is likely to be wasted.

As a result, many applicants will be well advised either to make more creative use of a year off before high school—i.e., to consider one of the other categories of activities listed above—or to go to a less desirable college and plan to transfer once a solid collegiate academic record is in place.

If you decide to pursue a PG year, note that you do have several options. One is to go to a private high school in your area that offers a postgraduate year. Another is to go to a boarding prep school in another area; many of the most famous, long established schools (especially those in the Northeast, such as Phillips Exeter, Deerfield, and Hotchkiss) offer PG years. Yet another option is to go overseas. British and Swiss schools are obvious possibilities. The former offer a thirteenth year as a matter of course because the British secondary school system is predicated upon a thirteen-year (rather than twelve-year) program. The Swiss private schools have long catered to those who needed extra help and had the money to pay (well) for it.

HOW TO CHOOSE THE RIGHT ACTIVITIES FOR YOU

The possibilities of what you might do are so numerous that you risk being overwhelmed by choice. Knowing why you want to take time off, and what you hope to gain from it, will help you select activities that will maximize your experience. If you are weighing numerous possibilities, or unsure of how to think about which activities will provide you with the greatest benefits, consider the following criteria:

- What personal skills and experience will you gain? For example, dealing with the public, supervising other workers, negotiating with people, learning how those from different socioeconomic or ethnic/racial backgrounds live, and so on
- What practical skills and experience, qualifications, and contacts will you gain?
- Will you be able to do something similar at college? Or, during vacations?
- Will it prepare you for other, better work at college?
- Will it help prepare you for work after college?
- Will you impress potential future employers with the nature of this job or your performance on it?
- Will you be able to explore potential career (or college study) options?
- Will it help you get ready for college coursework?

■ Can you do it in conjunction with other activities you would also like to undertake?

■ How much will you learn about yourself and others, about your community or another part of the world?

■ What level of satisfaction (and fun) will you derive from doing this job and doing it well?

The questions listed above are relevant whether you intend to take time off after having deferred entry to your chosen college or, instead, intend to reapply to schools during your year off. In the latter case, however, two additional questions should be considered:

■ Will your planned activities enhance your college application positioning effort (see Chapter 6)?

■ Will you make yourself more interesting, more unusual, and saddled with fewer negatives than you currently are?

The two stories at the end of this chapter illustrate the different situations faced by those who need to improve their chances of being admitted by top colleges via their year off activities, and those who have already been deferred by their chosen school.

START THE PROCESS EARLY

The most likely trouble you will encounter is failing to plan your year off and ending up wasting it. Many of the useful things you might do require substantial advance planning. For example, if you intend to travel or work abroad you may need to arrange for visas, some of which will take weeks or months—not days—to obtain. There is the same need for advance planning for courses you wish to take, jobs you hope to obtain, volunteer work you wish to do, and so on. Remember that although admissions officers and employers value the additional experience, maturity, confidence, and perspective that a year off can add, they are suspicious of those who have failed to take advantage of the possibilities a year off offers.

YOUR OPTIONS AT A GLANCE

The chart below is a quick-and-dirty guide to some of the likely potential advantages and disadvantages of different types of activities. The specific activity chosen will, of course, determine the actual benefits (and costs) you derive.

	Paid Job (U. S.)	Unpaid Intern- Ship	Paid Job Abroad	Volunteer (U. S.)	Volunteer Abroad	Travel (U.S.)	Travel Abroad	Short Courses	PG Yr.
Potential Advantages									
Earn Money	✓✓		✓						
Make Contacts	✓	✓	✓	✓				(✓)	
Gain Job-Specific Skills	✓✓	✓✓	✓	✓	✓			✓	
Gain Trans-ferable Skills*	✓	✓	✓	✓	✓			✓	
Learn How You Fit into Work World	✓✓	✓✓	✓	(✓)					
Learn about Life	✓	(✓)	✓	✓	✓	✓	✓		
Explore Possible Future Careers/ Gain Foothold	✓	✓✓	(✓)	✓				✓	
Learn other Language/ Culture		(✓)	✓	(✓)	✓		(✓)	(✓)	(✓)
Demonstrate Independence	✓		✓✓		✓		✓		(✓)
Help Others		(✓)		✓	✓				
Learn to Value What You Have					✓	✓		(✓)	
Academic Learning								✓	✓✓

(cont'd.)	Paid Job (U. S.)	Unpaid Intern- Ship	Paid Job Abroad	Volunteer (U. S.)	Volunteer Abroad	Travel (U.S.)	Travel Abroad	Short Courses	PG Yr.
Potential Disadvantages									
Hard to Find Worthwhile Jobs	✓	(✓)	✓✓						
High Costs				(✓)	✓	✓	✓	✓	✓✓
Viewed as for Spoiled Rich Kids		(✓)		✓	✓		✓✓		✓
Homesickness/ Loneliness		✓			✓		✓		✓
Emotional Exhaustion				✓✓	✓✓		(✓)	**	
Danger					✓		(✓)		

*Such as communication, negotiation, teamwork, leadership, or time management skills
**Can feel like you never left school, if the course is too long or too academic

COMBINING PURSUITS

Fifteen months—the period between finishing high school and starting college a year later—is a long time, offering you the opportunity to do more than just one thing. One common approach is to travel in a relaxed fashion for the first month or two out of school, in order to wash high school out of your hair, then settle down for a time to study, work, or volunteer (or some combination thereof). It is fine to leave certain periods unspecified and unplanned for, such as designating a six week period for loose-jointed travel in whatever direction the first train takes you, but be careful not to leave the whole effort unplanned. The greatest risk of wasting a year is by waiting until graduation without having planned anything with the expectation that "something will turn up."

FUNDING YOUR YEAR OFF

It is important to budget for your year off very carefully and realistically. Some efforts may not require funding—working and living at home, for instance—but others will require more money, or at least more money up front, than you may have assumed. Thus even if you have a job lined up in another city, whether in the U.S. or abroad, you can expect to need money to get under way. Just getting there, arranging for a place to live, and paying for food until your first pay check arrives are likely to require more than you might expect if you have never done something comparable.

Work out a sensible budget for your planned year. The following chart may help:

| | Range of Estimates | |
	High	Low
Expenses		
Travel (to and from)	_____	_____
Room	_____	_____
Board	_____	_____
Entertainment	_____	_____
Local travel (bus pass, e.g.)	_____	_____
Holiday travel	_____	_____
Fees (for volunteer projects, courses, etc.)	_____	_____
Other	_____	_____
Subtotal		
Sources of Cash		
Savings	_____	_____
Earnings between now and starting	_____	_____
Earnings during year off	_____	_____
Contributions	_____	_____
Subtotal		
Total	_____	_____

Whether you need a little or a lot of money will probably determine how you try to raise funds. The following is a brief look at the possibilities:

You can pitch your parents (or grandparents, or favorite aunt and uncle, and so on). Do not take their financial support for granted. They will respond best if you have a carefully thought out plan and budget to present to them, complete with well-stated rationales for undertaking whatever you propose. Two cautions: first, be clear as to the precise amount you want from them, so that they do not feel that they are going to have to contribute endlessly if they make this initial payment. Second, be sure to ask at an appropriate time, when your parents can think calmly and clearly about your proposition.

Work hard senior year and/or immediately upon graduation. Funding yourself will give you a great deal of pride in your own abilities; it will also impress college admissions officers and potential future employers

Arrange sponsorship with a local business or charity. Local businesses may be willing to put up some money for you if they can be persuaded that you will provide them with a worthwhile marketing or publicity opportunity. For example, if you plan to hike the Andes, consider approaching a camping equipment company to help you based upon the newspaper coverage you will get, the stories you will write for publication in specialist magazines, and so on. They may donate the equipment you need and even provide you with flights to and from Latin America. A similar approach could be made to a large, local sporting goods retailer or camera shop. If you were hiking to publicize the plight of a certain species of bird in the Andes, you might be able to get an American birding organization or wildlife charity to contribute to your expenses.

A NOTE FOR PARENTS

Taking time off before college is not for everyone. Too few people in our experience, however, take advantage of an opportunity to explore the world and themselves at a time when the costs of doing so are quite low—when they have no mortgage payments to make or careers that cannot be interrupted—and when the rewards are potentially immense. College admissions officers, especially those who have been in the business for a substantial period of time, strongly believe that time off, when pursued constructively, is beneficial for virtually all who try it. Separating the process of becoming a (somewhat) independent adult from that of starting college can be useful. The personal growth of those taking time off helps prepare them to get the most out of their college experience. They are more inclined to pursue their college studies with a purpose and less likely to be distracted by the frivolous (and even the potentially dangerous) aspects of college than they would be had they gone straight from high school.

"YEAR OFF"' SUCCESS STORIES

APPLYING TO COLLEGE AFTER HIGH SCHOOL: JOSH'S STORY

Josh started interning (without pay) at a local political consulting firm after his junior year in high school. He filed, copied, input data, and so on. As he became more and more interested in what he saw the senior consultants doing, he decided to pursue political consulting as a possible career.

Following the senior consultants' advice, he took every math course he could during his senior year: calculus, statistics, and math for computer science. He also enrolled in a data analysis course at his local community college. As his understanding of relevant mathematical techniques and computer programs progressed, he was allowed to do more and more of the initial data analysis for clients.

DECIDING TO REAPPLY TO COLLEGE

Because he had goofed off during his early years of high school, Josh was unable to get into his top college choices. He decided that rather than go to his back-up choice, which failed to inspire him with enthusiasm, he would reapply the next fall. He reasoned that he would look like a much more interesting and accomplished applicant at that point, with his budding political consulting career being further advanced, and another year of strong academic effort under his belt.

He pitched his parents and was delighted to find out that they were in agreement. They did, however, condition their acceptance of his plan upon his commitment to attend college a year later. Josh next arranged an offer of full-time work after high school; his firm was pleased to have him, given the good attitude he had demonstrated in addition to his on the job growth.

GETTING THE MOST OUT OF SECOND SEMESTER SENIOR YEAR

Josh got recommendations from his favorite math teacher at the end of the year, when his teacher had the time to do a particularly careful job and after the teacher had seen him perform very well in several courses. Josh had recognized the value of these courses and worked hard in them; his work in the political consulting realm meant that he had wonderful real-life examples that he could use in doing class projects. He had presented his results to each class with real enthusiasm. This performance was, of course, much more impressive and far more interesting than that undertaken by any of his classmates. His teacher was therefore able to recommend him extremely enthusiastically, with detailed stories about the work he had done, the way he had enjoyed presenting it to his classmates, and their positive response to his enthusiasm.

JOSH'S WORK EXPERIENCE AFTER HIGH SCHOOL

Josh worked hard for his consulting firm, and also took several related community college courses. As Josh developed his understanding of the business as well as his technical skills, he was given increased responsibilities. For example, he frequently did background research on the needs of potential clients; he also did the initial "situation assessments" for new clients. He eventually attended client meetings to be available to answer clients' requests that depended upon in-depth knowledge of the statistics and methodologies underlying the firm's presentations.

APPLYING TO COLLEGE THE FOLLOWING FALL

Josh had learned a great deal about what he wanted in a school. He knew that he wanted a school with strong political science and statistics departments, with a chance to double major in the two subjects. He wanted the opportunity to take highly quantitative courses within the political science department and to write a thesis under the supervision of a recognized authority on applying quantitative methods to political science issues.

Josh took advantage of his year off to bolster his positioning. He became clearly identifiable as "the politico." He contacted political science professors teaching American politics or data analysis courses, explained what he was doing, and discussed at length with them how their courses could be of benefit to him. In several cases they ended up marketing their respective schools to him, going so far as to write strong letters on his behalf to their admissions directors. Josh also got a very strong supplemental recommendation from his boss, who had never before had a high schooler make such an impact. Josh was further helped by the fact that his senior year grades were good, as were his community college grades during and after his senior year.

Armed with his improved credentials and positioning, Josh got into two of the schools that had previously rejected him and two others to which he had not previously applied. He went to one of the latter, and enjoyed remarkable success there; this included capitalizing upon his political consulting experience both in and out of the classroom.

WORKING DURING COLLEGE

Josh began by working as a pollster for his college newspaper freshman year, producing bi-weekly articles (always with his own byline). He ultimately managed to "quintuple dip," that is, get five benefits from his efforts. He got the credit for his newspaper articles, which turned him into a well-known figure on campus by the end of his first semester. Second, he published only some of his data, thereby creating the opportunity to sell some of his insights to student politicians running for office. Third, he contributed modified versions of his campus writings to the city newspaper nearby, for which he was also paid. Fourth, he eventually started consulting to politicians interested in attracting the student vote at his campus. He was a more credible source of information for them about students than were their usual consultants. And fifth, he generally managed to use his survey data for political science and data analysis courses he was taking.

Long before he graduated, Josh was working nearly full-time as a pollster and consultant. He had the choice, upon graduation, of further developing his own consulting business or of joining an established firm as a junior partner.

DEFERRING COLLEGE: FABIANNA'S STORY

During her senior year Fabianna had been admitted to an Ivy League college. She had intended to go straight to college, but had been convinced to take time out beforehand. Her parents and grandparents were concerned that she was too serious about everything, had pushed herself too hard in high school, and had not yet seen enough of the world and learned enough about herself to head straight into an academic pressure cooker. Her maternal grandparents, both born in Tuscany, suggested that she spend time in Italy getting to know her relatives,

Fabianna liked the idea of improving her rather poor Italian, which she generally spoke only with the two of them. She also proposed that she pursue a new interest of hers—cooking. She investigated the possibilities in Italy and was delighted to learn that several well-regarded schools offered cooking instruction in English. She figured that she could at least start in such a school while she improved her Italian, then switch to a cooking school offering courses only in Italian.

During the summer following high school, Fabianna lived with one set of her relatives while attending cooking school and taking Italian language lessons at the local university. By September she felt ready to step out on her own. She moved to Rome to enroll in a cooking school conducted solely in Italian. She took classes for two months, then spent several more months interning in a local restaurant, a position that the school arranged for her. After that she spent the winter working as a cook at a ski chalet in Cortina, in the Dolomites (in the Italian Alps). During the late spring and summer she worked as a chef aboard a yacht in the Mediterranean. In between each of these efforts, and on many of her weekend breaks, she spent time traveling around Italy with the people she met studying or working.

Fabianna's Results

At the end of her year off Fabianna knew that she could celebrate several accomplishments. Her command of Italian had soared, going from poor to native in fifteen months, as had her knowledge of Italy. Equally important, she had become a truly professional cook, able to put together a very wide range of meals at a moment's notice, to work as part of a team of professionals in a restaurant kitchen, to design a menu to various cost and taste specifications, and to supervise lesser skilled helpers in cooking for private parties. During college she would of course be able to work part-time (and on an emergency fill-in basis) for excellent wages at any of the Italian restaurants in the area. She planned to investigate setting up her own catering business as well. During holidays she figured to work again as a private chef in ski or summer resorts, except this time she would be able to command a higher salary, given her demonstrated skills and experience (along with the recommendations she had from her prior employers). As a result of this year, Fabianna knew full well that she would be able to make her own way in the world wherever she found himself. A bonus was that she had also greatly improved her skiing and learned a great deal about sailing, thereby advancing two personal hobbies.

Fabianna's parents and grandparents were relieved that she had started to view life as more than an academic exercise. They believed that she would be less likely to overcommit herself prematurely to a career path in her freshman year. They figured that she would instead be more inclined to sample different educational and career possibilities, given her greater self-awareness and broader base of experience upon which to draw. As a result of this—and of her having gotten to know some of her relatives and having had a delightful year—they considered their money extremely well spent.

THE ADMISSIONS OFFICERS TALK ABOUT TAKING TIME OFF BEFORE COLLEGE

WHAT IS YOUR OPINION ON TAKING TIME OFF BEFORE COLLEGE?

"We think it's a good idea if *the candidate* thinks it's a good idea."
—*Michael Goldberger, Director of Admissions, Brown University*

"I think it's great. There's no reason you have to go to college right after high school, just as there's no reason you have to go for four straight years."
—*Dan Walls, Dean of Admissions, Emory University*

"We think it's a great idea! For perhaps a decade we've been putting a statement into the admit letter to the effect that 'We hope you'll consider taking a year off before coming to Harvard.' We really do want students to think about it—we believe it's in their best interest. We also want parents to see that we think it's not only okay, but even a very good thing, supported by the college. We don't want parents discouraging their children from taking time off before college."
—*Marlyn McGrath Lewis, Director of Admissions, Harvard University*

"We encourage taking a year off. We don't explicitly suggest it to students, though, except in special cases—such as home-schooled applicants who are sixteen and need some maturing."
—*John Hanson, Director of Admissions, Middlebury College*

"Taking a year off is often a very good idea. Many students who do this come back refreshed, more focused, more in charge of their own education."
—*Jonathan Reider, Senior Associate Director of Admissions, Stanford University*

"We still don't see that many admitted students wanting to defer. I think this is because our applicant pool is a bit different—really research-oriented, academically-oriented kids who are excited to get here right away. It's also not common for us to see kids who are applying during a year off."
—*Marilee Jones, Dean of Admissions, Massachusetts Institute of Technology*

"I encourage taking a year off. It's a great way to spend a year."
—*Nanci Tessier, Director of Admissions, Smith College*

WHAT ARE THE BENEFITS OF TAKING TIME OFF BEFORE COLLEGE?

"The need to simply reinvigorate before diving into college is a very good reason to take a year off."
—*Richard Shaw, Dean of Undergraduate Admissions and Financial Aid, Yale University*

"A year off can be great for a student—especially if there is a concern about maturity. Service projects conducted during a year off are always looked upon favorably."
—*Barbara-Jan Wilson, Dean of Admissions and Financial Aid, Wesleyan University*

"We have a strong viewpoint on the idea of taking a year off. First, it's better to be more mature and focused when arriving at this demanding place. We also think being older by a year, in and of itself, is usually beneficial—an extra year before you start college can only be a good thing. We also encourage students to take time off from college while they are here."
—*Marlyn McGrath Lewis, Director of Admissions, Harvard University*

WHEN IS IT BENEFICIAL FOR A CANDIDATE TO WAIT UNTIL AFTER GRADUATING FROM HIGH SCHOOL, DURING A YEAR OFF, TO APPLY TO COLLEGE?

"Applicants who take time off and then apply to college can be very appealing—they've often done very interesting things during that year off. But making yourself more interesting won't make up for a so-so high school record—applicants should keep that in mind."
—*Karl Furstenberg, Dean of Admissions and Financial Aid, Dartmouth College*

"One young woman applied here and was waitlisted. Instead of going to college somewhere else, she went to Europe to vagabond around. There was no growth, no meaning to what she was doing. So when she applied again the next year, we didn't even put her on the waitlist. We didn't see how her candidacy was improved by her year off. We like it much better when students do something valuable with their time."
—*Jonathan Reider, Senior Associate Director of Admissions, Stanford University*

"I suggest that students apply here while in high school, and then defer to take the year off. Very seldom does a year off change one's chances of being admitted to a school like ours—the fundamentals are the high school grades and the test scores, and those won't change during a year off. Occasionally doing something really phenomenal during a year off can change a student's perspective or give her something exciting to present in the application, but it's rare that that might color our decision."
—*Richard Shaw, Dean of Undergraduate Admissions and Financial Aid, Yale University*

"When see applications from students who have done well in school and have great potential but have not yet been through a rigorous academic experience, we suggest that they apply to a program called the Transitional Year Program, or TYP, at Northfield Mount Herman [a college preparatory school] for a year. We ask them to reapply to Wesleyan during that extra year. There's no *guarantee* that they'll be admitted to Wesleyan, but if they do well in the program, we always admit them."

—*Barbara-Jan Wilson, Dean of Admissions and Financial Aid, Wesleyan University*

WHEN IS A POST-GRADUATE (PG) YEAR BENEFICIAL FOR A STUDENT?

"A PG year can be good if students are going to *do* something with it—they really need to be able to hit the ground running, though. They need to be able to adjust quickly to a new academic and social life. Students should put a lot of thought into doing an extra year of high school—don't do it thinking that it will be easy to boost your chance of admission, because that's not always the case."

—*Eric Kaplan, Director of Admissions, University of Pennsylvania*

"A PG year *can* be beneficial but this one year does not erase the rest of an applicant's high school record. It can only do so much. It's usually helpful for those who got a late start in terms of performing academically or for potential athletic recruits who need more college preparation and a slightly better record."

—*Karl Furstenberg, Dean of Admissions and Financial Aid, Dartmouth College*

"We think the PG year can be a really good thing—it's especially terrific for athletes who need an academic boost. PG students don't necessarily have a harder time in our admissions process. The problem is when a student decides to do a PG year and doesn't do well. That sometimes happens—with students from non-rigorous high schools who get to a demanding prep school and can't do as well as they wanted to. The PG year will only hurt them in this case."

—*Barbara-Jan Wilson, Dean of Admissions and Financial Aid, Wesleyan University*

IS IT GENERALLY MORE DIFFICULT FOR A PG STUDENT THAN A REGULAR HIGH SCHOOL STUDENT TO GAIN ADMISSION?

"A PG year doesn't drastically increase a person's attractiveness—but it's also not looked at negatively if there was a reason for doing it."

—*Karl Furstenberg, Dean of Admissions and Financial Aid, Dartmouth College*

"PG students usually have a harder time being admitted because if they're doing a PG year in the first place, there's probably a reason for it—a weakness of some sort in their regular high school record."

—*Eric Kaplan, Director of Admissions, University of Pennsylvania*

WHAT REASONS ARE CONSIDERED LEGITIMATE FOR ALLOWING SOMEONE TO DEFER MATRICULATION?

"Kids who apply, get in, and then want to defer a year can do anything they want to except go to another college. Full-time study at another institution is not allowed."

—Jonathan Reider, Senior Associate Director of Admission, Stanford University

"There are often good reasons for deferring a year—travel, getting out of the lockstep of school, that kind of thing. Students don't have to promise not to go somewhere else in the end—that's usually not a problem because they all show up here eventually."

—Lee Stetson, Dean of Admissions, University of Pennsylvania

"I think it's great when students want to take a year off before college. Those who apply here and defer can do anything except go to college somewhere else for that year. They can take courses somewhere—at a college overseas, dance classes, language classes, whatever—they just can't go full-time for regular college credit."

—Christoph Guttentag, Director of Undergraduate Admissions, Duke University

"Deferring is fine as long as it's to do something worthwhile and a student doesn't enroll at another college."

—David Borus, Dean of Admission and Financial Aid, Vassar College

"Our expectation is that the student has a plan—a reason for the year off. As long as this is the case, we say 'Go ahead.'"

—Nancy Hargrave Meislahn, Director of Undergraduate Admissions, Cornell University

"We grant deferrals, but not if it's to do other schoolwork. We like students to have a plan—to work on a kibbutz, sail around the world, take care of a health problem or illness."

—Marilee Jones, Dean of Admissions, Massachusetts Institute of Technology

"Deferring a year to 'hang out' is not a good idea. I don't consider that a legitimate reason for taking time off."

—Richard Shaw, Dean of Undergraduate Admissions and Financial Aid, Yale University

3

DECIDING WHERE TO APPLY

— KEY POINTS —

Colleges vary tremendously in atmosphere, educational philosophy, course offerings, student body, and a host of other potentially critical characteristics
—*Some schools are likely to fit your needs well, others surely will not:*
you need to figure out which are which
■

The process of choosing colleges is complex
—*There are a lot of good schools and a lot of different criteria to consider*
—*Choosing colleges requires projecting yourself and your needs*
five or six years into the future
■

Start early
—*Expect the process to take a great deal of time and effort (and anxiety)*
■

Choosing the right colleges starts with analyzing yourself
■

Learn about colleges by reading college guidebooks and other literature, looking at Web sites, meeting with college representatives, talking to alums and students, and visiting campuses
—*See Appendices I and II to learn more about how to optimize your use of the college rankings and your college visits*
■

Expect to apply to approximately eight schools
—*Three or four "stretches," two or three "possibles," and two "safeties"*

INTRODUCTION

Your selection of schools will be driven by two interrelated activities:

1. Analyzing yourself to determine your needs and desires, and
2. Investigating colleges thoroughly to find the best fits for you.

The more you analyze yourself and your needs, the more you will learn about what you require in a college; likewise, the more you investigate colleges, the more you will learn about yourself and your needs. Thus, you should conduct these two activities simultaneously in order to do the best job possible of choosing colleges that are ideal for you. You will find that with each successive round of investigation, you develop better and more precise ideas about the kind of institution you would like to attend. This iterative process can be arduous and time-consuming. Do not think you will read a few college catalogs on a Saturday afternoon and have all the answers. It will take months (for some students, years) of investigation.

To set in motion the iterative process just described, first analyze yourself, your needs and goals, and who you aim to become in college and beyond. Next, based on your desires and needs, determine what qualities are important to you in a college. Then use a variety of resources to research and investigate the colleges to decide where to apply. In the end, after hearing from each of your target colleges, you must make a final decision about where you will matriculate in the fall.

AVOID THE COMMON PITFALLS ASSOCIATED WITH CHOOSING COLLEGES

There are two major errors that many students make when looking at colleges:

1. They focus on the "best" colleges rather than those that best fit their needs and goals.
2. They focus on one single "perfect" college.

Yes, you should aim to get into the best college possible, but you should also want to get into the best college possible for *you*. There are many excellent colleges to choose from, and they are not all the same. You should investigate carefully to be sure you are choosing schools that fit your needs, desires, and aims, rather than hoping to be accepted at a school just because of its rank in *U.S. News & World Report* or the prestige that it commands in your hometown. Students who apply to and ultimately accept an offer at one of "the best" schools without examining how that college fits their personal needs often end up unhappy. When you have so many great selective colleges to choose from, there is no excuse for applying to a college for the wrong reasons.

To avoid the second mistake, resist going into the college selection process with the idea of "choosing *a* college." Even if you are the most talented and interesting person in America, there is never a guarantee that you will get into a particular college. For this reason, train yourself from the very beginning to think of the selection process not as one in which you deem one school "the favorite" and the rest completely unacceptable, but as one in which you determine general features of importance to you, and then match a set of schools to those features.

It is certainly all right to determine that one college fits your needs and desires a bit better than any other. As discussed at length in Chapter 5, most applicants in fact benefit from applying to a college Early Decision, a binding commitment that requires, among other things, that you have deemed that college your top choice (of the colleges at which you have a fair chance at admission). Even after applying to a college Early Decision, though, you must remember to spread your enthusiasm and energy sufficiently among all of the schools to which you will eventually make applications, in the event that this Early application is not successful. Be sure that no matter what college you deem your favorite, you continue to acknowledge the exciting possibilities that your other target schools pose.

In sum, the process of selecting appropriate colleges is a narrowing down or focusing exercise, but only to a certain degree. You want to be able to picture yourself at each of the colleges to which you apply—and picture yourself being happy and satisfied at each of them—rather than allowing yourself to become fixated on one particular school to the exclusion of all others. This way, you will prevent yourself from suffering the pain that many high school seniors needlessly put themselves through when they set their sights on one and only one college—and then are not accepted. If you conduct the college selection process thoughtfully and carefully, you should not experience any serious disappointments in the end.

ANALYZE YOURSELF TO DETERMINE YOUR NEEDS AND DESIRES

You should analyze yourself in an attempt to make some decisions about what you are and are not looking for in a college before you begin visiting your target schools. Then, as you start visiting campuses and learning more about schools, you can refine and change your list of needs and desires as appropriate. There are several ways of going about the self-examination process. You might try one of the following exercises:

■ Take half an hour or so to concentrate on your high school experience. Determine what was good and bad about your high school and make lists of each. This will help you decide what you should look for again in a college and what you should avoid. For example, if the intimacy of your 45-person graduating class shows up in the "good" column, you can assume that you will probably be happiest at a small college. (See the sample self-evaluation below.)

A SAMPLE SELF-EVALUATION: AN EVALUATION OF MY HIGH SCHOOL CAREER

WHAT WAS GOOD	WHAT WAS BAD
➤ I know every person in my 53-person class fairly well—feels intimate and cozy	➤ All-girls school—I want to attend a coed college
➤ Great art and drama departments	➤ Not enough diversity—too many students of my same background
➤ Beautiful campus—nineteenth-century architecture; pretty, rural surroundings	➤ Not enough focus on computing or technology
➤ Teachers are always there for us—I can ask for help at any time and receive plenty of individualized attention from them	➤ High pressure to succeed—students are too competitive with one another
➤ School's educational philosophy stresses importance of a balanced lifestyle	➤ Terrible food!

The student who wrote this self-evaluation might determine, for example, that she should attend a fairly small college, with an accessible faculty, in an appealing rural environment. It would ideally boast good performing and visual arts departments as well as state-of-the-art technology resources. The diverse and active student body would be concerned with more than just getting top grades. (In a perfect world, the on-campus dining facilities would also offer quality food, but this is likely to be one of the least important factors on the list.)

■ Engage in a fantasy process, whereby you try to picture how you would be most satisfied and happy in the world, regardless of what you have experienced so far in life. After you have described your fantasy world, try to extract meaning from the outlandish portions of the description. Bringing your desires down to a level of reality can help you to determine what you should be looking for in the place in which you will spend the next four years of your life. For example, perhaps in your dream world it snows 365 days of the year and you have enough time to hit the ski slopes every afternoon. You can assume that you might be happiest at a school in the northeast corner of the United States, where winter can last half the year and skiing is a way of life.

■ Make a list of your values and needs. In the "values" column, cite what philosophies, principles, and lifestyle choices are important to you. "Close contact with my siblings" might show up in the values column; in this case, you might consider looking at schools fairly near to your home. In the "needs" column, list the circumstances, tangible objects, and other things that you require in your daily life. If you list "sunshine" here, you can probably rule out most schools in the Pacific Northwest. (See the sample values and needs evaluation below.)

A SAMPLE SELF-EVALUATION: MY VALUES AND NEEDS

VALUES	NEEDS
➤ Quality time with family and friends	➤ A lot of sleep
➤ Honesty and personal integrity	➤ Stimulation and intellectual challenges from peers and teachers
➤ Independence and freedom—little constraint on personal desires	➤ Community service options
➤ Contributing to the community	➤ Water sports

The student who wrote this self-evaluation should most likely attend a college with a strong residential system, best for maintaining close relationships and becoming a significant part of a tight-knit community. He might be especially attracted to schools with an honor code and colleges that offer significant community service programs. He would probably be happiest at a school with a very flexible curriculum, rather than one with strict core curriculum or distribution requirements. He would want to look at selective schools with bright and intellectual students, but maybe not somewhere like MIT—where he might not be able to get a good night's sleep on a regular basis. He would want to look at schools located on either coast or near rivers and lakes so that he could be sure to continue participating in water sports while at college.

■ Start by visiting a few easily accessible or local colleges. It does not matter if they are the right caliber or style for you. The point is to visit a campus, talk to some students, and pick up admissions materials—doing so will trigger your thoughts about college. Visiting a school will likely encourage you to imagine what qualities you will be investigating when you look at the schools that *do* interest you. You might not even realize, for example, before visiting a local university what it really feels like to be at a "suitcase school" on a Saturday afternoon. When you feel how dull and quiet the campus is with everyone away at home for the weekend, you will be sure to inquire about such circumstances at other schools you visit.

■ Use the following self-evaluation to begin thinking about your needs, goals, values, educational philosophy, and where you want to be in the future. Thinking about the ideas presented in this evaluation will help you to determine what you are looking for in a college.

A SELF-EVALUATION TO HELP YOU IN THE COLLEGE SELECTION PROCESS

As you explore colleges to determine which are most suitable for you and your needs, you will realize that a thorough understanding of yourself will help you in the college selection process. Describing yourself, your habits, and your goals will help you begin to determine what is important in a college. The ideas presented in each of the eight sections of this self-evaluation will help you to identify what is and is not important to you:

➤ By identifying your needs regarding **educational philosophy and academic environment,** you can determine what kind of intellectual atmosphere you want; what level of academic difficulty and pressure you are willing to accept; the degree of flexibility you desire in a college curriculum; and the degree to which you want to follow a broad liberal arts curriculum versus focusing on a particular field.

➤ By identifying your needs regarding **academic particulars,** you can determine what departmental strengths you seek; the level of emphasis on reading or writing you desire; what kind of interaction with faculty you would like; and the class size and type (lecture, seminar, independent study, tutorial) you prefer.

➤ By identifying your needs regarding **overall environment and atmosphere,** you can determine how important it is to you that you attend a prestigious institution; and whether or not you want to be immersed in a culture that particularly values politics, sports, community service, or internationalism.

➤ By identifying your needs regarding **social environment,** you can determine the degree of diversity you seek; how small or large a student body you want; the degree to which a conservative or liberal bent is desirable to you; and what type of social life you prefer.

➤ By identifying your needs regarding **location,** you can determine whether you want to attend an urban, semiurban, or rural institution; how close to home you want to be; and what kind of climate and culture are best for you.

➤ By identifying your needs regarding **physical features and facilities,** you can determine how important the quality of the various buildings and facilities on campus is to you.

➤ By identifying your needs regarding **future goals,** you can further determine how much flexibility you desire in a curriculum; and whether you want to follow a broad liberal arts curriculum or focus on a particular preprofessional field.

➤ By answering several **miscellaneous** questions, you will further clarify why you are going to college; what of your high school career you want to repeat and avoid; and what it is you are looking for in college.

Respond to the statements as truthfully as possible—this is to be used only by yourself in your quest to make the smartest decisions regarding college. The purpose here is not to figure out ways to market yourself to colleges but to determine for yourself what you are really after, so being dishonest will only hurt you down the line. In each selection, you should either circle one of several alternative statements or finish the single given statement in your own words.

EDUCATIONAL PHILOSOPHY AND ACADEMIC ENVIRONMENT

➤ I am more interested in learning and feeling intellectually engaged than I am in getting good grades.

I care more about my performance in class than I do about feeling intellectually stimulated.

➤ I am independent and like to make decisions on my own, without help from parents or other adults.

I am not yet able to make decisions on my own and would rather have guidance from my parents, teachers, or other adults in doing so.

➤ I would rather take a lot of different subjects than focus on one subject.

I would rather focus on my favorite subjects than take a lot of courses in areas that are not important to me.

➤ I like to do extra projects and go beyond what is expected of me in the classroom.

Even when I am interested in the subject matter, I tend to do the bare minimum in a class rather than produce extra work.

➤ I am ready to start thinking about my career and life after college.

I am not ready to start thinking about my career and life after college.

➤ I like to be challenged and work on my weaknesses.

I would rather stick to improving my strengths than working on my weaknesses.

➤ I am good at making my own decisions.

I am bad at making my own decisions.

➤ I do best when I feel confident that most of my peers are not as intelligent as I am.

I do best when challenged by peers who are more intelligent than I am.

➤ I do best in an environment in which students are preoccupied with their studies and there is pressure to perform well.

I do best in an environment in which students are relatively relaxed about their studies and there is no external pressure to perform well.

ACADEMIC PARTICULARS

➤ I participate heavily in class discussions and do not learn well if I am not an active contributor.

I do not participate much in class and learn just as well (or better) when not required to contribute to discussions.

➤ It is very important to me to be able to seek attention and help from my teachers.

It does not matter very much to me whether or not I am able to obtain personalized attention from teachers.

➤ I enjoy and benefit from hearing other students' ideas and opinions in class.

I do not especially enjoy or benefit from hearing other students' ideas and opinions in class.

➤ I am motivated on my own to do my schoolwork.

I only do my schoolwork when reminded or badgered by my parents or teachers.

➤ I love to write and feel confident in my writing abilities.

I love to write but do not feel confident in my writing abilities.

I do not love to write but feel confident in my writing abilities.

I do not love to write and do not feel confident in my abilities.

➤ I love to read.

I do not like to read.

I do not particularly like to read but am willing to do it for educational purposes.

➤ When I do not understand something or feel confused in class, I am not afraid to ask the teacher for help.

When I do not understand something or feel confused in class, I am afraid or uncomfortable asking the teacher for help.

➤ I perform my best when motivated by "positive" reinforcement (i.e., praise for my strengths and accomplishments rather than criticisms of my weaknesses and failures).

I perform best when motivated by "negative" reinforcement (i.e., criticism of my weaknesses and failures rather than praise for my strengths and accomplishments).

➤ It is important for me to get to know my teachers and feel that they care about me and my progress.

It does not matter to me whether or not my teachers play a role in my life or seem to take an interest in my progress.

➤ I am a better and more motivated learner when I know I am being monitored and watched over by teachers.

I am motivated to learn on my own and do not need the reinforcement of teachers watching over me in order to do my best.

➤ I like to speak in front of others in class, even when I am not confident about my opinions and ideas.

When I am confident of what I am saying, I like to speak in front of others in class.

I do not like to speak in front of others in class, even when I am confident of what I am saying.

➤ I am afraid to take a stand on something if I think that others disagree with me.

I am unafraid to take a stand on something, even if I think that others disagree with me.

➤ My favorite subjects in school are …

➤ It is important that any school I attend have a strong department in …

OVERALL ENVIRONMENT AND ATMOSPHERE

➤ I would find it acceptable to attend a college with a prestigious name even if it were not the ideal place for me and my goals.

Prestige is not very important to me—I would rather attend a school that is best for me than go somewhere with a better name.

➤ I enjoy community service and need to have a wide range of volunteer activities available to me.

Community service is not very important to me.

➤ I read newspapers and news magazines regularly.

I do not read newspapers or news magazines regularly.

➤ I like to play and watch sports.

Sports are not a big part of my life.

➤ The "work hard/play hard" philosophy is appealing to me.

I would rather work hard than play hard.

I would rather play hard than work hard.

➤ An educational experience involving only academics (and no extracurricular activities) would not appeal to me.

An educational experience involving only academics would appeal to me.

➤ I am attached to one or more special causes and feel my life would not be as full without my involvement in them.

I am not particularly attached to any special causes.

➤ It is important for me to live within an international and globally oriented community.

It is not important for me to live within an international or globally oriented community.

➤ My favorite extracurricular activities are …

➤ If I suddenly had an extra year in my life to do anything I wanted to, I would spend it …

➤ The ways in which I spend my free time include …

Social Environment

➤ I am most comfortable and happy when surrounded by people like myself.

I thrive when surrounded by people who are different from me.

➤ I am happiest when surrounded by highly politicized people.

I am uncomfortable with or indifferent to being surrounded by highly politicized people.

➤ I like socializing in small groups with just a few intimate friends.

I like socializing in large groups with both friends and people I do not know.

➤ I prefer a calm social scene, where most socializing is done in small group gatherings and is confined to weekend nights only.

I prefer a wild and crazy party scene, with social options every night of the week.

➤ The best social atmosphere for me is one in which I am a member of an exclusive club or organization.

The best social atmosphere for me is one in which I am not a member of any special club or organization but free to socialize as I please, although I do not mind if others around me are members of such exclusive clubs.

The best social atmosphere for me is one in which no one is a member of an exclusive club or organization.

➤ It is important for me to feel recognized and acknowledged by my peers and community, not an anonymous face or a number in a system.

Recognition and acknowledgment from others are not important to me—I would rather be an anonymous face in a large crowd.

➤ I like being around others and do not enjoy being by myself.

I like being alone and do not enjoy being around others.

I value both time alone and time spent with others.

➤ I am religious and maintaining my devotion is important to me.

I am religious but maintaining my devotion is not particularly important to me.

I am not religious and do not like being around people who are.

I am not religious but do not mind being around people who are.

➤ I adhere to an alternative lifestyle (in terms of sexual preference, a particular environmentalist stance, devotion to a certain cult or religion, etc.) and would do best in an environment that supports alternative practices.

I do not adhere to an alternative lifestyle but would like to be part of a community that supports alternative practices.

I do not adhere to an alternative lifestyle and would feel uncomfortable in a community that supports alternative practices.

➤ I want to be in an environment in which different racial and ethnic groups interact rather than merely living side by side.

It does not matter to me whether or not different racial and ethnic groups interact in my environment.

LOCATION

➤ I like to be in an urban environment, surrounded by crowded city streets and plenty of cultural attractions.

I like to be in a semiurban environment, not in a city itself but near enough to one to be able to enjoy it on occasion.

I like to be in a peaceful, rural environment where there is plenty of natural beauty and perhaps limited access to cultural and entertainment venues.

➤ Attending cultural and entertainment events of national or international stature is important to me.

Attending cultural events of national or international stature is not very important to me.

➤ Weather and climate are important to me—they affect my moods and productivity.

Weather and climate are not important to me—they do not affect my moods or productivity.

➤ I am looking forward to being independent and have no reason to stay close to home when I leave for college.

I am looking forward to being independent but need to stay fairly close to home when I attend college (for one reason or another).

I am not looking forward to being away from my family and friends and want to stay fairly close to home when I attend college.

➤ My ideal home would be in …

Physical Features and Facilities

➤ The way my surroundings (architecture, landscape, etc.) look and feel is important to me.

The way my surroundings look and feel is not important to me.

➤ It is important to me that the library I use is in top condition.

It does not matter to me whether or not the library I use is in top condition.

➤ It is important to me that the computing facilities I use are in top condition.

It does not matter to me whether or not the computing facilities I use are in top condition.

➤ It is important to me that the science labs I use are in top condition.

It does not matter to me whether or not the science labs I use are in top condition.

➤ It is important to me that the athletic facilities I use are in top condition.

It does not matter to me whether or not the athletic facilities I use are in top condition.

➤ It is important to me that the performing arts facilities I use are in top condition.

It does not matter to me whether or not the performing arts facilities I use are in top condition.

➤ It is important to me that the dining halls where I eat my meals are in top condition.

It does not matter to me whether or not the dining halls where I eat my meals are in top condition.

➤ It is important to me that my living quarters are in top condition.

It does not matter to me whether or not my living quarters are in top condition.

Future Goals

➤ I view college primarily as an opportunity to prepare for my future career rather than as an opportunity to explore intellectual interests.

I view college primarily as an opportunity to explore intellectual interests rather than as an opportunity to prepare for my future career.

➤ I know exactly what I want to do in my future career.

I have no idea what I want to do in my future career.

I have some ideas about what I want to do in my future career, but I am not certain about which ones I will pursue.

➤ I am more interested in pursuing a successful career than I am in having a fulfilling personal and family life.

I am not as interested in pursuing a successful career as I am in having a fulfilling personal and family life.

➤ My possible future careers include …

➤ My general short- and long-term goals are …

MISCELLANEOUS

➤ The reasons I want to go to college are to …

➤ I am most looking forward to … in the future.

➤ I am most afraid of … in the future.

➤ One bad decision I made in high school that I would like to avoid in college is …

➤ One good decision I made in high school that I would like to repeat in college is …

REMEMBER TO BALANCE IDEALISM WITH REALISM

It is important to balance idealism and realism when engaging in the college investigation process. You might dream that in a perfect world, your college would allow all athletes to forego classwork during their varsity season—this is, of course, not something you will find at any college, so you have to remember to tone down your expectations when the real search begins.

A PROCESS OF MATCHMAKING

Once you have some ideas about what you are looking for, the process of deciding where to apply is a little like matchmaking. You need to start investigating colleges, keeping in mind the key qualities discussed later in this chapter, and then identify which institutions fit your desires and needs best.

The problem is that there is no matchmaker to do the job for you. There is no one who can perform the tasks and make decisions for you, precisely because the process requires knowing yourself well in addition to understanding what the various colleges are all about. You should not expect to find a matchmaker among all those people who may be contributing to your college selection process. You may think that your independent counselor, high school guidance counselor, older brother, or parents are going to do the matchmaking job by coming up with the perfect fit for you. Or you may think that, even though you disagree with them, you should follow their advice because they are older and wiser. But it is you who must do the work. If you do not do it yourself, you may end up satisfying other people's wishes or ideas without satisfying your own. Your independent counselor, high school guidance counselor, big brother, and mom are all likely to read you and understand some of your needs well—so you should certainly listen to what they have to say. But be sure that you are the final judge of what schools fit your needs, goals, and lifestyle concerns.

LET GO OF FALSE IMAGES

There are many ways to go about starting your investigation of the colleges themselves. No matter what process you choose, you should first do one thing: Try as best you can to let go of all the unsubstantiated images and ideas you have in your mind about certain colleges. This is not to say that everything you read in books, see in movies, and hear through the media or the rumor mill is false—even far-fetched rumors are often based upon some sliver of reality. For example, you might have heard that Princeton is full of snooty rich kids and is no place for a person, such as yourself, from a low-income background. In fact, Princeton attracts more low-income and disadvantaged students than most schools because of its generous financial aid budget. There was certainly a time when only the wealthy elite attended Princeton. But you should not rely on images from F. Scott Fitzgerald's *This Side of Paradise* for a realistic picture of Princeton at the turn of the millennium.

Start by giving every college a fair chance. If you do not assign a neutral position to all schools before examining them for yourself, you may prevent yourself from considering a school that could be ideal for you—just because your mother heard from her friend who heard from her daughter's piano teacher who heard from one of his students whose cousin went to the school that it is an awful place for anyone who does not passionately love football. Likewise, do not let Hollywood or the media shape your view of what colleges are like. Make informed decisions about schools based on your own research and observation rather than on hearsay or impressions you get from the television or movie screen.

RESEARCH THE SCHOOLS

First you should develop knowledge about colleges in general. You can do so by reading about the characteristics of colleges beginning on page 53; spending a few hours in your high school guidance counselor's office looking through college viewbooks and other materials; perusing college Web sites; or reading several publications devoted solely to the idea of how to choose colleges. If you are a top student whose grades and scores place you in the running for admission to the best colleges, then it is smartest to limit your explorations to the top 50 or 100 schools (see Appendix I for help in using college rankings), whether they be large public universities, national private universities such as the Ivy League institutions, or small private colleges.

You should be able to generate a list of about 20 preliminary schools that interest you for one reason or another. This does not mean that you have to look seriously at each one—but if you cannot come up with a large number of schools that interest you based on your initial searches, you may be confining or limiting yourself unnecessarily. Now you need to begin to investigate the schools more closely:

1. Look at the information contained in guidebooks to colleges. You should have at least one of these at home for quick reference. *The Fiske Guide to Colleges* (Times Books, updated each year) is a good one to have on hand. These kinds of reference books should help you narrow down your most important criteria.

2. Get information from the schools themselves. Call, write, or E-mail each school to get its brochure, course catalog, and application materials. Here you can discover basic information about a college, such as the composition of its incoming class (by ethnicity, geographic origin, SAT scores, high school class rank, etc.), the majors and special programs it offers, or its graduation requirements.

3. Visit college Web sites. Instead of remaining sheltered within the admissions pages, jump around to find course offerings, look at the student newspaper, or become a participant in chat rooms for student groups. By perusing a school's Web pages, you can tune in to the pulse of the campus and all it has to offer. You can also subscribe to a college's newspaper, another good way of learning as much as possible about a school.

4. Learn when you can meet the school's traveling representatives. Most schools travel to college forums, gatherings held in cities around the country to introduce high schoolers to a variety of colleges. The colleges set up booths and give out information about their programs. You can meet representatives from the schools at these affairs, although they are often too crowded to get any decent conversation going. Colleges also send their representatives to individual schools around the country. These information sessions are often less hurried than are the larger forums, thereby providing the opportunity to question representatives and get more detailed feedback.

5. Talk with alumni of each school. Schools are generally glad to give you names of alumni in your area who have volunteered to discuss their colleges with prospective applicants. Recent alumni in particular can be good sources of information about the college's current atmosphere, strengths (and weaknesses, if they are willing to be honest), and the types of students who are happiest there. Remember that alumni referred to you by the

admissions office are always ardent supporters of the school. They will provide you with one perspective, and it may be biased—after all, they see it as their job to convince prospective applicants of the greatness of their school. Still, alumni can be a source of valuable opinions and information—just remember that what they say represents only one perspective among many and is not the final word on a college.

6. Visit the schools. Visiting a school is an important part of your research. You should not visit only your top "stretch" schools; becoming comfortable with the atmospheres at your "possible" and "safety" schools is just as important. (See the next section for a discussion of these three types of schools.) Visiting a school allows you to tap into its pulse in a way no other method of investigation can. See Appendix II for more detailed information on how to conduct campus visits.

CREATING YOUR FINAL LIST OF TARGET SCHOOLS

By this time, you should have a pretty good impression of what your original 20 or so colleges are all about. Now it is time to narrow down your list, so that you can come up with approximately eight final target colleges. Sometimes fewer is fine; sometimes more is fine, too—it all depends upon how certain you are of what you want and how far you are reaching in terms of your chances for admission at each. You should spread your applications to schools representing a range of selectivity. Thus, your final list should probably include

- Three to four stretches,
- Two to three possibles, and
- Two to three safeties.

A stretch (sometimes referred to as a reach) is a school at which acceptance is possible but not at all certain. A possible is a school at which you have a better than 50% chance of being accepted. A safety is a school at which you are almost certain to be admitted.

The best way to determine the likelihood of your gaining admittance to a particular college is to look at the statistics on its most recently admitted freshman class. Look at GPA figures, rank-in-class figures, and standardized test scores—looking at the average, median, or range of numbers for each—and then compare yourself with those in the freshman class. Remember that the very best schools deny far more applicants possessing their average grades and scores than they admit. If your credentials place you among the college's averages for admitted students, you will probably have to market yourself exceptionally well or possess something valuable aside from academics—a special talent or athletic skill, for example—in order to get in. If your grades and scores place you below the average matriculated candidate, then the school is a stretch for you. If your grades and scores place you at or above the middle of the freshman class, then the school is likely to rank as a possible. If your grades and scores place you in the top quarter or so of the most recently entered class, then this college is probably a safety.

Adjust your determination up or down a notch if you have taken a particularly challenging or particularly unchallenging courseload. For example, if your grades and scores place you above the average student but they have been achieved in easy classes (especially if your school offers Advanced Placement [AP] and honors classes, but you have generally opted not to take them), you cannot assume you will easily be admitted because other candidates with lesser grades will likely be favored over you. Similarly, if you have very stellar or very limited extracurricular involvements or accomplishments, you will want to adjust your determination of the likelihood of your acceptance at a college up or down a notch.

The likelihood of your being accepted at a given school is generally improved if one or more of several factors are working for you. If one or more of the following statements are true of your relationship with a certain college, then you can assume that your chance of being admitted is somewhat better than would be indicated based on scores and academics alone:

- You are an athlete being recruited by a coach at the college.
- You are a legacy applicant (whose mother, father, or other relative attended the school).
- You are a "development" case, meaning that a prominent or wealthy relative of yours has offered the college significant resources or funding if you attend the school.
- You fall within the college's mid to upper range of average admitted candidates *and* will apply Early Decision.

The spread in applications (among stretches, possibles, and safeties) will prevent several terrible things from happening. It will prevent you from missing a special opportunity, which might happen if you were to refrain from applying to any stretches. Refraining from applying to stretches might keep you from attending the best college possible. (You should always remember, however, that the most competitive school is not always the best one for you.) Spreading out your applications will also prevent you from not going to college at all, which could happen if you do not apply to some safeties.

It is acceptable to have as few as one stretch as long as you are not setting your sights on attending that one school. In other words, if your several top picks happen to be colleges at which you are likely to be accepted, then do not worry about not having any stretches on your list. You should, however, worry if you do not have at least two safeties and at least one possible. You need to apply to at least two safety schools that you would be happy to attend. They should not be schools you merely throw onto your list to satisfy the demands of this book or your guidance counselor at school. Your safety choices require at least as much (if not more) thought as your stretches and possibles required. There is a strong possibility that you might attend one of your safeties, so you should visit them and examine them with as much enthusiasm as you did your top picks. You should also remember to continue to picture yourself at your safety schools, just as you might daydream about stepping into your top-choice school next fall.

AVOID THE USUAL PITFALLS WHEN MAKING
YOUR LIST OF TARGET SCHOOLS

1. Start the process early. You do not want to feel so rushed that you start eliminating schools because of time constraints or fail to investigate colleges thoroughly.

2. Do not take the rankings too seriously. They are no better than rough proxies for a school's quality and reputation. They also do not help you to determine which colleges are the best fits for you based on an analysis of yourself and your needs. (See Appendix I for more advice.)

3. Be aware that your interests may well change as you go through the search process and learn more about what different colleges are like. Recall the discussion on page 36 about the iterative nature of the college selection process.

4. Be aware that your academic interests may change during college. You should not pick a college based solely on its strong history department, for example. Even if you do stick with history, all the top colleges have strong offerings in each area, so there is no need to pick a school on this criterion alone if the school's other aspects do not meet your needs.

5. Do not be swayed by spiffy college brochures or fancy Web sites. The quality of a school is not directly related to its admissions materials. After a while, you will begin to see that they all look more or less the same anyway.

6. Do not be swayed by one particularly warm or cold admissions officer, alum, or tour guide. Colleges are full of different personalities, and one person should not determine your ideas about an entire campus population.

APPLYING TO UNIVERSITIES WITH MULTIPLE SCHOOLS

Many universities have a whole set of undergraduate schools, some of which are much easier to get into than are their sister schools. At Cornell, for instance, only a small minority of those entering the Hotel Administration School score 700s on their SAT Is, unlike those entering the Engineering School. This does not mean, however, that you should try to get into the Hotel School if you intend to be an engineer! (Note, too, that universities permit you to apply to only one program in a given year.) It is generally not easy to transfer from one school to another, especially if the programs are as unrelated as are these two. It is also notoriously difficult to perform well in a program that does not interest you, and transfer evaluations are typically based largely upon your college academic performance.

The strategy of trying to get into a prestigious university via a back-door needs to be considered in light of your other options. Only if you are unlikely to be admitted to a university roughly comparable in reputation (and interest to you) should you even consider the back-door approach. Even then, you should probably consider this route only if you intend to pursue a subject that is offered in different versions in more than one school at a given university. (The two most obvious areas are economics, which may be on offer in a liberal arts school and a business school, and languages, which may be available in a liberal arts school and in a foreign service or diplomacy school.)

For each university and program, consider the following factors before deciding to try to get your foot in the door at a university by applying to one of its less selective programs:

➤ The ease of getting into each program (for you in particular, given your profile)

➤ The likelihood of truly enjoying each program

➤ The closeness of each program to your current interests

➤ The ease of taking a substantial number of courses in other schools or programs

➤ The number of required courses that you might otherwise prefer to avoid

➤ The extent to which a degree in this field will help or hinder your pursuit of your ultimate career goals

➤ The ease of transferring to your chosen program

➤ The likelihood of being able to get grades good enough to help you transfer.

CHARACTERISTICS TO CONSIDER WHEN EVALUATING COLLEGES

There are whole books devoted solely to helping prospective college students identify the characteristics that make an educational institution a good fit for them. The main goal of this book is to help you prepare your application and get into those ideal colleges once you identify them. We believe, however, that it is critical that students spend a significant amount of time and energy thinking about their college choices and selecting institutions that are best for them. We aim to help prospective college students gain acceptance to the "best" colleges possible, but we hope that those colleges are best not only in an objective or generic sense, but also in a way appropriate to the needs of the individual student. Hence, the rest of this chapter discusses (in as much detail as is appropriate, given the scope of this book) the various characteristics to examine when choosing target colleges.

Some of the basic characteristics you will want to consider when determining what kind of colleges you should be looking at include size, location and climate, proximity to urban or rural resources, safety issues, public versus private, personality (political bent, social tendencies, etc.), and academic and extracurricular strengths. Some of the categories we mention here are also discussed and dissected in Appendix I. Again, be sure to examine each school carefully. The following discussions offer general ideas about certain kinds of institutions, but these categories are not absolutes. You might find that a particular school does not act as you would expect it to according to a certain characteristic. A rural school nowhere near a big urban center might have a wonderfully diverse and international population, despite one's expectations of homogeneity and provincialism given the school's location. Use the material here as a guideline, but do your own detective work for each school you are interested in.

SIZE

One of the most basic decisions you should make concerns the size of the institution you want to attend. Colleges range in size from a few hundred students at the smallest schools to nearly 50,000 at the largest universities. Generalities relating to an institution's size are often accurate, but be sure to examine each school yourself to gain a complete picture of how its size affects academic and social dynamics. Be warned against taking a simplistic view of large versus small.

You should not automatically assume, for example, that a large university will not give you any feelings of intimacy whereas a small school will provide a super-friendly environment. On the contrary, some large schools do everything they can to make their students feel more at ease, for example, by doing things such as grouping them in small living clusters so that students get to know a small segment of the population well and do not feel lost among the masses. Similarly, some small schools may not take special precautions to make their students feel at home, thus making social adjustments harder than they would be at a larger school.

LARGE UNIVERSITIES

Larger schools often project an abundance of perceived school spirit to the outside world because they tend to be well-known institutions with popular sports teams. But school spirit does not always equal a feeling of community within the campus itself. It is more difficult for a school with a large population to foster the same intimacy, common identity, and sense of community that a smaller school often does. The size of a larger university makes it possible to remain anonymous if that is what you desire. It also offers you the possibility of running into new people at every juncture in your four-year journey. If you find that you need a wealth of social opportunities to keep from becoming bored, a larger school is probably for you.

Large schools tend to be universities with a lot of graduate students. Thus, despite an impressive roster of senior faculty, a university may offer poor or suboptimal quality in terms of undergraduate level teaching, because the graduate students do a large portion of it. At some universities, graduate students tend to teach the introductory courses whereas at others they tend to teach the smaller discussion and seminar classes. Be sure to find out at all target schools who does the teaching in all fields of interest to you.

Large schools tend to offer more courses and majors from which to choose. The breadth of options is usually better at a larger university than it is at a small liberal arts college. If you know that you are going to major in something with a very narrow specialization (such as ocean engineering or Slavic literature), you will probably want to look at larger schools to find what you need because small colleges might not offer the same range of courses. But sometimes the size and structure of a university can prevent students from enjoying the breadth of options. Courses listed in the university's catalog may not be open to all students. At many large universities, access to certain classes is, for example, limited to those in the appropriate major. Access to certain classes, professors, and activities can also be constrained at larger institutions because students have to fight for limited space.

Similarly, bigger schools can offer you less and more all at the same time in terms of extracurricular activities. A larger student population generally requires more outlets and organizations than does a smaller student body; a larger number of students and their individual interests also encourage breadth in the kinds of activities offered. Because there are, however, so many students on a big university campus, it might be more difficult to earn a space on a sports team or to become the editor-in-chief of the newspaper there.

You have to be a self-starter to fare well at a large school. You have to be ready to fight for professors' attention, keep yourself on track in classes where you might not get much individualized help, and stick yourself out socially rather than waiting for opportunities to come to you. An active personality is key to survival at a large university: Passive or lazy students tend to get lost academically and socially at a big school.

SMALL COLLEGES

Small schools usually foster intimacy and a solid sense of community. Williams College may not project an image of special vitality and school spirit to the outside world because of its tiny size and stance as an NCAA Division III school—but if you walk onto campus and talk to a few students, their passion for the school and sense of common identity is palpable. At a school of only several thousand students you are likely to recognize most faces in your class by the time you graduate. If you thrive on intense relationships with a small number of people rather than on the breadth of your social sphere, you will do fine at a small school. On the flip side of the intimacy equation, the tight nature of a small school can mean that your business is everyone else's business. If you need to be able to hold a degree of privacy in your life, an especially intimate collegiate atmosphere might frustrate or discomfort you. Similarly, if you are constantly searching for new hands to shake, you might feel stunted or confined—that your social options remain static—if you attend a smaller school.

The quality of teaching and caliber of faculty with whom undergraduate students have ongoing contact are often better at smaller schools, especially those schools without graduate programs. At a small college with no graduate facilities, you will generally have plenty of contact with professors and faculty because they teach their own classes rather than relying on graduate assistants to do the work for them. Most of the big cheeses at smaller colleges actually teach courses—even small discussion-style classes—and keep regular office hours so that you can seek their wisdom or advice on a regular basis. Similarly, at a small school you will usually have fewer large lecture classes and more intimate classroom settings. You will not often be able to get away with hiding when you have not completed your assignments. At the same time, you will not have to aggressively jockey for attention or time with a professor.

Smaller private colleges usually offer fewer courses than public universities. The range of offerings at a small college might not match that of a public institution in the same city. Yet at the same time, small schools usually offer better access to classes for all students. Students at small schools rarely find themselves "stuck" in classes they do not want to take for lack of better options or because they are unable to secure a spot in a class of interest.

Smaller schools can also allow students to get more involved in activities—especially those in which they are novices or are not especially experienced—because competition for a place in an organization or group is not so fierce. Activities themselves, however, may be limited. A smaller campus population may not feature enough interested parties to put together a mime troupe or a classic Indian dance ensemble. A smaller campus may have two a capella singing groups rather than the ten at a bigger university.

PUBLIC VERSUS PRIVATE

Whether an institution is public and maintained by the state government or private and independently operated often shapes its character and the quality of its facilities.

PUBLIC INSTITUTIONS

Public universities were originally founded to educate state citizens and are subsidized by taxpayers' money. They are thus subject to state political currents, such as the Proposition 209 legislation in California, which banned affirmative action from admissions on state campuses. Furthermore, public institutions must obey certain state protocols, thus subjecting all campus decisions to a lot of red tape. Dealing with the bureaucracy at a state institution can be extremely difficult. For example, getting a requirement waived at a state institution may require not only the college registrar's approval, but also signatures from the entire board of regents and other state officials. It can take months (maybe even years) to get responses from state institutions, whereas the same problem at a private college might be handled by one person within a matter of days.

Public universities have far lower tuitions than do private schools, especially for state residents. Prospective college students should realize that along with low tuitions must come somewhat lower expectations. At some public institutions, you all too often get what you pay for. In other words, some of the facilities and resources at public universities do not always equal those at their private counterparts. Libraries may have fewer books (or not enough books to service the larger student population), technology and computing services may be of less than optimal quality, gyms and playing fields may not be kept up as well as expected, and clubs may not receive as much institutional support. This is, of course, not always true of resources at public institutions. The University of California at Berkeley, for example, has a superb gym with state-of-the-art equipment and a healthy offering of fitness classes, more impressive than athletic facilities at many private institutions.

Public institutions tend to have more breadth in terms of course offerings, as well as preprofessional programs and honors programs for undergraduates. Because public schools service a wider and more academically diverse group of people, they have more to offer. Because of the large size of these schools, though, classes are more difficult to get into than they are at smaller private schools. At many public universities, certain classes are limited to students in the appropriate major.

Public universities also do not attract the same caliber of students that top private schools do. Even the flagship state universities—which, of course, attract some stellar students—do not across the board boast the high-quality students that the very top private colleges do. Compare, for example (see the accompanying box), the ranges of SAT scores for the middle half of the freshman class (the scores achieved by those in the twenty-fifth to seventy-fifth percentiles) at the very best flagship public institutions against those at some of the top private schools. The range of the middle half of the class is significantly lower at the best public universities than it is at the top private schools.

As a result, most solid public institutions command respect within the state, but not as much clout outside of the immediate area. Only the top flagship institutions, such as the University of Michigan or the University of California at Berkeley, also command respect outside of the state. Still, even the very best public universities do not inspire the same kind of awe or command the same prestige that the top private colleges often do.

Public schools also do not feature the same wealth of geographic diversity that private colleges do. After all, public institutions are constrained by the need to choose most applicants from within their own states.

SAT RANGE OF THE MIDDLE HALF OF INCOMING CLASSES AT PUBLIC FLAGSHIP UNIVERSITIES VERSUS PRIVATE COLLEGES

SOME TOP PUBLIC INSTITUTIONS

The University of California, Berkeley (580–710 V; 620–730 M)
The University of Virginia (590–700 V; 610–710 M)
The University of Michigan, Ann Arbor (560–660 V; 590–700 M)
The University of Wisconsin, Madison (520–650 V; 550–670 M)

SOME TOP PRIVATE INSTITUTIONS

Harvard University (700–790 V; 690–790 M)
Princeton University (670–770 V; 680–780 M)
Dartmouth College (660–760 V; 680–760 M)
Amherst College (660–750 V; 670–740 M)

PRIVATE INSTITUTIONS

Private schools, on the other hand, tend to be everything that public institutions are not. They are governed by their own internal politics, like any institution, and not by state political currents. Their trustees and administrators have free reign to make changes and institute their own rules. The bureaucracy at private schools is less cumbersome than it is at public universities, so that students and faculty have much more power to force change upon the school or move the college in a new direction.

Private schools charge high tuitions. (Note, however, that the top private colleges have very healthy need-based aid programs to cover nearly all the need of admitted students.) At most private colleges, students get what they pay for. The top private colleges maintain top-notch facilities: Their libraries are impressive, their computing centers are excellent and offer free laser printing, academic buildings and dormitories are well maintained, and organizations are subsidized so that their members can travel for special events and make necessary purchases.

Smaller private colleges usually offer fewer courses than public colleges. The range of offerings at most private colleges may not match that of a public institution nearby. Students at private colleges generally have better access to all courses, though, because private schools tend to be smaller. Private institutions also generally do not offer honors programs or preprofessional undergraduate majors, such as business, although these omissions have more to do with educational mission and philosophy than they do with the public or private designation of the school.

Private colleges can admit whomever they choose. Thus, student populations tend to be diverse in every way: ethnicity, socioeconomic background, geographical origins, personal and family backgrounds. You will not have to fear that you will end up sharing a room with two other people from your home state at one of the top private schools. It is instead likely that you will come into contact with the widest range possible of students if you attend one of the top private colleges.

EDUCATIONAL MISSION AND PHILOSOPHY

All educational institutions have their own mission and philosophy about the purposes and goals of higher education. (For a more in-depth discussion of educational philosophy and how it affects many of the top schools in their admissions processes, turn to pages 158 through 160 in Chapter 5.) Philosophical concerns dictate the manner in which each institution chooses to educate its students. Some schools believe strongly that every student should be educated in the classics, and thus require all students to take courses in the "Great Books" or ancient civilizations. Some schools think that every student should know something about the developing world, and thus require everyone to study a third-world culture. Most colleges have a foreign language requirement, so that every graduate has had at least minimal exposure to a language other than English. Many schools are heavily influenced by their religious roots, requiring everyone who receives a B.A. to have taken at least one theology course.

The most crucial and basic of all of the educational philosophies is an institution's stand on the relationship between education and future goals (i.e., whether higher education should direct a student toward one specific future career or merely provide a student with a strong foundation upon which to build any future career he or she chooses). Some universities allow undergraduates to follow a preprofessional track, focusing nearly exclusively on business, architecture, communications, nursing, engineering, or another career-related field; other colleges require that every student, no matter what his or her major, follow a broad liberal arts curriculum.

PREPROFESSIONAL DEGREES

Public universities and some larger private universities offer preprofessional bachelor's degrees for undergraduates. At many of these universities, prospective students apply to a particular college within the university to follow a specialized degree, in business or engineering, for example. Students are not required to take the broad range of classes that students of liberal arts colleges must finish in order to graduate. Instead, they take a curriculum heavy in courses of direct relevance to their prospective careers. Applying to a particular non–liberal arts school means that as a high schooler you must be certain about what you want to do in your career, because the classes you will take in college may well have real value for only one type of future.

LIBERAL ARTS CURRICULUMS

At liberal arts colleges, in contrast, there are generally no preprofessional or specialized programs offered whatsoever (with the exception of classes that constitute premedical requirements, but these are taken as part of the liberal arts curriculum). The philosophy at these schools is that a liberal arts education teaches students how to think, read critically, analyze, reason, process complex ideas, and present opinions and facts through oral and written communication skills. These advanced skills, in turn, give students the strong intellectual foundation that will allow them to do anything they wish in the future, whether it be pursuing a job in finance or becoming a journalist. The benefit of the liberal arts curriculum is that it is valuable no matter what the future holds. Students attending liberal arts colleges do not have to decide at the age of 18 what they want to do in later life and can change careers many times in life, knowing that what they learned in college will be entirely relevant and valuable in all situations.

ACADEMIC STRENGTHS

Whether you want to follow a preprofessional or a liberal arts degree, if you have any inkling of what subjects are of interest to you, be sure to investigate the academic strengths of various colleges to be sure you will be getting the best quality possible in your given field.

DEPARTMENTAL STRENGTHS

Even the very best colleges have some departments that are weaker than others. You should know what the reputation of a department is before signing on to a college if you know what your major or fields of study will be. Balancing the quality of a department (assuming you know exactly what you will do in college) with the quality of a school overall is a tricky task. As an undergraduate, you do not want to sacrifice too much in terms of overall quality or reputation in order to have access to a better physics or English department—your future usually depends much more on the name of the college you attend and your overall performance there than it does on the education you receive in one area.

It is difficult to measure the strength of an academic department in terms of the education it provides to undergraduates—there is no surefire or accurate way to grade each department in a college. Considering several factors in tandem, however, can serve as the best possible proxy for such a grade of quality. First, if the college has a graduate program in the field, do some research to find out how strong it is. Generally speaking, the stronger the graduate program in a field, the stronger the undergraduate program is as well. Then find out about the undergraduate classes offered in the field. Examine what teaching structures are used as well as how big the classes are. How many classes with over 100 students are there? What about classes with fewer than 10 or 20 students? The greater the number of small classes, the better the education is likely to be. Are there opportunities to take small seminars and do independent studies? Look at the student–faculty ratios for all classes taught in the department. Look at the breadth of classes offered, as well as the depth that upper-level seminars reach. Get your hands on an "unofficial" student-published guide to the school. Such guides, often published by the student assembly or student union on campus, usually feature a section on academics in which polled students give candid opinions about classes and faculty members. The books usually give a good clue to the strongest departments and teachers on campus.

MAJOR AND GRADUATION REQUIREMENTS

You should also research the academic requirements at each school so that you are clear about what is necessary to graduate. At some schools, for instance, it is very difficult to double major because each major requires that nearly half of one's classes be devoted to it. For someone who is certain she wants to double major in economics and mathematics, such strict major requirements at one school might be a reason to consider different schools, where doing the same double major would be feasible because fewer credits are required for each.

Some schools, such as Dartmouth, offer no minors. At some colleges, some fields require that all candidates majoring in those areas write a thesis in order to graduate. Other schools, such as Princeton, require that all seniors in all fields write a thesis in order to graduate. Be aware what core curriculum, general distribution, and other graduation requirements exist at each of your target schools so that you can choose a college that best matches your own academic desires and needs.

SPECIAL PROGRAMS

Some colleges have special programs or academic features that are of great advantage to the right applicants. Brown and Northwestern, for example, both offer prestigious and competitive medical programs (Brown's is eight years, Northwestern's is seven years) in which students applying for freshman admission are also admitted unconditionally to the medical school. This is a great boon for strong high school students who know with certainty that they want to attend medical school and are interested in getting a jump start on their careers. Similarly, many of the public universities offer honors programs in which admitted students get special and exclusive educational benefits to help them get ahead in their careers even before graduating from college. Honors program benefits often include independent study opportunities, research opportunities, internship opportunities, contact with top tenured professors, attendance at guest lecture series, and financial rewards. Be sure to inquire at all colleges that interest you about special opportunities in your fields of choice, and read all college materials closely to learn about academic opportunities offered.

NONACADEMIC STRENGTHS

Just as each college boasts particular strengths in academic fields, each school also possesses certain nonacademic strengths. Some schools are known for the power of their women's ice hockey teams, others for their wonderful theater productions, others for their provocative newspapers or literary magazines, still others for their talented stand-up comedy acts. If you have a special hobby or activity you want to pursue further during college, be sure to find out about the existence of such an organization on target college campuses.

LOCATION

CLIMATE AND WEATHER

Do not underestimate the influence of geography on a campus's desirability or fit with your needs. The location of a college obviously dictates the climate and weather patterns that prevail there. If you are someone who is affected mildly or seriously by weather and climate, you should definitely make location a primary consideration when choosing colleges. Consider whether you want to live in a place—most likely in the Northeast or Midwest—with four distinct (and perhaps severe) seasons. If you love winter weather, you might want to be far north so that you can enjoy the cold and snow for longer periods of time each year. Or perhaps a mild climate with little seasonal change is what you most desire, making colleges on the West Coast particularly attractive to you. If you are strongly partial to warmth and sunshine (and suffer swings in mood and productivity when you lack access to the sun's rays), consider the weather patterns in the locations of your target colleges before setting your heart on any of them. Four years is a long time to spend in longjohns if you hate the cold.

LOCAL CULTURE

Location also affects an institution's cultural values, which you should take into account in your investigations. Be well aware before making your college visits that there are distinct regional differences in the United States. Plan to look into these differences and how they affect campus life during your travels.

The prevailing stereotypes of people in each region are not entirely accurate, although a visit to each area of the country will most likely assure you that there is some truth to them. The Northeast tends to have an intense atmosphere, often featuring people who are competitive with others and unafraid to demonstrate anger or frustration in public. The Midwest is friendlier, and people there tend to be more neighborly and helpful. In the South, people can be polite to a fault and generally refrain from displaying strong emotions in public. The West Coast tends to be relatively "laid back"; emotions and situations are rarely volatile. Time moves much more slowly in the South (and usually in the West as well) than it does in the Northeast. You should be sure that you can handle the cultural differences between North and South if you plan to go from your Boston high school to college at the University of Virginia, Duke, or Vanderbilt. It is likely that the academic atmosphere will be more relaxed, the people will be more homogeneous and conservative in their views, and students might dress up on Saturdays to attend football games. If you are not anxious to fall into a culture of this sort, you will want to rethink your college choices.

Remember, as always, to keep an open mind when starting the process of looking at schools in different areas of the country. Do not automatically resort to a "nothing west of the Mississippi" stance if you have never even been west of the Mississippi to judge for yourself what it is like! Begin your college search with an adventurous spirit until you examine issues on your own to determine what is right and wrong for you.

PROXIMITY TO URBAN OR RURAL RESOURCES

Along with thinking about a school's general geographic location, you must also consider how a college is shaped by its immediate surroundings. A college located in an inner city will feel a lot different from one located in the mountains, two hours away from the nearest urban center. Apart from how an urban or rural location shapes a school's personality and determines the kinds of students it attracts, location also influences the realities of daily life on a campus. There are top-notch colleges located in urban areas (University of Pennsylvania, University of Chicago, Columbia), semiurban areas (Berkeley, Harvard), suburban areas (Northwestern, Wellesley), and rural areas (Bowdoin, Dartmouth, Middlebury). Each school is molded (both positively and negatively) by its civic and natural surroundings.

Urban and Semiurban Locations

A college in an urban center is likely to be throbbing with vitality. Urban areas— and usually semiurban areas as well—offer students a wealth of social and cultural opportunities and the chance to escape the confines of the campus environment. Urban areas also offer a range of internship and work opportunities for students embarking on career discovery. Similarly, a host of urban problems can inspire the growth of a diverse range of community service outlets.

It is difficult to feel stifled in a large city, where the social sphere may start within the campus walls but inevitably extends far into the larger urban outpost. Students at city universities and semiurban schools have more and better cultural venues—such as theater, performing arts, or museums—to enjoy, more restaurants to choose from, and more opportunities to meet people outside the school environment. But often the energy on a city campus feels a bit diffused, because the attention is focused not only on campus life but also on what goes on outside.

Going to college in a city or in a semiurban area also affects one's practical living situation. If you are a fashion hound, you will be happier with easy access to Boston's Newbury Street than you would be living three hours away from shopping of equal caliber. It is difficult to maintain a position at the peak of fashionability when most of your shopping takes place in the far reaches of Vermont. Generally speaking, urban areas offer more access to all goods, whether they be clothes, athletic equipment, furniture, or ethnic foods.

Suburban Locations

A suburban campus may have the best of both worlds—urban and rural— because it is located somewhere in between. At the same time, however, a suburban school can feel somewhat lacking in personality. Just as a suburb itself can feel rather characterless and nondescript because of its attempt to straddle itself halfway between an urban center and an attractive natural landscape, suburban universities can feel this way, too. If you are comfortable with this half-full, half-empty personality, though, a suburban campus can be a perfect answer to finding proximity to diverse cultural outlets along with adequate access to the beauty of the outdoors.

RURAL LOCATIONS

Rural schools often evoke a strong sense of community among their students and faculty because of their positions as oases of intellectual and cultural vibrations. The beauty of rural campuses is what first attracts many students. Access to the great outdoors and all that one can do in it—hiking, canoeing, skiing, camping, even simply running in a peaceful setting—is often what makes the final case for attending a school far away from an urban center. Taking advantage of all that a rural setting offers can be what makes a student's collegiate life so special—especially for those who end up spending the rest of their lives sweating it out in a skyscraper on Wall Street.

Students should be warned, however, that there are also limits to life in a country setting. College towns often have only a handful of restaurants, one pharmacy, one grocery store, and one movie theater. Access to clothes and serious shopping is often limited, and cultural opportunities may be few and far between as well. This is not true in all rural towns, of course. Hanover, New Hampshire, for example, boasts cultural venues that surpass those of many cities because of the special programming at Dartmouth's Hopkins Center—which brings all sorts of entertainment, from the American Ballet Theatre to African drumming ensembles, to the woods of New Hampshire on a regular basis.

SAFETY ISSUES

IN URBAN AND SEMIURBAN LOCATIONS

Safety is a concern that is closely related to location. At urban universities, safety tends to be more of a concern than it is at schools that are not located in the midst of a metropolitan area. These days, urban campuses (and many nonurban campuses as well) are patrolled well, operate safety escort services for students who need to get across campus at night, and maintain secure dormitories for living. Columbia is one example of an urban university that takes its security very seriously and maintains a very safe environment in the midst of upper Manhattan. Still, safety is more of an issue at urban universities than it is at suburban or rural campuses. If you have never lived near an inner city, you should spend a few days learning what life is like on an urban campus (you will have to learn to lock your doors, keep your purse zipped and gripped tightly, and take taxis rather than walking alone at night) before deciding to attend a city school.

IN SUBURBAN AND RURAL LOCATIONS

Rural and suburban schools are often safer than city schools because of their sheer distance from most security risks. However, less attention to and awareness of security issues (from both students and campus administrations) can result in mishaps. Students should not be fooled into thinking that rural and suburban campuses are 100% safe and risk-free, although these kinds of schools tend to be safer than urban universities. Be sure to ask about safety concerns at all schools you visit.

COST OF LIVING

Cost of living is also closely related to location. Do not underestimate the degree to which the cost of living varies from one location to another across the United States. Visit grocery stores, look at rental and real estate sections in newspapers, and pass by some gas stations near the colleges you visit—a little of your own detective work will go a long way in giving you a sense of how prices differ from place to place.

IN URBAN, SEMIURBAN, AND SUBURBAN LOCATIONS (ESPECIALLY ON EITHER COAST)

Cities, semiurban, and many suburban areas—especially those located on the East and West Coasts—tend to be more expensive than small towns or rural areas. Rents are more expensive, gas is more expensive, groceries are more expensive— even movies are more expensive in large and cosmopolitan areas near big cities.

IN RURAL LOCATIONS (AND SOME NONCOASTAL AREAS)

In rural areas, as well as many noncoastal areas (whether they be characterized as urban or rural in nature), the cost of living is generally lower. You can save hundreds of dollars a month on rent if you attend college in Maine rather than in the greater San Francisco area, for example.

SOCIAL LIFE CONDUCTED ON OR OFF CAMPUS

IN URBAN OR SEMIURBAN LOCATIONS

A campus's location also has an impact on how social activities are conducted. At some schools, a lot of socializing takes place off the college property, and often in an environment far removed from the feel of the college setting. At urban and semiurban colleges, this is usually the case. Colleges located in urban or metropolitan areas are surrounded by restaurants, bars, night clubs, civic centers, concert halls, museums, sporting arenas, and other facilities common to large population centers. Students thus have a wealth of options available to them when planning weekend or evening entertainment. When not constrained to a campus's limited social venues, students tend to seek after-hours livelihood elsewhere, partially because it helps them to forget the stress associated with the campus, and partially because off-campus settings are simply more abundant and more glamorous. Some prospective college students relish such opportunities to socialize in a variety of locations, thus making urban or semiurban colleges more attractive options for them. Other students, however, find the lack of campus identity and spirit unnerving and would rather attend a college where few off-campus activities interfere with the pulse of campus life.

In Suburban or Rural Locations

At other schools, nearly all social activities take place on or near campus. At rural and suburban schools, students tend always to congregate and party on campus because there are not many off-campus facilities for holding social events. Some prospective college students find that they prefer to attend such a college, where there is an intimacy and a sense of community fostered through students' remaining on campus as much as possible. Other students feel bored or restrained when not presented with plenty of options and opportunities to get away from the tiny hub of campus life.

OPPORTUNITIES FOR EMPLOYMENT

Many students setting off for college—especially those who are not on financial aid or who do not need to work for wages during college—forget that higher education often becomes most valuable when accompanied by work experience. In order to best prepare for a successful life after college, many students find that they want or need to acquire serious work experience of a career-related nature while in school. Some students are satisfied doing so during summer vacations, when they are mobile and can go elsewhere to work; other students like or need the option of working when class is in session as well. Visiting the career services centers on college campuses can help you learn what kinds of opportunities are available locally for students on the campus.

In Urban and Semiurban Areas

In general, students attending colleges in cities and semiurban areas (such as Cambridge, Massachusetts or Palo Alto, California) have much better access to career-related (especially business- or law-related) jobs during their college years. Students at schools in urban or metropolitan areas can find a wealth of paying jobs and internships at law offices, consulting firms, banks, technology firms, museums, major nonprofit institutions, and other such employers. If you know that you intend to seek a professional career (especially in law or business) and want to work during college, this is something to consider.

In Suburban and Rural Areas

On the other hand, all areas—whether urban, suburban, or rural—offer limited opportunities to work at hospitals, schools, small businesses, local community service centers, and other such employers that are found everywhere, no matter the location. If you do not plan to attain significant work experience when class is in session, it may not matter if the area surrounding your college does not offer the same wealth of job options as would a different location.

RESIDENTIAL SYSTEM

Campus residential systems can affect how students interact with one another and the sense of community fostered on campus as well. Most colleges realize that the quality and type of housing arrangements on campus are important priorities for prospective students, so they are eager to share their housing options with you. If a school does not offer much information about housing and residential systems, definitely ask about it.

RESIDENTIAL HOUSE OR CLUSTER SYSTEMS

Some colleges, such as Harvard, place students (during either freshman or sophomore year) in residential "houses" (actually clusters of buildings that together form one residential unit) where they remain for the duration of their time in college. Students live, eat their meals, and socialize within the house, and much of campus life is focused on these small residential quarters.

These kinds of residential systems foster a unique social living experience in which students have the opportunity to get to know very well a small portion of their classmates (as well as students in other classes, too). Students at these schools tend to develop a strong identity rooted in their living clusters. Living in the same cluster with the same students year after year instills a sense of "home" and "family" that is impossible to create when students jump around from one living space to another over four years. At the same time, though, students who are not motivated to make social ties on their own may feel bogged down by these types of residential situations because they do not encourage students to make new friends during their later years of college or search out alternative social outlets. Some students may feel that the residential house system feels too cliquey, almost fraternity-like in nature, because it fosters an inward orientation rather than an outward or all-embracing orientation.

HIGHLY RESIDENTIAL CAMPUSES

At other highly residential colleges, students may not necessarily live in the same house or living cluster during all four years of college, but they are required or strongly encouraged to stay on campus throughout their education. Colleges that are highly residential in this manner often instill a real sense of community among their students, in the same way that colleges located far from urban or noncampus social resources do.

CAMPUSES WITH SIGNIFICANT OFF-CAMPUS RESIDENCY

Some colleges do not have strict campus residency policies. Some people appreciate being part of an administration that does not wish to constrain the choices of its students, instead letting them live, sleep, and eat as they please. A residency policy that is flexible regarding students' wishes to live where and how they desire can also foster a valuable sense of independence in students who choose to live off-campus. Students who have an opportunity while in college to deal with landlords and real estate companies, pay rent and utility bills, buy groceries, and cook their own meals often find themselves better prepared for "real life" than those who have never taken on such responsibility. In addition, students at colleges with lax residential systems may (if rents in the area are reasonable and the student knows how to cook for himself or herself) have more of an opportunity to save money on living expenses than those who are forced to remain in college dorms and on college meal plans throughout their entire four years. On the negative side, colleges that allow a large percentage of students to live off-campus also may feel lacking in school spirit. When students are diffused over a wide geographical area rather than concentrated within a small campus environment, they often become less connected to the school and more dependent on outside resources.

QUALITY OF LIFE ISSUES

If quality of life issues are important to you, gather facts about important aspects of living on each campus you visit. Find out about dorm living—living in a high-rise built in 1962 offers quite a different experience from living in a nineteenth-century brick building, your room adorned by a fireplace and a windowseat. Find out how many roommates you will have and whether or not there are special living options, such as smoking rooms or foreign language halls. Ask about dining options. What kinds of cafeterias are there? What are their hours of operation? Are there healthy alternatives to the usual college fare? Find out about the athletic facilities or exercise class options if those are important to you.

SOCIAL ATMOSPHERE

Find out as much as you can about the nonacademic side of things at every school you visit. The social experience you receive at college will be every bit as important as the academic experience. Spend a weekend at some of your target campuses to test out the goods. Find out if students go to fraternity parties or to off-campus events. Are there enough activities that are predominantly nonalcoholic? Do students go to cultural events together or do they head off to the bar as soon as dinner is over?

DOMINANT GREEK SYSTEMS

Colleges with strong Greek systems feel very different from those without fraternities and sororities. Schools with Greek life tend to be very cliquey, especially if the majority of students on campus belong to a house. The social life of such colleges is often dominated by Greek-sponsored parties, meaning large, loud, drunken bashes usually held in unglamorous (read "hot," "smelly," "dirty," "crowded") spots, such as the fraternity's basement. Fraternity and sorority life is attractive to some people and not attractive to others; you need to decide for yourself how much it appeals to you, or at the very least if you would mind attending a school that offers such options. Going to a school with a Greek system does not mean that you have to participate in it, but you should be aware that these are the kinds of events that many of your peers at such a college will be attending.

DOMINANT CLUB SYSTEMS

Some colleges feature exclusive clubs (called "eating clubs," "finals clubs," etc.) instead of Greek fraternities. The effect on the social life of a campus is largely the same, either way. Clubs sponsor the wild parties on campus and breed the dominance of cliques and small exclusive groups on campus. Again, some students desire to be part of such a formalized intimate group; others do not wish to be part of such a system but do not mind its existence; and yet others do not want to attend a campus that even offers exclusive clubs as a social option.

STRONG CULTURAL VENUES

At some schools, cultural entertainment is an important part of the social scene. If you would like to attend a school where most students check out a modern dance performance or attend a sculpture opening before letting loose for the evening party scene, try to catch a glimpse of the cultural events and get a sense of their dominance in the social life at each campus you visit.

ACADEMIC ENVIRONMENT

Find out about the academic environment at colleges you visit if that aspect of a school's personality is apt to influence you positively or negatively. Some students like to be in a pressure-cooker environment because it inspires them to perform well. Other students, on the contrary, dislike such an intense atmosphere because it makes them nervous and unable to relax or perform their best. Determine whether the competition at the school is cut-throat or whether students seem relatively easy-going about academics. Do premeds ruin other students' lab experiments in order to get ahead? Or do students seem cooperative and more interested in learning for learning's sake? What is the campus like during exam period? Are people bursting into tears at every desk or is there a positive energy generated by all those minds pushing forward through the last battle?

STUDENT BODY COMPOSITION

The composition of the student body is likely to influence your thoughts about a college. At each college you consider, you will want to investigate the gender balance; the number of minority, international, and out-of-state (at public institutions) students; the diversity of the population in other regards; and the degree to which the various groups on campus mix with one another.

A single-sex environment is, of course, going to feel very different from a coeducational one. If you are considering an all-women's college and have never before attended a girls' school, you should definitely visit the campus, ideally spending a weekend there. An all-women's environment is highly appropriate for some students, but not the right atmosphere for all women. You might find that the absence of a male viewpoint in some classes is a problem. Similarly, on the social scene, you may be disappointed if you sense that the focus of student life shifts to other campuses on the weekends. There are few coeducational schools where gender balance is a problem. The balance between men and women is relatively even at all of the top colleges.

If you are a minority or international student, you will want to confirm that you will feel welcome and comfortable at the school you attend. Although your status might serve you well in being admitted to the college if it attracts few students of your race, ethnicity, or citizenship, you may not feel comfortable being part of a particularly small group of students on a campus. You will want to get a good sense of how students like yourself live and learn on the campus, and whether or not they are happy and satisfied with their experience there.

No matter who you are, you likely have a good idea of how much diversity you want or need on campus. Some campuses are particularly diverse, featuring large percentages of certain American minorities or international students, whereas other campuses are much more homogeneous. International students on the leading college campuses make up as little as 2 to 3% of the population at a place like Carleton, but about 10% of the population at Cal Tech or 13% at Mount Holyoke. There are differences in the compositions of the undergraduate student bodies at the country's top schools, as you can see from those featured in the accompanying box.

Aside from looking at the numbers of various kinds of students featured in a student body, you should also closely examine relations among the various groups on a campus. At some campuses, even some that are not especially diverse in terms of numbers of minorities or international students, there is regular and frequent mixing among the various races and ethnicities. Students mix socially with those unlike themselves, interracial dating is common and accepted, and minority groups do not feel isolated. Some campuses, on the contrary, are very racially or ethnically segregated. Students nearly exclusively socialize with those of their own kind, interracial dating is uncommon or not widely accepted, and minority groups keep to themselves. This can be a problem, even at schools where the numbers paint a picture of diversity. Diversity does not benefit a student if he or she has no access to or interaction with those who are different.

STUDENT POPULATIONS AT SELECT TOP COLLEGES (CLASS OF 2002)

CARLETON COLLEGE

527 students in the Class of 2002

46% men / 54% women

47 states and 9 countries represented

17.5% American minorities

(African American, Asian American, Hispanic/Latino/Chicano, or Native American)

3% international

HARVARD UNIVERSITY

1652 students in the Class of 2002

53% men / 47% women

37% American minorities

9% African American

19% Asian American

8% Hispanic/Latino/Chicano

1% Native American

6% international

65% public school   35% private/parochial school

UNIVERSITY OF PENNSYLVANIA

2414 students in the Class of 2002

50% men / 50% women

48 states and 62 countries represented

36% American minorities

6% African American

5% Hispanic/Latino/Chicano

25% Asian American

< 1% Native American

10% international

57% public school   37% private school   6% parochial school

THE UNIVERSITY OF VIRGINIA

2908 students in the Class of 2002

47% male   53% female

66% in-state   34% out-of-state

46 states and 71 countries represented

22% American minorities

10% African American

10% Asian American

2% Hispanic/Latino/Chicano

< 1% Native American

4% international

76% public school   24% private or parochial school

WESLEYAN UNIVERSITY

721 students in the Class of 2002

47% men / 53% women

27% American minorities

11% African American

11% Asian American

6% Hispanic/Latino/Chicano

5% international

55% public school   39% private school   5% parochial school

POLITICAL PERSONALITY

Although most college campuses are predominantly moderate to liberal, you should decide for yourself if you like the feel and tempo of a university's political atmosphere. Even if you are not politically active yourself, you might find that you value an open political atmosphere in which all groups are welcome, regardless of the dominant ideology on campus.

Some campuses are particularly liberal or feature vocal radical groups that give a certain flavor to college life. At a few schools, an excessive liberal edge might mean that conservative groups are marginalized, unwelcome to address issues in their own manner. A Stalinist might be allowed a podium whereas a moderate Republican would not feel welcome to express his or her views. For some prospective students this is not a problem; for others, even those who consider themselves liberals, the squeezing out of minority ideologies might be bothersome. Other schools lean farther into the conservative realm because of particularly vocal Republican or conservative groups. This flavor, similarly, might not feel right to some students.

Check out the number of liberal and conservative political clubs and publications. What is the reaction of most students on campus to those groups or publications? Are any groups (conservatives, for example) marginalized? Is there enough political debate on campus for your needs? Are there weekly rallies for local, national, or international causes at the campus center? Do students seem to care about what goes on in the outside world? What are their positions on certain issues?

RELIGIOUS OVERTONES

At most of the top colleges, religion does not play a significant role in collegiate life. The student body at most schools represents a broad spectrum of religions. At most colleges, there is no one dominant religious group, nor are there any particularly religious overtones to campus life. If you are devoutly religious, you will want to ensure that you will feel comfortable and have access to appropriate channels of worship at any of the schools to which you apply. A Mormon, for example, might feel especially uncomfortable at particularly liberal East Coast institutions and may discover that he or she has little access to religious connections at some of these schools. If religion is a concern in your life, be sure to inquire about the existence of fellow believers and talk to others like you about their experiences at the school.

Similarly, those applying to schools with religious roots, such as Georgetown, Notre Dame, or Brandeis, should be aware that these schools are still somewhat dominated by their founding philosophies. If you are not part of the majority religious group, you will want to talk to others like yourself on campus to get a glimpse of what it is like to be a religious minority there. (Remember, though, that there may well be positive implications for applicants to these schools who are not of the majority religion. Even the schools founded upon Catholic or Jewish doctrines are interested in achieving diversity in their student populations. A non-Jewish applicant to Brandeis may be particularly attractive to its admissions board, whereas Jewish or Hindu applicants to Notre Dame stand out in comparison to the rest of the pool.)

Some schools that are not religious by nature attract large or particularly active groups of people with certain religious ties. Schools with especially dominant or cohesive religious groups may be particularly attractive to some applicants and unattractive to others. At Stanford, for example, there is an especially active "born again" Christian population, which might make the school particularly desirable to devout Christians, who feel marginalized at many of the top colleges. As another example, the Jewish populations at the Midwestern Universities of Michigan and Wisconsin have long-standing connections with the East Coast Jewish establishment, making those schools especially attractive for Jews who want to stake their careers on the East coast. On the other hand, Jews and Catholics (and others) applying to southern schools, for example, should inquire about the existence of fellow religious minorities before committing themselves to attending. The South still cultivates a predominantly Christian Protestant ethos, often a surprise to Jews and Catholics from the northern or western parts of the country.

GENDER RELATIONS

Apart from the issue of gender balance on a campus is the issue of relations between the sexes. At some campuses, gender relations are peaceful and students seem generally satisfied with the prevailing dating and relationship networks. At other colleges, especially those featuring radical feminist organizations or a male-dominated Greek system (or both), a campus can feel like a war zone rather than like a solid community that happens to feature people of two different sexes. When such animosity between the sexes extends to the greater campus, it can infect the social atmosphere there in an unpleasant way. During your visits to colleges, talk with students and observe on your own (especially in social settings or on weekend sleepovers) to find out about the gender politics on campus.

Find out what the dating scene at each college is all about, too. At many colleges, students complain that there is not a lively dating scene; instead, students get to know one another in groups rather than going out one-on-one in order to form intimate relationships. Do students seem to have meaningful relationships or just casual sexual encounters? How do they meet one another and how are dates arranged? Do the men on campus flock to a nearby women's college for fun? Find out about the dating scene for gay students if that is a concern for you. Are there enough openly gay students to ensure the chances of forming positive relationships? Is gay social life integrated into the larger social life of the community or are gays marginalized, forced to socialize within their own clusters?

Women should also inquire about the legal and safety implications of gender problems. Ask about sexual harassment, for example, if this concerns you. Safety officers might have official information, but talking to students on campus might be just as informative when it comes to finding out about women's safety issues.

PERSONAL STYLE OF THE STUDENT BODY

Look at the students you see on each campus to determine how appropriate a school is for you. The dominant styles of behavior and dress differ from school to school. Some schools attract a large number of party-hearty kids who are social, even bordering on wild. Some colleges attract quiet and reserved types, often studious and intellectual. Some campuses attract a large number of athletic types. At some schools, the lazy "grunge" look dominates whereas at other campuses, many students go so far as to dress up for class. The students on some campuses are very fashion-conscious and chic, whereas the students on another campuses seem unconcerned about appearances (or perhaps they are merely dressing to accommodate negative weather patterns or athletic priorities).

WHAT THE ADMISSIONS OFFICERS HAVE
TO SAY ABOUT CHOOSING COLLEGES

"It's very important that prospective students investigate the colleges carefully and make wise choices. We are all very different from one another. Yale, for example, is a very community-oriented place that offers a highly residential experience for undergraduates. A student would get a very different atmosphere at other kinds of schools. Candidates need to know what they are looking for."

—*Richard Shaw, Dean of Undergraduate Admissions and Financial Aid, Yale University*

"Students need to look for schools whose programs and environments match their interests, lifestyles, and goals. A school should stretch them and force them to reexamine their current thinking. Students shouldn't be swayed by the hottest college. A college should fit a student's individual needs. Students should start by looking at themselves, and then reflecting their needs against a school's offerings."

—*Richard Avitabile, Director of Admissions, New York University*

"We see kids visiting earlier and earlier each year. We joke that soon we'll have seventh graders asking us for viewbooks. It's part of the trend toward Early Decision and a general acceleration of the college search process."

—*David Borus, Dean of Admissions and Financial Aid, Vassar College*

"I went to college without even visiting the school! Today students are much more serious about choosing schools and doing their applications. People come to visit the campus a few times rather than just once, for example. Applicants are really doing their research on Brown so they know what we're all about before applying, which is to their advantage."

—*Michael Goldberger, Director of Admissions, Brown University*

"We advise applicants to think not only about the commonalties among schools, but also about the differences between them. The question we most like to hear from prospective students is 'How is Middlebury unique?' We want applicants to see meaningful differences in our school. We may be rural and small like many similar institutions, but we're also different from them—we're very international, we emphasize writing and language, we're highly residential."

—*John Hanson, Director of Admissions, Middlebury College*

HOW HAS TECHNOLOGY CHANGED THE WAY PROSPECTIVE STUDENTS LEARN ABOUT AND CHOOSE SCHOOLS?

"The Internet has really helped students look at colleges. There are virtual tours, and prospective students can look at our student newspaper and class information over the Web. This is a wonderful source of information."

—*John Blackburn, Dean of Admissions, University of Virginia*

"The number of applications we receive has been growing steadily each year. This is partially because students are applying to more colleges, but also because the Internet is giving information and access to students who might not have previously thought about Wesleyan. This has been a great way for us to spread our message."

—*Barbara-Jan Wilson, Dean of Admissions and Financial Aid, Wesleyan University*

Appendix I

USING THE RANKINGS

The purpose of *How to Get into the Top Colleges* is not to rank schools nor to place one particular school on a list of "top" colleges and relegate another school to a list of second-tier institutions. Other publications devote substantial effort to evaluating and ranking colleges, and the field will be left to them. This appendix examines some of the rankings available, discusses the methodologies they employ to reach their conclusions, and suggests how you can use the rankings without being misled by them.

U.S. News & World Report is now the most important source of college rankings. It began publishing its annual rankings in a special issue in 1987 and has been enjoying the resulting controversy and sales—this is routinely its top-selling issue—ever since. The other sources of rankings included here are guidebooks to colleges: *Barron's Guide to the Most Competitive Colleges; The Fiske Guide to Colleges;* and Cass and Birnbaum's *Guide to American Colleges.*

These guides take different approaches to rankings. *U.S. News,* for example, gives a numerical ranking for schools. Thus it lists a number one school, number two, and so on. The three guidebooks, on the other hand, put schools into tiers, with the top tiers being labeled "most competitive," "five star," or "most selective," respectively.

USING THE RANKINGS

The ranking and rating of colleges is a very uncertain science. Organizations that undertake such evaluations are confronted by daunting methodological problems. For example, how important is it to have a library of 20 million volumes rather than 10 million volumes? How about median SAT I scores of 1400 rather than 1360? Is the school with 20 million volumes and SAT averages of 1360 better than, equal to, or worse than the school with 10 million volumes and SAT averages of 1400? It is not obvious how the two schools should be compared, even when two relatively simple quantitative measures are employed. The problem is made infinitely more complicated when numerous other factors are considered, especially because many of these are inherently subjective rather than accurately and objectively quantifiable.

SOME WARNINGS

Rankings are useful as a rough guide to the reputation and quality of different schools. Most people take them far too seriously, however, when considering where to apply. It is inappropriate to take the latest *U.S. News* rankings and limit yourself to the top five schools in one of their lists. The various schools differ enough in their goals, philosophies, academic strengths, and atmospheres that a person who will be well served by one may be very poorly served by another. To take an obvious example, an applicant interested in becoming an actor rather than a nuclear physicist should probably put Yale, Northwestern, and Carnegie Mellon before Princeton, Cal Tech, or Chicago because the first three also have top-flight theater training available. The latter threesome is an exceptionally good set of schools—but for quite different purposes and thus quite different students.

Chapter 3 lists many criteria that are relevant to choosing the right program. Not all are equally significant and, admittedly, reputation is critically important. But it would be silly to opt for a school ranked fourth by *U.S. News* over one ranked eighth solely because of these rankings. If the college ranked fourth had an unsuitable atmosphere, had weak departments in your areas of interest, or suffered from one of many other critical weaknesses relevant to your educational and personal goals, then it would not make much sense to choose it over one that was listed below it. There is no precision to the rankings; the same publication might even reverse the rankings of the same two schools next year! (In fact, the volatility of its rankings helps *U.S. News* sell magazines, which is its underlying motivation.)

RULES TO REMEMBER WHEN CONSULTING COLLEGE RANKINGS

1. Use rankings primarily to determine the approximate level of a school's reputation.

2. Note that a ranking of a school is not the same thing as the ranking of each department and program within the school, and some departments and programs within a school will be substantially better than others.

3. Consult multiple rankings, rather than just one, because the consensus view tends to be more valuable than any one ranking.

4. When rankings are suitably detailed, as is true of the *U.S. News* rankings, examine them to see what questions are raised in addition to what answers might be provided. For example, if a school has a substantially lower graduation rate than its peers, you should investigate what underlies the disparity.

5. Since you should be looking for the best college to meet your specific academic and extracurricular needs, with an atmosphere in which you will thrive, the rankings should play only a modest part in helping you to determine the best schools for you. They have little to say, after all, regarding which school will provide the courses that you will find most useful or the social environment that will most stimulate you.

6. More important than the rankings is the research you conduct to evaluate particular colleges and their offerings, as discussed in detail in Chapter 2.

The Rankings: National Universities

	U.S. News* (Top 25/50)	Barron's (Top 25)	Fiske (Top 22)	Cass & Birnbaum (Top 15)
Cal Tech	1	+	5	+
Harvard	2	+	5	+
MIT	3	+	5	+
Princeton	4	+	5	+
Yale	4	+	5	+
Stanford	6	+	5	+
Duke	7	+	5	
Johns Hopkins	7	+	5	+
University of Pennsylvania	7	+	5	+
Columbia	10	+	5	+
Cornell	11	+	5	+
Dartmouth	11	+	5	+
University of Chicago	13	+	5	+
Brown	14	+	5	+
Northwestern	14	+	5	
Rice	14	+	5	
Washington University	17		4	
Emory	18		4	
Notre Dame	19	+	4	
University of California, Berkeley	20		5	
Vanderbilt	20		4	
University of Virginia	22	+	5	
Carnegie Mellon	23	+	4	
Georgetown	23	+	4	+
University of California, Los Angeles	25		4	

	U.S. News* *(Top 25/50)*	Barron's *(Top 25)*	Fiske *(Top 22)*	Cass & Birnbaum *(Top 15)*
University of Michigan, Ann Arbor	25		5	
University of North Carolina, Chapel Hill	27		5	
Wake Forest	28	+	3	
College of William and Mary	29	+	5	
Tufts	29	+	4	
Brandeis	31		4	
University of California, San Diego	32		4	
University of Rochester	32		4	
Case Western Reserve	34		4	
Lehigh	34		4	
New York University	34		4	
University of Illinois, Champaign	34		5	+
University of Wisconsin, Madison	34		5	
Boston College	39	+	3	
Georgia Institute of Technology	40	+	4	
Pennsylvania State	40		3	
University of California, Davis	42		4	
University of Southern California	42		3	
Tulane	44		3	
University of California, Santa Barbara	44		3	
University of Texas, Austin	44		4	
University of Washington	44		4	
Yeshiva	44			
University of California, Irvine	49		3	
University of Florida	49		4	

*The top *U.S. News* category was considered to include only the top 25 schools (actually 26, given the joint ranking of two schools at number 25), to make it more readily comparable to the other three rankings, which include fewer schools in their highest category.

Others receiving top rankings (from *Barron's*) include the United States Air Force Academy, United States Coast Guard Academy, United States Military Academy, and United States Naval Academy.

The following chart is intended to reflect the consensus view of the rankings above regarding which schools should be considered among the real elite of American universities. Using another set of rankings would, of course, alter this list. The point is not that this list represents a definitive view of which colleges are or are not to be included, but rather that it is closer to such a listing than a list from any one single source would be. Readers are encouraged to put together their own listings using whichever guides have appealed to them as most appropriate for their own needs—and even then, they should not rely too much on the conclusions!

Ranked in top category* by all 4	By 3	By 2
Brown	Duke	U. California, Berkeley
Cal Tech	Georgetown	Carnegie Mellon
University of Chicago	Northwestern	University of Illinois, Champaign
Columbia	Rice	University of Michigan, Ann Arbor
Cornell	University of Virginia	Notre Dame
Dartmouth	William & Mary	
Harvard		
Johns Hopkins		
MIT		
University of Pennsylvania		
Princeton		
Stanford		
Yale		

The Rankings:
Liberal Arts Colleges

	(Top 20/40) *	*(Top 17)*	*(Top 11)*	*(Top 13)*
Swarthmore	1	+	5	+
Amherst	2	+	5	+
Williams	3	+	5	+
Wellesley	4	+	5	+
Haverford	5	+	5	+
Middlebury	5	+	4	
Pomona	7	+	5	+
Carleton	8		5	
Bowdoin	9	+	4	
Wesleyan	10	+	5	+
Davidson	11	+	4	
Grinnell	11		4	
Smith	13		4	
Claremont McKenna	14	+	4	
Washington and Lee	14	+	4	
Mount Holyoke	16		4	
Vassar	17	+	4	
Bryn Mawr	18		5	+
Colby	18	+	4	
Colgate	18	+	4	
Hamilton	18		4	
Trinity	22		4	
Bates	23	+	4	
Macalester	24		4	
Barnard	25	(included within Columbia)		
Colorado College	25		4	

The Rankings:
Liberal Arts Colleges (cont'd.)

	(Top 20/40) *	*(Top 17)*	*(Top 11)*	*(Top 13)*
Connecticut College	25		4	
Oberlin	25		5	
University of the South	25		4	
Bucknell	30		4	
College of the Holy Cross	30	+	4	
Kenyon	32		4	
Lafayette	33		4	
Union	33		4	
Franklin and Marshall	35		4	
Scripps	35		3	
Whitman	35		4	
Sarah Lawrence	38		4	
Dickinson	39		4	
Bard	40		4	
Lawrence	40		4	
Occidental	40		4	

Others receiving top rankings are as follows: from *Barron's:* New College of the University of South Florida, Webb Institute; from *Fiske:* St. John's (Maryland and New Mexico); from *Cass and Birnbaum:* Cooper Union, Harvey Mudd, Reed, St. John's (Maryland and New Mexico).

Ranked in top category * by all 4*	*By 3*	*By 2*
Amherst	Bryn Mawr	Bowdoin
Haverford		Carleton
Pomona		Claremont McKenna
Swarthmore		Colby
Wellesley		Colgate
Wesleyan		Davidson
Williams		Middlebury
		St. John's
		Vassar
		Washington and Lee

*The *U.S. News* category was considered to include only the top 20 schools (actually 21, given the joint ranking of four schools at number 18), to make it more readily comparable to the other three rankings, which include fewer schools in their highest category.

U.S. NEWS & WORLD REPORT

In this section, we analyze the *U.S. News* rankings (rather than those of the three guidebooks) because its methodology is the most sophisticated and detailed and includes both subjective and objective elements, and it is the most influential of the various rankings. As such, it provides the right vehicle for understanding issues critical to any college rankings.

METHODOLOGY
OVERVIEW

U.S. News & World Report's rankings involve a three-step process. The colleges are separated into their different categories based upon groupings determined by the Carnegie Foundation for the Advancement of Teaching. The two groups of schools whose rankings we list here are the "National Universities," which offer a full range of undergraduate majors plus master's and doctoral degrees, and the "National Liberal Arts Colleges," which offer almost exclusively undergraduate education.

Second, *U.S. News* gathers data on sixteen indicators from these institutions. It uses seven main categories, all given different weights in the final rating, in evaluating each school: academic reputation (25% weighting); retention of students (20%); faculty resources (20%); student selectivity (15%); financial resources (10%); alumni giving (5%); and graduation rate performance (5%).

Third, *U.S. News* inserts the data into a series of formulas to rank each college against others in its category.

THE SEVEN RANKING CATEGORIES

U.S. News computes each institution's *academic reputation* score by surveying the administrations at other colleges and universities in the same college category. Responders to questionnaires are required to rate each of these other schools in various programs, on a one-to five-point scale. The responses for each school are then averaged.

The *retention of students* figure refers to a combination of two separate indicators: the percentage of students graduating within six years of entry (80% of the retention score) and its freshman retention rate (i.e., the percentage of freshman returning to the school; 20% of the score). Retention is used here as a proxy for several hard-to-measure underlying factors, including student happiness with academic and nonacademic situations.

The *faculty resources* score takes several indicators into consideration: class size, which is the proportion of classes with fewer than 20 students to classes with more than 50 students (40% of the final faculty resources score); faculty salary, which is average faculty pay plus benefits (35%); proportion of professors with the highest degree in their field (15%); student–faculty ratio (5%); and proportion of faculty that is full-time (5%). The basic rationale for this score is that having relatively many professors, paid a lot of money, is meant to be a proxy for good teaching.

Student selectivity is calculated using several factors meant to measure the caliber of the student populations at the colleges: the SAT or ACT scores of accepted students (40%); the proportion of freshmen who graduated in the top decile of their high school classes (the top quartile of their high school classes for regional schools) (35%); the acceptance rate, or ratio of accepted students to total applicants (15%); and the yield, or ratio of students who enroll to the total number admitted (10%). (For the 1999 rankings, these figures were taken from the class entering college in 1997.)

The *financial resources* measure looks at the total spent upon student services, libraries, research, and various other educational items. (For the 1999 rankings, these figures were taken from the 1996 and 1997 fiscal years.) The underlying belief is that the more that is spent on students, the better the educational experience they must be having.

The *graduation rate performance* score measures the difference between the percentage of students who actually manage to graduate within six years and the predicted six-year graduation rate, using a recent class at the college. (For the 1999 rankings issue, for example, figures were computed for the class that entered college in 1991.) The predicted six-year graduation rate is calculated using a formula that rests on two variables: the "quality" of the incoming class, as based upon the class's average standardized test scores, and the amount of financial resources expended per student. If the actual graduation rate exceeds the predicted rate, *U.S. News* credits the school with "enhancing the students' achievement."

The *alumni giving* rate is the percentage of alumni who contributed money to their school in a recent one-year period, which is meant to reflect alumni satisfaction with the school.

Putting the Data Together

A score is calculated for each indicator within each of the seven categories. The schools with the highest value for each indicator are assigned a "grade" of 100. Then every other school's score for that indicator is calculated as a percentage of that highest value. The resulting scores are then weighted, as set forth previously, and totaled to determine the scores for each category. Those scores, in turn, are then weighted and totaled to determine a final score, rounded to the nearest whole number, for each school. Schools are then ranked according to those scores. When two or more schools receive the same overall (rounded) score, they are assigned the same ranking.

ADVANTAGES OF THE *U.S. NEWS* APPROACH

There are definite advantages to this approach. First, it looks at a host of factors to arrive at a ranking, rather than depending upon any single factor. Given the complexity of the education experience that *U.S. News* is trying to measure, no one factor is likely to suffice in arriving at a sensible ranking. Second, the statistics that the magazine uses are presented for scrutiny and possible manipulation by applicants and their advisors. Thus a reader can use this same statistical information for his or her own purposes, such as by reweighting factors to more accurately reflect his or her own needs. Third, the data is gathered each year, providing a useful time series for viewing schools' results. Fourth, the data-driven methodology restricts the ability of the magazines' editors to help or harm a school's ranking due to their subjective preferences.

In general, the *U.S. News and World Report* rankings are very helpful in suggesting the approximate level of a school's reputation and quality. This is no small matter: Knowing that a school is not ranked anywhere near the top of the liberal arts colleges' rankings, for instance, can alert you to a potentially disqualifying reputation (assuming that you are looking to attend a truly top college).

SOME LIMITATIONS OF THE *U.S. NEWS* APPROACH
FACTORS NOT INCLUDED

Innumerable factors that might be relevant to you are not included in this (or any other) ranking. For example, there is no direct measure of the actual quality of teaching or of faculty accessibility, no department-by-department analysis of each school, and so on.

NO ONE WEIGHTING OF FACTORS WILL APPROPRIATELY REFLECT ALL READERS' NEEDS

One of the major problems in producing a ranking of colleges is that different students want different things in a college. For example, George may prefer a school with a huge library but limited computer facilities to one with a small library but wonderful computer facilities, whereas Lisa may prefer the opposite. Producing one ranking, based upon whatever weighting of these two factors is chosen, cannot do justice to the needs of both George and Lisa. (To its credit, *U.S. News* now recognizes this problem. It suggests that students consider doing their own ranking of schools by determining what weight to give to each factor *U.S. News* has calculated. This can be done on their Web site.)

This problem of determining what weight should be given to each factor is potentially very important. For example, consider Johns Hopkins and Brown. Johns Hopkins was recently rated number seven among *U.S. News's* Best National Universities whereas Brown was rated number fourteen on that same list. The following chart summarizes the *U.S. News* rankings of the schools, with a + indicating that a school received a better ranking on the given factor and a = indicating that the two were given equal scores.

Factor	Johns Hopkins	Brown
Academic reputation	+	
Freshman retention		+
Graduation rate performance		+
Faculty resources	+	
Class size	=	=
Student–faculty ratio		+
Full-time faculty		+
Selectivity: SAT scores		+
Selectivity: Top 10% of high school class		+
Selectivity: acceptance rate		+
Financial resources	+	
Alumni giving		+

A quick glance reveals that although Johns Hopkins was rated above Brown, a slightly different weighting of the various factors might have reversed the rankings. Even if you decided that *U.S. News* was considering all the relevant factors and assessing them perfectly—matters about which the rest of this section should raise very serious doubt—it is clear that two students could weight the various factors differently, resulting in one favoring Brown, the other, Johns Hopkins.

POTENTIAL IRRELEVANCE OF DATA

Some of what *U.S. News* evaluates may be quite accurate, but that does not mean that it will pertain to you. For example, even though small classes are generally preferable to large ones, seeing that College X has 20% of its classes with 50 or more students whereas College Y has only 10% with 50 or more students does not necessarily mean that even on this dimension College Y is the better choice for you. If you are going to major in history and not take any biology courses, for instance, the question becomes whether the history courses you would otherwise wish to take are large or small, not whether the biology courses are invariably large.

ACADEMIC REPUTATION

Two obvious markets exist for the graduates of top colleges: employers and graduate or professional schools. Unfortunately, *U.S. News* does not attempt to assess directly the market value of graduates of different schools, preferring instead to get the views of relatively uninformed, distant observers—undergraduate deans and presidents. These college administrators are not in a position to render sophisticated, up-to-date judgments about the value of other schools' outputs, but they *are* an inexpensive way for *U.S. News* to get some measure of school reputation. Thus, the magazine does not examine the hiring practices of the top management consulting firms and investment banks, publishing houses and newspapers, scientific research institutes and biotechnology firms, and so on. Neither does it survey those in charge of hiring at such companies. *U.S. News* similarly fails to examine the success of schools' graduates in getting into leading graduate and professional schools; neither does it survey those schools' admissions directors to understand their perspective on the quality of undergraduate institutions.

RETENTION

GRADUATION RATES

Having a high graduation rate is probably a good thing overall. Having few students graduate within five or six years would suggest that many who had been admitted found the work too difficult or the atmosphere too unpleasant to complete the required coursework. There is another possibility, however: Schools might be tempted to make it too easy to graduate by making sure that few failing grades are handed out. Having some students fail to graduate within six years therefore may actually be a good thing, indicating that a school is keeping up standards, which helps guarantee the quality of the degree conferred.

There is a second problem regarding very high graduation rates as a good thing. Should a school be penalized for students who leave after a couple of years of study to take advantage of great opportunities that were offered to them because the school prepared them so well in their fields? For example, consider an actress who is able to get a start on Broadway at 20. If she does not graduate until she takes a break from acting at age 35, it is certainly arguable that her college had actually done very well by her rather than failing her. The same is true for a fellow who leaves college after his sophomore year to start an Internet company. Cashing out three years later as a multimillionaire certainly looks like an affirmation of his college education.

Faculty Resources

The amount spent on the faculty may or may not correlate with faculty quality. There are a number of problems with this notion, however, some of which are dealt with under the "Financial Resources" section, later in this appendix. One problem concerns the fact that engineering and science faculty are more expensive to employ than are classics professors. Should a school such as Cal Tech be ranked above a school like Columbia simply because it has more science faculty than Classics faculty—due, of course, to its having a preponderance of science students? Another problem is that this measure inherently rewards slothful management: Schools that fail to minimize the amount they pay for a given quality of faculty are rewarded. For example, a school would be much better ranked this year than it was last year, due simply to doubling its faculty pay, even if it still has the same faculty, teaching the same courses in the same way.

Part-time Instructors Are Not Necessarily Evil

These rankings reward schools for having full-time rather than part-time instructors. This may be an appropriate standard when distinguishing between one lesser college and another, but it is highly inappropriate for distinguishing among the top schools.

Lesser colleges often try to hold down their expenses by using a large percentage of part-time instructors. A faculty filled with part-timers is likely to interact less frequently with students outside of class than a faculty brimming with full-time instructors. Similarly, such a faculty may face continuity problems, with a great deal of annual turnover among instructors, impeding students' planning for classes in future years. Therefore, a faculty with 80% full-time faculty will ordinarily be preferable to one with 20% full-time faculty.

The problem comes when looking at the top colleges. It is not at all clear that a faculty with 100% full-time instructors is better than one with 90% full-timers. Having no part-time faculty means that a school forgoes bringing in practitioners on the cutting edge of new developments in their fields, people who would never give up their practices in order to be full-time professors but would enjoy teaching now and again. This is more important in some fields than others, of course. Computer science or biotechnology professionals, rather than historians, are likely to be missed due to this policy. In practical terms, the schools located in major urban areas tend to utilize a larger percentage of part-timers than do schools in areas where there are few outside professionals working. Schools in small towns use few part-time faculty because no potential part-timers of interest to the school reside there.

Penalizing a school for having Bill Gates give a class on expected developments in information systems, or having Dr. Henry Kissinger lecture on diplomacy, or having Trevor Nunn discuss how to direct Shakespeare for modern audiences, seems perverse. The optimal percentage of full-time instructors is unclear, but it is clear that the appropriate figure is less than 100%. The *U.S. News* rankings therefore are rewarding schools for being hidebound and not looking for the best talent available, or for being so isolated that no talented would-be instructors reside in their area.

STUDENT SELECTIVITY
FRESHMEN IN TOP TEN PERCENT OF CLASS

There are numerous problems with this measure. First, it pays no attention to the quality of competition at different high schools. Graduating number 95 in a class of 1000 at a poor-quality school where few are serious about grades may be less of an academic accomplishment than graduating number 11 in a class of 100 at an intensely competitive, seriously academic school, but this measure takes no account of such distinctions. Second, this measure ignores how different high schools calculate class rank. Some give extra value to grades earned in difficult classes whereas other schools do not. (In the latter case, a student who takes only the easiest classes and avoids all advanced ones will not be penalized.) The result is another apples and oranges problem: It is hard to compare results when they are arrived at in such different manners. Third, it can be hard to determine whether some students are or are not in the top 10% of their classes, given that a very substantial number of high schools no longer calculate class rank.

ACCEPTANCE RATES AND YIELDS

Acceptance rates can be managed in a variety of ways. The key way to "game" the numbers these days is to try to determine which applicants are most likely to attend the school and then admit only them. This results in higher "yields"—the percentage of those accepted who actually matriculate—which allows schools to accept fewer applicants to fill the class. The result is that many strong applicants, including many who are better candidates than those actually accepted, may be rejected because the school did not believe that they would actually attend.

Schools can determine which applicants are most likely to attend by considering whether they visited the school (and how many times they visited!), interviewed, filled out the school's own application form rather than the Common Application, communicated by E-mail with school admissions officers, and so on. In the case of applicants from high schools with active college counselors, especially those that are well known to the college, admissions officers can have informal chats with the college counselor to learn whether their school is the applicant's first choice.

Schools often use the waitlist to placate those with strong credentials suspected of intending to go to another college. In prior years, schools have also used the waitlist to figure out an applicant's intentions: If the person stayed on the waitlist and campaigned hard to get into the school over the summer, she would be admitted on the assumption that she really did intend to attend. This has not been the case in the last year or two because higher than expected yields at the strongest schools have left them unable to take anyone from the waitlist.

Another unfortunate aspect of the emphasis placed upon acceptance rates is that admissions offices are under pressure to push up the number of applicants to their schools, so as to push down the acceptance rate. This all too often results in encouraging people to apply even when they have absolutely no chance of being accepted, because this helps the schools' numbers. Basing any ranking upon the number of unqualified and unrealistic applicants to schools is essentially meaningless.

There is one other obvious difficulty with acceptance and yield data. Some universities, such as Cornell and NYU, are made up of a set of "schools," such as Industrial Relations, Arts and Sciences, Hotel Administration, and so on. Some of these schools are much harder to get into than are others. Using admissions data applicable to the whole university (i.e., aggregating the data for each constituent school) risks distorting more than it reveals about the different schools clustered together under the umbrella of this university.

FINANCIAL RESOURCES

The financial resources measure used by *U.S. News* is inherently subject to problems. First, schools that prepare a large number of science and engineering students tend to need more expensive facilities, such as laboratories, to provide a suitable education than a school educating a greater proportion of Classics majors. Thus Cal Tech, MIT, Stanford, and Johns Hopkins, all of which are famous for their focus upon science and engineering education, are atop the Financial Resources lists. If, hypothetically speaking, Cal Tech provides $250,000 worth of laboratory facilities per science and engineering student and Cornell does the same, should Cal Tech receive a higher ranking simply because a higher percentage of its students are indeed science and engineering students?

Second, consider the following case. Imagine that College X built a marvelous library in 1948, with many plush reading rooms and other useful extras, whereas College Y is currently building a trashy library without sufficient space to house its book collection, let alone such extras as marvelous reading rooms. Because College X has long ago ceased paying for its plush building (or even depreciating it on its financial statements), but College Y is currently spending money for its trashy building, the latter will be ranked higher on this measure.

Thus, a school's accounting policies, such as the means of depreciating different capital assets (e.g., buildings and laboratory equipment) is but one example of the arcane matters that can affect these rankings, potentially adding substantial volatility to a school's ranking. (Further discussion of the fine points of financial accounting is beyond the scope of this discussion.)

Third, where buildings and other matters are concerned, a school might have to pay more for any given product if it is in a high-wage, highly unionized area than another school would in a different labor environment. The same is true regarding *when* it has work done. Building during a boom period may necessitate spending more for hard-to-obtain resources than would be necessary during a recession, but the resulting buildings would not necessarily be any better for students.

The major problem with input measures, especially financial measures, is that one can spend money well or poorly. As many a major league baseball, basketball, or football team could attest, it is not difficult to spend a fortune and fail to win a championship. The academic market is a much more opaque one than the sports market, so it is likely to produce even weaker correlations between spending and actual results. In general, these input figures say nothing about the quality of spending (i.e., whether much or little has been wasted).

GRADUATION RATE PERFORMANCE

The difference between predicted and actual graduation rates is arguably the single weakest element of the *U.S. News* rankings. The predicted rate is based upon only two factors: the standardized test scores of incoming students and the amount of money that the school spends upon them. That rate is then compared with the actual graduation rate. The difference between the two is assumed to be due solely to the quality of the school's education. This assumption is heroic, indeed.

Other possible causes of students graduating or failing to graduate in six years are legion. A few of the innumerable other possible causes are:

- Taking chances on applicants from weak high schools. These candidates are more likely to drop out than are those from tried-and-true feeder schools, even though taking such chances can produce a more interesting, diverse class.

- Recruiting a disproportionate number of students from far away. These students may drop out more often because they cannot readily go home when struck by homesickness. A geographically diverse class is ordinarily considered beneficial but could work against a school's ranking.

Numerous other factors affecting graduation rates could, of course, be offered. Suffice it to say that using only two factors to predict graduation rates—and considering any variances from the predicted graduation levels to be something to be held for or against the school—borders on the absurd.

ALUMNI GIVING RATE

Using the alumni giving rate as a proxy for alumni satisfaction with their alma maters is by no means absurd, but it suffers from some serious drawbacks. First, it looks at whether someone donates at all rather than the amount donated. If College X has 50% of alumni donate $10 apiece, it fares better in the rankings than College Y, which has 40% of its alumni donate $1000 each. In other words, the strength of alumni feelings is not incorporated in this measure. Second, it ignores the fact that some people donate substantial amounts in major "pledge years" and nothing in between. This causes a degree of volatility in this measure from year to year that does not reflect shifts in alumni feelings. Third, it is substantially biased against public universities, the alumni of which tend not to donate money in the belief that these schools are meant to be funded by taxpayers' dollars.

CONCLUSION

The discussion of the limitations of the various rankings, and in particular that of *U.S. News & World Report,* should not be viewed as harsh criticism. Instead, this is meant as a caution, to keep you from misusing these rankings. In fact, these rankings offer a great deal to prospective applicants. We urge you to consult these and other rankings both to "put you in the picture" regarding what schools might meet your standards for reputation and other matters, and to raise (and settle) issues that might otherwise elude your attention.

SOURCES

James Cass and Max Birnbaum, *Guide to American Colleges* (1996), 17th ed.

Barron's *Guide to the Most Competitive Colleges* (1998).

Edward B. Fiske, *The Fiske Guide to Colleges* (1999).

U.S. News & World Report, *America's Best Colleges* (1999).

Appendix II

THE COLLEGE VISIT

INTRODUCTION

Visiting a college is an important part of your research. The visit brings to life a campus that has heretofore been only an imaginary place fashioned by rumors, hearsay, viewbook pictures, Web site information, guidebook blurbs, and statistics. Visiting colleges impresses upon a student that the college experience is minimally about grades and scores and far more about interactions with people, involvement in a multitude of activities, and the pursuit of intellectual endeavors.

In addition to partaking in the usual introductions to campus (a tour, an information session, an interview), a prospective student should attempt to experience the life of students at the campus. This can be done by sitting in on a class, meeting with a professor, reading the school newspaper, hanging out where students tend to congregate (the student union, library, cafeteria, or dorms), attending an extracurricular event, or spending the night in a dorm. While you probably will not have time to do these things at every college you visit, you should attempt to do many of them at the colleges in which you are most seriously interested.

WHY VISIT A CAMPUS?

➤ A visit can jump start the college application process and provide you with the energy necessary for getting through its anxieties. It makes the college admissions process a reality (if it was previously not at the forefront of your mind) and makes you excited rather than bored about diving into the task.

➤ A visit puts a face on something that was previously only about average SAT scores and GPAs. It can make a competitive college seem more human, thus reducing your fear of the admissions process.

- ➤ A visit gives you your first taste of college life. By spending some time on a college campus, you can learn what it will be like to be far away from home, live in a dormitory with roommates, interact with a diverse group of people, and eat all your meals at a dining hall rather than in the comfort of the family kitchen.

- ➤ A visit helps you in the application process because it gives you a better sense of what the school is about and what it is looking for from its candidates.

- ➤ A visit signals your interest in the college to the admissions officers. Admissions offices record the visits of prospective students; unless you have a good reason for not visiting (because you lack the financial resources or you live particularly far away), admissions officers will doubt your true interest in a school if you do not investigate it thoroughly.

- ➤ A visit gives you an opportunity to make a positive impression on admissions officers (if you interview while on campus) as well as professors or coaches, which could positively influence your chances of being admitted.

- ➤ A visit to a school you particularly like inspires you to continue performing well (or to buckle down).

- ➤ A visit to a school that you were not very attracted to based on its publications or description in guidebooks can prove beneficial by demonstrating it to be a much better place in reality.

WHEN TO VISIT

Ideally, you should visit colleges during the spring or summer of your junior year or early in the fall of your senior year. Visiting as close as possible to the beginning of the admissions process in the fall of your senior year will best help you determine to which schools you should apply. However, there is no reason you cannot begin looking at colleges a lot earlier if you want to—even as early as your freshman year. For example, if you are vacationing in close proximity to a college that might interest you, take advantage of the opportunity to see it.

Although often difficult for high schoolers to manage, it is best to visit a college when school is in session so that you can get the right feel for campus and student life. If at all possible, try to visit schools when classes are in session, but not during exam period. Attending campus when school is in session will give you an opportunity to interact with students, who are the best reflection of a school and what it is all about. At exam times, however, you may get a poor impression of the school because students may be stressed out; they will have no interest in (or time for) talking to prospective students. Furthermore, if you visit during exam time, you will see students holed up in the library but will not get to see the usual dynamics of the campus—there will be few student soccer games taking place on the playing fields, students lounging around and laughing together in the common areas, or students participating in rallies or public activities.

You should also try to visit a campus on a weekday in order to get the best sense of the school. Weekday visits will allow you to see students interacting and to attend a class. Visiting Monday through Friday will also ensure a visit with admissions staff, even if you do not have an interview. Staying for a weekend night is a good idea if you have the time to spare but should be secondary to seeing the school when regular classes and activities are going on. Remember that at college, when students are no longer under the watchful eyes of their parents, social activities take place all nights of the week—not just on Fridays and Saturdays. So there is a good chance you will get to attend a social activity or two if you are staying overnight during the week rather than during the weekend.

Spring or summer break might well be the only time when you can get away to visit schools. If this is the case, bear in mind that you are unlikely to get an accurate impression of a school when the campus is void of activity. During spring and summer vacations, the campus is likely to contain only the limited energy of a handful of postexam students who wish they were in Bermuda with their more fortunate classmates, or to vibrate with the pulse of teenagers attending a campus summer program. If you can visit a school only during a break, of course it is better to visit at that time than not at all—you will at least be able to talk to admissions officers, see the facilities, and picture yourself living and studying there.

It is not a bad idea to revisit schools you are seriously considering after you have been accepted in order to arrive at a final decision. This is especially true if your original visit was during your freshman or sophomore year. You will want to be sure as a high school senior that the college fits your current needs, which may well have changed during your four years of high school.

A NOTE ON MAKING PLANS TO VISIT COLLEGES

FOR COLLEGE APPLICANTS AND THEIR PARENTS

Although you may be tempted to let your parents organize your trips and interviews, you really should be the one who makes many of the arrangements, at least the ones that involve the colleges themselves.

It is usually best for prospective college students to be in charge of the college application process and to practice taking control of their own lives. You, not your parents, will be going on the interview, interacting with the students and admissions officers, and—ultimately—attending college as well. You should take care of the college-oriented details so that you have the logistical elements fresh in your mind and will not miss out on anything important. (For example, let us assume that your mother is doing all the work for you and an admissions staff member informs her over the telephone that anyone interested in seeing the athletic facilities should go on the morning rather than the afternoon campus tour. If your mother does not think seeing the gym is important, she might not remember to tell you this detail, thus making you miss out on something that may be meaningful to you.) Organizing college visits can also give you your first taste of what it will be like to take responsibility for your own life arrangements in the near future. You should start getting used to having to arrange your own appointments and keep your own datebook. Mom and Dad will not be there at college to do these things for you!

The benefits that high school students receive from arranging college trip details, however, are tempered by the reality that most 17-year-olds have never before organized such a trip on their own. Thus, sometimes it is best if students take care of the college details (arrange for interviews, find out what time campus tours begin, inquire about and sign up for an overnight stay) while parents take care of the travel and logistical details (make hotel reservations, obtain road maps, buy airline tickets, rent cars, get directions). This makes the most sense for many families because it allows students to begin taking responsibility while also ensuring that nothing serious goes awry. After all, you want to ensure that your trip is well planned and that no last-minute problems will occur, so some parental involvement in the travel plans and logistical details is often best.

FOR PARENTS OF COLLEGE APPLICANTS

Some parents will find that their children—even the best and most motivated of students—have trouble gearing up for the college application process, often out of fear for its consequences. In this case, you may have to take care of the visiting details yourself (the only other option being to not visit colleges at all, since your child refuses to make any calls or take any action). Parents of these kinds of students often find that their arrangements help to get their kids rolling. Once these students take a small step into the circle of researching, choosing, and applying to colleges (a step arranged and provided for by Mom or Dad), they often warm up to it and can continue on with less prodding.

BEFORE THE VISIT

Follow the guidelines recommended in Chapter 3 regarding the kind of research you should do before visiting colleges. By the time you start out on your college trips, you should have completed the following tasks in order to get the most out of your visits.

- Plan to visit a range of colleges. If you are not certain what you are looking for, this is extremely important. Visiting different kinds of schools is a smart move even for those who think they know what they want. You might be certain, for example, that you want to attend a large university because your high school felt too small and limiting—but actually visiting a range of schools might help you to see that you would feel lost at a really big place. Visit small and large schools; public and private colleges; urban and rural schools. Also, be sure to visit a range of colleges in terms of selectivity. You need to visit not just your reaches, but also your likelies and your safeties.

- Familiarize yourself thoroughly with the colleges you will be visiting—use college guidebooks, check out the school's Web page, contact students you know on campus, browse the school's brochures and viewbook. You should be familiar with all the basic facts about a school before getting to the campus, where your job is to refine your impressions and conduct a more detailed investigation. Start a college notebook, allotting a few pages to each school you will visit. Record all the basic data as well as any questions you have about the school so that you will have it on hand when you are on campus. Leave blank pages for each college so that you can record your impressions and answers to questions after the visit.

- Plan your trips thoroughly. Make sure that you take care of all the logistical details before getting into the car or onto the airplane. Reserve rental cars and airplane seats ahead of time. Map out car trips before hitting the road: Be sure to have both general highway maps and detailed ones of each college town. Get specific directions to each campus from the college admissions office—most Web sites and viewbooks give detailed information about how to get there from any direction. Make all hotel reservations or arrangements to stay with friends before setting out. Do not assume that it will be easy to find a hotel once you get to a small college town or even a big city—with many prospective students on the road, a constant flow of visiting parents, and the various conferences that take place on college campuses, hotels are often booked far in advance. Ask admissions office staff for their recommendations on inexpensive overnight options.

  When making your arrangements, be realistic about the number of activities and travel you can cram into one day. You should ideally visit only one school per day if you want to explore thoroughly and get the best sense of the college's environment. Visiting two schools per day is fine if necessary, but visiting three schools in one day becomes a waste of time.

Allow at least three to four hours per campus if you are attending an information session, going on a campus tour, and being interviewed. Allot even more time if you have arranged an additional meeting with a professor or a student. Contact the admissions office to determine times of tours and information sessions. Enlist the help of the receptionist in determining how much time to allow on campus and for traveling to neighboring schools. Do not hesitate to talk to the staff at one school about how to get to other nearby campuses. They realize that students visit a number of colleges on one trip and will not be offended to know that you are interested in more than just their own school!

- Arrange for formal or informal (depending on the school) interviews with admissions officers. Call to schedule an appointment as far as possible in advance, especially for formal admissions interviews.

- Arrange meetings with individuals in areas of interest to you—coaches, instructors in the performing arts, and professors. Professors are especially good contacts if you have an interest in a major that is less popular on a particular campus—faculty in these fields are always looking for interested applicants to bolster their programs and might even become your advocate in the admissions process if you convey genuine enthusiasm for their discipline. The admissions office is usually helpful in tracking down E-mail addresses or phone numbers of such people.

- Arrange to speak with a financial aid officer. Again, the admissions office can help you in contacting someone with whom you can speak about financial aid and overall college financing concerns.

- Create a list of questions to ask in order to get a comprehensive and honest view of the school. See page 108 for suggestions.

- If possible, arrange to stay overnight with a friend on campus or contact the admissions office to inquire if they have an overnight program in which you can arrange to room with a student.

WHILE ON CAMPUS

While you are on a college campus, you have a lot of options in terms of what to do to get the best feel for the place. The basics include taking the campus tour, attending an information session, and going on an interview or meeting with an admissions officer. There are plenty of other things you can do while you are there to make the experience that much more beneficial. Here is a full range of activities you might consider doing on any given campus.

TAKE THE CAMPUS TOUR

The campus tour gives you a feel for the college landscape and facilities. The better ones also introduce you to the college's history, philosophy, academic offerings, and other special features. The tour gives you a chance to walk around and see some typical scenes from "a day in the life" at the college. You can check out the kinds of students the campus attracts and notice if they appear to be happy or dissatisfied, stressed out or generally at ease. Tours typically last between forty-five minutes and an hour, depending upon the size of the campus and the level of detail the tour covers. Tours are almost always led by students who are trained by the admissions office. Take advantage of this opportunity to ask them questions, but bear in mind that these students are salespersons for the school and might not always be completely forthright in their responses. If you are interested in particular buildings on a campus (the performing arts center if you are an actress, for example), ask the guide at the beginning of the tour if the building will be included in the walk. If it is not, get directions so you can find it after the tour.

ATTEND AN INFORMATION SESSION

Basically, a group information session is a school's sales pitch. It is, however, a useful tool for gaining basic information about a school. Instead of wasting precious time (and giving the impression that you are uninformed) during interviews with admissions officers with your questions about fields of study and admissions requirements, attend a group information session, where these questions will be answered. Usually led by admissions officers or students who work in the admissions office, these sessions give a student an overview of the school's tradition and philosophy as well as the multitude of academic, extracurricular, residential, and other opportunities available on the campus.

Although admissions officers often lead these sessions, this is usually not a time to try to stand out from the crowd by impressing them. Most admissions officers report that they very rarely have an opportunity to take note of prospective students at these meetings, which often include a few hundred high schoolers and their parents at one time. Applicants who try to dominate sessions or gain attention with too many questions that are not of interest to everyone are frowned upon by admissions officers.

VISIT THE ADMISSIONS OFFICE

At many campuses, you can visit the admissions office and ask to speak with an admissions officer, even if you have not prearranged an interview. An officer might be willing to give you a few minutes of his or her time to answer questions and address concerns. Express your interest in the school and ask questions that show you are serious. If you have a special interest in a particular area (and you have not already prearranged a meeting with an individual in that area), ask the admissions officer whom you might contact to discuss pursuit of this interest.

Here you have the chance to impress the admissions officer in a way that might benefit you, so be on your best behavior and be sure that your questions and comments show your overall knowledge of the school and your general intelligence. Stanford's admissions officers, for example, say that they often take note of students with whom they talk in brief informal meetings that occur when they are on the road giving presentations or when a student pops into the office while visiting the campus. If a prospective student really impresses one of them or seems particularly intelligent, they might slip a note into the student's file so that their impressions become part of the admissions record. This can be especially helpful in admission at places such as Stanford, where there are no interviews.

VISIT THE FINANCIAL AID OFFICE

In speaking to a financial aid officer you will get a better sense of how financial aid works at a school, if there are any packaging policies that might benefit you, and if there are any special opportunities or awards you should apply for; you can also gain a sense of the financial aid package that will be offered to you if admitted. Students should not let their parents attend the financial aid office appointment on their own. You should show a college that you are serious about your future and concerned about your own financial affairs (as well as those of your family) by sitting in on the meeting. There may, of course, be details that are best left up to your parents. If this is the case, you might try to take advantage of this opportunity to separate from them for a while to explore the campus on your own. If you think this might be the case, you can inquire of the financial aid officer before beginning the discussion if it would be appropriate for you to leave at a certain juncture in the conversation. Simply explain that you think it best if you took some extra time to wander through parts of the campus you have not yet seen while your parents discuss the financing details with which they are most concerned.

ATTEND A CLASS

Upon contacting the admissions office to arrange your visit, ask about the possibility of sitting in on classes. This is a great opportunity to get a feel for professors, students, and the quality of teaching at the school. If you have time, you might want to try to sit in on a variety of classes: different subjects, different teaching contexts (e.g., a lecture course, a small group discussion, a participatory seminar), and different faculty members.

SPEND THE NIGHT WITH A FRIEND OR STUDENT

It is always a good idea to spend the night at a school. Some schools arrange for overnight stays with students on campus; or you might already know a student with whom you could stay. Your host should ideally be someone who lives on campus in a regular dormitory, rather than off-campus in an apartment with just a few other people. This is a great opportunity to sample college life, particularly the social aspects, as well as to get an honest assessment of the school from students. Try to go to a campus party if you can, or at least have a meal with a group of students. Attend a guest speaker event, participate in an evening dorm activity, or go out to the late-night pizzeria—anything you can imagine yourself doing as a student once you get to campus and at which you will have the opportunity to talk with a variety of students.

EAT IN A CAMPUS DINING HALL OR CAFETERIA

You will almost certainly have a chance to see the campus eating facilities and sample the food if you stay overnight. But even if your visit is just a day trip, you should consider taking a meal in one of the college's student dining halls. This will allow you to sample some of the food (remember that campuses often have a variety of dining options so one place is not necessarily representative of all the facilities on campus) and observe students in an informal setting.

VISIT THE GYM OR ATHLETIC FACILITIES

If sports and physical exercise are important parts of your lifestyle, you will want to check out the athletic facilities at your target campuses. Many colleges will allow you to use the equipment or facilities if you tell them you are a prospective student. Look at the athletic fields and fitness rooms, observe or participate in an exercise class, take a look into the locker room. A visit to this area of campus can tell you a lot about the student population as well. You will see at a glance if the students seem to be healthy and physically active, if they seem to be dedicated to maintaining a well-balanced lifestyle, or if they appear to be overly concerned with fitness and body image.

PICK UP A COLLEGE NEWSPAPER AND CHECK OUT CAMPUS BULLETIN BOARDS

To discover the real pulse of a campus, read the college newspaper and look at various bulletin and message boards, usually located in the student center, near the student mailboxes, in dining facilities, and in the library. The newspaper will alert you to current campus issues as well as any negative aspects of the college that administrators and students might otherwise be hesitant to voice. For example, the newspaper is sure to let you know about crimes committed on campus; distasteful activities of various college organizations (such as a fraternity's dangerous hazing rituals); unpopular moves by the administration (such as a ban on the possession of alcohol in campus housing); and problems with certain faculty members or departments (such as a popular professor's failure to receive tenure). Bulletin boards are full of announcements about campus activities—they let you know what kinds of things take place at the school as well as giving you an opportunity to actually attend an activity if you so desire.

GO TO THE LIBRARY

Visit the main library on campus. You can either sit quietly somewhere to observe students and soak in the atmosphere, or you can wander around from room to room. Visit the various study halls; check out the online library catalog; inquire about whether the library maintains "open" or "closed" stacks. If the stacks are open to student perusal, duck into them to see what a huge college library is all about.

VISIT THE BOOKSTORE

Most prospective students make a trip to the bookstore to pick up college gear before heading home. But you should also take the opportunity to look at the textbook section of the campus store. Most campus bookstores post listings of required reading for all courses in session in the textbook section—you can check out some of the materials you might be using once you get to college. Keep in mind, however, that many college courses publish their own compilations of collated reading materials or require students to use library reserve materials rather than purchase their own texts, so the limited number of books on sale for a certain course does not necessarily indicate anything about its actual workload. Take note, also, that some stores maintain minimal stock of textbooks after the first few weeks of school, so it may not be possible to get a good idea of course reading requirements at all campus bookstores.

THE ROLE OF PARENTS ON THE CAMPUS VISIT

The practical realities of traveling to colleges usually require that students go with a parent—and there is no reason your parents should not want to sample schools with you and give you their input. Parents are preparing to go through as much of a transition as you are, and college visits often help them to ease into the idea of your leaving home. It is important that you remain as sensitive to *their* emotions during the college application and preparation process as they are trying to be of yours. Furthermore, you should be appreciative of all the help they are giving you in this difficult and logistically complex process. Ideally, though, you will have ample time to explore college campuses by yourself or with a friend in order to get a true feel for being on your own in the college environment. Spending time on your own also lets you avoid being too influenced by your parents' opinions about a school.

It can be a little tricky balancing your own needs with those of your parents during college visits. You both want to see the campus and determine how appropriate it is for you, but your parents are likely to have different concerns than you do. You will probably want to have some time on your own at a campus, whereas your parents might not want you to stray too far, fearing that you will get lost, be late for your next appointment, or develop ideas about the school to which they cannot relate because they missed out on a certain experience. All parties need to try their best to understand and respect one another's needs on these visits.

Instead of planning to ditch your family as soon as you arrive on campus, you should discuss beforehand your mutual expectations of how your parents will act and what role they will play. Try to draw a compromise between spending time on your own and tackling the visit with your parents. In other words, you might decide to take the campus tour with your parents, and maybe even take them with you to a class. But also try to spend some time apart from your parents if possible, exploring the campus and interacting with students and professors on your own. Staying overnight on campus—while Mom or Dad stays in the motel down the highway—is often the most convenient way to do so.

Admissions officers are used to parents accompanying their children on campus visits. But parents should be careful not to dominate conversations with admissions officers or faculty. And a parent never should try to enter the meeting room with his or her child when the student goes into an interview. College officers want to know that students themselves are serious enough about the school to prepare their own questions—and they are interested in knowing more about a prospective student from herself, not from her parents' point of view.

BE AWARE OF YOUR PREJUDICES

Many things can skew your impressions of a campus for better or for worse, thereby affecting your ability to evaluate it. Therefore, pay attention to these points:

- Do not let your like or dislike of a single person (tour guide, admissions officer, student, professor) influence your overall impression of a school.
- Bear in mind that weather is a transitory thing and you might be visiting a school on the rare sunny day or the rare rainy day.
- Remember that depending on when in the term you visit (i.e., at the beginning of the term or during midterm exams), students might be more or less engaging.

■ Do not let the presence of local eccentrics color your view of a school, no matter how annoying or strange they may be. Many schools feature a local loonie who has taken up permanent residence in a public space in order to warn passersby of the coming of the end of the world.

■ If you sit in on a class, recognize that the material is likely to be far more advanced than in high school. Hence, do not be discouraged if you are unable to follow along.

■ Remember that part of a school's goal is to attract students. Thus, official school representatives might try to sell you. The more people you talk to (particularly students, because they are not as concerned about attracting more students to the school), the better able you will be to sift through the embellishments.

■ Even though a school might have a prestigious name, it is not necessarily the best school nor the best school for you. Remember to determine what is important to you in a school before visiting most campuses (and certainly before making final decisions about where to apply). During the visit you will then be better able to analyze how well the colleges you visit match up to your needs and desires. Remember that college decision making is an iterative process—as you visit and examine schools, you will learn more about your own needs and as you learn more about your own needs, you will make further decisions regarding which colleges are best for you.

■ Appreciate and observe the school for what it is rather than obsessing about your chances of admission there. If you focus too much on the latter, you will limit your ability to accurately assess the school.

THINGS TO NOTE ON YOUR CAMPUS VISIT

➤ The school's appearance: Is it clean and well kept? Are the facilities functionally modern? What kind of architecture predominates?

➤ The diversity of the student population: Is the student population homogenous or does there appear to be a good mix of people? Do different ethnic and racial groups interact?

➤ The students: Do they appear happy or glum? Stressed out or at ease? Engaged or apathetic? (Remember that the timing of your visit can affect the ways students are acting.)

➤ The professors: Do students and professors interact? (Look outside of classrooms, in cafeterias, and at the student union for faculty–student interaction.) Do professors, especially older ones, seem weary and bored with their material or are they energetic and uplifting?

- ➤ The pulse of the campus: What sorts of activities and events are advertised on bulletin boards? What issues are important to students? (You can discover the latter by talking to students, listening to conversations in eating facilities or dorms, and reading the school newspaper.) What is the overall "feel" of the campus?

- ➤ The computer labs: Are there enough computers to support the student body or is a personal computer a better bet? Is free laser printing available? Is the equipment state-of-the-art?

- ➤ The library: Are students utilizing it? Is it attractive? Does it offer both private study carrels and areas for group meetings? Is there an area with comfortable chairs for light or less intense work? Is the atmosphere conducive to studying?

- ➤ The dining facilities: Are they clean and attractive? Do the menus offer enough variety? Are there healthy options at all meals? Are the dining halls open at convenient hours?

- ➤ The dormitories: Is there variety in living arrangements? Do dorms have common areas and common kitchens? Are bathrooms single-sex or coed? Are bathing facilities clean and modern? Are there singles? What is the greatest number of students living in one room? Are the rooms spacious? Is the furniture comfortable? Is there room for privacy within shared living quarters? Is it possible to ask for a room in a quiet area?

UPON LEAVING CAMPUS

RECORD YOUR IMPRESSIONS

Keep detailed notes of the colleges you visit. Buy a notebook for your campus visits and allot a few pages to each school, noting the basic facts you gain from your initial reading and research as well as any questions you have for each school before visiting. Then, after your visits, record your impressions of campuses and responses to questions you ask as soon after your visit as possible. It is best to make these notes at the end of the visit but while still on campus (this can be a great opportunity to sit at a campus cafe or in an easy chair in the library for a few minutes) or in the car immediately after leaving. Do not wait until the end of a trip—or even the end of a multicampus day—to record your impressions. By the time you have gone to even one other campus, some of your memories from a previous site are bound to have faded. And even your most enjoyable campus visit might become a blur by the time you get home, having visited eleven other schools in the meantime.

SEND THANK-YOU NOTES

Send thank-you notes to key people with whom you interacted. This can include interviewers, financial aid officers, professors or other faculty who took time to chat with you, and students who hosted you. It is not necessary (or worth your time and effort) to send notes to people who conducted large information sessions or tours—these people are not likely to remember you and there is no reason to send a note to thank someone for this kind of routine group treatment. It is the individualized treatments that need to be addressed with letters of appreciation. Be sure to note the names, titles, and addresses of individuals while on your visits—and be sure to get all the spellings correct. If you are unsure of any spelling details, you can always call the admissions department (for the names of admissions officers and interns), the student telephone directory (for the names of students), or academic department offices (for the names of faculty or administration members) to make sure you are correct. While sending thank-you notes will not guarantee your admission, it is nevertheless a nice gesture and will be appreciated by the recipients. See page 467 for more details on writing thank-you notes.

QUESTIONS TO ASK WHILE ON CAMPUS

You should use your campus visit to ask as many questions of admissions officers, administrators, students, and faculty as possible. Asking the same question of a variety of people will often give you different perspectives on an issue. For more ideas about questions to ask (especially of admissions officers and faculty who might influence your chances of admission), see "Intelligent Questions to Ask Your Interviewer" on page 465. You will also want to ask any questions that have been raised while perusing the college's Web site or admissions materials. These sources often contain bare-bones information that needs clarification in order to be fully understood. These sources can also serve to spark questions about related aspects of college life, which you should be sure to have answered during your visits.

➤ Who does the teaching here? (Many large or research universities use teaching assistants or graduate assistants to teach undergraduate courses while professors are off doing research or teaching graduate or upper division courses. Find out who teaches the core or distribution courses typically taken by freshmen and sophomores.)

➤ What do you particularly like and dislike about the university? What do you see as its benefits and shortcomings?

➤ If you could change one thing about your school, what would it be? (This question is especially useful in gauging the honesty of the person responding and is probably best directed toward students and tour guides who have a fresh perspective on the school. Even a student who adores his school should be able to come up with one negative aspect (e.g., he thinks the freshman academic advising program needs improvement, or he resents having to waste his time fulfilling distribution requirements, or he dislikes the inflexibility of the dining options).

➤ Is it common for students to have close relationships with their professors? What opportunities exist for students to foster relationships with professors?

➤ What do students do for fun? What is a typical weekend like? Is the social life primarily relegated to on-campus activities? How prevalent is the Greek system? Will you have a social life if you're not involved in the Greek system?

➤ How big do freshman classes tend to be? (Many freshman introductory courses are very large. If this is a concern for you, ask questions to determine the amount of one-on-one attention that will be available to you through the professor's office hours or the use of teaching assistants and tutors.)

➤ What campus and world issues are most important to students?

➤ What do you feel are the strengths of this school relative to its competitors? (To students only:) Why did you choose this school over other schools?

➤ What are the most popular majors?

➤ What are the most popular extracurricular activities?

➤ What sort of advising services—overall, academic, career, health, mental health— are available to students?

➤ What special academic programs—overseas study, research opportunities, seminars, independent study, etc.—are available to students?

➤ What are the strongest and weakest departments?

➤ I'm interested in X as a major—how strong is the program here? Are there any special opportunities available to students in this major?

➤ What if I'm undecided about my major—will I get an opportunity to explore various disciplines before choosing one?

Do Not Ask ...

➤ Avoid asking questions about admissions requirements for GPA and SAT scores or any other questions that you can find the answers to on your own by simply reading admissions brochures and publications.

➤ Avoid asking admissions officers to compare their college to another specific college. Instead, ask a more open-ended question (e.g., How does your school compare to its competitors?).

➤ Avoid grilling an admissions officer only about the school's weaknesses. Asking about weaknesses shows that you are doing serious investigation work and that you are concerned about your future, but remember also to be positive and ask about strengths as well.

4

ATTENDING A BRITISH UNIVERSITY

— KEY POINTS —

Some students should consider attending a top British university, especially Oxford, Cambridge, or the London School of Economics and Political Science (LSE)

■

British university education is not for everyone, though

■

Those who should contemplate British university include applicants who:
—Know what specific field they want to study
—Are independent and mature, able to study far away from friends and family, and in another culture
—Are academically prepared to "hit the ground running" in their chosen field

■

The rewards of study at a top British university include:
—Top flight instruction, often of a very personal nature
—Completion of a B.A. in three years
—The opportunity to study law, medicine, and other professional fields directly after high school, thereby permitting much earlier entry into such professions
—Lower tuition payments
—Immensely prestigious credentials

INTRODUCTION

There is no reason you have to limit yourself to the United States when thinking about college. If you are bilingual (or intend to become bilingual after further study of a language) and want to live abroad during your adult life, you have a world of universities open to you. If you want to attend a university where the language of instruction is English, your choices are a bit more limited. Although all English speaking countries can claim their share of universities with excellent *national* reputations, there are few foreign universities that enjoy a reputation within the U.S. equal to those of our own top colleges. If you plan to live and work in the U.S. in later life, you should not consider (as an alternative to a first-rate American college) attending any but the finest and most renowned universities abroad. For this reason, this chapter focuses only on England, whose very best universities claim reputations in the U.S. equal to or better than those of top-tier American schools.

There are many benefits to going to a British university (see the box below). Some American teenagers and their families may be overlooking an attractive and unique option by ignoring this possibility.

The British university system is radically different from our system of higher education. The criteria necessary for successful admission to a university, the expectations of first-year university students, the methods of teaching, and the means of academic evaluation in England are all dramatically different from our own. An average American student would have difficulty trying to transition from high school in the U.S. into one of England's institutions of higher learning, but the very best American students preparing to go to the top colleges may be well-suited to the British alternative. The option of going to university in England is one very much worth exploring, but only if you feel—after closely examining the British university model—that it is suited to you and your needs.

THE BENEFITS OF ATTENDING A BRITISH UNIVERSITY

➤ An undergraduate B.A. takes only three years to complete, allowing a student to enter the workforce or graduate school one year earlier than in the U.S.

➤ The three-year plan saves a family (at the very least) a full year of tuition and expenses (generally around $33,000 at the top schools in the U.S.). In addition, attending university in England can save a family $5,000–10,000 a year on annual tuition, for a possible savings of some $50,000–60,000.

➤ Oxford and Cambridge confer honorary master's degrees on their first-degree candidates three years after graduation. A student essentially earns two degrees in three years of actual study in the Oxbridge system.

➤ There is enormous prestige attached to the names of universities such as Oxford, Cambridge, and LSE, giving a graduate of one of these schools a secure foundation upon which to build a future.

➤ The focused programs, one-on-one tutorials, and general intensity of the academics provide a student with excellent preparation for graduate study.

➤ Certain subjects are best pursued in England. European history and Classics, for example, have strong departments at British universities. LSE has some of the best undergraduate departments in the world in fields such as international relations, politics, and economics.

➤ Law, medicine, and other professional fields can be studied as first degrees in England, allowing for entry into a professional career at a much younger age than is usual in the U.S.

➤ A student at a British university learns to become more independent and mature than his or her counterparts who remain on American soil throughout college.

➤ Attending university in another culture enhances a student's worldliness.

➤ Proximity to continental Europe allows for remarkable travel opportunities and cultural stimulation.

There are hundreds of institutions that grant degrees of higher education in England. But for most ambitious Americans—someone whose educational alternatives are the top colleges in the U.S.—only a few are worth considering. If you plan to return to the U.S. in later life, you will want to attend a university that not only provides a quality education but also carries strong name recognition and clout beyond the borders of the United Kingdom. Therefore, for the purposes of this chapter we focus on the University of Oxford, the University of Cambridge, and the London School of Economics and Political Science (LSE), which is one of several colleges within the University of London. (The former two, when referred to together, are often called "Oxbridge" in this book, as they are in their home country.) There are, of course, other famous and reputable institutions in England, including some of the other colleges within the University of London system, such as Imperial College, King's College, and the School of Oriental and African Studies (SOAS). Still, Oxbridge and LSE are the British options most worth exploring because they offer both a high-quality education and a very strong reputation overseas.

OVERVIEW OF THE BRITISH EDUCATIONAL SYSTEM

It is important that anyone thinking about applying to university in England understand how the educational system there works and what is expected of students at the upper levels of study.

SECONDARY SCHOOL EDUCATION

At the age of 16, British students who plan to pursue a higher-level academic (as opposed to vocational or arts-related) education take GCSE (General Certificate of Secondary Education) examinations in five to ten subjects. After taking their GCSEs, students must decide what subjects to study for the next two years, depending upon the field of study they intend to pursue at university. (Note that what we call "colleges" in the United States are called "universities" in the U.K. "College" has a different meaning altogether in Britain—it refers either to what we would call a preparatory high school or to a smaller residential and academic institution within the umbrella of a large university.) In other words, *British students are asked to narrow their focus very early—at the age of sixteen—about four years before American students are usually required to choose a major in college.* Furthermore, in Britain, no coursework is done in outside fields after beginning university. At an American college, by contrast, usually one- to two-thirds of a student's coursework is done outside of the major.

A-LEVELS

For those who will attend university, the last two years of high school are spent preparing for A-levels (General Certificate of Education, Advanced Level). The level of schooling at which students prepare for A-levels is referred to as the "sixth form." A-levels are subject exams required for admission into university and are graded on a scale, with A being the highest grade and E being the lowest. Students are generally required to have first passed GCSEs in the subjects in which they will take A-levels.

Students can continue to study for their A-levels at the same school they previously attended (whether state-funded or independent) if it offers the sixth form, or they can attend a sixth form "college," the equivalent of a preparatory school in the U.S. *The standard pre-university education in England, including the final two years studying for A-levels, requires thirteen years of school rather than our twelve.*

Each A-level is a subject-specific test, in the same way that our SAT IIs are subject-specific tests. Candidates for admission to a British university must apply to study a certain major or field and are admitted only into that area of study, on the basis of their success on A-levels. Success on A-levels requires an extremely high level of knowledge, so students generally study for two, three, or four exams, rather than pursuing a broad range of subjects in the sixth form.

A-levels are sometimes supplemented by STEP papers, subject-specific examination papers used to assess an applicant's aptitude for study at university. The response written by a student for a STEP paper (unlike the material completed in an A-level exam) is available for view by universities, so it can be very helpful in helping admissions committees evaluate students' true strengths and weaknesses. Cambridge in particular is known for requiring students in certain subjects to complete STEP papers for admission.

APPLYING FOR UNIVERSITY-LEVEL EDUCATION

Students apply to all British universities through the Universities and Colleges Admissions Service (UCAS). The UCAS application is due by December 15 of the year before a student plans to enter university. If a student is applying to Oxford or Cambridge, the form must be received by UCAS two months early, by October 15. A student (whether resident or overseas) can apply to only six universities in a given year. Furthermore, a student can apply to *either* Oxford *or* Cambridge, but not both. Although UCAS facilitates the admissions process for all British universities, the individual schools make their own admissions decisions.

When a student is given an acceptance, it will almost always be a "conditional" offer. Most applicants have not yet taken their A-levels when applying to university. Admission committees therefore make conditional acceptances to their candidates, requiring that they perform to a certain standard on A-levels. If a university notifies a candidate that it grants her a conditional AAB offer, for example, it means she must get at least two As and one B on her A-levels. Each university makes its own offer, so one student may receive different prescriptions from different universities.

When a student is notified of all universities' decisions, she can accept two offers. One is referred to as a "Firm Offer," which she makes to the university she prefers most. The Firm Offer guarantees a university that she will attend if she meets the conditions of her offer. The other acceptance is referred to as an "Insurance Offer," to a school whose conditional offer she is nearly certain to meet, in case she does not meet the standards of the more selective school.

UCAS operates "the Clearing System" during the summer to place unsuccessful candidates—including those who did not meet the conditions of their offers—in open spots at universities for the fall semester.

UNIVERSITY-LEVEL EDUCATION

A bachelor's degree in the U.K. is called a "first degree" and generally requires three years of study to complete.

A COMPARISON OF BRITISH AND
AMERICAN UNIVERSITY EDUCATION

Attending university in England is entirely different from going to an American college. The academic expectations of first-year university students, the methods of teaching, and the means of academic evaluation in England do not resemble the way things are done in the U.S. Because there is a mismatch between the educational systems of Britain and the U.S., it is often difficult for American students to be admitted to the top universities in England and, more importantly, to succeed once they are there. Attending a British university is an excellent option, but only for those who have the right academic qualifications, personal habits, and personality features.

DEPTH VERSUS BREADTH IN ACADEMICS

Applications to British universities are made for study in a particular subject matter. This presents a mismatch between our students and England's university system. American students often do not know when applying to college what field they want to study. We give our students two or even three years during college to try out different subjects before forcing them to choose a concentration. Many American 18-year olds would be hard-pressed to apply to British university because they simply have not yet decided what field they want to study. Making a haphazard decision is not advisable, because it is difficult at British institutions to change your field of study once you are enrolled.

American students are usually one year behind their British peers in preparation for college because of our twelve-grade (as opposed to thirteen-year) system. In addition, British sixth formers, as mentioned earlier, study only three or four subjects during their last two years of school. This means that when they arrive at university, they have already built a wealth of knowledge in their chosen fields. Even the brightest and best-schooled Americans might feel they are behind when first arriving at universities in the U.K. They might feel unprepared to compete with their British classmates who have long since focused on a particular area of study.

TEACHING AND EXAMINATION SYSTEMS

The teaching and examination systems are different in England as well. There is more small-group interaction in England and less emphasis on large classes and lecture-style learning. The Oxbridge system is based upon a one-on-one method of teaching. These sessions, called "tutorials" at Oxford and "supervisions" at Cambridge, are weekly meetings between a student and a supervisor where most of one's learning takes place. Tutorial sessions involve one teacher and two or three students. In some subjects at Oxbridge, there are essentially no classroom attendance requirements other than tutorials or supervisions. Other British universities also use private tutorial sessions, but not as exclusively as do Oxford and Cambridge.

The tutorial system requires that students at Oxbridge not be afraid to engage seriously in the learning process. Students cannot sit back and watch while others do the thinking; they are required to be active participants in their own education at all times. Students must be confident and able to conduct prolonged discussions with faculty members. In addition, the small-group emphasis in classrooms requires that students in the Oxbridge system facilitate their own social interactions. It is not as easy to meet people and make friends when you do not regularly attend classes with a lot of other students. To find happiness and fulfillment at Oxbridge, you must be able to reach out on your own to meet people and become part of the social fabric.

University students in Britain are tested infrequently, although frequently required to write papers. They are not systematically encouraged or required to keep up with their work through tests at regular intervals on smaller amounts of material. In some subjects, students are examined only at the end of each year—and sometimes only at the end of the first and third years. These tests are the only evaluations upon which a student's final diploma award is based. Students must be able to steer themselves through an entire year (or more) of self-study in preparation to ace final exams at the end of the year.

CHARACTERISTICS NECESSARY FOR ATTENDING A TOP BRITISH UNIVERSITY

If you are considering applying to Oxbridge or LSE, you should possess most or all of the qualities listed here—they are necessary for both gaining admission to a British university and becoming a success once you are there:

■ *A superior academic record:* You need to have stellar academic credentials to be admitted to the schools discussed in this chapter, especially Oxford and Cambridge. Your main selling points should be your academic gifts rather than extracurricular or personal accomplishments and roles.

■ *Evidence of intellectual vitality:* You need to be able to prove that you have gone beyond the requirements of American high school education in pursuing your academic interests. Study in the British system requires self-motivation and the ability to follow curiosities on your own, without much direction from faculty members.

- *A firm understanding of what field you want to pursue and why:* When applying to a British university, you must apply to study a certain field or major. You are admitted to university on the basis of your demonstrated interest in and potential for success in that field of study.

- *Independence:* You must show that you can think and work on your own rather than being guided step-by-step through your studies. You must also show that you are ready to live on your own in a foreign country, far away from your family and friends.

- *Maturity:* You must be prepared to immerse yourself in an altogether new culture and academic setting.

- *Confidence:* You must demonstrate that you are confident in your own academic and presentation abilities. You must be able to both work through material alone and function in the tutorial mode, often one-on-one with faculty members, which can be daunting to those who are timid or unsure of their abilities.

- *Superior organizational and motivational skills:* You must be able to manage your time wisely and structure your own study habits rather than waiting for someone else to tell you what to do next.

- *The ability to reach out socially:* You must be able to form friendships easily and know how to get involved in group activities with your peers. Lack of constant classroom interaction means that friendships and peer groups do not form as naturally as they do on American campuses.

- *Secure finances:* Although British universities are less expensive than U.S. colleges, they have very limited funds for overseas undergraduate students. Overseas students can sometimes obtain small bits of financial aid from the British Council, the universities themselves, and other sources to cover small gaps in funding—but an American undergraduate cannot obtain a great deal of merit- or need-based aid in order to attend a British university.

OTHER REASONS TO STUDY AT A BRITISH UNIVERSITY

If you possess most or all of the traits listed in the previous section, you will likely be able to handle attending a top British university, but that does not mean you should head off to England just yet. Those who fit the categories listed here are the ones who will profit most from a British university education:

■ *Want to study particular subjects.* British universities often have strong departments and instruction in certain subjects, such as European history, English literature, international relations, and the Classics.

■ *Plan to enter graduate school and a career in academia.* Those interested in pursuing graduate study at the master's or doctoral level after a B.A.—whether in the U.S. or overseas—would benefit from going to a leading school in England. The rigor of the instruction, the independent learning, the one-on-one interaction with professors, and the frequent writing assignments better prepare students for graduate school and careers in academia than do most elite American schools.

■ *Want to enter a professional career as early as possible.* In the British system, students pursue the professional fields (medicine, veterinary medicine, dentistry, law, etc.) as first degree or bachelor's degree subjects. Going to university in England means that a student may be able to enter a professional career much sooner than his or her American counterparts, who must undergo four years of college and many more years of graduate school before beginning the same career. Generally speaking, only students studying architecture and engineering can earn first degrees in their fields in the U.S.

■ *Lack strong extracurricular records.* British universities generally admit students on the basis of academic credentials alone. An American student with top academic performance but little in the way of extracurriculars has only a modest chance of being accepted at the top U.S. colleges, but does have a good chance (if he or she possesses the right academic record and capabilities) of getting into Oxford, Cambridge, or LSE.

■ *Want to save money.* Although the British schools generally do not offer financial aid to foreign students, they do offer a bargain for those who can pay on their own. Each year of education costs significantly less than a year at a top college in the U.S., with the total cost of attendance ranging between about $23,000 and $28,000 (based on the £1 = $1.55 exchange rate in effect as this book went to print) within the Oxbridge and LSE programs, as compared to about $33,000 at the top U.S. colleges. Most Americans attending British universities can thus expect (assuming they would be paying "sticker price" at an American college) to save between $5,000 and $10,000 per year. Furthermore, an undergraduate degree in Britain takes only three years to complete, saving Americans an additional full year's tuition and expenses at an American school ($33,000 or more), for a total savings of between $48,000 and $63,000 on the entire college education, or a cost reduction of about 35 to 45%. Furthermore, if you consider that you receive an honorary master's degree from Oxford and Cambridge after several years, you are really getting two degrees for the price of one (or less than one).

AMERICAN COLLEGE VS. BRITISH UNIVERSITY

	American College	British University
Apply to ...	School at large	Particular college and field of study
Accepted on Basis of ...	Academic and other criteria	Academic criteria
Acceptance Is ...	Unconditional	Usually conditional
Academic Focus	Study many subjects	Study one subject
	Choose major after 1–3 years	Enter major field immediately upon arrival
Can Switch Majors or Departments ...	Readily	Almost never
Most Classes Are ...	Interactive group classes	One-on-one tutorials OR large lecture sessions
Testing	Frequent testing	Infrequent testing
Degree Earned	After four years	After three years

THE THREE FEATURED BRITISH UNIVERSITIES AT A GLANCE

University of Oxford
10,823 undergraduates
4,413 postgraduates
5% overseas or foreign
60:40 male:female
39 colleges (30 house undergraduates) and 6 private residence halls

University of Cambridge
11,223 undergraduates
4,688 postgraduates
6.3% overseas or foreign
56:44 male:female
31 colleges

**London School of Economics and Political Science
(a college within the University of London)**
2,698 undergraduates
2,537 postgraduates
51.7% overseas or foreign
55:45 male:female

Note that it is difficult to talk of either Oxford or Cambridge as one institution, because student life at both universities is governed by the individual colleges rather than the larger umbrella university. Colleges are independent and self-governing entities responsible for accommodating and feeding students as well as providing sports, entertainment, and activity facilities, giving them a social focus, and overseeing their academic and personal well-being. The characters and personalities of the various colleges differ depending upon location, history, academic or nonacademic strengths and weaknesses—and thus the kinds of students they attract—just as individual universities and colleges in the U.S. do.

ADMISSIONS OF OVERSEAS STUDENTS AT OXBRIDGE AND LSE: AN OVERVIEW

Foreigners applying to the Oxbridge schools have a more difficult time getting in than do home students because admissions officers find their credentials difficult to judge. At LSE, however, which admits the highest numbers of overseas students of the three schools discussed here, admission for foreign students is much less competitive than it is for British students. Whereas the admissions rate for British nationals is about 7% of those who apply, generally about 40% of overseas applicants are admitted. Foreign students at all three schools are evaluated by the same people who admit British students, but are evaluated based upon different criteria because they generally have not taken Britain's A-level exams.

All candidates to Oxford, Cambridge, or LSE apply for admission to a particular subject. When applying to Oxford or Cambridge, you also apply to a specific college (this does not apply to LSE since it *is* a single college within the University of London.) Applying to Oxford or Cambridge requires a separate application form (in addition to the usual UCAS application), which is sent directly to the school rather than to UCAS. LSE, however, requires no extra material beyond the UCAS application from its candidates.

At each Oxford or Cambridge college, as well as at LSE, academic faculty evaluate and admit candidates in their own fields. These faculty members read the admissions files individually as well as meet with others in their departments to discuss their decisions. There are no official ranking systems, although individual faculty members might have their own personal ways of evaluating and ranking candidates. Most candidates are evaluated by at least two people. Because of the faculty role in decision making at British universities, applications can and should be as sophisticated as possible in terms of their academic and intellectual content.

At the Oxford and Cambridge colleges, the admissions officers pass on any attractive candidates for whom their colleges have no space to other colleges within the university for consideration. At Cambridge's St. John's College, for example, which gets a large number of applicants due to its popularity and academic strength, about a third of all applicants are denied from St. John's but sent on for consideration at other Cambridge colleges.

SPECIAL ADMISSIONS CONSIDERATIONS

Oxford and Cambridge do not accept transfer students. An overseas student possessing an undergraduate degree can apply to Oxford or Cambridge to acquire a second bachelor's degree in only two years, though, in effect becoming transfer students who enter the second-year classes. At LSE, foreign students without degrees can be considered for transfer entry into the second year of study. The Law department does not, however, take transfer students. All Law students must complete four years at LSE rather than the usual three required for other graduates.

AVOID THE OPEN APPLICATION

If you do not want to indicate a college preference at Oxford or Cambridge, it is allowable to complete an "Open Application," whereby the university will place you in a college if you are accepted into your field of study. This is not necessarily an advisable means of applying to either university, though. The more popular houses do not usually have room for Open applicants, so it is often impossible to be admitted to them through the Open system. Since you could end up anywhere when applying this way, unless you have really investigated each and every college and like all of them (highly unlikely, since they are all very different in terms of personality, atmosphere, architecture, size, and numerous other factors), it is not a wise move. Completing an Open Application also forces you to relinquish control of your marketing efforts. Overseas applicants especially need to prove to the admissions tutors that they know what they are looking for and have what it takes to do well at Oxford and Cambridge academically and socially. Being able to target a particular college as ideal for one's needs, as well as meet and interview with the tutors at the college, can thus be crucial. The Open Application does not allow for this kind of targeting.

DEGREE OF DIFFICULTY IN ADMISSIONS VARIES BY COLLEGE AND FIELD

The degree of difficulty of being admitted to Oxford, Cambridge, or LSE differs by college at the first two universities and by field of study at all three universities. Applying to an unpopular college or an unpopular field of study within a particular college can be much easier than running up against many other candidates for a coveted place somewhere. In other words, there are ways of getting around the competition. See the chart below to see how the various fields of study within King's College at Cambridge differ in their admissions rates.

Oxford, Cambridge, and the University of London (the umbrella university to which LSE belongs) publish annually numbers of applicants and accepted students for each college. Doing your own research will tell you which colleges and subjects of interest are easier to get into than others. This does not mean you should apply to Oxford's St. Hilda's (an all-women's college, which does not receive nearly as many applications as the coed colleges) if you do not want to live and study with only women. You might be easily admitted to a place like St. Hilda's, but would not be satisfied with your experience once there.

Choosing a field of study requires utmost caution because it is difficult to switch subjects once at a British university. While it is nearly impossible to switch fields after arriving at Oxford or LSE, Cambridge offers a bit more flexibility, allowing many students to change (or combine subjects) after the first year. For example, some students do English for two years and history for one year in a sequential mode of study. With this in mind, some students might consider applying for a field that has higher admissions rates, with the plan to add or switch into another field at a later time. If you plan to take this route, you should investigate the possibilities thoroughly and beware that it may be risky. It might be difficult in the first place to fake enthusiasm for a subject you do not want to study, and switching subjects later on might become more difficult than you had anticipated.

KING'S COLLEGE, UNIVERSITY OF CAMBRIDGE
RATE OF ADMISSION BY SUBJECT FOR 1999 ENTRY

This table shows that rates of acceptance vary dramatically from one field of study to the next. The numbers here reflect applications made to King's College, Cambridge for 1999 (or deferred 2000) entry. From left to right, the numbers represent the total number of applicants to King's in a subject; the number accepted by King's; the number accepted by another Cambridge college (upon referral by King's); and the success rates of candidates offered acceptances by King's and by all Cambridge colleges.

Subject	Applicants	Accepted by King's	Accepted Elsewhere	Rate of Admission
Archeology/Anthropology	16	6	3	38%/56%
Architecture	16	3	2	19%/31%
Classics	12	8	1	67%/75%
Computer Science	23	4	0	17%/17%

Economics	36	7	2	19%/25%
Engineering	35	6	1	17%/20%
English	81	9	5	11%/17%
Geography	15	3	2	20%/33%
History	21	8	1	38%/43%
History of Art	5	2	0	40%/40%
Law	18	3	0	17%/17%
Mathematics	69	9	6	13%/22%
Medicine	49	8	1	16%/18%
Modern Languages	24	8	3	33%/46%
Music	25	10	1	40%/44%
Natural Science (Bio)	38	9	2	24%/29%
Natural Science (Physical)	33	9	0	27%/27%
Oriental Studies	4	4	0	100%/100%
Philosophy	30	5	6	17%/37%
Social/Political Science	60	9	6	15%/25%
Theology	6	2	0	33%/33%
Total	**616**	**132**	**42**	**21%/28%**

EVALUATION CRITERIA FOR OVERSEAS STUDENTS: ACADEMICS AND STANDARDIZED TESTS

The problem that the British universities have in admitting American students is that none of our testing options are comparable to A-level performance. Furthermore, American high schoolers have not focused aggressively on one or two fields as English students applying to university have. The colleges like to see candidates' SAT I and SAT II scores (APs are even better for their purposes), but even the best SAT and AP scores do not guarantee you a place at one of the top British universities.

American students thus have several options in submitting academic criteria for admission to British universities:

1. The preferred option is for American students to have followed an IB curriculum in high school. Students who have completed an International Baccalaureate are at an advantage because these courses are recognized by the British system as indicative of the ability to do university work.

2. The next best option is for American students to prove their academic preparedness for British university by submitting not only high SAT I and II scores (applicants need to score at least 675 on each section to be competitive), but also strong performance on AP exams. Applicants generally need to report three or four tests with scores of 4 or 5 on each to be competitive. The subjects of the AP tests should correspond with the field to which an applicant is applying.

3. The next option is to take a one-year cram course in England to prepare for A-levels. The candidate would then apply to British universities based on his A-level performance, like British home candidates.

There are two additional options for students wishing to apply to LSE:

1. American applicants can complete one year of study at a U.S. college with a strong GPA and then apply to transfer in to LSE. The GPA itself is of more interest to LSE than the caliber of the school.

2. A final option for American students wanting to attend LSE is to take what is called a Bridge or Foundation Course in England, a thirteenth year of study. At its completion, a student would take LSE's entrance exam (the single exam given to applicants in all subjects who have taken neither A-levels nor AP exams, nor received an IB).

The last two options for those considering LSE are least preferable because they do not allow an American student some of the main benefits of attending British university, namely the ability to save a great deal of money and time. The last method of gaining entry is also risky because an applicant could potentially waste an entire year. There is no guarantee of admission to candidates planning to succeed this way.

All overseas applicants to Oxbridge or LSE should contact the proper admissions office for advice on how to prepare for the application. This is especially important for those who plan to go to England to take a Bridge or Foundation course before applying. Such programs are not all alike, and many of them are considered inadequate preparation for entry into a top university.

THE NONACADEMIC PROFILE LACKS IMPORTANCE

The nonacademic profile is not as important to admissions at British universities as it is in the U.S. It is for this reason that academically competitive American students with little extracurricular activity should consider applying to British schools. The admissions officers agree that extracurricular activities make a student interesting, but it is the academic profile that really counts.

SUPPLEMENTAL ADMISSIONS MATERIALS

Most courses of study at Oxford and Cambridge require supplemental application materials. For example, in modern languages at Oxford, candidates must submit two pieces of recent work for each of the languages they are currently studying. At least one piece should be written in the candidate's target language of study. No matter what field of study an applicant plans to pursue, supplemental materials should generally be pieces marked with teachers' corrections and comments. The colleges generally note that they want to see applicants' own work, not something that has been rewritten and perfected with obvious help from teachers and tutors.

Applications to many subjects at Oxford and Cambridge also require tests or exams to be taken when candidates come to interview. Modern language applicants to Oxford, for example, are required to sit for 30-minute tests in each language.

INTERVIEWS

Admissions tutors at Oxford and Cambridge strongly recommend that overseas applicants do all they can to increase their visibility and improve their chances of getting in by coming for an interview, even though it is not required. Interviews are held during a specified admissions period called "Open Days" each year—usually in May or June—although overseas students can often arrange to come at a different time.

Interviews at Oxford and Cambridge colleges are intense and quite different from the relaxed situations encountered by college applicants in the U.S. Each applicant generally sits through two or three interview sessions, all conducted by experienced members of the faculty rather than by administrators or school alumni. They focus on knowledge of a subject area rather than on general information or a getting-to-know-you type of discussion. They require a student to be able to think on his or her feet, feel confident in the face of challenges, appear well-read and prepared in a field of study, and make impressive oral deliveries of information. Interviewers will evaluate how applicants think, develop ideas, and present them to others.

Oxbridge applicants should definitely seek assistance in this regard before the interview. They should meet with teachers or get in touch with nearby college professors to seek help in preparing for an intense academic interviewing experience. Reviewing test materials in their field of study as well as conducting extra reading is also essential to enter an interview well prepared to share knowledge and demonstrate intellectual interest in a subject beyond basic classroom learning.

Many admissions officers note that the interview helps them to identify those with superior intellectual passion and gifts as well as those who will be successful under the tutorial teaching method. The one-on-one interview with a faculty member is itself, after all, somewhat like a tutorial. Thus, the admissions interview at Oxbridge, unlike at U.S. colleges, frequently makes or breaks a candidacy. (There are no interviews for admission at LSE except in the case of older students who are applying after some time out of school.)

RECOMMENDATIONS

A reference from a teacher (often called a "referee" for admissions purposes in England) is required at all three institutions. Admissions officers at Oxford, Cambridge, and LSE primarily want hard academic information, including predictions of final grades if the course is still in session, rather than stories about a candidate's personality or interaction with others in the classroom. Recommendations from supervisors other than academic teachers are discouraged. It is most helpful if the writer of a recommendation is familiar with the British university and its system of education so that he or she can address the student's potential for success in this unique environment. Recommenders writing letters for LSE should also make a realistic assessment of the student's ability to cope with London, a huge international city.

Generally in England the "head teacher" writes the recommendation, pulling together material from all other teachers, as our guidance counselors do in the U.S. Thus, for the purposes of applying to British universities, it is advisable for American students to do one of two things:

1. Include a supplemental recommendation from your guidance counselor along with a teacher recommendation.

or

2. Ask an academic teacher to write a reference that includes the information gathered from other faculty members that your guidance counselor compiled. Your guidance counselor should understand your concern and agree to hand over her notes or letter for the teacher's use.

Either way, despite the lack of explicit instructions requesting a general guidance recommendation, British university colleges expect to receive this type of letter on candidates' behalf, so you should prepare to submit one. Whether you have your counselor or a teacher do this for you is up to you.

BRITISH UNIVERSITY ADMISSIONS OFFICERS
TALK ABOUT OVERSEAS ADMISSION

WHAT IS THE MOST IMPORTANT ADVICE YOU HAVE FOR OVERSEAS APPLICANTS?

"Look at the coursework before applying. People think studying here will be just like being at Harvard—it's not true. You need to look at what you'll be expected to do in your first year. Also, students should know that there are very few subjects you can start at Cambridge—you have to be well into the knowledge of a field to enter university here."

—*Simon Goldhill, Director of Studies in Classics/Admissions Tutor, King's College, University of Cambridge*

"Prospective overseas applicants may wish to E-mail or call us in advance for advice regarding their plans. Every overseas applicant is different, so our advice is tailored to each individual's needs."

—*Louise Burton, Admissions Officer, London School of Economics and Political Science, University of London*

"We operate differently than American schools, and applicants should realize this. American students like to know what's expected of them right away, and to get results right away—which is not how things work here!"

—*Ray Jobling, Senior Tutor/Former Admissions Tutor, St. John's College, University of Cambridge*

IS THE OPEN APPLICATION A GOOD IDEA?

"The Open Application is not a smart idea. We at St. John's end up taking those who didn't mark us as their first choice in only a small number of cases, because there are just too many strong John's applicants. Talk to people and find out which college you want. You should always apply to a particular college in my view."

—*Ray Jobling, Senior Tutor/Former Admissions Tutor, St. John's College, University of Cambridge*

HOW IS EXTRACURRICULAR INVOLVEMENT EVALUATED?

"We're interested in this sort of thing, but quite frankly, we're much more keen on academics."

—*Michael Allingham, Admissions Tutor, Magdalen College, University of Oxford*

"No personality or extracurricular features will get you in here."

—*Simon Goldhill, Director of Studies in Classics/Admissions Tutor, King's College, University of Cambridge*

SHOULD OVERSEAS CANDIDATES INTERVIEW?

"Americans are told they are not required to come for an interview. But quite honestly, an American student would have a very hard time being admitted if he or she couldn't make him- or herself available for an interview."
— *Anne Daniel, Admissions Officer, Christ Church College, University of Oxford*

WHAT ARE YOU LOOKING FOR IN THE INTERVIEW?

"The interviewers want to see that you can think, how you develop ideas on your own, that you can form an opinion, defend it, revise it, and so on."
— *Anne Daniel, Admissions Tutor, Christ Church College, University of Oxford*

"You must be able to talk about your subject and related materials, and talk about them intelligently. Your experience and intelligence must go beyond the curriculum you've been assigned at school."
— *Simon Goldhill, Director of Studies in Classics/Admissions Tutor, King's College, University of Cambridge*

WHAT ARE YOU LOOKING FOR IN RECOMMENDATIONS?

"It's very important that the teacher knows the student very well. The reference also needs to be very distinctive. Teachers need to recognize we're looking for academic *potential,* not just a past show of success."
— *Ray Jobling, Senior Tutor/Former Admissions Tutor, St. John's College, University of Cambridge*

"We want hard academic information here, not touchy-feely stuff."
— *Anne Daniel, Admissions Officer, Christ Church College, University of Oxford*

"It is important that the writer is familiar with Cambridge and what it takes to make it here. Please, no references from tennis coaches! That doesn't cut it here—we want academic information only."
— *Simon Goldhill, Director of Studies in Classics/Admissions Tutor, King's College, University of Cambridge*

ARE EXTRA RECOMMENDATIONS EVER HELPFUL?

"It is rare that a reference from someone other than a teacher could really shed light on academic potential, on a candidate's qualifications to study at Oxford."
— *Anne Daniel, Admissions Officer, Christ Church College, University of Oxford*

"If you're working for someone in your field, in a potentially preprofessional job, then occasionally a reference from this person could help your standing."
— *Ray Jobling, Senior Tutor/Former Admissions Tutor, St. John's College, University of Cambridge*

WHAT DIFFICULTIES DO AMERICAN STUDENTS USUALLY
HAVE WHEN ARRIVING AT A BRITISH UNIVERSITY?

"Our experience is that American students may have trouble when they first get
here because they simply aren't used to focusing. They're used to breadth
rather than depth."

—Anne Daniel, Admissions Officer, Christ Church College, University of Oxford

"The cultural differences are often hard for American students to digest—
just because we both speak English doesn't mean we're the same. Learn to
enjoy that fact!"

—Ray Jobling, Senior Tutor/Former Admissions Tutor, St. John's College,
University of Cambridge

WHAT KINDS OF STUDENTS SHOULD APPLY TO A BRITISH UNIVERSITY?

"You have to be independent-minded, able to organize your life carefully, and
mature. We cannot necessarily discern these qualities when admitting a student,
so the student needs to decide for himself whether or not British university is
right for him."

—Michael Allingham, Admissions Tutor, Magdalen College, University of Oxford

"Our degrees are much more specialized than those in the U.S. so only those who
really know what they want to study should apply. If you're going into maths
you'll be entering alongside hundreds of freshers [freshmen] who have specialized
in maths over the last several years. So you must be ready to work really hard and
make some serious adjustments very quickly, which can be quite difficult."

—Ray Jobling, Senior Tutor/Former Admissions Tutor, St. John's College,
University of Cambridge

"We're looking for students who can cope with a different method of studying plus
cope with living in the middle of London for the first time. We especially need kids
who've shown initiative—we want to be confident that they'll get up and do something when they get here instead of holing up in their rooms out of fear."

—Louise Burton, Admissions Officer, London School of Economics and Political Science,
University of London

A COMPARISON OF THE APPLICATION PROCESSES
AT OXFORD, CAMBRIDGE, AND LSE

	Oxford	*Cambridge*	*LSE*
How to Apply	Through UCAS	Through UCAS	Through UCAS
Application Deadline	October 15	October 15	December 15
Apply to …	College and Subject	College and Subject	Subject (LSE = one college)
Supplemental Materials	Yes	Yes	No
Interviews	Yes (Recommended)	Yes (Recommended)	No
Recommendations	One required	One required	One required
Ability to Transfer In	No	No	Yes
Overseas Funding	Essentially none	Essentially none	Essentially none

A GENERAL PRESCRIPTION FOR SUCCESS
IN BRITISH UNIVERSITY ADMISSIONS

1. Follow an IB curriculum, if at all possible.
2. If you do not follow an IB curriculum, take as many AP exams as possible.
3. Score well on your SAT Is and IIs. Submit your scores to British universities, even if they are not required.
4. Focus on the field to which you will apply for undergraduate study. Take all available classes in this area at your high school. If possible, take additional classes at a nearby college, special institute, or summer program. This is especially important if you are applying to study a subject that is not offered at the high school level in the U.S. For example, if you are applying to study Astronomy, be sure to take all the science classes available at your high school, but also pursue an introductory course in Astronomy at a community college. In addition, take summer classes before arriving at the British university in order to be prepared for the curriculum there.
5. Participate in a study abroad program during high school, if at all possible. This will allow you to better understand whether or not you want to attend college overseas, and will help you to explain to British admissions officers how you are prepared for the experience.

6. Go for an interview, even if it is not required. Assure that you are prepared for the hard academic nature of British university interviews by reviewing materials in your subject area and practicing with a teacher in your field before sitting for the interview.

7. Assure that your teacher and guidance counselor understand the British university's structure and requirements before they write your letters of recommendation. Sit down with them to discuss the university to which you are applying, the field that you will study, the nature of study at British universities, and the criteria upon which your candidacy will be evaluated, to ensure that they can do the best job possible in writing your recommendations.

8. Show in your application materials and during the interview that you understand what the university's structure, academic life, and culture are all about.

OTHER THINGS TO KNOW ABOUT ATTENDING UNIVERSITY IN THE UNITED KINGDOM

HEALTH CARE

An added benefit to attending university in England is that you are entitled to excellent health care during your stay free of charge, as if you were a British citizen. All full-time students in programs that last six months or longer receive medical treatment under the National Healthcare Service (NHS). Most services are free; more serious problems may require payment, but fees are relatively inexpensive. Prescriptions are subsidized and dental care is available for a small fee.

EMPLOYMENT

Overseas students are prevented by law from working full-time in Britain, but working part-time or during vacations may be allowed. A work permit will be granted only if the student can show proof from his or her university that such employment will not interfere with studies and if there is no suitable British citizen or resident available to fill the position.

A DISCUSSION WITH AN AMERICAN UNDERGRADUATE AT CAMBRIDGE

David Waddilove of Grand Rapids, Michigan, recently entered St. John's College at Cambridge as a first-year student. David applied to Harvard, Yale, Princeton, the University of Michigan, and Cambridge—and chose Cambridge after being accepted at all of them.

Did you tailor your high school experience in anticipation of applying to a British university?

I knew I wanted to go to Cambridge after I spent a month here in the summer of 1995—at the Cambridge Prep Experience, an on-campus summer program for high schoolers. I knew all along that I would have to make my high school program fit certain criteria here. I knew I would have to take a lot of AP courses and exams—more so than if I were applying only to American colleges. [David submitted five total AP results, four scores of 5 and one score of 4.]

How is gaining entry to Cambridge different from the admissions process we know in the U.S.?

Most importantly, the interviews here are serious and pretty tough. I didn't go on an interview, which is rare for an overseas candidate, but I know all about them from friends. One interviewer at St. John's is famous for taking what you might call a "maximum intimidation stance."

Since I didn't come for an interview, I was sent two supplemental questions to answer after I applied. These are the kinds of questions I would have been asked to discuss and write about during the day of the interview, had I come. The first was simple: "Why do you want to come to Cambridge?" The second was, "Is inflation ever a good thing?" These were given to me in place of my coming for interviews.

What has been your initial reaction to studying in Britain?

The systems are shockingly different. I knew this before I came here, of course, but I've still been surprised. For example, there are a lot of "supervisions," which are almost always one-on-one sessions with a faculty supervisor, rather than classes as we know them. The exam system is daunting. I have major exams at the end of each year, but that's it. You have to be very motivated and self-starting to master the system here.

Are all Cambridge colleges created equal when it comes to being admitted?

No! It's *definitely* easier to get into the less popular colleges and subjects. The newer colleges are known to be much easier to get into—New Hall and Robinson are probably the least competitive. John's is one of the more difficult—it has an excellent reputation and its popularity is based on a lot of different qualities. It is the second wealthiest college at Cambridge, so we have access to a lot of resources, we're good in sports, it's a beautiful campus and you can "live in" [live in the residential halls] all three years.

5

Understanding Admissions at the Top Colleges

— KEY POINTS —

A thorough understanding of how admissions works
—including the terminology used, the priorities of the admissions department,
the various admissions cycles, and the way in which decisions are made
—will help you to fare your best in the application process

∎

Understanding the various cycles of admission will allow you to make the critical
decision of whether to apply Early Decision or Early Action at a particular college

∎

Admissions committees examine your academic potential, nonacademic pursuits,
and personal attributes to evaluate your candidacy

∎

Colleges seek diversity and want to craft a "well-rounded" class, which is not
necessarily composed of "well-rounded" individuals
—*They seek to balance a class, making sure that it includes students representing a
wide range of academic and nonacademic talents, educational and career goals, personal and family backgrounds, ethnic and racial identities, and geographical and
socioeconomic origins*

∎

Colleges have different educational philosophies and values, which play a role in
admissions, as well as different methods of evaluating candidates for admission

INTRODUCTION

A thorough understanding of how the top colleges make their admissions decisions is essential for you to do the best job possible in completing and submitting your applications. This chapter will help you to understand the basics of college admissions. You will learn about the various application timing options (Early Action, Early Decision, Regular, and Rolling), which will help you to determine whether or not you should apply early to a college. The chapter will also teach you what criteria the college admissions committees evaluate, who is involved in the evaluations, and how these evaluations are performed.

The way in which admissions departments at the top colleges are organized and the way in which their decision procedures are carried out share many of the same features. At the same time, however, there are differences in the admissions operations at the leading colleges. Some of these differences lie in logistical or procedural methods, whereas other differences lie in philosophical approach. Our aim in this chapter is not only to introduce you to the ideas behind college admissions, but also to share our findings about how the different approaches to admissions at the various schools shape their decisions.

THE ROLE OF ADMISSIONS

The job that a college's admissions department performs has more bearing on the school's future than most other activities on campus. It may well have more overall impact on the future direction of the college than the work of Nobel laureates, the construction of new libraries, the donation of large sums of money by benefactors, or the employment opportunities snatched up by its recent graduates. The work performed by the college admissions department is so important because it leads to all of the above and more. The candidates chosen for the next class will be members of the college community for life, thus adding to the value of the college with their own Nobel-quality work, presence in campus activities, monetary contributions, and future career successes. The quality of the candidates admitted and enrolled at the college determines the college's appeal to future applicants. The talents, strengths, and diversity of each incoming class help to create the campus's success, reputation, and appeal to others. The admissions department thus plays a critical role on the campuses of the top colleges.

Admissions departments play a dual role. They are responsible for selling the college to prospective students and evaluating applicants for admission. Admissions officers are meant to be ambassadors of the school, bestowing prospective applicants with positive information about the college and its offerings. Most travel the country and the world in order to publicize their schools and stir up interest in attending them among future college entrants. These same officers work together, beginning in November each year and continuing through the winter months until April, to read applications and make decisions about which candidates to admit.

ADMISSIONS PRIORITIES

Before reading further in this chapter, it is important that you command an overview of the various priorities that admissions committees must juggle when evaluating students. Obviously, the top colleges want students who will be successful in college and beyond. As discussed later in this chapter (starting on page 151), the three fundamental criteria upon which you will be evaluated for admission to a college are your academic potential, your nonacademic pursuits and talents, and your personal attributes.

Admissions committees must also, however, fulfill specific needs of the college. They must first of all ensure that the college maintain or enhance its "profile," which is the information submitted to the public about the college. Colleges know that the public judges their quality based on information such as the college's rate of acceptance in admissions, the SAT I scores of the most recent incoming class, and the college's yield on accepted applicants (the percentage of accepted applicants who decide to attend the college). For this reason, colleges want as many applications as possible (so that they can push down their rate of acceptance), they look for students with high SAT I scores, and they want to accept students whom they believe are most likely to attend their institution.

Colleges have other priorities as well. They look to diversify their classes as much as possible, which means that they are concerned not only with each applicant as an individual but also with how each applicant will add to the college's composition, often referred to as the "composite." Most colleges set targets for the numbers of minority or international candidates they want to accept, for example. See pages 154 through 157 for an in-depth discussion of diversity's role in college admissions.

Colleges also must abide by certain policies set by the college's administration, in conjunction with a board of directors or other decision-making bodies. The most important of these policies might concern, for example, the need to compose a high-performance hockey or basketball team or to satisfy wealthy contributing alumni by admitting their offspring at higher rates than other applicants. One of the most important policies that govern college admissions concerns the college's ability to admit students who cannot afford its cost. This refers to a college's stand on need consciousness in its admissions process.

NEED CONSCIOUSNESS IN COLLEGE ADMISSIONS

Perhaps the most important policy governing admissions is a college's approach to evaluating candidates with financial need. Most of the top colleges have financial aid budgets strong enough to allow them to evaluate applicants without concern for their financial situation at all. Such a system, called a "need-blind" admissions policy, means that a college's admissions officers evaluate a candidate without having any information about his or her financial situation available to them. If the candidate is admitted, the financial aid office then puts together an aid package and presents it to him or her upon receipt of the acceptance letter from the college. (Note that not all colleges that are need-blind also agree to meet the full need of all students admitted. A college can admit a student need-blind, but then offer him or her an aid package that is not sufficient to cover the costs of attending the school.)

Most of the colleges whose admissions officers we interviewed for the purposes of this book are need-blind. In other words, at almost all of the top colleges, an applicant's ability to pay for college is not taken into account at the time the admissions decision is made.

At the more selective colleges that are *not* fully need-blind, the majority of applicants are admitted without regard to need; it is only those applicants who are at the bottom of the list of possible admits that are looked at with some consideration of their ability to pay for college. When admitting the last students in a class, the admissions committees at schools that are not fully need-blind (often referred to as having "need-aware" or "need-conscious" admissions policies) will admit students with little financial need over those with great financial need. Thus, if you are an extremely well-qualified applicant, likely to be highly desirable to the college and stronger even than most of those who will be admitted alongside of you, then it will not matter—even at need-conscious schools—if you have great financial need. If you have great financial need and are at the bottom of the college's list of possible admits, though, then your weak financial situation might play a part in seeing that you are denied admission to the college.

THE FOUR POSSIBLE OUTCOMES OF AN ADMISSIONS DECISION

The decision that an admissions committee makes regarding your application will be one of four possibilities: admit, deny, waitlist, or defer.

To **admit** an applicant is to offer the student a place in the incoming class. To **deny** a candidate admission is to notify the candidate that, though he or she may be qualified to attend the school, it is not offering him or her a place in the class. To **waitlist** an applicant is to notify the candidate that he or she is not being offered a place at the school at the present time, but there is still a possibility of being admitted in the future if there is space in the class after all admitted applicants notify the school of their decisions. To **defer** a student is essentially to put the applicant "on hold." Deferring an applicant delays a final decision until more information about the student can be evaluated or until the admissions committee can better compare the student against other applicants. Deferring a student does not occur in Regular Admissions cycles, but only during Rolling Admissions, Early Decision, or Early Action cycles.

THE FOUR TYPES OF ADMISSIONS CYCLES

Generally speaking, there are four different types of college admissions cycles, which govern the timing in which applications are submitted and evaluated. These four cycles are: Regular Admissions, Rolling Admissions, Early Decision, and Early Action.

REGULAR ADMISSIONS

Regular Admissions is the standard admissions evaluation cycle, which requires an applicant to submit the application by a particular deadline (usually in early to mid-January of the year in which he or she wants to attend college). After the deadline, the admissions team begins to evaluate all applications at the same time. All students are notified of the college's decision several months later (usually in late March or April), at more or less the same time as other candidates, whether the decision be to admit the student, deny the student admission, or waitlist the student. Because of concern for the composition of the class as a whole, most decisions are not finalized until all applications have been reviewed. Most schools notify students who applied for Regular Admission in late March to early April and stand by the Candidates' Common Reply Date (set up by the Ivy League) of May 1. This means that students applying to most of the top colleges are not required to notify schools of their decisions to attend or not attend until May 1, allowing them to receive notification from all target colleges before being forced to make a decision.

ROLLING ADMISSIONS

Rolling Admissions is an admissions evaluation cycle that allows applications to be reviewed and decided upon as they arrive in the admissions office. A Rolling Admissions policy might, for example, open its season on October 1, requiring only that all applicants get their applications in by a certain deadline in the winter or spring. (For Rolling Admissions, it is generally beneficial for the applicant to get his or her application in as soon as possible.) Under most Rolling

Admissions policies, a candidate is notified of the college's decision four to eight weeks after receipt of the application. Rolling Admissions cycles are generally used only at large public universities, such as the University of Wisconsin or the University of Michigan. Many of the other flagship public universities, however, do not conduct Rolling Admissions, abiding by a Regular Admissions cycle instead.

EARLY DECISION

Early Decision is a policy offered by most of the top colleges for students who know what their first-choice college is by the beginning of the senior year. In Early Decision, a student applies to the college under a *binding contract* early in the fall (the deadline is usually November 1 or 15), is notified several months later of the college's decision, and is *obligated* to attend the school if admitted. A student applying Early Decision to one school cannot apply Early Decision or Early Action to any other school.

EARLY DECISION II

A few schools, such as Bowdoin, Wesleyan, Middlebury, and Colby, now conduct two rounds of Early Decision, one with applications due by the early November deadline and another with applications due by a January deadline. "Early Decision II," as it is often called, using the January deadline, is still a binding contract in which candidates are obligated to attend the school if accepted. They are notified within a month or two, before regular January applicants are notified.

     The benefit of the ED II policy is that students have more time to investigate colleges and think about where they want to go before committing themselves, yet still get the benefit of proclaiming that a school is their definite first choice (a plus for your candidacy in the eyes of admissions officers). The drawback to ED II is that students cannot wait until hearing of the decision before completing applications to other colleges, so the option does not save candidates any work or energy. (As yet another option, Wellesley offers something it calls "Early Evaluation" in addition to Early Decision. Early Evaluation is not binding, but it is also not a final decision. Wellesley merely tells a candidate asking to be evaluated early in the fall—at the same time as the Early Decision process—whether it is "likely," "possible," or "unlikely" that she will be accepted in the spring.)

EARLY ACTION

Only a few colleges have Early Action rather than Early Decision policies. Early Action also allows a student to apply to a college early and be notified from the school a few months later. It differs from Early Decision in that it is not a binding contract. Those who apply Early Action are not obligated to attend the school if they are accepted but can wait until hearing from other schools (during the Regular Admissions round) to make a final decision about where to attend. The most notable examples of colleges with Early Action rather than Early Decision policies are Boston College, Brown, Georgetown, Harvard, and MIT. The Early Action policies now allow a student to apply to other colleges' Early Action programs but prohibit an applicant from applying to any Early Decision program.

THE BENEFITS OF THE EARLY OPTIONS FOR COLLEGES

Because one is a binding policy and the other is not, Early Decision and Early Action confer quite different benefits upon the colleges' admissions committees. Early Decision is beneficial for colleges because it helps them choose good candidates to form a foundation for the upcoming class, knowing for certain that those students will attend the school. This helps them to improve their "yields" (the percentage of accepted students who decide to matriculate at the college) because they know that the students admitted Early will attend. Early Decision also benefits the college by ensuring that a portion of the class is extremely enthusiastic about attending the school, declaring it their first choice early on. Every college wants to be sure that its students are happy, motivated, and productive. When a large portion of the entering class strongly supports the college, the feeling can be contagious, thus boosting the morale of everyone on campus.

An Early Decision policy gives colleges a great deal of control over class composition, knowing for certain that students admitted Early will matriculate at the college. Early Action, on the other hand, is not as beneficial for colleges because it does not allow them to admit a student knowing for sure that he or she will attend. Early Action does not give colleges as much control over their future classes. (It is important to note, however, that colleges usually get a better yield from their Early Action applicants than they do from their regularly admitted applicants.)

Because of the ways in which they benefit the colleges, Early Decision and Early Action are very different in terms of the strategies that students can and must use when abiding by them. Applying somewhere Early Decision generally requires much more thought and strategy on the part of applicants than does applying Early Action. On the other hand, the admissions advantages for the applicant who aims for the right target are generally greater for those applying Early Decision than Early Action.

THE BENEFITS OF THE EARLY OPTIONS FOR APPLICANTS

The real question is how beneficial Early policies are for applicants. Most of this discussion focuses on Early Decision, since an application under this binding policy involves much more thought and commitment, and confers more benefits upon an applicant who chooses an ED target wisely, than does an Early Action application.

Over the past decade, the top colleges have continued to fill greater and greater portions of their freshman classes with Early Decision (and Early Action) applicants. Most of the top colleges fill between 33 and 40% of their freshman classes with Early applicants, although some have gone as far as to fill half the class Early in recent years.

The acceptance rates (the percentage of applicants who are admitted to the college) at nearly all the schools is higher among Early Decision (and Action) applicants than it is among Regular Admissions applicants. Naturally, high school students are now concerned that they need to apply somewhere under an Early Decision or Action policy in order to boost their chances of acceptance. The result has been a huge surge in the number of Early applications that the top colleges receive each year—a kind of mad frenzy among high school seniors to decide on a favorite college and apply Early in the fall.

College admissions officers and high school counselors alike are worried about the repercussions of this trend toward applying Early, especially under Early Decision policies. It means that many students are applying under binding contracts to colleges that may or may not end up as their first choices. Many students are simply not ready by the very beginning of their senior year to make a final decision about their top-choice school, and yet they are applying Early Decision to colleges despite this uncertainty, for fear of not being accepted in the Regular Admissions round.

The unfortunate fact is, there is good reason for the frenzy around Early applications. It is indeed much easier for students of certain profiles to gain admission Early Decision (and often Early Action as well). As an added benefit, if you are accepted under a college's Early Decision or Action policy, you will not have to commit as much time to the application process as you would if you were to apply to a large number of schools. You can breathe easily for the rest of the year in a way that other seniors do not have the luxury of doing.

THE IMPORTANCE OF INVESTIGATING THE EARLY OPTIONS

These days, applying Early should be considered a near necessity for many savvy prospective college students. Most students will not want to miss out on this opportunity. This is one of the reasons that it is more and more important that you start the college research and investigation process early on and complete your visits by the end of the summer before senior year begins. Deciding on a first-choice school at the beginning of your senior year so that you can apply under an Early Decision (or Early Action) policy will enhance your prospects of going to the best college possible, assuming you apply the right strategy (something that is admittedly difficult to do without the help of a very knowledgeable college counselor).

It is important that you aim for the right school if you are going to apply somewhere Early Decision or Early Action. If you decide to go Early Decision, you have only one shot at this option. You have to be sure you are aiming for the right target so that you do not blow your chances. In other words, you have to be certain you are applying to the best possible college (and the best possible one for *you,* given your needs) but do not aim *too* high, for a college that will probably not accept you Early. If you mistakenly aim too high, you forfeit your chance of admission at the school one notch below, to which you *should* have been trying for an Early Decision acceptance. On the other hand, if you do not aim high enough, you will be relegated to attending a college that is one notch below others at which you could have been admitted. Similarly, if you decide to apply to a school (or several schools) under an Early Action policy, you are losing your opportunity to apply to one of the Early Decision schools, so you must choose wisely. Applying somewhere Early requires that you work with an expert college counselor who can help you make important decisions about your options.

WHO SHOULD APPLY EARLY

As mentioned previously, a majority of applicants would be wise to apply early to some school or another, assuming that they can choose the right college. Those who should be particularly ready to apply Early, especially Early Decision, include two types of candidates:

1. Applicants with particularly high SAT I scores and weaker high school records (when compared to those of most admitted students at the particular college); and

2. Solid performers (within the context of the particular college's applicant pool) with no extra-special offerings

Applicants with Particularly High SAT I Scores and Weaker High School Records

For students with high SAT I scores but academic records that are a bit weaker than the average accepted applicant at a particular college, Early Decision (and sometimes Early Action as well) is a smart way to go. Most colleges want to boost their SAT profiles (the published SAT scores of their incoming classes) enough to overlook some less than ideal performances in high school in order to gain students whose scores will enhance their image. Some of the top colleges that normally accept only students with A/A– grades have in recent years consistently admitted high SAT I performers with A–/B+ grades during their Early Decision policies in order to ensure under a binding contract that these students (and their great scores) matriculate at the college. If your SAT I scores are exceptionally high and you have made a few blunders or performed only at a B+ level in high school, you should definitely prepare to apply under an Early Decision policy. You often have a better shot at Early Action admission as well, but the necessity of applying Early Action to those colleges that offer it if you have this high test score and lower grades profile is not as compelling.

Solid Performers with No Extra-Special Offerings

The top colleges readily admit that during the Early Decision (and sometimes Early Action) process they fill their classes with many solid students who have good or very good records but might not fare well in the Regular Admissions process simply because their backgrounds are not unique or because nothing sets them apart from other similar applicants. The top colleges will inevitably be admitting some of these solid but not unusual students anyway, so it is best for them to admit them Early rather than waiting until later on. Admitting these kinds of students Early Decision allows the colleges to be certain of their attendance (thus improving their yields) and to ensure that a certain portion of the incoming class is particularly enthusiastic about the school.

Students who fall within the category of being good academic performers with nothing extra-special to offer should definitely consider applying to a college Early Decision. These types would be wise to dig into the college investigation and visiting process early on in their high school careers so they are prepared to make decisions and submit an application early in the senior year. If your high school record is strong, your test scores fall around the median of those submitted by a college's last incoming class, and your extracurricular involvement and leadership are healthy—but you do not possess any special status or trait (by virtue of your race, ethnicity, geographical origins, personal background, legacy status, athletic recruit status, etc.) that will set you apart from other similarly strong candidates—you are substantially more likely to be accepted at the school Early Decision (and, to a somewhat lesser extent, Early Action) than if you apply later on.

WHO SHOULD NOT APPLY EARLY DECISION

There are three types of students who should not apply to a college under a binding Early Decision policy, although it is perfectly fine for them to apply to a college under a nonbinding Early Action program.

1. Those who have not identified a single top-choice college by the senior fall;
2. Those who are likely to benefit in college admissions from their academic or nonacademic performance during senior fall; and
3. Those who want to be able to compare financial aid packages (and perhaps bargain) before deciding which college to attend.

Those Who Cannot Clearly Identify a Top-Choice College

Students who cannot identify which college is best for them should not apply anywhere Early Decision. Because the policy is binding, it should be used only by those who know for certain which college is their top pick. As mentioned earlier, most students can benefit from applying to a college Early, so high schoolers are wise to begin the college investigation process during sophomore or junior year so that they are able to grasp the opportunity that Early application offers. Students who have not yet completed the college research and investigation process should not rush into an Early Decision move (Early Action is fine since it is not a binding agreement to attend) if they are unsure what they are looking for, though.

THOSE WHO ARE LIKELY TO BENEFIT IN COLLEGE ADMISSIONS FROM THEIR ACADEMIC OR NONACADEMIC PERFORMANCE DURING SENIOR FALL

Late bloomers and others who are predicted to boost their chances of admission through their senior fall performances should not rush into Early Decision either. Late bloomers and other students whose records have progressively improved throughout high school (and are expected to continue through senior fall) will look better to the colleges when they have one more strong semester of grades or test scores to show for their maturity. If you have gone from being a poor or mediocre student in your freshman year to a fantastic student by the time you reached junior year, you should probably wait another semester—making sure to give a stellar performance during senior fall—before applying to colleges.

Similarly, if you expect to perform extremely well during your senior fall in a key nonacademic area, you should wait to apply to colleges. If, for example, you are a strong swimmer destined for college-level competition and your summer-before-senior-year performance suggests that you are likely to set state records in the butterfly come December or January, it will probably be worth your while to wait until regular admissions to apply to colleges, in which case all schools will see you as being that much more valuable.

If the improvement to your profile during your senior year will outweigh the benefits of applying to a college Early, the best advice is to wait. The more information affirming your capabilities that colleges have in front of them, the more likely they are to decide that you have what it takes to succeed on their campuses.

THOSE WISHING TO COMPARE FINANCIAL AID AWARDS

Many students applying for financial aid have been told not to apply to any of their top choice colleges under a binding Early Decision policy because they will be cheated out of the best aid package possible if they are admitted this way. This can certainly be true at schools that give merit-based aid, design preferential packaging policies based on merit, or do not guarantee that the full financial need of all students is met. Schools that provide financial assistance based on merit, give some students better financial aid packages than they give others, or do not fulfill the need of all their students might be tempted to design less desirable packages for students who apply Early Decision because they know they are bound to attend their institutions no matter what. It is not a good idea to apply to these kinds of schools under an Early Decision policy if you need substantial financial aid. It is, however, generally fine to apply to a school Early Action if you fit a financially needy profile, because you are not bound to attend.

The truth is, though, that few of the top colleges fall into these categories of colleges. Almost none of the most competitive schools grant any financial aid based on merit. All eight of the Ivy League institutions, as well as most of their rival top colleges, grant financial aid based on need alone. These schools use certain methodologies to determine how much financial assistance to give each admitted student, as well as what form that assistance will take. These methodologies apply to every admitted student, based on the information he or she submits to the college about the family finances, and therefore would compute the same aid package for a student applying Early Decision as they would for the same student applying under Regular Admissions. Although there is room for some negotiation about financial aid even at these schools, such maneuvering generally improves packages by a matter of hundreds of dollars rather than the thousands that are likely to change a decision about whether or not to attend the college.

Several of the top colleges do, however, use preferential packaging policies that benefit students based on merit. Most of the preferential policies confer minor rather than substantial benefits to those rewarded (an additional $500 each year in grant rather than loan, for example), so you might consider waiting to apply to these schools if you are financially needy, because there is always a chance that you would receive a better package from the school in the spring.

The Ivies, as well as most of their competitors, also agree to meet the full need of every admitted student, meaning that their financial aid policies cover full need for everyone admitted. They do not generally shortchange less desirable students after accepting them to the college. All of this means that if you apply to this type of school Early Decision, your aid package will probably look little different than if you were to apply in the regular round, because packages are essentially determined using predetermined packaging methods.

If you will need financial aid to go to college and have a clear-cut first-choice college, first check to see what that college's financial aid program is like. If it is a need-blind institution, fulfills the need of every student admitted, and grants financial aid based on need alone, with no preferential packaging policies, you might, with careful consideration, decide to apply under the Early Decision policy. You will probably receive a similar package Early as you would receive as a Regular Admissions applicant; even if the financial aid package is not exactly the same, the difference is likely to be a slight rather than significant one.

The problem with applying Early if you need financial assistance comes when you or your family decide that financial considerations will play a part in your decision about where to attend college. If, for example, Columbia is your first choice but you would consider attending Penn State instead if it gave you a "full-ride" scholarship, then you should not apply Early Decision to Columbia because doing so would not allow you to compare packages before making a decision. If you are a very needy but also very talented student, chances are that you will be able to secure a very desirable financial aid package—maybe even a full ride—to attend an average, less competitive institution. It is up to you to decide whether you would rather take on some hardship and debt in order to attend a much better institution, which will likely pay you back with much better earnings and great rewards in the future, or attend a lesser college for free.

If you have not yet come to a conclusion about how much hardship you are willing to take on in order to attend the best school possible, you should not apply to one of the top colleges under an Early Decision policy. Applying under a binding Early Decision agreement will not allow you to compare the financial aid packages you will get at the top colleges (most of which are need-blind, give aid based on need alone, and cover full need—yet require that every aid recipient take on some bit of debt) with the more lucrative packages less selective schools are likely to offer you.

THE ADMISSIONS OFFICERS TALK ABOUT EARLY DECISION

"The reason we started Early Decision II was to provide an Early Decision option for students who haven't known about Wesleyan all along, who discover us during the fall of the senior year. The regular Early Decision pool is very homogeneous— mostly white, affluent, East Coast kids who have heard about Wesleyan for a long time, usually visited once or twice before senior year, and known others who have attended. We draw a better mix of students with ED II."

—*Barbara-Jan Wilson, Dean of Admissions and Financial Aid, Wesleyan University*

"Early Decision candidates are telling us that their interest in Northwestern is very high. In light of this strong and well-informed interest, we offer admission to all those we can. If we cannot offer admission to a candidate, we say so rather than offer to defer for later consideration. This is different from what other schools with Early Decision do."

—*Sheppard Shanley, Senior Associate Director of Admissions, Northwestern University*

"We're worried that the numbers admitted Early are too large. This year without intending to we took 38% of the class Early. I don't like to see this, but at the same time I don't want to cap the number artificially. My worry is that if the number of Early Decision applications keeps going up, it will begin to appear to everyone that the only way to get into Bowdoin is to apply through Early Decision and I believe that would send a message we don't want to send."

—*Richard Steele, Dean of Admissions, Bowdoin College*

WHAT THE ADMISSIONS OFFICERS SAY ABOUT EARLY ACTION

"The yield on our Early Action applicants is generally somewhere between 85 and 90%. The yield for regularly admitted applicants has been somewhere around 70 or 80%. Even though Early Action applicants are not bound to come here, they are for the most part choosing us over others in the end, at a greater rate than do regular admits."

—*Marlyn McGrath Lewis, Director of Admissions, Harvard University*

"In applying to our Early Action program, a student cannot apply to any binding Early Decision program at the same time—but Early Action applicants are allowed to apply to other Early Action programs if they choose."

—*Barbara Bergman, Associate Dean of Admissions, Georgetown University*

"The number of Early Action applications has nearly doubled in the last five years."

—*Michael Goldberger, Director of Admissions, Brown University*

"The shift in the last few years toward Early applications is enormous. The number of our Early Action applications has doubled in five years."

—*Marilee Jones, Dean of Admissions, Massachusetts Institute of Technology*

WHAT AN APPLICATION REQUIRES

THE ELEMENTS OF THE APPLICATION

Applications to the top colleges generally require six elements, which together provide the entire set of criteria upon which you will be evaluated for admission:

1. A high school transcript
2. A high school profile
3. Standardized test scores
4. The written application (including activity lists, short answers, and essays)
5. An interview
6. Recommendations from teachers and a guidance counselor

The **high school transcript** is the official record of all of your classes and grades over three years; grades from the senior fall are also evaluated (except in the case of Early Action and Early Decision applicants) once they arrive in the admissions office.

A **high school profile** is provided by the guidance counselor at your school; the profile contains a description of your high school and its students, as well as offering information about your school's course offerings and grading systems.

Standardized test scores are the results from your SAT I, SAT II, and ACT tests; the various colleges have different standardized test score requirements and options. (Advanced Placement [AP] and International Baccalaureate [IB] test results will also be evaluated by the colleges if provided.)

The **written application** consists of several pieces. All applications, including the Common Application, ask for lists of your nonacademic activities and information about them, including your specific roles, the amount of time you dedicate, and the length of your participation. Some applications also require short answer responses. All written applications also require at least one longer essay or personal statement; some schools require several different essay responses.

Most (but not all) of the top colleges offer **interviews** to their applicants. Admissions officers incorporate the results of the interview into their decisions by using the information provided on an interview evaluation form that the interviewer fills out after meeting with you.

All colleges require at least two **recommendations.** They ask for one letter of recommendation from a guidance counselor at your high school, which is usually compiled from that person's discussions with many of your teachers and supervisors over your high school career. Colleges also require at least one recommendation from a teacher. Some of the top colleges require or allow other kinds of recommendations as well.

Each of these important pieces of the overall application is discussed in far more detail in the chapters in Part II.

OBJECTIVE CREDENTIALS VERSUS SUBJECTIVE PRESENTATION

The high school transcript, high school profile, and standardized test scores together make up your academic credentials. (The information contained within your transcript, supplemented by the information contained in the profile of your school, creates your high school academic record; your high school academic record and the standardized test scores together create your academic credentials.) Academic credentials are bits of hard, objective information that, for the most part, you can do little about changing after the fact of your performance. There are ways in which you can overcome the impact of a negative grade or negative test score, or compensate for a weakness in your record, but there is nothing you can do to change the original record itself. (See Chapter 8 for further details on how to make up for academic weaknesses after the fact.)

The credentials you bring to the application are one thing, but your presentation of them is another. Your presentation, which is conveyed through the written application, the interview, and the recommendations, matters a great deal for several reasons. Most important, you have the opportunity to color the interpretation of all the objective data—your academic credentials—by providing a context and explaining how all of the different pieces fit together. The objective data can look quite a bit different when viewed through a subjective lens. Strong credentials lose their ability to impress when the supporting presentation is not compelling. Weak credentials are boosted when the supporting presentation is particularly powerful.

In addition, sharp admissions officers will cross-check the information provided in the various parts of your application for consistency. They will compare your essay assertions, for example, with what you say (and how you say it) in your interviews, to get as honest a picture of you as possible. This means that your presentation must be meaningful and fine-tuned.

Your total presentation (delivered through the written application, interview, and recommendations) also provides information that is important to admissions decisions yet not evidenced by the objective credentials. This subjective information is crucial to the overall picture that is created. The essays, for example, reveal your writing ability and your ability to sustain a closely reasoned argument. The recommendations reveal the extent to which you have impressed your teachers and also qualities such as intellectual passion. The interviews reveal your personality, oral communication skills, and maturity, among other traits.

Although it is always easier to make an impressive presentation when your substantive credentials are strong, the extent to which you take full advantage of the opportunity to present your case as effectively as possible can change how the admissions officers think about you. Because of their role in your presentation, we regard the written application (particularly the essays, but also including the nonacademic activity presentation and short answer responses), the interview, and the recommendations as your three main marketing vehicles. Each of these marketing vehicles is discussed in further detail in Part II of the book.

MIT EXPLAINS THE GOALS OF ADMISSIONS COMMITTEES AT THE TOP COLLEGES WELL IN ITS ADMISSIONS MATERIALS

"The goal of the admissions process is to create a community that bubbles with motivated, passionate students. We start with people we know can handle the work, then mix in an unpredictable blend of interests, talents, and activities. There's room for all types, from the kid whose main hobby is cloning dinosaurs to the jazz pianist to the captain of the All-State soccer team. That means we don't have a magic formula for the perfect applicant. We look for intellectual commitment and potential, creativity, and character. Those are not exactly quantifiable but we can tease them out of the information you supply."

"Most of our applicants have top-notch academic credentials, so we look beyond the numbers. We base our more subjective evaluation of your personal character-istics on the application itself and the letters of recommendation, secondary school report, and interview. The application forms are designed to allow you to describe what makes you tick: use them to describe your activities, personality, interests, and dreams. Your activities list gives us a sense of how you spend your time outside the classroom, while teacher references offer insight into how you do in the classroom and school community."

Application for Freshman, Admission and Financial Aid. Published by the Office of Admissions, Massachusetts Institute of Technology, 1999. Page 4.

THE EVALUATION CRITERIA

Through these many materials—from the high school transcript down through the letters of recommendation—a college's admissions committee can gather all the information upon which they examine their candidates. The top colleges are most concerned about your academic record, but it is important to recognize that this is only one piece of the complete picture they will take from your appli-cation. The most fundamental criteria upon which admissions officers at the top colleges evaluate prospective students are:

- Academic and intellectual potential,
- Nonacademic pursuits and talents, and
- Personal attributes.

These main elements that they seek are evidenced in different ways and to different degrees by the six elements of your application discussed previously. The following chart explains where the admissions committees look to find out whether you have the academic potential, nonacademic pursuits, and personal attributes they desire.

Criteria	*Primary Sources*	*Secondary Sources*
Academic/intellectual potential:	High school transcript High school profile Standardized test scores Recommendations	Written application Interview
Nonacademic pursuits/talents:	Written application	Interview Recommendations

Personal attributes:	Written application
	Interview
	Recommendations

ACADEMICS

In terms of academics, the most selective colleges of course want to see top grades and scores. They also look for students who have consistently performed well or improved academically over time; the selective schools are not inclined to admit students who provide evidence of strong academic performance in the past but have regressed over time. Just as importantly, though, the top colleges require that you challenge yourself by taking the most rigorous courseload available to you. Admissions committees also learn about certain aspects of your personality through academics. The top colleges are looking for students who like to challenge themselves intellectually, test their limits, expand their knowledge, and investigate their curiosities. They like students who express enthusiasm for the learning process and passion for particular subject areas. See Chapter 8 for further information about the academic credentials colleges value most.

NONACADEMICS

In terms of nonacademics, the colleges are most interested in seeing how you spend your time outside of the classroom and what kind of person you are, as demonstrated by what you do. If you have a special nonacademic talent, then the level of your accomplishment in that activity can substantially help you gain the attention of admissions officers. For others without particularly advanced or specialized nonacademic talents, it does not matter what worthwhile activities you enjoy, as long as you demonstrate commitment to certain ones among them (through the length of time you have participated in them and the number of hours you devote to them) and can discuss *why* these endeavors matter to you above others. Colleges also generally want to see that applicants have taken full advantage of the opportunities given to them.

Excellence in and special commitment to certain activities is important, while trying to demonstrate that you do a little bit of everything is not ideal. Still, some versatility is advisable. The colleges are looking for students who possess particular strengths but are also complex, multidimensional human beings. One-dimensional candidates—even talented one-dimensional candidates—appear dull and unimpressive when matched against candidates with a multitude of orientations, values, and pursuits. A brilliant computer whiz kid who devotes every spare moment to working in computer labs and designing software does not match up to a brilliant computer whiz kid who also publishes poetry or raises seeing-eye dogs for the blind. See Chapter 9 for more information on how to build an impressive profile of nonacademic pursuits.

PERSONAL ATTRIBUTES

Just as with academics, college admissions committees can learn about your personality traits by the way you describe and discuss your extracurricular activities and other life experiences. Some of the personal traits colleges tend to look for in prospective students include the following:

Passion	Devotion
	Commitment
	Enthusiasm
	Energy
	Dedication to learning
Perseverance	Follow-through
	Ability to overcome obstacles
	Fortitude
Compassion	Kindness
	Humanity
	Generosity
	Selflessness
	Community awareness
	Tolerance
Interpersonal Skills	Leadership
	Teamwork
	Cooperation
	Sense of humor
Creativity	Entrepreneurism
	Originality
	Innovation
	Imagination
Maturity	Independence
	Judgment
	Thoughtfulness
Honesty	Integrity
	Honor
	Morality
Curiosity	Adventurousness
	Willingness to take calculated risks
	Inquisitiveness

Before applying to colleges, you will need to think about which of the preceding characteristics you possess (and which are most clearly emphasized through the evidence you can make available to admissions officers). It is important to make your most desirable personal attributes well known through the academics, extracurricular activities, and life experiences you present in your applications. There is no one prescription or formula that you can follow in order to give the admissions committees what they are looking for. The reason for this is quite simple: The top colleges are not looking for one particular type of applicant.

The most selective colleges want to include in their classes as many different kinds of people as possible—people who, despite being different in their backgrounds and strengths, are nonetheless similar in that they are all talented and special in some way. The top colleges desire well-rounded *classes*, meaning classes composed of a wide range of individuals. They do not, however, necessarily want to populate those classes with well-rounded *people*, contrary to popular myth. Successful applicants are not those who show evidence of doing or being a little bit of everything. Successful applicants are instead those who show that they excel and surpass others, whether it be with their academic pursuits, nonacademic talents, personal attributes, or some combination of the three. Attaining such excellence nearly always requires the kind of focus that prevents one from doing or being many other things. The most successful applicants are those who can prove to the admissions committees that their excellence—attained in as few as one, two, or three areas—will allow them to better contribute to and benefit from an education at a top college than other applicants would.

THE ROLE OF DIVERSITY IN ADMISSIONS

Admissions decisions are more complicated than the three basic admissions criteria suggest because the desire for diversity is thrown into the mix. The top colleges are all extremely committed to the virtues of diversity. The kind of diversity they desire goes beyond creating a community that is merely well-rounded in terms of the academic talents, nonacademic pursuits, and personal characteristics contained therein.

The leading institutions of higher education strongly uphold the value of incorporating a wide variety of people in their communities in order to spread the value of higher education; create learning environments that are representative of a wealth of ideas; improve the number and strength of academic and nonacademic pursuits on their campuses; and increase communitywide tolerance for differences in thought, belief, or culture. In diversifying their classes, the colleges want to include not only students who represent a wide variety of academic talents, nonacademic pursuits, and personalities, but also students who represent a wide variety of races, ethnicities, nationalities, geographical locations, family backgrounds, and personal histories.

In creating an environment that supports a diversity of ideas, the college admissions officers are looking for students of all shapes and sizes—this includes a variety of minority students and international applicants, those from single-parent households as well as from large united families, those from the inner city as well as from remote rural areas, and those with unique religious or philosophical outlooks. Some admissions officers focus on looking beyond superficial labels (such as "Latino" or "resident of California") to find *real* diversity. In other words, if you claim a certain background or label but do not evidence any sort of connection to it, you may not be considered as valuable to the college as someone who clearly identifies with that background or label. You cannot rely only upon brief tags and labels in order to convince an admissions committee that you will add to its desired mix of students.

The desire for diversity means that each candidate is judged not only as an individual, but also as one of many individuals who make up a class and a community. Each candidate is evaluated on the basis of how he or she can contribute to campus life and complement the virtues of the others admitted alongside him or her. A candidate whose academic potential is deemed not as strong as others in the applicant pool might be admitted over others because he hails from a small town in Arkansas, a state with little representation in the applicant pool, and is a fine trombone player, desperately sought by the college's marching band. Another candidate might be regarded especially highly by the admissions committee because, alongside her strong academic record, she represents the first generation in her Ukrainian immigrant family to attend college. Another candidate might rise above other upper-middle-class white males from the Northeast because of his particular draw as an All-State hockey champion and his leadership as the head of a community society for the prevention of cruelty to animals.

Thus, the admissions committees weight criteria differently depending upon the applicant. They do so in order to admit a wide variety of individuals into their classes, with the goal of improving and enhancing the education and experience that each member of the collegiate community receives.

WHAT THE ADMISSIONS OFFICERS SAY ABOUT DIVERSITY

"If we're looking at a candidate with a Muslim background but there is no practice of the religion, what of that background would the student really bring to Williams? If there is no practice and honor of the religion, we cannot really think that the student would be adding to our diversity with it. A true cultural heritage is much more important than just the fact of being able to identify oneself with a certain group."

—*Philip Smith, Dean of Admissions, Williams College*

"We aim to make our enrolling class as diverse as possible. We look for academic strength combined with diversifying factors such as race, socioeconomic background, geographical origin, academic and nonacademic interests. Because of our location in the nation's capital, we may even look for diversity among the political views held by our students. This makes for very interesting conversations."

—*Barbara Bergman, Associate Dean of Admissions, Georgetown University*

"Our pool is so diverse in the first place that we don't have to worry about creating diversity here."

—*Marilee Jones, Dean of Admissions, Massachusetts Institute of Technology*

"A diversity of ideas is what we're after. We're looking for students who will add something to the class: kids from single-parent households, students from small rural schools, others from big inner-city schools, students who have overcome serious challenges, original thinkers."

—*John Blackburn, Dean of Admissions, University of Virginia*

"We look to bring all perspectives, interests, opinions—especially those that are not well-represented in mainstream communities—to our campus. We are interested in all facets of diversity, including diversity of political views or sexual orientation. Often, however, certain unusual or rare aspects of a person's experience or way of looking at the world are not brought to our attention, so we are not in a position to take them into account in evaluating a candidate."

—*Katie Fretwell, Director of Admissions, Amherst College*

"I find it important to look beyond the superficial labels to find *real* diversity. Someone whose family has for generations lived in southern Florida is very different from a candidate who now happens to live in Florida but just moved there a year and a half ago from Long Island."

—*Nancy Hargrave Meislahn, Director of Undergraduate Admissions, Cornell University*

"We don't move into the admissions process with some overall game plan, but we *do* want to make sure we get a balanced class. We think part of a student's growth at Yale comes from being exposed to different kids with different backgrounds and experiences. The girl who grows up on a sheep ranch in Wyoming provides a nice contrast with a suburban boy from New Jersey."

—*Richard Shaw, Dean of Undergraduate Admissions and Financial Aid, Yale University*

"We're very conscious of building pools, so that we are never in the position of accepting a candidate just because she's the only one of her kind—let's say the only student from South Dakota—in the pool. We want diversity but we also want to keep our options open."

—*Katie Fretwell, Director of Admissions, Amherst College*

"We don't have to engineer our incoming class to include students of different backgrounds. That takes care of itself through the range of applications we receive."
—*Sheppard Shanley, Senior Associate Director of Admissions, Northwestern University*

"We have a very multicultural pool so we don't have to search very hard to make our class diverse along the lines of race and ethnicity."
—*Janet Lavin Rapelye, Dean of Admissions, Wellesley College*

"We want a class that represents a good cross-section of America."
—*Dan Walls, Dean of Admissions, Emory University*

STANFORD WARNS APPLICANTS IN ITS ADMISSIONS MATERIALS THAT THE SCHOOL'S AIM OF SHAPING AN ENTIRE CLASS MAY MEAN THAT SOME FACTORS IN ADMISSIONS ARE BEYOND THE REALM OF YOUR CONTROL

"Bear in mind that at the same time that we are focusing on each applicant, we are also putting together a class that cuts across a number of dimensions. Consequently, many factors may enter into the process over which individualized candidates have no control. A high proportion of those applying are capable of succeeding scholastically at the University, and many more academically qualified students apply each year than we have places for in the class."
Stanford Today 1999. Published by the Office of Undergraduate Admission and Financial Aid, Stanford University, 1999. Page 41.

THE ROLE OF "FIT" IN ADMISSIONS

Each college also possesses its own distinct personality and educational philosophy, which in turn governs the way in which its admissions committee evaluates applicants. Many applicants overlook the fact that schools of a similarly high quality are in fact very different places, and thus may have different emphases in terms of what they are looking for in their future students. These emphases play an even greater role in admissions as applicant pools grow and, more significantly, as the number of equally qualified students in those applicant pools increases. When forced to choose between several candidates of equal talent, a college's admissions team often looks for the best "fit" between a candidate and the school in order to make the best decision.

A fit or match between a student and a school can exist as a result of many different factors. Chapter 3 discusses many of the academic and nonacademic qualities you should examine before deciding which schools best fit your needs and where to apply. Fully examining these many characteristics when looking at colleges will help you not only to determine which schools represent the best fit for you, but also to communicate this fit to the admissions committees. Admissions officers are pleased and impressed by an applicant who can provide evidence that their particular college offers the most ideal circumstances for the applicant's goals. An inner-city candidate wanting to attend Bowdoin or Dartmouth, for example, might write an essay about working as a Fresh Air Fund counselor in a small rural town. In showing how this experience helped him to discover new skills and personal attributes, he can also incorporate a discussion of how he aims to build upon these attributes by spending the next four years in a similar type of setting, thus providing evidence of a match between the school and himself.

THE ROLE OF EDUCATIONAL PHILOSOPHY IN DETERMINING "FIT"

A college's educational goals and philosophy represent the primary qualities with which admissions committees yearn to match applicants. MIT is a prime example of a college with a very distinct value system, which comes across clearly in its admissions procedures. MIT's culture is initiative-oriented. In order to succeed there, students have to be willing both to take risks and even occasionally to fail at their endeavors. The admissions officers thus look for applicants who have demonstrated not only leadership and self-initiative but also resilience. The admissions committee wants students who are independent and who can claim responsibility for their own development and actions.

MIT's emphasis on initiative in admissions came about as a way in which to distinguish the most appropriate applicants from the rest of the talented pool. MIT sees an extraordinary number of very bright and capable applicants, including many first-generation students whose families have immigrated to the United States from other parts of the world. Some of the students who apply to MIT tend to have been pushed by their parents to succeed rather than creating goals and dreams of their own, which is something the school frowns upon. Applicants to MIT, keeping the school's values and educational philosophy in mind, will do themselves a great service by showing that they are capable of self-starting and risk taking.

The phrase Stanford's admissions officers use to describe the special quality that matters most to them is "intellectual vitality." Stanford relies upon this value so much that during the 1998–1999 application season it adopted

"Intellectual Vitality" as one of the areas in which all applicants are rated (on a scale from one to six) in the admissions evaluation process. A successful application to Stanford nearly requires that you be able to provide clear evidence of passion for intellectual endeavors, whether it be through discussing intellectual pursuits outside of the classroom, soliciting recommendations from teachers who can attest to your stimulation and initiative in pursuing academic subject matter, or writing an essay about a special academic commitment.

As another example, Amherst's admissions officers describe the college as a "very verbal place." Amherst's educational philosophy relies heavily upon the importance of the written word, and this is emphasized in its admissions process. Amherst leans very heavily upon the essays when evaluating applicants and does not interview candidates for admission at all. Candidates for admission to Amherst should take the school's particular emphasis on the written word to heart when completing its application.

Brown's method of education places a great deal of responsibility on the student through the lack of core curriculum and distribution requirements. Brown's admissions officers thus look closely at applicants to ascertain whether or not they can handle the academic independence and benefit rather than fall to pieces in a flexible academic environment. Any student applying to Brown should try as best as possible to give positive proof of intellectual independence (discuss independent projects, outline classes taken outside of school, or demonstrate your intellectual creativity) as well as demonstrate maturity and sound decision-making skills. Show the admissions officers that you are capable of succeeding without an academic roadmap and are prepared to steer your way through academic endeavors on your own.

Columbia's educational philosophy, on the other hand, is nearly the opposite of Brown's. Everyone at Columbia takes the Core Curriculum, a structured set of small seminar classes. The admissions officers thus look for candidates who demonstrate that they are well-suited to both the relative structure in the undergraduate curriculum and the educational philosophy that governs that structure. Applicants should be able to demonstrate that they seek an education that is, in part, somewhat inflexible and emphasizes traditional learning—i.e., studying the classics of Western literature and world civilizations.

Columbia's New York location is also an important factor in its educational philosophy. The city's cultural resources are used to create a unique learning experience in many classes. Students applying to Columbia would thus benefit from making any possible connections between their own backgrounds and a future immersion in the opportunities that New York's institutions offer—for studying subjects such as art and music or for merely experiencing life as an inhabitant of the world's most vibrant cultural capital. A student coming from a very different small-town environment—one that offers no such opportunities—

could contrast her present situation with what she would expect at Columbia; an applicant from Chicago might draw upon his experiences learning from the cultural wealth in his own city while sharing what he would get out of Columbia.

Dartmouth is committed to finding students who exhibit adventurousness, curiosity, and risk-taking ability. Dartmouth also demonstrates a commitment to honoring student perspectives—something crucial to the learning environment at any of the top colleges—in the admissions process. It does so by requiring a peer recommendation (a recommendation written by another student rather than by a teacher or adult supervisor) of all candidates and using current Dartmouth students as interviewers.

It is important to realize that, although the top schools are looking for many of the same general traits in their candidates, some also look for prospective students who possess particular characteristics deemed necessary to fulfilling the school's educational mission and goals. By doing your homework and knowing a school well, you can determine on your own what a particular college claims as its educational philosophy and communitywide values. Understanding what is fundamental to the life of a school will help you to decide if that college is right for you as well as help you to fashion your application with the proper foundation and ideals in mind.

A college's educational mission, philosophy, and personality usually come across in admissions materials and brochures, campus Web sites, and conversations with admissions officers. If you are unsure what values are most important to a certain school, you can always discuss the matter with an admissions officer. Take care to do so tactfully. Do not, for example, ask an officer to tell you what to write in your essay. Instead, have a conversation with him or her about the kinds of impressions you have gained from the college's official materials and what you have determined to be the unique features of the school from your outside perspective. Ask the officer if your impressions about what is most important to the college are correct, positioning the conversation as a way in which to gather information for your own decision-making purposes.

FIT WITH THE COLLEGE VERSUS ENTHUSIASM FOR THE COLLEGE

All colleges report that demonstrating fit with the school can be very important, especially for borderline applicants competing against other borderline applicants for spots in the class. Although showing fit is always important, gushing with enthusiasm for a school is not necessary. Schools are concerned with their yields (the percentage of admitted applicants who opt to matriculate at a college), and therefore put some thought into admitting those students whom they believe will decide to attend. However, colleges also realize that most applicants are savvy enough to know they need to show some interest in the school, and thus schools take displays of enthusiasm somewhat lightly. The bottom line is that you should show interest and knowledge of a school, but you do not need to tell the admissions officers that you dream in the school's colors every night.

Although desire to attend a college is generally not an important factor (except in waitlist decisions, as discussed in Chapter 15), admissions staffs are often persuaded to deny a candidate admission if he or she shows a particular *lack* of enthusiasm for the school. A sloppy presentation, mistakes in the application, failure to show up for an interview, or failure to visit a school if you live in close proximity to it, all indicate a minimum of genuine interest in the school.

THE ADMISSIONS OFFICERS TALK ABOUT WHAT IMPORTANT ISSUES CANDIDATES SHOULD CONSIDER WHEN COMPLETING COLLEGE APPLICATIONS

How Important Is It That a Student Demonstrate Fit with a Particular College?

"We definitely look for fit. If someone tells us they want to be a business major, something we don't offer, we would wonder how much they know about Middlebury. Many students dazzle us in their applications with how much thought they've put into how they would fit in here—the absence of this can reflect negatively on an application."

—*John Hanson, Director of Admissions, Middlebury College*

"We are always, in every single admissions case, looking for signs of self-initiative. MIT is a full-strength experience and only those with great initiative will fit in here. We want to know that kids have done what they have done because of their own will and curiosity."

—*Marilee Jones, Dean of Admissions, Massachusetts Institute of Technology*

"'Fit' is critical to us. It is important that a candidate fits with Cornell's overall culture as well as with the program to which he or she applies."

—*Nancy Hargrave Meislahn, Director of Undergraduate Admissions, Cornell University*

"If we feel that an applicant does not know Brown, or states a determination to do something we don't offer here, chances are we might not take him."

—*Michael Goldberger, Director of Admissions, Brown University*

"Most kids we see have high grades and test scores, and have done all the right things. But to discover what makes a candidate different and special and appropriate for Stanford, we ask ourselves, 'Do our faculty want to teach this student? What does this student's work mean to him or her?' This is a high priority for us."

—*Jon Reider, Senior Associate Director of Admissions, Stanford University*

"Amherst is a very verbal place—we're very committed to the written word. And this is emphasized in our admissions process. We look for students who we think appreciate and can contribute to our ideals."

—*Katie Fretwell, Director of Admissions, Amherst College*

"'Fit' is a complex issue. We want to know, if a candidate attends Yale, how will he or she play a role in who we are? The residential college system makes this a community-oriented place, music is everywhere, community service is important to us—we want to measure how well candidates match our focus and atmosphere."

—*Richard Shaw, Dean of Undergraduate Admissions and Financial Aid, Yale University*

How Does Your School's Institutional and Educational Philosophy Play a Role in Admissions?

"Everyone on campus—even the maintenance crew—knows what our mission is and can recite it on command: 'To provide an excellent education to women who will make a difference in the world.' We are very committed to the ideals embodied in our mission, and it really comes through in our admissions process. We want students who will make a difference in the world."

—*Janet Lavin Rapelye, Dean of Admissions, Wellesley College*

"Our curriculum puts more responsibility on the student. There is no core curriculum, there are no distribution requirements. So we need to look closely at applicants to be sure that we think they are prepared to take on this kind of independence and responsibility."

—*Michael Goldberger, Director of Admissions, Brown University*

"From our perspective, we offer a unique education. Everyone at Columbia takes the Core Curriculum, which is a structured set of small seminar classes. Our intellectual atmosphere and our location in the city of New York also create a very unique learning experience. It's very important to us that students be able to articulate that there is a match between themselves and Columbia."

—*Eric J. Furda, Director of Undergraduate Admissions, Columbia University*

"The Jesuit philosophy provides the framework and foundation of the Georgetown education. The Jesuits focus on educating the whole person; learning about and exploring one's values and ethics. This type of education and introspection comes in part from learning about others and their backgrounds. These values come through in our admissions process—we really have a commitment to bringing in a mix of students who will learn from one another."

—*Barbara Bergman, Associate Dean of Admissions, Georgetown University*

"MIT has a very unique culture—it's very initiative-oriented. You have to be willing to fail if you want to come here. So we want to find kids with resilience, because *everyone* gets bumped around here, no matter how smart they are. You've got to be tough and resilient to make it here."

—*Marilee Jones, Dean of Admissions, Massachusetts Institute of Technology*

How Important Is It That an Applicant Show Enthusiasm for Your College in the Application?

"Desire to attend Penn doesn't *drive* our decisions but it can certainly on occasion *inform* our decisions."

—*Eric Kaplan, Director of Admissions, University of Pennsylvania*

"We've had applicants tell us they would crawl through broken glass to come here, and then not show up, so this can't play a big role in our decisions. We care more about fit than we do about how much a candidate screams that she wants to come to Yale."

—*Richard Shaw, Dean of Undergraduate Admissions and Financial Aid, Yale University*

"Early Decision is for those with a really compelling interest in Duke. Otherwise, the desire to attend Duke is not really a factor in admissions. We're interested in attracting the best possible students. We don't want to sacrifice the quality of the students for the sake of yield."

—*Christoph Guttentag, Director of Undergraduate Admissions, Duke University*

"We treat everyone who has applied as if they want to come to Brown. There are, however, things that can turn us off on a candidate because they signal a *lack* of care for our application—a poorly thought out presentation or misspellings, for example."

—*Michael Goldberger, Director of Admissions, Brown University*

"We assume reasonable interest in Middlebury by dint of the fact that a student has applied. But if there is an obvious lack of interest—say, for example, a student lives within easy driving distance of the school and has never visited—we might wonder why. We would perhaps take the application less seriously."

—*John Hanson, Director of Admissions, Middlebury College*

"We keep a record of a student's contacts with Cornell, so we know in the admissions process how the student became interested in the school and what is fueling her decision to apply. This is not something that is factored into the admission decision formally, but it does help us to know how a student came to know and have interest in Cornell."

—*Nancy Hargrave Meislahn, Director of Undergraduate Admissions, Cornell University*

"We have a question on our application asking applicants how they became interested in Northwestern. The details, language, and slant of the answer can be important, but we do not use enthusiasm for Northwestern as an admissions criterion. If a student lives nearby we find it strange if she doesn't visit the campus. Obviously, if a candidate lives in Bangladesh, we won't necessarily expect a visit."

—Sheppard Shanley, Senior Associate Director of Admissions, Northwestern University

"Years ago, I would have said that it's helpful. But in this day and age, applicants are very savvy and some will approach each school's application in a manner that implies it is their top choice. Therefore, we don't place great weight on this information and it doesn't impact admissions decisions. In most instances we take great enthusiasm with a grain of salt."

—Barbara Bergman, Associate Dean of Admissions, Georgetown University

"A candidate's enthusiasm for the school is irrelevant in our decision-making process."

—Karl Furstenberg, Dean of Admissions and Financial Aid, Dartmouth College

"It is not at all important."

—Jonathan Reider, Senior Associate Director of Admissions, Stanford University

"Showing particular enthusiasm is not that important in the regular admissions process, but it does become crucial if one is waitlisted and wants to be admitted."

—Marilee Jones, Dean of Admissions, Massachusetts Institute of Technology

"It's not a factor."

—John Blackburn, Dean of Admissions, University of Virginia

"It's less gushing enthusiasm that we're looking for and more demonstration that a student understands what kind of institution we are."

—Eric J. Furda, Director of Undergraduate Admissions, Columbia University

"Doing an interview expresses particular interest in us. In general, though, enthusiasm for the school is never as important as grades or high school curriculum."

—Barbara-Jan Wilson, Dean of Admissions and Financial Aid, Wesleyan University

"Enthusiasm for Penn is reasonably important. We ask students in a short-answer essay question how they became interested in us."

—Lee Stetson, Dean of Admissions, University of Pennsylvania

"Is the applicant's desire to attend important? I don't let my staff ask this question. We're up against a lot of different great colleges. I don't want to get into playing the game of guessing who's going to come here."

—Richard Steele, Dean of Admissions, Bowdoin College

> "A student's enthusiasm is nice, but it doesn't really make a difference until we get to the waitlist."
>
> —*Janet Lavin Rapelye, Dean of Admissions, Wellesley College*

THE CANDIDATE EVALUATION PROCESS

WHO EVALUATES APPLICATIONS FOR ADMISSION
ADMISSIONS OFFICERS

The employees in a college admissions department include the senior admissions officers (directors, deans, and their associate or assistant counterparts); junior admissions officers; and the administrative staff. Senior admissions staff generally oversee the activities of others in the office and make final decisions about candidates when there is no consensus. They also usually take part in some or all of the duties of junior officers, which include talking to prospective students on campus; visiting high schools and attending college events in particular geographical areas; and evaluating candidates' files. The admissions offices generally divide up the United States (by state or region) and the world (by country or region), assigning particular noncontiguous areas to each active admissions officer. An officer might be responsible, for example, for the following five geographical regions: Oregon-Washington; Florida; Illinois-Indiana-Ohio; the greater Los Angeles metropolitan region; and all the African nations. Responsibility for a geographical region requires that an admissions officer visit its high schools, getting to know the various guidance counselors and talking to students; attend college consortiums, fairs, and other regional events as a representative of the school; become the in-house authority on the area's high schools, communities, and culture; and oversee the applications from the region, making sure that they are evaluated properly during the admissions decisions.

Contrary to what some other recent publications have asserted, the senior admissions officers at the top schools are intelligent, perceptive, impressive people who, for the most part, attended leading colleges themselves. Many of them teach on their college campuses in addition to serving as admissions officers, have graduate degrees, and publish articles in industry journals and magazines. They are interested in both general educational issues and the educational priorities of young people. Most college admissions committees also include some junior staff members who are recent graduates of the college (or one of its peers). At many schools, acquiring one of these limited postgraduate positions in the admissions department is considered a very prestigious honor, one for which many seniors and other recent graduates compete. Thus, you can be sure that those reading your applications will be highly capable and well aware of what qualities make a successful student at a demanding college.

The officers at the top colleges are experienced in admissions and talented at evaluating all kinds of candidates, no matter what their particular strengths or selling points. They may or may not have advanced knowledge of a given subject—whether it be Swahili, gene therapy, or tap dancing—but that does not mean that they are incapable of evaluating a student with an interest or talent in it. After all, many food critics cannot cook.

You must therefore fashion your application so that it is impressive to an intelligent reader, but comprehensible to someone unschooled in your particular areas of discussion. You need to explain anything that is not common public knowledge but should not make the mistake of "talking down" to your readers. If you simplify your ideas too much, you risk appearing unintelligent or unsophisticated yourself. Do not turn a serious subject into the "lite" fluff version in fear that a sophisticated discussion will befuddle your readers. These people are not dummies and they desperately want to be impressed by you. Furthermore, admissions officers defer to the opinions of faculty experts, when necessary, in evaluating candidates whose special talents they cannot measure themselves.

Seasonal Hires

In addition to regular admissions department administrators, many admissions offices hire seasonal application readers to help evaluate candidate files during the busy winter months. Stanford, for example, usually hires four or five temporary additional readers each season. These extra readers are hired with care—they are highly educated and chosen for their ability to evaluate the kinds of top high school students who apply to Stanford—and thoroughly trained by experienced admissions staff. They are often retired admissions officers of other top colleges, spouses of Stanford faculty, local high school guidance counselors, visiting lecturers, or Stanford graduate school students.

Faculty and Students

Some schools also include faculty or students on their selection committees. At Cornell, for example, there is faculty involvement in each of the committees responsible for admitting freshmen to the seven undergraduate schools. At Bowdoin, about five faculty members, all appointed by the academic dean, sit on the admissions committee each year. At some schools, faculty input is sought when evaluating students interested in studying particular academic fields. At Duke, engineering faculty help in the selection of engineering candidates but are otherwise not involved in admission. At Columbia, math and science faculty sit on the admissions committees to help select students with strengths in those areas. Other faculty are invited to participate in Columbia's admissions process if they wish, but are required to read at least sixty candidate folders before being allowed to sit in on committees and vote on candidates.

At some schools, such as Georgetown, Wellesley, and Wesleyan, students are involved in the admissions selections. At Wesleyan, some of the "senior interviewers"—students in the senior class who conduct interviews on behalf of the admissions office—also conduct "first reads" (initial in-depth readings and evaluations) of applicant folders. At Georgetown, each of the separate admissions committees from the four undergraduate schools contains one student, who gets a vote equal to that of the deans, faculty, and admissions staff. Wellesley's admissions board includes the admissions staff plus ten to twelve representatives from each of three groups: the faculty, the administration, and the student body. The students on the admissions board are elected by their fellow students and serve for two years; a student vote on the committee equals that of others on the board.

THE EVALUATION PROCESS: A GENERALIZED DESCRIPTION

Each college has a slightly different procedure for evaluating admissions files. At most schools, the process approximates the following scenario, with minor differences from school to school:

The evaluation process begins soon after the application deadline with a "first read," which is a thorough reading of everything in a candidate's file, of every application submitted. At some schools, the first reader of a given application is the admissions officer responsible for the geographical area in which the student lives; at other schools, files are divided alphabetically or sorted randomly between all the first readers. First reads are the longest and most careful evaluations of candidates; most schools ask their officers to spend between fifteen and thirty-five minutes when acting as the first reader of an applicant's folder.

First readers are usually responsible for filling out a sheet of paper, which is then attached to the front of the file, with hard data and basic information about the candidate. These data sheets, often called "workcards," will provide information at a glance to the readers who visit the file after the initial evaluation. Workcards often include information such as rank in class, standardized test scores, an applicant's race or ethnicity (if provided on the application), and any special status information (if the candidate, for example, is a legacy applicant or a recruited athlete, or possesses a special talent). The workcard usually also includes ratings determined by the first and subsequent readers in a number of different areas, such as academics or extracurricular involvement. Almost every school uses numerical ratings so that readers of an application can make judgments of candidates in a variety of areas, which become useful for purposes of comparison against other applicants.

At the end of a first read, the initial reader has the opportunity to indicate whether he or she thinks the candidate should be admitted, denied, or discussed further. Files generally then go to a second reader. The second reader also looks over all material in the file thoroughly and provides his or her own opinion as to whether the candidate should be admitted or denied, or falls somewhere between the two extremes. At most schools, if the first and second reader agree wholeheartedly that a candidate should either be admitted or denied, the folder generally does not go to a committee for further discussion. It instead usually gets passed to a dean or director of admissions, who authorizes the decision to admit or deny the candidate. At most of the top colleges, only the borderline applicants (usually a large majority of the applicant pools) are discussed in a committee setting.

The files of all applicants who fall somewhere between the "certain admit" and "certain deny" categories, as well as those who received inconsistent evaluations from the first two readers, generally go to a committee for further evaluation. Committees are made up of several people, who present candidates to one another, talk about the applicants together, and then vote on whether to admit, deny, or waitlist each. As the admissions process moves ahead, the department usually keeps track of the entire pool of admitted candidates to determine what it looks like as a whole. At the end of the committee's decision-making process, the admissions department ensures that the class composition is ideal for its own diversity needs and goals before letters of acceptance are sent out. Sometimes last-minute adjustments or changes are made, for example, if there is a great gender imbalance or if the class is not deemed adequately diverse.

THE EVALUATION PROCESS: FEATURES UNIQUE TO PARTICULAR COLLEGES

The extent to which each school follows the basic pattern just described in its admissions evaluations differs.

READERS AND COMMITTEES

At some schools, more than two reads occur before a file is either decided upon or sent to committee for further evaluation. For example, the University of Virginia has a three-reader system, where each file is read by three initial evaluators. Only those with inconsistent votes after the third read go on to committee for discussion and group evaluation. Those files that receive consistent evaluations (whether they be admit or deny decisions) in the first three reads are never seen by the group committee but are considered final after the three close evaluations.

At Middlebury, all candidates who are probable or possible admits, in the eyes of the first two readers, go to committee for evaluation. No one is admitted to Middlebury without a committee's agreement, although candidates can be denied without being discussed by the committee. Even so, all denied applicants are seen by at least four admissions staff members before the decision is made. Middlebury encourages disagreement among members as a way in which to ensure that each applicant is evaluated fairly, from a variety of perspectives.

Taking the group-decision philosophy to its extreme, some schools send *all* files to committee so that all candidates are discussed among many individuals before being admitted or denied admission. At Wellesley, for example, after the first two or three reads are completed, every candidate is discussed in committee and voted upon. Harvard similarly makes no admissions decisions before sending a candidate's file to a committee discussion for final vote. No applicant to Wellesley or Harvard is accepted or rejected before being discussed and evaluated by a group of officers.

Some schools, on the opposite end of the spectrum, do not use formal committees or group decision-making structures at all. At Northwestern, for example, all officers read files individually. First or second readers hand all files—whether deemed probable acceptances or denials—to senior officers for final decisions. Four of the senior officers do nothing but make final decisions on candidates. Stanford also avoids evaluations by committee. Officers read files by themselves and then pass folders on to the next reader. The workcard at Stanford becomes the historical account of each reader's thoughts.

Stanford's evaluation process is also unusual in that the first read is not a careful, in-depth evaluation but a quick skim intended to cut the applicant pool down to a more manageable size. This first step in Stanford's evaluation process is called "sorting." Only very experienced readers take care of the sorting round, in which brief reads result in denials for a large percentage of the applicants (usually about 60%). Over half of the applicants to Stanford are rejected on the basis of this one person's opinion.

The very top applicants—usually about 5% of the total applications—are creamed off during the sorting phase and go to a second reader for a close, in-depth evaluation in which the workcard is filled out. As long as the second reader agrees that the applicant should be admitted, the file is then sent to the dean to be signed off for acceptance. The other applicants that make it through the sorting process but are not certain admits—usually about 35% of the applications—also go to round two reads. Each round two reader gets a stack of 100 files and explicit instructions about how many of these applicants should be denied admission, how many should be admitted, and how many should swim (meaning to receive a deferred decision until after another round of discussion.) Like the sorter, the second reader thus has full responsibility for denying admission to certain applicants. Several more rounds of reading are conducted before final decisions are reached. Informal mini-committees are often used to discuss the last few admits when there is great indecision.

Applying to Stanford is a very risky, even somewhat arbitrary business, because applicants can be denied on the basis of one reader's decision. Furthermore, the denial can be contingent upon not only that reader's personal subjective opinion, but also, if you make it to the round two read, which particular ninety-nine files you are being judged against.

RATING SYSTEMS

The way in which each school rates its candidates also differs tremendously from school to school. Harvard, for example, assigns two codes to every applicant, one based on academics and the other based on personal criteria, which takes into consideration extracurricular involvement, special talents, and personal attributes. The ratings Harvard assigns are not used to put candidates in an order from most desirable to least desirable, but are only guidelines. At Amherst and Williams every candidate is rated in two ways, one based on academics and one based on nonacademics. Both schools intentionally devised their two ratings on different scales so that there would be no way to average them together in evaluating candidates.

While the schools discussed previously uphold the idea of providing ratings that cannot be combined in any way to provide definite or foolproof overall judgments or rankings of candidates, other schools do just that. At MIT, for example, all applicants are evaluated in two ways in order to be placed on a graph or table that determines their desirability as candidates for admission.

First, the admissions staff calculates a Numeric Index, or NI, for each candidate, using an algorithm that takes a student's grades, rank in class, and standardized test scores (SAT Is and IIs) into account. The NI is a number between one and five, with five being the best rating possible. Each candidate also gets a subjective rating—also on a one through five scale, with five being the best score—that is based upon his or her cocurricular activities (learning-oriented activities outside of the classroom), interpersonal skills, and extracurricular activities. The objective rating is mapped backward on an *x*-axis and the subjective rating is mapped backward on a *y*-axis, so that every candidate ends up being placed in a "cell" on this table, with those located in the lower left-hand corner representing the admissions committee's top candidates. (See the accompanying graph.)

	1.0					
	2.0					
y-axis:	3.0					
subjective rating	4.0					
	5.0					
		5.0	4.0	3.0	2.0	1.0

x-axis: objective rating = Numeric Index

THE ADMISSIONS OFFICERS EXPLAIN HOW THEIR CANDIDATE EVALUATION PROCESSES WORK

"An outsider would consider our admissions process a very inefficient system; we are painstakingly thorough."

—Marlyn McGrath Lewis, Director of Admissions, Harvard University

"We are probably not as score-driven as many of our peers, and no part of our approach is quantifiable. We spend a disproportionate amount of time looking at essays and reading what a student has to say. We're a little plodding in the way we go about it."

—John Hanson, Director of Admissions, Middlebury College

"Everybody from one area, from each high school, is presented together. This is not to compare kids against others from the same school. The purpose is so that we can get to know the high schools—their courses, teachers, grading systems—really well. Applicants are not competing against others from their high school, though."

—Michael Goldberger, Director of Admissions, Brown University

"Our evaluation process is rather complex because we need to adjust our thoughts for four different undergraduate schools, as well as for in-state and out-of-state applicants."

—John Blackburn, Dean of Admissions, University of Virginia

"There is no single criterion by which we admit applicants, just as there is no single criterion by which we discount or eliminate applicants in the process."

—Richard Shaw, Dean of Undergraduate Admissions and Financial Aid, Yale University

"Our process is cumbersome, but we feel we really know the candidates by the end."

—Richard Steele, Dean of Admissions, Bowdoin College

"We spend most of our time on the middle group of candidates—not the best ones, who are sure admits, or the worst cases, who are easily denied, but those in the middle."

—Delsie Phillips, Director of Admissions, Haverford College

"There's still an art to admissions. You can't capture the process through a formula."

—Dan Walls, Dean of Admissions, Emory University

"We first make tentative decisions about our class. Then in mid-March we do a number of reviews to see what various subgroups of the class look like. We try to do some shifting at that time to make the overall class look the way we want it to."

—David Borus, Dean of Admission and Financial Aid, Vassar College

"We look at the candidate evaluation process from a positive perspective. We look for reasons to admit students, not for reasons to reject them. I always remind people that I am the dean of *admissions,* not rejections."

—*Karl Furstenberg, Dean of Admissions and Financial Aid, Dartmouth College*

"The 'sorter'—the person responsible for doing the brief first reads of applications—sorts alone. So it has to be an experienced reader."

—*Jonathan Reider, Senior Associate Director of Admissions, Stanford University*

"At the very minimum, each applicant has two readers plus myself look at his or her application."

—*Barbara-Jan Wilson, Dean of Admissions and Financial Aid, Wesleyan University*

"Occasionally an applicant whose file went into the deny drawer will be salvaged in the end and admitted—if we found out there were extenuating circumstances that accounted for poor grades one semester."

—*John Hanson, Director of Admissions, Middlebury College*

How Do Your Evaluation Committees Work?

"The regional representative for an applicant's hometown is responsible for representing that student to the admissions committee."

—*Lee Stetson, Dean of Admissions, University of Pennsylvania*

"We pride ourselves on the fact that every file comes to committee. Before it comes to committee it's read carefully by at least two people—three if you are an athletic recruit, an eight-year medical program finalist, an engineering applicant, or someone who has received very different reads from the two original readers."

—*Michael Goldberger, Director of Admissions, Brown University*

"Each of the readers of a case writes notes all over the applicant's file, then we discuss every case in committee and make a decision by majority vote after a series of excruciating comparisons. I think you could call this 'the lunatic fringe of democracy.'"

—*Marlyn McGrath Lewis, Director of Admissions, Harvard University*

"Each of our four undergraduate schools has its own admissions committee—featuring representatives from the dean's office, faculty, admissions, and current Georgetown students. Each member of the Committee has an equal vote. Our method brings together many different perspectives to the admissions process."

—*Barbara Bergman, Associate Dean of Admissions, Georgetown University*

"We're different from most schools. Every decision is made jointly by a small committee of readers—there are representatives of the administration, of the admissions department, of the faculty, and of the students on all committees. Everyone gets an equal vote."

—*Janet Lavin Rapelye, Dan of Admissions, Wellesley College*

"Our process is fairly straightforward. We review all candidates randomly, one candidate after another. Each applicant is usually evaluated by two readers before coming to me for a final read. I see all applicants except for obvious denies—and even those are seen by the Director of Admissions before a final decision is made. We use a committee at the end of the process for candidates who receive different evaluations from the various readers."

—*Karl Furstenberg, Dean of Admissions and Financial Aid, Dartmouth College*

"The regional officer is the first reader of a file and is responsible for presenting the best candidates from the region to the committee for further evaluation. The regional officer is a kind of advocate for applicants in his or her area. Our admissions officers have a lot of responsibility in that they provide quality control before bringing up files for discussion in committee, so that we don't have to discuss every case there."

—*Richard Shaw, Dean of Undergraduate Admissions and Financial Aid, Yale University*

"We pass files among ourselves to arrive at a consensus—rather than by group discussion and vote. There are no committee meetings here."

—*Sheppard Shanley, Senior Associate Director of Admissions, Northwestern University*

"We are distinct. We don't have a committee method at all. We read privately in our offices, then pass folders on to the next reader. The workcard becomes the historical record—a kind of running tape of each reader's thoughts."

—*Jonathan Reider, Senior Associate Director of Admissions, Stanford University*

"We have a three-reader system. The first reader probably does about thirty-five first reads per day. He or she rates each file: offer, waitlist, or deny. It gets passed on to a second reader and then to myself or an associate dean for the final read. If there's no consensus, the file goes to committee."

—*John Blackburn, Dean of Admissions, University of Virginia*

Are Students or Faculty Involved in the Selection of Candidates?

"Faculty are involved in the selection of our engineering candidates, but otherwise they are not involved in admissions."

—*Christoph Guttentag, Director of Undergraduate Admissions, Duke University*

"Faculty are involved in our admissions decisions. About one-fifth of the applicants are evaluated by faculty members—these are generally applicants with interests or strengths in math and science. Faculty in the arts also review portfolios and evaluate recordings of musical talent."

—*Eric J. Furda, Director of Undergraduate Admissions, Columbia University*

"Faculty sit on the committees of all seven undergraduate colleges. The strength of our process is that each faculty can look for the different qualities they deem important in students."

—*Nancy Hargrave Meislahn, Director of Undergraduate Admissions, Cornell University*

"Some of our senior [student] interviewers do first reads of applications for us. They are highly trained before doing so."

—*Barbara-Jan Wilson, Dean of Admissions and Financial Aid, Wesleyan University*

How Do Your Reader Evaluation Cards Work?

"Our Reader Rating Sheet is a composite of the opinions of each reader who looks at an applicant's file. Each reader records impressions on this sheet and offers an opinion on whether admission should be 'likely,' 'possible,' or 'unlikely.' The vast majority of the applicants—usually about 65%—fall into the 'possible' range."

—*Eric J. Furda, Director of Undergraduate Admissions, Columbia University*

What Kinds of Rating Systems Do You Use to Evaluate and Compare Candidates?

"We use codes to rate applicants in several different areas—academics, extracurricular contributions, and personal qualities—but we don't combine them together afterward to come up with any kind of definite ranking or ordering system."

—*Marlyn McGrath Lewis, Director of Admissions, Harvard University*

"We intentionally devised our two ratings on different scales so that there would be no temptation to average them together to come up with a pat way of categorizing candidates."

—*Philip Smith, Dean of Admissions, Williams College*

"We rate students on many different aspects—academics, nonacademics, teacher recommendations, the interview evaluation. But the ratings are not used in any formulaic way to help us decide definitively who gets in and who does not. These scores are markers only."

—*Richard Shaw, Dean of Undergraduate Admissions and Financial Aid, Yale University*

"There are six types of numerical ratings here. We give ratings on strength of curriculum, performance in class, standardized tests, extracurricular activities, the essay responses, and the letters of recommendation and the interview combined."

—*Christoph Guttentag, Director of Undergraduate Admissions, Duke University*

"We use two scales for student ratings. One is an academic rating, which is driven by objective criteria. We basically use the Academic Index to come up with this score, but admissions officers can use their own judgment, altering the number a bit with a plus or minus to further differentiate between candidates. The other scale is for personal qualities, based upon personality plus extracurricular activities, teacher comments, and the student's essay."

—Eric J. Furda, Director of Undergraduate Admissions, Columbia University

"We rate students on three scales: in academics, in nonacademics, and in intellectual vitality. On all the scales, a 'One' is the highest rating and a 'Six' is the lowest. Our ratings are a guide only. There are plenty of 'Academic Ones' who are not admitted, just as there are some 'Academic Sixes' who are admitted."

—Jonathan Reider, Senior Associate Director of Admissions, Stanford University

"We don't use numbers to rate students anymore."

—John Blackburn, Dean of Admissions, University of Virginia

"We have three ratings. One is for academics; one is for involvement and recognition in extracurricular activities; and one is for what we call 'Self-Presentation'—which evaluates the applicant's skill at completing the application."

—Sheppard Shanley, Senior Associate Director of Admissions, Northwestern University

"We rate two different aspects of a student's file: academics and nonacademics. There are three components to the nonacademic profile: cocurricular activities, which are learning-oriented activities outside of the classroom; extracurricular activities; and interpersonal skills."

—Marilee Jones, Dean of Admissions, Massachusetts Institute of Technology

"All applicants are given two separate numerical ratings: one reflects a student's academic achievements, the other a student's nonacademic achievements. Each of the two readers assigned to a candidate rates the applicant and prepares a narrative assessment. The ratings themselves are *descriptive*, not *prescriptive*.

—Katie Fretwell, Director of Admissions, Amherst College

"We don't use an algorithm or quantitative formula for any of our ratings, but all applicants get rated in five different categories: academic achievement, intellectual curiosity, commitment, personal qualities, and extracurricular performance."

—Barbara-Jan Wilson, Dean of Admissions and Financial Aid, Wesleyan University

"We rank applicants in five categories: academics, extracurriculars, teacher evaluations, counselor evaluations, and essays."

—Lee Stetson, Dean of Admissions, University of Pennsylvania

"We don't use ratings here—mostly because of how small we are. We do a narrative evaluation of every candidate."

—James Bock, Director of Admissions, Swarthmore College

"The Academic Index is a measure that was devised by the Ivy League to rate or compare academic credentials of recruited athletes. It has no decisive role in our decision-making process."

—Marlyn McGrath Lewis, Director of Admissions, Harvard University

CONCLUSION

The admissions procedures at the top colleges are, as you can see, somewhat complicated. It is important that you have a thorough understanding of the over-all admissions picture at the top colleges in order to make the right decisions and use the correct strategies while completing your own applications. Furthermore, each school is different from the next. These differences in the ways that prospective students are evaluated can affect the likelihood of your being admitted to one school over another. Be sure to understand everything there is to know about a college's admission procedures before applying.

ONE TOP COLLEGE'S WORKCARD

The following card is the workcard that one of the top colleges uses in its admissions process. Such a card is filled out by the first and subsequent readers of an applicant's file and then attached to the front of the file. It becomes a running record of each reader's opinion on the candidate. The terms used on the card are described. Similar types of cards are used by all the colleges in order to place certain crucial information and ratings of a candidate in one location so that they can be easily accessed by other admissions officers.

Explanation of Terms

Explanations of words used on one of the top college's workcard are given for the nonobvious terms, starting with those in the upper left corner of the card, continuing down the left column, and then moving to those in the upper right corner of the card and continuing down the right column.

Affiliation = Affiliation. Comments on an applicant's relation to a current student, alum, or employee of the university.

12th & 1st = Twelfth Grade and First Semester PG Year. Refers to a candidate's academic performance during senior year as well as the first semester of any additional postgraduate study the candidate has performed.

Rank in Class U W = Rank in Class Unweighted or Weighted. One of the two terms after Rank in Class is circled to indicate how the rank is calculated.

7 = Seventh Semester. Refers to the fall semester of senior year (the seventh of eight semesters of high school).

GPA-SSR/Transcript = GPA-Secondary School Report/Transcript. The candidate's GPA (either found on the secondary school report or on the candidate's own transcript—the reader circles the source).

% to 4 yr = The percentage of seniors at the candidate's high school who attend four-year colleges.

C COMPETITIVE = Readers are asked to place a "C" in all the spaces in which the candidate would be considered especially noteworthy or competitive.

NC NONCOMPETITIVE = Readers are asked to write "NC" in all the spaces in which the candidate would be considered especially deficient or noncompetitive.

Program = The quality of the high school and academic curriculum that the candidate has followed.

PQ's = Personal Qualities. A candidate's personality and other characteristics.

Support = Teacher or guidance counselor recommendations.

Self-Presentation = Essays.

Solid All Around = Refers to a candidate's stance as a "solid" or "well-rounded" person.

Use of Resources = Refers to whether or not a candidate has taken advantage of available opportunities.

Glue = Refers to candidates who are especially spirited or well-liked (i.e., those loved by everyone, with great interpersonal skills, to whom others turn for support and help).

Yrs. in U.S. = Years in the U.S. Refers to how long the candidate has lived in this country, if he or she immigrated from somewhere else.

Home Lang. = Home Language. Refers to the language a candidate speaks at home with his or her family.

Academic Program: Avg AA Rg MRA = Academics: Average or Above Average Regular or Most Rigorous Available. Readers must circle one of the choices to indicate the candidate's academic curriculum.

HSR = High School Record.

AC: = Academic Rating. Readers must rate the candidate on overall academics.

JIL = Joy in Learning. Readers must rate the candidate on his or her demonstration of "joy in learning," also sometimes called intellectual curiosity.

Athletics: B R _____ = Athletics: Blue-Chip or Red-Chip _____. Readers are asked to circle whether or not a recruited athlete candidate is a "blue-chip" recruit, meaning a high-priority athletic recruit, or a "red-chip" recruit, meaning a low-priority athletic recruit. The space is for noting the sport.

Work: HPW = Work: Hours Per Week. Indicates how many hours of paid work the candidate performs per week.

NONAC: Nonacademic rating. Readers must rate the candidate on overall nonacademics.

EL = Enthusiasm Level. Indicates an admissions reader's enthusiasm for the candidate.

RECOMMENDATION_____ A H D = Recommendation_____ Admit or Hold or Deny. Refers to a reader's opinion on what the decision on the candidate should be. "Hold" means to defer the decision and send the candidate's file to another evaluator.

Unusual circs./Q's = Unusual Circumstances or Questions. Readers make any notes or ask questions they would like answered about the applicant's candidacy.

RAD = Regional Admissions Director. A space for the officer responsible for the student's region of the country or world to make comments.

A H D WL 7 DEF = Admit or Hold or Deny or Waitlist or Seventh Semester or Defer. Refer to the decision made on a candidate.

FRESHMAN

Round 2 Reader _____ Date _____ ED: ____

Academic: Avg AA

Program: Rg MRA 7th:

AP's/Awards:

Tests 1 2 3 4 5 6 _____

HSR + N M — _____

AC: 1 2 3 4 5 6

JIL 1 2 3 4 5 6 _____

Nonacademic: Work: HPW _____

Athletics: B R _____

Art: _____

Dance: ____

Drama: ____

Music: ____

NONAC: 1 2 3 4 5 6 _____

Self-Pres. + N — _____

Support + N — _____

PQ: + N — _____

EL + N — _____

RECOMMENDATION _____ A H D

Unusual Circs./Q's

Round 2 Comments

Ethnicity: ___ ___ Decline to State☐ Citizenship _____

Permanent Resident: Financial Aid:

Gender:

Affiliation:

	A's	B's	C's	D's	F's	P's	GPA	Rank in Class U W
Transcript 10th							.	(of ___)
11th								7 (of ___)
10th & 11th								GPA-SSR/Transcript
12th & 1st								U W

Test Scores | % to 4 yr ___

____ ____ ____ ____ ____ Date: _____

____ ____ ____ ____ ____ Date: _____

Round 1 Reader _____ Date _____

C COMPETITIVE

____ Academic Record ____ Use of Resources

____ Rank in Class ____ Background

____ Program ____ Area/Geography

____ Scores ____ Diversity/Mix

____ Intellectual Vitality

____ Nonac.Achieve ____ Special Circumstances

____ Special Talent ____ Glue

____ PQ's

____ Support ____ Other _____

____ Self-Presentation

____ Solid All Around

NC NONCOMPETITIVE

____ H.S. Record

____ Rank in Class

____ Program

____ Scores

____ Nonacademics

____ PQ's

____ Support

____ Self-Presentation

____ Not Outstanding

____ Other _____

Search: Clear Admit _____ Estimated GPA _____

Round 1 Comments

Yrs. in U.S. _____ Home Lang. _____

Major/Career: ☐M

☐O ☐V ☐S ☐U ☐F

☐L ☐D _____

RAD

Hold Round Comments _____ | Date _____

XYZ

Dean Comments

AC	JIL	Non-Ac	A	H	D	WL	7	DEF

Figure 5-1. Workcard.

Appendix III

College Preparation and Application Timetable

FRESHMAN YEAR

THROUGHOUT THE YEAR

- With the help of an advisor or counselor, tentatively plan out your curriculum for the next four years, making sure to take challenging (albeit manageable) classes. In general, top colleges like to see four years of English; three to four years of a foreign language (preferably the same language throughout); three to four years of math (algebra I, geometry, algebra II, and an advanced math course such as calculus); three to four years of natural sciences (physical science, biology, chemistry, and physics); and three to four years of social science classes (history, government and politics, ethics, etc.). Furthermore, top schools like to see that you've taken advantage of available AP, IB, or other honors programs. See Chapter 8 for more details on high school curriculum planning.

- Get seriously involved in a few extracurricular activities, planning to maintain your commitment to one or two of them throughout the next four years. It is best if these activities also allow for growth or change in your role over time. Remember that sustained commitment to at least one or two extracurricular activities is critical for admission to a top college. Feel free to sample a number of endeavors at this time so that you can find two or three you really like. Also note that at some point during your high school career you should partake in some sort of community service work. It does not have to start during your freshman year, but do not let it slip through the cracks over the next three years.

- Plan for a meaningful summer experience—employment, volunteer work, extracurricular programs (such as athletic and/or other recreational theme camps or art programs), summer school or academic enrichment programs (to get a jump start on the following year or to explore new areas of academic interest).

- Take advantage of opportunities that may arise to visit colleges—just to start getting a feel for them. Check out local colleges or visit campuses convenient to family vacation spots. It is not yet necessary to be overly evaluative on these visits; it is merely helpful for a student to have a feeling for what college campuses are like before starting the self-assessment and research process during junior year.

SOPHOMORE YEAR

THROUGHOUT THE YEAR

- Continue to follow a challenging curriculum.
- If you have not already committed to one or two extracurricular activities, do so now.
- Continue to visit colleges when the opportunity arises. You may want to attend a college fair or a multicollege consortium to look at a few campus publications, listen to current applicants' questions, and get a feel for what kinds of things will be important to you when you start to look more seriously at colleges.

OCTOBER–DECEMBER

- Take the October PSAT in preparation for the junior year PSAT/NMSQT. The results you receive on your first set of practice PSATs will let you know what your weak spots are so that you can start to better prepare for future standardized tests.
- Students who plan to take the ACT should take PLAN as a practice run.
- Start to plan for a meaningful summer experience. Continue in an activity in which you were involved the previous summer if there is a way to advance within it or do something new.

JANUARY–MARCH

- Students and parents should at this time familiarize themselves with the nuts and bolts of college financial aid. You should also take a preliminary look at FAFSA and PROFILE forms to prepare for the kinds of information you will be required to offer. (Parents: You must begin to prepare this early for financial aid applications, because you have to allow time to make any and all legal adjustments to your financial situation before January of your child's junior year of high school. The year that runs from January of the junior academic calendar year to December of the senior academic calendar year is the one upon which all college financial aid considerations are made.)

- Students and parents should discuss and assess the need for special services such as a standardized test prep course or an independent college consultant.

MARCH–JUNE

- Assess your needs and interests against the curriculum at your high school. This is the time to start thinking about whether or not you would benefit from taking a course at a local community college during your junior or senior year. Talk to your guidance counselor and teachers about the possibilities open to you.
- Take the SAT II in subjects you complete sophomore year.
- Take AP exams in AP courses you complete sophomore year.

JUNIOR YEAR

Junior year is generally considered the most critical year in terms of your admission to colleges. Therefore, you need to start the year off prepared to give your best performances in challenging classes as well as assert yourself in extracurricular activities (ideally, those in which you have been involved since freshman year). You also need to make any final moves toward preparing for the college application process, such as arranging for testing improvement courses or hiring a private college advisor or consultant.

THROUGHOUT THE YEAR

- Continue to follow a challenging curriculum.
- Continue to commit yourself to extracurricular activities. If you have not yet participated in substantial community service activities, you should plan to do so now.
- Buy a basic guidebook to the colleges if you have not already done so.
- Do some preliminary self-assessments in order to formulate ideas about what you are looking for in a college as well as what your positioning efforts might be. Use the guidelines provided in Chapter 3 in doing these self-assessments.

- Continue to inform yourself about colleges. Speak with friends in college and alumni of colleges in which you are interested. Take advantage of gatherings with adults and college-age students to learn what you can about various schools—holiday parties, church or temple events, and neighborhood happenings are good opportunities for doing this. Also learn about colleges by attending college fairs or information sessions with college representatives, surfing the Web, and reading guidebooks.

- Develop a preliminary list of appropriate colleges for you based on your self-assessment and college research.

- Examine any application forms you can get your hands on, even if they are a year out of date, to get an initial feel for what the application process will involve.

- Create a resume of accomplishments and experiences. It will be useful when it comes time to solicit recommendations, go on interviews, and write your applications.

- Start filling out the Personal Organizer in Appendix IV to get a jump on the application process.

- Reassess your needs and interests against the curriculum at your high school. Decide (with the help of guidance counselors and teachers) whether or not you would benefit from taking a course at a local community college.

- Take advantage of any opportunities to interview (for jobs or volunteer positions) in order to develop interviewing skills.

SEPTEMBER–OCTOBER

- Register for and take the PSAT/NMSQT. The PSAT qualifies you for National Merit Scholarships and prepares you for the SATs.

- Register for and take the fall ACT if your performance on the PSAT has been less than optimal. As you compare your ACT and PSAT/SAT I performance, you will be able to determine which testing option is going to be best for you.

- Determine whether or not you would benefit from a class to improve your standardized test scores and arrange to take it before the spring tests.

- Start to plan for and arrange college visits for the spring of this academic year.

- Students and parents should take care of any adjustments or changes to the family financial situation that will need to be made for financial aid consideration purposes before the beginning of the next calendar year.

NOVEMBER–DECEMBER

■ Start to plan for an especially meaningful summer experience. Many college applications ask you to write about your past summer, so you will want what you do between your junior and senior years to be something from which you can extract a lot of meaning. Many interviewers also ask college candidates about their past summer experience.

■ Start to consider who should write recommendations for you. If there are junior year teachers who you will want to write your recommendations, then you should continue to foster your relationships with them, especially if they will not be teaching you at all senior year.

JANUARY–JUNE

■ Take the SAT I (and the ACT, if you choose to do so).

■ Take the SAT II in subjects you complete junior year.

■ Take AP exams in AP courses you complete junior year.

■ Complete arrangements for spring and summer college visits.

■ Complete arrangements for a meaningful summer experience.

■ Meet with your high school guidance counselor for preliminary talks and planning, even if your school does not require you to do so at this time.

■ Start to think about any supplemental application submissions you will want to make for special talents in the performing or fine arts. Consult with a teacher or instructor about your best work and how to go about preparing it for college submission purposes. Continue to work on the planning and execution of these materials throughout the summer and senior fall.

■ Register with the National Collegiate Athletics Association (NCAA) Clearinghouse once the junior academic year is complete if you are an athlete who intends to be recruited by Division I and II schools. (The NCAA needs an academic record containing six semesters or three full years of high school study in order to register a student for Division I or II recruiting, so you must wait until after your junior year grades are processed to do so.)

■ Reassess the need for a prep course to improve your standardized test scores and arrange to take it over the summer, before your final testing opportunities in the fall of your senior year.

■ Reassess the need for an independent college consultant. If you decide you would benefit from working with an independent counselor, make the contact as soon as possible. Junior year is not too late to begin working with a counselor, but the earlier you start, the more you will benefit from outside services.

SENIOR YEAR

Students need to remember that, despite the primary importance of the junior year, senior year is no time to slack off! Colleges look closely at academic records from the fall of the senior year and often contact high schools during the spring decision-making process to inquire about continued performance.

THROUGHOUT THE YEAR

- Continue to take a challenging courseload.
- Continue to commit yourself to extracurricular activities.
- Continue to inform yourself about colleges by speaking to alumni, attending college fairs and information sessions, and surfing the Web.

SEPTEMBER–OCTOBER

- Formalize your list of target schools.
- Request applications from schools to which you are considering applying. Many schools are inefficient about sending out materials, so start this process early!
- Acquire the Common Application in the event that you will be applying to any schools that accept it. (See page 334 for our recommendations on using the Common Application.)
- Start a college application organizational system. Allocate a corner of your bedroom or the den for all the college publications and flyers you receive. Keep a folder for travel and logistics information about college visits you are planning. Keep another folder for the Master Application Organizer in Appendix IV, which notes details about all the applications you will file. Use the Individual College Application Organizer in Appendix IV to make notes about each particular college's application details. Start a filing system in which you maintain separate folders for each college in which you are particularly interested. Each file should contain the Individual College Application Organizer and other notes on that school as well as the college's brochures, publications, and application.
- Decide whether or not you will be applying Early Decision or Early Action to any school.
- *Early Decision and Early Action candidates:* Applications for ED and EA are due on November 1 or 15. (A few colleges now have a second round of Early Decision called ED II, for which binding-commitment applications are due in January.) All Early Decision and Early Action applicants must both initiate and finalize all aspects of the application process for their ED or EA

application college during these two short months. All application details for that one application (soliciting recommendations, completing the essays, filing financial aid forms, etc.) must be done during September and October rather than in the later months indicated on this timeline. Note that you should continue to follow the timeline regarding applications to other colleges. Do not wait until late December, when you will hear from the Early application school, to move forward with other applications; if you are deferred or rejected from the college to which you applied early, you will have a lot of work to do while also suffering from a waning confidence level.

- Register for and take (during September, October, November, and December) the SAT I, ACT, and SAT II.
- Take any AP tests you have not yet taken (only for completed AP courses).
- Start rough drafts of essays and personal statements. The sooner you complete a rough draft of an essay, the more time you will have to rework it to get it into its best shape.
- Continue to visit schools.
- Arrange for interviews at schools that require or recommend them.

OCTOBER–NOVEMBER

- *Rolling Admissions candidates:* If you are applying to a school with rolling admissions, submit your application as soon as the school will start accepting them. The sooner you get it in, the better chance you have of being admitted. Rolling admissions candidates generally receive a reply from the school four to eight weeks after the submission of the application. Note that you should continue to follow the timeline regarding applications to other colleges.
- Approach recommenders and request recommendations. Give them at least a month in order to write you the best recommendation possible. The more time you give a recommender, the more willing he or she will be to support you—you do not want to get off on the wrong foot here!
- Request your high school transcript and review it to verify that all information is correct.
- Continue to revise and complete final drafts of application essays.
- Complete final drafts of application forms.

DECEMBER–JANUARY

- Most regular admissions applications are due to college admissions offices in December or January. Complete and submit applications with December and January deadlines.

- *Early Decision and Early Action candidates:* Early Decision and Early Action candidates generally receive their notices of admission, rejection, or deferral in December. If admitted, send in your reply along with your deposit. (Early Action candidates should reply positively and send in their deposits only if certain they will attend the school.)

- Check with teachers and your guidance counselor to confirm that recommendations and transcripts have been sent to target schools.

- Request FAFSA and PROFILE financial aid forms. Complete the forms and return them as soon as possible after the first of January.

JANUARY–FEBRUARY

- Submit final applications.

- Contact schools that have not yet acknowledged that your file is complete.

- File any remaining FAFSA and PROFILE forms as well as any other financial aid forms required at particular colleges.

MARCH–JUNE

- Notify schools of any new information, such as awards, honors, and scores, that might benefit you in the admissions process.

- Continue to perform well academically! Do not slack off, especially if there are schools from which you have not yet heard. Admissions committees often call schools for updates when they are forced to make tough decisions or to choose among two candidates.

- Most schools notify candidates of admissions decisions by April 1.

- Visit schools you have been admitted to in order to make your final decision. Take advantage of yield enhancement events and prospective student weekends offered at schools to which you have been admitted. These give you a comprehensive view of the school's academics, extracurricular offerings, and social atmosphere, as well as an opportunity to room with current students.

- Notify your recommenders of schools' admissions decisions and tell them what college you plan to attend. Thank them again for their assistance.

- Notify the schools of your acceptance or rejection of their admissions offers. Most schools require replies from their admitted candidates by May 1. Send in your deposit to your school of choice.

- If you have been put on the waitlist at a school, notify it that you would like to remain active on the waitlist if you still want to be considered for admission. Write a letter reiterating your interest in the school, send in any additional information that will help your case, and request recommendations from those who can support your interest in the school.

WHERE ARE THINGS MOST LIKELY TO GO ASTRAY?

You should be aware of two different types of problems: those that are partially outside your control (but not your influence) and those that are within your control.

Problems That Are Partially Outside Your Control (But Not Your Influence)

1. Some schools fail to send out a substantial percentage of applications upon first request, or do so with lengthy delay. The obvious solution to this is to start requesting applications early and stay on top of the situation. If you are having problems obtaining an application, try requesting it through different media—telephone, fax, letter, online.

2. Your recommenders are another source of likely trouble. They are busy people who, despite their best intentions, may still need reminding or prodding to get the recommendation turned in on time. You will want to make their jobs as easy as possible, and then stay on top of the situation. If the situation becomes dire, you may want to ask your school guidance counselor to step in to address concerns on your behalf.

Problems That Are within Your Control

1. The U.S. Postal Service is sometimes unreliable. To avoid delays or lost applications, simply avoid using the postal system. Instead, use Federal Express, UPS, DHL, or any other more reliable carrier when sending your application materials to colleges. Urge your recommender to use this same approach, offering to pay the expenses, especially if you are getting close to a deadline.

2. Your essay writing is likely to fall behind schedule because of academic and extracurricular commitments. It is easy to push college essays to the backburner when you have no external deadlines to meet. Start the essay writing process early and continue to give yourself time, on a regular basis, to work on your essays. You must be disciplined about this if you want to maximize your chances of success.

Appendix IV

THE APPLICATION ORGANIZER

This appendix contains two different forms that will help you to stay organized while you complete the college application process. You may make copies of these forms from the book or create your own similar versions of them by hand or on a computer.

The Master Application Organizer is a chart on which you can record basic organizational and scheduling information about all the schools to which you will apply. There is room here to include information for up to six schools, but you may make your own form larger if you will apply to more than six schools, as we suggest that most applicants do.

The second form is the Individual College Application Organizer. You will need to make a copy of this for each college to which you will apply. Here you can record more detailed information about your application to each particular school. File each Individual College Application Organizer in a separate folder where you keep other information about the college.

GETTING ORGANIZED

Many high school students have trouble getting started when it comes to organizing themselves for the college application process. You are not alone if the prospect of requesting materials, reviewing them, organizing them, and ensuring that everything gets done on time seems like a drag. When receiving application and college materials at home, do not feel as if you have to look at them the day they arrive. It is probably better if you review them when you are fresh and have time to read through them thoroughly. Keep unperused materials in one pile. Then, after looking at the materials, separate them into two piles: one for colleges you might be interested in, and one for colleges you are almost certainly not interested in. (We suggest you keep all college materials until the application process is over—you never know when you might change your mind about a school or want to look at a college's materials for comparative purposes.)

When you start making decisions about the colleges to which you will apply, take some time to review each school's application procedures and materials, marking down the necessary information on the organizers. Keep the application materials for each college in a folder or envelope along with its Individual College Application Organizer. You might want to use a different color folder for each college. As you near the end of the application process, you also might want to use sticky notes or index cards to indicate on the outside of each folder what steps you have left in completing that particular application. That way, as you near the end of the process for each school and have a few scattered tasks left to do, you will be sure not to omit one of them accidentally.

MASTER APPLICATION ORGANIZER

	1	2	3	4	5	6
School						

APPLICATIONS

Application deadline

Target mailing date

Actual date sent

Interview date

APPLICATION FORMS/BROCHURES

Date requested

Received (Make a check here when received.)

SAT I SCORES

Date taken

Date score report requested

Received by college (Make a check here when college notifies you of receipt.)

SAT II SCORES

Subject

Date taken

Date score report requested

Received by college (Check here.)

School | 1 | 2 | 3 | 4 | 5 | 6

SAT II SCORES

Subject

Date taken

Date score report requested

Received by college (Check here.)

SAT II SCORES

Subject

Date taken

Date score report requested

Received by college (Check here.)

TOEFL SCORES (for overseas applicants only)

Date taken

Date score report requested

Received by college (Check here.)

TRANSCRIPTS

Date requested

Received by college (Check here.)

ESSAYS

Target completion date of rough drafts

1   2   3   4   5   6

School

Editor/reader reviews completed

Target completion date of final drafts

Final drafts completed (Check here.)

RECOMMENDATIONS

Recommender 1:

   Date requested

   Date briefing completed

   Received by college (Check here.)

Recommender 2:

   Date requested

   Date briefing completed

   Received by college (Check here.)

Recommender 3:

   Date requested

   Date briefing completed

   Received by college (Check here.)

FINANCIAL AID

FAFSA

   Date forms requested

   Received (Check here.)

   Deadline

School	1	2	3	4	5	6
Target mailing date						
Date sent						
PROFILE						
Date forms requested						
Received (Check here.)						
Deadline						
Target mailing date						
Date sent						
College and other forms						
Date forms requested						
Received (Check here.)						
Deadline						
Target mailing date						
Date sent						

NOTES:

INDIVIDUAL COLLEGE APPLICATION ORGANIZER

COLLEGE

APPLICATION DEADLINES

Application deadline

Financial aid/scholarship deadline

ADMISSIONS AND APPLICATION DETAILS

Admissions address

Admissions telephone number

Admissions fax number

Admissions E-mail address

Admissions and information Web site

Admissions director

Admissions officers contacted

   Under what circumstances

Application fee

Application fee check made out to

APPLICATION TASKS

Date application and materials requested

   Received (Make a check here when received.)

Secondary research completed (Make a check here when completed.)

Date transcript requested

   Received by college (Check here.)

Date SAT I scores requested

Received by college (Check here.)

Date SAT II scores requested

   Received by college (Check here.)

Date ACT scores requested

   Received by college (Check here.)

Recommender 1

    Date requested

    Date briefing completed

    Date recommender's progress checked (if necessary)

    Received by college (Check here.)

Recommender 2

    Date requested

    Date briefing completed

    Date recommender's progress checked (if necessary)

    Received by college (Check here.)

Recommender 3

    Date requested

    Date briefing completed

    Date recommender's progress checked (if necessary)

    Received by college (Check here.)

Application data form completed (Check here.)

Application short answers and activity lists completed (Check here.)

Application essays

    Essay 1 topic

        Rough draft completed (Check here.)

        Editor/reader reviews completed (Check here.)

        Final draft completed (Check here.)

    Essay 2 topic

        Rough draft completed (Check here.)

        Editor/reader reviews completed (Check here.)

        Final draft completed (Check here.)

    Essay 3 topic

        Rough draft completed (Check here.)

        Editor/reader reviews completed (Check here.)

        Final draft completed (Check here.)

Essay 4 topic

    Rough draft completed (Check here.)

    Editor/reader reviews completed (Check here.)

    Final draft completed (Check here.)

Essay 5 topic

    Rough draft completed (Check here.)

    Editor/reader reviews completed (Check here.)

    Final draft completed (Check here.)

Application photocopied (Check here.)

    Date application sent

    Method of delivery

    Routing or confirmation number (of deliverer)

    Interview status

    Date requested

    Date of interview

    Location of interview

    Interviewer's name

    Interviewer's title

    Interviewer's address (for thank-you notes)

    Date school notified me of file completion

FINANCIAL AID/SCHOLARSHIP TASKS

FAFSA

    Date FAFSA requested

    FAFSA received (Check here.)

    FAFSA completed (Check here.)

    Date FAFSA mailed

PROFILE

    Date PROFILE requested

    PROFILE received (Check here.)

    PROFILE completed (Check here.)

Date PROFILE mailed

College financial aid forms

Date financial aid forms requested (if necessary—generally included with application materials)

College financial aid forms received (Check here.)

College financial aid forms completed (Check here.)

Date college financial aid forms mailed

Date financial aid office notified me of financial aid file completion

NOTES:

Part *II*

APPLYING TO COLLEGE

6

Marketing Yourself: General Principles

— KEY POINTS —

Understand how you compare with the competition

∎

Learn how admissions officers will view your candidacy based upon their expectations of people from your educational and personal background

∎

Capitalize on your strengths, while minimizing your weaknesses

∎

Show how you bring unique value to the school
—*Learn how to "position" yourself so that you stand out relative to others*
—*Maximize your reward/risk ratio*

∎

Use themes to focus your marketing effort

INTRODUCTION

When you apply to college, you are essentially selling yourself. This may sound crass (after all, we once thought of marketing as something we perform only regarding cars, clothes, books, and other *things,* but not people), yet it is true! Just as the sales representative of a software company must develop specific strategies and selling points to market the newest products, so you must develop strategies and themes to present yourself to colleges. Do not think that a fly-by-the-seat-of-your-pants, haphazardly concocted message will produce optimal results. You need a carefully constructed plan.

To come up with a selling strategy, you need to decide *before* putting together any materials, writing essays, handing out recommendation forms to teachers, or interviewing with college officers what you are going to emphasize in your application. What will your thematic focus be? Your focus will depend upon what each particular school wants, what your competition offers, and your relevant strengths and weaknesses as compared to the competition. You need to be able to capitalize on your strengths and minimize weaknesses to make the greatest possible argument for your acceptance.

CREATING A MARKETING STRATEGY

To begin the process of putting together a successful marketing strategy, you must first closely examine all the schools to which you will apply. You already know from Chapter 5 what schools are generally looking for in candidates. They want brains. They want special artistic, athletic, and other kinds of talent. They want leadership potential. They want independent thinkers who can also perform well within a community or group. They want students who take initiative, make things happen, and follow through.

But you must also gather relevant data about each school to which you will send an application so that you can be sure to effectively tailor your message to each one. School and entering class profiles can usually be found in the information packages schools send out about themselves; they can also be found on college Web sites, in college guidebooks, or in your high school's college counseling office.

You will want to examine the following data on the most recent incoming freshman class of each school:

- Average SAT and ACT scores
- Average high school GPA
- Distribution of geographic origins

- Percentage from public versus private schools
- Percentages of various ethnic groups

You also need to know about the school's strengths and requirements, and facts about the student body at large:

- What are the school's strong departments or fields of study?
- What departments or fields of study are undersubscribed?
- What kind of foreign language and/or foreign culture requirements are there?
- What kinds of study abroad programs does the school offer?
- What varsity and club sports teams does it field?
- What kinds of newspapers and special publications does it offer?
- What kinds of art, music, or drama programs does it feature?

You need to get a real sense of what a school is looking for as well as what it already has enough of. This will allow you to refine your message to meet the school's specific needs and interests.

MAXIMIZING STRENGTHS, MINIMIZING WEAKNESSES

With this information in hand, it will be easier to see how you stack up against your competition for each school. In analyzing your situation, you need to determine what an admissions officer is likely to see as your strengths and weaknesses. Then you need to capitalize on your new understanding of yourself as one college applicant amidst a huge pool of competition.

Admissions officers would like to get to know their applicants as well as possible when making judgments about them; they will certainly view your entire application with as much care as they can (given time and energy limitations) to make decisions about who you are and how you compare with other applicants. If you follow our guidelines in this and the following chapters, your message will be sophisticated and multifaceted, yet crystal clear. You will thus not be merely a "category" to the admissions people you are trying to impress; you will become an individual. In other words, you will not be just "a jock," but "the fantastic field hockey player and shot-putter who also volunteers at an animal shelter and wants to become a veterinarian."

TRANSCENDING CATEGORIES

In order to transcend the boundaries of any categories in which you might fit, though, you should understand how admissions departments might view you given some basic information about you. There is no denying that people can, consciously or unconsciously, make snap judgments based on little information, and admissions officers are no exception to this rule. Although admissions officers certainly realize that not all "children of immigrants" are the same, they probably have some basic presumptions about what a child of immigrant parents is like, what strengths and weaknesses he or she might bring to the college. Keep in mind that your strengths and weaknesses when compared to those of the rest of the applicant pool might be valued differently from school to school. Columbia, located in Manhattan and attracting a generally sophisticated and ethnically diverse crowd (over 30% of the undergraduate population are American minorities), might not place as high a value on your cosmopolitism or your Hispanic roots as does Colby, a small school in rural Maine where minorities make up only 10% of the student population.

The chart presented here is intended to make this process of identifying where to focus your efforts a bit easier by showing likely presumed strengths and weaknesses of different categories of applicants. These may give you some ideas for things you can emphasize as strengths, while also showing you what weaknesses you might want to think about disproving. Remember that a single applicant can certainly embody more than one category or type.

CATEGORY	STRENGTHS	WEAKNESSES
Academic Superstar	Intelligent, focused on academics, career-oriented	Dull, no sense of humor, poor interpersonal skills, not necessarily a leader, quiet loner type
Jock	Dynamic and energetic, strong team player, strong interpersonal skills, strong leadership skills	Less intelligent, not focused on academics
Student from a Disadvantaged Background	Strong work ethic, determination, unique or underrepresented perspective	Culturally unsophisticated and unsavvy, unprepared for rigors of college, difficulty fitting in
Student from a Wealthy and/or Advantaged Background	Rich experiential knowledge, culturally sophisticated and savvy, prepared for rigors of college, future success nearly inevitable	Arrogant, weak work ethic, spoiled
Artsy Type	Creative, culturally sophisticated and savvy	Poor analytical and quantitative skills, romantic dreamer rather than pragmatist, postcollegiate employability and potential for success uncertain
Verbal/Language Type	Strong communication and writing skills, dynamic, creative	Poor analytical and quantitative skills, postcollegiate employability and potential for success uncertain
Math/Science Type	Strong analytical and quantitative skills	Poor communication and writing skills, uncreative, dull and undynamic, nerdy

CATEGORY	STRENGTHS	WEAKNESSES
City Kid	Culturally sophisticated and savvy, ability to relate to diverse classmates	Arrogant, tendency toward boredom in collegiate environment
Suburban Kid	Solid and grounded	Ordinary or lacking in uniqueness, spoiled
Rural Kid	Unique and underrepresented perspective, solid and grounded, strength of character	Culturally unsophisticated and unsavvy, unprepared for rigors of college, difficulty fitting in
Immigrant/Child of Immigrant Parents	Unique or underrepresented perspective, strength of character, strong work ethic, determination	Weak English language skills, too focused on academics (lack of interest in extacurricular aspects of college), unwilling to take risks, difficulty fitting in
Elite Private or Boarding School Student	Prepared for rigors of college, focused on academics, career-oriented, future success nearly inevitable	Arrogant, spoiled
Physically Handicapped Student	Strength of character, strong work ethic, determination	Difficulty fitting in
Learning Disabled Student	Strength of character, strong work ethic, determination	Unprepared for rigors of college, poor analytical and quantitative skills
Older, Nontraditional Student	Rich experiential knowledge, career-oriented, focused on academics	Lack of energy, unwilling to take risks, difficulty fitting in, inability to work and associate with fellow students, lack of interest in extracurricular aspects of college

HOW TO PREPARE YOUR MARKETING STRATEGY

After examining how you stack up against a school's competition and how the admissions officers might view you, given your profile, you must figure out how to market yourself. Start by making a list of general ideas or facts about yourself, ignoring the ideas of "positive" and "negative" or "strength" and "weakness" for the moment. You can make the list yourself or you can fill in our Personal Profile Worksheets, provided in Appendix V, which essentially ask for the same information. If you are making your own list, divide it into five categories: academics, extracurricular activities, work experience, summer activities, and personal background. First write down everything you can think of to say about yourself in the area of academics: your academic interests, what kind of grades you receive in various areas, how your grades have changed over time in various areas, special projects you have done, any awards you have won, etc. Do the same for each category, basically attempting to make a list of data that would cover nearly every aspect of your life, whether or not you deem it important.

When you are through, you need to take each piece of information and regard it objectively, to determine whether you should characterize it as a strength or a weakness. Remember that a strength is not necessarily the same thing as "a positive situation" and vice versa. You must look at each piece of data the way an admissions officer would, rather than simply judging whether the experience has *felt* positive or negative to you. In other words, you may think that the experience of growing up in a poor, rural area has been nothing but negative; you would rather have grown up advantaged, with a lawyer rather than a dairy farmer as a father, and wearing Stussy surf gear rather than overalls. But remember that from an admissions standpoint, your background gives you no negative points. It is a strength, or can easily be pitched as a strength; for example, performing farming chores to help support the family has given you a strong work ethic and taught you the meaning of responsibility. Similarly, taking the cinch English class instead of the challenging (but doable) AP variety might have affected you positively in the short term, giving you an easy A grade and fewer papers to write each semester, and thus more time to spend with your girlfriend. But to an admissions officer, this piece of data would be a weakness: You took the easy way out rather than challenging yourself.

You need to turn each piece of information around in your head to envision what it will look like (or what you can make it look like) to the admissions committee. You might well need a college counselor, a friend, or a teacher to help you in this exercise. First, you must be sure that you have included every piece of information possible on your five-category list. This is often difficult to ascertain on your own. After all, from your own internal perspective, certain parts of your life might escape your attention or be deemed unworthy of mention because they have become so commonplace to you. For example, if you have cared for your now 3-year-old sister for several hours every day after school since she was born, that is a significant piece of information. But because this aspect of your life has become so ordinary, perhaps even tedious, you may neglect to realize its value as material in a college application.

After making your lists of strengths and weaknesses, you need to mold them into a strategy. First, you will want to support any obvious strengths. You can relate stories in your essays, for example, that demonstrate these strengths. You will choose recommenders who are likely to provide supporting examples of your best assets as well. The interviews give you a further opportunity to amplify your strengths. The following chapters show you how to use these three communication vehicles most effectively. Next, you must do whatever you can to minimize your weaknesses, or, better yet, show that you do not suffer from them. Once again, it is a matter of addressing them through each of the vehicles at your disposal: the essays, recommendations, and interviews.

MAXIMIZING YOUR REWARD–RISK RATIO

To maximize your reward–risk ratio, place all of your strengths (the rewards a college will reap if it gains you as part of its student body) on the top of the ratio equation, or as the numerator of a fraction; then place all of your weaknesses (the risks a college assumes if it decides to accept you) on the bottom of the equation, as the denominator. Rewards include academic strengths, athletic talent, leadership potential, social skills, a unique geographical background, and the like. Risks include the possibility of your failing academically, dropping out of school, having disciplinary or substance abuse problems, or simply being unhappy and "needy" as a student. You want the rewards to far outweigh the risks, thus making the ratio or number as large as possible. This is what we refer to as maximizing your reward–risk ratio. Schools want students who will make major contributions to their programs without involving substantial risks of academic failure or other kinds of failure. The higher the reward–risk ratio, the better your chance of appealing to a school.

A popular and well-rounded student with an A– GPA but nothing particularly unique to offer has a far different task in maximizing the reward–risk ratio than does a right-wing political aficionado whose grades are mediocre but who has founded a thriving forum for archconservative speakers in his community as well as run local election campaigns. The well-rounded good student is likely to be regarded as someone who would do fine and fit in with her classmates, without being much of a risk. She brings solid academic skills and experience to the school. It might look as if it would be an absolute cinch for her to gain admission because of her steady and solid record. But her problem is that she is but one among thousands of solid, well-rounded students applying to the school, all of whom bring similar qualities. In other words, she poses no risk to the school, but she also brings no readily identifiable rewards.

To improve her chances of admission, she must show that she is quite different from other adequate but not unique students. She can do so by showing the extreme consistency of her work over time and across disciplines, a dedication to a certain area of academics, the breadth of her capabilities, or perhaps even a sophisticated portrayal of her future career ambitions.

The right-winger is in a nearly opposite situation. In his case, the problem is not what he brings to the program or how he is unique. His unpopular politics (and self-confidence in expressing them) are rather unusual within most college environments today, which are populated for the most part with moderate to liberal-minded students. His initiative in creating a speaker's forum for his community is impressive, as is his successful record in coordinating election campaigns at such a young age. He has considerable uniqueness value to start with. His problem involves the risk side of the ratio. An admissions director is likely to worry that he spends too much time on his political passions and not enough effort on academics, or perhaps that his mind for academic matters is simply not that sharp. As someone who has not proven himself academically, what if he were not able to handle the demands of the college? An admissions officer may also simply not like his politics and harbor an unconscious but powerful bias against him. Or she might worry that his politics will be distasteful to most of his peers and perhaps alienate him in some way. In other words, this candidate brings high rewards *and* high risks.

To improve his chance of admission, he must strive to use the three main admissions vehicles (the essays, the recommendations, and the interview) to his best advantage to show maturity, sensibility, and academic capability. He must discuss his views in ways that do not offend others and are easily and logically supportable. He should demonstrate that he understands that the general atmosphere of the campus may not be conducive to his particular views and activities. He must be able to "prove," perhaps through a discussion of one of his extensive extracurricular activities, his brainpower in order to make up for the brilliance not demonstrated in his academic record. He might want to show a sense of humor to take the edge off his profile and provide some comic relief to an otherwise serious set of application considerations.

The well-rounded student would make a terrible mistake if she were to concentrate on the risk side of the ratio; she must instead focus on the reward side by showing her unique value. The right-winger would make a terrible mistake if he were to concentrate on the reward side of the ratio; he must reduce the risk he poses.

FIT IN–STAND OUT

No matter who you are or where you are applying, tailoring your message depends first and foremost on one idea: the "fit in–stand out" issue. Fitting in means that you will be able to handle the coursework, you will subscribe to the school's mission and overall philosophy of education, and you will be accepted by your peers and get along well with them. In other words, you will be happy and thrive at the school and will best benefit from the resources it offers. Standing out means that you bring something unique and special to the college, something that distinguishes you from other students. In other words, you will offer your resources to classmates and the greater community so that others may benefit from your talents.

Admissions officers view the relationship between an individual student and a college campus as a synergistic one. Admissions officers want to be sure that you will benefit from their school (thus, you want to show that you fit in), but they also want to know that the school community will be richer because of your presence (so you also need to prove that you stand out). Instead of merely throwing a bunch of your foremost accomplishments and qualities at the admissions officers, forcing them to imagine on their own how you might give back to the school if you matriculate there, it is better to be explicit about how you plan to contribute to the campus community. Many applicants, though they know they must impress admissions officers, concentrate more on showing a school how they will personally benefit from going there. This helps to show how you will fit in, but does not necessarily help you to stand out. Rather than discussing only that you want to attend a certain college because you would like to work on its award-winning daily newspaper, which will give you competitive skills for your future career in journalism, you also want to emphasize that the newspaper (or some other outlet you may even create on your own) will be better off with your input. Showing how your future contributions to the campus will be distinct will help to separate you from the crowd.

The trick is to fit in *and* stand out at the same time. It is not sufficient to do only one or the other. Arguing that you really fit in, that you look like a composite of all the other students, gives the school no reason to want you there because you bring nothing different or new. Saying that you really stand out, that you do not resemble the student body in any way, is similarly useless because you will be seen as too risky to invite into the community. Colleges do not want to matriculate unhappy or unsatisfied students; they need to keep their graduation rates up, their transfer rates down, their mental health clinics empty—and they want to produce successful alums whose positive memories of their college years will encourage them to donate money to the school in the future.

A good way to straddle the fit in–stand out divide is to fit in with regard to certain key dimensions and stand out with regard to other aspects. More people will fall on the "fit in" side than on the "stand out" side. Unlike specialized technical schools or graduate programs, most four-year undergraduate institutions offer a vast variety of programs, which also ensures that their student bodies are quite diverse. The majority of high schoolers—even those with fairly unique qualities—will not have to worry about showing that they fit in. The right-winger, on the other hand, does not have to put so much special effort into standing out; his problem is convincing admissions that he fits in. The right-winger is a rather special case. You probably do not need to worry about fitting in unless you can identify yourself as belonging in one of these risky "categories":

- The quiet and shy loner,
- The proverbial troublemaker,
- The distastefully rebellious or angry youth,
- The spoiled rich kid, or
- The fanatic with a singular passion.

The Quiet and Shy Loner

The quiet and shy loner is easily identifiable from his list of extracurricular interests and hobbies. He engages in individual rather than group activities. He plays chess or collects butterflies rather than engaging in interactive activities. If he's athletic at all, he probably runs cross-country or swims rather than participating in a team-oriented sport such as soccer or water polo. He might perform solo guitar at a local coffeehouse, but probably does not play an instrument in the school orchestra. He refrains from working on school committees or in group projects. He might be involved in activities that are more commonly associated with adults, such as working for the local election board, showing that he avoids fraternizing with kids his own age. If he writes, it is on his own and not as part of the editorial board of a school literary journal. You will give yourself away as a shy loner type if you claim yourself to be wildly passionate about your activities or hobbies without ever being involved in any group outlets devoted to them. The quiet loner can also usually be identified during an interview. Traits giving away this personality are often divulged (consciously or unconsciously) in teacher recommendations, and sometimes even in one's own essays.

This is not to say that you must change your personality if you are a shy, quiet person and enjoy being on your own rather than interacting in groups! You should simply be aware that some admissions officers might stereotype you as antisocial or unfriendly in some way; they would be more confident about admitting you if you can show that you have the positives of the quiet, shy personality without the negatives. In fact, you may even be able to play up this aspect of your personality for all of its strengths (introspection, strong sense of identity, peaceful by nature, etc.). But it is probably best if in at least one way you can prove yourself to be capable of interacting with others and performing well in a group setting.

You can inspire confidence in your sociability in one of several ways. You can write an essay that shows you in a communicative and social role, even if it is with only one other person. For example, in writing about an event that significantly changed your life, you could write about tutoring younger children from your community in reading; caring for a sick grandparent; or befriending your newly immigrated neighbors and helping them adjust to life in the United States. You can similarly ask teachers who are writing recommendations to be aware of issues concerning your personality type, perhaps documenting your involvement in team or group activities and otherwise assuring your friendliness or ability to interact with your peers.

It would also be wise to go against your natural instincts and become involved in one serious and committed activity in which you interact with others. Sometimes such an activity can appear (on paper) to be a group or team effort, when your role or contribution is still fairly independent. In other words, it might serve to erase any worries regarding your sociability on the part of admissions officers yet not prove too painful or uncomfortable for you. For example, you could become part of the Golden Key society that gives tours of your high school and promotes it to outsiders, something that is widely assumed to require interactive skills, if not a bubbly cheerleader personality. But you could join specifically to edit the group's newsletter or to develop its Web site. In joining a group activity, you might even find you like the team spirit involved. Anybody can demonstrate social ability or ease in communication by merely showing a link, however insignificant in terms of real interaction, between himself or herself and a group of people.

If you are painfully shy, become nervous easily, or are worried about how you will come across in a college interview, you should make efforts to improve your interviewing and discussion skills. Professional college counselors can coach you and help prep you for interviews of many kinds; sitting through several mock interviews and receiving feedback from a professional or even a school advisor can help you to improve your ease and grace in communicating with others. You can also have a friend, parent, or advisor videotape you, so that you can watch yourself in action to determine what features of interviewing you need to improve. (For more on interviewing, see Chapter 14.)

THE PROVERBIAL TROUBLEMAKER

The proverbial troublemaker is spotted by his school (or civil) record of disturbance and misbehavior. Any formal citations against your behavior (probations or suspensions from school, serious arrests) will be evident from your official record. But even informal infractions and questionable behavior are often conveyed to college admissions officers through a school guidance counselor or teacher recommendation. A high school counselor is ethically obligated to pass on behavioral information about you; so even if you were only reprimanded by the principal rather than formally suspended for playing hooky or getting caught tying underwear to the flagpole, it might be transmitted to colleges.

It is difficult for troublemakers to convince college admissions officers of their worth if their record is particularly heavy with blemishes and those blemishes have continued on through senior year of school. But if you have only one infraction of the rules counting against you, or have demonstrated that your pattern of disturbing behavior improved or stopped by senior year, you may be able to save yourself. First, you need to come across as maturely and properly as possible during your interview. Dress particularly well, be clean, arrive early, be particularly polite. If you have a logical, mature, and sincere way of addressing your behavior in the interview or in an essay, certainly do so—but do not whine, blame others for your mistakes, or carry on too long about your past. And certainly do not offer additional details that will not be revealed elsewhere! Second, and better yet, you can have a teacher that you know and trust write you a recommendation, specifically addressing the bad behavior. You will want someone who likes you and seems to have understood and forgiven your transgressions to do this job. Discuss the issue with the teacher to see if he can offer a plausible and positive way to evaluate your past mistakes. Ask him if he would be willing to go out on a limb and predict future good behavior and maturity.

THE REBELLIOUS OR ANGRY YOUTH

The distastefully rebellious or angry youth gives herself away in interviews as well as in essays or teacher recommendations. This type, unlike the proverbial troublemaker, does not necessarily have any formal charges lodged against her by authorities. It is not her official record but the attitude she conveys that dooms her. Acting hostile or seriously disgruntled, or showing a general lack of enthusiasm for life, will probably not win you many friends in the admissions department. These types convey their angry, rebellious attitudes through sloppy dress or adorning themselves in black leather, chains, and a mohawk for the interview. Similarly, they might show a lack of respect for the interviewer and the admissions process through a late arrival (worse yet, a late arrival without apology), a slumped posture or otherwise impolite body language, or rude behavior toward the admissions staff. You will probably gain loads of respect from admissions if you can demonstrate impeccable manners and politeness when showing up in your crazy rebellious teenager gear. Going the extra mile by writing a thank-you note after the interview would not hurt, either. You also demonstrate rebelliousness and anger if you voice particularly vicious disapproval of authorities or generally accepted sociopolitical systems, either in your interview or in your essays. You are allowed to have opinions, even strong ones about unpopular subjects, but be sure to back them up and convey them in ways that will not alienate others. For example, if you support the legalization of marijuana and feel compelled to discuss this for some reason (probably not a smart idea in the first place) in your essay or the interview, avoid bashing those who oppose drug legalization; use a rational argument backed with solid information rather than emotional appeals to state your case.

THE SPOILED RICH KID

Spoiled rich kids are not necessarily risky in that they will "stick out" at college (all colleges have their fair share of the well-to-do), but many admissions officers simply do not like them! Your family's wealth and opportunity is readily evident through your application (as is discussed elsewhere in this book)—even if you are not applying for financial aid—and you cannot change that. But you can make sure that if you come from privilege you do not come off as ungrateful for your opportunities, spoiled rotten, or unaware of the circumstances of those who are less fortunate. You would appear to be spoiled and unlikeable if you wrote an essay about your family's trip to Greece and concluded with a caustic remark mourning the plight of fellow classmates who had to stay home in Indianapolis to work for wages over the summer.

The simplest and easiest way to combat your "disadvantageously advantaged" profile is to make sure you are involved in serious community service throughout your entire high school career. This means volunteering in a capacity that truly helps those less fortunate, not simply performing something called "volunteer work" by taking pictures free of charge for the community newspaper. (This kind of thing is perfectly acceptable and beneficial for your profile as a general activity, but will not count as service to those in need.) You can also readily acknowledge the advantages with which you've been blessed in an essay or the interview. When asked in an essay about her favorite childhood story, one young woman we know used Dr. Seuss's "How Lucky You Are" as her response, incorporating a discussion of how her parents taught her to be grateful for all the special opportunities she had enjoyed.

COMBATING A PRIVILEGED IMAGE

Do:

➤ Conduct community service.

➤ Show that you have taken advantage of all opportunities.

➤ Demonstrate that you have crossed social and other divides or experienced the plight of (and sympathize with) others who are less fortunate.

Don't:

➤ Discuss shopping, expensive trips, or glamorous events you have attended.

➤ Describe your parent as managing partner of Chicago's largest law firm—"lawyer" will suffice as a description.

➤ Sound arrogant, spoiled, or unappreciative of your opportunities.

THE FANATIC WITH A SINGULAR PASSION

It is, generally speaking, always a good idea to show admissions officers that you are passionate about and devoted to your activities and studies. But you must be careful not to overdo it here, especially if you have a singular activity to which you commit most of your time and that activity's value could be considered questionable by others. For example, you do not want it to become apparent in your application that you spend every minute of your free time playing Dungeons and Dragons or logging on to your favorite chat room on the Web. Dungeons and Dragons can certainly develop useful skills (strategic thinking, etc.) in its players. Likewise, becoming a frequent contributor to a Web site devoted to human rights or amateur investing can be a valuable experience worth noting to admissions officers. But these kinds of activities on their own do not instill the full range of qualities that an admissions officer wants to see in an applicant. You do not want to come across as a true fanatic with a singular passion that prevents you from devoting energy and time to other valuable activities if that passion is of questionable or minimal worth.

Note that if your single extacurricular activity is playing tennis and you are ranked as the number three singles player in the United States in your age group, this is a different story. Here, devotion to your sport, for which you have superior proven talent, would quite naturally prevent you from doing a lot of other things with your free time. In this case, your tennis career requires not only passion, but also a willingness to forgo other activities. Furthermore, there is no question about the value of this talent. Your athletic skill will likely be one of your most attractive qualities to colleges; commitment to a sport and a team, as well as the social and life skills tennis can teach, will also become valuable parts of your profile. In this case, a near fanatical devotion to the activity would not detract from your overall application.

ADMISSIONS OFFICERS TALK ABOUT THE KINDS OF STUDENTS THEY ARE RELUCTANT TO ACCEPT

"We don't like students who back away from challenges or are super-competitive with others. We also are not attracted to candidates who are antisocial—I don't mean in a shy or loner kind of way, but in a way that is disruptive to others. We don't like kids who use their brains to do things like shut down the school's Web server for a day or play cruel, harsh jokes on others."

—*Marilee Jones, Dean of Admissions, Massachusetts Institute of Technology*

"Students who are overly committed and zealous about only one thing—to the detriment of other areas of development—worry me. I'm talking about the kid who may be really bright and started his own computer business, but he hasn't done much outside of computers. Passion is always a very good thing, but one-dimensionality is not."

—*Nancy Hargrave Meislahn, Director of Undergraduate Admissions, Cornell University*

"Grade grubbers and zealous perfectionists are what we don't like to see. When I say 'perfectionist,' I don't mean kids who get all As, but those who risk more important things to be 'perfect' in severe dimensions—you see this thing in extreme anorexics, for example."

—*Jonathan Reider, Senior Associate Director of Admissions, Stanford University*

"Kids who are poorly prepared for a demanding college are always risky. If we see a student who has done well but in a terrible school system, we might struggle over whether to admit him. This can be a difficult situation. We often feel that many of these kids *deserve* to be admitted, but we're not sure if they can handle it here."

—*Barbara-Jan Wilson, Dean of Admissions and Financial Aid, Wesleyan University*

"We're very intrigued by students who have made a remarkable turnaround—kids who were awful students in the eighth and ninth grades, maybe even into tenth grade, and then suddenly show remarkable improvement. We often agonize over decisions about these kinds of applicants—the ones who've shown only eighteen months of good grades, but the teachers all attest to how wonderful and brilliant they are. Students like these really make me believe in the qualitative approach—it allows us to take risks in admissions."

—*Nancy Hargrave Meislahn, Director of Undergraduate Admissions, Cornell University*

MAXIMIZING THE IMPACT OF YOUR APPLICATION

The admissions director of a top college is confronted with thousands of applications for each class. She is meant to read far too many lengthy folders on these candidates, containing data sheets, lists of schools and extracurricular activities, transcripts, essays, recommendations, interview write-ups, and so forth. As if this onslaught were not enough, every time an admissions officer ventures into a public forum, there are applicants trying to grab her attention. Most of these applicants are qualified, meaning that they could successfully complete the work at the college. If you are not careful, you will remain part of this undifferentiated mass of applicants. The key to standing out from the crowd is positioning yourself well.

POSITIONING

Positioning is a marketing or sales concept that is meant to deal with the problem of too many applicants (or products) trying to capture the attention of admissions officers (or buyers). To cut through the haze, you must have a sharp and clear image that is readily noticed, valued, and remembered.

Let's look at an example of how this works. There are many different manufacturers of ice cream, even premium ice cream. But a number of ice cream products are distinctively positioned in the market to stand out and attract the attention of consumers. For example, Ben and Jerry's offers premium ice cream made from "all natural" ingredients and "the milk of Vermont cows." The ice cream markets itself to consumers who consider themselves healthy and wholesome; although the regular ice cream (as opposed to the low-fat varieties, yogurts, and sorbets) carries all the fat and calories of other ice creams, it is made naturally, with no artificial flavorings or preservatives.

The company heavily publicizes its commitment to various social causes and world peace through the Ben and Jerry's Foundation, into which 7.5% of the company's pretax profits are funneled; Ben and Jerry's Peace Pops even carry a "1% for Peace" slogan on their labels. Similarly, the company advertises that it opposes recombinant bovine growth hormone, pledging that the cows used to supply it with milk are not scientifically treated. The various flavors are given wild and crazy names, some even commemorating famous icons of liberalism: Cherry Garcia, for example, is named after the leader of the Grateful Dead. The recently redesigned colorful cartons promote the notion that the company is "fun" and "zany," as do its various unique marketing ploys, such as the annual Free Cone Day and the sponsorship of Vermonster eating contests. Although the ice cream is expensive relative to ordinary brands, its community-oriented and hippie-ish founders (whose faces are featured on the original cartons) have positioned it uniquely to attract civic-minded, humanitarian, and socially liberal consumers.

Haagen-Dazs, on the other hand, markets itself as a food product for the socially refined and sophisticated. The company has given itself a Dutch name and advertises its product essentially as a dessert for snobs with high standards. The consumers targeted by Haagen-Dazs's positioning efforts are not asked to care whether the money spent on their favorite dessert is going to support family farmers or the European aristocracy. Flavor names are sophisticated in their austere simplicity: Coffee, Vanilla, Chocolate. The company caters to those who need no gimmicks when choosing a product that will satisfy their refined culinary sensibilities.

These two products—Ben and Jerry's and Haagen-Dazs—compete in the very high end of the ice cream market, yet each is positioned to be completely unique. Their marketing efforts aim to make it very clear what key attributes they possess, and they are very successful. Both are held in extremely high regard by serious ice cream lovers, although they are considered somewhat unrelated to one another. The result is that each may claim a premium price for its distinctiveness that would be impossible were they positioned head-to-head. In other words, both may exist and succeed in the market at the same time because both are positioned so favorably.

How does this apply to you and your college applications? You must distinguish yourself from others in the applicant pool. Even if you are of "undisputed" high quality as far as college applicants go, there are many other applicants out there just as qualified as you are. You need to position yourself so that you can compete head-to-head with others like you.

College applicants are not all the same; your job is to show your uniqueness. By appearing unique, you increase your value. After all, if you are the same as the 15,000 other applicants, what school will really care if it gets you or someone else just like you? By making yourself unique, you also make yourself more memorable. Remaining anonymous will not help you. Far better if an admissions committee remembers you, perhaps even having a shorthand expression used in discussing you. Being the "girl who started a business refurbishing antique rocking chairs" means that you are remembered and can be discussed as a unique person. Contrast this with the sort of person who is referred to as "Which one is that? I don't remember her ..." And, by the way, it is not necessary to have started a business refurbishing antiques to make yourself memorable. You can distinguish yourself even if, at a glance, your resume does not seem to offer anything that is extraordinarily unique. You need to learn how to create uniqueness out of the ordinary.

DIFFERENT POSITIONING TACTICS FOR DIFFERENT SCHOOLS

To what extent should your positioning differ from school to school? Most serious four-year colleges are fairly similar, but none are identical. Thus, you might want to position yourself differently for different schools. For example, let's suppose you are a stellar mathematician *and* an accomplished actor, and you are applying to both MIT and Yale. You would want to rely strongly on the math skills to distinguish yourself from the crowd of applicants at Yale, where the world-renowned drama department probably sees its fair share of serious thespians; but you would want to emphasize your theatrical skills more in your application to MIT, since math whizzes are a dime a dozen there. Acting and math would be important pieces of both applications, but the emphasis would change according to the school. The difference is merely in focus.

But markedly different applications for each school is a lot of extra work. Not only would you need to start from scratch when writing each batch of essays, but you also might need to use different recommenders. You also would have to be pretty savvy in coaching yourself to perfect your image for each interview. You might not want (or realistically have time) to go overboard on completely changing your message for each of the schools to which you apply. Instead, take a modified approach if you need to differ your positioning efforts at all. Have a general positioning strategy that you can fine-tune to fit the needs of specific schools without making major changes in your application. Emphasize different aspects of your experience for a given school rather than trying to re-create yourself for it. This assumes you will not be applying to one school in order to concentrate on one subject and another in case you want to focus on something completely different. (If you are unresolved about what kind of focus you are looking for, then you will obviously have to prepare very different applications for different schools.)

ADMISSIONS OFFICERS REVEAL WHAT TYPES OF APPLICANTS THEY ARE ESPECIALLY INTERESTED IN ATTRACTING

"I personally have a vision of what I would love to see more of at MIT. I'm always looking for more 'policy wonks,' humanitarians, communicators, and classic leaders. By classic leaders, I mean those with real charisma, who can draw others to their causes."

—*Marilee Jones, Dean of Admissions, Massachusetts Institute of Technology*

"We're always looking for more female scientists, particularly female physicists. We would also like to see more students interested in studying Russian and German, as well as those who study Classics. Students from the southwestern U.S. are generally in demand as well."

Barbara-Jan Wilson, Dean of Admissions and Financial Aid, Wesleyan University

"The states of South Dakota and Wyoming are often underrepresented in our pool. We're always looking for students interested in anthropology and linguistics—we have a great linguistics department, but most 17-year-olds have no experience with this yet. There are lots of ebbs and flows in what we're after, though. For the next few years, for example, our band leader has notified us that we need more brass players."

—Lee Stetson, Dean of Admissions, University of Pennsylvania

"We're committed to ensuring we have a good representation of kids from the Carolinas—we generally want 15% of the class from the states of North and South Carolina."

—Christoph Guttentag, Director of Undergraduate Admissions, Duke University

"We're always looking for more Hispanic and Latino students, as well as black students—there aren't as many of these minorities in Virginia as there are in other areas of the country. I am personally interested in finding students who have overcome challenges or are original thinkers."

—John Blackburn, Dean of Admissions, University of Virginia

"We're always looking for more musicians and artists—when I came here I determined to make that a priority for us. We're also always looking for kids who represent the first-generation-to-college and students from small rural high schools— I call them the 'tiny towners.'"

—Richard Steele, Dean of Admissions, Bowdoin College

"Native Americans—it's very hard to recruit them, and we'd love to do better at attracting them here."

—Janet Lavin Rapelye, Dean of Admissions, Wellesley College

"We would love more classics majors, but we're not going to lower our standards just to get classics people to come here."

—Nanci Tessier, Director of Admissions, Smith College

THE MECHANICS OF POSITIONING: USING THEMES

Positioning is meant to provide a method for presenting a very clear picture of you. A simple way to achieve this is to use several themes to organize your material. When writing the essays, for example, relate all or at least most of your material to your chosen themes. If your material is organized around three or four themes, your positioning will be very clear and easy to grasp. In other words, with strong themes you can better guide the way in which admissions officers will think about you. You will have more control over the application process and reach better outcomes.

The themes you use will be different from those that your next-door neighbor will use. Nevertheless, as noted before, all colleges are looking for a few of the same general features in their candidates. They want students who will accomplish things, despite any obstacles in their way. They want students who are relatively mature and have begun to explore their identities and their futures with seriousness. They want people who are determined, willing to work hard and persevere in order to attain goals. Remember these generalities when fashioning your themes, but do not focus only on such broad ideas. Many astute applicants have by now figured out that these are the qualities colleges want, so there will be a lot of competition clamoring for attention as hardworking leaders who are prepared to accomplish a lot in their futures.

Instead, keep those general positive qualities in the back of your head while coming up with ways to modify them to fit you more particularly or to become especially memorable to administrators. For example, rather than using the theme of "leader," you can go a few steps further. Instead of merely showing yourself to be an all-around leader, you can show that you are actually an initiator of new ideas and events. You create new ideas, are successful at persuading others to rally around them, and can guide a group to accomplish the task that you originally set out to attempt. Or you can show that you are someone who has taken advantage of skills learned through formal leadership roles to apply them even in situations involving informal leadership. In other words, your leadership is such that you can take the bull by the horns in any situation you encounter, even when no one has specifically designated that you be in charge.

Here are some examples of the kinds of themes others have used:

- Warm, loving, good citizen type: Started a neighborhood baby-sitting service, volunteers in a senior citizens' home, and comes from a strong, close-knit family of eight.

- Polyglot: Speaks three languages fluently and has been a part of many different cultural influences as the daughter of a French mother and an Egyptian father.

- From an unusual background: Grew up on a ranch on the Texas–New Mexico border, living 21 miles away from the nearest neighbor.

- Risk taker or adventurer: Studying for a pilot's license, went on an animal safari to Africa last summer, and participated in an exchange program with a troubled inner-city school during junior year.

- Determined youth from a disadvantaged background: Grew up in a housing project with a single mother and works after school at a grocery store to help care for three siblings.

■ Change-the-world type: The community's junior United Way chairperson, spearheaded the school's recycling efforts, and plans to become a social worker.

■ Quiet, introspective type: A knowledgeable bird-watcher who goes out alone at dawn on Saturdays to do fieldwork, has kept a journal since first grade, and plans to get a Ph.D. and go into academia. (As mentioned earlier in the chapter, this type can be viewed positively or negatively, so you must take precautions to prove that you carry the strengths of this type without the weaknesses.)

There are practical limitations to the number of themes that will help you. If you use too few, you have very little maneuvering room in writing your essays because everything has to fit into just one or two organizing themes. If you use too many, you end up doing no organizing whatsoever and your positioning will no longer be clear. (Using too many themes is the equivalent of not devising themes at all.) The trick is to provide a balance. Using about three themes is generally appropriate because with that number, you do not constrain your efforts so much that you appear boring, but you are focused enough that admissions committees reading your applications will know what you are about and remember you. The key is that they should be able to summarize your positioning in three or four short phrases. If this is what a committee comes away with, they have you pegged in the way that will serve you best: You will become an individual to them, yet one whom they can get a handle on.

As discussed before, you have three primary vehicles for getting your message across to colleges: essays, the recommendations, and interviews. You will need to be consistent within and across all three vehicles to gain the maximum positive impact. The following chapters show how to make the most of each.

A SIMPLE POSITIONING EFFORT

"My love for science began when I developed a bug collection for a first-grade science project. I somehow persuaded my parents and my three older siblings (one of whom is now studying for his doctorate in organic chemistry) to help me dig around in our backyard for beetles and crickets. My passion for the biological sciences grew over time, as did the number of antfarms, aquariums, and hamster cages cluttering our garage. As a sophomore in high school, I led a team of five to the state Science Fair finals with our study and report on the Human Genome Project; in my junior year I began to volunteer in the emergency room of a local hospital to receive more exposure to science in the form of medicine. Over the last several years, my focus on human biology has deepened (though I do still maintain a 300-gallon fish tank at home!) and I have begun to shape plans to follow a premedicine curriculum in college. My plans to become a doctor took on more meaning last year when my mom was diagnosed with breast cancer. In an effort to find the best treatment possible and help her cope with her condition, my entire family has engaged in extensive cancer research. Despite my lifelong love of science, I never would have guessed that I would be opening a medical textbook at the early age of sixteen."

That paragraph represents a no-frills positioning effort. It is not meant to be a realistic college essay. Instead, it is meant to illustrate that it is possible in a short space to develop some important organizing themes. We know, in just a few short lines, that this candidate has a passion for science, especially biology. We know that she is serious about academics as well as accomplished in her field. We know her family is important to her and seems to have encouraged her to develop strong values; she cares not only for her own family but also for the well-being of others. This mini-portrait shows several clear themes: a deep-rooted passion and aptitude for biological sciences; a conviction about developing a future in medicine; and strong family ties. It is a fundamental but powerful positioning effort.

CONCLUSION

The penalty for failing to capitalize on your strengths and to prepare a powerful application is, all too often, rejection. Schools have plenty of qualified applicants who took the time to study the process and submit a well-written application. Failure to do these things suggests that you are not able to do so or that you did not take the college application process seriously. In either case, you are unlikely to be viewed as showing high potential.

Your application to a top college will be read differently than was the photocopied one-sheet application form you had to fill out to become a cashier or hamburger flipper last summer. You are competing with the best and the brightest applicants from all over the country (and other countries as well, although they are generally viewed as part of a separate admissions pool). The competition for these positions is intense, and the colleges feel justified in expecting high-quality applications, especially from students who come from college-educated parents or attend high schools (public or private) generally known for the quality of their college preparatory programs. Given your stated desire to begin your adult life at one of the top institutions of higher learning in the world, the colleges will expect that you have already begun to figure out how to be savvy in marketing yourself. They also expect you to treat the process seriously, insofar as the program will take up four years of your life and affect your personal development and career success as no other endeavor you have yet undertaken has.

ADMISSIONS OFFICERS STRESS THE IMPORTANCE OF PROVIDING AS MUCH CONTEXTUAL INFORMATION AS POSSIBLE WHEN MARKETING YOURSELF

"Build a three-dimensional case for yourself—a richer picture comes through if you make connections between the various pieces of your life."

—*Eric J. Furda, Director of Undergraduate Admissions, Columbia University*

"We always try to ask ourselves—in every part of the admissions process—are we being fair? How can we understand a student in relation to his background? If there is immigrant status, a different language background, or a need to work, we evaluate a student in relation to these circumstances. We have different expectations of different students depending upon the context of their development and education."

—*Jonathan Reider, Senior Associate Director of Admissions, Stanford University*

"Context is absolutely important. Understanding the context of a student's family situation and community is critical, so applicants must paint a complete picture for us."

—*Nancy Hargrave Meislahn, Director of Undergraduate Admissions, Cornell University*

"Everything needs to be explained and placed in a context. As an example, it can look like you're not involved if you have to commute long distances to school, which often prevents students from participating as much in extacurriculars. This kind of thing should be noted in the application so we can understand."

—*Dan Walls, Dean of Admissions, Emory University*

"If I have one piece of advice for applicants it's that they must point us in the right direction at all times. For example, if they're working, why? Is it to support family? Is it because of a drive to create a career in computers? They need to explain everything so that we can determine where they are coming from."

—*Richard Avitabile, Director of Admissions, New York University*

Appendix V

PERSONAL PROFILE WORKSHEETS

ACADEMIC PROFILE

High school curriculum and grades (List all courses taken and grades received.)

Course	Grade 9	Grade 10	Grade 11	Grade 12
English				
Math				
Science				
Social science				
Foreign language				
Performing/Fine arts				
Other				
Other				
Overall GPA		**Class rank**		

Other academic work (List all institutions, courses, dates of attendance, and grades received.)

	Course	Institution	Dates of attendance	Grade
Course I:				
Course II:				
Course III:				
Course IV:				

Standardized test scores (List all scores and circle the best for tests taken more than once.)

Subject	Score 1	Score 2	Score 3
SAT I			
ACT			
SAT II			
SAT II		.	
SAT II			
SAT II			
AP			
AP			
AP			
AP			

Awards and honors (List all awards, institution granting award, date of receipt, and basis of award receipt.)

	Award	Institution	Date of receipt	Basis of award receipt
Award 1:				
Award 2:				
Award 3:				
Award 4:				

EXTRACURRICULAR ACTIVITY PROFILE

List all extracurricular activities performed in high school, your role, the number of hours per week you spent (spend) on the activity; check years of participation. You may choose to include volunteer work and community service here or in the Work Experience section.

	Activity	Your role	Hours/week	Grade 9	Grade 10	Grade 11	Grade 12
Activity 1:							
Activity 2:							
Activity 3:							
Activity 4:							
Activity 5:							
Activity 6:							

Activity   Your role   Hours/week   Grade 9 Grade 10 Grade 11 Grade 12

Activity 7:

Activity 8:

Activity 9:

Activity 10:

Choose up to four activities to describe in detail here. These activities should be those in which you have demonstrated the most commitment (in terms of years of involvement and/or importance of your role) or those that are most important to you.

Activity 1:

Detailed description:

How has your role changed over time?

What has your involvement taught you?

Have you shown leadership in this activity? If so, explain.

Why is this activity special or important to you?

Do you plan to participate in a similar activity in college and/or beyond? If so, explain.

Activity 2:

Detailed description:

How has your role changed over time?

What has your involvement taught you?

Have you shown leadership in this activity? If so, explain.

Why is this activity special or important to you?

Do you plan to participate in a similar activity in college and/or beyond? If so, explain.

Activity 3:

Detailed description:

How has your role changed over time?

What has your involvement taught you?

Have you shown leadership in this activity? If so, explain.

Why is this activity special or important to you?

Do you plan to participate in a similar activity in college and/or beyond? If so, explain.

Activity 4:

Detailed description:

How has your role changed over time?

What has your involvement taught you?

Have you shown leadership in this activity? If so, explain.

Why is this activity special or important to you?

Do you plan to participate in a similar activity in college and/or beyond? If so, explain.

WORK EXPERIENCE PROFILE

List all work performed in high school, your role, the number of hours per week you worked; check years of participation or list specific dates. You may choose to

include volunteer work and community service here or in the Extracurricular Activity section.

Job	Your role	Hours/week	Grade 9	Grade 10	Grade 11	Grade 12
Job 1:						
Job 2:						
Job 3:						
Job 4:						

Choose two or three jobs to describe in detail here. These activities should be those in which you have demonstrated the most commitment (in terms of years of involvement and/or importance of your role) or those that are most important to you.

Job 1:

Detailed description:

Why did you take this job?

How has your role changed over time?

What has this job taught you?

Have you shown leadership in this job? If so, explain.

Do you plan to continue in this line of work in college and/or beyond? If so, explain.

Have you managed a project, a budget, or other people in this job?

How have you contributed to the organization's overall success?

Job 2:

Detailed description:

Why did you take this job?

How has your role changed over time?

What has this job taught you?

Have you shown leadership in this job? If so, explain.

Do you plan to continue in this line of work in college and/or beyond? If so, explain.

Have you managed a project, a budget, or other people in this job?

How have you contributed to the organization's overall success?

Job 3:

Detailed description:

Why did you take this job?

How has your role changed over time?

What has this job taught you?

Have you shown leadership in this job? If so, explain.

Do you plan to continue in this line of work in college and/or beyond? If so, explain.

Have you managed a project, a budget, or other people in this job?

How have you contributed to the organization's overall success?

SUMMER EXPERIENCE PROFILE

Discuss various summer activities and experiences from each of your high school years. You do not need to repeat information included elsewhere in the worksheets, such as material on jobs or extracurricular activities.

Summer between freshman and sophomore year:

Summer between sophomore and junior year:

Summer between junior and senior year:

PERSONAL LIFE PROFILE
Childhood and Family Life

Write about a favorite childhood memory.

Where were you born, where have you lived during your life so far, and how have these places shaped who you are today?

Write about a favorite memory that involves a place in which you have lived.

Write about your family here. Include details about how your family composition has changed over time, the people who make up your immediate family, and other relatives.

Write about a favorite recent occurrence that involves you and one of your family members.

Describe your upbringing: what your parents do, what kinds of activities you enjoyed as a child, what kinds of activities your family performs together, what values have shaped you, etc.

EDUCATIONAL PROFILE

Elementary schools attended:

Middle schools attended:

High schools attended:

How has your particular education—including schools, teachers, educational philosophies, and other school-related influences—shaped who you are today?

Describe your "ideal college class."

Under what circumstances do you perform your best academically?

TRAVEL PROFILE

Talk about your favorite travel experience. The experience need not be exotic—many people have not had the opportunity to travel very far from home in their lives. You can discuss visiting your grandmother's town, for example.

Discuss any significant travel experiences that are not discussed elsewhere in the worksheets.

PERSONAL INTERESTS

Besides your formal extracurricular activities, what do you like to do in your leisure time?

What is your favorite book and why? (You may answer this question for second- and third-favorite books as well if you wish. …)

What is your favorite movie and why? (You may answer this question for second- and third-favorite movies as well if you wish. ...)

Describe how an ideal Saturday would be spent.

OVERALL PROFILE

Based on everything you have written about so far on these Personal Profile Worksheets (as well as anything you have not yet included), think about the following questions and answer them accordingly.

Who are the three or four people who have most influenced you?

What are four or five qualities you most admire in others?

What has been your greatest accomplishment? Why do you consider it an accomplishment?

What has been your greatest failure? Why do you consider it a failure? What did you learn from it?

What is your greatest leadership experience?

What is your greatest fear?

What fear have you overcome?

What hardship have you overcome?

What are the four or five key words that best describe you?

What do you think your friends and family most like and dislike about you? (In other words, what are your strengths and weaknesses?)

What is your most important value? Can you give an example of how you uphold this value?

What events or time periods in your life represent turning points or inflection points (i.e., points at which you experienced significant change or new beginnings)?

In what way are you different from five years ago?

What are your future goals, including both personal life goals and career goals?

OTHER COMMENTS OR NOTES:

7

MARKETING YOURSELF: SPECIAL CASES

— KEY POINTS —

The following types of applicants are sufficiently unique to warrant special attention:

—*Transfer Applicants*
—*International Applicants*
—*Older Applicants*
—*Minority Applicants*
—*Home-Schooled Applicants*
—*Learning Disabled Applicants*
—*Physically Disabled Applicants*
—*Legacy Applicants*
—*Recruited Athlete Applicants*

INTRODUCTION

There are nine types of applicants that are different enough from the majority of candidates at the top schools to warrant special attention here. The purpose of this chapter is to help you understand the benefits of your position as well as the pitfalls you need to avoid in your applications. All applicants—regardless of their special case status—should first read Chapter 6 to understand how to market and profile themselves on a general level before reading the section in this chapter appropriate to their individual positions.

TRANSFER APPLICANTS

SPECIAL CASE STATUS

Transfer applicants are handled a bit differently than are regular applicants for admission to the freshman class. If you are a transfer candidate, your application is not evaluated along with the freshman applications but is placed in a pool of other candidates wishing to transfer to the college from another school. You compete only against other transfer applicants. Because there are fewer transfer applicants against whom one must compete, it is in one sense easier for transfers to make a strong case for themselves. On the other hand, the transfer pool is a bit more diverse than the regular pool, including older applicants who have had substantial careers before going back to college and students from a wide variety of other personal and educational backgrounds. This means that, in another sense, it is more difficult to make oneself appear unusual or unique as a transfer applicant.

At most colleges, the set of criteria by which transfer applicants are evaluated is slightly different from that by which regular candidates are examined. There is much more emphasis on a transfer applicant's college performance than on his high school performance (at some colleges a high school record is not even required for application to transfer). Students who do well in college can apply to transfer to colleges that may not have taken them for freshman admission based upon their high school records. Transfers have another great advantage in that they can generally get by with far lower standardized test scores than can regular applicants. The test scores of transfer students are not considered in the calculations of incoming class averages that become part of a college's profile (to be publicized in books, magazines, and other written materials). This means that colleges are much more willing to take transfer students with low standardized test scores than to take regular applicants with poor scores.

PERCEIVED STRENGTHS OF YOUR POSITION

If you are applying to transfer into a college from a four-year institution or a community college, you have several things working in your favor. First, taking the bull by the horns by applying to transfer to a different college rather than simply accepting your lot requires the kind of initiative that colleges find appealing. They will be impressed with your desire to improve yourself and steer yourself onto the correct path in life. (Simply applying to college as a senior, an act that many students perform simply because it is expected of them—a "given" in the life of a high school senior—does not require as much self-awareness and initiative.) Second, transfer students have the benefit of more life and academic experience, which generally allows them to show that they have a good idea of what they want to do in college and beyond. Having a wealth of self-knowledge and the ability to lay out a life plan is always to your advantage when applying to college.

PERCEIVED WEAKNESSES OF YOUR POSITION

There are not any significant weaknesses inherent in a transfer's profile. If a transfer student is applying to move from a college that is severely inferior to the one she desires to attend, though, the quality of her collegiate education thus far may be perceived as a weakness by the admissions committees. If a transfer applicant is applying from a college that is radically different from the target school (which is often the case), there is the possibility that the admission committee might be tempted to consider the candidate a poor judge of his own needs for having selected that college in the first place. This is easily rectified, though. Transfer applicants can simply acknowledge the poor judgment call made in youthful ignorance and use the difference in philosophy or style of education to their advantage by highlighting the need for transferring and the suitability of the target school.

APPLICATION TIPS

First, even if it is not explicitly asked of you, you must discuss in your application why your current college is not right for you as well as why the target school is a much better fit. Be as specific as possible to convince the committee that a move to its college is right for you. Acceptable reasons for applying to transfer to a college include needing a different academic orientation or curriculum, teaching methods, educational philosophy, location, size, or campus atmosphere. All transfer applicants should find some academic basis for the transfer, even if other nonacademic reasons are cited as well. Proximity to a girlfriend and better cafeteria food are not acceptable reasons for wanting to transfer!

If you originally applied to the target school, were accepted, and declined the offer, it is even more important that you show why your original choice of schools was not right. Acknowledge that you made a mistake the first time around and try to explain as best as possible why you thought you were making the right decision for freshman year. If you originally applied to the target school but were not admitted, take advantage of this by showing the school that it had interested you all along. If possible, discuss your original application with an admissions officer to get feedback on what went wrong and how you can avoid the same mistakes this time.

Take advantage of the perceived benefits of your status. Use self-awareness and initiative as some of your defining personal characteristics. Show that you now have a better and more complete life plan than you did when applying to colleges as a high school senior. Be as specific as possible about how you have come to realize you need a change and in showing how the target school's curriculum, academic and nonacademic offerings, philosophy, personality, atmosphere, and location match your personal and career needs.

If you are applying from a far inferior institution (in which case you will have had to receive stellar grades in order to be accepted at the target school), show that you have taken advantage of every opportunity possible to extract the most value from it. Try to show that you have studied the most difficult curriculum or been taught by the best professors there.

Take advantage of any special programs, research opportunities, internships, or other offerings that you can before applying to transfer. Such experiences will allow you to provide evidence of your initiative and success in college, as well as give you a forum in which to develop more meaningful relationships with professors for recommendation purposes. If possible, take classes with small numbers of students and try to develop substantial relationships with professors so that your recommendations will be as meaningful as possible. Getting the most from recommenders can be trickier for college students than it is for high school students because they generally have less contact with faculty than do high schoolers.

Last, retake standardized tests if you need to in order to be competitive with the college's applicants, remembering that transfer applicants are often accepted with lower scores than are freshman admits. If you are sure that you cannot do any better on your SAT Is than you already have and your scores represent the college's average or not far below, you can probably disregard them and assume that they will not keep you out of the school.

WHAT ADMISSIONS OFFICERS SAY ABOUT TRANSFER STUDENTS

"The standards that we maintain for transfer student admission are indistinguishable from those we use in freshman admission."

—*Marlyn McGrath Lewis, Director of Admissions, Harvard University*

"In the transfer admissions process, we often accept students who we did not accept for freshman admission—but we also reject students we originally accepted for freshman admission, so it can work both ways."

—*Michael Goldberger, Director of Admissions, Brown University*

"Transfer application is extremely competitive—we get about 150 applications for about 5 spots. Some years we take none because we have no room."

—*James Bock, Director of Admissions, Swarthmore College*

What Criteria Do You Evaluate for Transfer Admission?

"We do require test scores for transfers. Standardized test scores are relatively less important for them than they are for regular freshman admits, but transfer applicants can take tests again if their scores were low."

—*Sheppard Shanley, Senior Associate Director of Admissions, Northwestern University*

"We evaluate each transfer differently depending on the context of the application. Many of these people really bombed in high school. If they've really made a comeback that terrible record can actually influence our decision *positively* by showing us where the student has come from."

—*Marilee Jones, Dean of Admissions, Massachusetts Institute of Technology*

"With transfer admission, the decision is based on grades in college. We don't even require the high school record, but we have a college GPA cutoff of 3.0—you have to have at least a 3.0 at your undergraduate institution to come here as a transfer."

—*Delsie Phillips, Director of Admissions, Haverford College*

What Kinds of Applicants Show Up in the Transfer Pool?

"Our transfer applicants come from all walks of life—we get cab drivers who have done some work at community colleges, people serving in the military, students at other top four-year institutions."

—*Marilee Jones, Dean of Admissions, Massachusetts Institute of Technology*

"We have a large transfer program, taking about 500 students each year. Many have applied to UVA for freshman admission, were denied, and attend another school for a year before reapplying."

—*John Blackburn, Dean of Admissions, University of Virginia*

"Our transfers can basically be divided into three sets: those from larger universities, often prestigious ones—the students feel they are missing out on faculty interaction; those from women's colleges; and those who were originally on our waitlist but didn't get off of it to come here freshman year."

—*Richard Steele, Dean of Admissions, Bowdoin College*

INTERNATIONAL APPLICANTS

SPECIAL CASE STATUS

Overseas student admission is an important priority for all of the top colleges. Because the top colleges want to create student bodies that are as diverse as possible, international students possess a very valuable status. You are a treasure in that you bring a unique perspective, background, and cultural heritage to the campus. You are also a special case because of how you are treated in admissions.

You will become part of a separate overseas applicant pool and will be evaluated largely against other international students rather than against U.S. citizens or residents. Most colleges have notional targets dictating how many overseas applicants they will admit in any given year (generally a certain percentage of the freshman class). International students need to realize they are generally competing not only against all other applicants in the overseas pool, but especially against those from the same country or region of the world. The main objective in the admission of international students is to create a diversity of backgrounds, cultures, and perspectives on campus, so each college wants to avoid stuffing the international group with too many students from the same background. If you are applying from India or Argentina, countries from which the top colleges generally receive many applications each year, you might face stiffer competition than if you were applying from Sierra Leone or Finland, countries that are not well-represented on American college campuses. (Note that colleges have their own particular recruiting priorities and international connections, so each college will differ in its number of applicants from various countries or areas of the world.)

Overseas applicants at almost all colleges are admitted according to different admission and financial aid policies than are regular U.S. applicants. Most colleges do not extend their need-blind admission policies (see Chapter 5 for an explanation of need-blind and other policies relating to financial aid) to overseas students because they do not have enough international aid to cover all the students they would want to admit. Colleges also generally do not guarantee that admitted overseas students will receive full financial aid. Again, each college has its own policy.

You will be evaluated in a context particular to your background, educational history, and nationality, based upon what the admissions officers know about the life, educational systems, and cultural norms of your area of the world. Most other cultures do not provide the same extracurricular and leadership opportunities to high-school-aged students as do the schools and communities in the United States, for example. Admissions officers know this and do not expect international applicants to have achieved the same recognition or success in nonacademic activities as have their American counterparts. Like regular American applicants, you will be evaluated for how you have utilized the opportunities open to you.

PERCEIVED STRENGTHS OF YOUR POSITION

As an international student, you enjoy a coveted position as a candidate with an easy and clear way to position yourself in the applicant pool. Your status as a foreigner is a real blessing as far as admissions go. The problem that most American students have in applying to the top schools is finding a way to make themselves stand out in the admissions pool so that they can claim that they bring something special to the campus. You do not need to dig for any distinguishing features because they are inherent in your international status. Because of your particular background, no matter what country or part of the world you come from, you invariably can claim a unique perspective, background, and cultural heritage.

Just as you can claim a strength simply through your being "different," you can also claim a strength through your being "better," if your national and cultural heritage allow for it. It is likely that a particular aspect of your background gives you a desirable skill or characteristic. For example, if you have been educated in England, thus having focused on a few subjects for the past few years before taking your A-level exams, your extensive knowledge in those areas is of value to American colleges. Similarly, if you have been raised in a large agricultural family on Sumatra, as one of nine siblings who helps your father with the rice harvest each year, you probably possess personal qualities that many others in the admissions pool could not claim. Such a lifestyle could be positioned as having cultivated traits of responsibility, family values, and selflessness.

PERCEIVED WEAKNESSES OF YOUR POSITION

The weaknesses of your position really depend upon your individual case as an international student. Sometimes the weakness in an international applicant's profile can be a result of belonging to a large group of applicants from one particular region, thus preventing him or her from seeming as unique as possible. If you are a Chinese student competing against many other Chinese applicants in the pool, for example, it is more difficult to win a place in the class over others like you. Your weakness as an international applicant may result from your educational background, which may not have been as rigorous as the preparation that most applicants to the college have had. Your cultural background may be so different—if you are a female who has lived a sheltered existence in a very conservative Islamic society, for example—that admissions officers may be unconvinced that you would be happy and fit in on the campus. Your weakness may lie in your English language proficiency.

There may also be problems inherent in your financial situation. Most colleges do not give full financial aid to all overseas applicants, thus forcing them to pick international applicants who can afford the college on their own rather than more qualified applicants who cannot pay their own way.

APPLICATION TIPS

The most important thing for you to remember when putting together your college applications is to develop a profile that suggests you will be able to fit in and stand out at the same time. You need to highlight your strengths while minimizing your weaknesses. In other words, you should show that you can be comfortable in the college's environment and be successful there, but you also need to play up your uniqueness in order to sell yourself.

To show that you will fit in to a certain degree, you need to demonstrate that you are academically talented, proficient in the English language, and able to live your life in an American environment. You can instill confidence in your ability to live and learn on an American college campus by discussing any experiences abroad (especially if they were in the United States) or showing what you have learned from interacting with Americans or other foreigners. As part of your research, talk to each college's international admissions officer to find out more about the school's environment and what qualities are generally considered crucial for obtaining a place there.

More important than showing how you will fit in, you should use the inherent way in which you will stand out to your utmost benefit. Rather than play down your differences, you need to do just the opposite. American colleges want as many different types of people as possible to populate their communities, so you should take advantage of your uniqueness. Be sure to demonstrate how you alone can add certain benefits to the college that no other applicant can bring, remembering that you are up against other applicants from your country or area of the world. Whereas in some other cultures conforming to a certain norm and showing that you fit a certain mold are the best ways of demonstrating your fitness for an educational opportunity, it is just as important to show what differences you can bring to the mix at one of America's top colleges.

WHAT ADMISSIONS OFFICERS SAY ABOUT INTERNATIONAL STUDENTS

"In 1999, we admitted 15% of our domestic applicants and only 7% of the international applicants—it's more difficult to get in as an overseas applicant."

—*Jonathan Reider, Senior Associate Director of Admissions, Stanford University*

"We think of ourselves as a very international place. We were one of the very first liberal arts schools to offer such a range of languages, and we have remained very committed to the international community. We are one of two or three American colleges that treat overseas students exactly as we do domestic applicants. We are need-blind in international admissions *and* those candidates receive full need if accepted."

—John Hanson, Director of Admissions, Middlebury College

"We have the largest international population of any American university. Thirty percent of our undergraduates are overseas students."

—Richard Avitabile, Director of Admissions, New York University

"We're very proud of our involvement with international applications. We now visit three continents—South and Central America, all of Europe, and East Asia. We're preparing to add more to this list eventually. And we're excited to be able to offer international applicants without an ability to pay for an education the chance of a lifetime to come here."

—Richard Shaw, Dean of Undergraduate Admissions and Financial Aid, Yale University

WHAT CRITERIA ARE EVALUATED IN THE ADMISSION OF OVERSEAS STUDENTS?

"Usually international students don't present much in the way of extracurriculars so they don't come across with great leadership or community service experience. We tend to rely more heavily on academics for international admission."

—John Blackburn, Dean of Admissions, University of Virginia

"The way we view standardized test scores from international applicants varies according to their language ability."

—Sheppard Shanley, Senior Associate Director of Admissions, Northwestern University

"We are well aware that TOEFL [Test of English as a Foreign Language] exam scores vary tremendously from country to country. It is very difficult for a Turk to score well on TOEFL, for example, and not as hard for a student from France to do well on it. As with other variations in applicants' backgrounds, these things are taken into consideration."

—Jonathan Reider, Senior Associate Director of Admissions, Stanford University

"We really try to calibrate the use of recommendations for overseas students relative to what we know about the culture and educational system there. For example, in England, teachers are very honest—to the point of being harsh. They often discuss shortcomings as much as they do positive attributes. In many countries there is absolutely no grade inflation, and it is actually much tougher to get top grades than it is in our schools. We take all these things into account when reading recommendations for international applicants."

—Karl Furstenberg, Dean of Admissions and Financial Aid, Dartmouth College

---

OLDER APPLICANTS

SPECIAL CASE STATUS

Older (sometimes referred to as "nontraditional") students are a fast-growing segment of the college population. Although the majority of the colleges in the United States report surges in the numbers of applications they receive from candidates who have been out of high school for several or many years, the top colleges have not felt the trend as strongly. This is to your advantage if you are planning to apply to some of the nation's leading schools, because it means that you can stand out more clearly in the admissions pool.

Each college treats older applicants differently. While some colleges have special programs for applicants who are 25 and older or have been out of the educational system for a given length of time (such as Wellesley's Davis Scholars program), other schools treat them as part of the regular admissions pool. Some colleges take older students only through their transfer programs, requesting that anyone who has been out of the educational loop for five or more years start at a community or other college first, and then apply for admission to the sophomore or junior class. Colleges differ as to the criteria upon which they base the admission of older students as well. While some schools require standardized test scores and high school transcripts from older applicants, other colleges base their admission of older applicants on an entirely different set of criteria from that upon which regular freshman admits are judged.

PERCEIVED STRENGTHS OF YOUR POSITION

As an older applicant you are in a position of strength in that it is easy for you to show how you stand out among other applicants. You are quite naturally different from most applicants and bring something interesting to add to a college's mix of perspectives and personalities.

Older students are seen as being more mature and more directed than younger applicants. Because they have spent time in the working world and have grown into adulthood, they generally know what their life goals are and what kind of a career or focus they would like to follow. They know themselves better than do 17-year-olds (a result of having more time to ponder their own existence as well as the ability to do so from the perspective of an independent adult) and can often speak from a strong position of self-awareness.

Applying to college after a long time out of the educational system requires the kind of initiative that admissions officers like. Older applicants intent upon going to college at an untraditional age tend to have an appreciation for learning and education that younger applicants do not. Whereas many high schoolers apply to college merely because they are following what is assumed and expected of them, older applicants who either lacked or missed the opportunity to go to college directly out of high school know exactly why they want to go to college. The kinds of people who apply to college at an untraditionally older age tend to have a strong work ethic and demonstrate great motivation.

Most important, older applicants possess a wealth of life experience—whether it be from working, raising a family, traveling, or a host of other activities—that younger applicants cannot possibly have. They provide a perspective in academic and nonacademic situations that is particularly valuable on campuses where student bodies tend to be diverse in every way except for age.

PERCEIVED WEAKNESSES OF YOUR POSITION

Your difficulty in the admissions process is not in demonstrating how you stand out but in showing how you fit in. First and foremost, admissions officers worry that people who have not been in an academic environment for a long time will have a hard, perhaps ultimately unsuccessful, time settling in at a rigorous educational institution. After all, the requirements for doing well in tough classes are often very different from the requirements for doing well in many careers and occupations. This can be an especially daunting obstacle for those who did not perform well in high school but are applying to top colleges after years of developing as a successful person in other realms of life. Colleges also worry that adults—who often have children to care for, spouses to support, and adult-level problems to contend with—will not have time or energy to contribute to campus life. The schools want to know that you want and will be able to live, learn, associate, and communicate with your peers, who will be much younger and generally different from yourself. Many adults do not have enough patience to deal with the naiveté and inexperience of college-aged students; other adults cannot add to the campus environment because they are prevented from doing so by their personal responsibilities.

APPLICATION TIPS

You need to do your best, like all applicants, to maximize the rewards and minimize the risks inherent in your profile. To maximize the benefits of your special status, concentrate on the wealth you bring because of your age and experience. Show through your essays, recommendations, and the interview that you are mature, self-aware, focused, and goal-driven. Discuss in detail how have you gotten where you are today, tracing the major developments that have affected you since you left high school. Make sure that admissions officers can evaluate your application in the proper context by explaining why you have taken the route that you have, how you have grown through your various jobs or endeavors, and what motivates you to seek a college degree at this point in your life. Demonstrate what unique perspectives, ideas, and life experiences you will bring—try to describe them in ways that make it clear that no other applicant can add what you will add to the class.

To minimize the risks inherent in your profile, you should first attempt to make the admissions committee as confident as possible of your academic ability. This is especially true if you had a less than stellar high school record. To ensure the best possible success in college admissions, it is a good idea (even if your high school record is unblemished) to take classes at a nearby college. If you have done well in recent college-level classes, you are providing the college with that much more evidence that you have what it takes to succeed there.

You also need to show your target schools that you can fit in and become an active and valuable member of the college community. Try to provide evidence that you are tolerant of others' perspectives and that you are capable of occupying a unique position of difference in a largely conformist community. Demonstrate that your family or other burdens will not in any way prevent you from spending significant time and energy studying for your classes as well as participating in campus organizations and events.

WHAT ADMISSIONS OFFICERS SAY ABOUT ADMITTING OLDER STUDENTS

"We have a special program for students twenty-five or older, who have been out of the educational system for five years or more—the Resumed Undergraduate Education (RUE) program. Some of the applicants have really abysmal high school records—we ask to see them, but mostly because it's helpful to see how far they've come since that period in their lives. Poor high school records don't really hurt these applicants. We don't require standardized test scores from these candidates, either."

—*Michael Goldberger, Director of Admissions, Brown University*

"They really add to the mix. They're some of the most interesting applicants."

—*Richard Shaw, Dean of Undergraduate Admissions and Financial Aid, Yale University*

"For older students, it's better that they come to us from a community college first, as transfer students. We want some proof or evidence of success in higher-level academics."

—*Jonathan Reider, Senior Associate Director of Admissions, Stanford University*

What Criteria Do You Evaluate When Students Have Been Out of the Educational Loop for a Long Period of Time?

"We don't look at the high school record of older applicants. Instead, life experience becomes a very important factor in admission for these people."

—Karl Furstenberg, Dean of Admissions and Financial Aid, Dartmouth College

What Liabilities Might Older Applicants Bring with Them to Campus?

"In order to survive on a traditional college campus, older students have to be patient enough with younger people who don't have the same experiences they do. They can't resent the smooth sailing that has characterized the life of many of the younger students."

—Delsie Phillips, Director of Admissions, Haverford College

"Our older, nontraditional applicants tend to be really interesting, accomplished people. But occasionally there is the problem of an older applicant not being able to handle the particular rigors of the collegiate environment, a problem shared by many traditional applicants, too, of course."

—Marlyn McGrath Lewis, Director of Admissions, Harvard University

What Special Positive Qualities Do Older Applicants Generally Exhibit?

"Maturity, life experience, focus, specific goals—these are the positive traits that older applicants bring."

—Marilee Jones, Dean of Admissions, Massachusetts Institute of Technology

"They provide perspective in the classroom because of their tremendous life experience. They also show appreciation for learning and a positive work ethic."

—Barbara-Jan Wilson, Dean of Admissions and Financial Aid, Wesleyan University

MINORITY APPLICANTS

SPECIAL CASE STATUS

The recruitment of minorities—especially African Americans, Hispanics, and Native Americans— is a top priority at all of the top colleges. If you have performed well in academics as one of these kinds of minority candidates, you stand a good chance of doing very well in the college admissions process. Asian Americans, on the other hand, are at a disadvantage in relation to other minorities in the applicant pools at most of the top colleges because the number of strong Asian American students has grown tremendously over the past few decades. Whereas being an Asian American once gave an applicant a distinct edge in admissions, at some colleges (those where Asian American pools are huge), such a status can actually be a disadvantage. The colleges do not actually maintain quotas for the numbers of minority applicants they take, but no top college wants overrepresentation of any type of group, be it students from Connecticut, females over males, or Korean Americans.

PERCEIVED STRENGTHS OF YOUR POSITION

Minority applicants benefit from being in a position of great value to the colleges. In their efforts to bring the greatest amount of diversity possible to their communities, colleges seek American minority students in significant numbers. Your status as part of a minority is valuable in and of itself, and it can become more beneficial if you show that you possess certain perspectives, ideas, or strengths because of it. Minorities are generally perceived as having great fortitude and strength of character for having to endure systematic discrimination. Those minority applicants who live in situations of poverty and in communities where educational and other resources are inadequate are seen as having great perseverance for having to overcome obstacles in order to live and learn and find success.

PERCEIVED WEAKNESSES OF YOUR POSITION

There are no inherent weaknesses in your position if you are an African American, Latino American, or Native American applicant. If you are an Asian American applicant, you may face a challenge stemming from the fact that you are competing against many other very talented and bright students of similar background in the admissions pools at the top schools. A weakness that can arise as an *indirect* result of minority status is a lack of academic preparation stemming from the type of school you have attended. Those minorities attending school in poorer public systems that do not offer AP classes, SAT preparation, and other similar opportunities may do well in school yet still be regarded as less successful and less prepared for a top-tier college than are applicants who have done well in much more rigorous curriculums. This would be true of Caucasian (nonminority) applicants coming from the same poorer school systems.

APPLICATION TIPS

First, it is important that you note your minority status in order to benefit from it. Make sure when taking standardized tests and filling out college applications that you check the right box to notify the colleges of your particular status.

You can also use your background as a profiling point, making it one of the ways in which you position yourself in the application. Make sure when doing so to avoid clichés or sounding as if you are trying to manipulate the colleges with your status. Do not resort to trite statements such as "By persevering through extraordinary prejudice, I have become a stronger person." This is a fine theme to use, but you need to tell detailed stories full of self-analysis and meaning in order to make the theme come through without actually stating it. Do not make your minority status into something it is not, either, because the admissions officers will probably be able to sense when you are stretching the truth. If you live at a fancy address in Brentwood and your parents are professionals (both pieces of information are readily available to admissions officers from your application data sheets), do not write an essay about the poverty and difficulty you have endured as a black male growing up in Los Angeles. Last, be sure to show that you have taken advantage of every opportunity available to you and done as best as you can given the resources available to you if you have gone to school in a less than ideal public system.

> Colleges want minorities for two reasons, one pragmatic and the other more idealistic. The pragmatic reason is that colleges face difficulties with many of their constituencies if they have inadequate minority representation. On a more positive note, colleges hope that minorities will contribute valuable perspectives. The latter consideration suggests that the most valuable minority students will be those who bring a different perspective, have not been homogenized, but are also going to mix well with other types of people (not just members of their own minorities). Demonstrating that you are such a candidate can be tricky but of substantial value in the admissions game.

ADMISSIONS OFFICERS SPEAK ABOUT MINORITY APPLICANTS

"We are always looking for more African American and Latino students as well."
—*Christoph Guttentag, Director of Undergraduate Admissions, Duke University*

"Twenty-one percent of our population consists of students of color, but we are always looking for more minorities."
—*Nanci Tessier, Director of Admissions, Smith College*

HOME-SCHOOLED APPLICANTS

SPECIAL CASE STATUS

The trend toward home-schooling is one that has been felt in certain pockets of American society but not yet had an overwhelming effect on admissions at the nation's top colleges. Most of the leading schools receive a handful of applications from home-schooled applicants each year and have developed guidelines (whether formal or informal) for these applicants but have not yet made home-schooled admissions a real priority or area of concern for their staffs. Although a few admissions departments assign a particular officer to oversee applications from candidates who currently learn at home or have been home-schooled for some portion of their high school careers, the great majority deal with each home-schooled applicant on a somewhat improvised basis.

Home-schooled applicants are special cases in that they must be careful to do all the right things when preparing and applying to colleges, or they risk faring poorly in the process. Most colleges want home-schooled applicants to approach their applications a bit differently than do regular applicants. Home-schooled applicants are warned by all the top colleges that their standardized test scores will count very heavily in their evaluation. They are encouraged to submit more than three SAT II scores and to take AP exams to prove their academic preparation for college. Many colleges want them to submit detailed information about the curriculum used in their classes. Home-schooled candidates are always advised to sit for an interview, with an admissions officer rather than an alum if that is available at the school, even at colleges that do not necessarily put a large emphasis on the interview for other applicants. The colleges also generally hope that a home-schooled applicant has taken some classes at a nearby school or community college, so that there can be the benefit of a recommendation other than one written by the parent.

PERCEIVED STRENGTHS OF YOUR POSITION

Some of the differences inherent in your position are generally viewed as strengths from an admissions officer's point of view. Home-schooled applicants are generally thought to be remarkably independent, capable of learning and pursuing topics on their own. They demonstrate the kind of entrepreneurism and intellectual curiosity that schools love. They are seen as being mature, motivated, diligent, and self-aware. Many home-schooled students have benefited from being able to pursue particular interests (often academic ones that are not available at most high schools—a particular language or the study of architecture, for example) to a depth far beyond what the average applicant has accomplished. They have often begun to focus on a particular field or subject matter at a young age and have even benefited from jobs or internships in those fields, giving them a bit of life experience that other high schoolers do not possess.

PERCEIVED WEAKNESSES OF YOUR POSITION

Although most applicants who demonstrate that they are different from the usual candidate benefit from showing their uniqueness, some of the differences inherent in a home-schooled applicant's profile are considered weaknesses rather than strengths. Many schools worry that students who have learned at home, through their parents' teaching methods, are ill-prepared for a top college curriculum. Because they cannot be certain that a home-schooled applicant has covered all the material that is studied by a student in public or private school, admissions officers often feel less than confident about a home-schooled applicant's academic readiness for college. They also wonder if the student can follow a class with rigorous and inflexible requirements after getting used to learning what and when he wants to study.

Colleges are enormously concerned about home-schooled applicants' social and communication skills. The top colleges employ curriculums that require a lot of interaction between students inside the classroom. They are also for the most part residential communities where students must cooperate and live peaceably with one another. Many admissions officers are wary that home-schooled applicants will have a hard time adjusting to living and learning with other students after spending so much time on their own. Many of the admissions officers view home-schooled applicants as academically mature but socially immature. This becomes a more obvious pitfall for those home-schooled applicants applying to college at the age of 15 or 16.

APPLICATION TIPS

First, all home-schooled applicants must contact the admissions committee of each of their target schools to discuss their candidacy and what they can do to ensure the best treatment in the admissions process. This is crucial for all candidates applying to colleges from a current home-school status as well as those applying to colleges as regular high school seniors who have been home-schooled at some point in their high school careers. Each school has different recommendations for home-schooled applicants, so you need to talk with someone at each college—this will help to put you on their radar screen as well as clue you in as to what you need to do when applying.

Be sure to follow all of the colleges' guidelines. If a college tells you and your parents that it wants a curriculum list, take the request seriously. Do not send some Post-It notes with the names of books scribbled down on them! Call your local school system to see what a curriculum guide contains and how it is put together. Send the colleges a formal printed list containing substantial and detailed information. It is a good idea for all home-schooled applicants to offer curriculum lists, even when they are not requested. Be sure to follow each school's testing requirements. It is best if you can take (and do well on) as many SAT II and AP exams as possible.

It is also in every home-schooled candidate's best interest to take classes at a school or community college, not only for the objective grades you can then show for yourself but also for the teacher recommendations you will be able to solicit. Joining activities and organizations in the community or at a school is a smart way to ensure that you receive recognition for your pursuits and to extinguish any thoughts on the part of admissions officers that you are antisocial or unable to work well with others. You should always sit for an interview, on campus with an admissions officer if the school offers such interviews, if you are a home-schooled applicant. Because one of the concerns that admissions officers have about you is regarding your social, interaction, and communication skills, the interview is an ideal way in which to put their fears to rest. It also gives you an extra opportunity to elaborate on your experiences and provide the proper context for an evaluation of your candidacy.

Capitalize on your strengths as much as possible. Your independence, self-motivation, intellectual maturity, and passion for learning should become critical aspects of your profile. If you have a particular interest that you have been able to pursue in depth through your unique education, use that material in your essays. By doing your best to prove that you have none of the weaknesses inherent in your profile and playing up the unique benefits of a home-school education, you can win over the admissions committees and find a place in their hearts (and in their incoming classes).

WHAT ADMISSIONS OFFICERS SAY ABOUT HOME-SCHOOLED APPLICANTS

"Home-schooling is certainly a growth industry. Every year we see and take a few more home-schooled students than the year before."

—*Marlyn McGrath Lewis, Director of Admissions, Harvard University*

"It always involves a bit of a leap of faith to take them, but some of them are superb."

—*David Borus, Dean of Admissions and Financial Aid, Vassar College*

"There has been enough rise in the number of home-schooled applicants to warrant our changing our application one year ago. Our application now offers 'home school'—along with public, private, and parochial—as one of the choices for applicants to check off when describing the school they attend."

—*Lee Stetson, Dean of Admissions, University of Pennsylvania*

WHAT ADVICE WOULD YOU GIVE TO HOME-SCHOOLED APPLICANTS?

"We prefer that home-schooled applicants take five SAT II subject tests instead of the usual three."
—Eric J. Furda, Director of Undergraduate Admissions, Columbia University

"The best thing for home-schooled students to do is to reach out—join social activities at church, participate in community activities, that kind of thing. Otherwise there is no evidence of what kind of person the applicant is, no evidence of how they interact with others."
—Philip Smith, Dean of Admissions, Williams College

"I would suggest that all home-schooled students interview as well—we try to be sure they do if they are nearby."
—Christoph Guttentag, Director of Undergraduate Admissions, Duke University

"The more SAT II subject tests home-schooled applicants can take, the better—take a dozen if you can."
—Richard Shaw, Dean of Undergraduate Admissions and Financial Aid, Yale University

"I want some organization in a home-schooled student's curriculum. I don't like these setups where there is a month of Jane Austen, a month of studying birds—that kind of jumping around isn't ideal. I'd rather see a serious curriculum with breadth. I want to see that these students have studied a topic from its beginning to the end, not just history of the Civil War and some ancient Greece. Home-schooled students still need to study a foreign language, and also need substantial math."
—Jonathan Reider, Senior Associate Director of Admissions, Stanford University

"It's much easier for us to evaluate a home-schooled student if he or she has gone to community college or taken some classes at local schools—especially when recommendations come from these outside sources."
—Michael Goldberger, Director of Admissions, Brown University

"I tell students who are schooled at home to get as much external validation of their abilities as possible—especially in math and science. Taking AP exams and SAT IIs is the best way to do so."
—Nancy Hargrave Meislahn, Director of Undergraduate Admissions, Cornell University

"Because of the nature of their grades, we like to see as many SAT II scores as possible from home-schooled applicants. We also hope that they've taken a few courses at a local school or college. We urge them to come for an interview. Here's where an interview at UVA might matter."
—John Blackburn, Dean of Admissions, University of Virginia

"Balance is especially important. They need to have studied what we require as prerequisites for admission. We don't like it when they've concentrated on one subject and neglected others."

—Janet Lavin Rapelye, Dean of Admissions, Wellesley College

"We like to have something other than a parental evaluation. It's not that I don't believe them, but parents tend to be cheerleaders. Community college instructors can be good, but they generally can't compare the student to the kinds of students we're used to—we need someone who knows what the really top kids are like in the classroom."

—Delsie Phillips, Director of Admissions, Haverford College

"We require that the student have participated in an educational plan reviewed by the state educational department—an approved home-schooling curriculum."

—Richard Avitabile, Director of Admissions, New York University

ARE STANDARDIZED TEST SCORES MORE IMPORTANT FOR HOME-SCHOOLED APPLICANTS?

"Standardized tests inevitably count more in the evaluation of home-schooled students—how could they not?"

—Jonathan Reider, Senior Associate Director of Admissions, Stanford University

"Test scores are often the only way to measure them academically and in comparison with other applicants."

—Barbara Bergman, Associate Dean of Admissions, Georgetown University

"Here is where we suspend our admissions philosophy of subordinating quantifiable criteria. We have to look at test scores carefully with home-schooled applicants. We can't avoid it—we don't know what their grades mean."

—John Hanson, Director of Admissions, Middlebury College

"Standardized tests take on a greater weight for home-schooled students."

—Christoph Guttentag, Director of Undergraduate Admissions, Duke University

"We just changed our policy in regard to testing for home-schooled applicants. We still don't *require* that they submit test scores, but we highly recommend that they submit as many scores as possible. We end up not taking students if we can't see test scores and the only grades and recommendations are from parents."

—Richard Steele, Dean of Admissions, Bowdoin College

WHAT ARE YOUR BIGGEST AREAS OF CONCERN WITH APPLICANTS WHO HAVE BEEN HOME-SCHOOLED?

"It's harder to get a handle on them. We might have concerns about how they are going to fit in—both with other students and in the classroom setting. How do they interact with others? Can they handle a class with a set structure, syllabus, and traditional means of evaluation?"

—*Barbara Bergman, Associate Dean of Admissions, Georgetown University*

"It's hard for us to evaluate the credentials of home-schooled candidates, so we often don't know if they're really prepared for the rigor of Wesleyan."

—*Barbara-Jan Wilson, Dean of Admissions and Financial Aid, Wesleyan University*

"My biggest concerns about home-schooled students have to do with their sense of narrowness, or their tolerance level—many of these kids have been very sheltered and wouldn't do well in our diverse environment. Also, I wonder if they have what it takes to sit in a classroom all day with others and do the nitty-gritty that college coursework demands. That kind of work is a lot different from doing special internships with the friends of parents and designing your own curriculum."

—*Marilee Jones, Dean of Admissions, Massachusetts Institute of Technology*

"Our greatest concern with home-schooled applicants is regarding their social maturity. They often apply to college at a very young age and don't have the experience of interaction in the classroom that others have."

—*Richard Shaw, Dean of Undergraduate Admissions and Financial Aid, Yale University*

"My biggest concerns with home-schooled kids are regarding social interaction and maturity. Engagement with fellow learners is critical to higher education, and we need to know that our students can hold up their end of the responsibility here."

—*Nancy Hargrave Meislahn, Director of Undergraduate Admissions, Cornell University*

WHAT SPECIAL POSITIVE ATTRIBUTES DO HOME-SCHOOLED STUDENTS TEND TO EXHIBIT?

"They tend to be very mature and independent."

—*Karl Furstenberg, Dean of Admissions and Financial Aid, Dartmouth College*

"Home-schooled students tend to show great intellectual vitality—which fits Stanford's admissions criteria wonderfully. It fits our desire for 'student as entrepreneur' types. I endorse home-schooling as long as it is approached the right way."

—*Jonathan Reider, Senior Associate Director of Admissions, Stanford University*

"Home-schooled applicants have the ability to show really extended development in one area—that's the draw. They can often go farther in music or science— whatever they're into—than other students can. But they also need to have some balance."

—*Sheppard Shanley, Senior Associate Director of Admissions, Northwestern University*

LEARNING DISABLED APPLICANTS

SPECIAL CASE STATUS

If you have been diagnosed with a learning disability, you should treat your college admissions situation as a special one, even though it will not be seen as such by the schools themselves. Colleges cannot legally require you to disclose information about a disability. Nowhere on the college application forms will you be asked about such problems. If you have a disability that has affected your academic performance, though, and you have a way to discuss it without whining, you should let the colleges know. By way of providing the colleges with as much contextual information as possible, you enable them to have more confidence in your ability to perform there. For example, if a learning disability helps them to understand why your grades in math have fluctuated dramatically, despite your having done consistently well in all other subjects, then you need to make them understand the situation. This way, they can be certain you will perform well once given the opportunity to choose your own areas of study (which, you might remind them, will not include math or physics!).

PERCEIVED STRENGTHS OF YOUR POSITION

The only significant strength of your status is what you can claim from having battled a problem, come to terms with it, overcome it, and found ways to live your life around it. Showing that you sought help for a learning problem and worked to overcome it indicates initiative and the ability to persevere.

PERCEIVED WEAKNESSES OF YOUR POSITION

The weaknesses of your position stem from the limits imposed by your disability on your academic capabilities. Learning disabled students who have performed well after the diagnosis was made and attempts to solve the problem were carried out largely escape any problems associated with their position. If you have already proven that you are capable of doing well by using certain coping mechanisms, then you will not suffer much. Learning disabled students who have *not* performed well in spite of diagnosing the problem and applying particular study tactics may have a hard time convincing admissions officers that they have what it takes to succeed at a demanding college.

APPLICATION TIPS

As mentioned previously, you should definitely offer the admissions committee as much information as possible about your problem and, if possible, provide evidence that when applying the right coping mechanisms, you can perform well.

Colleges are not concerned with what strategies you use to achieve something, they merely want to see that you can achieve your goals and that you are capable of doing the work that will be expected of you.

The question is not *whether* to disclose information about the disability, it is *how* to disclose that information. Colleges have slightly different opinions about this. Most schools agree that a guidance counselor is often best able to provide appropriate information in a way that does not sound like an excuse for poor performance and is accompanied by some amount of perspective on the problem. Some schools also want candidates or teachers to address the issue, whereas others prefer that the problem not take up too much of the application's focus. You should contact each target school to ask an admissions representative's advice on how to go about the application.

Whereas it is usually appropriate for candidates to grasp onto the strengths inherent in their positions and play them up in their applications, the personal strength you have gained from battling a learning disability is not one you should necessarily highlight. Being as succinct as possible in dealing with this kind of disability is usually more effective than harping upon it and allowing it to be the only message that comes through in your application. You do not want to be known as the girl with the learning disability; you want to be known as the great candidate who has the best record in her league for the 400-meter run—oh, yes, and also happens to have a learning disability that she has fought and overcome. Find other positive qualities and strengths with which to position yourself.

ADMISSIONS OFFICERS TALK ABOUT APPLICANTS WITH LEARNING DISABILITIES

"We often don't know about learning disabilities during the admissions process. But if a student has taken the SAT untimed, or there is evidence of a disability, the student should tell us more so that we understand something about the conditions under which the candidate has succeeded."

—*Katie Fretwell, Director of Admissions, Amherst College*

"We are interested in *performance*—how a student has performed over time. We're not so interested in the strategies a student has used to achieve that performance as we are in the end result itself. Learning disabilities in and of themselves do not discourage us from admitting an applicant."

—*Marlyn McGrath Lewis, Director of Admissions, Harvard University*

"Any kind of disability—whether it be a learning disability or a physical affliction—is probably a big part of a student's life—so we would want to hear about it, in whatever depth an applicant feels comfortable talking about it."

—*Philip Smith, Dean of Admissions, Williams College*

"We tell applicants with concerns about a disability to be in touch with the campus coordinator for students with disabilities while applying to Cornell. All conversations with that office remain confidential—records of the contact do not go to the admissions committee. I recommend full disclosure of disabilities, though—students who do the best job of presenting themselves give us a full context in which to make our decisions."

—*Nancy Hargrave Meislahn, Director of Undergraduate Admissions, Cornell University*

"We think it's to a student's advantage to tell us about a learning disability. It allows us to understand them better."

—*John Blackburn, Dean of Admissions, University of Virginia*

"If we need to know something in order to be confident about your ability to handle our work and courseload, by all means tell us."

—*Janet Lavin Rapelye, Dean of Admissions, Wellesley College*

Is It Best for an Applicant, a Teacher, or a Guidance Counselor to Disclose the Disability?

"It can be helpful if the student addresses the disability and a teacher or guidance counselor do the same in a recommendation—so we get a few perspectives on the issue."

—*Nancy Hargrave Meislahn, Director of Undergraduate Admissions, Cornell University*

"I don't suggest that the disability come through in every part of the application. If everyone—the student, the counselor, a teacher—discusses it, it starts to become the only thing we see."

—*Sheppard Shanley, Senior Associate Director of Admissions, Northwestern University*

"Disclosing a learning disability is a tricky thing to do. It is sometimes handled better by a guidance counselor."

—*Barbara-Jan Wilson, Dean of Admissions and Financial Aid, Wesleyan University*

PHYSICALLY CHALLENGED APPLICANTS

SPECIAL CASE STATUS

If you have a physical disability, you should treat your college admissions situation as a special one, even though it will not be recognized as such by the schools themselves. Colleges cannot legally require you to disclose information about a disability. Nowhere on the college application forms will you be asked about such situations. All of the schools, furthermore, have offices for students with disabilities and provide assistance for those in need of help in performing academically, living comfortably on the campus, and contributing to the campus community. You will find students possessing every kind of physical disability—from blindness to multiple sclerosis—on the campuses of the leading colleges.

If you have a disability, even if it has not affected your academic performance whatsoever, you should by all means let the colleges know. By providing the colleges with as much contextual information as possible, you enable them to understand and appreciate your situation all the more.

PERCEIVED STRENGTHS OF YOUR POSITION

You derive enormous strengths that can benefit you in the college admissions process from coping and living with a physical disability. Living with a disability and caring for the burdens of a health problem show that you possess great inner fortitude. If you have a serious disability and have still managed to perform well academically and reach your goals, you demonstrate an ability to bound over obstacles and deal with an affliction quite unique among the college applicant pool. You are also seen as possessing strength of character through facing discrimination and marginalization.

PERCEIVED WEAKNESSES OF YOUR POSITION

There are no weaknesses inherent in your position, unless your academic performance suggests that you might for some reason not be able to live and learn on the college campus because of the limitations of your physical disability.

APPLICATION TIPS

Discuss your disability situation as part of your profile, but do so with great care. You cannot afford to appear as if you are "using" your position to gain sympathy from the admissions staff, nor can you risk sounding crass, angry, or resentful of others. Discuss your disability in a meaningful way, do not whine, and avoid using clichés to show how you have been formed by your life experiences. It is also a good idea to contact each target school's office for disabled students. You will need to start preparing to live in a new environment, but contact will also be helpful for your own fact-finding purposes. Discussions with the office for disabilities can teach you more about the school and how it conforms to your needs and desires as a special student. This information can in turn be used in your admissions materials to demonstrate your fit with the college. In addition, a counselor in the disabilities office may even become a supporter of your case in the admissions process.

ADMISSIONS OFFICERS DISCUSS APPLICANTS WITH PHYSICAL DISABILITIES

"Physical disabilities are very important to discuss—students shouldn't hide them! A discussion of a disability often gives us a very good picture—a positive impression—of the candidate. We want to know what obstacles an applicant has overcome, what makes that applicant unique, what affects the day-to-day life."

—*Karl Furstenberg, Dean of Admissions and Financial Aid, Dartmouth College*

"Discussing a physical disability helps us know who a person is. Doing so could only improve our respect for a candidate, so there's no reason not to be truthful here."

—*Barbara-Jan Wilson, Dean of Admissions and Financial Aid, Wesleyan University*

LEGACY APPLICANTS

SPECIAL CASE STATUS

All schools treat legacies as special cases. Whereas some colleges define a "legacy" as someone whose parent attended the school, other colleges' definitions are broader, including applicants whose siblings, uncles, aunts, or grandparents attended the school. Most admissions committees work in conjunction with their development offices and offices of alumni relations to make decisions about which legacies are most important for the school's needs (i.e., which legacies' relatives are most important to keep happy). Some schools place legacies in a separate applicant pool so that they are treated with special care. Other colleges look at legacy applications alongside all the others, but make sure to give them additional consideration or have the director of admissions look at each one to ensure proper evaluation.

PERCEIVED STRENGTHS OF YOUR POSITION

There are two strengths that you are thought to exhibit by way of your legacy status. The first is that you are often more likely to attend the school than others in the applicant pool who do not have family ties (i.e., have not been wearing the school's sweatshirts since the age of two). Your admission thus contains the possibility of a "sure thing" attendance (equivalent to the "sure thing" attendances that colleges get when they take Early Decision applicants), which increases the school's yield for the year. The second strength of your profile is that of your connection with alums of the school. By admitting you, the school keeps a contributing and supportive alum happy, which helps the college maintain the health of its bottom line. Unhappy alums do not donate money, especially not in large library-constructing sums.

PERCEIVED WEAKNESSES OF YOUR POSITION

There is no inherent weakness in your position as a legacy.

APPLICATION TIPS

As a legacy applicant, you should do everything in your power to make the admissions committee confident that your interest in the school stems not only from your family connection but also from your own research and investigation. Although admitted legacies generally attend colleges in higher numbers than do nonlegacies, admissions officers are also aware that there are plenty of legacies who have applied to their colleges to use them as safety schools. Many students end up applying to mom's and dad's alma maters not because they really want to attend them but because they think that they might have an easier chance at getting into those colleges than they do at other schools. You should thus show to the admissions officers that you have substantial and mature reasons (i.e., reasons other than the fact of your perfect football game attendance record since the age of five) for wanting to attend the school and that you would choose it even without the family push.

Make sure to solicit materials from the school, visit its Web site, and make a formal prospective applicant visit, even if you think you already know all there is to know about the school. You are bound to discover something new, which you can use to show your fit with the school in your admissions materials. You also need to confirm your serious interest in the school to admissions officers, who have no way of knowing that you have been reading Dad's alumni magazines and staying in the dorms during alumni reunion weekends all your life.

There is not much else you should do as a legacy applicant. The admissions committees will look with special care at your case if your parent or relative is a big donor to the campus or occupies a position of leadership in an alumni organization. If your alumni relative is not an important priority to the college, your application will still be treated with great care by the admissions committees, but you may not get much of an edge over other applicants in the process.

WHAT ADMISSIONS OFFICERS SAY ABOUT LEGACIES

"Our alumni are our taxpayers, so we can't ignore them. There is some level of preference for alumni children who come to us in Early Decision. Those in the regular admissions pool get little preference, though."

—*Lee Stetson, Dean of Admissions, University of Pennsylvania*

"Legacy candidates are evaluated along with everyone else—they are not placed into a separate pool or anything like that. And, as at other schools, being a legacy can become a plus when a student is right on the border."

—*Karl Furstenberg, Dean of Admissions and Financial Aid, Dartmouth College*

"As with other special categories of students—those with fine arts talent, for example—legacies are looked at separately. All legacies receive a modest benefit in the process if everything else is substantially equal. In addition, the development office tells us ahead of time what legacy cases it considers important. We look with special attention at legacy applicants whose Stanford connections are important to the school."

—*Jonathan Reider, Senior Associate Director of Admissions, Stanford University*

"There is a tacit agreement at MIT that we admit only the absolute best. You might call our attitude toward legacies 'Preference at the same cost.' A legacy status only comes into play if we are deciding between several equally qualified candidates and one happens to be a legacy."

—*Marilee Jones, Dean of Admissions, Massachusetts Institute of Technology*

"We of course accept a greater percentage of legacies than of nonlegacies. But that's really not so terrible as some people make it out to be. If an applicant has a parent who went to Amherst, we would expect that he or she grew up in a home where reading is valued, good books are always around, and intellectual pursuits are common. So there is probably more likelihood of that student being a good fit with Amherst anyway."

—*Katie Fretwell, Director of Admissions, Amherst College*

"How do we treat legacies? With incredible respect! All legacies get a third look by me before they are denied admission if that's the direction their files are headed."

—*Barbara-Jan Wilson, Dean of Admissions and Financial Aid, Wesleyan University*

"Our Quaker roots obligate us not to give preferential treatment to legacies—our alumni all respect this policy."

—*James Bock, Director of Admissions, Swarthmore College*

"Tradition and connections are especially important at small schools, so extra weight is given to legacies. We give a legacy folder an especially careful read."

—*David Borus, Dean of Admissions and Financial Aid, Vassar College*

"We don't have a legacy target. We don't reserve places. All other things being equal, we'd give a legacy a nod."

—*Richard Avitabile, Director of Admissions, New York University*

RECRUITED ATHLETE APPLICANTS

SPECIAL CASE STATUS

Athletics is a big part of collegiate life and virtually all schools pay a great deal of attention to athletes in the admissions process. If you are a high school athlete looking to attend a world-class institution, it would be a mistake—and a potential opportunity lost—to assume that this emphasis on athletics is found just at "jock schools." Few colleges have deemphasized athletics; the Ivy League schools, for example, are heavily invested in winning at each of the many varsity sports they play.

Many of the top colleges, including the Ivy League schools and the liberal arts colleges, do not grant athletic scholarships. They do, however, seek talented athletes and are willing to stretch to admit less able students who are gifted athletes. The Ivy League, for example, maintains minimum standards of admission for recruited athletes, calculated by something known as the Academic Index (AI). The AI score is the sum of the average of your two SAT I scores, the average of your three SAT II scores, and your Converted Rank Score, which is based upon your rank in class and high school performance. The potential range of scores is 1 to 240, with 240 being the highest (and approximately 170 the cutoff for recruited athletes). The typical scores of admitted nonathletes are 200–220; for recruited athletes, averages are perhaps in the 180s, with many in the 170s.

PERCEIVED STRENGTHS OF YOUR POSITION

Simply stated, top academic institutions are looking for accomplished student athletes. Even if you are not in the top 10% of your high school class, the combination of a solid academic record and your athletic prowess may prove to be a combination that you can leverage into a top-school acceptance. The opportunity for self-promotion is stronger for the ambitious, accomplished student athlete than it is for almost anyone else in the admissions pool.

Part of this is due to the impact you may have upon a college team's prospects. Part of your value, however, resides in the personal qualities you are assumed to possess. Being the successful captain of your outstanding soccer team, for example, indicates personal attributes such as perseverance, leadership, teamwork, and the ability to juggle many different responsibilities at once.

PERCEIVED WEAKNESSES OF YOUR POSITION

There are two potential weaknesses that you may need to overcome, depending upon the sport you play as well as your own profile. If you are a male, playing one of the "macho" sports—football, ice hockey, basketball, wrestling, and perhaps track and field (albeit not distance running) or baseball—you risk being stereotyped as an inconsiderate, even potentially violent fellow, if other aspects of your candidacy also point in the same direction. For example, a wrestler who has been suspended from school for drinking will need to counteract this. (This is particularly true if there is even a hint of trouble in his file regarding the treatment of young women.) The other potential problem is that you may be viewed as not entirely up to the intellectual mark.

APPLICATION TIPS
DETERMINING YOUR VALUE

Begin by assessing your value to schools. Ask your coaches, rival coaches, and other experts familiar with your abilities how you compare with athletes playing for your target schools. Emphasize that you are seeking their honest, informed opinions. If they mislead you about your value to schools, you may end up missing substantial opportunities, so be certain that they are not sloughing you off with well-intended exaggerations of your worth.

Note that you will be much more valuable to some schools than others. Your value depends upon the value the college places upon your sport and your ability to help the team win (or at least garner publicity). Colleges tend to value the "money sports," such as football, very highly. Each college also has historical favorites, those sports in which it has traditionally been successful. A look at the past success of the school's teams or a quick chat with a few students will reveal which sports are close to a given school's heart.

As for your ability to help a team win, several factors will be determinative (in addition to your own ability level). First, there is the level of competition at which this team plays: Is it a national contender or a perennial, small-time loser? Second is the importance of your position. A quarterback will be regarded as playing a more important position than that of tight end. Similarly, if you are a sprinter and thus able to run the 100 meters, 200 meters, 4×100 relay, and perhaps long jump, you will be considered more valuable than one event participants such as shot-putters. Third is the availability of substitutes for you. If your school already has a marvelous quarterback, or has a set of them currently applying, your value is proportionately lower.

Coaches have the ability to influence a number of admissions decisions. Depending upon the sport and the school, a coach can probably have five to ten applicants considered as top recruits (although for football the number is likely to be thirty to fifty). The higher you are on the coach's list, the more impact it will have on the process. Note, however, that if someone above you on the list plays your same position, your fate may depend upon whether that person decides to attend the school. Thus, find out from the coach where you stand overall and as to your position. Track your situation over time, too, because coaches submit updated lists each month.

MARKETING YOURSELF

Unless you are a consensus All-American, you are likely to need to market yourself rather than simply respond to schools' recruiting efforts. The first step is to make sure that you come to the attention of your chosen schools. You can do this by participating in very high-profile tournaments or attending high-profile camps. For many, however, the easiest route is to contact the schools directly.

The appropriate way to initiate contact is to send a package of materials about yourself to the coaches at your chosen schools. This should include:

- A cover letter, explaining your interest in the program (and the coach) and the school.

- A sports resume, with a brief look at your academic record (including test results), extracurricular and outside of school achievements, and your athletic accomplishments. Include your height and weight, your key statistics (and show your progress over time), and your honors and awards.

- Recommendation letters from your coach, an opposing coach, or another expert, focusing upon your ability, attitude, and potential.

- Clippings from newspaper coverage of you.

- A schedule of your upcoming competitions, in case a coach or interested alum will be able to see you perform.

- An offer to send a video of your performance, if you are involved in a sport (lacrosse or ice hockey, for instance) in which this will be helpful.

Have your high school coach contact the coaches at colleges of interest to you. Brief him or her in advance so that he or she knows what to emphasize, including how you will fit into a given school's program. In addition, be sure to visit the school and arrange (in advance) to meet with the relevant coach or coaches.

The impact of being considered an athletic recruit depends upon both your athletic value to the college and the extent to which a college will have to stretch academically to admit you. The better the academic credentials you possess, in other words, the less a school will have to stretch for you and the better your chances of admission.

SHOULD YOU TRADE DOWN IN SCHOOL QUALITY FOR A SCHOLARSHIP?

It is easy to take a full scholarship to play basketball at Stanford or Duke rather than attend Swarthmore or Williams, given that the former are both among the academic (as well as the athletic) elite. The harder question is whether to take an athletic scholarship to play for Villanova or the University of Texas at El Paso. Given that few can earn a living playing basketball or any other sport, the question for most applicants should not be whether a given athletic program will maximize their chances of making it to the "big leagues" or onto the professional circuit. Instead, the question is whether the scholarship money warrants giving up the better education. For a more detailed discussion of why choosing the better school may be worth your while, turn to Chapter 1.

Note, however, that there is an additional drawback to accepting an athletic rather than academic scholarship. Your time may be more your coach's than your own at many schools. Partly due to this, the graduation rates of athletes (particularly in the "money sports," such as basketball and football) at some schools are minuscule. Thus, all too often athletes get a second-class education even at schools that are otherwise highly regarded.

WHAT ONE ADMISSIONS OFFICER HAS TO SAY ABOUT RECRUITED ATHLETES

"There are definitely different expectations for recruited athletes. They don't necessarily have to be in the most demanding courses available. If you do B work and one of our coaches wants you, you'll probably do fine in admissions."

—*Barbara-Jan Wilson, Dean of Admissions and Financial Aid, Wesleyan University*

8

ACQUIRING STRONG
ACADEMIC CREDENTIALS

– KEY POINTS –

Both components of your academic credentials are critically important at
the top colleges:
—*Your high school record*
—*Your standardized test scores*

■

It is essential to understand that a good high school record consists of more
than good grades

—*The strongest candidates are those who take the most challenging courses, especially in
the "solid" subjects*

—*Advanced Placement (AP) offerings and International Baccalaureate (IB) curriculums
represent ideal selections*

—*Failure to take the most rigorous courses places candidates at a
substantial disadvantage*

■

Schools tend to look at academic performance first and test results second

—*This does not mean, however, that the most competitive schools are willing to sacrifice
much in the way of test results to get strong academic performers: they can get both.*

275

INTRODUCTION

Your academic profile consists of two parts: your high school record and your performance on standardized tests. These data together function like a key that can open the gateway of possibility for admission to a top college—but if the key does not fit, the door will most likely remain closed to you. There is no way of getting around the fact that for almost all candidates, intellectual ability is the most important criterion upon which you will be evaluated for college admission.

You should realize by now, of course, that the top colleges are looking for students who bring a lot more than just brains to their campuses. But academic potential, except in special admissions cases such as recruited athletes, is still the number one concern of admissions officers at the top schools. The way to prove one's future academic potential is, quite obviously, to provide evidence of superb past academic performance. Admissions committees generally examine the hard facts first, and anyone who passes muster on his or her academic credentials is then passed through the entryway in order to be investigated at closer range as a potential student. If you do not satisfy basic academic expectations, then (in most cases) you will not be considered for admission based on your other characteristics and strengths.

WHICH IS MORE IMPORTANT, THE HIGH SCHOOL RECORD OR STANDARDIZED TEST SCORES?

The top colleges generally consider both academic indicators—the high school record and standardized test scores—important. Furthermore, the most competitive schools have so many fantastic applicants that they do not need to make compromises by accepting students who have excelled in one or the other, but not both. Still, the top colleges differ slightly in their messages, contained within their procedural methods, about which is *more* crucial, a great high school record or great test scores. The basic story from all of the most competitive schools is that you cannot completely override poor SAT I or II scores with a great high school record, just as you cannot completely compensate for a poor high school record with good scores. Both count for something and, depending upon which schools you apply to, they vary in their value.

Most schools prefer to see great high school grades rather than great standardized test scores. Strong test scores and a poor high school record suggest that, though a student might be intellectually gifted, she is lazy and lacks determination to succeed—no college is looking for candidates with these qualities.

On the other hand, poor test scores and a strong high school record suggest that a student can succeed when he works really hard and that he is indeed willing to work really hard. He might not be an intellectual powerhouse, but he has proven that he can do well by applying himself. Colleges generally reason that students who are lazy in high school will continue to be so in college and that hardworking high schoolers will continue to work as diligently in college. Therefore, in many cases they prefer good high school performers over good test takers.

At the same time, there are limits to the extent that colleges will overlook test scores. For one thing, SAT I scores are considered evidence of an applicant's intellectual firepower, and no school wants students who will have to struggle to do the more demanding work a rigorous college requires. For another, a college knows that the public perception of its caliber and quality rests on several important factors in its profile, one of which is the SAT I scores achieved by its incoming freshmen. Along with a low admission rate and a high yield on accepted applicants, colleges want to show that their students have the best SAT I scores because this helps them to gain a more favorable impression in the public eye. For both these reasons, high SAT I scores are inevitably important to the colleges.

Because of the importance of high SAT I scores, many schools use academic ranking methods that systematically take test scores into account. Applicants with better test scores thus receive a better academic rating or ranking than those with worse scores, all other things being equal. So even if the admissions officers at these schools "like" what they see in your file despite less-than-optimal scores, and believe you to be a candidate worth accepting, your academic ranking (based on your test scores) might prevent you from winning out over another candidate with better scores.

Stanford, for example, assigns to every applicant an academic rating ranging from one to six (with one being the best rating) that is initially based almost purely on SAT I scores and then adjusted slightly according to high school performance. Applicants who score 750 and above on each portion of the SAT are "Academic Ones" (called "Ac Ones" in Stanford admissions lingo); those who score between 700 and 750 are "Academic Twos"; and so on. Anyone who scores below 550 is an "Academic Six," the lowest rating possible.

After initial numbers are assigned, the rating can then be adjusted if the high school performance is better or worse than the initial ranking indicates. For example, if a student who scored very high on his SAT Is, thus being assigned an initial Ac One rating, were not in the very top of his class at school, then his rating would be knocked down a notch and he would become an Academic Two. The academic ratings at Stanford, like at other schools, are not hard-and-fast rules but merely signals that make the admissions committee's job easier. Like other schools, Stanford uses its ratings only as general guidelines. There are no stringent rules regarding what ratings warrant an acceptance and what ratings warrant a denial. There are Academic Ones who are not admitted, just as there are occasionally Academic Sixes who are admitted.

Dartmouth and the University of Pennsylvania rely mostly on the Academic Index (AI) to determine the academic ranking of their applicants. The Academic Index is a formula that was developed by the Ivy League schools to ensure that all recruited athletes meet certain minimum academic expectations in order to be admitted to their institutions. It combines the average of an applicant's SAT I scores, the average of the applicant's SAT II scores, and the Converted Rank Score (CRS), which is an indicator derived through one's rank in class (RIC) and grades, to come up with a number between 1 and 240, with 240 being the best figure attainable. Although the AI was intended to be used for evaluating athletes only, it has become the tool by which some (not all) of the Ivies base their academic rankings of all applicants. Dartmouth and the University of Pennsylvania base their one through nine (with nine being the best ranking) academic rankings of applicants on the 1 through 240 figure calculated through the AI.

MIT computes an algorithm that it calls the Numeric Index to assign academic ratings to its applicants. The formula takes into account rank in class, high school grades, SAT I scores, and SAT II scores. Based on the algorithm, all applicants are assigned a one to five rating, with five being the best.

Other schools, in contrast, assign academic rankings that do not rely on inflexible calculations using test scores or grades. Amherst, for example, assigns an academic rating to each candidate but does so completely subjectively. The academic rating at Amherst is done on a scale of one to seven, with one being the best rating. It is not at all "calculated" in the strict sense of the word. It is arrived at through a file reader's own discretion after looking at all the academic criteria when it is presented together. Harvard and Wesleyan similarly assign academic ratings that are not based on hard calculated facts but on readers' impressions, gathered after reading over an entire folder. Both pieces of the puzzle—grades and standardized test scores—matter to these schools, but a student can probably get by more easily with lower standardized test scores at colleges that assign academic ratings subjectively rather than objectively.

At Brown, the most important academic criterion is a student's performance in high school, including the nature and caliber of classes taken, not test scores. After looking at a student's high school record, the admissions officers at Brown look for fit with the school's educational philosophy, which holds students largely responsible for their own development because of the lack of core requirements. The last factor that comes into play when evaluating a candidate's academic appropriateness for the school is standardized test scores. Brown does not compute an Academic Index or any other evaluation figure that relies upon standardized test scores for anyone other than recruited athletes.

THE HIGH SCHOOL RECORD

A student's high school record provides information about his or her intellectual ability and willingness to work hard. But having a strong high school record is not as easy as simply having a high GPA—even the minimally talented could manage a high GPA taking the easiest courses available at a noncompetitive high school. Colleges look closely at the rigor of the school you attend, the classes you have taken over the past four years, including the number of honors or accelerated courses you have opted to take, and where you stand in relation to your classmates. Some schools, as indicated previously, indeed use formulas that plug a candidate's GPA and test scores into an equation in order to compare him or her academically against other applicants. But schools will alter the GPA portion of your equation if they have reason to believe that the number assigned to you by your school is not a true representation of your performance. Furthermore, even the schools that utilize some sort of academic formula look beyond it to peer into the details of your record before allowing themselves to be duped by the formula's numbers.

THE HIGH SCHOOL PROFILE

All candidates are evaluated alongside a high school profile, which gives college admissions officers important information about the school you attend. The profile gives detailed information about your high school's curriculum, lists all classes available to students, explains how the grading and grade point average system work, and sometimes provides average or median grades for each class. The profile also tells admissions officers what percentage of the previous year's graduating class went on to attend a four-year college and what colleges recent graduates attend, to provide a picture of the context in which you were taught.

The bad news is that the high school profile makes it difficult for you to fool admissions committees into thinking that you are a better student than you really are. You cannot, for example, trick the admissions committee into thinking that you are brilliant and ambitious (because of your straight-A record) if you have taken only the easiest classes available at your school. The high school profile also, however, provides a fair playing field for those operating in strenuous high school environments or challenging themselves with the toughest options.

Admissions officers will know from your high school profile whether or not you have taken the most challenging courses available to you. If you are a very good student who has opted to take no honors classes despite their existence at your school, then a college will assume you are lazy and not intellectually motivated. A college will also know not to penalize you for the lack of advanced or AP courses on your transcript if your high school does not offer any. A high school profile lets admissions officers know whether or not the high school calculates weighted or nonweighted GPAs. If your high school "weights" more advanced classes by increasing their grade assignment before calculating a GPA, then a college knows that your numbers account for the fact that you have taken difficult classes. On the contrary, if your high school explains that it does not weight classes when calculating GPAs, a college might decide to boost your GPA when it sees that your courseload has included some really tough classes that have likely handicapped your GPA.

The rigor of your high school and the context in which you were educated can tell an admissions officer a lot about you. Admissions officials recognize that a mediocre student at a very tough high school will probably be more academically prepared than a top student at a very easy high school. Likewise, however, they recognize that if you have performed extremely well and pushed yourself at a high school where only 10% of the graduating class goes on to college, you must be particularly determined and goal-oriented, possessing real strength of character. They recognize that it is far easier for a student from an affluent suburb, where life is fairly easy and everyone is *expected* to go to college, to keep her head in the books than it is for an inner-city student who has had to overcome the norms of her neighborhood's teenagers—criminal behavior, dropping out of school, teenage pregnancy—in order to stay focused on academics.

Because admissions officers are looking for students from a variety of backgrounds, it is not imperative that you attend the best public or private high school available in order to be admitted to a top college. Admissions committees recognize that money and location often prohibit students from attending strong college preparatory schools. The colleges generally want to see that you have taken advantage of those opportunities given to you, but will not penalize you for not having had the same experiences that others with better opportunities have had.

IS YOUR HIGH SCHOOL'S PROFILE HELPING OR HURTING YOU?

Most students never see their high schools' official profiles, nor do many even know such a thing exists. The profile is a document full of public information and should be available to you upon request. Ask to see it! This piece of evidence will accompany your applications to colleges and you certainly have a right to know what your high school communicates about itself.

If you do not attend a high school that is known as a solid public or private college preparatory school, you have even more reason to take a look at the profile that is sent to colleges. Although there are not likely to be any explicit errors on a high school profile, there are liable to be omissions of information that could greatly help your case—especially if you attend a high school that is not particularly strong in preparing to send its students to top colleges.

For example, if you have taken classes called "Track 2" at your high school, yet your high school profile does not explain that "Track 2" is accelerated while "Track 1" courses are standard options (colleges are likely to assume the opposite is true), your high school profile might be hurting you! Or perhaps you took a science class during your sophomore year called "Marine Biology" as an alternative to regular "Biology." Colleges will assume that this is the easier "fluff" biology course in your school, taken by those who fear the rigors of regular lab sciences. If "Marine Biology" is actually considered an advanced class with one of the toughest teachers in the school—a lab science just as rigorous as regular biology and not its simplistic cousin—then colleges need to know this. If this information is not communicated on your high school profile, then you need to do something about it.

Review the two examples of thorough, well-crafted high school profiles starting on page 282. If you recognize that your school's profile does not measure up because it is misleading (in ways that might hurt you) or lacks important information, you have two options:

1. You can schedule a meeting with your school's college advisor or guidance counselor and bring your concerns to his or her attention. Ask if the situation can be remedied by including the information that will help you on the high school profile. If the general school profile cannot be changed (because of necessary approvals from the school board or for another reason), ask if the guidance counselor will at least augment the high school profile that will be sent to your target colleges. Ask that the new profile be sent to you so that you can confirm the changes made.

2. Option one is usually the best one because, coming from the high school itself as part of its academic profile, information seems more objective and will be taken at face value. But if your high school does not comply with your wishes, you can always take the matter into your own hands. Write a note to colleges, citing the information you wish to convey as simply and concisely as possible. The nature of your note is important—you do not want the college to think that you are a desperate "grade-grubber." Make your point in one or two sentences and do not blame or criticize your high school for its omissions or errors.

NOBLE AND GREENOUGH SCHOOL

10 Campus Drive
Dedham, Massachusetts 02026-4198
781-326-3700
C.E.E.B. Code: 220-680
FAX: 781-320-1329
Web Page: http://www.nobles.edu

Richard H. Baker
Headmaster
Michael K. Denning
Co-Director of College Counseling
Michael_Denning@nobles.edu
Michael A. Johnson
Co-Director of College Counseling
Mike_Johnson@nobles.edu

1999–2000 Profile

DESCRIPTION: Founded by George Washington Copp Noble in 1866, Noble and Greenough School is a co-educational, non-sectarian day and boarding school for students in grade seven (Class VI) through twelve (Class I). Co-educational since 1974, Nobles has grown to a current enrollment of 521 students—including 266 girls and 255 boys, 32 of whom are five day boarders.

DIPLOMA REQUIREMENTS: The standard and expected academic load of every Nobles student is the equivalent of five credits in each semester. Three is a petition process by which students may be granted permission to take a sixth full credit course. Please refer to our Curriculum Guide for comprehensive course descriptions.

DEPARTMENT	MINIMUM REQUIREMENTS FOR GRADUATION	HONORS AND ADVANCED PLACEMENT
English	Eight semesters	Elective Program No designated AP or Honors sections
Mathematics	Six semesters (through Class II)	Honors Algebra, Geometry, PreCalculus; AP Calculus (AB, BC)
Foreign Languages	Completion of level III: French, Spanish, Latin or Japanese	French III, IV Honors; Spanish III, IV Honors; AP French, AP Spanish, AP Latin (Vergil, Lyric)
Science	Four semesters: Biology and either Chemistry or Physics	No designated Honors Sections: Biology, Quantitative Chemistry and Quantitative Physics require permission of the department, a strong background in mathematics and the ability to formulate problems in mathematical terms. AP Biology, AP Physics, AP Chemistry
History and Social Science	Four semesters: (two in U.S. History and two in History of the Human Community)	No Honors Sections: AP U.S. History, AP European History, AP Economics
Computer Studies	Through Computer Proficiency IV	AP Computer Science
Visual and Performing Arts	One semester each in Visual Arts and Performing Arts	AP Drawing
Community Service	Eighty hours	

Figure 8-1. School Profile.

GRADING SYSTEM:
Noble and Greenough has a semester system. Grades are given on a scale of 0–11, in January and June.

11 = A	Highest Distinction (Honors)	5 = C	Satisfactory
10 = A–	Highest Distinction (Honors)	4 = C–	Less than Satisfactory
9 = B+	High Distinction (Honors)	3 = D+	Poor
8 = B	Distinction (Honors)	2 = D	Poor
7 = B–	Commendation	1 = D–	Poor
6 = C+	Satisfactory	0 = E	Failing

RANKING SYSTEM: Nobles uses o form of Class Rank and no differential weighting of courses.

CLASS OF 2000 ENROLLMENT: 102

Distribution for Class of 2000 of six semester unweighted cumulative GPA's on 0–11 scale as of June, 1999.

10.5–11.0:	2%
10.0–10.49:	5%
9.5–9.99:	8%
9.0–9.49:	14%
8.5–8.99:	21%
8.0–8.49:	15%
7.5–7.99:	12%
7.0–7.49:	17%
6.5–6.99:	5%
6.0–6.49:	2%
5.0–5.99:	1%

AP TEST PERFORMANCE, CLASS OF 2000

Seventy-one members of the Class of 2000 (70% of the class) took 129 AP tests during their junior year. Approximately 80% of AP's taken in the junior year are in U.S. History, English Literature, and foreign languages.

- 88% of the scores were 3 or higher
- 61% of the scores were 4 or higher
- 23% of the scores were 5.

During the senior year, Class of 2000 students will take AP courses and exams in the following subjects: AB and BC Calculus, Chemistry, Physics, Biology, Computer Science, Microeconomics, Macroeconomics, Statistics, European History, Art History, Government and Politics.

STANDARDIZED TESTING SUMMARY, CLASS OF 2000

SAT I Performance Summary of Class of 2000 through June, 1999

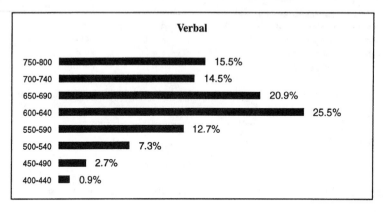

Verbal

750-800	15.5%
700-740	14.5%
650-690	20.9%
600-640	25.5%
550-590	12.7%
500-540	7.3%
450-490	2.7%
400-440	0.9%

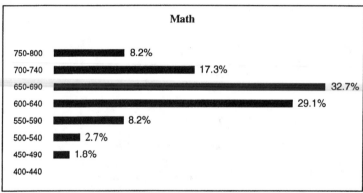

Math

750-800	8.2%
700-740	17.3%
650-690	32.7%
600-640	29.1%
550-590	8.2%
500-540	2.7%
450-490	1.8%
400-440	

SAT II Performance Summary of Class of 2000 through June 1999

SAT II Test	# of Students	Average Score
Physics	19	694
Writing	88	692
Math Level IIC	65	655
French (reading)	12	652
Literature	11	618
Biology	48	613
Chemistry	39	611
Spanish (reading)	12	595
American History	49	590
Math Level IC	35	582

MATRICULATION LIST, CLASS OF 1999

Boston College	4	Amherst	2
Colby	4	Boston U.	2
Georgetown	4	Connecticut C.	2
Harvard	4	Emory	2
Middlebury	4	NYU	2
Trinity	4	U. Pennsylvania	2
Tufts	4	Princeton	2
Bowdoin	3	Stanford	2
Brown	3	Syracuse	2
Dartmouth	3	Wesleyan	2
Skidmore	3	Williams	2
U. Wisconsin	3		

One student matriculated at each of the following institutions: Bard, Barnard, Brandeis, Carnegie Mellon, U. Chicago, Columbia, Cornell, Drew, Eastman School of Music, Harvey Mudd, Holy Cross, Johns Hopkins, Lehigh, Miami U., Notre Dame, Oberlin, Reed, Rensselaer, U. Richmond, Roger Williams, Smith, U. Texas, Union, Vanderbilt, U. Virginia, U. Washington, Wellesley.

MATRICULATION LIST, 1994–1999

The following institutions have enrolled 3 or more Noble and Greenough graduates:

Harvard	29	Wesleyan	10	Vanderbilt	6
Brown	28	Colgate	9	U. Vermont	6
Trinity	28	Duke	9	Barnard	5
U. Pennsylvania	21	Emory	9	Bates	5
Georgetown	20	Johns Hopkins	9	Boston U.	5
Bowdoin	18	NYU	9	Union	5
Dartmouth	17	Princeton	9	U. Virginia	5
Colby	15	Amherst	8	Colorado C.	4
Middlebury	14	Cornell	8	Kenyon	4
Connecticut C.	13	Wellesley	8	Swarthmore	4
Boston College	12	Northwestern	7	Tulane	4
Tufts	12	Yale	7	Haverford	3
Williams	12	Columbia	6	Vassar	3
Skidmore	11	Holy Cross	6	Villanova	3
Stanford	10	Syracuse	6		
U. Wisconsin	10	U. Michigan	6		

1998–1999 Profile
Thomas Jefferson High School for Science and Technology

Geoffrey Jones, Principal
Shirley Bloomquist, Director of Student Services

Mission

Working with the belief that science and technology constitute a process that blends human functions and needs with knowledge, tool use, and skills, our school has a fourfold mission:

◆ offering programs that provide enthusiasm, exploration, and academic excellence in an evolving economic and scientific/technological community.

◆ serving as a laboratory school examining and developing new methods and materials in curriculum innovation and reform.

◆ fostering a broad exchange of ideas and programming through outreach in teacher training, enrichment for students K-12, and networking.

◆ serving as a model for private sector and public education partnerships.

Curriculum

All courses are taught at the gifted/talented or honors level.
The rigorous college preparatory curriculum provides students with the opportunity to achieve in all disciplines, with an emphasis on the sciences and the technology of applied sciences. All students are enrolled in an eight-period program designed to satisfy the 26* credits required for graduation.

English	4
Mathematics (including Calculus)	5
Science (Biology, Chemistry, Physics, and Geoscience)	4
Social Studies	3**
Foreign Language (in the same language)	
Health and Physical Education	2
Science Technology Research	2
Computer Science	1
Fine Arts or Humanities	1
Additional Mathematics, Science, Technology, or Computer Science	1

*27 credits for the Class of 2002 and beyond
**4 credits for the Class of 2002 and beyond

Technology Laboratories

The learning environment is enhanced with specialized technology laboratories equipped by business and industry to support programs in the sciences. These laboratories are:

Astronomy
Chemical Analysis
Computer Assisted Design
Computer Systems
Energy Systems
Geoscience
Industrial Automation and Robotics
Life Sciences and Biotechnology
Microelectronics
Oceanography
Optics and Modern Physics
Prototyping and Engineering Materials
Video Technology and Communications

Mentorship Program

Students in the mentorship program complete graduate-level research projects in scientific and engineering labs throughout the Washington, D.C. metropolitan area. They are supervised by mentors who are recognized scientists and engineers. Many students have published in national scientific and engineering journals. More than one hundred organizations have participate din this program including National Institutes of Health, Georgetown University Hospital, Naval Research Laboratory, Smithsonian Institution, U.S. Geological Survey, The MITRE Corporation, TRW, and Wang Federal, Inc.

Advanced Placement

Advanced Placement courses offered.

English Literature	Physics
English Composition	Biology
United States History	Chemistry
United States Government	Psychology
European History	French
Computer Science	German
Calculus AB	Spanish
Calculus BC	Latin
Statistics	

Post-Advanced Placement courses offered:
Artificial Intelligence
Multivariable Calculus
Linear Algebra
Computer Architecture
Differential Equations
Organic Chemistry
Complex Variables/Differential Equations
These courses receive an additional .25 (semester) or .5 (full year) quality point in the grade point average.

Student Selection

Students are selected to attend TJHSST in a competitive process that evaluates admission test scores, academic achievement, personal essays, teacher recommendations, and self-reported interests and activities. Applications are reviewed by independent selection committees composed of counselors, teachers and school administrators. For the 1998–99 school year, 18 percent of the applicants to TJHSST were accepted.

Figure 8-2. School Profile.

Achievement

Of the 393 students in the class of 1999, 141 are **National Merit Semifinalists,** 9 are National Achievement Semifinalists and 8 are Hispanic Scholars.

1997–98 SAT Scores

	Verbal *mean*	Mathematics *mean*
TJHSST	712	731
NATION	505	512
VIRGINIA	507	499

AP Grades

Of the 858 students who sat for **2,023 Advanced Placement examinations,** 96 percent earned scores of three or higher.

Test	% of 3(+) Scores
Biology	100
Chemistry	98
Computer Science AB	91
Economics: Micro	85
Economics: Macro	100
English Lang. and Composition	99
English Lit. and Composition	100
European History	100
French Language	98
French Literature	100
German Language	67
Gov. and Politics: United States	97
Gov. and Politics: Comparative	93
Latin: Vergil	71
Latin Literature	100
Mathematics: Calculus AB	97
Mathematics: Calculus BC	99
Music Theory	50
Physics B	75
Physics C: Mechanics	100
Physics C: Elec. and Mag.	86
Psychology	100
Spanish Language	98
Spanish Literature	100
Statistics	100
United States History	96

Class Rank

Because TJHSST students are selected in a competitive admissions process that evaluates aptitude, achievement, and interest in the study of mathematics, science and technology, all academic programs are designed and taught at the accelerated or enriched levels. Thus, specific courses are not labeled honors, accelerated, or enriched, nor is class rank computed. The class of 1999 GPAs range from a high of 4.136 to a low of 2.217.

Scholarships

The class of 1998 earned a total of $8,768,780 in scholarship awards separate from any financial aid based on need.

	Offered	Accepted
Military	$1,715,925	686,325
College sponsored	5,435,228	908,950
Privately sponsored	1,617,627	1,946,612
Total:	$8,768,780	$3,541,887

Senior Counselors

Mr. Newberry 703-750-8344
Ms. Simmerman 703-750-8349

Dr. Williams 703-750-8348
Ms. Johnson 703-750-8345
Mr. Peck 703-750-8346
Mrs. Taylor 703-750-8343
Mrs. Doff 703-750-8347

Class of 1998 College Acceptance Data

(Schools are listed if five or more students applied)

	Percent of TJHSST applicants accepted
Amherst College	44
Boston University	92
Brigham Young University	100
Brown University	15
Cal Tech	33
Carnegie Mellon University	91
Case Western Reserve	75
College of William & Mary	72
Columbia University	43
Cornell University	51
Dartmouth University	38
Duke University	53
Emory University	71
Florida A&M University	100
George Mason University	87
George Washington University	92
Georgetown University	39
Georgia Tech	82
Harvard-Radcliffe Colleges	18
Harvey Mudd College	88
James Madison University	73
Johns Hopkins University	55
Mary Washington College	80
Massachusetts Inst. of Technology	41
New York University	84
Northwester University	69
Oberlin College	100
Penn State	100
Princeton University	28
Radford University	33
Rice University	60
Spelman College	80
Stanford University	27
Swarthmore College	38
Syracuse University	100
Tufts University	63
United States Air Force Academy	100
University of California - Berkeley	80
University of California - Los Angeles	100
University of Chicago	71
University of Delaware	100
University of Illinois-Urbana	86
University of Maryland-College Park	100
University of Miami	100
University of Michigan	81
University of North Carolina - Chapel Hill	25
University of Notre Dame	71
University of Pennsylvania	60
University of Pittsburgh	100
University of Rochester	100
University of Southern California	83
University of Virginia	82
Vassar College	40
Virginia Commonwealth University	100
Virginia Tech	91
Wake Forest University	86
Washington University	76
Williams College	75

Fairfax County public schools are accredited by the State Board of Education and the Southern Association of Colleges and Schools

FOLLOWING A SOLID CURRICULUM

It is absolutely imperative that you take the strongest curriculum possible at your high school in order to gain admission to one of the top colleges. College admissions officers know that although you may not be able to control your ability to attend the best schools available, you at least have access to all the courses offered at your high school. The top colleges maintain standards that are far higher than most high schools' graduation requirements. You cannot expect to take what is minimally necessary for graduation at your high school and still get into a stellar college.

A strong high school record shows four years each of five or more "solid" courses. Academic solids are classes that prepare you for college in the following subjects:

- English
- Math
- Hard sciences
- Foreign languages
- Social sciences

Most high schools follow a particular pattern with regard to solid studies. At most schools, for example, the math sequence is as follows: Freshmen take algebra I, sophomores take geometry, juniors take algebra II, and seniors take calculus. Most high school science curriculums similarly require freshmen to take a lab or physical science, sophomores to take biology, juniors chemistry, and seniors physics.

It does not matter that you follow a particular order with regard to your solid courses, but you do need to be sure that you are fulfilling most colleges' standard prerequisites for admission. The top colleges vary slightly in their particular requirements regarding solid high school transcripts. Williams, for example, recommends that its applicants take "English and mathematics in four-year sequences; one foreign language for three or, preferably, four years; and three years each in social studies and laboratory science." MIT's recommendations are slightly different: "Recommended preparation: four years of English, two or more years of history/social studies, mathematics through calculus, biology, chemistry, and physics, and a foreign language." Because of MIT's particular emphasis, the requirements regarding social studies and foreign languages are less stringent, but the admissions committee states particular preferences in regard to math and science preparation.

You will likely apply to a variety of colleges. Therefore, you should not decide as a sophomore to stop taking Spanish just because the college you think you most want to attend does not require more than one year of foreign language preparation. It is best if you follow the standard menu of four years of five solids through senior year, since you will likely be applying to colleges with different prerequisites.

BEYOND THE SOLIDS

Semisolids are courses that are related to the solid curriculum but are not necessary as preparation for college-level work or are supplemental to the regular high school curriculum. Courses in psychology, ethics, journalism, or art history are considered semisolids. An earth science or astronomy course, rather than regular senior year physics, would also be considered semisolid work.

On top of the solids and semisolids are electives such as art, music, dance, woodshop, home economics, and computer science (this is sometimes considered a semisolid rather than an elective). Colleges generally do not request that their applicants take electives, nor do they ask for specific electives, but they play an important role on your transcript by showing that you have outside interests. Electives and semisolids can help you to develop special talents or extracurricular passions, so you should not decide to let them go in lieu of concentrating on your grades in solid courses.

WHICH YEARS OF HIGH SCHOOL ARE MOST IMPORTANT?

All colleges look at the junior and senior years more closely than the first two years of high school. Generally speaking, colleges will overlook mistakes made during the freshman year of high school as well as pay attention to overall growth and development rather than viewing each year individually. For most colleges, it is the overall trend and growth over four years that is most important, with most of the emphasis placed on the junior and senior years.

Admissions officers disagree a bit on which year—junior or senior—is really the most crucial. Some colleges, like Williams, weight the junior and senior years heavily and lean especially toward performance during the senior year. Amherst looks particularly closely at senior year performance because the admissions officers believe that it is the best predictor of the kind of work a student will do at college. Other schools, however, contend that the junior year is generally most important in terms of your academic performance. Wesleyan places the most focus on the spring semester of junior year when evaluating candidates' academic performance.

WHAT ADMISSIONS OFFICERS SAY ABOUT THE ACADEMIC PROFILE

"Everything is a trade-off. If a student is academically weaker than the majority of those we admit, he'll have to compensate for it in another area."

—Christoph Guttentag, Director of Undergraduate Admissions, Duke University

"Success in the classroom and the rigor of the courses a student takes is still the foundation upon which our decision rests. The academics are the most important part of the overall picture."

—Richard Shaw, Dean of Undergraduate Admissions and Financial Aid, Yale University

"Our choices are made very much on the basis of academic potential—but other factors come into play as well."

—Karl Furstenberg, Dean of Admissions and Financial Aid, Dartmouth College

"When I counsel students I tell them that if there are hiccups in the record— whether it be a bad semester or year, or something else—to address it somewhere in the written application. A student should speak to any obvious weakness or aberration in the record so that we know what went on."

—Nancy Hargrave Meislahn, Director of Undergraduate Admissions, Cornell University

WHICH YEARS OF HIGH SCHOOL ARE MOST IMPORTANT?

"We weight very heavily the junior and senior years, and lean especially toward what is going on senior year. There was a kid this year we really wanted because of his status as a recruited athlete—but he's getting a D during his senior fall— we will not take him with that D!"

—Philip Smith, Dean of Admissions, Williams College

"We look at all four years but nearly discount a student's performance freshman year. It's really the overall trend and growth over four years that is most important."

—Marilee Jones, Dean of Admissions, Massachusetts Institute of Technology

"We really don't pay that much attention to what went on during the freshman year."

—Barbara-Jan Wilson, Dean of Admissions and Financial Aid, Wesleyan University

"We weight the junior and senior years very heavily."

—Eric Kaplan, Director of Admissions, University of Pennsylvania

"Senior fall is the best predictor of the kind of work a student will do here at Amherst if accepted. We look at it very closely—it is absolutely critical that a student do well senior fall."

—Katie Fretwell, Director of Admissions, Amherst College

"Spring semester junior year is the most important semester in terms of applying to Wesleyan."

—Barbara-Jan Wilson, Dean of Admissions and Financial Aid, Wesleyan University

"We definitely weight the junior and senior years more heavily—but that doesn't mean you can have totally rocky freshman and sophomore years and still be admitted."

—Janet Lavin Rapelye, Dean of Admissions, Wellesley College

How Important Is a Challenging Curriculum?

"When we look at the high school record along with the profile, we are disappointed if we see a student is not really challenging him or herself."

—John Blackburn, Dean of Admissions, University of Virginia

"The high school curriculum is probably the least understood part of the application process by college candidates. Kids don't understand that a good GPA isn't all there is."

—Dan Walls, Dean of Admissions, Emory University

"One thing I see applicants doing wrong all the time is not continuing with a demanding curriculum during their senior years—blowing off math or science or foreign languages. We see a lot of senior programs that are fluffy. The strength of the program all the way through senior year is critical."

—David Borus, Dean of Admissions and Financial Aid, Vassar College

PURSUING THE MOST CHALLENGING OPTIONS AVAILABLE

On top of maintaining a high school transcript that is full of solid courses (as well as the right balance of semisolids or electives), you must also show colleges that you have pursued the most rigorous options available to you. The most competitive schools expect that you will choose challenging options over standard classes in all or most cases in which you have a choice. This means taking any courses that are labeled "honors," "accelerated," "advanced," or "Track 1" ("Track 2" if your school assigns the higher number to the more rigorous track) courses, as well as Advanced Placement (AP) courses. Following an International Baccalaureate (IB) curriculum is another way of pursuing the most challenging option, if it is available in your community.

Advanced Placement (AP) Courses

AP courses are those sponsored by the College Entrance Examination Board (CEEB), allowing advanced high schoolers to take college-level classes. Students can take just one AP course if they so desire, or they can take a plate full of AP courses. Students are encouraged to take the AP exam in their subject after completing a course in order to provide evidence of accomplishment and learning. AP exams are offered every May in a range of subjects and are graded on a scale of 1 to 5, with a 5 being the best score. Most of the top colleges regard only 4 and 5 AP scores as significant indicators of advanced learning. Many colleges give college credit for classes in which AP exams have been taken (with scores of 4 or 5). Such credit can allow a student to place out of requirements, thereby having more time to pursue other academic interests, or sometimes even graduate from college a semester or two early.

INTERNATIONAL BACCALAUREATE (IB) OFFERINGS

Though not very common a few years back, International Baccalaureate (IB) programs are becoming more prevalent in American high schools. The IB curriculum was originally created to prepare American students for study at universities across the globe and was thus offered mostly overseas, at American high schools and other schools, for the children of diplomats and other expatriates.

The IB is a rigorous two-year curriculum designed to meet the requirements of higher institutions of education throughout the world. Unlike AP courses, which can be taken individually, the IB is a single set curriculum covering a range of subjects. Students who opt for it follow the entire program, not just a course here and there, taking distribution requirements in each of six general subject areas: Language A1 (courses in the student's first language); Language A2 (a second modern language); Individuals and Societies (includes history, geography, philosophy, etc.); Experimental Sciences; Mathematics; and Arts and Electives. In addition, a student must fulfill two special IB requirements: Theory of Knowledge (TOK), an interdisciplinary course that teaches critical reflection, and Creativity, Action, Service (CAS), which requires immersion in extracurricular events. All students must also undertake original research to write an extended essay in order to graduate from the IB program.

Students who have taken the IB curriculum take six (sometimes seven) IB exams, three of which are preliminary tests, called standard level (SL), and three or four of which are higher level (HL) exams. The exams are graded on a scale of 1 to 7, with 7 being the highest score. The six scores are then added together, with three extra points available for completion of TOK, CAS, and the essay, for a total of 45 possible diploma points. Individual subject scores of 6 and 7 are generally considered worthy of recognition by the top college admissions offices. Again, some colleges recognize IB exam achievement with college credit.

AP and IB curriculums and test results provide evidence that a student is serious and willing to challenge himself or herself, as well as capable of handling college-level work. Furthermore, the higher the student's scores on AP and IB exams, the more inclined an admissions officer will be to dismiss lower scores elsewhere. These tests are generally considered truer measures than SAT scores of a student's intelligence, knowledge, and ability to perform critical thinking and reasoning skills.

FOR MORE INFORMATION ON THE AP CURRICULUM AND EXAMS

The Advanced Placement program is administered by the College Board. The Board oversees the curriculum and teaching of AP-designated college-level courses in a variety of subjects in high schools around the country, as well as the administration of AP exams in the subjects. For more information, see your high school guidance counselor or contact:

The Advanced Placement Program
The College Board
45 Columbus Avenue
New York, NY 10023
(212)713-8066
www.collegeboard.com

FOR MORE INFORMATION ON THE IB CURRICULUM

For more information about the International Baccalaureate, contact the International Baccalaureate Organization at its headquarters in Switzerland or the North American regional office:

Organisation du Baccalaureat International
Route des Morillons 15
1218 Grand-Saconnex
Geneva
Switzerland
Tel 41 22 791 77 40
Fax 41 22 791 02 77
IHBQ@ibo.org

International Baccalaureate North America
200 Madison Avenue
Suite 2301
New York, NY 10016
Tel (212)696-4464
Fax (212)889-9242
IBNA@ibo.org

ADMISSIONS OFFICERS TALK ABOUT AP
AND IB PROGRAMS AND TEST RESULTS

"The International Baccalaureate is the best preparation for entering a liberal arts college you can get. There is breadth *and* depth there, and it's a difficult program. If students do well in it, it's hard to imagine they would have trouble at a demanding college."

—*Nanci Tessier, Director of Admissions, Smith College*

"AP results are really a very minor element in our admissions process. Not every student has access to AP courses—we want to see that a student has taken the toughest courses, so we like to see APs and IB curriculums on a transcript. But not everyone has the opportunity to take these kinds of classes." ·

—*Karl Furstenberg, Dean of Admissions and Financial Aid, Dartmouth College*

"We absolutely look closely at AP and IB results. But we don't penalize students who don't present them because not everyone has access to AP or IB courses."

—*Katie Fretwell, Director of Admissions, Amherst College*

"We have found that SAT IIs, AP results, and IB results are the three main predictors of success on our campus."

—*Philip Smith, Dean of Admissions, Williams College*

IMPROVING YOUR HIGH SCHOOL RECORD AFTER THE FACT

If you have any truly egregious gaffes on your high school transcript, you might want to think about doing something to compensate for them before applying to college. Although your options will not remedy your high school GPA, your efforts and results can show admissions officers that you care about improving yourself and that you are more capable of doing good work than your high school record shows.

The way to partially overcome a particularly poor grade is to retake the class (or a very similar one) to improve your performance. Chances are that your high school will not allow you to retake a class (and that you will not have time to do so during regular high school hours because of other solid curriculum require-ments). What you must do instead is look into summer schools or night and weekend classes at community colleges.

To achieve the maximum benefit of retaking a class, you need to commit your-self to getting a good grade. You should not waste time that could be spent con-centrating on your current academic commitments with a duplicate class unless you know that you can do well. If you had extreme difficulty with chemistry, for example, and your poor performance did not result from personal problems or lack of effort, you might consider whether or not a retake is worth your time. You might decide that your performance in chemistry is simply a weakness you should contend with by performing especially well in English and the humanities—especially if strength in the sciences is not one of your marketing points anyway. Or, if you do decide to retake the class, you might want to consider hiring a tutor for extra attention and help so that your effort pays off in the end.

STANDARDIZED TEST SCORES

Standardized test scores make up the other half of the academic profile. Standardized test scores provide admissions officers with a standardized measure to use in assessing all candidates. Although the tests are imperfect, they help officers to compare students from different educational backgrounds and to assess those from backgrounds about which they know very little.

Over the past several years there has been much debate over the value of standardized test scores, whether or not some groups of students are discriminated against in standardized testing situations, and whether or not colleges should require test scores of their applicants. Even though there is always talk that the top colleges are on the verge of deciding not to require standardized test scores of their applicants, the SAT, SAT II, and ACT scores remain important pieces of the admissions puzzle at most schools. There are, however, some selective schools that do not require applicants to submit any standardized test scores; these include Bowdoin, Bates, and Hampshire Colleges.

Most colleges will tell you that standardized test scores are not quite as important as the high school record. This is indeed usually the case when officers are looking subjectively at a candidate's overall application. However, as mentioned in the beginning of this chapter, a college's reputation depends upon the strength of its profile, which includes the SAT I scores achieved by its incoming freshmen. Many admissions committees thus are compelled to take students who have earned the highest SAT I scores. It is for this reason that some schools' academic ranking formulas rely more on standardized test performance than they do on the high school record, as already discussed.

Today there are more testing options from which candidates can choose than there were years ago. The majority of the top colleges require applicants to submit either SAT I scores and three SAT II scores *or* ACT scores (in place of both SAT tests). Some schools' policies are slightly different. For example, Harvard requires the SAT I and three SAT IIs *or* the ACT and three SAT IIs. Stanford requires either the SAT I *or* the ACT and does not actually require SAT IIs, although it highly suggests that students submit them. (For further advice regarding your decision to take the SAT I or the ACT, see page 300.)

Although the SAT II tests do not provoke as much anxiety and discussion as does the SAT I, do not underestimate their importance in the admissions process. As mentioned earlier, the SAT II scores are often factored into colleges' academic rating formulas. Furthermore, many admissions officers consider them the foremost indicator of academic potential.

Be aware that some colleges require or prefer certain SAT IIs over others. Many of the top colleges ask for SAT IIs in math, writing, and one other subject. At MIT, one SAT II must be in math, one must be in science, and one must be in writing or a humanities field. Since each program has its own SAT II requirements, you should be sure to look into individual college and program requirements as early as possible so that you can be prepared to take all necessary SAT IIs at the proper time in your high school career.

THE SAT I (AND THE PSAT)

The SAT I (Scholastic Assessment Test I—Reasoning Test) is the most widely administered standardized college admissions test in the United States. The SAT I, until 1994 known simply as the SAT (Scholastic Aptitude Test), was created and developed by the College Board; the test is administered by the Board's affiliate company, Educational Testing Service (ETS), throughout the country on seven Saturdays, during the months of October, November, December, January, April, May, and June.

Besides modifying its name ("Aptitude" was changed to "Assessment" and the "I" was added), the SAT has undergone other changes in the past decade. The Verbal section now focuses more on reading interpretation than on vocabulary while the math section now features some non-multiple-choice questions, for which test takers must produce their own answers. The scores were "recentered" in 1995 so that average national scores on both the Verbal and Math sections would equal 500. (That means that a 650 in Verbal from before 1995 is not necessarily worse than the 700 you received this year; the scores are probably about equal.)

The exam consists of seven sections, each separately timed. There are three Verbal sections, three Math sections, and one "wild card" section, in either Math or Verbal, which is used later as a research tool by the College Board. (Test takers do not know which of the seven sections is the one that will not count toward their scores and therefore must put equal effort into all of them.) Verbal sections focus primarily on vocabulary and reading comprehension (sentence completions, analogies, performing critical reading on given passages) and are entirely multiple choice. Math sections focus on applied mathematics principles and problem solving rather than on technical computations; a calculator is allowed in the exam. Within every section, whether Verbal or Math, questions start out easier and become increasingly more difficult. The entire test takes about three hours.

Scores are totaled by calculating one point for all correct answers and then subtracting a fraction of a point for each incorrect answer. (One-fourth of a point is subtracted for questions that offer five choices; one-third of a point is subtracted for questions that offer four choices.) No points are gained or lost for unanswered questions, nor are any points gained or lost for giving incorrect answers on the student-produced responses in the Math section. Thus, students who can identify one or two answer choices as being incorrect are encouraged to make educated guesses; if a student has no basis upon which to eliminate any of the answers as incorrect, it is generally not advisable to guess randomly.

All Verbal and Math sections are combined to produce two raw scores (one Verbal, one Math). The raw scores are then changed into a "scaled" score (through a statistical process called "equating") on a scale of 200 to 800, with 800 being the best possible score. The two scores are then added together to produce an overall SAT I score (with 1600 and 400 being the best and worst possible scores, respectively).

Students receive their scores approximately three to four weeks after the test date. When a student takes any SAT I test, his or her scores automatically become part of the ETS record and cannot be eliminated. A student cannot actually submit to colleges only his best scores on the SAT I, because all scores tallied show up on the record. Colleges thus see every SAT result, although they "use" only the best scores in their final decision-making processes. Most schools, in fact, consider your highest Verbal and Math scores, even if they were not achieved on the same testing day. Recalling that colleges want to be able to report the highest possible SAT I scores for their incoming class, you can see why it is to their advantage to consider only your best Verbal and Math scores, regardless of whether they were achieved at the same time or not.

FOR MORE INFORMATION ON THE SAT I, SAT II, OR PSAT

To obtain further information on tests developed by the College Board and administered by Educational Testing Service (ETS), contact the following:

The SAT Program
P.O. Box 6212
Princeton, NJ 08541-6212
(609)771-7600

The PSAT Program
P.O. Box 6671
Princeton, NJ 08541-6671
(609)771-7300

ETS
Rosedale Road
Princeton, NJ 08541
(609)921-9000

The College Board
45 Columbus Avenue
New York, NY 10023-6992
(212)713-8000
www.collegeboard.com

The PSAT (Preliminary Scholastic Assessment Test) is merely a practice exam for the SAT. It mimics the format and scoring of the SAT I exactly, but scores do not count toward college admission. The PSAT is typically administered to sophomores and juniors so that they can prepare for the SAT I under realistic conditions and test-taking circumstances. It is given only once a year, in October. The PSAT-NMSQT exam is the same exam as the PSAT (although it is restricted to juniors only) but is also the National Merit Semifinalist Qualifying Test. Performance on this particular PSAT determines the National Merit Semifinalists from each state (the top one-half of the top 1% of performers in each state qualify as National Merit Semifinalists). National Merit Finalists are then selected from the Semifinalist pool based upon an application and a student's academic record. Although the National Merit Finalist designation makes a student eligible for various scholarships at many colleges, most of the top colleges do not honor National Merit finalists with financial rewards, basing their aid on need rather than merit.

FOR MORE INFORMATION ON THE NATIONAL MERIT SCHOLARSHIP PROGRAM

To obtain information on the National Merit Scholarship program, contact:

National Merit Scholarship Corporation
1560 Sherman Avenue Suite 200
Evanston, IL 60201-4897
(847)866-5100

THE ACT (AND PLAN)

The ACT (American College Testing) Assessment is administered by the American College Testing Program and is most popular in the Midwest, Southeast, and Southwest. The ACT consists of subject-based tests that measure a person's knowledge, understanding, and skills acquired throughout high school. There are four sections—English, Math, Reading, and Science Reasoning. Because the ACT is subject-based, just like the SAT II, in-school preparation is key for success. It is thus recommended that students not take the test until spring of the junior year and fall of the senior year.

Each section of the ACT is further broken down into subsections as follows:

English	Usage/Mechanics
	Rhetorical Skills
Mathematics	Pre-Algebra
	Elementary Algebra
	Intermediate Algebra and Coordinate Geometry
	Plane Geometry
	Trigonometry
Reading	Social Studies
	Natural Science
	Prose Fiction
	Humanities
Science Reasoning	Data Representation
	Research Summaries
	Conflicting Viewpoints

Questions in each section do not progress from easiest to most difficult as they do in the SAT I. The entire test itself takes about three hours (three hours and forty-five minutes with breaks).

Each section of the ACT is scored on a scale of 1 to 36, with 36 being the best score. The scores are then averaged to produce an overall score between 1 and 36. Only correct answers count toward the score, and students are not penalized at all for wrong answers. Thus, on the ACT, even random guessing is better than leaving answers blank.

The PLAN Assessment test is the preliminary test drive for the ACT, much like the PSAT that prepares students for the SAT I. It is identical to the ACT except that its scores do not count toward college admission.

FOR MORE INFORMATION ON THE ACT AND PLAN

To find out more about these tests, contact:

ACT Registration
P.O. Box 414
Iowa City, IA 52243-0414
(319)337-1270

HOW TO CONVERT AN ACT SCORE INTO ITS SAT EQUIVALENT

There is no official method for converting ACT scores into SAT equivalents. But if you are not used to thinking on a 1 to 36 scale and you want to get a rough feel for what your ACT score means, try this unofficial formula:

([ACT score] × 40) + 110 = Combined SAT I score

For example, if your ACT score is 30, you can figure that it is roughly equivalent to a 1310 combined Math and Verbal SAT I score.

SHOULD YOU TAKE THE SAT I, THE ACT, OR BOTH?

All students should start by taking the SAT I. If performance on the SAT I is very good, or at least likely to improve with review and practice, there is no reason to take the ACT as well. Almost all schools now accept either the SAT or the ACT, but most admissions officers subconsciously (or consciously) prefer the SAT. Admissions officers are more familiar with the SAT, it affects a college's public profile in a way that the ACT does not (ACT scores achieved by an incoming class are published but not regarded with great importance by the public), and the SAT is considered to be a more difficult test. The SAT I is meant to measure a student's innate ability to think critically, reason, analyze, and apply knowledge, whereas the ACT measures learned concepts, or how much information a student has stored after studying a subject in school. Many admissions offices formally or informally convert ACT scores to the SAT scale so that officers can better compare an ACT-submitting applicant to the rest of the applicant pool.

Take the ACT if you have done poorly on the SAT I. Many students perform better on the ACT than the SAT I because the ACT measures knowledge that you are likely to possess if you have been in math, science, and English classes throughout your high school career. Although it is true that colleges tend to prefer the SAT to the ACT, they prefer higher scores to lower scores even more so. If you score significantly better on the ACT (and this score is likely to improve with time because of accumulated knowledge), then you should submit only your ACT scores to colleges that accept them in lieu of SAT I scores.

THE SAT II

The SAT II (Scholastic Assessment Test—Subject Test) tests, once called "Achievement Tests," are developed by the College Board and administered by ETS. These one-hour exams measure academic achievement in a variety of subjects; in other words, they test a student's learned knowledge of a subject. SAT IIs are administered across the nation on six different Saturdays, in October, November, December, January, May, and June—the same days on which SAT Is are administered, minus the April SAT I testing date. The two tests—the SAT I and the SAT II— cannot be taken on the same day, but a student can take up to three SAT II subject tests on a single test day. Not all SAT II subject tests are necessarily given at all locations on all dates, so you should be careful when registering for the exam.

The SAT II subject test should be taken immediately after a student has finished a course in that subject. The Writing test is generally best mastered at the end of the junior year or beginning of the senior year, since high schoolers generally improve their writing ability dramatically throughout high school. SAT II subjects include English Literature, English as a Second Language, Writing, Math Levels I and II, American History, World History, Biology, Chemistry, Physics, certain "Reading only" language exams (French, German, Modern Hebrew, Latin, Italian, Spanish), and certain "Reading and Listening" language exams (English Language Proficiency, French, Chinese, German, Japanese, Korean, Spanish).

The SAT II subject tests are scored similarly to the SAT I exam. Correct answers receive one point and a fraction of a point is subtracted for incorrect answers. (One-fourth of a point is subtracted for questions that offer five choices; one-third of a point is subtracted for questions that offer four choices; and a half of a point is subtracted for questions that offer three choices.) No points are gained or lost for unanswered questions. Like on the SAT I, students who can identify one or two answer choices as being incorrect are encouraged to make educated guesses. The raw score is then changed into a "scaled" score, on a scale of 200 to 800, with 800 being the best possible score.

The Score Choice option allows a student to wait until after seeing SAT II results to decide which scores to add to his official ETS record, thus controlling which SAT II scores are reported to colleges and which are withheld. (Note that this option applies to SAT II scores only and cannot be used for withholding SAT I scores.) Once a score is "released" onto the record, however, it becomes permanent and cannot be removed in the future. When taking SAT IIs, students should *always* forfeit the initial free score report option and wait to see scores before deciding to place them on their records. Once a poor score is placed on the record, it can never be removed. Since students need to submit only three

SAT II scores to colleges, they should wait to see which scores they want to make public and which they want to withhold.

TOEFL, TWE, AND SAT II: ELPT (FOR FOREIGN STUDENTS ONLY)

The TOEFL (Test of English as a Foreign Language), TWE (Test of Written English), and ELPT (SAT II—English Language Proficiency Test) are tests administered to non-native English speakers to measure English proficiency.

TOEFL is administered by Educational Testing Service (ETS), the same organization that administers the SAT I and II tests. Most colleges require TOEFL scores from overseas students (except native English-speaking American citizens living overseas) and those who have lived in the U.S. for fewer than a given number of years. If you are a non-native English speaker but are not required by a particular college to take the TOEFL, you should take it anyway if your SAT I Verbal score is low. Colleges know that non-native English speakers tend to score lower on the Verbal portion of the SAT, so admissions officers will look for other indications of English ability. If an admissions officer sees a high TOEFL score, he will be much more inclined to disregard a low Verbal score on the SAT.

There are two TOEFL formats: the original paper format and the new computer version. The paper format is scored on a scale from 200 to 677, while the computer version is scored on a different scale, with 300 as the best possible score. The TOEFL consists of three parts: Listening Comprehension; Structure and Written Expression; and Vocabulary and Reading Comprehension. The top colleges are generally looking for a minimum score of 600 on the standard TOEFL (250 on the new computerized version), but higher scores are preferred.

The TWE (Test of Written English) is a supplement to the TOEFL. You do not need to register for it separately, although you should realize that it is not offered every time the TOEFL is offered. The TWE is not commonly requested of overseas applicants, but you should talk to admissions officers at your target schools to see if they recommend that you take it. The TWE is a short essay exam that is scored on a scale of one to six.

The ELPT is not valued as highly as the TOEFL in college admissions because it is considered an easier test and ineffective for assessing the more sophisticated English skills critical to success in highly selective colleges. Students attempting to make up for low SAT I Verbal scores or low TOEFL scores should, however, consider taking the SAT II ELPT to see if they can perform better on this test.

FOR MORE INFORMATION ON THE TOEFL

To find out more about the TOEFL exam or register for it, contact:

TOEFL
Educational Testing Service
P.O. Box 6151
Princeton, NJ 08541-6151
U.S. A
(609)921-9000

GENERAL TIPS ON PREPARING TO ACE STANDARDIZED TESTS

➤ Read, read, read. The only sure way of preparing for the SAT I Verbal tests as well as other reading and comprehension related exams is through lifelong reading of fairly serious literature. This does not mean that you need to read *only* National Book Award or Booker Prize winning novels or nonfiction from Pulitzer Prize contenders, though trashy novels, self-help books, and pedestrian magazines will not usually provide the necessary rigor. Any semisophisticated adult literature—fiction, nonfiction, journalism of the highest variety—will do.

➤ Familiarize yourself with the tests by taking preliminary ones (PSAT, PLAN) and plenty of sample tests. Review the answers that you miss. Make sure that, at the very least, you know exactly what to expect in terms of a test's format—what each section asks you to do, how long each section is—before going in. That way you will not waste time reading directions or panicking, and will be able to concentrate on your performance.

➤ After taking the PSAT, contact ETS to get your actual test back with the correct answers so that you can review better for the SAT I.

➤ Take care of your health and get enough rest for at least two nights before taking standardized tests.

➤ Be organized on the day of the test. Be prepared to bring Number Two pencils and a calculator to the exam site. If the site is not familiar to you, be sure that you have precise directions to it and know exactly how long it will take to get there, allowing for traffic or unexpected delays. Arrive at the testing site ten minutes early so that you have time to go to the restroom and calm yourself down.

➤ Be prepared to take a test more than once, continuing to prepare and review before the second (or third) shot.

➤ Take SAT II, ACT, and TOEFL tests at the most opportune time. Any SAT II subject exam should be taken as soon as the subject has concluded or as soon as you have the most advanced knowledge of a subject (i.e., during your fourth year of a foreign language rather than after the second year). ACT exams also depend upon classroom learning. TOEFL takers should take the exam after a period of immersion in an English language environment or at an advanced period within English language learning.

➤ Make vocabulary lists and notecards with basic math principles to take with you for reviewing whenever you have a spare moment.

➤ Buy test prep guidebooks and CD-ROMs if you need practice.

➤ Take a test prep course if you are not disciplined enough to practice on your own. (See page 306 for more details on test preparation courses.)

SHOULD YOU RETAKE A TEST? HOW MANY TIMES IS TOO MANY?

If your initial round of scores on the SAT I or ACT are superb, do not bother to take it again, hoping to reach perfection! You get no brownie points for having taken a standardized test more than once. Furthermore, you risk your score decreasing (it happens all the time), and both scores will be reported to the colleges. Although they will still officially consider only your best score, they will nonetheless see all of them.

If your standardized test scores will not help get you into a college of your choice, however, then you will need to retake them. Review your PSAT results and your practice tests again to determine where your weaknesses are. Then work on those specific weaknesses; for example, if it is clear that a limited knowledge of vocabulary has hurt you, work extra hard on that. Buy practice books and put yourself on a self-induced study schedule or enroll in a test prep course if you need to.

Do not take the SAT or ACT more than three times. Two or three times is ideal. Although studies show that students perform better on admission tests when taken more than once, admissions officers start to look skeptically at applicants who submit too many scores. If your scores increase, admissions officers will likely overlook the number of sittings. If your scores do not change significantly, though, submitting more than three scores for the same test makes you look like a greedy grade-grubber and might force admissions officers to wonder if your priorities are in place (i.e., questioning why you are spending your time and energy agonizing over your numbers).

HOW TO OVERCOME BAD TEST SCORES IN THE COLLEGE ADMISSIONS PROCESS

There are a few things you can do to overcome poor standardized test scores when applying to college. These will not, of course, erase your standardized test record, but they can help you to boost your chances of admission if your record contains scores that are less than optimal. Your options include:

■   *Counter a bad score on the Verbal or Math portion of the SAT I with strong performances on the SAT II, AP exams, or IB exams.*

If you do poorly on the Verbal or Math section of the SAT I, a strong score on the English or Math SAT IIs, respectively, will indicate to admissions officers that you are academically capable in these areas and make them more inclined to disregard poor scores in either section. You can also help your cause if you do well on an AP or IB exam that tests the area in which you were weak on the SAT I. If SAT I scores go into a formula that calculates your academic ranking, then your bad score will still harm you, but admissions officers can override what the numbers tell them if they see information that sways them in another direction. Schools that do not use formulas for calculating academic ratings are even more apt to view your SAT II (or other) scores with generosity when SAT I scores are not ideal.

■   *Counter poor scores in one area by marketing yourself in a way that does not require those particular strengths.*

Do not market yourself in a way that requires strengths that you clearly do not possess. If your scores on the Math section of the SAT I are weak, for example, you will benefit by marketing yourself as something other than a math wizard or future engineer. You want your profile to match your strengths and weaknesses on the standardized tests so that admissions officers are inclined to believe that a deficiency will not minimize or harm your future contributions to the college or society. If you are pushing yourself as a future journalist or poet whose talents lie in the humanities, a college will not need to worry that poor math skills will prevent you from reaching your potential at college or meeting your future career goals.

■   *Use ETS's Score Choice option for submitting SAT II scores.*

Score Choice is a good option to exercise when applying to highly selective schools, because one low SAT II score can negatively impact your admission. Score Choice allows a student to review his SAT II scores before deciding which ones will go on his official ETS record, i.e., which ones he wants to submit to colleges. Some students take more than the required number of SAT II exams, and thus can decide to suppress certain scores that they do not want publicized to colleges. (You can also take any SAT II more than once, thus suppressing the bad score and reporting only the better one.) Once a student decides which scores to submit, he must contact ETS to release selected scores and have them sent to colleges.

■ *Apply to some schools that abide by the FairTest policy.*

The FairTest policy was developed for candidates who need to minimize the weight of SAT or ACT scores in order to do well in the admissions process. The top colleges generally do not subscribe to the policy, but you can look into applying to a college that recognizes it if you feel you need to. There are five categories within the FairTest policy:

1. SAT/ACT used only for placement and/or academic advising.
2. SAT/ACT required only for out-of-state applicants (at public state universities).
3. SAT/ACT required only when minimum GPA or class rank is not met.
4. SAT/ACT required for certain programs only.
5. SAT I/ACT not required, but SAT IIs required.

ARE TEST PREP COURSES WORTH THE MONEY?

Many college applicants wonder at some point in their high school careers whether or not a test preparation course will be worthwhile. Such courses can be beneficial for the right student, but are neither ideal nor necessary for everyone. Students need to examine their own studying and learning techniques, as well as be honest with themselves about how motivated they are to obtain better scores. Any student can prepare on his own just as well as he can in a course that costs upward of $1000. The learning materials are easily obtained without attending a special class (identical practice tests, vocabulary lists, and the like are available in many different kinds of test prep books you can buy in your local bookstore), the prep methods are not difficult to master, and the test prep instructors are notoriously undertrained anyway. The benefits to preparing on your own are that it is low-cost, offers you complete scheduling flexibility, and allows you to tailor your preparation to suit your own particular needs.

The problem is motivation. Students who are organized, diligent, persistent, and determined will do just as well on their own—no course needed. You just have to be able to set aside the right number of hours per week (perhaps six to eight hours a week for eight weeks) and stay on yourself to keep up with the work, not slacking off and supplanting SAT prep time with TV time after the second week.

On the other hand, it is much easier to follow through with SAT preparation work when you are forced to go to a class and follow someone else's instructions, especially when you feel guilty about all the money your parents are spending to help you. A test prep course forces you to start preparing early, offers you a resource (although not a particularly expert one) on call when you have questions, and gives you an opportunity to study with others who are serious about doing well. The price and inconvenience are often outweighed by the higher scores test prep courses will produce.

You have to decide for yourself whether you have the motivation and the confidence to teach yourself the techniques or whether you would benefit from being under the watch of a supervisor who could better whip you into shape. The appropriate choice for you will depend upon the kind of person you are, your study habits, your financial resources, and your goals. Those who should probably think about taking a test prep course if it is possible include:

➤ Those who tend to score below their ability level on standardized tests;

➤ Those who lack the self-discipline necessary to do basic preparations and review trouble spots; and

➤ Those who need substantial help on more than one aspect of the exam.

CHOOSING A TEST PREP COURSE

Test prep courses tend to cost a lot of money, so be sure that you will get what you pay for. The best value, and best instruction, may not come from the nationally known firms. Look carefully at their smaller competitors before handing over $1000 or more that the name-brand companies demand.

There are several reasons to look at the full range of test prep companies rather than opting for the default choice of one of the famous providers. First, the major companies' claims that they have ultrasophisticated materials, embodying the otherwise unknowable secrets of the exams, are spurious. The fact is that employees of each company, large and small, monitor the efforts of their competitors and readily incorporate their best ideas. Thus, courses are more alike than different. Second, although the major companies can boast enormous libraries of materials on which to practice, few students utilize more than a modest fraction of these materials. Third, the major companies inevitably (given the huge numbers they employ) take on many instructors of average intellect and test-taking talent (including out-of-work actors, waiters, and so on), provide limited training, and suffer from high instructor turnover. The best of the smaller companies can avoid this difficulty. By the same token, if you do opt for one of the major firms, be careful to select the specific course on the basis of the instructor teaching it. To do so, inquire of others who have already taken courses there and check with the firm's clerical staff, too; you are likely to hear that one or two of their instructors are highly sought after.

THE ADMISSIONS OFFICERS TALK ABOUT STANDARDIZED TESTS

How Important Are Standardized Test Scores?

"They are pretty crucial. Our academic rating is initially assigned based upon an applicant's SAT I score alone, and then adjusted up or down according to performance in the classroom. But we certainly don't admit a student on that basis alone."

—*Jonathan Reider, Senior Associate Director of Admissions, Stanford University*

"The *last* thing we look at is standardized test scores—no one believes this, but it's true! Our students have high test scores because they are great overall applicants, but their scores are really the least important component of the academic record to us. We just don't look at them as heavily as other schools do."

—*Michael Goldberger, Director of Admissions, Brown University*

What Are the Standardized Test Requirements or Options?

"We offer the choice of submitting scores for the SAT I or the ACT. We don't prefer one or the other, but very few students submit ACTs."

—*Philip Smith, Dean of Admissions, Williams College*

"We look only at a student's best scores, even though we are given access to all of them."

—*Karl Furstenberg, Dean of Admissions and Financial Aid, Dartmouth College*

"Our emphasis is on *achievement,* so SAT Is are not required. We do require SAT IIs, though, and like to see AP tests and other achievement-oriented scores as well."

—*John Hanson, Director of Admissions, Middlebury College*

"We require the SAT I or the ACT. We strongly recommend that applicants submit SAT II scores, but it's not absolutely required."

—*Jonathan Reider, Senior Associate Director of Admissions, Stanford University*

What about the SAT II?

"We tell students to submit as many SAT IIs as possible because they are such predictors of success."

—*Philip Smith, Dean of Admissions, Williams College*

"We ask that there be one SAT II in math and one in writing—the final SAT II can be in a subject of the student's choice."

—*John Blackburn, Dean of Admissions, the University of Virginia*

"Everyone must submit a Writing SAT II score."

—*Eric J. Furda, Director of Undergraduate Admissions, Columbia University*

"We require the SAT II in Writing. I have one thing to tell students taking this exam: Finish the test completely, and write a concluding paragraph. You can't get a good score on this exam if you leave the essay without a conclusion because of how it's graded."

—*Janet Lavin Rapelye, Dean of Admissions, Wellesley College*

CAN STRONG SCORES ON ONE TEST OFFSET WEAK SCORES ON ANOTHER?

"AP and IB results *can* offset poor standardized test scores. I think evidence from four years of work is often more compelling than evidence from three hours of work!"

—*Christoph Guttentag, Director of Undergraduate Admissions, Duke University*

"AP scores don't really have the ability to offset poor SAT or SAT II scores."

—*Karl Furstenberg, Dean of Admissions and Financial Aid, Dartmouth College*

"Our Numeric Index, calculated for each student, takes both SAT I and II scores into account, so great SAT II scores can never completely compensate for weaker SAT I scores. Similarly, competitive scores on APs or IBs are a good thing, but they don't go into the NI formula at all, so they can't change the objective rating we give to a candidate."

—*Marilee Jones, Dean of Admissions, Massachusetts Institute of Technology*

"There's a lot of balancing that goes on when we look at test scores. We *do* use test scores, we think they're important. But if you've done really well on your subject tests, or AP exams, even New York State Regents or AIME tests, yet you haven't done well on the SAT I, then we might focus more on those other scores, and not as much on the SAT."

—*Richard Shaw, Dean of Undergraduate Admissions and Financial Aid, Yale University*

"We tell students who want to offset a low verbal SAT score to submit a graded English paper. That can really help give us more confidence in the student's English language ability."

—*Nanci Tessier, Director of Admissions, Smith College*

"A strong SAT II really can compensate for weak SAT scores—especially in our process, since we use no algorithms or formulas to rate students. AP scores can also override weak SATs, for that matter."

—*Barbara-Jan Wilson, Dean of Admissions and Financial Aid, Wesleyan University*

DOES NATIONAL MERIT FINALIST DESIGNATION
HELP A CANDIDATE IN COLLEGE ADMISSIONS?

"Being a National Merit finalist is, of course, a good thing. But it is so very common among our applicants that it doesn't give applicants to MIT a leg up in the admissions process."

—Marilee Jones, Dean of Admissions, Massachusetts Institute of Technology

"We don't even record whether or not a student is a National Merit scholar—we see it on practically every other application we receive. It's too common to be a distinctive factor in our decision"

—James Bock, Director of Admissions, Swarthmore College

HOW MUCH DO LOW TEST SCORES HURT AN APPLICANT?

"We don't have test score cut-offs, but we start to worry if we see a verbal score under 600. If there is a reason for it—if English is a student's second language, for example—then we understand, but otherwise we would be concerned about a student's ability to perform at Amherst, which is a very verbal place."

—Katie Fretwell, Director of Admissions, Amherst College

"If a student were interested in engineering and had low scores and skills in math, that would be a problem. But this rarely occurs, because most students' interests lie in their strengths."

—Eric Kaplan, Director of Admissions, the University of Pennsylvania

HOW DO YOU REGARD APPLICANTS WHO TAKE TESTS TOO MANY TIMES?

"If an applicant has taken the SAT more than three or four times, it looks odd. But we wouldn't really hold that against him or her."

—Eric Kaplan, Director of Admissions, the University of Pennsylvania

"We feel sorry for the student who takes the SAT eight times. We also note the student who scores a 1580 the first time and takes it over again three times trying to do better. That's putting your priorities in the wrong place."

—Dan Walls, Dean of Admissions, Emory University

DOES AN OPTIONAL TESTING POLICY SUGGEST THAT A SCHOOL
DOES NOT CARE ABOUT STANDARDIZED TEST SCORES AT ALL?

"Some students jump to the conclusion that we don't care about how a student does on standardized tests since we don't require score results. That's a leap they shouldn't make. Test scores certainly help students who do well on them. We now even recognize National Merit scholars, partly to signal that we *do* care about test scores. We do not require them, however, and we know we can make informed decisions by evaluating applications, transcripts, and recommendations carefully."

—*Richard Steele, Dean of Admissions, Bowdoin College*

What Do You Think about Applicants Who Take Test Prep Courses?

"We almost expect that students have taken some sort of SAT prep course, given the way that college admission is treated these days."

—*Barbara-Jan Wilson, Dean of Admissions and Financial Aid, Wesleyan University*

"If we saw a *really* radical change in an applicant's test scores—a rise of 200 or 300 points—then we might wonder whether or not the student took the exam himself. We might call the College Board and look into the case. But I would find it hard to penalize a student for preparing to take the SATs."

—*Lee Stetson, Dean of Admissions, the University of Pennsylvania*

"We assume these days that many of our applicants have taken [test prep courses]. We make allowances for kids from poorer socioeconomic backgrounds when we're looking at their test scores—we might assume that their scores would be a bit higher if they had an opportunity to take a prep course as many other students do. We would never, however, let the test prep assumption work negatively upon a candidate from a background full of opportunities."

—*Michael Goldberger, Director of Admissions, Brown University*

"Wouldn't you prepare the best you could? I really get frazzled when people talk about how evil test prep courses and independent counselors are. Why shouldn't kids do everything in their power to do better in the admissions process?"

—*Marilee Jones, Dean of Admissions, Massachusetts Institute of Technology*

9

SHAPING YOUR NONACADEMIC PROFILE

— KEY POINTS —

Few candidates will be accepted at the top colleges on the basis of academic credentials alone
—What you do outside of class is critically important

■

There are five areas of nonacademic involvement:
—Intellectual pursuits outside of the classroom
—Extracurricular (school and outside-of-school) activities
—Community service
—Work experience
—Summer experiences (which might include any of the above)

■

Commitment and depth are more important than the number of activities you pursue
—The longer you are involved and the more active you are in an organization, the better
—Similarly, the greater the responsibility you shoulder, the more leadership you exert, and the greater the impact you have, the better

■

Your nonacademic pursuits thus become a critical part of your positioning effort
—What you do outside of the classroom can help admissions officers understand who you are, what values you hold, what motivates you, what special attributes you will bring to campus, and the way they should view your objective academic credentials

INTRODUCTION

By now most smart high school students know that academics alone will probably not get them into a top college. As explained in Chapter 8, an excellent academic record will put you in the running for admission at a top college. It is usually the rest of the material presented in the application, however, that determines whether or not a prospective student is actually admitted over others with similarly impressive academic records at the best schools. This "other" material includes one's overall nonacademic record; one's particular ethnic, geographic, or personal background; and any special admissions appeal one possesses because of a particular talent, legacy status, and the like. This chapter explores the five main facets of a student's overall nonacademic profile: (1) intellectual pursuits outside of the classroom, (2) extracurricular (school and outside of school) activities, (3) community service, (4) work experience, and (5) summer experiences.

There are two important concepts that students still generally fail to realize regarding their overall nonacademic records. The first is that colleges are not looking for the proverbial well-rounded student. Colleges want well-rounded or diverse *classes* of students, not students who themselves are well-rounded.

A strong and diverse class of students requires that each student be exceptional, but perhaps only in one or two areas. The large number of students in a class takes care of ensuring that all possible strengths that contribute to well-roundedness are covered. It is basically impossible for one person to excel to the greatest degree possible at many different things—after all, there are only so many hours in the day to dedicate to one's endeavors. If a student is accomplished academically, then he or she may only need to stand out in one or two nonacademic arenas in order to be competitive at the top schools. Colleges are thus looking for students who are particularly strong in a few areas, devoting the majority of their time and effort to becoming standouts in perhaps two or three ways. Aiming toward becoming well-rounded will lead to mediocrity rather than excellence.

The second truth that many students fail to realize is that a lack of strength in traditional extracurricular activities may not hurt them if they have spent time outside of school doing other worthwhile things (e.g., working at a paid job, performing community service, or caring for siblings or elderly relatives). In other words, college admissions committees want to see that you are spending your time wisely, but they do not expect miracles. If you have had to work at nights and on weekends to help make ends meet for your family, a college will not blame you for failing to dedicate the 15 or more hours a week necessary to play a varsity sport. If you have helped to take care of your elderly grandparents after school, that counts for something—it is not lost or wasted time as far as college applications go.

Your nonacademic record becomes a large part of your overall positioning effort. The way in which you spend your free time, the talents and skills you have developed, and the personality traits you exhibit through your nonacademic activities all contribute heavily to your overall profile. You need to tailor your pursuits and the way you present them to colleges in a way that will add to (rather than detract from) your main marketing efforts.

Remember that the placement of the material that makes up your nonacademic profile does not matter too much. You can choose to include your community service under an application's "Extracurricular Activities" list or "Work Experience" list; it is up to you to determine whether you want to discuss your summer enrichment experience at a physics camp under "Summer Experiences," "Extracurricular Activities," or "Coursework Conducted Outside of the Classroom."

The important thing is to include everything that will help you improve your presentation and to do so in a way that makes you appear to be focused, yet also not deficient in any one area. Thus, if you have never worked for pay and have plenty to discuss under "Extracurricular Activities," you will want to place your volunteer service in the "Work Experience" category—to avoid appearing as if you have never lifted a finger or exerted yourself in labor.

INTELLECTUAL PURSUITS OUTSIDE THE CLASSROOM

There was a time when it was not very common to hear of students participating in academic pursuits outside of regular classroom learning. Even the best students vying for places at the most competitive institutions of higher learning were satisfied to do the best they could within their high school curriculums, spend time outside the classroom on nonacademic activities, and wait until college to further pursue special intellectual interests. Now, however, there are many opportunities for high school students with special interests to get beyond the basics learned in high school, prepare themselves for future training in a subject, or explore possible college majors and career options ahead of time. Taking part in intellectual activities outside of the classroom has one other very important benefit: It can help you to get into a top college.

Colleges have always liked to see that students show particular affinity for learning by finding ways to supplement their classroom education. Admissions committees have for a long time looked hard to find students whose teachers say that they enjoy "learning for learning's sake" and show evidence of special intellectual interests. But recently this trend has become even more pronounced. With growing numbers of applications per year and growing numbers of high-quality applications as well, colleges are constantly thinking about how to make admissions decisions when there are too many desirable candidates in the pool.

Some of the most competitive schools now look for special intellectual passion in applicants as another way of distinguishing between superb candidates and more-than-superb candidates.

It has in fact become nearly imperative to show special intellectual prowess beyond classroom participation to be admitted to some of the top schools. MIT, for example, rates all applicants on a scale of 1 to 5, with 5 being the best rating, in four separate areas: Academics, Cocurricular Activities, Extracurricular Activities, and Interpersonal Skills. Cocurricular Activities are described as "learning-oriented activities that take place outside of the classroom." Applicants must be able to show that they participate in academic pursuits beyond what is required of them at school in order to stay in the running for admission at MIT.

For the 1998–1999 admission season, Stanford added a component called "Intellectual Vitality" to its original two areas upon which every candidate is given a numerical rating, "Academics" and "Nonacademics." Stanford's decision to create this category was based on the fact that most applicants they see have good grades, high test scores, and impressive talents. The school needed to develop a way to differentiate between strong candidates and stellar candidates. The admissions officers thus made it a priority to select candidates who have demonstrated special intellectual passion and commitment beyond regular expected classroom participation.

ADMISSIONS OFFICERS DISCUSS THE IMPORTANCE OF INTELLECTUAL PASSION

"We now rate each applicant in a category we call 'Intellectual Vitality.' Most kids we see have high grades and test scores, and have done all the right things. But to discover what makes a candidate different and special, we ask ourselves, 'Do our faculty want to teach this student? What does this student's work mean to him or her?' This is a high priority for us. "

—*Jonathan Reider, Senior Associate Director of Admissions, Stanford University*

"We conducted a study with our faculty, asking them to pick their three favorite students and describe what they like about them. Far above intelligence was 'enthusiasm for learning.' This is what we are looking for—students who are not particularly engaged in learning shouldn't be at Bowdoin."

—*Richard Steele, Dean of Admissions, Bowdoin College*

We thus highly recommend that you pursue some outside learning in an academic activity with special meaning for you if there are opportunities available. If there are not opportunities readily available, try to create them yourself. You do not need to wait for an organization or institution to invite or summon you to join in an intellectual activity—in fact, creating these kinds of opportunities yourself is what "intellectual vitality" is really all about. Expand your thinking and do not feel limited by what has been done before in your school or community. Just because your community newspaper has no student contributors at present does not mean that it would not welcome an opinion piece from you. Academic pursuit is often conducted alone rather than in groups, so do not feel that you have to "become part of something" in order to show your spark.

HOW TO PURSUE INTELLECTUAL INTERESTS OUTSIDE OF THE CLASSROOM

➤ Participate on a model United Nations team.

➤ Participate on a debate team.

➤ Participate in a mock trial group.

➤ Write an editorial (or a regular editorial column) for your town's newspaper.

➤ Contribute to a newspaper or Web site on a topic that interests you.

➤ Conduct special projects for submission to science contests and fairs.

➤ Submit original fiction, poetry, or drama to writing contests.

➤ Write a play and then direct it, putting on a show for your school or community.

➤ Take classes at a community college or in an enrichment program.

➤ Take classes at a special performing arts or technical school.

➤ Attend a special summer program at a boarding school or college to pursue subjects of interest to you.

➤ Attend a writing workshop.

➤ Start a Web magazine or journal.

➤ Conduct a special research project under the supervision of a teacher.

➤ Take place in Civil War reenactments.

➤ Organize an event at school to celebrate and teach others about a person or topic in which you are particularly interested. For example, if you are interested in Oscar Wilde, ask a teacher or school administrator if you can hold a special event on his birthday. You might give a talk about the dramatist and stage *The Importance of Being Earnest.* If you are interested in the Long March on which Mao Zedong led his staunchest Chinese Communist Party followers in 1934–1935, ask your world history teacher if you can plan a special lecture for class on the topic. Decorate a bulletin board outside the classroom with photos, a data sheet about the journey and its participants, excerpts from journalist Edgar Snow's discussions with Mao, and a map demonstrating the route.

EXTRACURRICULAR (SCHOOL AND OUTSIDE OF SCHOOL) ACTIVITIES

Extracurricular activities include everything from playing on high school sports teams to taking part in religious festivals. It is here where most college applicants fail in presenting themselves. A college would much rather see that you have put many hours of valuable work over several years into two activities than joined every club in school, playing very limited roles. Quality matters much more than quantity. In fact, a long list of activities merely dilutes the overall impression that your extracurricular profile gives an admissions officer.

Remember that anything and everything can "count" as part of your profile here—it does not have to be sponsored by your high school, or even anyone at all! Let us assume, for example, that you are interested in a certain period in American history and have spent time at antique shows and auctions augmenting your collection of furniture and other pieces from the era. This way of spending your Saturdays can certainly become fodder for extracurricular material, whether it be merely mentioning it on an activity list or incorporating it into your essays somehow. Be sure to put an appropriate spin on whatever you are claiming as an "activity." In other words, it is better to present the antique collecting as part of your interest in a certain period (especially if history is a strength that you are marketing) than as a mere "shopping habit." Likewise, if you read philosophy to your grandfather and his roommate at the nursing home once a week, you would want to present it as something more serious and meaningful than just "visiting Grandpa."

Extracurricular activities are important to admissions officers for many reasons. They show how you choose to spend your time away from school; demonstrate special talents and skills; provide evidence of personality and character traits; and complement ideas presented within your academic profile. In sum, they give admissions officers an idea about how you might contribute to the college environment if accepted.

The admissions officers are not looking for any particular activities on a student's palette of extracurricular involvements. Except in cases in which a special talent is a selling point for a candidate, they do not much care whether you are editor-in-chief of the yearbook or director of your school's environmental and recycling team. They are, however, looking for students who have been involved in a few activities for a good length of time, showing commitment and passion. A bit of a balance is usually ideal, so that a student does not appear one-dimensional, but in general showing commitment and focus is better than being the "all-around" kid.

Extracurricular activities help to show your personal qualities. Admissions committees at the top schools tend to look for students who have taken on substantial responsibilities within their organizations, demonstrating (most importantly) leadership, initiative, and a positive "can-do" attitude. Dartmouth likes to see evidence of "adventurousness, a willingness to take risks, and curiosity"—along with the other usual traits of commitment and leadership. Amherst likes to see "perseverance and follow-through" evident in extracurricular activities. The University of Pennsylvania notes that all schools need good leaders, but they also need their fair share of good *contributors* as well. In other words, you do not have to have the star role in everything you do—solid contributions to organizations and groups are also valued.

Although it does not really matter what activities you choose, keep in mind these important points about your extracurricular record:

- *Depth of involvement:* Show that you have been committed to one or more activities for a length of time, preferably three or more years. Show that you have advanced within at least one activity and consistently devoted substantial time to it over several years.

- *Leadership:* Show that you have taken on an important leadership role in at least one activity. This means founding a club or group, becoming an appointed or elected high officer of a group, or directing a group's efforts in one area. Show that you can motivate others around you to contribute their best efforts to a common cause.

- *Something unusual:* Not everyone has the talent or resources to do something really out of the ordinary. But everyone can find a way to use his or her abilities to get involved in something that stands out from the usual student council, yearbook, and varsity sports activities that show up on college applicants' rosters. Doing something a bit unusual can be beneficial because it will expand your own mind, exposing you to something you might not have run into without special effort, as well as make you a bit more memorable to college admissions officers. Training seeing-eye dogs, leading nature hikes, participating in a communitywide choir, becoming a glassblower, joining a "neighborhood watch" association to fight crime, or playing in a Korean drumming ensemble are examples of activities that are distinctive but within reach of high school students with the right ambition and prerequisite skills.

- *Possession of at least two dimensions:* You want to present yourself as a focused individual with a memorable profile, not someone who dabbles in everything without much commitment to any one particular activity. But avoiding the tag of "well-rounded student" does not mean you should become one-dimensional. Be sure that there is at least one activity you can point to that stands out as not fitting into your main marketing scheme. For example, if you are presenting yourself as a future biologist who is strong in the sciences, works at the city aquarium, and leads children's nature hikes at a nearby park, make sure to get involved in at least one activity that is completely unrelated to your interest in the biological sciences—painting classes at an art institute or playing on the tennis team, for example.

WHAT ADMISSIONS OFFICERS SAY ABOUT THE NONACADEMIC PROFILE

HOW IMPORTANT IS AN APPLICANT'S NONACADEMIC PROFILE?

"After we determine there is a match between a student and Harvard in terms of academics, then we're basically looking to find out who you are, what makes you tick—to flesh out the other sides of you."

—*Marlyn McGrath Lewis, Director of Admissions, Harvard University*

"We want to see what kind of recognition a student has received from the community, school, or peers for his or her various contributions and activities. Looking at 'recognition' allows us to feel a candidate's real impact on those around him or her."

—*Christoph Guttentag, Director of Undergraduate Admissions, Duke University*

"About eighty to ninety percent of our applicants are academically qualified for admission. This means that we look very closely and carefully at nonacademic areas as well. Personal strength is looked at significantly in the admissions process."

—*Barbara Bergman, Associate Dean of Admissions, Georgetown University*

"We assign an extracurricular rating using an A-B-C scale. As are those who are really stars at something. Bs are good, well-rounded students—maybe a president of a club or a captain of a team. Cs are those who sit inside playing Dungeons and Dragons all day."

—*David Borus, Dean of Admissions and Financial Aid, Vassar College*

WHAT ACTIVITIES "COUNT" AS PART OF THE NONACADEMIC PROFILE?

"If a student has demonstrated a high commitment to a sport but is clearly not qualified to play at the college level, then the sport won't be considered a major piece of the application as it would for a recruit or a very good player. But it still indicates to us how the student spends his time, that he is a committed team player, and so on, so it is useful."

—*Philip Smith, Dean of Admissions, Williams College*

"We know you have friends and like to hang out with them. That's not an activity you should be describing on the application."

—*Delsie Phillips, Director of Admissions, Haverford College*

"People really overestimate the importance of summer programs at colleges and prep schools. I don't like the idea that students and parents see them as factories—people think that if you go to these programs, you'll automatically be accepted into the best colleges. These programs are fine, but I'd rather see students focus on a single activity—go to computer camp or music camp or work for Mother Teresa's organization in India."

—*Richard Shaw, Dean of Undergraduate Admissions and Financial Aid, Yale University*

"It's clear that students thrive when they are most engaged and passionate. They shouldn't do something just to impress colleges—in the end, that probably won't serve them well. Students need to be able to tell us *why* something is important to them, what value it has had for them."

—*Eric J. Furda, Director of Undergraduate Admissions, Columbia University*

WHAT PERSONAL QUALITIES, EVIDENCED THROUGH THE NONACADEMIC PROFILE AND ELSEWHERE, DO ADMISSIONS OFFICERS MOST LIKE TO SEE IN CANDIDATES?

"Part of what we're looking for is passion and commitment, and how those things have developed. Leadership, character, integrity also come into the mix."

—*Nancy Hargrave Meislahn, Director of Undergraduate Admissions, Cornell University*

"Passion, maturity, civic-mindedness. These are some of the things we look for."

—*John Blackburn, Dean of Admissions, University of Virginia*

"We are committed to finding students who show adventurousness, willingness to take risks, and curiosity."

—*Karl Furstenberg, Dean of Admissions and Financial Aid, Dartmouth College*

"Self-initiative, commitment, social skills, and leadership are what we are looking for."

—*Marilee Jones, Dean of Admissions, Massachusetts Institute of Technology*

"Perseverance and follow-through are important. Quality over quantity of activities is also key."

—*Katie Fretwell, Director of Admissions, Amherst College*

"We have stressed maturity quite a bit in our admissions process. We give our students quite a bit of freedom here, and we want to know they can handle it. Honesty is also a big factor for us because of our honor code."

—*Richard Steele, Dean of Admissions, Bowdoin College*

"We are always, in every single admissions case, looking for signs of self-initiative. MIT is a full-strength experience. We want to know that kids have done what they have done because of their own will and curiosity."

—*Marilee Jones, Dean of Admissions, Massachusetts Institute of Technology*

"We have a real commitment to Philadelphia here so we need students who will be able to contribute, who have shown real involvement in the community."

—*Lee Stetson, Dean of Admissions, University of Pennsylvania*

"Duke's admissions committee often uses the word 'impact' when discussing candidates for admission. We look for evidence of impact and having made a difference. We ask ourselves 'What has this student done with the opportunities given to him?'"

—*Christoph Guttentag, Director of Undergraduate Admissions, Duke University*

How Important Is It to Show Commitment and Follow-Through?

"It's not about joining, it's about what you do with your involvement. Having a sustained commitment to something is important. We're looking for depth and passion."

—*Richard Shaw, Dean of Undergraduate Admissions and Financial Aid, Yale University*

"'Significant follow-through' is a term coined by my colleague Phil Smith at Williams. This is very important to us. We don't care if a student does piano lessons or wrestles or sits on the student council, but we want to see a student pursue something and stick with it. Success in life requires diligence, cooperation, the ability to stick with something—we like to see evidence of this."

—*John Blackburn, Dean of Admissions, University of Virginia*

"Follow-through is a notion that is very important to us when looking at what a student does with his or her spare time. We like to see commitment to an activity, evidence that a student has gotten significantly involved and stuck with a group, an organization, or an activity."

—*Barbara Bergman, Associate Dean of Admissions, Georgetown University*

Which Is Better, Breadth or Depth?

"Level of commitment is very important, but that doesn't mean that students shouldn't experiment a little and make changes in their extracurricular schedules when it's appropriate. We expect that there will be growth in many different directions."

—*Eric J. Furda, Director of Undergraduate Admissions, Columbia University*

"Some versatility is advisable. This doesn't mean that we don't like someone of Olympic stature who does nothing else but train in his or her spare time. But for the most part we like students who are focused, yet still somewhat versatile."

—*Sheppard Shanley, Senior Associate Director of Admissions, Northwestern University*

"The faculty on our admissions committees tend to be very impressed with the 'angular' student—a student who has a specific focus academically or a significant talent in something like music, for example. The students on our committees tend to be more impressed with well-rounded students."

—*Barbara Bergman, Associate Dean of Admissions, Georgetown University*

"We really want to see depth and focus in extracurricular activities."

—*Eric Kaplan, Director of Admissions, University of Pennsylvania*

COMMUNITY SERVICE

Most college applicants should be sure to have some sort of volunteer or community service to show for their four years in high school. As an exception to this general rule, those who come from very low-income families or are required to work a great deal to help support the family should not feel that they need to add community service to their high school activity lists. If it is clear that you spend a substantial amount of energy working for wages necessary for your or your family's survival, you will not be expected to have donated your limited free time to charity work.

Other college applicants, however, should at the very least have on their activity lists (or work experience lists) a mention of running an event at a Special Olympics function or raising money for a local charity. As with other areas of one's nonacademic profile, more depth in a community service project is always better than these kinds of single instances of volunteerism. Thus it is much better if you can show that you worked for a cause for a length of time rather than showing up for one Saturday or participating in a single weeklong campaign.

WHAT KIND OF COMMUNITY SERVICE?

Again, as with other kinds of activity, it is not particularly important what group or cause you help with your time and effort. An admissions committee will be impressed whether you have helped blind children to learn Braille, contributed to an effort to save the seals, or served meals to hospice patients with AIDS. You should try to be as directly involved in your cause as possible rather than performing work that is only attached to the cause indirectly. Volunteer to work with patients at a hospital rather than shuffling papers in the administrative office, for example. Being directly involved with the people who need your help or in fashioning efforts to solve a community problem will teach you much more (in terms of both hard skills and life lessons) than raising money to support a cause or doing office work for a community organization. These other indirect tasks might become part of your job, but try to allot at least some of your time for hands-on experience with the "service" component of the work.

Community service can also be used to show leadership, initiative, drive, creativity, or an entrepreneurial spirit. Your volunteer efforts in a service project will be that much more powerful and useful to you in college admissions if you can go beyond the standard effort to contribute more meaningfully to a cause. For example, rather than merely joining a group that protects the natural habitat in your community's park systems, you might consider going one step further by spreading the group's efforts to the next town, thereby becoming the head of the task force for another community. Or you might create a new program for the existing service organization—perhaps a monthly educational meeting for community residents or a kids' task force, to encourage young children to join the service. You might even create an entirely new organization by taking something in which you have helped a single individual and spreading the impact to many others. One upstart we know had helped an elderly woman in the nursing home in which he volunteered learn how to use E-mail to communicate with her grandchildren. When the college applicant saw how effective he had been in helping one woman to improve her life, he decided to take the effort a step further. He founded an organization to teach senior citizens how to use E-mail and to make computer systems available for such purposes at libraries, community centers, and nursing homes.

What counts most with community service is that you prove your commitment to caring about something other than yourself. Some schools look particularly carefully for evidence of volunteer service. The University of Pennsylvania, for example, looks for students whom it can depend upon to contribute to volunteer functions because the school is committed to improving Philadelphia and the surrounding community. Personality traits that are attractive to college admissions officers can show up through volunteer service as well. Involvement in community service can help demonstrate compassion, appreciation for one's own fortunes, maturity, special talents, leadership potential, and responsibility for others' well-being. Volunteer service can fit nicely into one's overall marketing efforts, but it also does well standing alone as a tribute to your humane character, communal spirit, and energetic initiative.

IMPORTANCE OF COMMUNITY SERVICE FOR ADVANTAGED APPLICANTS

Community service is especially important if you come from a wealthy or even moderately well-off family and have never had to work for paid wages. If it is evident that you have enjoyed many advantages in your life, you should make an effort early in your high school career to find a service or cause that excites you and devote substantial energy to it over the next few years. When it comes time to apply to colleges, try your best to provide evidence that you have contributed your energy to something that helps those less fortunate than yourself or serves community interests in some way.

In the case of the advantaged applicant, something in the way of volunteer service is usually better than nothing at all. There are instances, however, when a tiny contribution to community service—when viewed in comparison to energy spent on other activities—might seem crass rather than admirable. For example, if a student from an extremely wealthy family were to throw in a mention of a one-day commitment to United Way after including loads of information about numerous travels abroad with the family, expensive soccer camps, and special summer programs, he might come across as disingenuous to an admissions officer. If you fear that you might appear insincere—as if you are merely trying to win over the admissions officers—by including information about limited community service efforts on your application, ask a college counselor or other objective reader to look over your materials to gain another opinion. If others agree that the mention shows poor taste or judgment, leave it out.

WORK EXPERIENCE

Many candidates for college discount the value of the experience they have gained working for wages—often because the jobs high schoolers have might not seem to be worthy of discussion in an application to a top college. Candidates may think, "How can I prove that I'm Princeton material when I flip french fries for a living?" Yet the truth is that work counts for a lot in college admissions, and it often does not matter what kind of work is being performed. Work for wages is generally viewed by college admissions offices as being just as important as extracurricular activities, depending upon the context in which you have worked and the nature of the work.

WHAT KIND OF WORK "COUNTS"?

All schools, quite obviously, value the basic ideas of "work" and "responsibility" that come with paid labor. But some schools admit they maintain a double standard with respect to the value they place upon the nature of paid work experience. All colleges report that for students from low-income backgrounds, it absolutely does not matter what the paid work experience is. If a student is working because he has to in order to support himself or his family, no thought is given to whether or not the job is particularly worthy, meaningful, or enlightening. For students who come from upper-class or upper middle-class backgrounds, and can choose whether they want to work or spend their time doing something else, the nature of the work generally matters to admissions officers.

Admissions officers prefer that someone who does *not* have to work takes advantage of the best opportunities for success rather than work in an unskilled job just for cash. Schools would rather see a student in a leadership position or doing something that will better enrich him than working at a job that most likely will contribute little to personal growth. This often means that leadership activities or substantial work experience count more in college admissions than do "meaningless" paying jobs for those candidates who do not have to work. Still, Harvard, for example, believes that all paid work experience at least shows energy and commitment and gives information about what a student is doing with her time.

If you come from a disadvantaged or low-income background and must work to support yourself or your family, do not worry about what job you are performing. Take the job that will best contribute to your expenses—and then do the best you can to stick with it long enough so that you can move up in your role or take on added responsibility. The more you can show colleges that you have utilized your work experience to the best of your potential and extracted all you can out of the experience, the better off you will be. Be sure to explain thoroughly on your college applications why you work, how much you contribute to your own basic needs or those of your family, and the reason you took the job that you did.

For those who do not have to work for pay but choose to do so, be careful about the choices you make. It is not unwise to work for pay, but if you have the leeway to be picky about what you do, take time to be sure you are getting all you can from your paid job. Ask yourself these questions to ascertain that the job you choose will not only contribute to your bank account but also contribute to your overall growth and the record you are building for college preparation purposes:

- What kinds of responsibilities and skills will I gain from the job?
- Is there room for growth and development within the job once I master my original tasks?
- Will my performance and learning in this job contribute at all to my future academic and career plans?
- Will this job help me to make crucial decisions about the direction of my academic focus or future career?
- Will I gain valuable contacts in this job to help me in later life?

You should choose a job that balances the best pay and the most enjoyment with positive contributions to your future.

WHAT ADMISSIONS OFFICERS SAY ABOUT WORK EXPERIENCE

"Paid work experience shows energy and commitment—and also helps to tell us what a person does with his or her time."

—Marlyn McGrath Lewis, Director of Admissions, Harvard University

"If a candidate works forty hours at a fast-food restaurant to help support the family, it doesn't matter that it's fast-food. It's impressive."

—Philip Smith, Dean of Admissions, Williams College

"We don't place greater value on extracurricular involvement than on work experience. We look at how the student has spent his or her free time in the context of the background and interests. Often we see students who have no choice, who must spend their free time working to help support themselves. Clearly this is very valuable experience. The context is very important."

—Barbara Bergman, Associate Dean of Admissions, Georgetown University

"All work experience—even if it's working in a convenience store—is life experience and involves responsibility. We value all of it—and wouldn't expect as much extracurricular involvement from a student who has to work."

—Karl Furstenberg, Dean of Admissions and Financial Aid, Dartmouth College

"We're looking at the reflection of the employment on the student—how has it impacted him?"

—Jonathan Reider, Senior Associate Director of Admissions, Stanford University

"We don't make judgments on the types of jobs applicants carry. It's not what they do but what they do with it that matters."

—Marilee Jones, Dean of Admissions, Massachusetts Institute of Technology

"As an example of how we regard an application in its context, if a student has no paid work experience and no community service record either, but has been living overseas in an expat community where those things are impossible to have achieved, we need to be considerate of that."

—Nancy Hargrave Meislahn, Director of Undergraduate Admissions, Cornell University

"If the child must work for family support, the type of work does not matter. But if the student chooses to work, then the type of work performed might matter more."

—Barbara-Jan Wilson, Dean of Admissions and Financial Aid, Wesleyan University

"The way we look at work experience depends on the context. Internships can be great, but they are often handed down by a friend of Mom or Dad—and sometimes don't amount to much substance."

—Lee Stetson, Dean of Admissions, University of Pennsylvania

"Work is evaluated in a contextual way. For someone who doesn't have to work but still chooses to work twenty hours a week, the job should have some sort of cumulative effect. If it doesn't, we'll wonder what moves this person. We want to see how a student establishes priorities outside of school."

—Sheppard Shanley, Senior Associate Director of Admissions, Northwestern University

"Anyone who has to work should not feel badly about this or worry about what it will do to his extracurricular profile. But again, like other nonacademic activities, work is an opportunity. We want to see what a kid has done with this opportunity, whatever it may be."

—Christoph Guttentag, Director of Undergraduate Admissions, Duke University

"We certainly honor work experience and do not expect as much after-school activities involvement from those who are employed systematically and meaningfully."

—John Hanson, Director of Admissions, Middlebury College

"One of the first factors we look at when looking at the nonacademic profile is if the student is working."

—Richard Steele, Dean of Admissions, Bowdoin College

"Does the nature of the work experience matter? No—not to me, at least. I do occasionally find students who work too much when they don't need to and have no other interests—to support a car, for example. How important is the car relative to schoolwork or pursuing other things? We ask ourselves this."

—Delsie Phillips, Director of Admissions, Haverford College

"It's one thing if the student has to work, it's another if he just wants gas money for his Mustang."

—David Borus, Dean of Admissions and Financial Aid, Vassar College

"For us the commitment to a job is more important than what the job is. If you've had a newspaper route for seven years, I'm impressed. If a job just began six months ago, it probably won't matter that much on the application."

—James Bock, Director of Admissions, Swarthmore College

"We'd miss out on some great students if we denied admission to otherwise great, smart, capable kids who spend the summer waitressing. Students often feel a need to make their own money, even if they don't have to. We don't place our own judgment on which is better, doing an activity or working."

—Nanci Tessier, Director of Admissions, Smith College

SUMMER EXPERIENCES

Summer experiences, especially what you choose to do between your junior and senior years, can become significant contributors to the nonacademic profile you create for your college applications. The summer experience is not really a new category of nonacademic involvement, but is rather another way in which to include one of the first four categories of nonacademic activity on your high school record. In other words, a summer can be spent pursuing intellectual endeavors outside of the regular high school classroom; immersing yourself in an extracurricular activity; doing a community service project; or working for pay.

Although it is not necessary that you spend your first summer in high school doing something particularly impressive, your summers should be fairly substantive the closer you get to the college application process. This does not mean that you need to attend expensive private institutes each summer or travel the world in search of meaning. A meaningful summer can consist of working full-time for pay, or doing volunteer community service along with training intensively for your sport. Participating in an enrichment program in an academic subject, attending a camp to improve a special talent, or going on an organized trip in the United States or abroad are other ways of spending your summers wisely. The content of your summers does not matter; but you should be sure that at least part of one (and preferably two or all three) of your high school summers is spent doing something that a college admissions officer would call "worthwhile." See the first four sections of this chapter to learn more about how your choices will affect your overall application and how you should best plan your time during the summer months.

COMPLETING THE
WRITTEN APPLICATIONS

— KEY POINTS —

Choose whichever type of application is best for you:
—Standard printed applications
—Downloaded applications
—Online applications
—Software-generated applications

■

Although the essays are the most critical part of the written application, you cannot afford to be lackadaisical in putting together the rest of your materials
—Sloppiness says you do not care about the application
—You need to take advantage of all opportunities to fully support your positioning effort
—This is a unique opportunity to paint a complete picture of your high school career, since your essays will focus on no more than a couple aspects of your candidacy

■

Supplemental materials can be of great value to some applicants, especially those with special talents in the performing and visual arts

■

Eschew gimmicks

INTRODUCTION

Although the essays are inevitably the most important (and worrisome) part of the written application, you must also be cautious when filling out the other portions. Completing the other parts of the written application requires attention to detail as well as attention to your main marketing and positioning efforts. This chapter discusses how to organize and complete your applications most effectively.

CHOOSING YOUR APPLICATION FORMAT

First you will have to decide what method you will use for submitting each college's written application. Whereas a decade ago applicants had no choice but to file a standard printed application form obtained from the college's admissions office, there now exist several different kinds of computer-based application formats. Not all application formats are offered by each school. You will have to check with each of your target colleges to see what your options are.

It is best if you try to stick to one or two formats to reduce your efforts and make the entire process more efficient. You will notice that after you fill out a few applications, you become accustomed to the process, making it easier to complete the remainder of the forms. There are different instructions for filling out each kind of application, making it difficult to hit a rhythm if you are utilizing three or four different methods of application. Furthermore, there is a greater chance that you might make a procedural mistake or omission if you are following different application approaches for each college.

The application formats currently available are:

■ *Standard printed application.* You obtain the printed application from the college's admissions office and fill it out with pen and/or electric type and mail it to the college.

■ *Downloaded application.* You download the application from the college's Web site and, after filling it out on your computer screen, print out a hard (paper) copy and mail it to the college.

■ *Online application.* You fill out an online application produced either by the college itself or by a company [CollegeLink, Embark (formerly known as College Edge), Apply, ExPAN, Next Stop College, etc.] that produces college applications for you once you submit the information needed by each school. In the former case, you send the application to the college electronically rather than mailing a hard copy. In the latter case, the company sends your applications to the appropriate colleges electronically after you have paid the company's required fees.

■ *Software-generated application.* You order software from the college itself or one of the college application companies, which allows you to reproduce the application on your computer at home. After filling it out on your computer, you either print out a hard (paper) copy and mail it to the college or send the diskette (now with your personal application on it) back to the college.

Each application filing approach has advantages and disadvantages. Factors you will want to consider when looking at your options include:

■ *Cost:* Each college requires a nonrefundable fee for filing an application. The college application services will charge you additional fees on top of the required expense for each college. Sending applications by mail (particularly if you know you are a procrastinator and will be doing so at the last minute) can also be quite costly. If this is a concern, investigate the options and their relative costs thoroughly before choosing a filing method.

■ *Overlap usage for other colleges:* Filling out each individual college's application will require you to complete similar yet not identical forms many times over. When using the college application service companies, however, you will need to enter basic pieces of data into the database only once. The services will then take your information and process it for inclusion on each college's application, saving you time and energy.

■ *Ease of filling out the forms:* Some application methods require more work than others. Each method varies in terms of the amount of information you must provide on the application form and the user-friendliness of the forms. Look at each method to decide for yourself if the directions are easy to understand, if there is enough space allotted for the answers, etc.

■ *Ease of filing the forms:* Again, some application methods require more energy than others. Investigate each option to ascertain the simplicity with which it allows you to transmit the application to the college's admissions staff. Sending applications to a college online (or sending your information to an application service, which will then process the material onto individual applications for you) is generally much less time-consuming than gathering various application pieces into an envelope, taking it to the post office, and then standing in line in order to send it off.

■ *Flexibility and adaptability:* Whereas you can always make a standard printed application conform to your own needs by adding sheets of paper or writing outside of the boxed areas provided, some of the online services will not allow users any additional space for answering questions. If this is a concern to you, you should investigate the flexibility of each option before choosing a filing method.

■ *Readability:* You want to be sure that what you submit to colleges is presented well (i.e., that it is neat, legible, and well-organized). If you fear that you will not do a good job filling in standard printed applications neatly, you should consider using one of the online or computer-generated application methods, so this will not be a potential problem.

ELECTRONIC APPLICATIONS

One of the hassles of applying to college is filling in the little boxes on the application forms. (Who still has an old typewriter around for completing them?) Most colleges now offer several good alternatives. First, some colleges allow you to download their applications from their admissions Web sites. To do so, you usually must use an application such as Adobe Acrobat Reader to view, fill out, and print the forms; these technology applications are generally available free of charge from sponsoring company Web sites. The college will let you know what technologies or computer applications you will need and where to find them. Second, some colleges allow you to apply online with secure Web forms or to order application software from a variety of services, such as CollegeLink, Embark (formerly known as College Edge), Apply, ExPAN, or Next Stop College. When using any of these services, you may still have to submit your transcript and letters of recommendation through the mail, the old-fashioned way. Colleges will give you detailed instructions in their admissions materials.

THE COMMON APPLICATION

The Common Application is exactly what its name suggests. It is a single application that is accepted by a substantial number of schools in lieu of their own applications. In other words, you can fill out this one application and use it to apply to a number of colleges. Each school's application materials will let you know whether that particular college accepts the Common Application or not.

Some colleges, such as Amherst, Wesleyan, and Harvard, use *only* the Common Application (often with a special supplement generated by the school), whereas others offer it as an option to their own individualized questionnaires. All schools that have their own applications but also accept the Common Application *claim* that they give the latter equal weight in the admissions process. But some admissions officers admit that they believe the most interested applicants go the extra mile and complete the college's own particular application. If a college is at the very top of your wish list, you are better off taking the extra time to fill in its own application forms—just in case. This is a strong signal to the college that it is important to you. Taking the time and effort to fill out a college's own application materials will show that you are not just "tacking it on" to your original target list of colleges and that you are genuinely serious about wanting to be admitted. If you choose to fill out the Common Application rather than a school's own form, *always* choose to complete any optional supplemental essays or questions provided.

WHAT ADMISSIONS OFFICERS SAY ABOUT THE COMMON APPLICATION

"We don't take the Common Application because it doesn't address our values as an institution. Our own written application is crucial to us in that it addresses the ideas of passion and initiative."

—*Marilee Jones, Dean of Admissions, Massachusetts Institute of Technology*

"Over half of our applicants use the Common Application—it doesn't make it any harder to get in using it."

—*Philip Smith, Dean of Admissions, Williams College*

"We don't take the Common Application. I'm not a subscriber to the approach behind it. We're not at all like many of our competitor schools, so it wouldn't make sense for us to evaluate our future students using the same questions and application materials that another college requests."

—*Richard Shaw, Dean of Undergraduate Admissions and Financial Aid, Yale University*

COMPLETING THE BASIC DATA FORMS

PREPARING THE MATERIALS AND PAYING ATTENTION TO THE BASICS

No matter what format you will use to fill out your applications, you should take the following initial step before doing anything else. Take a blank sheet of paper and use it as your master list for recording the stock information (name, address, Social Security number, parents' occupations, etc.) you will be asked to fill in on all the applications. Make sure when producing your master list that all your information is accurate and that spellings are correct—if you get it wrong here, it will be copied incorrectly onto everything you turn in. Have your parents check it over for accuracy—they most likely know the answers to these questions as well as (if not better than) you do. You will refer to this master list as you fill in each application form.

If you are filling out a standard printed paper application by hand or electric type, by all means make at least two copies of the blank form before beginning. (Similarly, if you are downloading an application from a Web site, print out a few copies of the form.) Making extra copies will ensure that if you make mistakes in the application process, you can use another clean page to start over again. Even after you have compiled your master list of data and basic information, you should make a rough draft on one of the copies to be sure that the information fits in the allotted space. If it does not, you will have to be creative in the positioning of your type or edit down the entry. If you are filling in an electronic application you do not need to worry about this step, because you can edit everything before sending it to the college or printing it out.

Remember when filling out your applications that neatness counts. An application's appearance is called "self-representation" in college admissions lingo, and it symbolizes an applicant's interest in the institution and care for the application process. A poorly planned presentation, misspellings, grammatical errors, or a failure to follow directions make admissions officers think that a student is little concerned about an application.

It is still acceptable to fill out the basic data portion on a paper application in your own handwriting, but if you take this route, be sure your handwriting is neat and legible. Never use pencil; use only black or blue pens, and stay away from ink that will smear. Longer answers and essays should be typed or computer-generated if at all possible, even if the application says that you can do them by hand. It is difficult for a tired admissions officer to read even the most legible handwriting for any extended period of time.

Be consistent. Use the same pen and color of ink, and do not mix handwriting styles. Your name should be written the same in each entry (and should be the same name that appears on your standardized test scores and transcripts). Do not mix "William" and "Bill," for example, even if you go by both names in your personal life. Refer to school names, clubs, and the like consistently. Readers will not know that your school often refers to the "Big and Little Sister Program" as "Sibs" if you do not explain.

ADMISSIONS OFFICERS TALK ABOUT THE IMPORTANCE OF THE WRITTEN APPLICATION'S APPEARANCE

"The seriousness with which the student has treated the written application is important. Misspellings and that kind of thing really hurt a student—because they show a lack of care, sloppiness."

—*Philip Smith, Dean of Admissions, Williams College*

"The written application's appearance—we call this 'self-representation'—can be pretty important. It can represent a student's interest in the institution and care for the application process."

—*Eric Kaplan, Director of Admissions, University of Pennsylvania*

"I call the super-glossy, professionally printed applications from kids of ad executives 'Plastic Fantastic'—this kind of thing doesn't help an ounce."

—*Philip Smith, Dean of Admissions, Williams College*

"Failure to follow directions is a real turn-off. If an applicant staples a resume of activities instead of answering our question about what activities are most important to him, we've got to make the assumption that he just doesn't care about this application very much."

—*Michael Goldberger, Director of Admissions, Brown University*

ANSWERING THE QUESTIONS

Most of the questions on the data forms are fairly straightforward. You do not have very many decisions to make before you get to the extracurricular activity and award lists or short answer portion of the application. Your answers on the basic data forms matter, so give some thought to what you are doing.

For example, if you are asked to state your intended major, be keen but reasonable. Do not write down the first interesting idea that pops into your head. Instead, remember your marketing and positioning strategy when answering questions about what you will study at the college. You will want your answers to the basic data sheet questions to remain consistent with your general profile. It is often a good idea to list a major that is consistent with your previous achievement and success in that field, whether you think it will be your actual field of study or not. (Refer back to Chapter 6 for more specific information on positioning yourself.)

If you are considering several possible majors, be strategic about which one to list. Remember that a school with a particularly good reputation in one area most likely maintains especially high standards with regard to applicants interested in that field. Thus, you might not want to divulge to Johns Hopkins, for example, that you are planning to follow premed studies if your excellent performance in English suggests you might help the school in its quest to beef up its humanities programs. (It is generally more difficult to get into Johns Hopkins as a premed student because of the strong reputation of its medical school.) You will not be held to what you state as your intended major on the application if you are admitted to the school, so you can always change your mind later on. If you know that a college has put a lot of effort into recruiting good students for its Anthropology major over the last few years and this response fits with the rest of the information you provide on the application, there is no reason you cannot write "Anthropology" even if you are not sure that is what you will major in. On the other hand, if you have never taken Greek or Latin and are not strong in languages in general, do not write "Classics" just because you know that the college is looking for Classics majors! You can only stretch as far as the underlying facts and supporting ideas will allow you to. Do not worry if you have no clue as to what major you want to follow. Admissions directors note that writing "Undecided" in no way harms your application.

WHAT ONE ADMISSIONS OFFICER HAS TO SAY ABOUT CITING "UNDECIDED" AS YOUR INTENDED MAJOR

"'Undecided' is the most commonly cited major of our successful applicants. It is perfectly okay for an applicant to tell us she does not know what her major will be."

—*Janet Lavin Rapelye, Dean of Admissions, Wellesley College*

COMPLETING EXTRACURRICULAR ACTIVITY AND OTHER LISTS

REMEMBER YOUR POSITIONING EFFORTS

When filling in lists of extracurricular activities, jobs, awards, and the like, be sure to read the college's directions. Most schools ask you to list activities from most important to least important (rather than chronologically). Although you should be honest, you also need to make sure that your answers support your marketing or positioning efforts. If in your heart you enjoy playing on the soccer team more than anything else, but have played for only a year, serve no supplemental roles on the team, and are not a very good player, then soccer should not be listed as your "most important" activity. If your long-term commitment to community service on an AIDS hotline is a crucial piece of your marketing effort, then this might be what you list first instead—even if you have suddenly found you have a lot more enthusiasm for the soccer team. Activities in which you have evidenced serious leadership (through your particular role or position) or time commitment (in terms of both length of involvement and hours of dedication per week or month) are generally those that should be listed first.

QUALITY OVER QUANTITY

Because quality over quantity is what counts when listing your activities, being part of 12 different groups or teams will not mean a thing to the admissions committee if your involvement in each is minimal. Admissions committees frown upon "serial joiners" who do not amount to much in any of their organizations. Instead you need to show that you play an important role in what you do.

Do not feel the need to mention every committee you are part of here, even if you think that the strength of your most important activities will make up for the weakness of the stragglers at the end of the list. Too long a list will merely dilute your message. Include things that might bear relevance to your positioning efforts (if you state that your intended major is physics and talk about it as being your favorite subject, you might want to tack on your involvement in the Science Club, even if the club's presence in your school is minimal)—but consider leaving off other minimal and unimportant involvements. There is no reason the college needs to know that you show up for French Club meetings once a month to get the *pain au chocolat* served or helped wash cars for an hour last spring to raise money for the school's foreign exchange program. By the time the reader gets to the bottom of your long list, he will have forgotten all about your first entry mentioning your impressive role as founder of the school's Writing Resource Center.

Grouping related activities together under a category heading, such as "Athletics" or "Environmental Efforts," can be very helpful for your marketing efforts. This is an especially beneficial way of listing items if you want to include many minimally important activities on your list, because it will allow you to create focus and order out of what would otherwise appear haphazard. If you choose this option, list the category headings (rather than the individual activities, each of which will now be included under one of your subject headings) in order of importance to you.

A student might, for example, first list "Literary Activities" (which would include her position as editor-in-chief of the school's fiction and poetry magazine, her attendance at a special by-invitation-only writing camp, and her job as a writing tutor at a neighborhood grade school), "Religious Activities," (which would include her position as an advisor for *bat mitzvah* candidates at her synagogue and her role as an editorial writer for a local Jewish community newspaper), and "Athletic Activities" (which would include her position as a coxswain on the women's crew team as well as a cocaptain position on a coed Ultimate Frisbee League team). Note that the position as contributor to the Jewish paper could be listed under "Literary Activities" or "Religious Activities." This particular student would be wise to include it in the latter in order to "create" another positioning tag for herself as someone dedicated to learning about and studying Judaism— her writing category is already full of substantial contributions without a fourth addition, while the single advisory role to *bat mitzvah* candidates alone would not merit an entire category devoted to religious endeavors.

Remember that anything and everything is fair game here, as long as it is an activity to which you devote time and effort. Do not forget to list volunteer work or community service; service as an acolyte or teacher at your church, temple, or religious group; and employment (if there is no separate space for its inclusion). Be sure to provide a brief (one phrase or sentence is usually sufficient) description of any activity, award, or program whose meaning will not be obvious to someone outside your school or community. For example, if you say you are a "member" of "The High Rollers" without elaborating, the admissions committee will never guess that you are the tenor in a six-man *a cappella* singing group chosen from over 200 auditioners in your high school each year. You will have lost a real opportunity to say something about your unique talent, your passions, and how you spend your time. Give meaning and detail to awards so that their significance is clear. Instead of simply listing "Recipient of the Firestone Award," which will not tell admissions officers anything, explain: "Recipient of the Firestone Award. Award given annually by faculty to one junior who exhibits highest commitment to improving the community. Cited for excellence in directing the High Hopes literacy program and running an environmental awareness colloquium on Earth Day."

WHAT ADMISSIONS OFFICERS SAY ABOUT
EXTRACURRICULAR ACTIVITY LISTS

"Serial joining is certainly not what we're after. We want to see that applicants have invested themselves in a few activities rather than joined a bunch of organizations on which they've had only a marginal impact."

—*Marlyn McGrath Lewis, Director of Admissions, Harvard University*

"The activity list is not a scorecard—one activity or work experience is not worth more points than another."

—*Dan Walls, Dean of Admissions, Emory University*

"All too often we see little boxes filled out but not enough explanation as to what those activities or jobs mean. This type of information is important—candidates need to provide as much supporting information as possible so that we can best understand their nonacademic side."
—*Richard Avitabile, Director of Admissions, New York University*

SPACE CONSIDERATIONS

Sometimes the space that colleges give you for making extracurricular lists and answering short-answer questions is not very generous. If you need to, you can certainly attach an extra sheet of paper where necessary or complete the entire answer on a separate attachment. Be sure that wherever you do this, you indicate in the space provided where the supplemental material can be found. Simply write, "Please see attached page, headed 'X'" or "Continued on attached page." In addition, head all attachments with appropriate titles or response numbers and always remember to put your name and Social Security number on every piece of paper attached, just in case they become separated from your application or fall out of your file.

RESPONDING TO SHORT-ANSWER QUESTIONS

When responding to short-answer questions (such as Brown's "Tell us about the academic areas which interest you most and your reasons for applying to Brown" or Stanford's "Jot a note to your future college roommate relating a personal experience that reveals something about you" or Dartmouth's "What was the highlight of your summer?"), take the time and make the effort to polish your material. These short-answer responses can be as important as the essay questions in helping readers gain a sense of who you are and how you compare to others in the admissions pool, so do not consider them lightly. Do not expect to write a quick response and be done with it. Write "drafts" just as you would for lengthy essays. Start working on them when you begin to work on the longer essays, put them down for a while before editing and revising them, and do not finalize your effort until you have all the pieces of an application planned. You will want to be sure that the various short and long answers are tightly integrated so that together they form the best application possible, with constant themes but no redundancies. See Chapters 11 and 12 for more detailed information on how to address various essay topics and how to write effective essays.

ADMISSIONS OFFICERS DISCUSS THE IMPORTANCE
OF THE SHORT-ANSWER QUESTIONS

"The short-answer questions on our application are fairly important. We can determine what a student's focus is from them, and gain insight into the student. They also give an applicant the opportunity to add insight to his academic profile."

—*Karl Furstenberg, Dean of Admissions and Financial Aid, Dartmouth College*

"Short-answer questions can be important—our current one, 'How would someone who knows you well describe you?' tells us a lot of personal information."

—*Eric Kaplan, Director of Admissions, the University of Pennsylvania*

SUPPLEMENTARY MATERIAL FOR SHOWCASING SPECIAL TALENT

Sending in supplementary material for evaluation is generally fine *if you are certain that your talent is significant and will help your chances of admission.* Most schools advise that you should not send in "ordinary" work such as writing samples, poetry, research papers, projects assigned at school, or computer programs you have designed. Stanford states in its admissions materials, "We would prefer that you and your recommenders describe your special academic pursuits and talents on our application forms." But if your work has won an award or you have reason to believe it demonstrates extraordinary talent, it will not hurt you to send it in.

Do not go overboard. Choose one piece that best showcases your talent rather than sending in multiple pieces. The admissions officers will only be exasperated and annoyed if they are buried underneath a stack of poetry you have composed between the ages of five and seventeen. The admissions committee and faculty evaluators from various academic and performing arts departments will not have the time, patience, or faith in your judgment to sort through a whole bunch of original music compositions or slides of your artwork. If you send them too many pieces, they may never even get to your best work in order to examine it. Do not expect the admissions officers and their faculty colleagues to sort through your material—you need to make their task as simple as possible and show that you have the sense and talent to spot your own best work. Furthermore, as mentioned in the section on activity lists, a large number of items usually dilutes what could have been a strong message.

Most schools list specific guidelines for submissions of extra materials to demonstrate fine arts (art, music, drama, or dance) talent. If you are an extraordinary artist, you should by all means submit slides or prints of your work (most schools specifically ask candidates to refrain from sending original work); an extraordinary musician, a recording of your work; an extraordinary actor or dancer, a videotape or resume of your training and performances. If you are an extraordinary athlete, it is sometimes appropriate to send in a videotape of your performance (with a data sheet describing your skills and record or a letter from a coach). (See the section for Recruited Athlete Applicants in Chapter 7.) It is likewise sometimes appropriate for you to send in evidence of original scientific research. Your supplemental material should showcase *your* talent, not someone else's. Do not, for example, send in recordings of your school's 40-piece orchestra simply because you are one of the percussionists. Nor should you send in anything of less than exceptional quality, just to prove that you are involved in an activity. This is a waste of the admissions committee's time and will only hurt your chances of admission, because it will show that what you view as impressive is merely mediocre when compared to the talent of students enrolled at the college.

You should follow each college's instructions when submitting supplemental admissions materials. Most colleges publish guidelines in their application instructions. If you are uncertain about a college's policy, call the admissions office and ask where to send your supplemental materials (you might be asked to pass them directly on to an appropriate faculty evaluator). Do not send anything directly to a department or faculty member unless you are told to do so by the school. Be sure to label every piece you send in with your name, Social Security number, and a brief description of the material. (For example, "Samantha Regis. SSN 287-00-0555. Performance as Laura in Tennessee Williams's *The Glass Menagerie.* Trinity High School. April, 1999.")

WHAT ADMISSIONS OFFICERS SAY ABOUT APPLICANTS WITH SPECIAL TALENTS

"I spend a few days with the head of the music department each fall or winter. He looks over the docket of talented musicians in the candidate pool, rates all the recordings he receives from them, and tells me what the music department needs to fill the groups in the upcoming year—oboes, violins, whatever. This is how we in the admissions department are alerted to what kind of talent warrants our special attention."

—*Philip Smith, Dean of Admissions, Williams College*

"We ask that candidates send their supplemental materials to the admissions department first so that we can pass them on to the appropriate faculty members for professional assessment."

—*Katie Fretwell, Director of Admissions, Amherst College*

"We receive a lot of videotapes, Web page locations, and CD-ROMs from applicants—many of which just aren't necessary or helpful. It's true that the basic application is geared toward people who can articulate what they need to say in *writing*, which may not seem particularly fair to those who can't express their talents well in this medium. But it's really only appropriate for those with *extra special* talents to be sending us videos or cassettes."

—Eric J. Furda, Director of Undergraduate Admissions, Columbia University

"We try to discourage kids from sending us too much material for their files. We try to give everything in the file at least a cursory look, though, and we send special talent contributions to the appropriate faculty members for evaluation."

—Richard Shaw, Dean of Undergraduate Admissions and Financial Aid, Yale University

"We're a little different in how we deal with special talents here. I recommend that students applying here correspond via E-mail or phone with an appropriate person on the faculty. Faculty on campus can become real advocates for students in admissions."

—Dan Walls, Dean of Admissions, Emory University

ADMISSIONS GIMMICKS

It is difficult to cite a hard-and-fast rule about admissions gimmicks and quirky efforts at catching the attention of the admissions committee. The problem is that over the years, the admissions committees have seen it all: chocolate cakes with "Admit Me!" messages on them, blow-up life preservers that read "Keep Me Afloat!" from applicants on the waitlist, CD-ROMs featuring interviews with a student's parent or best friend talking about what a major contribution he would make to the school. Most schools are eager to publicize that there is nothing impressive about admissions packets that look as if the annual advertising budget for Coca-Cola has been spent producing them. Glossy, lavishly produced admissions materials do absolutely nothing to help a candidate's chances of success. Do not bother making your application stand out aesthetically. This is not what counts in college admissions. The effort will only make it seem as if you do not stand out enough on your own merits and are trying all too hard to make up for that fact.

When there is real creativity at work *and* the admissions folks have never seen the idea used before *and* the effort contains something more valuable and meaningful than just a clever "Please admit me" message, a quirky gimmick *might* work. It will never change the committee's mind about a candidate who would otherwise be rejected, but it can push a borderline applicant into good favor or make an already "in" candidate especially memorable. The problem here is that most efforts, although they may seem brilliant and original to you, are tired and stale to the admissions teams.

A reasonable rule of thumb is: If the gimmick actually says nothing more than "I am trying to be creative to catch your attention so that you will let me in," do not use it. If, on the other hand, it harbors within its creativity a valuable message about you, it might work. For example, a candidate to Dartmouth worked as a painter at an original fabric design company. She asked the owner of the company to write her a "recommendation" on the back of one of her originally designed shirts. The message praised the applicant's responsibilities as one of the young entrepreneurs at the company. More important, it noted her talent and craft, saying that she would be a wonderful ice sculptor at Dartmouth's Winter Carnival in the coming years. It was most likely not this gimmick that got the candidate admitted to the school, but it made sense as an admissions effort because it did more than just show the applicant's ability to think of something cute. It showcased a talent and made a highly specific connection between the candidate and the college.

AN ADMISSIONS OFFICER OFFERS HIS OPINION ON GIMMICKS

"A gimmick is a gimmick. We've seen it all. Every year we get someone who sends us chocolate chip cookies with a note—we eat the cookies, but these things are never factored into our admissions decisions."

—*John Hanson, Director of Admissions, Middlebury College*

THE FINAL STRETCH

As with every other piece of your application, you should have a third party read your data and short-answer sheets before sending them off. The data sheets and short-answer questions need to be examined carefully in order to catch mistakes of all sorts (typos, grammar problems, spelling errors, inconsistencies) and to ensure that everything is readily comprehensible. Before slipping all the pieces into an envelope to send to the admissions committee, read over the college's application checklist to be sure that you have included everything and not misplaced anything. Make copies of everything before sealing your envelope. If you are sending in a diskette or applying online, save all of your work on your computer's hard drive and print out hard (paper) copies as well.

Get the application in on time. Some books will tell you that colleges receive so many applications near their deadlines that they cannot possibly know which reach the campus on time and which are a few days late. But at some schools, administrative assistants do record arrival dates on packages or make a note on folders that arrive late. Though a few days of tardiness will probably not matter, you should not risk your college career on a silly mistake. You will only feel relief that much sooner if you send your materials in on time.

BASIC RULES FOR COMPLETING THE WRITTEN APPLICATION

1. Neatness counts.
2. Be consistent in your positioning efforts, descriptions, and style.
3. Make copies of all blank forms before filling them in.
4. Follow each school's directions carefully.
5. Remember your positioning effort—it is important not only in writing essays but also in completing data sheets and short-answer responses.
6. Treat short-answer responses seriously. Make drafts and plan out your entire application before finalizing any answers.
7. Make copies of all pieces of your application before sending it in.
8. Get the application in on time.

Understanding the Key Essay Topics

— KEY POINTS —

Familiarize yourself with the topics you need to address

■

You will be evaluated on your choice of topic as well as your writing style

■

Be leery of the approaches that are all too common

■

Be sure to use the essays to further your positioning effort

INTRODUCTION

Yale explains the importance of the college application essays in the following way: "There are limitations to what grades, scores, and recommendations can tell us about any applicant. Please use the following two essays to help us learn more about you. We hope that in writing these essays you will reflect on your attitudes, your values, and your perception of yourself." That last line sums up well what most colleges are looking for when they read your essays. They do not want regurgitations of information about your academics or awards that can be found elsewhere in the application. They are seeking to discover more about *who you are.*

The essay portion of the written application offers you the chance to show schools who you really are as well as to demonstrate your writing ability. The essays will, after all, be evaluated for both content and writing style. Take advantage of this opportunity and use it to further your marketing or positioning efforts. Do not write what you think the committee wants to hear or go for a "safe" topic—such approaches usually produce tired and stale essays that sound like thousands of others the committee has read. You need instead to tell your audience something special and particular about you. You do not have to come across as the smartest, most talented, or most glamorous applicant in doing so—an essay about looking for shells on a beach with your little brother can be as telling and enlightening as one discussing an immigration journey from Guatemala to the United States.

It is crucial that you use the essay portion of the written application—the first of the three marketing vehicles available to you in the application process—to do things that the other two vehicles cannot. Recommenders can show only a part of who you are, since most recommendation writers are teachers or other adults who know you in a single context. Similarly, interviews are not under your control to the same extent that essays are. Essays can be created over time with great thought poured into them. They can be rewritten and reexamined to make sure that "the real you" (as well as "the best you") is presented.

This is your chance to choose which parts of your past and yourself to highlight, and to determine how people should view them. This is also a precious opportunity to color the reader's interpretation of all the objective criteria included elsewhere in the application. Your essays should thus present a clear picture of who you are, but they do not need to tell all. Sketching in the critical main points with appropriate stories full of detail—rather than covering every possible point with little supporting narrative—is always the best solution. Whenever possible, try to tell a story rather than write an essay. The task will seem lighter, more enjoyable, and easier to accomplish.

Furthermore, visualize your audience in a way that encourages you to be forthright and creative rather than in a way that frightens you into creating something commonplace and cliché. Imagine that a pleasant man or woman is sitting down with a cup of hot tea in an easy chair examining your essays, hoping to find something that distinguishes you and makes it possible to know you, even without having met you. That more accurately describes how your audience will approach your essays than the nightmarish visions (perhaps a stern librarian-like figure with reading glasses peering down at your application with disdain) you have likely conjured up for yourself. The admissions officers want to find reasons to admit you rather than reasons to keep you out of their college. They bring a feeling of hope and a genuine love and understanding of students your age to the table when sitting down to read your application materials.

This chapter analyzes the most common essay questions, including the "free-for-all" Common Application question. The next chapter will show you how to go about writing the essays. There are also fifty examples of actual student essays to the top colleges in the back of this book, in the section entitled "Application Essay Examples."

THE COMMON APPLICATION QUESTION

The Common Application asks students to submit a personal statement of 250 to 500 words on a topic of their choice or on one of three suggested topics.

QUESTION:
Please write an essay on a topic of your choice or on one of the options listed below.

(1) Evaluate a significant experience or achievement that has special meaning to you.

(2) Discuss some issue of personal, local, national, or international concern and its importance to you.

(3) Indicate a person who has had a significant influence on you, and describe that influence.

WHY THE QUESTION IS ASKED

The Common Application question, like the essay questions on many schools' own individual applications, is open-ended. Even the three topical suggestions offered are exceedingly vague. The colleges are being deliberately inexplicit because they want you to provide them with what they call a "personal statement." They want you to write something that best speaks to who *you* are, something that will allow readers to know and want to admit you to their colleges. All college applicants are different, and therefore most college application questions are fairly broad, allowing each responder ample opportunity to develop an essay that is personal and meaningful.

Thus, vague questions do not and should not command vague answers. Your responses to the Common Application question and others like it should be as detailed and specific as possible, offering plenty of poignant and unique information about you. Essays having a narrow focus are nearly always more effective than those that are broadly construed, even when answering a question that lacks specificity.

Since all three of the topics suggested in the Common Application show up frequently in colleges' own applications, we treat each one separately in the pages to follow, under "Frequently Asked Essay Questions." The three Common Application topics are covered first.

FREQUENTLY ASKED ESSAY QUESTIONS

QUESTION:
Evaluate a significant experience or achievement that has special meaning to you.

WHY THE QUESTION IS ASKED

One's personal character and outlook on life are often shaped by pivotal experiences. Such experiences can make for interesting narratives, if retold convincingly. Admissions committees are hoping that applicants are capable of the kind of self-reflection required to think back on their lives and identify meaningful moments. Being able to do so indicates maturity as well as self-knowledge. Admissions officers also ask this question because they want to see what your values are. By identifying something that has had meaning for you, you are pointing to a personal value.

You have several major options in answering this question. For example, you can answer it by identifying any one of the following: an epiphany, an immersion in the unknown, an achievement, a leadership experience, a failure, or an ethical dilemma. We will examine each of these approaches individually in the pages to follow. Note that the first two options are covered because they are not discussed in detail in the context of other essay questions. The latter four approaches (an achievement, a leadership experience, a failure, and an ethical dilemma) are discussed within the context of other frequently asked questions.

AN EPIPHANY: THE TYPICAL APPROACH

Describing a life-changing experience or realization can be an effective way to get at one's character and current state of being. The problem with this approach is that describing an epiphany can often sound contrived and theatrical rather than honest and forthright. The applicant who describes a single moment in his life that suddenly and unexpectedly changed his entire course or perspective on something is seldom believable. The story may seem too convenient or dramatic to be true. Applicants who describe a single event as being life-changing without backing up the statement with plenty of convincing detail risk appearing naive and childish, if not sycophantic and dishonest.

A BETTER APPROACH

An epiphany can be an ideal way to bring up the story or anecdote you have otherwise been unable to fit into your application, if you go about it the right way. Treat the experience intelligently but lightly. Keep it in perspective. Do not resort to dramatic overtures or exaggerations of impact. A single event rarely changes everything all at once. Do not, for example, claim that as an affluent white you never realized what it is like to be a minority in this country until reading Richard Wright's *Black Boy,* after which you forged an identity with the black man, thus changing your outlook on social injustice. A book can change lives, but it seldom does so on its own or all in one sweep. Instead, you might discuss how the initial reading of the book got you thinking about race relations; as you discussed what you read with others your ideas solidified further, eventually allowing you to approach your relations with minorities differently; you now continue to examine your new perspectives through other readings and activities to educate yourself further.

ADVANTAGES OF THIS APPROACH

Following our approach to describing an epiphany can allow you to use a poignant yet perhaps not particularly exciting event (such as reading a book or taking care of an ailing parent) to make yourself better understood. Our approach allows you to use such an event without seeming naive or dishonest, or tending toward exaggeration. Such a story can make you more interesting as well as help show what your real values are.

AN IMMERSION IN THE UNKNOWN: THE TYPICAL APPROACH

An immersion in the unknown is a convenient way for applicants to answer a question about a significant life-altering experience while also revealing what makes them unique and different. It often allows applicants to tell compelling or humorous stories. This topic is ideal for students who have lived, studied, or traveled in foreign countries; conducted community service projects in environments previously unfamiliar to them (such as the inner city); or experienced things that many others have not, such as undergoing serious and potentially traumatic surgery or working on a vineyard for a summer.

The problem here is that many applicants *think* that they have done or discovered something really special, yet the written effort conveys something far from unique. Too many students talk about how they "learned how to appreciate other cultures" by traveling or "learned to value human life and not take things for granted" after having experienced serious health risks. Such statements are trite and unsophisticated. (Of course you learned to appreciate other cultures while traveling around the world! Of course you value your life more after nearly losing it!) This kind of essay will seem superficial if you cannot discuss your immersion in the unknown with particular detail and zeal, and make it unique to you, not like everyone else's immersion in foreign territories.

A BETTER APPROACH

Use this topic only if you can penetrate it and go beyond the superficiality of "experiencing something new." We all experience new things all the time, but that does not mean they are worth discussion in a college essay. Talking about the new and unexpected situations is meaningless if you cannot bring real insight to the topic.

THE ADVANTAGES OF THIS APPROACH

Discussing an immersion in the unknown can help show several appealing characteristics. First, it allows you to demonstrate that you are adventurous, curious, and willing to take calculated risks. Colleges like these traits and consider it important that some portion of their incoming classes exhibit such adventurous personalities. As mentioned earlier, describing this kind of situation often lends itself to offering bizarre, unique, or humorous details that can make a story particularly compelling. Stories about new and different experiences may also help candidates distinguish themselves from others and show what new perspectives they may bring to the incoming class.

QUESTION:

Discuss an issue of local, national, or international concern that is important to you.

WHY THE QUESTION IS ASKED

Colleges want students who contemplate big life questions and who tackle important issues plaguing society. They want to know that the students they admit are well informed about the world around them, and that they will contribute significantly to answering questions and solving problems in their future careers. This question is designed to find out whether you have thought about issues beyond the scope of your own daily life, and whether or not you have the ability to discuss and analyze a complex topic in a sophisticated fashion.

THE TYPICAL APPROACH

Most people discuss the most headline-grabbing item they can think of. In recent years, these subjects would have included global warming or ethnic cleansing of any one of numerous groups of people around the world. Most applicants' discussions, moreover, tend to resemble the headlines of tabloid newspapers: "Global disaster forecasted! Major changes needed immediately!" No research informs the essay and it is full of broad moral imperatives. The other bad approach—all too often seen as well—is that of too obviously cribbing from a recent lead story in an issue of *Newsweek* or some other news magazine. This makes it seem as if you have no original opinions and can only regurgitate common ideas on the matter. Both of these mistaken approaches also usually fail in that they provide no clue as to why the topic is of importance to the applicant, thus not helping to develop her profile or make a case for her admission.

A BETTER APPROACH

If you realistically have firm beliefs to discuss, especially if they at all relate to your positioning effort, do so. For example, if you are selling yourself as both a feminist and a future doctor, you might want to discuss the need to introduce better women's reproductive health clinics as part of a greater health care movement, either here in the United States or elsewhere in the world. Most applicants do not have such a clear-cut opinion on any issue. Instead, they have some not overly informed opinions about a handful of topics, any one of which could fit well here. If this is your case, choose the topic that shows you to the best advantage. It should enable you to express sensible but not blindingly obvious ideas, enhance your positioning, show you to be intelligent and analytical, and demonstrate your interest in societal matters. You may not be able to satisfy all those criteria at once, but aim for as many as possible.

Does it matter what topic you choose? Yes and no. It matters that you choose something that strikes admissions committees as being quite important—at least after you have explained why it is important. But what is likely to matter more is how you discuss the topic you have chosen.

When discussing any topic, remember to follow the usual rules: Be as specific as possible, be upbeat rather than defeatist (avoid wallowing in the demise of a certain species of bullfrog, for example). Instead of looking at the negative side of change, try to look at the issue from all angles. Analyze the opportunities and challenges that might follow in the wake of change, whether it is negative or positive. You should be able to give a sophisticated treatment of your subject, but this is likely to be the case only after you have done some reading. Look at issues of respectable magazines or books to find out more about the issue and develop a serious position on it.

ADVANTAGES OF THIS APPROACH

This topic is sometimes a godsend in that it can allow you to further your own positioning efforts while ostensibly discussing an abstract concept. You can show, for example, that you have a real desire and need to study in a top political science department by discussing your views on a matter and relating them to your future goals in the field of politics or international relations. At the same time, you will show that you have given real thought to a complex matter. If your objective criteria fail to indicate superb intelligence and analytical skills, this is a golden opportunity to set the record straight and show your mental capacities. A great essay will not change the objective data, but it can convince potentially skeptical admissions officers that you are on the right track and worth a spot in the class.

QUESTION:
What one person has had the most significant influence on your life?

WHY THE QUESTION IS ASKED

This question allows colleges to discover more about your personality, your values, and how you interact with others. Colleges like to know that the students who will populate their campuses are capable of sustaining meaningful relationships, working with other people, and learning not only inside the classroom but also outside of the classroom, through life experiences.

THE TYPICAL APPROACH

Many candidates use relationships with others in order to demonstrate their personal values or show an important life lesson they learned through interacting with someone else. The problem here, especially for those who choose to discuss a relationship with a mentor or a special relative such as a grandparent, is that writers often end up discussing the other person more than themselves. Candidates often write entire essays praising and eulogizing those they admire, but end up failing to show anything important about themselves in the essay.

A BETTER APPROACH

Remember that *you* are applying to college—not your grandfather, your older sister, or your sixth-grade teacher. When answering any question on a college application, even about a relationship, the focus of the discussion should always be on yourself. That is not to say that you should take a self-important or cocky attitude, shouting "me, me, me" in all your discussions of interactions with others. However, the impact of all activities and situations on you must be at the center of everything that you write. It is imperative that you use the other person as a foil in this case—the person should ideally reflect what is most impressive about *your* interests, *your* values, *your* achievements, and *your* goals.

ADVANTAGES OF THIS APPROACH

Discussing a relationship with someone else does several good things for you. It shows that you are mature and receptive to the knowledge and input of others. You can also demonstrate that you find relevance in the lives of others and consider learning from interactions with people (even people who are not your teachers)—a crucial component to one's life education.

QUESTION:
What is your greatest achievement?
Why do you consider this an achievement?

WHY THE QUESTION IS ASKED

This question allows colleges to ascertain how impressive you are and how you might contribute to the life of the college, based on your past performances. The question also allows colleges to learn more about you and your values insofar as you must explain why you consider something to be a substantial accomplishment.

THE TYPICAL APPROACH

Most applicants use the whole of the essay to demonstrate that their accomplishments are impressive. They focus on their accomplishments and not on themselves. The achievements discussed by most applicants also tend to be things like making the high school basketball team or being elected to student council, which can be learned by taking a brief look at the applicant's data sheets. Another mistaken tendency is to list a string of accomplishments rather than to explain one accomplishment (or two, if the question asks for "accomplishments") in detail.

A BETTER APPROACH

This question obviously gives you the chance to "toot your own horn." You can brag a bit about what you have accomplished in life, but what is more important is that you put your own spin on what you have done. A particular accomplishment is all the more impressive when you explain the obstacles you have had to overcome to succeed. You should be sure to give the full context of your accomplishment so that its importance comes to life for your readers.

Some accomplishments are of obvious significance. Other accomplishments are much more personal in nature. It is perfectly fine to discuss an achievement that may not be obvious to others. For example, if you stuttered as a youth and finally ended your stuttering during high school, after resorting to a strenuous program of speech therapy, this might be an extremely significant event for you personally. You have probably done things that have had more impact upon the rest of the world, but for you this accomplishment might loom larger. Besides, it is not something that is mentioned on your data sheets, so the essay can add new information and a whole new dimension to your application. You will want to talk about your achievement as an example of your determination and desire to improve yourself, as well as describe all the work that went into achieving your goal of stutter-free speech. Even if you just discuss accomplishments of a more public nature that can be acknowledged from other parts of your application, be sure to personalize them in such a way that they take on greater significance than they would as one item in a list.

The first step is to determine which accomplishment you will discuss. Choose one that furthers your positioning effort, highlights something unusual, and is interesting for admissions committees to read about. An achievement in which you can discuss your values (as part of the explanation of its importance to you) will also benefit you. You may also want to choose an example that meets one of these criteria:

- You had to overcome major obstacles, showing real determination in doing so.
- You learned more about yourself.
- You used real initiative, perhaps by pushing a bureaucracy to respond or bypassing one altogether.
- Your success was unexpected.
- You worked extremely hard toward a clear goal.
- Your impact can be seen clearly.

Go into sufficient detail to bring events to life, but do not stop there. Discuss why you consider this a substantial achievement, why you take pride in it, and what you learned from it. Did you change and grow as a result? Did you find that you approached other matters differently after the event?

ADVANTAGES OF THIS APPROACH

This question gives you a lot of latitude. Most particularly, it gives you an opportunity to discuss matters that are unlikely to be listed on your data sheets or mentioned by your recommenders. Using it to show more of the real you will help you to avoid the usual problems people create for themselves in developing this essay. Following our advice will allow you to show you have overcome challenges that matter to you, achieved something useful in your life, and are prepared to achieve greater things in the future.

QUESTION:

What was your most significant leadership experience?

WHY THE QUESTION IS ASKED

Top schools expect to produce society's future leaders in all fields. They are looking for applicants who have already distinguished themselves as leaders, since past performance is the best indicator of future performance. Learning about your leadership skills also allows a committee to see how you interact with others, whether or not you are effective in group situations, and how determined you are to succeed.

THE TYPICAL APPROACH

All too often, applicants discuss being part of a group that achieved something noteworthy without making it clear that they themselves were leaders in the effort. Other applicants, seeing this question as similar to the substantial accomplishment essay, focus on the end result or achievement rather than homing in on the leadership aspect. Other applicants discuss roles in which they were designated as leaders through a title (such as Captain or Editor-in-Chief) but then fail to show how they approached the role and that they did a good job with the task. Claiming a leadership title and doing something spectacular with that role are two different things.

A BETTER APPROACH

This question is indeed deceptively similar to the substantial accomplishment essay. The substantial accomplishment essay, as noted earlier, asks you to describe an achievement (and often what it means to you). The leadership essay, on the other hand, is not looking so much for an achievement as it is for an understanding of how you led an effort to reach the end result. In other words, your emphasis should be on your leadership of other people rather than on the accomplishment itself.

To write this essay, you must understand what leadership is. One obvious example is managing or guiding others in a group effort when you have a formal title (such as Captain or Editor-in-Chief) that identifies you as the leader. Less obvious examples involve pushing or inspiring nonsubordinates to do what you want done. This can be done through leading by example, relying on your influence as a perceived expert in something, relying on others' respect for you, influencing through moral suasion, or influencing by personal friendship. Whether your leadership was formalized or influence-based, you should describe your methodology in depth. What was your approach and what strategy did you employ? Why? You may not have been deliberate or extremely self-aware in your actions, of course, in which case you might wish to discuss what you learned from the effort and how you would use those same newly found leadership skills again. What problems did you confront? Would other strategies have worked? Have you developed a philosophy of leadership as a result of the incident?

Your leadership qualities should be those of a mature adult leader: thoughtfulness, sensitivity to others, empathy, determination, valuing other people's input, the ability to influence or communicate with different kinds of people, the ability to integrate disparate parts into a unified whole, honesty, and personal integrity.

ADVANTAGES OF THIS APPROACH

Viewing this question as concerning your understanding of leadership, and the ways in which you yourself lead, will result in an essay with the appropriate focus. This will help you to demonstrate your method of approaching and resolving leadership issues, which is what concerns the admissions committee. If you show yourself to be aware of the leadership issues inherent in your situation, and include some suitable comments regarding what did or did not work, and why, you will have the core of a good essay. Furthermore, the piece will show off one of your most valuable and positive traits.

QUESTION:
What has been your greatest failure?
Why do you consider it a failure and what did you learn from it?

WHY THE QUESTION IS ASKED

This question is basically asking whether or not you are mature enough to admit that you make mistakes and whether or not you can extract meaning from past errors. The question also helps admissions officers to see how you have changed and grown in recent years.

THE TYPICAL APPROACH

Many admissions officers like to see applicants write about failures or weaknesses, as long as they are treated in the right way. If you choose to discuss a failure voluntarily without being required to do so (for example, if you talk about a failure in your answer to the first topic suggestion in the Common Application), you must be especially certain that the story is going to work for you. After all, if it does not do a superb job of showing positive qualities and expressing thoughtfulness, then you might as well avoid it altogether and discuss an achievement, if given the choice.

The problem is that many applicants write about failures without being able to show how the event has turned out to be helpful in their growth or development. Applicants often talk about failures by simply retelling the story of what happened. They focus more on the mistake than on what they learned from it. The typical applicant does himself a disservice by not analyzing *why* he failed, what he could have done differently, what he learned, and how he would approach the situation if faced with it again. Other applicants make fools of themselves by discussing trivial failures that are incapable of instilling life-changing thoughts or feelings, such as forgetting to mow the lawn or arriving late to a test. (Failing to find the perfect prom dress would also constitute a poor choice in topics!) This merely shows the admissions committee that you are immature, hoping to convince them you have never had any greater failures in life—something they know is not true.

A BETTER APPROACH

Whenever you are discussing a failure, but especially when doing so voluntarily rather than because you are explicitly asked to talk about one, you must use an experience that you can show has affected your subsequent actions and decisions. It should be a failure to which you can attach a story of another incident to demonstrate that, when presented with a similar situation a second time, you succeeded. One implication of this is that the failure probably should be something that occurred not last week but at least a year ago. We generally need time to learn from our mistakes.

Do not belabor a description of the failure itself. Although details always make a story more interesting, in this case too much detail might make you look bad. Remember that it is what you learned from the failure that is critical here, not the situation itself. Consider what you learned from the experience concerning yourself, your education, your work ethic, your attitudes, your opinions, or your relationships.

ADVANTAGES OF THIS APPROACH

A sensible approach to the statement about a failure places an emphasis on your development. We learn more from our mistakes than we do from our successes, which is why it is legitimate to discuss failures, even when not asked to do so. A willingness to admit mistakes is one sign that you have reached adulthood. It is also the hallmark of someone who will benefit from higher education at a top college. Even the best students are sure to suffer some failures at a demanding college—admissions officers like to know that admitted students are prepared to handle such challenges and can benefit from mistakes rather than being sunk by them. Furthermore, addressing a failure shows that you are honest and a person of good character.

QUESTION:
Describe an ethical dilemma you faced and how you resolved it.

WHY THE QUESTION IS ASKED

Educational institutions are often concerned with ethics. Colleges are, after all, attempting to educate their students not only in academic subjects, but also in life itself. Thus, this question is often a sincere attempt to understand your moral grounding. The question helps admissions officers evaluate your level of honesty and maturity. Sometimes, though, the question is less about ethics and more about finding out what makes you tick. Readers can learn more about your thought processes and how you relate to the greater world around you through your answer to this question.

THE TYPICAL APPROACH

Most people have trouble finding something to discuss here, so they end up choosing something trivial. In discussing it, they think that a question about ethics must call for a holier-than-thou stance, so they end up sounding disingenuous, or like the leaders of a New Age conference. Another common mistake, which could single-handedly kill your chances of admission, is to describe a situation in which you made a very serious moral transgression or in which you seriously considered doing something terribly wrong. For example, you would not want to discuss stealing of any kind or the serious consideration you gave to helping your friend blow up the principal's office.

A BETTER APPROACH

The toughest part of this essay is finding something suitable to discuss. Here are some possible topics:

- *Personal gain versus community benefits.* Discuss a situation in which you had to choose between gaining a reward for yourself versus helping a group achieve a reward. For example, perhaps you once agreed to work with four classmates in a science competition that requires teams of five. After two weeks working on the project, with only one more week left to go until judgment day, a different group asks you to join them, and you believe its project has a much better chance of winning first prize. You need to decide whether to honor your commitment to the first group (who will not have enough time to find a fifth partner if you bail out on them, thus losing a shot at the prize) or whether to sign on with the second group, in which case you might win big.

- *Loyalty to a friend versus loyalty to an ideal.* College admissions officers value loyalty to friends, but they also want students of high moral integrity. It is therefore appropriate to discuss a situation in which a good friend asked that you lower your moral standards in order to help him or her out. For example, perhaps you see your best friend, who has trouble in math classes but is desperate to do well in order to attend a good college, cheating on a geometry exam. You need to decide whether to remain loyal to your friend but act against your school's honor policy, which requires students to report one another when transgressions occur, or to uphold the honor policy and betray your friend.

- *An opportunity to take advantage of someone else's weakness.* You can discuss a situation in which you stood to gain from someone else's problem, lack of knowledge, or lack of ability. Perhaps, for example, a wealthy customer of your landscaping company asks to purchase a fertilizer treatment that you know is bad for the long-term health of her lawn. You need to decide whether to sell the product to an unsuspecting customer who is willing to fork over a lot of money, at a substantial profit for your company (and yourself), or to tell the customer the truth about the product, thus sacrificing financial gain.

Remember that the fact that the situation you describe is a "dilemma" means that, although you may have eventually managed it well, there was no clear-cut answer or surefire way to handle it. You cannot describe a situation and then claim that you never hesitated about doing the right thing, because then it could not be described as a dilemma. You want to show that there was a dilemma, at least on a surface level. You will probably want to show that you explored and investigated the nature of the problem, turning it around in your mind, since you were no doubt reluctant to make a snap decision when it appeared that any decision would have generated adverse consequences. You will want to show that you explored every option and did your best to minimize the negative impact, whatever your decision.

The tone of this essay must be just right. If you sound like an innocent 7-year-old who believes it is always wrong to lie, you will not seem believable. You will also not appear tough enough to handle the real world, where people constantly have to make hard decisions with rotten consequences for some. On the other hand, if you sound like a Machiavelli, for whom the only calculus depends upon personal advantage and for whom the potential suffering of other people is irrelevant, you will be rejected as a moral monster. You need to be somewhere in the middle, someone who recognizes that the world and the decisions it requires are seldom perfect, but that it is appropriate to try to minimize adverse consequences as best one can.

ADVANTAGES OF THIS APPROACH

It is critical to find a subject that you can get your teeth into. Our essay examples at the back of the book help you find such a subject, one with layers of detail and dilemma. If you go into depth in exploring your subject, without sounding like a naive child or a totally cynical manipulator, turn it about and examine it from different angles, and weigh the various options thoughtfully, you will show yourself to be top college material.

QUESTION:
What will your fellow students learn from you as a result of your experiences, background, values, or personality?

WHY THE QUESTION IS ASKED

Schools want to know that if they admit you, you will bring something special to the campus. They want to know that you will benefit from the college, but they also want to be assured that the college will benefit from you. Colleges are concerned about their "composites," or the composition of the class as a whole, and similarly about ensuring that each class admitted features a good mix of skills, strengths, backgrounds, and experiences. This essay is your chance to show what you bring to the mix.

THE TYPICAL APPROACH

The typical applicant writes an essay that is dull and dry, expressing basic ideas that neither show how he is unique nor convince admissions officers that he will help peers to develop in any way. First, he claims that he is a very hard worker. Then he says that he will try to contribute to class discussions and that his strengths in a certain academic area will enhance the experiences of others in his classes. Last, he mentions that he is a friendly guy who gets along with everyone, someone whose company will be enjoyed by one and all.

A BETTER APPROACH

The main goal here is to show that you would add something valuable and unique to the operations of the school. You can emphasize characteristics that are important in or out of class. The usual things that applicants discuss (personal characteristics such as humor or determination, for example) are worth noting in passing, but the focus should be on something more compelling. Unusual items worthy of focus include:

- *A different perspective.* If you are from an unusual part of the world (or country) as compared to most of the student body, discuss this. Perhaps you have had an unusual personal history (for example, if you grew up sitting in the front of a taxi cab with your dad while he drove the streets of Chicago).

- *Knowledge of an unusual academic field.* If you have done extensive research in quantum physics or have studied African cultures, you can explain how your expertise will benefit others in the classes and activities you intend to pursue.

- *Specialized outside interests.* A person who has started her own business, has published her written work in a national magazine, or is a superb jazz musician can discuss how her experience or knowledge will be of use to others on campus.

- *Special personal qualities.* It is difficult to convince admissions committees that you possess certain important qualities, such as the ability to listen well to help others resolve problems, to a degree that surpasses other applicants. If, however, you have stories, examples, or anecdotes to back up your claims of superlative personal characteristics, you can by all means emphasize these in your essay.

The last component of the essay is to show that you are the kind of person who will share knowledge with others at school. You should try to show that you are accustomed to interacting and exchanging ideas with others. Demonstrate that you are able to work well on a team, within an organization, or with a project group. The best way to validate that the traits you have mentioned will have value for your future college classmates is to demonstrate that you have already influenced peers at high school or in your community.

ADVANTAGES OF THIS APPROACH

Knowledge of what distinguishes you from other applicants is crucial in order for an admissions officer to want you over other applicants. You can use this question to appeal to schools to diversify their student bodies by accepting you into the class.

QUESTION:

Describe the impact that a secondary school teacher has had upon your intellectual development.

WHY THE QUESTION IS ASKED

Colleges, especially small ones where students have the opportunity to receive much individualized attention from professors, want to know that you will take advantage of all the learning resources made available to you. They want to know that you appreciate your teachers, interact with them on a regular basis, feel grateful for all that they have done for you, and are prepared to forge meaningful relationships with faculty at the college you choose to attend.

THE TYPICAL APPROACH

Many applicants start with a trite, "My favorite teacher is …" While it is fine if the teacher you discuss here happens to be your favorite, the more important focus should be on the impact a teacher has had upon you. This essay can just as well be on a teacher whom you once disliked, especially for his challenging nature, but then grew to respect because of the way in which he forced you to expand your mind. The other mistaken course that many applicants take is simply to list all the wonderful things the teacher has taught them without explaining *how* they have been taught, the *methods* that the teacher uses, or in *what way* he has been so effective. Other applicants write about a teacher whom they value because they particularly enjoy the subject matter learned in the class. While intellectual content can certainly be a part of this essay, the emphasis should be on the teaching skills and methods and your interaction with the teacher.

A BETTER APPROACH

First remember that this essay does not have to involve the nicest teacher in your school, or the one who has given you the best grades, or even the best faculty member. It should focus on someone whose unusual teaching habits or philosophy of education has changed or inspired you the most. Think about the secondary school teachers you have had and choose one for whose special teaching skills you can provide anecdotes and supporting evidence.

It is ideal, although not absolutely necessary, if you can show that this teacher has affected your development inside and outside the classroom. In other words, if at all possible, show interaction with the teacher on an intellectual or academic level and on a personal level. Remember to focus on how he teaches, not what he teaches. As mentioned previously, it is often appropriate to discuss a teacher you did not (or still do not) even like that much. By demonstrating that you learned a lot and gained respect for someone you did not particularly like, you will show outstanding maturity. If you go with this approach, remember to temper your opinions and do not sound too negative or bratty.

ADVANTAGES OF THIS APPROACH

If you write this essay correctly, you can easily show that you possess great intellectual vitality, passion for the act of learning, and appreciation for those who devote their lives to teaching. Furthermore, this essay provides more information on your values and the way you interact with those around you.

QUESTION:
What academic areas interest you most? Why?

WHY THE QUESTION IS ASKED

It is fairly obvious why admissions officers ask this question. Although they can see your grades and the list of classes you have taken from the rest of the application, they also want to know what most interests you. They want to know that you are intellectually engaged, that you do not just perform well in school because you want to get good marks, and that your interests are such that you will be able to continue them at college.

THE TYPICAL APPROACH

Many applicants make the mistake of discussing academic *strengths* here, merely recounting grades and academic accomplishments instead of piercing the heart of the matter. Your strengths in an academic subject may come into play here, but that is not the point. Too many applicants also make trite remarks that could easily be made by anyone possessing even remote familiarity with the subject matter discussed. For example, an applicant might write something such as, "I love math because I am obsessed with numbers. I like the challenge of looking at an equation and having to work through it until my response works." This kind of thing tells the admissions officers nothing about what makes you tick, nor does it hint at what you might do with your academic interests once you get to college and thereafter.

A BETTER APPROACH

First, be sure that your choice of subjects matches your positioning effort. If you are selling yourself as someone particularly interested in foreign trade and hoping to study at the school's program in Geneva, you might consider discussing French as your favorite subject. Although your greatest academic interest does not necessarily have to match your greatest academic strength, it is a good idea to demonstrate that you are talented in your favorite subject matter. After all, if this is what you are planning to focus on and share with others, then it is more helpful if you are particularly good at it.

Try as best as possible to dig deep into the subject matter here to get at what it is about this subject that most interests you. In other words, the *fact* of loving history does not matter so much as *why* you love history, or what about it is so fascinating to you. Remember that the number of topics that can be discussed here is limited (there are only so many subjects that are studied at the high school level). The admissions officers will receive thousands of responses based on the same basic subject that you choose to write about. You have to take special precautions to avoid cliché or stale statements and you need to show that you really know something special about the matter or bring a fresh perspective to your work in the area. If possible, it is always good to allude to how you will continue your study of the subject in college.

ADVANTAGES OF THIS APPROACH

Using our approach will enable admissions officers to identify you as someone with particularly strong intellectual zeal and a real yearning for academic stimulation. You will also show yourself to be someone who has thought a bit about how you might incorporate your interests into your future.

QUESTION:
What extracurricular activity is most important to you? Why?

WHY THE QUESTION IS ASKED

As with the similar question about academic interests, it is fairly obvious why admissions officers ask this question. Although they can see the list of activities you have participated in over the years, they want to know more detail about those activities and what they say about you. They want to know that you are stimulated by what you choose to do in your spare time and that you have a balanced life. They want to know you are someone who will add to the community at the college, not just to the academic atmosphere.

THE TYPICAL APPROACH

Many applicants do not take this question seriously and end up merely listing a few favorite activities, doing nothing more than what they have already done in the activity data sheets. Furthermore, a lot of candidates mistakenly discuss too many activities rather than focusing attention on one or two. Many applicants also make the mistake of discussing nonacademic *strengths* here, merely recounting extracurricular accomplishments or pointing out leadership positions instead of digging deeper. Just as with the academic interest question, your strengths may come into play here, but that is not the point.

A BETTER APPROACH

Start by thinking about things you really enjoy. To choose one for discussion, use these guidelines:

- The activity aids your positioning effort.
- Its value is apparent.
- You know a lot about it and can discuss it intelligently.
- You have something distinct and different to say.

First, be sure that your subject matches your positioning effort. If you risk being pigeonholed as an antisocial loner, discuss an activity (even if it is the only one on your list of this type) in which you can point to interaction with others. Although your greatest extracurricular interest does not necessarily have to be one in which you have racked up loads of honors, it is a good idea if you can show some promise through your performance. If you are not particularly talented at the activity, at least show that you are working at it for a good reason. For example, you do not have to be preparing to swim the English Channel if you want to discuss swimming in this essay. You could just as well talk about how you have been a rotten swimmer your entire life, a source of real embarrassment to you, but are currently training for a swim-a-thon to improve your skills and raise money for a charity all at the same time. You should show that the activity has had some value and meaning in your life.

Since an activity is what you do in your spare time, it should inspire you with special enthusiasm. Try to capture this as much as possible. As mentioned earlier, the *fact* of loving basketball does not matter so much as *why* you love basketball, or what about it is so fascinating to you. The other key to your essay is to show that you are knowledgeable about the endeavor. The more unusual the activity the better, but you can make a discussion of anything at all distinct if you bring a fresh perspective to it.

ADVANTAGES OF THIS APPROACH

Choosing an activity that furthers your positioning effort has an obvious payoff in making your application more cohesive and your marketing points more thorough and believable. Discussing your pursuits enthusiastically permits you to build committee members' enthusiasm for you. Taking this approach also allows you to show knowledge about something outside of academics, which may not be possible on all applications.

QUESTION:
Why do you want to attend this particular college?

WHY THE QUESTION IS ASKED

Colleges ask this question for several reasons. First, they want to see that you have "done your homework" and that you care enough about the school that you have bothered to learn all you can about it. They want to determine whether you are a good fit for the college, and they want to know how you value their school relative to other schools you might be considering.

THE TYPICAL APPROACH

Most applicants make one of several mistakes here. Some make the error of discussing why they want to attend college in general, rather than talking about the school that is asking the question. Other applicants reveal (perhaps unintentionally) that they do not really know what they are looking for in a college experience. This can happen when an applicant discusses very general features of the college, such as the dormitory living environment, which are shared by most other schools as well.

Another mistake is for a student to state a reason for wanting to attend that is simply unacceptable to the college. An applicant might, for example, chalk up his interest to the fact that he has "always wanted" to go to the school. Or he might state "Brown is simply the best" or discuss the prestige factor, neither of which say anything intelligent about the school's appropriateness to the candidate as an individual. Another error is to say that you want to go to a school primarily because your parent is an alum or because a current boyfriend or girlfriend is in attendance. These are shallow, illegitimate reasons to want to attend a school; moreover, they show you to be uninformed and cause you to lose an opportunity to market yourself.

A BETTER APPROACH

Start by discussing your goals, desires, and needs, as identified when you started the college investigation process. Then relate what you are looking for in a college, showing that this particular school fits your needs. Be specific and detailed, referring to information you have gained from the college's publicity materials or Web site, and, more important, from discussions with admissions officers, faculty, alums, and students. Show that you want to attend the college because of the educational and nonacademic experience it will give you, not because of its prestige or the resume value of attending it. Refer to the discussion in Chapter 3 about deciding where to apply to refresh your memory on how to do this.

ADVANTAGES OF THIS APPROACH

This approach will help to make it clear that you are serious about college, that you are interested in finding a place that is a good fit for you, and that you have researched the school to find out what it offers. It shows you to be a sensible decision maker for having done your research and made the choice based on your findings. It shows that you value the school and are excited about attending. Your enthusiasm about and valuation of the school can be important for gaining admission since schools are concerned with their yield rates—they want to admit students whom they believe will attend the school rather than decide to go somewhere else.

BRIEF NOTES ON OTHER ESSAY QUESTIONS

QUESTION:
How did you spend last summer?

This is a fairly straightforward question, but remember to give your answer spark and life. If you spent the summer working, taking classes, traveling, or doing a community service project, you have no legitimate worries about what to say. If you traveled, make sure to avoid sounding spoiled (an extravagant trip can make you appear less than ideal). Instead, show that you have taken advantage of all the opportunities available to you. If you worked, talk about the job, how it instilled responsibility in you, and what you learned.

QUESTION:
Select a short text, formula, or visual image created by someone other than yourself and respond to it.

This is a license for creativity if ever there were one. This does not mean that your answer must be bizarre or off-the-wall. It is perfectly fine to select a passage from Jane Austen if you so choose, but be sure that you provide ideas or a viewpoint that is yours alone rather than a redigested version of some other source's analysis. Admissions officers do not want to read one more stale analysis of the mythological allusions in Botticelli's "Birth of Venus."

If possible, heed your positioning efforts in your choice of topics. Note that this can mean *either* using a topic that would aid a marketing effort that needs a boost, *or* choosing an analysis that shows something totally removed from your marketing efforts if you fear appearing too overprocessed or pat. For example, if nearly all your materials allude to your political ambitions and your desire to be a future president of the United States, you may want to write about something other than a passage from one of the Founding Fathers or FDR.

QUESTION:
If you had the time and resources to develop one skill, what would it be?

Use your head when answering this one. Remember that if in your positioning efforts you have claimed to be talented or particularly interested in a field, you should probably not discuss a skill relating to this area. If you are truly fascinated and moved by it, then you should already be doing something about developing yourself in that regard. Do not forget to discuss *why* you are interested in developing these skills.

QUESTION:
What are you most hoping for in a roommate?

It is pretty difficult to avoid sounding cliché here, but try to make some sort of statement about yourself with this one. You could, for example, talk about the homogeneity of your present school, saying that you are hoping to benefit from the diversity of the college by having an international roommate or someone with a very different background. You could talk, on the other hand, about your best friend and the characteristics that make him or her a decent, respectable person. Whatever you say, remember that committee members are looking at your answer to see what it says about your values.

QUESTION:
If you were a college admissions officer, what would you look for in candidates?

Again, it is difficult to avoid sounding like other responders here, but try not to be too cavalier. Do not, for example, say that you would completely disregard test scores and grades (especially if you yourself have scores and grades that are lower than the school's published averages).

QUESTION:
Attach a small photograph of something important to you and explain its significance.

Here is another question that begs for creativity, so use it. The photo needs, obviously, to be of something tangible, but you can use an object to represent an idea or intangible value if you want. For example, you can use a photo of your town hall to stand for the importance of the community in which you have lived all your life and the value you place on all it has done for you. Whatever you use, even if it is an object you appreciate for its own self, you must also talk about *why* it is important to you. You need, in other words, to say something about your values here.

QUESTION:

If you were to write a book, on what theme or subject matter would it be based and why?

In order to find an appropriate topic for discussion here, you might want to follow the suggestions made in "What academic areas interest you most?" (page 364), "What extracurricular activity is most important to you?" (page 366), "Discuss an issue of local, national, or international concern that is important to you" (page 352), or "What one person has had the most significant influence on your life?" (page 354). Another idea is to discuss a favorite or provocative nonfiction title and discuss the book you would like to write in response or as a follow-up to it. This is a real free-for-all, but you have to say something intelligent.

QUESTION:

Assume you are in a position to ask a question of college applicants. What would that question be? Now answer your question.

This is another chance for you to stretch your creative limbs. Many applicants simply substitute a question that they have had to answer for another college's application to save themselves the task of having to do extra work. If the question you are using is very common or broad, this is usually fine—it will legitimately seem to be something you consider important to ask college candidates. Avoid using a question that is too specific to another school, such as "What do you want in a roommate?" asked by Stanford. It will be obvious that you are being a bit lazy and may appear crass. If you desperately want to use an essay you have written for another school because you think it is particularly good, disguise the question a bit and modify the essay appropriately. For example, "What are you looking for in a roommate?" could become "Please tell us a little about a new friend you plan to meet at college next year." Whatever you do, make sure that your own answer matches your positioning efforts. Use this question to include the material or anecdotes you have not yet been able to discuss in the application.

QUESTION:

You have just completed your autobiography. Please submit page 201.

Remember that pages in books do not necessarily begin at the beginning of a paragraph and end at the end of a paragraph—your page may well begin in the middle of a sentence. Be creative yet thoughtful here. You want to do something catchy but also express something important about yourself. One good idea is to use this essay to discuss a future goal, here discussed as something that occurred in the past. It might even be something that happened during college.

QUESTION:

Cite a first experience that you have had and describe its impact on you.

Here you basically have one of two options. You can discuss a first situation that had great meaning, following the suggestions made in "What is your greatest achievement?" (page 355). Or, using a different approach, you can extract meaning from the details of a seemingly mundane "first," such as the first time you went to a real barber at the age of five or the first time you were allowed to baby-sit for your younger siblings.

QUESTION:

Describe an occasion when you took a risk. Was it the right thing to do?

Why? What did you learn from it?

You have many options here. You can discuss a physical, emotional, academic, or personal risk. You can show that it was or was not the right thing to do. No matter your subject choice, the important thing here is to show that you weighed each of your options against one another and took the risk based on some sort of judgment criteria. If you choose a situation in which the risk was not worth it and you did not meet your objectives, make sure to show that you learned from the situation.

QUESTION:

Discuss an opinion that you have had to defend or an incident in your life that placed you in conflict with the beliefs of others and explain how this affected your value system.

Like the "ethical dilemma" question, the most difficult part of this one is usually finding an appropriate topic. You need to avoid sounding too prissy or holier-than-thou, but you also want to choose a topic that will highlight your values and morals. Whatever you do, be sure to show that you believe *strongly* in your values—that you hold firm convictions and do not back down when opposed by others—or, at the very least, that you learned to do so through this incident.

QUESTION:

Write a note to your future college roommate relating an experience that reveals something about you.

See "Evaluate a significant experience or achievement that has special meaning to you" on page 350.

QUESTION:

Discuss an experience that helped you to discern or define a value that you hold.

See "Describe an ethical dilemma you faced and how you resolved it" on page 360.

QUESTION:

What work of art, music, science, mathematics, or literature has most influenced your thinking or most intellectually stimulated you?

See "Select a short text, formula, or visual image created by someone other than yourself and respond to it" on page 369.

QUESTION:

What book has had the most impact on you?

See "Select a short text, formula, or visual image created by someone other than yourself and respond to it" on page 369.

QUESTION:

If you could bring only one thing with you to college next year, what would it be?

See "Attach a small photograph of something important to you and explain its significance" on page 370.

GENERAL RULES FOR APPROACHING ANY ESSAY

A thoughtful approach is required when confronting any essay. Remember that a question does not exist in a vacuum. Instead, it is part of the whole application and should be answered in the context of how you wish the whole package to read.

Chapter 12 will describe in further detail how to go about writing your essays. It will also offer tips for producing the best and most effective written material possible. The most basic rules of thumb to follow to ensure that your essay works are:

➤ The story is interesting.

➤ The story is detailed and specific.

➤ The story helps your positioning effort.

➤ The story does not stand in contrast to anything else in the application (including information provided in a recommendation).

➤ You reveal something unusual or unique.

➤ You reveal something not revealed elsewhere in the application.

WHAT ADMISSIONS OFFICERS SAY ABOUT CHOOSING ESSAY TOPICS

WHAT TOPICS SHOULD APPLICANTS AVOID WHEN WRITING THEIR ESSAYS?

"Don't talk about someone other than yourself in the essay! And no sexual experiences; those usually don't work."

—*Michael Goldberger, Director of Admissions, Brown University*

"Suicide attempts, cutting oneself as an act of destruction, sex, anorexia and bulimia are not appropriate essay topics for showing the best side of you."

—*Janet Lavin Rapelye, Dean of Admissions, Wellesley College*

"The least successful essays are the ones that look like all the others or are variations on one sort of gimmick or another. These things don't work—they show an absence of judgment and originality."

—*John Hanson, Director of Admissions, Middlebury College*

"It's difficult to cite a hard-and-fast rule about what essay topics to avoid. Insightful applicants and good writers can craft wonderfully effective essays from seemingly dull or inappropriate material."

—*Marlyn McGrath Lewis, Director of Admissions, Harvard University*

"An applicant's first sexual experience is not an appropriate topic!"

—*Barbara-Jan Wilson, Dean of Admissions and Financial Aid, Wesleyan University*

IS IT EVER APPROPRIATE OR BENEFICIAL FOR AN APPLICANT TO DISCUSS A WEAKNESS IN AN ESSAY?

"Discussing a weakness in an essay can be a good thing sometimes—it demonstrates 'taking a risk,' a quality we highly value."

—*Karl Furstenberg, Dean of Admissions and Financial Aid, Dartmouth College*

"If it's honest, discussing a weakness can allow a student to reflect appropriately on how he has coped with it. A weakness that might *not* work, though, would be 'The day I stopped being a grade-grubber.' This kind of thing might be unappealing even if the point were to show that the student had changed."

—*Jonathan Reider, Senior Associate Director of Admissions, Stanford University*

"Everyone sitting around the committee table has a weakness. We understand that students have weaknesses, and essays about this kind of thing can be wonderfully expressive."

—*Eric Kaplan, Director of Admissions, University of Pennsylvania*

"My personal opinion on this is not shared by everyone in admissions. I think the essay is an opportunity to talk about your strengths. Recently we've really seen the 'Oprah effect,' where students talk about too many really personal and problematic issues. Essays on suicide attempts don't seem appropriate to me. I tell applicants, 'Remember, you are applying to college. You want to instill confidence in you. If you are now on top of a trying situation, talk about it intelligently. Otherwise, maybe the subject is not appropriate for college essays.'"

—*Janet Lavin Rapelye, Dean of Admissions, Wellesley College*

"I have admiration for those who have overcome something, but I don't want to hear whining. If a student is speaking from a position of strength, having gone through something and come out the other side, then I think it is fine to discuss it. But I caution students about sharing too much of a serious problem if there's nothing else to let us know that things are being taken care of."

—*Delsie Phillips, Director of Admissions, Haverford College*

"Discussing a weakness is perfectly fine. We like this—and, frankly, it's pretty common among the kinds of students we attract. They tend to be humble even though they are brilliant."

—*Marilee Jones, Dean of Admissions, Massachusetts Institute of Technology*

"I have advised students in the past to discuss weaknesses when appropriate. We want information, though, not excuses or whining."

—*David Borus, Dean of Admissions and Financial Aid, Vassar College*

"Taking a risk on the application *can* be a great thing, but applicants have to know when and where it is appropriate. We had one home-schooled applicant, for example, who wrote a piece about the problems inherent in her home-style curriculum. She said that what her mother called 'mechanical engineering' meant going to work pumping gas for the car mechanic down the street. 'I really don't think I've learned much in that class' is what she basically said. By being so forthright and honest, she really won us over and actually improved her case."

—*John Hanson, Director of Admissions, Middlebury College*

12

WRITING EFFECTIVE ESSAYS

— KEY POINTS —

Keeping your positioning efforts in mind, sift through your possible topics and choose those that will allow you to establish your most effective themes

■

Plan before writing: think about, outline, and draft your essays
before writing them

—*When a school requires more than one essay, make sure that they complement one another before finalizing any one of them*

■

There is no excuse for basic foul-ups: misspellings, grammatical mistakes, factual errors, or inserting the wrong school's name into an essay

■

Remember the tenets of good writing

■

Allot substantial time for reorganizing, redrafting, and soliciting the input of others: Remember, "There is no such thing as good writing, just good rewriting"

INTRODUCTION

Dartmouth's admissions brochure makes it clear that the quality of a candidate's essays is of great importance to the overall success of the application: "Most Dartmouth applicants present very strong academic credentials. The personal statement portion of the application goes beyond test scores, transcripts, and recommendations and tells us, in your own words, a little bit about what makes you an individual and how you differ from the other applicants in your background, values, interests, experiences, and significant accomplishments." In other words, if you intend to rely upon your grades and test scores, chances are that you will not be admitted. The top colleges are so competitive that an exceptional record alone is seldom enough to ensure acceptance. In fact, the better the school, the more likely it is that the objective data in your file will not determine your fate and that the essays in particular will weigh heavily in the decision.

Admissions officers will judge you on the basis of what your essays reveal about your writing ability (including your ability to persuade, structure, and maintain a well-reasoned argument, and your ability to communicate in an interesting and sophisticated manner). They will also look at your essays for revelations about your honesty, maturity, personality, uniqueness, understanding of what the college offers and requires, future contributions to the campus, and thoughts on where you are headed in the future.

This chapter is designed to help you actually write your essays. You have learned from prior chapters the types of things you are likely to want to get across in your essays. Now it is time to master how to go about putting what you want to say on paper. In addition to reading this chapter, you can learn about successful essay writing by examining some of the many examples provided at the end of the book.

THE WRITING PROCESS: GETTING STARTED

THINK ABOUT YOUR AUDIENCE AND YOUR OBJECTIVES

Before you start to write, you should dwell once again on your audience and the admissions criteria, pledging to keep both of these in mind while fashioning your essays. This does not mean, however, that you should forget who *you* are or write what you think "they" want to hear.

Your audience is the set of admissions officers who will read your application. These admissions officers are generally intelligent, astute people who review thousands of college applications from bright and accomplished individuals every year. In other words, you should aim high and be sophisticated. Admissions officers are generally "people oriented" and want to see you in a positive light; they are looking for information that will make you shine, not searching for material that will disqualify you from the game. Therefore, you should be open and honest, even about any apparent weaknesses; if you offer good explanations for them, you will be better off than if you hope your mistakes will rest undiscovered. Admissions officers are dedicated to their jobs and extremely conscientious but also undeniably overwhelmed by the volume of material they need to read each season. You need to make a strong impact with a small amount of material; do not be subtle or vague.

Admissions officers are highly familiar with the determinants of success in college and life after college. They will examine your application for convincing evidence of your intellectual ability, your potential as a leader and contributor to your community, your personal characteristics, and your future goals. They want applicants who clearly value learning and education. You will need to provide evidence that you make the most of opportunities, whether large or small. Remember also to think about what each particular school values when creating your essays (as when putting together the other components of your marketing effort).

By communicating effectively—showing that you understand what the admissions officers are looking for, presenting your material in an organized and logical fashion, and seeming mature yet honest—you will gain credibility as a reliable source of information about yourself. Remember that as important as it is to be sure you are addressing the committee's concerns, your essays should reveal your true self and convey an honest sense of who you are as a person. Colleges are looking to admit *people*, not numbers. They want to create their classes so that they are full of interesting, compelling people, not just brains who do well in class or jocks who can perform on the athletic field.

PLAN BEFORE WRITING

It is important to plan your essays before writing a word. Planning—which includes both developing and organizing your material—forces you to think about what you will write before you get tied up in the actual writing process. Too many people take the opposite approach, writing random paragraphs, hoping to be able to glue them together later, or trying to write the whole of an essay before thinking about it. The results of these approaches are all too predictable. The material included is a haphazard selection of what might be presented and the writing is not necessarily organized and coherent. No amount of editing will cure this problem, because it is not merely a problem of word choice or transitions. The greatest problem with the write-before-thinking approach is that, after expending great energy, writers are disappointed with the results and must go back to what should have been the starting point—thinking about what they should say.

DEVELOP YOUR MATERIAL

All too many essays sound the same. The poor admissions officer who has to read thousands of essays gains no understanding of an applicant who writes something that could have been written by any of another 500 applicants to the school. Your goal is to develop materials that will help you to write stories unique to you, stories that no one but you could tell.

Failing to develop your own material or examine yourself thoroughly will lead to dull generalities and mark your application with a deathly ordinariness and lack of sophistication. You will not do yourself any favors by writing the following kinds of things, which are not only tired and worn clichés stating the obvious but also are very ordinary observations that could be made by nearly every candidate:

- ■ "My travels broadened my horizons by exposing me to different cultures."
- ■ "The experience taught me that with hard work and determination I can reach any goal I set my mind to."
- ■ "Working with a variety of classmates from different backgrounds, I learned the true value of diversity."

Statements like these do not merit space in your essays if you want to dazzle the admissions committee.

Pulling together the relevant material for your application essays takes substantial effort. You probably do not even realize now how complex you really are and how much material you have access to! The material that might be relevant to your essays can virtually come from any time in your life, any episode, any experience.

The best way to start the process of generating material is to fill out the Personal Profile Worksheets in Appendix V. Try to fill them out over a period of time, because you will be unlikely to remember everything they call for in one sitting. You may want to reread personal diaries or journals to refresh your memory. Looking at family photograph albums, school yearbooks and report cards, as well as any resumes you have made might also help to jog your mind. Consider keeping a notebook or computer notebook handy for jotting down ideas, stories, or details about your past or your goals for the future. When you have completed the Personal Profile Worksheets, you should have far too much material to use in your essays. You should feel that you have a wealth of material from which to pick the most appropriate items.

ORGANIZE YOUR MATERIAL

Once you have generated your raw material, what will you actually say? If you have read Chapter 6, you have already determined what your main themes will be. Now is a good time to check that they still make sense in light of the information you have available. Do you have good stories that illustrate your adaptability to a variety of learning situations, if that is one of your themes? Do you have good grades in the courses you are highlighting as evidence of this adaptability? If not, now is the right time to reconsider your positioning. Think in terms of what would be appropriate organizing themes considering the information that you have.

After you have generated information, you must organize it. You will do so by recalling your overall marketing or positioning efforts, as well as determining what other important themes or messages emerge from your material. Then choose the pieces of your material that are most useful for answering the various essay questions posed by your target schools. Determine what your core message in each essay should be. In other words, what key points should you try to make? If you can state these, the next step is to group your supporting material according to the appropriate points.

OUTLINE YOUR IDEAS

To organize your thinking effectively, it is generally a good idea to outline your essay. This will save you time because the outline will make it clear whether you have too much or too little material and will provide a logical means of organizing your material. It will also allow you to make changes early in the process, rather than working on something that does not belong in the essay only to eliminate it after squandering time on it. In other words, the outline serves as a check on your thinking.

HOW TO MAKE AN OUTLINE

There are several outlining methods commonly used. All follow the same general rule, listing primary organizing ideas against the left-hand margin, with supporting materials indented to indicate their subordination to a larger idea.

INFORMAL OUTLINE, USING BULLETS AND DASHES

➤ Primary idea
  – Subordinate idea
  – Subordinate idea
    – Sub-surbordinate idea
➤ Primary idea
  – Subordinate idea
    – Sub-subordinate idea

FORMAL OUTLINE, USING ROMAN NUMERALS, LETTERS, AND NUMBERS

I. Primary idea
   A. Subordinate idea
   B. Subordinate idea
      1. Sub-subordinate idea
      2. Sub-subordinate idea
         a. Sub-sub-subordinate idea
         b. Sub-sub-subordinate idea
      3. Sub-subordinate idea
II. Primary idea
   A. Subordinate idea

It does not matter which outlining method you use. It only matters that it can perform the important functions necessary: Pull together related material, show how idea groups relate, and make evident which ideas are primary (i.e., which ideas are main themes) and in what ways supporting ideas should be subordinated. You may even find that you start with an informal outline and progress to a more formal or complex one as your ideas become clearer.

REVIEW BASIC WRITING AND GRAMMAR RULES

It is usually a good idea, especially for those who are not accustomed to writing a great deal (although this should not be the case if you are applying to the top colleges, where you will inevitably have to write a lot, no matter what your major field of study), to review the elements of good writing usage and style. We suggest perusing Strunk and White's *Elements of Style,* paying special attention to the principles in Chapters 1 and 5. It is a good idea to have a book like this on hand as you write and rewrite, in case you need to check up on your grammar or word usage. Another good grammar and usage reference is Patricia O'Conner's *Woe Is I,* which also happens to be a fairly entertaining read. William Zinsser's *On Writing Well* is an excellent guide to developing good writing style—it elaborates on many of the basic tenets set forth in this chapter. You should definitely have someone with the requisite knowledge of the English language (an English teacher or college consultant) review your essays before sending them off, no matter how polished your grammar and writing skills. Still, reviewing the basic rules before writing will set you up well for starting on your initial drafts.

THE WRITING PROCESS: PEN TO PAPER

WRITING THE ROUGH DRAFT

The next step in the writing process is to produce a rough draft. Be sure that you are not too demanding of yourself at this point. Even though you want to do a good job, perfection at this point can be your worst enemy. If you are unwilling to write down anything less than final-draft quality, you are highly likely to be unable to write anything at all. Rather than take this perfectionist approach, be sure to limit your goal to that of producing a rough draft that incorporates most of the basic points you want to make. Do not be concerned if the order you had planned to follow no longer seems to work well, or if you cannot quite express your thoughts, or if your word choice is awkward. Get something reasonable down on paper as a starting point.

If you have difficulty writing, do not think you are alone. Writing is not something that comes easily to most people. The ability to write exceptionally well is a talent, not a trade that can easily be taught. But there are several main tenets of good writing that can be learned and practiced by even the most unskilled writers. If you take them to heart and practice using them, your college essays will be that much stronger and more effective.

THE TENETS OF GOOD WRITING

- *Simplicity.* Every sentence should be stripped down to its basic components. Every word that is redundant or does not add meaning should be removed. Writing improves when you pare it down and eliminate unnecessary words or phrases. For example, "a friend of mine" is better as "my friend" or "a friend." "Hideously ugly" is better as simply "ugly" or "hideous."

- *Precision.* Be as detailed and specific as possible at all times. Details bring authenticity to your writing. If your readers see the word "car," their minds are left with a fuzzy, forgettable image. But if they read "rusted-out, pea green '78 Dodge," they are left with an indelible picture. Similarly, "The cat looked angrily out the window at me" is not as compelling or descriptive as "The soggy-eyed cat behind the window, ears splayed out behind him as if prepared to launch grenades at the next trespasser, warned me away with his scowl."

- *Show rather than tell.* Rather than tell readers what a situation is like, show them the situation (i.e., describe it in detail) and they will sense on their own what you want them to feel. For example, do not tell readers, "I was very sad and lonely when my older brother left for college." Instead, describe the twisted feeling you had in your stomach as you sat on his bed while he packed his things; recall the last few minutes of nervous conversation the two of you had before he slipped out the back door; describe the tears you shed as you watched the car pull away; talk about sitting at the breakfast table all alone with your parents for the first time; explore the feelings of abandonment you sensed when he called home but never asked to speak to you. By showing the situation, you will more powerfully convey to your readers how lonely and sad you really were.

■ *Choose your words carefully.* Do not follow the masses; avoid clichés and common phrases whose "understood" meanings could be conveyed more effectively using different words. Clichés will dull your reader and make you sound unimaginative or lazy. Phrases such as "blind as a bat" or "it was like looking for a needle in a haystack" can be better and more precisely conveyed in your own original words.

■ *Stick to one style and tone.* Decide before writing what kind of style and tone you will employ and stay with it throughout the entire essay. If your tone at the beginning of an essay is light-natured and humorous, do not switch to a somber or stern voice midway through the piece. If your essay is meant to be fashioned as a personal diary entry, do not suddenly start preaching to an outside audience.

■ *Alter the lengths, styles, and rhythms of your sentences for variety.* Your writing should contain some very long sentences as well as some especially short ones for greatest effect. You should not rely too heavily on any one or two types of sentence construction, but weave many different sentence forms and structures into your essays.

■ *Forget what you learned in grade school.* Every essay does not have to have the kind of "introduction," "body," and "conclusion" that you learned about as a kid. Your writing *does* need to be organized and unified, but organization and the development of ideas take on more sophisticated meanings once you have mastered the basics of writing. Your introduction does not have to have one single "topic sentence," nor does it have to summarize everything that will follow in the body of the essay. Your conclusion does not have to restate the topic sentence. Using the first person ("I") is entirely appropriate and necessary for college essays. Throw out the old rules of thumb if you have not already done so.

GET YOUR CREATIVE JUICES FLOWING

The difficulty with college essays is that they fall somewhere between "fact" and "fiction" in terms of the stylistic approach you must use when writing them. On the one hand, you must be truthful because these are meant to be honest expressions of who you really are. The "facts" must be solid and accurate. On the other hand, you want your writing style to be compelling and your language energetic; you want to come across as creative and perceptive. This is not like writing a chemistry lab report! You must therefore balance the facts with fresh prose.

There are many ways of triggering your creativity if you know you have trouble writing crisp and energetic prose. First and foremost, you must read! No talented writer ever became such without a voracious appetite for reading. Reading the works of talented authors, especially those who have produced what we might call "creative nonfiction," will prepare you to let loose your own creative juices for the sake of writing your college essays. A few suggestions if you would like to read brilliant personal memoirs or autobiographical accounts: Ernest Hemingway's *A Moveable Feast;* Zora Neale Hurston's *Dust Tracks on a Road;* Jill Ker Conway's *The Road from Coorain;* Vladimir Nabokov's *Speak, Memory;* Penelope Lively's *Oleander, Jacaranda;* Maxine Hong Kingston's *The Woman Warrior;* Andre Aciman's *Out of Egypt;* Vivian Gornick's *Fierce Attachments;* any autobiographical essay by Calvin Trillin or John McPhee.

In addition, here are five exercises you can use to practice your writing skills and creativity. They will not always be useful in generating writing for your college essays, but are good practice nonetheless for getting your writing mind in gear and bringing forth interesting images and vocabulary.

1. Do a timed stream-of-consciousness writing exercise. Make yourself write for a certain length of time (15 or 20 minutes is adequate) on any subject. The rules are that you must keep your hand moving at all times (whether you are using pen and paper or a keyboard) and cannot edit or cross out things as you go. Do not try to think or apply logic—just write! Ignore all spelling, grammar, and punctuation rules. Suspend your judgment. Do not worry about whether your topic is a good one to write about or if you are writing well. Allow yourself to write about things you might find distasteful or inappropriate if that's what comes to your mind. Let yourself be awkward or strange. No one else has to read this! This is a great way to capture your inner thoughts and force yourself to write by using your senses rather than your rational mind.

2. Pick any situation, event, or object (the ongoing clashes of the Tutsis and the Hutus, a milk carton, your high school prom) and use a full sheet of paper to write about it as if you love or support it. Then turn over the piece of paper (or go to the next page on your computer screen) and write about it as if you hate or condemn it.

3. On a single day, pick three different locations and write at each, describing your surroundings, for half an hour or so. The locations can be anywhere: your little sister's sandbox, a pizza parlor, your basement, the locker room at school, the side of a road, the backseat of a car.

4. Write about an obsession. It does not matter what it is, or if it is not a topic that would ever find its way into your college essays (which should be the case if you are obsessed with Brad Pitt or starting fires). Writing about something for which you feel genuine passion should make you realize what it feels like to be powerful on paper.

5. Look around the room and list ten nouns or objects in a vertical column on the left side of a sheet of paper. Fold the paper lengthwise in half so that you can write a new column of words without looking back at the first column. Here you should make a list of ten verbs. To trigger your mind to think of interesting verbs, pick one of these methods: Think of an animal and then describe ten of its actions; pick a profession or career and describe ten tasks associated with that profession; or turn on the television and describe ten actions performed by a particular character or figure. Now open the piece of paper. Write a sentence linking each subject and verb, no matter how strange the combinations seem. For example, if your first noun is "radiator" and your first verb is "nuzzle" (perhaps you were describing the actions of a deer or calf) then you might write, "The radiator nuzzled the umbrella standing next to it, as if begging some extra appreciation for its heat."

There are many books on writing that can suggest further exercises and strategies for unleashing your creativity. Consult, for example, Natalie Goldberg's *Writing Down the Bones* or Anne Lamott's *Bird by Bird* for other ideas.

HOW TO START WRITING AN ESSAY

Once you are confident that your writing juices will flow, there are a number of different strategies you can use if you simply do not know where to start in writing a college essay. No one method is recommended above others. This is very much a matter of personal preference. You can use any of these methods or invent your own; choose any method that gets you started on the road to producing a reasonably complete draft.

■ *Start with the introduction:* When an introduction lays out clearly what will follow, in effect it controls the body of the paper. Some writers like to start with the introduction in order to make sure that they have a grip on the body of the paper before trying to write it.

■ *Start with the conclusion:* Writers who use this method feel that they cannot write the body of the essay until they know what they are leading up to.

■ *Start with any of the paragraphs of the body:* Some writers like to pick any self-contained part of the body of the paper and write it, then move on to another part, and then another. These writers like to build the substantive pieces of the paper first and then provide an introduction and conclusion based upon this substance. Many people take this approach because they know certain aspects of the subject well and can write about them easily, but require more thought to fill in the remaining pieces.

■ *Write several different drafts, starting in different places:* This approach involves taking one perspective or starting point for writing a draft, then plowing through the entirety. Then the writer does the same thing from another perspective or starting point. Later, the writer can choose one draft or another, or cut and paste using pieces of each.

REVISING YOUR ROUGH DRAFT

Remember that "the only good writing is rewriting." When you start to edit your rough draft, you are embarking upon the first part of the crucial revision process. Even the very best and most practiced writers rewrite and revise over and over before reaching a finished product that is acceptable.

One of the most important aspects of the editing stage is its timing. Neglecting to take a break between the drafting and the editing stages will limit your insight into the flaws of the first draft. You will not see where you skipped a needed transition or explanation because you are too close to the original writing. If you can take a break—preferably at least a few nights, better yet a week or a few weeks—you will be better able to read your draft from the perspective of an outsider.

Make sure that you have edited your draft for substance—for what points will remain and what points will be eliminated—before you start editing the language. Otherwise you will devote time and effort to polishing the wording of material that might be discarded. (And, even worse, you are likely to keep the unnecessary pieces in your draft if you have gone to the trouble of making them at least sound good.) This chapter assumes that you will revise your essay three times. In fact, if you are a good writer and have taken the time to think through an essay before doing your first draft, you might well need to edit only once or twice. By the same token, if you are struggling with an essay it might require more than three revisions to sort out problems.

One very important warning: Do not view editing as taking the life out of your essay. Editing should clear out the dead wood, simplify your statements, and make your important points stand out, in effect adding more energy to an essay. Editing should not, however, necessarily make your writing more formal, serious, journalistic, or adult-friendly. In other words, do not think that the rules for creating a unique and personalized essay—one that really speaks from your heart—should suddenly be discarded during the editing process.

Your initial revisions to the rough draft should focus on the essay as a whole. The initial editing should focus on four areas:

- *Revise to accomplish your objectives.* Make sure that your essay directly answers the question and that your main ideas are clear.

- *Revise for content.* The typical rough draft may have too little and too much material, all at the same time. It might have just touched the surface of some portions of the essay without providing explanation or convincing detail. At the same time, it may have discussed things that do not contribute significantly to your major points. A good essay eliminates extraneous material while including all of the information necessary to make your point. Your reader needs sufficient evidence to accept what you are saying, so be sure that you have adequately developed and supported your main ideas. Material that does this belongs, while material that is unrelated to the main idea should be eliminated. Finally, avoid belaboring the obvious (an admissions officer knows what the catcher on the softball team does) but also do not assume that readers have any more technical knowledge than does the general public about certain activities. For example, if you are discussing your favorite hobby of collecting and studying insects, do not assume that the average admissions officer will know the difference between the order Coleoptera and the order Diptera; you will have to make it clear (if it is important to the point you are making or to understanding the essay) that the former describes the beetle family while the latter describes the fly family.

- *Revise for organization.* A well-organized essay will group similar ideas together and put them in the proper order. To be sure that your draft is in appropriate order, try to outline it from what is written. If it is easy to produce an outline from the draft and there is a clear logic to the flow of the material, you can be reasonably certain that you have a well-ordered essay. Otherwise, reorder your material.

- *Revise for length.* Be sure that your essay is approximately the right length. It is always best, of course, if an essay is under the prescribed word or page limits. If it is substantially longer than the stated word or page limit, then consider how to reduce the supporting material without losing exciting detail or life. If it must go beyond the limit, a good rule to follow is to avoid lengths 20% more than the stated limit. In other words, if there is a 1000-word limit, try not to write more than 1200 words. If your essay is shorter than the allowed length, consider whether to leave it be (which is always the right thing to do if the essay successfully communicates your main points) or to expand it by making additional points or providing further supporting material. If the essay is significantly shorter than the suggested length, you probably need more depth to your answer. If you feel you have nothing more to say, you might consider rethinking your choice of topic.

REVISING YOUR SECOND DRAFT

Assuming that you have successfully revised your first draft and the content is as you wish it to be, turn your attention to the individual components of the essay: the paragraphs, the sentences, and the individual words.

- *Revise paragraphs.* A proper paragraph should make only one major point. If a paragraph is part of a first-person narrative or reflective piece, it may seem as if it contains more than one idea, but all of these ideas should coalesce together to form one greater whole. The easiest way to organize a paragraph is to start with a topic sentence—one that makes the major point of the paragraph—and then to explain or illustrate that point in the following sentences. Creative writing certainly does not have to follow a basic "topic sentence" structure, but each paragraph should communicate a single idea, no matter what style of writing you are using.

- *Revise the length of your paragraphs.* Most writers tend to one extreme or the other regarding paragraph length: Either all of their paragraphs are very short or all are very long. A mixture of lengths is ideal. If you do not know what is an appropriate paragraph length, aim for between 30 and 150 words. The occasional paragraph that is substantially longer or shorter than this is fine, but follow this guideline as a general rule. The reasons for this are simple: Too many short paragraphs make you look simple-minded, unable to put together a complex idea or group related ideas, and they make your writing seem choppy. Long paragraphs will discourage reading by any but the most conscientious reader. Use short paragraphs for emphasis; use long paragraphs for discussion of complicated points or examples.

- *Revise for flow.* Even when you have well-written paragraphs placed in the right order, your writing may still be difficult to read because it lacks suitable transitions between ideas or other means of showing how the ideas relate. The most important method of relating ideas is using transition words and phrases. Some typical transitions include:

Purpose	Typical Transitions
Amplification	Furthermore; Moreover; In addition
Cause and Effect	Therefore; Consequently; As a result; Accordingly; Thus
Conclusion	As a result; Therefore; Thus; In conclusion
Contrast	Although; But; Despite; However; On the one hand; On the other hand
Example	For example; For instance; Specifically
Sequence	First, second, … finally

One other easy way to connect paragraphs is to make the beginning of one paragraph follow directly from the end of the prior paragraph. For example, if you say, "I needed the chance to show that I could lead the team without the coach's supervision" at the end of one paragraph, the next one could start with, "My opportunity to prove myself came when my coach wanted to schedule a special weekend drill session before the regional semifinals but was not able to attend himself because of a teachers' conference. He put the responsibility of organizing the entire two-day session in my hands." In this example, the relationship between the two paragraphs is ensured by having the second grow organically from the first.

■ *Scrutinize your introduction.* Make sure that it not only introduces your subject but also grabs the audience as much as possible. A good introduction is interesting as well as successful at conveying your main points or a notion of how you will be answering the question. In other words, it does not have to be an "introduction" of the variety learned in sixth-grade writing class (in which you write a topic sentence followed by a list of the main points you will make in the body of the essay, followed by a restatement of the topic sentence), but it should at least hint at the direction in which your essay will lead.

For example, let us assume you are answering the question, "What is your favorite hobby and why?" You do not need to open with the following kind of all-in-one-breath statement to summarize your entire essay: "Fly-fishing is my favorite hobby because I learned the basics from my grandpa when he was alive, and continued my study from a fishing journal he bequested to me upon his deathbed." Your essay would be far more compelling and meaningful if it were to lure in the reader at the beginning with a hint of what is to come, saving some of the exciting detail for later in the story. For example, your introduction could read, "On the morning of my seventh birthday, Grandpa Carl handed me a miniature fly-fishing rod and a brown paper lunch sack, and drove me out to the Flathead River for my first lesson. I noticed that day that Grandpa stopped every so often, taking a leather journal and ballpoint pen out of his trouser pocket, to make notes. I did not know at the time if he was recording the weather, remarking upon the river's yield, or making notes about his craft." Later in the story, the journal could resurface as Grandpa Carl's gift to you upon his death—perhaps a symbol of his love and the catalyst to your becoming committed to the sport.

Your introduction should appeal to the reader and set the tone for the whole essay. There are many effective ways to open an essay. You can state an interesting and relevant fact, refer to something currently in the news, lead in with an historical event, or discuss a personal experience. You can use an introduction to shock, disturb, or humor your reader. You may compare or contrast two different situations, present a paradox, or ask a compelling and thought-provoking question. You can also start an essay by simply beginning a story. A narrative naturally builds upon itself; as long as the first sentence is strong and the next few are equally compelling, it does not matter whether the lead statement is all-encompassing or merely a passageway into the real heart of the matter.

Do not restate the original question; it wastes valuable space and is a weak, plodding way to begin. Similarly, rarely should you use a quotation from someone famous to begin your essay. Mark Twain and Martin Luther King, Jr. both said a lot of very interesting and valuable things, but the admissions officers know that as well as you do. There is no reason you should quote them in your college essays. Unless the quotation, the speaker, and the context in which the remark was uttered all directly relate to the point you are making in your essay, you should not even consider beginning an essay with the words of someone else. This is *your* application to college; the admissions officers want to read what you have to say for yourself.

■ *Scrutinize your conclusion.* A good conclusion does one or more things:
  – Pulls together different parts of the essay.
  – Rephrases a main idea (without repeating anything word for word).
  – Shows the importance of the material.
  – Makes a recommendation.
  – Makes a forecast.
  – Points toward the future.
  – Gives a sense of completion.
  – Brings the story full circle, perhaps by echoing an idea mentioned in the introduction.

The conclusion should not follow a tired and belabored winding down. Instead, it should come abruptly, almost disappointing the reader in its appearance as the end of the essay. The conclusion should not make a new point that belongs in the body, nor should it sound tacked on. The concluding paragraph should develop naturally from the material that preceded it. Your very last sentence should be just as crisp and perfect as your first.

■ *Revise sentences and words.* Most essay writers pile on one long sentence after another. Avoid this by breaking up some of the longer sentences to provide variety. Use short sentences to make important points, long sentences to explain complex ideas or develop examples. Also, use a variety of sentence structures to maintain reader interest. Do not, for example, use a "not only … but also" construction in every other sentence! Eliminate sentences that sound awkward or choppy when read aloud.

■ *Edit your sentences to eliminate imprecise or wordy language.* For example, use "although" instead of "despite the fact that." Add vigor to your writing by eliminating all clichés, using fresh and interesting descriptions, and trying to write as much as possible with nouns and verbs rather than primarily with adjectives (which slow the pace and reduce impact). Similarly, write in the active voice.

■ *Revise for tone.* Your tone can be assertive without being arrogant. Your essay should sound confident, enthusiastic, and friendly. Be sure to avoid pleading ("I'd give anything to be a part of Amherst College next year") and whining ("I never do well on standardized tests and I believe it is unfair of colleges to use them as measures of intelligence"). One way to check the tone of your paper is to read it aloud. Read it first to yourself and then, once it sounds appropriate to you, try reading it to a friend. Ask her how easy it is to understand what the strong and weak points are, whether there are any mistakes in it, and whether it sounds like you. Does it reflect your personal style? The ideal essay should sound like your voice, but with repetitious and awkward phrasings and use of filler phrases such as "you know" and "like" eliminated. It should sound relaxed rather than formal but still flow smoothly.

■ *Use the first person.* Some applicants, remembering an old grade school textbook, try to avoid writing in the first person. In fact, it is not only appropriate to use "I" when writing your college essays, but also essential that you do so. You are being asked to give personal statements, so do not write in the distant and aloof third person.

REVISING YOUR THIRD DRAFT

■ *Revise again for style.* See the comments in the preceding section.

■ *Revise for grammar, punctuation, and spelling.* The way to spot grammatical errors and faulty punctuation is to read your essays over slowly, preferably after having put them aside for some time. Reading them aloud can also sometimes help this process. You should also have a copy of Strunk and White's *Elements of Style* or the *Chicago Manual of Style* on hand. Even if your sense of grammar is keen, however, you should always have a teacher or college consultant whose grasp of grammar is extremely good read over each essay. Spellcheck the final product.

■ *Check the length (again).* Most schools do not mind if you slightly exceed their limits—generally speaking, the better your writing, the more leeway they will give you. Greatly exceeding the limits, however, might strike even the schools that are liberal in this regard as unfair. Admissions officers have established these limits to aid themselves in the reading process and to provide a level playing field for the applicants. Someone who greatly exceeds the limits might be regarded as inconsiderate of the admissions committee, unable to follow the rules, or trying to gain an unfair advantage.

Three revisions is not a magic number, but will be a minimum for most applicants. There is nothing wrong with putting your work through more revisions.

GIVE YOUR ESSAYS TO SOMEONE ELSE TO READ

After you have edited the essays to your own satisfaction (or gotten stuck in the process of editing!) hand them to several people whose views on writing you respect and who know you well. They can provide you with an objective view that you may not be able to bring to the essays yourself. They can be particularly useful in determining whether your attempts at humor are working, whether the essays convey a true sense of who you are, and whether you have left out important connections or explanations. Pay attention to their opinions, but do not give up control of what are, after all, your essays, not theirs. Do not let them remove the life from your work.

PROOFREADING

Why proofread your essays if you have been careful in composing the final drafts? No matter how careful you have been, errors are still likely to crop up. Taking a last look at all essays before sending them off is a sensible precaution.

What are you looking for? Basically, the task at this point is no longer to make sure that the structure is correct, but simply to spot any errors or omissions. Errors tend to show up most often where prior changes were made. Combining two paragraphs into one, for example, may have resulted in the loss of a necessary transition phase. Grammatical mistakes can also live on, even after many pairs of eyes have combed over your essays. Be ready to spot any kind of mistake.

As with any editing task, your timing in proofreading is of the essence. Wait until you have already finished what you consider to be your final draft. If you can then put this draft away for a few days, you will be able to give it an effective last look. If not, you risk being unable to see mistakes because you are still too close to the writing. Another useful precaution is to have a friend proofread your essays.

A TIP ON FORMATTING

Use one of the following fonts to maximize the number of words you can fit on a page and readability at the same time: Abadi MT Condensed Light, Perpetua, Times New Roman, or Times.

SOME TIPS FOR GOOD ESSAY WRITING

■ Give yourself the time to do the essays right. Start early; it will take time to do the essays. The results will be better if you take time between steps rather than trying to finish an application in a hurry. Expect to spend ten to twenty hours getting ready for the effort, and then perhaps five to ten hours per essay, with the most difficult (and first) efforts taking longer.

■ Answer the question. Do not ever substitute an essay on another topic, even if it was your best essay for another school. The likely result of doing so is points off, either for your inability to do as directed or for laziness.

■ Use humor, but only if it works. Few people are as funny as Jerry Seinfeld. And even if you are hilarious in person, that does not always mean you can *write* humorously. If you can manage to write humorous prose or recount funny stories effectively, you will definitely distinguish yourself. To check whether you are successful at doing so, have several people (including someone who does not know you well and thus will not be biased or swayed by her familiarity with your in-person humor) read your essay to make sure that it works on paper.

■ Keep the focus on you. For example, do not get carried away in describing the outcome of your junior class community service project without showing how it relates to you and your efforts.

■ Favor a full and detailed description of one incident rather than listing or discussing several incidents briefly. It is generally better to describe one event or accomplishment at some length rather than mentioning a number of them without explaining the full range of details, such as why it occurred, what it meant to you, what the results were, and what you learned from it.

■ Be specific. The more detailed you make your writing, the more you personalize it and make it memorable. Generalizations ("I am very determined") without specific explanations and examples are weak and unconvincing. Examples and details add interest to generalities as well as make your point clear.

■ Refrain from casting everything in black-and-white terms. Readers will tend not to trust or believe you if your essays give only one side to an argument, tend toward overly dramatic conclusions, or categorize everything in the extreme.

■ Use bold type and italics sparingly. Resist overuse of these effects. Bold print and italics can be helpful for emphasis or in making your meaning clear if used moderately.

- Do not use headings, subheadings, or other dividers in your essays. The essays you are asked to write for college applications are much too short for these effects.

- Find someone to read and edit your work. Explain what you are trying to accomplish so that your editor can both determine whether you are meeting your objectives and correct your grammar and style. The test of your writing is what the reader understands, not what your intent may have been.

- Do not use your limited space to recite information that can be found elsewhere in the application.

- Do not give superficial answers. Take the essays seriously and remember that they are a crucial part of the college application.

- Do not pretend to be someone other than yourself. Doing so will not be supportable with your own history and will sound insincere or phony.

- Do not lie or exaggerate. Doing so will put all of your assertions into doubt.

- Do not think that an essay limit is a required length. Remember that length does not equal quality. On the contrary, the more concise you can make your writing, the more effective its message.

- Use an appropriate amount of space. It is generally acceptable to exceed word or page limits, but doing so without good reason suggests you are unable to follow directions or be reasonable.

- Do not use a minuscule type size or tiny borders to shrink an essay so that it fits a prescribed length or limit. Remember that your readers have to read thousands of essays and will not appreciate this inconvenience.

- Do not ever refer to the fact that you are writing an essay. For example, do not begin with "In this essay, I will ..." or state, "Before I explain why I undertook this project, let me tell you a little bit about ...."

- Do not use quotations unless they are perfectly and directly related to what you are saying. Too many people seem to have been taught to start everything they write with a cute or philosophical epigram, regardless of the fact that it may not fit the subject well and all too often does not match the intended tone of the essay.

- Do not use bullet points, lists, or other ways of conveying information without using full sentences.

- Do not use fancy vocabulary for its own sake.

- Do not preach. Provide support for your viewpoint but do not keep repeating your beliefs or take on a "high and mighty" tone.

REUSING YOUR ESSAYS

The top colleges all want to learn the same things about their applicants, so they tend to ask similar questions. This is good for you in that you can reuse some of your materials and cut down on the amount of work you have to devote to the essay writing process. On the other hand, few things annoy admissions officers more than to receive essays that were clearly first written to answer a question on another college's application (particularly if the other college's name is accidentally left unchanged!). It is possible to recycle your essays, but only as long as you do so intelligently.

Recycling is usually fairly simple to do when the question asked by a college is identical to one you have already answered for another school. Even so, you must remember that there are several situations in which you will have to make more of a change to a previously used essay than simply substituting the new school name. You might have to alter an essay even if a school's question is identical to one you have previously answered:

- If your positioning efforts for the two schools are different.

- If one of the schools requires one essay while the other requires several. For the school requiring one essay, you might have packed brief descriptions of many events into one piece. When writing for a school that requires more essays, you may want or have to spread these events throughout different answers. This might also require lengthening your descriptions of individual events. (The reverse process would be appropriate when changing an essay for an application with several questions to an essay for an application with just one essay.)

- If the length limits set by the two schools are different. In this case, you might have to shorten an essay, keeping your major points but reducing your elaboration of them. Alternatively, you might want to consider lengthening an essay if there were points or descriptions omitted from the first version because of space considerations.

Every once in a while, you can successfully recycle an essay to fit a question that is slightly different from the original one. For example, let us assume that in response to one college's question, "What is your favorite class and why?" you have written an essay that discusses your love of American history—because you are interested in human psychology and like to imagine yourself as various characters in the historical dramas you study, gauging your reactions to events from multiple perspectives. To answer a question on another application, "Tell us about a school project you particularly valued," you might recount a history project in which you compared testimony from Chief Sitting Bull, a lieutenant in General Custer's army, and a Montana prairie wife after the Battle of Little Big Horn—discussing many of your previously developed ideas about human psychology and the importance of examining varying perspectives in explaining why you valued the project so much. In this case, your recycling efforts will be somewhat complex and you will have to be extremely cautious that you satisfy the demands of the second question. Again, always have someone else read your essay to assess its ability to answer the appropriate question.

ADMISSIONS OFFICERS REFLECT ON APPLICATION ESSAYS

How Important Are the Essays?

"Amherst is a very verbal place—we're very committed to the written word. This means that the essay is of utmost importance to the application."

—*Katie Fretwell, Director of Admissions, Amherst College*

"Absolutely crucial."

—*Richard Shaw, Dean of Undergraduate Admissions and Financial Aid, Yale University*

What Recommendations Do You Have for College Applicants in Writing Their Essays?

"I recommend that applicants write an essay more than a month before the application deadline. Put it away in a drawer, don't look at it for a month, then take it out and ask yourself, 'Is this me?'"

—*Karl Furstenberg, Dean of Admissions and Financial Aid, Dartmouth College*

"It is crucial that applicants allow themselves to be as personal and self-reflective as possible when writing their essays. Avoid writing about something on a superficial level or resorting to a topic that does not reveal anything special about you."

—*Richard Shaw, Dean of Undergraduate Admissions and Financial Aid, Yale University*

"Essays that work tell us about the student, not the latest world crisis."

—*Richard Avitabile, Director of Admissions, New York University*

"Students should write about what they think is important, not what they think we want to hear."

—*Lee Stetson, Dean of Admissions, University of Pennsylvania*

"In the essays we're looking for a student's values, and how his or her mind works. We look for clarity of thought and clarity of expression—we want students who can demonstrate both. I tell students to try to reveal themselves—this usually produces a good essay."

—*John Hanson, Director of Admissions, Middlebury College*

"Overedited essays lose all their personality. Applicants shouldn't have a lot of different people—especially parents—give their input. This can really ruin an essay."

—*Karl Furstenberg, Dean of Admissions and Financial Aid, Dartmouth College*

MUST APPLICANTS ABIDE BY STATED WORD OR PAGE LIMITS WHEN WRITING COLLEGE APPLICATION ESSAYS?

"Our stated 500-word limit doesn't really matter. We would never, ever count words, and we don't care if a student writes more than we ask for. They can write as much as they want!"

—*Marilee Jones, Dean of Admissions, Massachusetts Institute of Technology*

"We don't really care about word or spaces limits, but one year we received an essay that was forty pages long—an unprecedented situation. It detailed the minutiae of the applicant's life from birth until present. Students should use common sense about these things!"

—*Sheppard Shanley, Senior Associate Director of Admissions, Northwestern University*

"Going over our limits by one-half is generally okay. After that, an essay is really too long."

—*Lee Stetson, Dean of Admissions, University of Pennsylvania*

"Some students think volume speaks loudly, but sometimes it speaks in the wrong tone."

—*Richard Avitabile, Director of Admissions, New York University*

13

Requesting Recommendations

— KEY POINTS —

Choosing the right recommenders is critically important

■

Approaching potential recommenders must be done carefully:
—*Give them a chance to say no*
—*Explain what your goals are and why you are applying to the target colleges you have chosen*
—*Explain your positioning effort so that they can do the best job possible in supporting your case*
—*Make suggestions as to what you would like them to write*
—*Emphasize telling relevant, rich stories*

■

Consider whether you will benefit from supplemental recommendations from adult supervisors or peers

—*If your recommender is not accustomed to writing such recommendations, be sure to emphasize their importance and be clear about what is expected*

■

Make your supporters' work as easy as possible

INTRODUCTION

Many high schoolers complain that recommendations are a waste of time because "everyone can find someone to say something good about them." These applicants are right to believe that most people *can* find a supporter, but they are wrong about the importance of the recommendation process.

Recommendations are probably the most overlooked and underutilized aspect of the college application. If someone writes a mediocre recommendation for you, your judgment will be questioned at the very least. It may even be assumed that you simply could not find people who would say something fantastic about you. A mediocre recommendation can be death to an application. A bad recommendation is eternal damnation. (Remember, though, that it is unlikely that a good recommendation alone would have the opposite effect. Good recommendations must be accompanied by good essays and a good interview to ensure a positive overall campaign.) Recommendations play a vital role in the big picture of the application and make up a crucial component of your marketing strategy. A good recommendation, by supporting your pitch with illuminating anecdotal evidence or by addressing critical issues of your candidacy, can be just the right added touch to set an applicant apart from equally qualified, or even more qualified, candidates. It is one of our top priorities at Degree of Difference to teach college applicants how to obtain successful recommendations like the ones you will see in this chapter.

To understand how crucial a recommendation can be, let us compare two applicants, Anand and Cindy. They are both straight-A students in schools with rigorous curriculums. Both have strong SAT I and SAT II scores and each is the captain of a varsity team. Both have presented solid, albeit somewhat bland, essays; both are in the running for admission. As is often the case in college admissions, officers might be faced with two such students but one slot for admission. In such a situation, when all else is equal, a recommendation can be the distinguishing factor in an acceptance. Compare and contrast these two letters of recommendation:

RECOMMENDATION FOR ANAND

I have had the pleasure of teaching Anand on two occasions: freshman English and senior year AP English. Given two years of experience with him in my classroom, I feel well qualified to address his candidacy to your school. One look at Anand's grades and scores and you will see why he is in the top 10% of his class and why I feel so confident in his ability to succeed academically at the college level. His 700 verbal score on the SAT I and his 710 on the Writing SAT II are proof enough of how strong his English skills are. He has never received below a B+ on a paper in my class, and I am considered one of the toughest graders at our school!

Anand is also quite a soccer player. Although I don't follow soccer very closely (tennis is my thing), I have been to a few games and Anand has always scored a goal. He is also very vocal, cheering on his teammates at all times and showing fine leadership as a captain. Truly, I can't say enough good things about Anand. He is an all-around great kid and would be a wonderful addition to your school.

RECOMMENDATION FOR CINDY

Cindy is special. In fact, a student like Cindy comes around only once or twice in a teacher's entire career. She excels at everything she does—academics, athletics, personal relationships, community service—but more importantly, she brings a real spirit and vitality to her endeavors, which comes from having a true passion for all that she does. I think this is what distinguishes Cindy from other "all-arounders" who are successful at many things. Cindy does not just go through the motions, she invests her soul into her studies and activities. When we studied *The Canterbury Tales,* she took it upon herself to check out instructional tapes in Middle English pronunciation from the library to learn how to recite Chaucer correctly; when she learned that her soccer team had an extra $200 in its funds for the year, she secretly designed a celebratory T-shirt to reward her teammates for a successful season.

I will not bother to repeat Cindy's fine scores and grades for you—they speak for themselves. Her A in my class can be partly attributed to her excellence in the basics—she writes, analyzes, and presents her ideas well. But what makes Cindy stand out in class is her insight and her unyielding pursuit of the truth. *Never* does she simply read a text. She is constantly trying to attain a deeper understanding— of human nature, of historical contexts, of her own world and values, of the philosophies held by particular authors. This dedication to discovering the truth makes her written work, as well as her contributions to class discussions, a learning experience for everyone, including myself. It is not uncommon for me to come away from a class discussion or one of Cindy's essays pondering a new dimension of a text I have taught for over twenty years. Just last week, I earned a new respect for Tessie Hutchinson, the rather unappealing and hypocritical lottery "winner" in Shirley Jackson's short story, "The Lottery," because of a unique but plausible interpretation of her character that Cindy provided in class.

The following is an excerpt from one of Cindy's in-class essays on Shakespeare's *Romeo and Juliet:* "Shakespeare suggests that love so deep for another—so deep that one would rather die than live without a certain companion—while tragic, may be the strongest, most pure kind of love there is. But to me, the idea of being bound to another to the point of losing one's sense of self is not love at all but obsession and co-dependence, emotions that are harmful and misguided. Furthermore, I see the kind of passion-induced suicide exhibited in *Romeo and Juliet* to represent not pure love, but rather pure selfishness. In taking one's own life, one is merely solving one's own problems by making another's life miserable: Do people who commit such acts not think of their parents, their siblings, those who have given up so much because of love for them?" As this was a response to a quick in-class exercise, it does not demonstrate the sophistication and polish that Cindy consistently applies when writing longer take-home essays or papers. But her boldness of opinion is a refreshing change from the timid conjectures of students who do not trust their own instincts and instead determine that what the Great Authors held to be true must be so.

If there is a weakness to be had in Cindy's English performance it may be that she is better at offering insight to her own thoughts and feelings "in relation" to a character in a book or an author's message than she is at evaluating her thoughts on their own, without using any comparative measures. While this may be a weakness, I believe part of the reason for this is Cindy's humility—as well as her awareness that she is but one player in a vast and diverse world. She is confident in her own abilities but constantly places her ideas and thoughts into a context, which often involves comparing herself to others.

Relating to this idea of Cindy's humility and her awareness of those around her, I would like to share an experience I had as faculty advisor for the "Thanksgiving Dinner for the Homeless" committee, chaired by Cindy and another student last year. I had heard from several teachers that I was lucky to have such a mature, responsible, caring person as Cindy for my student liaison, especially since her co-chair was not known for his sense of responsibility. Inevitably, I focused my attention on Cindy and left it to her discretion to assign responsibilities for the event, confident that her leadership would ensure a successful evening. During a conversation, though, Cindy politely said to me, "Thank you for having such confidence in my ability to run this event. I think, however, that it would mean a lot to Sam if he were in charge. It just seems that people are often discounting him to the point that he thinks he's worthless. I know this would mean a lot to him, and I have other projects in which to develop my leadership skills at the moment—whereas this is Sam's one big chance to prove himself in an extracurricular activity." Needless to say, the event was an astounding success, with Sam as the recognized leader and Cindy doing more than her fair share of the "back room" work. Sam was awarded the citizenship award that year and I learned a valuable lesson about mentoring and developing my students.

I do not want to take up more space than I already have. But let me reassure you that despite Cindy's athletic prowess, she fits none of the negative jock stereotypes. She is not shallow or one-dimensional. She is an intelligent, insightful, caring, mature, and balanced young woman who would add to your school in many ways. I feel well qualified to recommend Cindy to you. I recommended two students last year who are now members of your freshman class—even in comparison to these two stellar students, Cindy is a real standout.

Which one—Anand or Cindy—would you select? Cindy wins out easily, appearing to be the stronger candidate if we compare the two letters of recommendation. She may not, in fact, *be* the stronger candidate, but this finely executed recommendation tips the balance well in her favor. While Anand got his recommender to say good things about him, Cindy got a lot more mileage out of this recommendation. She chose the right person—someone who could share classroom as well as personal experiences about her, offer interesting anecdotes, and address her weakness in a sophisticated way. Furthermore, Cindy influenced the teacher to include the right information to support her own positioning effort. The letter offers insight that goes well beyond regurgitating already known facts and assumptions. The rest of this chapter is dedicated to helping you get your supporters to do the same for you.

WHAT ADMISSIONS OFFICERS SAY ABOUT THE IMPORTANCE OF RECOMMENDATIONS

"We pay very close attention to them. My feeling is that recommendations are very important in distinguishing between students of similar caliber."

—*Christoph Guttentag, Director of Undergraduate Admissions, Duke University*

"I have to be honest about this—the recommendations are *extremely* important. This is one of the most valuable parts of the application."

—*Richard Shaw, Dean of Undergraduate Admissions and Financial Aid, Yale University*

"There can be real strategy involved in recommendations. I don't think enough students realize this. With good, careful preparation, you can get a great recommendation. Bad recommendations are usually the result of poor planning or a cavalier approach to them. I tell applicants to take this seriously because it's important!"

—*Dan Walls, Dean of Admissions, Emory University*

"We pay quite a lot of attention to recommendations. I'm always fascinated by those from teachers of a class in which a student struggled, if the teacher saw the student overcome challenges and improve."

—*James Bock, Director of Admissions, Swarthmore College*

WHAT ADMISSIONS OFFICERS LEARN FROM RECOMMENDATIONS

1. *Your claims are true.* Recommendations are examined first for the extent to which they confirm and support your claims and your positioning. In some offices, the term "fit" is used to describe consistency between what you say about yourself and what recommenders say about you. If you claim, for example, that you often lead class discussions and are not afraid to speak up when you have something important to say, admission officers will look closely to see that this claim is supported by recommenders.

2. *You have many qualifications.* In looking at the teacher recommendation forms in the Common Application, you will see that teachers are asked to rate you in many areas—creativity, originality, motivation, independence, initiative, intellectual ability, academic achievement, written expression of ideas, effectiveness in class discussion, disciplined work habits, potential for growth—and then to expand on these ratings. Recommendations are an opportunity to provide more information about you, preferably in the form of stories and illustrations of general points the recommenders wish to make.

3. *There is more to learn about you than what is covered in the essays.* Because you are limited in what you can include in your application essays, it is difficult to present everything that might make you a desirable candidate. Therefore, it is important that your recommendations fill in the gap. For example, a short essay topic might ask the following: "Of the activities you have listed, which is the most meaningful to you and why?" If you are involved in two or three activities that you really care about, should you present a cursory description of all of them (rather than a meaningful discussion focusing on a single activity) or despair that you have room to talk about only one thing? Neither. Take advantage of your recommendations. By collaborating with your recommenders you can use their letters to elaborate on areas of your candidacy that you were not able to cover in your portion of the application.

4. *Your accomplishments have impressed others.* Admissions officers do not look favorably on an applicant who blatantly toots his own horn. This is especially true if a statement about you represents a subjective opinion rather than an objective fact backed up with concrete evidence. Saying you are "the funniest guy in the drama club" or "the one everybody looks up to" will be better received and more credible if offered by a recommender rather than by you. A recommender's positive comments show the admissions office that you have made an impression on others and ensure them that your own self-descriptions are valid.

5. *There are special circumstances that influence your academic or extracurricular performance.* Recommendations are a good place for shedding light on certain anomalies or special circumstances that might negatively influence your record. Teachers or guidance counselors can explain that your B– Spanish grade reflects the fact that you landed in the section with the toughest teacher, whose class average is actually a C rather than a B+, the class average of the other Spanish sections. They can discuss your performance over time if you are a late bloomer who did not do well during the ninth and tenth grades. They can also enlighten admissions officers on personal issues that might have gotten in the way of your performance, such as learning disabilities, health issues, or family problems.

6. *They learn information about your school and senior class, which helps to show how you are regarded and how you compare with others in your same environment.* Admissions committees look to the guidance counselor recommendation to get a sense of your high school and your class. This recommendation provides a context in which to evaluate you, thus giving admissions officers the ability to better assess you. A discussion of your class rank, the school's GPA weighting policy, level and breadth of your courses, your impact within the school, and your extracurricular involvement are commonly offered in this recommendation.

7. *You can accurately evaluate others and their perceptions of you.* If you end up choosing someone who writes a mediocre recommendation, your judgment will be questioned at the very least. It may even be assumed that you could not find people who would say something good about you.

One of the telltale signs that an applicant is not strong enough is that the recommenders and the applicant himself all tell the same few stories. This suggests that the applicant has achieved limited success.

WHO SHOULD WRITE YOUR RECOMMENDATIONS?

Selecting appropriate recommenders involves sifting many factors. Some colleges allow you great freedom to choose your recommenders, while others strictly limit your choice. Here are some general rules to be applied when choosing recommenders, whether they be teachers, guidance counselors, or nonacademic sources (who usually provide optional or supplemental recommendations). In general, you will be expected to submit recommendations from individuals who know you and are well placed to address the key issues concerning your candidacy.

1. *Choose those recommenders who know you well.* This rule may not apply to your guidance counselor's recommendation, because high schoolers typically have one assigned to them. Many teachers have the opportunity to get to know students well in an academic setting (if the class is interactive or if you spend time with the teacher outside of class) and in social or extracurricular settings (if they coach a sport, supervise a club, or perhaps have chaperoned class trips and functions). This serves you well because the better a teacher knows you in and out of the classroom, the more able he is to make the recommendation credible and powerful by illustrating points with anecdotes and lively details, and the less likely he will be to limit the recommendation to a discussion of your grades and scores. If your relationship with a teacher is relegated to the classroom, be sure it is a class in which you are very active and have frequent communication with the teacher. Your junior- and senior-year teachers are better able to give a current and detailed picture of you than are teachers from earlier in your high school career. Admissions committees will question the validity and pertinence of a recommendation from a freshman or sophomore teacher, unless you have a special reason for asking that person and that reason is made clear.

2. *Choose a recommender who can support your positioning.* If you are marketing yourself as a potential journalism major, for example, it would behoove you to get a recommendation from an English teacher who can attest to your writing ability and perceptiveness. In some cases, the teacher who best supports your positioning is one who can address your weaknesses and put a positive spin on them. For example, if your academic courseload has been unevenly distributed, with more time spent in humanities courses, and you want to shed light on your analytical and quantitative abilities, request a recommendation from a math teacher. If you risk being stereotyped (as "an athlete," "a genius," etc.) you will want your recommendations to address the weaknesses assumed of such types and, even more usefully, why you do not display such weaknesses.

3. *Choose teachers whose classes you enjoy and in which you have worked hard.* These are not necessarily classes in which you have received A grades. In fact, if a B or even a C grade is the result of much determination and enthusiasm, the teacher of the class can probably speak far more favorably about you than can a teacher who says you received an A in her class without having more than that to discuss.

4. *Choose a recommender who genuinely likes you.* It is rare that a teacher or supervisor would overtly dislike a student (in such a case, do not even think about asking for a recommendation, even if you do well in the class!), but it is fairly common to find teachers who are indifferent to some students. This indifference translates into a bland recommendation resulting from little time and little effort. Teachers who like you will take the time to write you a good recommendation and will provide examples to illustrate points made about you. This is impressive in its own right. A recommendation that looks as though it took only five minutes to write suggests that that is exactly how much time the recommender felt you deserved. In contrast, a recommendation that looks carefully written and well thought out suggests that the recommender is committed to helping you. One other reason for choosing someone who likes you: He or she will try to put a positive spin on your weaknesses, choosing examples that still manage to show you in a positive light. Someone who does not much care may well simply write the first thing that comes to mind.

5. *Choose recommenders who can address several of the key qualities colleges look for.* The key qualities include brains, character, leadership ability, and other talents and skills. Each of these qualities can be broken down into many smaller elements.

Brains

- Academic achievement
- Analytical ability
- Quantitative skills
- Originality
- Healthy skepticism
- Imagination and creativity
- Problem-solving ability

- Research skills
- Communication skills (written and oral)
- Effectiveness in class discussions
- Mastery of language
- Insight
- Thoroughness

Character

- Sense of morality
- Dependability
- Motivation and sense of initiative
- Sense of humor
- Involvement in relationships
- Sense of social responsibility
- Social skills

- Maturity
- Perseverance and work ethic
- Independence
- Discipline
- Potential for growth
- Open-mindedness

Leadership Ability
- Achievement in leadership positions
- Fairness
- Organization skills
- Respect for others
- Ability to motivate others

Other Talents and Skills
- Artistic talent
- Athletic talent
- Musical talent
- Acting talent
- Foreign language skill
- Technology and computer skills
- Other special talents and skills

In addition to these general rules, four additional criteria should also be considered when looking for recommenders:

1. *Seek out the voice of experience.* Many teachers have recommended students before you to the colleges of your choice. Therefore, these teachers have a sense of what the colleges are looking for, and they can compare you to those from your high school who are now attending a college to which you are applying. Admissions committees appreciate this kind of insight and will often become familiar with and look favorably upon particular recommenders who consistently promote good candidates. Note that this does not mean that a younger or first-year teacher will do a bad job when writing you recommendations. On the contrary, an energetic and young teacher, especially one in her first few years of teaching, is probably not as worn down from years of having to write college recommendations as other teachers are! She might do a better job than the average mid-career teacher simply because of the novelty of the task and the enthusiasm that she brings to her job.

2. *Timeliness counts.* Choose someone who is reliable and therefore likely to submit your recommendations on time. If you choose a teacher who tends to return assignments later than originally promised or seems to take an unusually long time to grade work, it will serve you well to stay abreast of his progress on your recommendation.

3. *Originality and sharpness count.* You want to choose teachers who bring originality and liveliness to their work, rather than those who appear to teach by rote, simply going through the same motions year after year or covering the material in the most basic way. Of course, it is usually a simpler task for an English teacher than a math teacher to make class "lively" simply because of the subject matter involved. Still, you should be able to ascertain which of your teachers are especially innovative or passionate, always going the extra mile to make class as interesting and original as possible, and which are

merely working right out of the textbook or giving the same dry lectures they gave to the Class of '78. Teachers who bring spirit and creativity to their classrooms will tend to bring the same qualities to the recommendations they write for their students.

4. *Learn where your teachers went to college.* Generally speaking, graduates of schools that are comparable in quality to your target schools can speak most convincingly about your relative abilities. Teachers with degrees from well-respected colleges, if they mention their alma maters in their letters, will become credible voices of reason in the eyes of the admissions committees. Note that this does not mean that you should avoid seeking a recommendation from a teacher whose alma mater you have never heard of if you know she is otherwise your best bet. People who themselves graduated from your target school are ideal, since they clearly know what is required to succeed in the program. On the other hand, you should be applying to numerous colleges, so this one recommender's advantage will not work across the board.

ADMISSIONS OFFICERS GIVE ADVICE ON HOW TO CHOOSE RECOMMENDERS

"We specify in our instructions on choosing recommenders that we want teachers from the eleventh or twelfth grade. It's important to us that the relationship between recommender and student be a recent phenomenon."

—*Jonathan Reider, Senior Associate Director of Admissions, Stanford University*

"You should pick a teacher who knows you well, and ideally someone who has taught you twice."

—*Barbara-Jan Wilson, Dean of Admissions and Financial Aid, Wesleyan University*

"Choosing the right recommenders is incredibly important. Go talk to the teachers you are considering asking, tell them what schools you are applying to, explain why you want a recommendation from each, let them get a feel for what you are after."

—*Michael Goldberger, Director of Admissions, Brown University*

"I suggest applicants choose recommenders who know them in more than one dimension if possible. This way, the writer has a greater frame of reference for speaking about the student. Also, make sure to give them enough time to do a good job."

—*Lee Stetson, Dean of Admissions, University of Pennsylvania*

"Don't be afraid to go to a teacher who hasn't given you the best grade if that person knows you best."

—John Hanson, Director of Admissions, Middlebury College

"I think there are three important things applicants should keep in mind when selecting recommenders. First, the teacher should write well. Second, the teacher should know them well. And third, the teacher should not be lazy. You wouldn't believe how lazy some recommenders are! We get all sorts of silly things—written by English teachers no less— statements like, 'There aren't enough expletives to describe this student' or 'So-and-so is of impeachable character.'"

—Philip Smith, Dean of Admissions, Williams College

"Sometimes teachers approach the recommendation with an attitude of 'They're not really going to read this.' We even see recommendations that are obviously form letters, with the wrong name substituted in for the applicant's name. Unfortunately, this can really harm the student. Applicants should be sure the recommenders they choose are prepared to do a good job."

—Richard Shaw, Dean of Undergraduate Admissions and Financial Aid, Yale University

"Candidates ought to choose recommenders who know them well. Also, it's usually best to get a recommendation from a recent teacher."

—Karl Furstenberg, Dean of Admissions and Financial Aid, Dartmouth College

TEACHER RECOMMENDATIONS

Come sophomore year, you should start considering which teachers would be best suited to write your recommendations. It is important to consider this because you will want to foster relationships with those teachers that will naturally transition into their writing you recommendations during your senior year. The more time you spend cultivating a relationship with the teacher, the more likely it is that he or she will have illuminating examples to support the points made about you.

Thankfully, the same things that ensure a good recommendation also help make you a good student: class participation, insight into the material, good behavior, diligence, well-executed and timely homework assignments, interest in the subject matter that goes beyond what is expected of you, willingness to assist the teacher, eagerness to approach the teacher on a regular basis (whether it is to chat or to seek help), and the ability to work well with your classmates on assignments.

Depending on the schools to which you are applying, you may have free reign to choose your teacher recommenders, or you may be restricted to recommendations from a math and an English teacher in an attempt by admissions committees to compare all applicants' academic abilities.

To the extent that you are given a choice, you will want to select teachers who will best support your marketing pitch and who will shed light on things that are not already presented in other areas of the application. For example, it does not serve you to choose a teacher in a subject in which you have strong grades and scores if that teacher cannot do more than reiterate your report card. Rather, you will want to select a teacher who knows you well enough that he is going to share insight about you beyond your academic record. Furthermore, you will want to choose teachers in core subjects (i.e., math, science, English, history, foreign languages) rather than noncore electives such as physical education or typing.

In order to be especially proactive, you should choose teachers who are able to minimize your weaknesses (or at least what admissions committees might view as your weaknesses) rather than merely hoping the college will not notice them. For example, if you did not do well on the math portion of the SAT I but have worked hard in your Calculus class and know your teacher well, you might request a recommendation from her. If, however, you are restricted to math and English teacher recommendations, it is important to make these letters work for you and support your marketing efforts. If an English teacher can address some or all of the following skills, she will provide an effective recommendation:

English Class Skills

- Ability to read literature critically
- Ability to disregard preconceptions
- Ability to explore and understand human behavior
- Ability to explore and understand a culture or historical era
- Ability to ascertain an author's intention
- Ability to compare and contrast writing styles, characters, cultures, etc.
- Ability to think critically about values, ethics systems, and rationality
- Communication skills (written and oral)
- Debating and persuasion skills
- Creativity
- Organization of thought processes
- Self-confidence and strength of convictions
- Enthusiasm for and enjoyment of subject matter
- Ability and interest in helping other students grasp material

Similarly, a math teacher should be able to address the following:

Math Class Skills

- Analytical ability
- Quantitative skills
- Ability to think independently
- Problem-solving ability
- Ability to explain the reasoning process used in arriving at solutions
- Ability to apply mathematical concepts to situations beyond the classroom
- Ability to persevere through periods of difficulty and lack of understanding
- Computer skill (in some cases)
- Enthusiasm for and enjoyment of subject matter
- Ability and interest in helping other students grasp material

Refer to the recommendation for Cindy (page 401) for an example of an effective recommendation from an English teacher. Here is an example of an effective recommendation written by a math teacher.

RECOMMENDATION FOR EMMA

Emma is one of the top three math students I have ever taught. This is an accomplishment in and of itself, but when coupled with the fact that Emma is succeeding despite odds against her (she was diagnosed with a slight learning disability during her sophomore year), her success is that much more impressive. To address her disability briefly, let me assure you that it has affected her analytical abilities hardly at all; the techniques Emma has studied to avoid misreading or reversing numerals have worked well. I admire her for confronting her problem and want to assure you that it should not make you lower your opinion of her academic quality whatsoever.

What makes Emma one of the best math students in my eighteen-year career? You can see for yourself the high achievement she has reached in my class. For the purpose of this recommendation I will focus on two of her many outstanding qualities.

First, she has the ability to project and utilize mathematical ideas and concepts beyond the confines of the classroom. The following situation occurred earlier this year: An article in our student newspaper reported that the school was contemplating the construction of a new senior parking lot, but due to high contracting costs, the plans had been discarded. After reading the article, Emma approached me and asked if I would supervise her effort to draw up some plans for the project. I myself found this to be a daunting project, but how could I, the teacher, say no?

Applying several concepts we had learned in class, as well as concepts she learned in her community college course, "Introduction to Engineering," Emma produced a plan for the lot. Not only did it include the 60 spots the school had requested, but it also included five extra spots for the school's sports vans, which to date have been located half a mile from school. She consulted several construction firms to confirm that her ideas were reasonable and even got some very rough estimates from them—estimates which were feasible given the school's budget. Emma presented her plan to our administration and Board of Directors and the school has now returned to the idea. I cannot say that her exact plan will be used for the construction of the actual lot, but it was an accurate and impressive assessment of and solution to the problem. More importantly, Emma's initiative provided the stimulus necessary for the school to go ahead with the project. And Emma doesn't even have a car! She didn't take this project on for selfish reasons, but merely to confront an interesting question and challenge herself.

Second, Emma's involvement in the predominantly male Math Club is notable. She is one of only three female members and was voted president this year by her peers. Not one to promote women by bashing men, Emma has made it a point to invite women who have been successful in the fields of math, engineering, and computer science to the school to speak. Emma feels it is important to expand young women's minds so that they do not buy into negative stereotypes regarding women's abilities in math and science. She has had a tough time grappling with just how to do so given the predominantly male membership of the club she heads. But never one to shy away from a challenge, she is collaborating with our counseling department on a "Women in the Workforce" assembly that will showcase women professionals in our area. She hopes that through this program she will reach a large number of young girls who have lowered their expectations or abandoned the idea of becoming successful in technical careers.

As Emma has indicated, she is interested in your engineering program. There is not a question in my mind that she will succeed. But more importantly, she will be a positive presence in your department and in your school. In an age when many women still shrink from entering technical fields, a student like Emma is a welcome breath of fresh air.

What do admissions officers learn from this letter that makes Emma such an attractive candidate?

- She has a passionate interest in math and learning in general.
- She has drive and initiative.
- She applies knowledge learned inside the classroom to other areas of life.
- She has made an impact at her school.
- She is community-minded.

- She enjoys challenges.
- She is interested in engineering (a major known for its low number of female students).

ADMISSIONS OFFICERS EXPLAIN WHAT THEY MOST WANT FROM TEACHER RECOMMENDATIONS

"'Why have you enjoyed teaching this candidate? Why is he or she a joy to teach?' are the crucial questions we are asking of recommenders. Comparisons with other students are helpful."

—Philip Smith, Dean of Admissions, Williams College

"The qualities a teacher should address in the recommendation include originality of thought, engagement, personality, how the student reacts to criticism, how she interacts with other students."

—Michael Goldberger, Director of Admissions, Brown University

"Some recommendations are boilerplate—from far too overworked and harried teachers. Then again, some teachers are very helpful and insightful. I wish more teachers would think about critical issues: When the student is presented with new material, how does she react? What is the student's mode of thinking and questioning? What has the development over time been like?"

—David Borus, Dean of Admissions and Financial Aid, Vassar College

"If a recommendation doesn't jump out at us because of the praise contained within it, we see a red flag. We're so used to ebullience in recommendations that a tepid one makes us wonder how great the student really is."

—Eric Kaplan, Director of Admissions, University of Pennsylvania

"When we have forty applicants from one school—one of our typical 'feeder' schools—we're looking for a comparative discussion. We need a way to distinguish between students."

—John Hanson, Director of Admissions, Middlebury College

"When we read the recommendations, we're asking ourselves, 'Is there brilliance of mind, or does this student just work hard?'"

—Marilee Jones, Dean of Admissions, Massachusetts Institute of Technology

"We're looking for comments that draw distinctions between a student and others in the classroom. We aren't looking for facts or data here—a teacher shouldn't waste space telling us about the student's grades or what he does outside of class."

—Sheppard Shanley, Senior Associate Director of Admissions, Northwestern University

"We ask teachers to discriminate, to compare students with others they've had during their entire teaching experience. We want to see outcomes in the classroom and interaction in the classroom. We want to see that there's intellectual depth beyond rote. Most kids get *grades;* we want to see *learning.* And that often comes best from a teacher's response."

—*Richard Shaw, Dean of Undergraduate Admissions and Financial Aid, Yale University*

"Whereas a guidance counselor recommendation often just confirms facts gained elsewhere, the teacher recommendations tell us things we can't learn anywhere else. They tell us how students are in the classroom, how they participate in the education of other students, what kind of insight they add to the class, and so on."

—*Lee Stetson, Dean of Admissions, University of Pennsylvania*

"What can be really damaging is a muted recommendation—one in which the teacher talks a lot about punctuality or attendance level, but never about real issues of importance."

—*Janet Lavin Rapelye, Dean of Admissions, Wellesley College*

"Sometimes a teacher damns a student with faint praise. Sometimes it's unintentional, and that's unfortunate."

—*Delsie Phillips, Director of Admissions, Haverford College*

"I tell applicants to choose recommenders who know them well and can give illustrations using examples. This is especially important when applying to the top schools because eight out of ten kids we see are 'the best in the class.' Those comments don't mean much to us. We need details."

—*Marilee Jones, Dean of Admissions, Massachusetts Institute of Technology*

GUIDANCE COUNSELOR RECOMMENDATIONS

Of all the recommendations, the guidance counselor's tends to be the one over which you have least choice. It also seems to be the greatest cause for concern among high school students. In most schools, students are assigned to a particular guidance counselor, or there is one who acts on behalf of all the seniors. Commonly, students have minimal interaction with their counselor—or minimal interaction until the end of junior year, when college application discussions start. The lack of choice and interaction, however, does not mean you cannot make this recommendation work for you. It does mean that you will need a well-planned approach to soliciting the recommendation.

The purpose of the guidance counselor recommendation is first and foremost to give admissions officers a context in which to place you. Admissions committees are trying to answer the question, "How does this student fit into his high school setting?" On an elementary level, the answer to this question lies within your class rank, a figure requested of guidance counselors. But to limit the answer to your class rank or grades and scores is wasting an opportunity to promote your candidacy. The most effective counselor recommendations provide a comprehensive picture of you that includes your academic record, your social impact, and explanations of any extenuating circumstances that may have affected your performance.

For example, your class rank may not indicate that you have taken a heavier courseload than students ranked higher than you. Or, maybe your mediocre scores on a particular SAT II exam are attributable to the fact that you had suffered from mononucleosis for the two weeks preceding the test. A guidance counselor can shed light on a rise or decline in your overall record or explain your lack of extracurriculars. She can explain that your poor performance during a particular semester was the result of the concurrent diagnosis of your mother's breast cancer. On a more positive note, if you are too humble to speak of the success of the food drive you organized at Thanksgiving time, a counselor can sing your praises for you.

Here is an example of an effective guidance counselor letter.

RECOMMENDATION FOR JASON

I am sure that a school of your caliber has the luxury of admitting an entire freshman class composed of students who ranked in the top decile of their senior high classes. I hope you do not, however, overlook Jason because of his second decile ranking. He is definitely a top-rate student, but because our school does not weight grades according to the difficulty of classes, his ranking does not accurately indicate his ability. He is taking one of the toughest courseloads among all the seniors—all APs, plus an independent study. A B+ in AP Chemistry and a B in AP Calculus put Jason in the second decile behind students who are receiving As in much easier courses.

Just one look at his test scores and you can see what strong potential he has. But Jason's strengths go far beyond academics. As Social Chair of the school, he has accomplished the impossible—he's actually lived up to his campaign promises while bringing respect to a notoriously "fluffy" position. As Jason said in his acceptance speech, "I want to impact the social life of this school beyond prom. I want to affect students' involvement in sports, clubs, performing arts ..." He has done just that. He determined that lagging club attendance (this pertains to all clubs) was due to students' wanting a hot lunch rather than the bag lunch we eat at our meeting tables on Mondays and Wednesdays. Because clubs meet during the lunch hour on those two days each week, students must choose between their dedication to a club and a "real" meal. Jason took the initiative to approach first our administration, then Food Services, to arrange for hot lunches to be delivered to meeting rooms—a seemingly simple gesture, but no one before him had taken the effort to do it. As a result, club attendance has increased dramatically.

Jason's presence is felt not only by students, but also by teachers, coaches, and even parents.

Mr. Robbins, our Chemistry teacher, said of him, "I have great respect for Jason for not shrinking away from classes like mine in order to protect his GPA, which was stronger going into senior year than it is now. He has a true love of learning, and I can't count how many times he has stayed an extra few minutes at the end of class to help clean up other students' experiments and keep our lab tidy."

Coach Wilkes, who oversees the basketball team, says, "While not a star player, Jason is nonetheless an integral part of our varsity squad because of his commitment to the team's spirit. Given our losing record this season, the morale of the team has tended to be quite low, yet Jason has brought real purposefulness to his position on the team. In fact, the team elected him 'Spirit Captain.'

The mother of one of his classmates once told me offhandedly, while we were watching a basketball game, that she always felt comfortable leaving her kids alone on a weekend evening or after school when Jason was around because he is so mature. She explained that Jason has proven himself trustworthy and considerate over many years of baby-sitting for her younger children.

You can be assured that Jason will bring the same maturity, initiative, and enthusiasm to your school as he has to ours.

What important information does this recommendation offer to make Jason an attractive applicant?

- He is a first-decile quality student, even if his actual ranking is in the second decile.
- He has a passion for learning as evidenced by his challenging courseload.
- He is a positive presence in school.
- He is a "doer" who takes initiative.
- He is mature, responsible, and considerate of others.

Here is another example of an effective guidance counselor recommendation.

RECOMMENDATION FOR JACKIE

Every now and then, I come across a student whose situation in life humbles me and gives me a healthy dose of perspective. Jackie is one such student. Her grades are not the best in the school, her extracurricular involvement rather ordinary. But her optimism in the face of hardship and commitment to improving her lot make her stand above other students with comparatively comfortable and easy lives.

Jackie comes from a single-parent family of six, she being the second eldest. Her father, an alcoholic, left her mother when she was quite young. If that wasn't enough, we have evidence that the man Jackie's mother later married physically abused the children, until she finally divorced him two years ago. Jackie's mother earns a very modest living, and the family finances forced Jackie into taking a job to help out. Interested in medicine, Jackie took a position at a hospital cafeteria, reasoning that if the work didn't stimulate her, at least the surroundings would. She wanted to find a way to meet professionals in medicine to learn more about her career possibilities. She has worked thirty hours a week for several years now, which explains her minimal involvement in activities at school.

As I mentioned, Jackie's overall grades are not the best, but her science and math grades have been consistently high. Jackie was selected to participate in a six-week hospital internship for accomplished high school students interested in medicine last summer, but had to decline because it conflicted with her work responsibilities. Still, the nomination itself is an acknowledgment of her talent.

In the face of all this, Jackie remains positive about her life prospects. In fact, her response to the missed opportunity at the hospital was, "I'll just have to be more diligent about learning from the doctors and med students that I meet at work." Never once have I heard her complain about her situation. Granted, she does not fit into the straight-A, multiactivity mold, but she has so much more to offer in other ways.

What information does this recommendation offer that makes Jackie such an attractive candidate?

- She has overcome enormous obstacles to get where she is.
- She has a positive attitude.
- She is mature and will likely be able to assist students with all sorts of problems at college.
- There is a fit between Jackie's dream of becoming a doctor, her selection for the special internship, her work in the hospital, and her strength in the sciences.

■ Her lack of extracurricular involvement can be attributed to her need to work nearly full-time to help support her family.

■ Given her background, she will add to the diversity of the student body.

■ She may be capable of much more than is evident from her record, which does not account for missed opportunities (such as the internship she had to turn down).

ADMISSIONS OFFICERS TALK ABOUT WHAT THEY MOST WANT FROM GUIDANCE COUNSELOR RECOMMENDATIONS

"We ask guidance counselors to explain any anomalies on the record. We also ask that they use tangible examples when possible—we like to see more than opinion on these recommendations, we like to see statements backed up by quotes from teachers."

—*John Blackburn, Dean of Admissions, University of Virginia*

"The best counselor recommendations come from those counselors who take the challenge seriously by starting early, talking with all the teachers, and getting to know the kids personally."

—*Richard Shaw, Dean of Undergraduate Admissions and Financial Aid, Yale University*

OPTIONAL AND SUPPLEMENTAL RECOMMENDATIONS

An optional recommendation is one included by the college in its application materials but not required of candidates. A supplemental recommendation is one that is not provided by the college. Rather, it is a recommendation that a student decides to submit in addition to the guidance counselor, teacher, and optional recommendations. Optional and supplemental recommendations can come from academic sources (if you feel another teacher can add further to your profile), but more typically they come from nonacademic sources. This includes coaches, instructors or tutors in nonacademic courses such as pottery or drama, employers, community service supervisors, music instructors, Scout leaders, alumni of the college to which you are applying, religious leaders, or peers.

Often, supplemental recommendations are looked upon unfavorably by admissions committees because they do not provide any new information or special insight about the candidate. In fact, there is a saying in admissions offices that shows disdain for useless supplemental recommendations and other unsolicited materials: "The thicker the kid, the thicker the folder." Optional recommendations are looked upon favorably (after all, the college offered you the option!) as long as they provide new information or add further critical support to claims made elsewhere.

How do you make optional and supplemental recommendations worthwhile? First and foremost, you should include only extra recommendations from people who can offer insight in ways that other recommenders cannot. Whenever possible, it is best to provide as much information as possible through the required recommendations rather than relying on additional ones to do the job, because admissions officers look closely and favorably at the required letters. In some cases, however, a supplemental recommender may be in a better position to offer solid, in-depth information about you.

For example, a guidance counselor might say that you work 30 hours a week at a software company and nothing more. If your interest in computers is a crucial selling point for you, then your guidance counselor's letter does not help you in that regard. Therefore, it would behoove you to request an additional recommendation from someone at the company suited to discussing your work—your supervisor or some other senior coworker.

Second, as with your teacher recommendations, select optional and supplemental recommenders based on their abilities to address critical issues. If you have conveyed a penchant for involvement in solitary activities (stamp collecting, playing an instrument, computer programming), your social skills might constitute a critical issue. Therefore it would benefit you to seek a coach, club advisor, or community service leader to write on your behalf, speaking about your team spirit, ability to relate to others, or the like.

A common mistake made by applicants is requesting a recommendation from an alumnus or a well-known person for the sake of impressing the college with her connections. Unless this person knows you well and can offer real insight, the only thing that you will impress upon the admissions committee in this case is your poor judgment. Do not seek letters of support from alumni or important people *unless there is a reason apart from their status* that supports their writing on your behalf.

When should you consider soliciting an optional or supplementary recommendation?

- If you have an extraordinary accomplishment such that admissions officers might not appreciate its significance because of lack of familiarity with it. Here we mean genuinely "extraordinary"—admissions officers already know what it means to be named an All-American or Eagle Scout. But if an achievement is really unusual, you should ask someone equipped to convey the importance and prestige of such recognition to write a recommendation.

- If you have overcome hardship in your activity (athletic injury, defeat in a music or debate competition) and in so doing demonstrated admirable traits, such as perseverance, drive, commitment, or optimism, select a recommender who can speak about this.

- If you have a unique dedication to an activity, such as religious instruction or community service, that goes beyond the regular student's commitment, select a recommender who can convey the depth of your commitment.

- If you have changed significantly over time (for example, if you have matured from a shy, reserved wallflower in the ninth grade to student body president in the senior year or were once a self-absorbed prima donna who now uses her opportunities to benefit others), then request a recommendation from a person who can attest to this growth and transformation.

- If you have a close relationship with someone who knows well the college to which you are applying (an alum, professor, or trustee), then request a recommendation that will explain why you are such a good fit for the school.

- If you have been limited to math and English teacher recommendations but your greatest strength lies in a different academic subject, request a recommendation from a teacher in that subject.

- If a family or personal situation has affected your high school experience or performance, request a recommendation from a family friend, psychologist, spiritual leader, or someone else who can shed light on the situation and its repercussions.

Keep in mind that in most of the aforementioned circumstances, a guidance counselor is capable of addressing the issue. Request a supplemental or optional recommendation only if such a recommender can offer new information about you or if he will do a significantly better job of marketing your strengths and minimizing your weaknesses than a guidance counselor would.

A NOTE ON PEER RECOMMENDATIONS

Some colleges, such as Dartmouth, require a recommendation from a "peer," meaning a friend or acquaintance of the candidate, generally someone of approximately the same age. Dartmouth asks that this recommender provide information about the candidate's personal and academic qualities, especially his or her maturity, ability to work with others, interests, special talents, and experiences. A candidate can choose a good friend or someone he or she knows through an activity or class (a soccer teammate or lab partner, for example). Follow these guidelines if you are required to select a peer recommender:

➤ Choose someone who knows you well and can tell interesting stories and anecdotes to support his her comments.

➤ Choose someone who possesses superior analytical thinking and writing skills.

➤ Choose someone whom you regard as honorable, not likely to want to jeopardize your chances of being admitted to the college. This is especially important if you are choosing someone who is applying to the same college—you need to trust that he or she will want to do the best job possible in aiding your application purposes.

A NOTE ON PARENT RECOMMENDATIONS

Some colleges, notably Smith and Tulane, now ask for a statement from a parent of each applicant. Colleges that ask for such a statement are primarily looking for extremely personal information, material that only a loving guardian who has known the applicant for seventeen or so years could provide. Applicants should not worry too much about a parent's analytical thinking or writing skills, nor should they worry about a parent's English language skills or sophistication. As you have learned from reading other sections of this book, college admissions officers are often very attracted to candidates from low-opportunity households or situations. Thus, a recommendation from a parent who is not college educated, does not possess solid English writing skills, or cannot create a sophisticated letter will not necessarily harm you—such a letter may even benefit you substantially, because it will help the admissions officers to see how well you have succeeded given the situation in which you have grown up. An applicant should simply ask his or her parent to provide an honest statement with as much detail as possible, perhaps highlighting the applicant's desire to attend the particular college or passion in pursuing his or her dreams. Other helpful areas for parents to address include weaknesses that the child has overcome, family problems or circumstances that may have affected the child's performance and outlook over the years, and areas in which the child has matured or grown in recent years.

ADMISSIONS OFFICERS DISCUSS OPTIONAL
AND SUPPLEMENTAL RECOMMENDATIONS

WHAT OTHER RECOMMENDATIONS, BESIDES THOSE FROM
TEACHERS AND GUIDANCE COUNSELORS, DO YOU REQUEST?

"The peer recommendation is very important to us. These tend to have a real freshness to them. We get to know a student on human terms, as a person. They're very valuable. The peer recommendation often crystallizes the whole case for me—I'm often in a position where I'm fairly certain I want to accept a student, then I read the peer evaluation and it does wonderful things for the candidate, making admission the clear decision in my mind."

—Karl Furstenberg, Dean of Admissions and Financial Aid, Dartmouth College

"We encourage peer recommendations, but they aren't required here."

—Barbara-Jan Wilson, Dean of Admissions and Financial Aid, Wesleyan University

"Yes, we recently began requesting a parental recommendation from our applicants. Parents have known their kids for eighteen years—they have a great perspective on personality and growth. They deal with an entirely different level than do teachers and guidance counselors. The parent recommendation makes the process more human."

—Nanci Tessier, Director of Admissions, Smith College

Is It Okay for Applicants to Submit Extra Recommendations?

"An extra recommendation is fine, as long as the applicant has thought about it. A candidate should ask himself, 'What new dimension is being added here?' before submitting extra letters of recommendation."

—Eric J. Furda, Director of Undergraduate Admissions, Columbia University

"Theoretically students can submit as many recommendations as they like. However, they should realize, that if they submit two or three, we will read them thoroughly, whereas if they submit fifteen, we'll skim them quickly."

—Barbara Bergman, Associate Dean of Admissions, Georgetown University

"We've seen excellent recommendations from employers—some of the best recommendations have also come from parents who have employed their own kids. Because we don't generally interview, the recommendations become very important."

—Richard Avitabile, Director of Admissions, New York University

"Extra recommendations are always fine. We like and welcome them, but students need to be judicious. An extra recommendation should have a purpose, make a contribution, and not reiterate what others have said."

—Nancy Hargrave Meislahn, Director of Undergraduate Admissions, Cornell University

"Only when there is a special arts talent do we recommend that an applicant get an extra recommendation."

—Katie Fretwell, Director of Admissions, Amherst College

"Remember the law of diminishing returns when thinking about adding extra recommendations to your file. More is not necessarily better."

—Lee Stetson, Dean of Admissions, University of Pennsylvania

"One extra recommendation is okay. After that the focus gets taken away. Students handing in additional letters should be sure that the recommendations provide additional information, information not found elsewhere in the application."

—*Barbara-Jan Wilson, Dean of Admissions and Financial Aid, Wesleyan University*

"Recommendations from bosses or employers occasionally can help a student, but letters from friends of family don't help."

—*Michael Goldberger, Director of Admissions, Brown University*

"We don't discourage additional recommendations. We like them, we're not fussy on this issue."

—*Richard Steele, Dean of Admissions, Bowdoin College*

"Supplemental recommendations—from rabbis, summer camp directors, employers—usually don't make much difference. Occasionally they work well, though."

—*Jonathan Reider, Senior Associate Director of Admissions, Stanford University*

HOW TO APPROACH A RECOMMENDER

The typical high school student's approach to a potential recommender involves a hurried interaction in the hallway or after class in which the student does little more than make a squirmish plea for a recommendation ("I'm wondering if maybe you could do me a big favor?") and then receives indifferent agreement from the teacher. (And sometimes then a sigh of relief from the student before she dashes off, late to field hockey practice!) This represents at best a completely wasted opportunity. In fact, it may prove to be worse than that.

THE MOST IMPORTANT GENERAL RULES TO KEEP IN MIND WHEN APPROACHING A RECOMMENDER

1. Give a recommender an opportunity to decline the request if she does not think she can write you a strong letter.

2. Allow your recommender enough time to write a good recommendation.

3. Provide your recommender with enough information to make her job easy and ensure an insightful letter of support.

Ideally, you should start the process about two months before the recommendation deadline. Begin your request to a potential supporter by scheduling ahead of time a 15-minute meeting with the person. The meeting should be face to face, not over the telephone, unless a meeting cannot be arranged. Arrive at the meeting well prepared to give information including:

- What colleges you are applying to and why,
- Why you have chosen this recommender,
- Your positioning effort, including strengths to be marketed and weaknesses to be addressed,
- How this person can help you, and
- Stories and examples you would like used as illustrations of your qualities.

It is best if you come to the meeting with a print-out of this information that you can give to the recommender, so she can use it to refresh her memory when sitting down to do the task. If the recommender is someone unassociated with your school and/or unaccustomed to writing letters of support on behalf of college applicants (perhaps a religious leader or art instructor), then you might also want to explain the level of competition you face in applying to your chosen schools, what is required in the admissions process, and how important the recommendations are. You of course need to do this carefully, not in a way that would seem condescending to the recommender. No adult wants to be treated as ignorant or less than capable by a high school student!

Next comes one of the most critical pieces of the process, which is often overlooked by high school students who feel desperate about merely finding recommenders rather than ascertaining that they will find the *right* recommenders: Make sure that each recommender is going to write a very favorable recommendation for you. The way to be sure of this is by giving the person an "out" if she feels unable to be highly supportive of your candidacy. Ask her if she believes she would be the right person to write a recommendation for you. If she feels at all uncomfortable because she knows that her honesty would prevent her from writing a highly favorable letter, then she will probably suggest that someone else might be more appropriate. If she declines, seems hesitant, or suggests using someone else, do not press her! You do not want to weasel a recommendation out of someone who is not eager to write one; it is bound to do you no justice. Thank her for her time and move on.

If, on the other hand, she agrees to write a letter, give her a further briefing in both verbal and written form. Tell her in more detail why you are applying to each particular school. Explain how you are trying to position yourself in general, and note any differences in positioning for particular schools if necessary.

Show her what questions she will need to answer about you and how you think these relate to your positioning. Suggest stories and anecdotes she can use. Provide her with enough detail to refresh her memory about the stories. If appropriate, ask her to address weaknesses.

This well-thought-out approach for procuring recommendations will prove helpful in a number of ways. First, it minimizes the chance that you will end up with a lukewarm recommendation. Second, you will have been highly organized and shown a serious attitude about your college applications, always a good impression upon the recommender. If you had followed the nervous, pleading, last-minute approach, she would likely deem you not quite as fit for Williams or Yale. Third, your organization and efficiency will avoid any resentment on the part of the recommender (which she might feel if she were asked at the last minute for the letter of support). Fourth, you know in advance what stories she is apt to tell and in what ways she will support your positioning. This means that you will retain some degree of control over the admissions process: You will know not to use the same stories yourself; you will know what qualities and traits she may not be able to address, in order to ensure that they are well documented elsewhere; you will know what points do not necessarily need to be included in other recommendations.

TACTFUL WAYS TO PRESENT YOUR MARKETING PITCH TO RECOMMENDERS

Here are some suggestions for presenting your marketing pitch without sounding presumptuous:

➤ "I have been researching colleges and it's clear to me that given the low acceptance rates at so many of the schools I'm interested in, I'm going to have to distinguish myself. I think that what will really count for me is ... Similarly, I think my biggest weakness is probably ..."

➤ "I know that, as an athlete (or whatever label), I might be stereotyped by admissions committees as being a 'jock.' I want to set myself apart from other athletes and avoid these stereotypes. I think the best way to do that is ..."

➤ "I have been working with my guidance counselor/college consultant to evaluate my overall profile and develop the best way to market myself. We have concluded that it is best for me to focus on ... while also ..."

MAKING THE JOB EASY FOR YOUR RECOMMENDERS

Try to do as much of the work as you can for your recommenders, to make their job as simple as possible. Your recommenders are undoubtedly busy people and probably have many other college recommendations to write, in addition to yours. Allow them plenty of time to write the recommendation (two months is optimal) and provide them with the following:

➤ The deadline for each application (and whether it is a postmark deadline or the day it must be in the admissions office)

➤ Stamped, addressed envelopes for each

➤ Several copies of each form, with the objective data about you (i.e., name, address, etc.) already filled in

➤ A list of the main points the person must discuss to satisfy the recommendation questions for all your target schools in a one-size-fits-all letter (see page 429 for more details on this)

➤ Copies of your own application essays

➤ A description of your positioning strategy, noting strengths and weaknesses

➤ Samples of work you have done for the person

➤ A list of your past and recent extracurricular activities (including employment) and what you have gained from them (this is especially important for your guidance counselor's recommendation)

➤ A list of experiences and stories the recommender can use to support your positioning

➤ A resume, if you have one

WHAT MAKES A GOOD RECOMMENDATION?

A good recommendation should show that you are an outstanding individual, one who is an appropriate candidate for a top college by virtue of having the brains, personality, special talents, and leadership ability such schools are seeking. It should also support your individual positioning strategy. A recommendation should:

■ Be well-written. It should be grammatically correct and reflect the thinking of a well-educated person.

■ Reflect substantial thought and effort on the part of the recommender. In other words, the writer shows he cares about you enough to spend the time to be as helpful as possible.

■ Show the writer knows you well. It should provide highly specific examples to illustrate points. These generally should not be the same examples you use in your own essays or that other recommenders note, although some overlap is acceptable. As with your essays, the use of illustrative stories and examples will make the recommendation credible and memorable.

■ Not mention things best handled elsewhere in the application. SAT scores, for example, usually have no place in a recommendation letter, unless the guidance counselor is mentioning them to explain extenuating circumstances that affected your performance.

■ Show you to be distinctive. The use of examples helps make you an individual rather than a type.

■ Discuss your growth and development over time.

■ Explicitly compare you to others who have gone to the college, if possible.

■ Show how you meet the requirements of the college and will add to the collegiate community.

Note that there are exceptions to the first requirement for a good recommendation letter, that it be well-written. For example, if you were to ask your student in an adult literacy program to write a recommendation for you, admissions officers would not expect it to contain perfect grammar and punctuation. On the contrary, part of the appeal of such a letter would be that it comes from someone outside the league of those with college-application know-how and that you are involved in helping that person, thereby improving your community. Similarly, if you were to ask an Outward Bound instructor to write you a recommendation, grammar mistakes and other imperfections would not be frowned upon by college admissions officers, because the purpose of this letter would be to address qualities not directly related to academics.

WORDS AND PHRASES TO AVOID IN RECOMMENDATIONS

Certain words and phrases can easily be misinterpreted by admissions committees as subtle criticisms of a student if not qualified or explained:

➤ "Diligent and conscientious": When referring to a student's academic capabilities, this can imply that she is a hard worker but not necessarily intelligent or insightful. If such a phrase is used to describe you when referring to academics and is left unexplained or without context, it might be considered indicative that your accomplishments have come only as a result of hard work and that your natural abilities and talents are limited.

➤ "Cares about grades": Implies that a student is a grade-grubber and not interested in learning for learning's sake.

Furthermore, if a recommender is overly exuberant about you but the critique does not fit in with your academic record, admissions committees might assume he is exaggerating at best, lying at worst, in order to protect or help you.

CAN RECOMMENDERS WRITE A ONE-SIZE-FITS-ALL RECOMMENDATION?

In an ideal world, all recommenders would take the time and energy to fill out each recommendation form for applicants' many target schools. In an ideal world, each day would contain thirty-six hours and each week eight days! Thus, although a few schools note that they much prefer recommenders to use the recommendation forms provided by the college, reality dictates that many teachers simply write one comprehensive letter to be sent to all of an applicant's target schools.

For the sake of efficiency, it is generally fine for a recommender to write a single letter of recommendation and attach it to the recommendation form for each school, *as long as it answers all of the questions that a school poses.* In other words, recommenders should not feel that they have to reinvent the wheel for each of your target schools, but they must be thorough and complete in performing their task. It is important that all recommenders realize the importance of explicitly answering all questions asked by each college. They must also fill out any required grids or checklists (concerning your qualities and abilities) that a school provides as part of its recommendation form if they choose to attach a one-size-fits-all recommendation letter.

In addition, there may be special cases in which a particular school should receive a slightly modified or amplified version of a recommendation letter. For example, if your positioning efforts are different for one of your target schools, you will want to ask your recommenders to keep this in mind (if it is appropriate, given their knowledge about you) for that school. Or if your recommender herself attended one of your target schools, she will want to make note of that in the recommendation.

HOW LONG SHOULD A RECOMMENDATION BE?

The recommendation forms provided by colleges often offer very limited space for a given response, but your recommender may want to write more. This space limitation should be treated differently from the limitations set out for your own application essays, *unless the recommendation form specifically asks that your recommender not go beyond a certain space or word limit,* which is rare. Recommenders are given more latitude in choosing how best to write a recommendation. It is generally acceptable for a recommender to write more than is permissible if he feels it is necessary in order to give the best letter of support. Of course, length does not always equal quality, and some ideas are best conveyed concisely. Acceptable length varies with the quality of the letter of recommendation. A recommendation that is a bit too long according to the prescribed standard will not count against you. This is one reason why it is appropriate to use the one-size-fits-all recommendation, which does not fit into the format provided.

TIMELINESS OF RECOMMENDATIONS

The schools can keep you informed as to whether a given recommendation has arrived. If it has not arrived and time is getting short, contact your recommender and ask very politely (not accusingly) how his effort is progressing and whether or not there is anything else you can do to make the process easier. This will tend to prod a recommender into action.

THE FOLLOW-UP

Be sure to send your recommenders a nice note thanking them for their efforts and stating that you will keep them informed of your progress. This is simple good manners and the least you can do to show appreciation in return for help in gaining admission to the college of your choice.

If you approach your recommender properly and on time, the chances are that he will submit your letters of support well before they are due. What should you do, however, if you call your schools and learn that a recommendation is missing? You can certainly approach a recommender to encourage him to submit it soon, as suggested previously. On the other hand, you can take a subtler tactic and send him a follow-up note explaining that you have completed the application process and are currently awaiting the schools' decisions. If he has not yet submitted your recommendation letters, this should spur him into action.

Keep your recommenders informed as to each school's decision. Also be sure to tell them what you have decided to do in the end. At this point it would not be inappropriate to send them a small, inexpensive gift (e.g., flowers, chocolates, a book). Very few people do this and it is certainly not required. High school teachers are generally accustomed to writing recommendations and consider it part of their job—they certainly do not expect students to buy them gifts in return. But considering, in the case of high school teachers, that their efforts perhaps are not as appreciated as they should be, such a small gesture might mean a lot to them. For an outside recommender, the opposite is true: Writing recommendations may be more taxing and not part of his usual job description—so a little extra appreciation might be especially welcomed.

Do your best to stay in touch with recommenders as you go through college, even if this means nothing more than dropping a postcard in the mail or sending them E-mail with news of your progress.

A SPECIAL NOTE FOR INTERNATIONAL APPLICANTS

If you have a potential recommender who is not able to write well in English, you can help matters greatly by writing up some stories for his use ahead of time. Furthermore, many schools are not averse to your translating the recommendation, as long as you include the original recommendation with your translation.

WAIVING YOUR RIGHT TO SEE RECOMMENDATIONS: THE BUCKLEY AMENDMENT

The Buckley Amendment allows every applicant access to a college's files containing his or her recommendations. Admissions committees look more favorably upon the recommendations of applicants who have waived the right to see them because they can be confident of the recommender's honesty and openness. Moreover, if you do not waive this right, admissions committees will question whether you have something to hide, doubt the fairness of your recommenders, or suspect that you have tried to bully your recommenders into writing what you want.

We encourage you to waive your right to access your recommendations. Waiving your right does not mean that you cannot ever see your recommendations. The Amendment concerns your relationship with the college and its files and has no bearing whatsoever on your relationship with your recommender and the letter he has written or has stored on his hard drive. In other words, if the recommender chooses to share a recommendation with you, it is perfectly acceptable and legal for you to see it, even if you have waived your right to access the college's files.

Appendix VI

The Recommendation Organizer

Recommender's Name _____

Title _____

Mailing Address _____

Telephphone: Work _____ Home _____

Fax: Work _____ Home _____

E-mail _____

Date to Make Contact _____

Date Contact Made _____

Schools for Which He/She Is Writing Recommendations

Materials Given/Explained

Further Materials to Be Supplied

Progress Checks and Results

Schools That Confirm Receipt

Note: This form can be copied or you can generate your own version to use for each of your recommenders.

14

INTERVIEWING

— KEY POINTS —

Establish your objectives: conveying a good impression, imparting your strengths, demonstrating your knowledge, and gaining information

■

Prepare yourself by:
—Learning the most likely questions
—Knowing yourself and your candidacy
—Knowing the school
—Formulating your own questions

■

Know what to expect from different types of interviewers:
—Admissions officers
—Alums
—Students

■

Practice via mock interviews

■

Familiarize yourself with the "do"s and "don't"s of interviewing

INTRODUCTION

Chances are that you will interview at most of the colleges to which you apply because most top colleges still firmly maintain the importance of a one-on-one session with their applicants. A few of the top colleges, such as Harvard and Georgetown, require an interview. Other schools, such as MIT, "highly recommend" that their candidates interview. Others still, such as Bowdoin or Yale, make interviews available in the hope that most candidates will take advantage of the extra opportunity to market themselves. At some universities with multiple undergraduate colleges, the interview policy differs from school to school. At Cornell, for example, interviews are required of candidates applying to the hotel and architecture schools, but not of candidates at other schools.

Most of the selective schools view the interview as important and want to interview most or all of their applicants for several reasons. One is the colleges' desire to admit outstanding *people* rather than just names attached to outstanding test scores and grades. An applicant's personality and social skills often "count." A related reason is that interviews offer schools the chance to learn more about applicants. Some things are not readily determinable without a face-to-face meeting. A high school student's interviewing ability can tell an admissions officer quite a bit about his presentation, maturity level, charm, confidence, sociability, and fit with the school. Thus, an applicant with good "paper" credentials will be less attractive to a school if she comes across poorly in an interview. Interviews also provide an opportunity to probe areas insufficiently addressed in the application itself.

A final reason for college admissions officers' love of interviews is that schools can market themselves better by meeting individually with applicants, even if the interview is conducted by an off-campus alum or a current student. This is particularly true for elite schools that compete for the best students each year. These schools welcome any chance to gain a voice through the interview, getting a jump on their rivals by better assessing candidates and promoting themselves to their top choices.

Not all colleges interview their applicants, though. Stanford, for example, does not conduct interviews, citing logistical difficulties in arranging them for its large applicant pools, as well as a belief that applicants are better judged on the basis of other application criteria. A few colleges, such as Williams and Amherst, have omitted the interview in recent years because they believe it to be an unreliable indicator of potential for success in college.

WHAT ADMISSIONS OFFICERS SAY ABOUT THEIR INTERVIEWING POLICIES AND THE IMPORTANCE OF THE INTERVIEW

"We want to talk to our applicants. Only in a rare case, if we have no alums in the applicant's area, would a student not interview—and even then, we usually try at the very least to do a phone interview."

—Marlyn McGrath Lewis, Director of Admissions, Harvard University

On-campus interviews are required at the hotel administration and architecture schools. At the other schools students can interview with alums in their area.

—Nancy Hargrave Meislahn, Director of Undergraduate Admissions, Cornell University

"We especially encourage home-schooled applicants, older or nontraditional student applicants, and other people with special concerns to come to us for an interview. We'd like to talk to applicants with special situations so that we can better understand their cases when it comes time."

—John Blackburn, Dean of Admissions, University of Virginia

"We do not require interviews anymore at Williams. Studies have shown that interviews are not accurate predictors of success or of anything else we would deem important in the admission process. We do offer forty-minute one-on-one sessions for applicants to ask us questions about the college, but these are not evaluative interviews of any sort."

—Philip Smith, Dean of Admissions, Williams College

"Our interview is required. It's only optional in areas where there is no alumni interviewer available."

—Barbara Bergman, Associate Dean of Admissions, Georgetown University

"The interview isn't required. It's more of an opportunity for the candidate to get to know Brown."

—Michael Goldberger, Director of Admissions, Brown University

"There are no interviews at all at Stanford. We just don't have the ability to interview a substantial portion of the applicant pool with our alums. We also think we learn enough from the rest of the application. We also think we learn enough from the rest of the application. Research has shown that interviews are easily prone to bias."

—Jonathan Reider, Senior Associate Director of Admissions, Stanford University

"We think interviews are more important for a student's evaluative purposes than for our own."

—John Hanson, Director of Admissions, Middlebury College

"We take it pretty seriously. The interview report becomes a formalized part of our admissions evaluation and gets a rating."

—Richard Shaw, Dean of Undergraduate Admissions and Financial Aid, Yale University

"Ninety-five percent of our applicants get interviewed. All interviews are by alums, though we will interview kids in the office if they are coming from abroad to visit MIT."

—*Marilee Jones, Dean of Admissions, Massachusetts Institute of Technology*

INTERVIEW PROCEDURES

Just as there is no one uniform interviewing *policy*, neither is there a singular interviewing *procedure* shared by the various colleges. Colleges have different systems for organizing and facilitating their interviews.

There are three different types of interviewers used by the colleges. Alums conduct interviews on behalf of colleges in their home locations across the United States and overseas as well. Admissions officers conduct interviews on campus and while traveling across the country on high school visits. (Note, however, that Directors of Admissions generally do not conduct interviews, except under very special circumstances.) Finally, some colleges have recently adopted the practice of using current college students to interview future candidates on campus. Some colleges use only one type of interviewer. Northwestern and the University of Pennsylvania, for example, use only alumni interviewers. The University of Virginia offers interviews only with admissions officers on campus. Most schools, however, use a combination of resources—alumni, admissions officers, current students—to conduct their interviews. When applying to Duke, Brown, or Wellesley, for example, an applicant can interview at home with an alum or on campus with an admissions officer. Dartmouth, Wesleyan, and Yale use all three kinds of interviewers—alumni, admissions officers, and seniors at the college—for interviewing.

CONFIDENTIALITY ISSUES

There is no reason to worry about sharing personal information or information contained within your application materials with the two varieties of "unofficial" interview administrators (i.e., alums and current students). The colleges understand concerns over privacy and have generally taken measures to assuage your fears. Many schools give interviewers nothing more than a briefing on an applicant prior to an interview. In other words, a non–admissions officer interviewer most likely does not have access to your test scores, grades, recommendations, or essays. Other schools have students and alums sign confidentiality agreements to ensure that they do not discuss the cases of the candidates they interview. All interviewers are expected to take the interviewing process very seriously and not to discuss candidates' private issues and concerns with other people.

Schools use interview results slightly differently. The great majority of the colleges give the interview no formalized weight factor in the evaluation process. A few schools, such as Yale, assign a rating to each candidate based on his or her interview results, though. Most colleges place the interview report as the last piece of information in an applicant's folder, so it is the last document a reader reviews in a file. The interview evaluation therefore often takes on the responsibility of sealing a case. Even at colleges that do not assign a particular weighted value to the interview in the admissions decision, the interview has the ability to significantly color the overall evaluation of an applicant, particularly when it is located at the back of the file as "the last word" on a candidate. At schools where admissions officers themselves interview applicants, the interview has even more power because the interviewer is present at committee meetings to act as an advocate or naysayer on behalf of the applicant. Most colleges confirm that the interview rarely "breaks" a case, but it can sometimes "make" one when a borderline candidate gets a rave review from an interviewer.

ADMISSIONS OFFICERS OFFER OPINIONS ON AN INTERVIEW'S ABILITY TO INFLUENCE A DECISION

"I believe 90% of interviews confirm what's already in the folder."

—*James Bock, Director of Admissions, Swarthmore College*

"The interview evaluation is the last piece of paper in the file, so it closes a reader's impression of the candidate. An interview could only break a decision if a candidate came in with a real attitude—this has happened, but it's quite rare."

—*Barbara-Jan Wilson, Dean of Admissions and Financial Aid, Wesleyan University*

"For the most part, they're positive. Few interviews are damaging."

—*Delsie Phillips, Director of Admissions, Haverford College*

"Interviews inform and supplement in an important way, but they are not a deciding factor."

—*David Borus, Dean of Admissions and Financial Aid, Vassar College*

"The interview is probably the first thing we'd discard in a file—if everything else pointed to a spectacular candidate but the interview was so-so, we'd probably ignore the interview report."

—*Richard Steele, Dean of Admissions, Bowdoin College*

SHOULD YOU INTERVIEW IF GIVEN A CHOICE?

If a school "strongly recommends" or even "recommends" that applicants interview, it is usually a mistake not to do so, as long as an interview can be conveniently arranged given your location or college visit schedule. Failing to interview (or at least to attempt to set up an interview) may be taken as an indication of a lack of interest in the school or a tacit admission that you do poorly in one-on-one situations. Wesleyan and Middlebury lean toward the feeling that failing to set up an interview is representative of a lack of interest in the school, unless there is a legitimate reason why a candidate cannot interview. Other schools, such as Brown, Yale, and MIT, however, hold that if a student declines an interview, it is simply an opportunity lost for the candidate. These schools say that it does not matter from an admissions standpoint whether or not a student interviews, but that applicants should know that frequently the interviewer becomes a very powerful supporter for the applicant. Most admissions officers thus agree that is usually a mistake to decline an interview.

There are often logistical considerations, of course, and schools are aware that it may not be realistic to expect you to travel 3000 miles for an interview, especially if you are from a low-income background or have already visited the campus. Logistical barriers are rare these days, though, because the top colleges generally send their representatives to major regions on a regular basis and have alums scattered throughout the country and worldwide.

Although it is almost always appropriate to interview, if you are certain you will make a poor impression, either take steps to improve your interviewing skills or maneuver to avoid an interview. The people who should probably avoid interviews include:

- Those who are pathologically shy (not just the ordinary variety of shy);
- Those whose English language abilities will crack under the strain of an interview;
- Those who feel they cannot change or modify any inappropriate behavior or presentation problems, such as a macho attitude or dressing like a neo-Nazi skinhead;
- Those who are so contentious that they will inevitably get into a verbal battle with their interviewer; and
- Obviously anorexic girls (or boys, although they rarely fit into the anorexic stereotype that troubles admissions officers).

The preceding types of college candidates should consider not interviewing if given a choice because their individual problems might get in the way of their performing well in an interview and impressing the interviewer. Those who are desperately shy or whose English language skills might cause problems in a nerve-wracking situation might stumble too much in an interview to do themselves any good. Those with inappropriate behavior or presentation issues, as well as those whose anger or contentiousness tends to get them in trouble in social situations, should avoid personal contact with those involved in the admissions process. Anyone who is visibly anorexic (not just "too thin," but worn down to the point that strangers often stare or make comments) might give the interviewer (especially an admissions officer) cause for concern over her general health, mental stability, and ability to stay in school while battling an eating disorder.

ADMISSIONS OFFICERS DISCUSS HOW APPLICANTS ARE VIEWED WHEN THEY CHOOSE NOT TO INTERVIEW

"Interviews are recommended, but it is not at all a problem if a student doesn't do one. If an interview evaluation is in the file, we look at it. The absence of an interview evaluation in a student's file is neutral, not negative."

—Christoph Guttentag, Director of Undergraduate Admissions, Duke University

"If an applicant chooses not to interview, it is an opportunity lost for that applicant—because frequently the interviewer becomes a powerful supporter of a candidate. We don't care if an applicant declines, though. It doesn't bother us, we just see it as an advantage lost for the applicant."

—Marilee Jones, Dean of Admissions, Massachusetts Institute of Technology

"Students who do not opt for them are generally seen as lacking real interest in and seriousness about Wesleyan—but sometimes there's a reason for not interviewing."

—Barbara-Jan Wilson, Dean of Admissions and Financial Aid, Wesleyan University

"We don't penalize an applicant for not doing an interview. What we don't like is if an applicant doesn't show up for one, or if he cancels and reschedules a bunch of times. Alums tell us these things, and this kind of behavior makes us wonder how serious the candidate is about Penn."

—Eric Kaplan, Director of Admissions, University of Pennsylvania

"If a student decides not to do an interview after being contacted by our alum, then it's always a good idea to tell us why. Write us a letter to the effect that, 'I think I communicated all my information well in the application. I have visited the school, and have no further questions. I'm having scheduling difficulties ...' If the applicant just doesn't call back the alum when contacted, then that reflects badly upon him or her."

—Eric J. Furda, Director of Undergraduate Admissions, Columbia University

PREPARING FOR THE INTERVIEW

The interview is important to the college for the reasons listed earlier. It is important for you, the candidate, as well—because it means that you have the opportunity to market yourself in a format in which many people do very little good for themselves. To be a good interviewee, you need to have prepared the points you want to get across, anticipate what questions will be asked, and understand how to enhance your presentation to satisfy your needs and those of your interviewer. In other words, you should analyze what you will confront and then practice performing under realistic conditions. Doing this will help you to avoid going blank, letting things you intended not to share slip out, forgetting to mention important points, or being unable to keep the interview flowing in a comfortable fashion.

Some candidates are afraid of the interview and set themselves hopelessly limited objectives for it. They hope to get through it without embarrassing themselves. Or they hope that the interviewer is simply "nice," smiling a lot and seeming to be mildly interested in the conversation. You have the chance to make a very positive impression that will further your marketing efforts, so it is up to you to seize it. Do not simply hope to survive the interview and extract pleasantries from your interviewer. Set higher goals for yourself: Be determined to achieve positive results. Use the interview to reinforce the positioning efforts you have used in your essays and recommendations.

You already have a marketing strategy in place, so go back to it when you are considering what you hope to accomplish in the interview. If you have positioned yourself as a virtuoso violinist whose talent has led him to an interest in late European music history, for example, this positioning strategy will help you think through the interview and how to prepare for it.

Ask yourself the following questions when beginning your preparations:

1. How do I want the interviewer to think of me? What specific impressions and information do I want her to carry away from our meeting?

2. How can I reinforce my strengths and address my key weaknesses?

3. How can I show that I know a great deal about the school—not only that I am extremely interested in attending the college, but also that I am prepared for the interview?

4. How can I learn whatever I need to know to decide what school to attend?

MENTAL PREPARATIONS

In mentally preparing for the interview, you need to know what to expect and set yourself up to do well once you are thrust into the spotlight. The discussion here is designed to help you anticipate and prepare for various aspects of your college interviews.

TYPICAL INTERVIEW FORMAT

➤ A welcome from the interviewer.

➤ A few chatty basic "warm-up" questions from the interviewer. These might include questions such as, "Did you find the interview location all right?" or "How are you?"

➤ A comment or two from the interviewer about the school, its future, and the admissions process.

➤ Detailed questions from the interviewer, which may lead to a back-and-forth discussion. Most interviewers start with some sort of general question, such as asking you to describe your personal background (including where you grew up, your family, etc.) and your high school education.

➤ An opportunity for the interviewee to ask questions.

➤ Conclusion. The interviewer might mention what the next step of the admissions process is; then there will be an exchange of thank-yous and a good-bye.

THE INTERVIEW FORMAT

A typical interview will last between 30 and 60 minutes, although if it is with an alum it may be even longer. The first few minutes of an interview may not involve substantive discussion, but they are still important in forming the interviewer's general impression of you. Therefore, do your best to appear confident and relaxed when answering initial questions, before reaching the heart of the interview. Doing so will give you confidence and momentum to carry you through the following parts of the interview.

THE INTERVIEWER

You can expect different things of an interviewer depending on whether he is an admissions officer, an alum, or a student. Here are some guidelines on what you are likely to encounter with each type of interviewer.

An interview with an admissions officer is likely to be the most formal, although not necessarily the most difficult, of the three types of meetings. Admissions officers will conduct themselves in a gracious and poised manner—their job is not only to find out more about you, but also to leave you with positive impressions of their schools. They are thus likely to consider an interview as much a public relations opportunity as anything else. Admissions officers have plenty of experience interviewing and socializing, so they should not leave you feeling uncomfortable or lead you astray in your discussions. In addition, college admissions personnel are accustomed to dealing with high-school-aged students—they generally like teenagers and understand teenage modes of behavior and dress, so you probably do not have to be as careful with them as you might with alumni interviewers, who likely do not interact with people your age on a regular basis.

At many schools, interviews with admissions officers are conducted only during the late summer and fall months, so that students interviewing with administration members will not yet have submitted any application information to the school. If you have already made an application to the college at the time of interviewing, though, admissions officers will know more about you and your background than will alumni or student interviewers, because they have access to all pieces of information in your file. Therefore, you need to be careful to prepare to expand on or supplement information included in your written application when interviewing with admissions officers, in order to avoid boring them with repetitious details.

Because interviewing applicants is a significant part of an admissions officer's job, you can be sure he will be extremely well prepared and thorough. This does not mean, however, that he will spend a great deal of time with you. On the contrary, an admissions staffer's busy schedule will probably keep an interview short rather than allowing it to run overtime (even if it is conducted while he is traveling to your high school or hometown), whereas alums and students may have more time to spend with you.

An admissions officer will want to gain some definite opinions about how your past experience and career goals suit you for his school's program, but that does not mean he will be uninterested in your personal life or in getting a feel for your general demeanor. Do not become a straight-and-narrow bore in front of the admissions folks! Be serious, but not overly so. Admissions personnel are concerned about filling their programs with lively candidates who offer more than just good grades and admirable future goals.

An admissions representative will obviously have the most thorough knowledge of the "official" aspects of the college, such as its opportunities for study abroad and its strongest departments or fields. But he will not necessarily know much about how to get involved in the college's annual animation festival or what life in the dorms is all about. Many admissions departments, however, now hire one or two of their recent graduates in order to improve their own perspectives, so this is not always true. A recent grad doing a stint in the admissions office can be a fantastic resource regarding all aspects of the program—formal and informal, academic and social. She essentially represents all three roles wrapped up in one: admissions officer, alum, and college student.

INTERVIEWS WITH ALUMNI

An interview with an alum is likely to be the most relaxed and easiest of the three kinds of meetings. (Obviously, this is not *always* the case. An occasional alum will approach her role with a hard-nosed determination to let only the best applicants shine—perhaps she is one of those who remembers "the halcyon days" of her alma mater with pride and wants to ensure that her school maintains high standards. Similarly, you may simply run into a personality clash with an alum, as with any other type of interviewer.) In most cases, alums who volunteer their time to interview applicants do so because they are personable, friendly types who like to meet new people and are basically interested in promoting their schools.

Alumni interviews generally take place in the alum's home, in the alum's office, or at a public meeting space such as a coffee shop. Interviews that are conducted in an alum's home tend to be more relaxed and perhaps a bit longer than those that take place outside the home. Interviews with alums in their offices might seem more formal because of the setting and the interviewer's naturally more serious demeanor while at the workplace. Some alums, particularly older ones, will be more sensitive to appearance and language than will admissions officers or students, both of whom are accustomed to being around college-aged students, with their sometimes radical dress codes and casual lingo. Err on the cautious side when dressing for an alumni interview—especially if you know ahead of time that the person is older—and be especially careful with your speech and behavior during the interview.

You can bet that the alum will have received some limited information about you, but her knowledge of you and your candidacy will almost surely be sparse. You should inquire of her or of the school's admissions office before the interview exactly what information she will have received so that you can bring appropriate materials with you to the interview to share and leave with her. You might want to bring a copy of your application or your resume for her. She will probably not have seen enough of your application to know what your weaknesses are, and thus will not challenge you on these points. By the same token, she will not know your strengths and positive attributes, so to make a good impression you might have to talk at length about ideas you have already expressed in your essays and supporting materials. It is certainly fine to ask your interviewer, if she does not offer the information herself, how much background material she has been given so you know what to talk about and what not to repeat.

Alumni interviewers are instructed to follow certain guidelines, so they will definitely ask some crucial questions—but most will not be as meticulous or sharp-shooting as an admissions officer or student interviewer. Alums tend to be chattier, more relaxed, and more interested in selling their beloved schools (or recounting their glory days for you) than they are in grilling you or using hardball tactics. An interview with an alum might feel more like a conversation with your Mom's friend at a holiday party than the intimidating or stressful experience you might conjure up in your nightmares. It will be unlike the casual conversations you have with friends your own age, yet it might not be scary or uncomfortable.

One drawback of having an alumni interview is that your interviewer will not be present in admissions committee meetings to personally push your case and, furthermore, might not know how to formulate a winning position to support your application. Although schools that use alumni interviewers take their opinions seriously, an alum can convey his opinion about you only through a written evaluation that he sends in to the admissions office after your meeting. Even with a favorable impression of you, if he is not an effective or convincing writer, his evaluation might not exude the necessary enthusiasm to make a serious impact upon the admissions committee when they sit down to review your file. He may be relatively unpracticed in the art of admissions and might not know what it takes to push an applicant from reject to waitlist status, or from waitlist to admit status. A professional admissions officer interviewer, on the contrary, will not only know how to convey a proper argument for a candidate, but might also be able to argue her case in person at an admissions committee session.

Another drawback of having an alumni interview is that those who have not been part of the school for some time will know the least about it. In other words, if you are hoping that your interview will provide a great opportunity to learn more about a school's program and how it compares to others, an interview with an alum who has been out of school five years or more might leave you unsatisfied. Even if an alum graduated fairly recently, it is likely that certain aspects of the school have changed since her time or are currently in the process of revision. If the alum graduated quite some time ago, she probably understands the current atmosphere and curriculum very little, even if she is active in the alumni association and tries to keep up to date from the outside.

INTERVIEWS WITH CURRENT STUDENTS

Student-led interviews are not yet common, but more and more schools are using them. Yale, Wesleyan, and Dartmouth are the leading examples. At Yale there are five seniors chosen to help admissions officers interview prospective students over the summer and about ten or fifteen more who give interviews during the school year. Students compete heavily for these coveted honorary positions on the campus and are thoroughly trained before having contact with applicants.

The schools that use student interviewers believe that candidates for admission regard interviews with students as being easier than other kinds—and that they may thus benefit from feeling "less pressure" in the interview session. But do not be fooled into thinking that an interview with a current student will be a cinch. As rookies, students tend to be less smooth in their interviewing tactics. They may not be well prepared, despite training in interviewing techniques. (If the busy college student is faced with the choice of studying for his Organic Chemistry midterm or preparing for an interview with a prospective student, how do you think he will spend his time?) A student interviewer may have trouble keeping the conversation flowing or thinking of things to say, in which case your job will be that much more difficult. He may even be just as nervous and ill-at-ease as you are. Of course, this is not usually the case. The students admissions offices recruit to conduct interviews of applicants are selected in part for their good communication skills and comfort acting as representatives of the school.

Student interviewers generally have very little access to your application file. Students are not privy to sensitive or confidential materials, so will know little about you going in. This will only serve to make matters worse if they are uncomfortable with the interviewing process in the first place. On the other hand, you might be able to control the conversation better with a student interviewer (a good or poor one) because of his lack of information. You will have more ability to take the ball and run with it, rather than waiting for specific questions or prompts. Like with alumni interviewers, it is usually a good idea to bring an extra copy of your application (if you feel comfortable sharing the entire thing with a current student of the college) or a resume for your student interviewer to review and keep as a reference when he or she is writing up your evaluation.

Students often ask applicants very tough questions. Sometimes they simply do not have enough perspective and life experience to realize what is and is not important. Furthermore, because they are so steeped in the intricacies of the college experience, they naturally have a lot of interview material at their immediate disposal. They know what life at the school is like, and thus can come up with very directed questions, maybe even ones that are so specific that they seem useless for obtaining relevant "big picture" information about you. This might especially be true if you and your interviewer have something in common, such as an interest in astronomy or talent in photography. When this is the case, your interviewer has even more interview material at his disposal. He might thus be tempted to ask you an extraordinary question such as, "Our renowned Professor So-and-So, as you probably know, just received the Nobel Prize for his research into gravitational collapse. As an ardent astronomer like myself, you must have your own ideas about how the pressure of thermonuclear reactions affects a star. How do you think Professor So-and-So's work will impact the research that other experts are currently conducting?"

There is no way to prepare for this kind of treatment. If this happens in your interview, just try to relax, appear calm and confident, and probe the interviewer for further explanation if the question is confusing or entails an understanding of theories or issues about which you know nothing. The interviewer is probably just trying to impress you (or himself) with his seasoned knowledge. Do not let it get to you; just tackle it as best you can and move on.

This, of course, does not always occur. Some student interviewers are likely to be as bouncy, friendly, and relaxed as alums—people with whom you will feel at home, with whom you could imagine becoming friends. You are fortunate if this is the case, but remember to be alert and serious; do not let your guard down just because you see a friendly and welcoming face in front of you. You want to match your interviewer's demeanor, but do not forget that this interview "counts," which means that you must sell yourself and why you should be admitted to the college. Selling yourself to a current student is a bit tricky, because you do not want to appear cocky or obnoxious. It is easier to market yourself aggressively with a more official administrator whose job it is to be impressed with you than it is to someone on a peer level.

An interview with a student is likely to be the most useful for your own fact-finding purposes. In fact, one of the reason Dartmouth supports the practice of using student interviewers is that it contends that candidates "can get a better feel for the school" through them. Because students are themselves involved in the day-to-day operations of the school, they will be able to give accurate answers to many of your most detailed questions. You will probably feel more at ease asking them about the nonacademic side of collegiate life as well, thus discovering more than you might have wanted to know about the quality of the food in the cafeteria or how often you can expect to get away to hit the ski slopes. But be astute about the types of questions you ask—by the end of the interview you will probably be able to sense whether or not your student interviewer will welcome the kinds of casual or odd inquiries that you would probably not dare to ask an admissions officer. If a student interviewer, for example, jokes with you about how wonderful he found the Pass-Fail option to be when he realized he was not doing well in an English class, it is probably fine to ask him how many times a student at the college is allowed to use the Pass-Fail option; on the other hand, if your interviewer seems particularly serious about academics or mentions that he thinks the grading scale at the college is too lax, it is not a good idea to ask him this kind of thing.

Here are some generalities that usually apply to interviews with the three kinds of interviewers:

ADMISSIONS OFFICERS TALK ABOUT THE VARIOUS KINDS OF INTERVIEWERS

WHO CONDUCTS INTERVIEWS?

"We have limited on-campus interviews with admissions staff provided on a first-come, first-served basis. But even if a candidate does one of these interviews on campus, he or she will normally also be invited by an alum in the hometown to do an interview."

—*Marlyn McGrath Lewis, Director of Admissions, Harvard University*

"We use admissions officers, a handful of chosen seniors, and about 4700 alumni all over the world in our interviewing process."

—*Richard Shaw, Dean of Undergraduate Admissions and Financial Aid, Yale University*

HOW ARE ALUMNI INTERVIEWERS USED?

"Our alumni interviewer is crucial to our admissions effort. They are our local contacts in the community and across the world. They hopefully can tell us something we can't gain from a written application—information about the applicant's family experience, the applicant's background, and more extensive information about the community he or she lives in. The alumni tend to be strong advocates for students in their areas and send us very helpful comments."

—*Barbara Bergman, Associate Dean of Admissions, Georgetown University*

HOW ARE STUDENT INTERVIEWERS USED?

"We choose a handful of Yale seniors to help us conduct interviews each year. It's taken very seriously—students compete heavily for these positions each year. They go through a formal training session to learn what we expect from our interviewers."

—*Richard Shaw, Dean of Undergraduate Admissions and Financial Aid, Yale University*

"We have twelve highly trained seniors who interview for us. I love this aspect of our admissions—the only problem with it is that parents sometimes think it's a second-rate interview, which is not the case at all. It's the real thing."

—*Richard Steele, Dean of Admissions, Bowdoin College*

"Using student interviewers seems to put less pressure on the candidate. I think applicants see them as being easier to talk to, and they probably get a much better feel for the school through them."

—*Karl Furstenberg, Dean of Admissions and Financial Aid, Dartmouth College*

	Admissions Officer	*Alum*	*Student*
Formality of Interview	High	Medium	Low
Ability to Influence Admissions Decision	Strong	Weak	Weak
Sensitivity to Appearance and Language	Medium	High	Low
Prior Knowledge of You	Great: Access to Entire Application	Little Knowledge	Little Knowledge
Knowledge of School	"Official" Knowledge (i.e., about Student Body, Majors Offered, Strength of Departments, Housing Options, etc.)	Little Knowledge (Unless Very Recent Graduate)	"Official" and "Unofficial" Knowledge (i.e., Info on Quality of Food, Social Options, etc.)

UNDERSTANDING YOUR INTERVIEWING OBJECTIVES

The University of Pennsylvania evaluation form In Figure 14-1 on page 469 may not capture everything that could be relevant in a candidate for college, but it suggests some of the ways in which a school will assess you. Other colleges, of course, have their own approaches, but they are similar to the approach that the University of Pennsylvania uses.

KNOWING THE COLLEGE

Chapter 3, "Deciding Where to Apply," examined many criteria relevant to the decision about where to attend. It also detailed how to find the information necessary for making a well-informed decision. Now that you are preparing for interviews, it would be a good idea to review the information you put together on each school with which you will interview. In particular, you should be extremely familiar with the information that the college publishes about itself. If you tell the interviewer that you plan to major in business, but the school offers no undergraduate business major, you will look foolish (not to mention looking like a bad fit for the college).

If you are going to interview on the campus itself, try to spend several hours in advance exploring the school and its environment. Talk with students in the cafeteria or student center, paying attention to the attitudes they evince. Are they generally happy there? Do they respect their professors? Is the social life adequate? Do they think the career services center does a good job of counseling students before sending them out into the real world? Are there any major issues, such as campus crime or lack of late-night library hours, that might matter to you? It always impresses an interviewer to see that you have taken the time and effort to examine the school up close rather than just reading some brochures or materials off the Web. Knowing what type of housing is available, or which courses students line up to get into, is the sort of thing that shows you to be determined, interested, and resourceful. It also helps you to develop good questions to ask the interviewer without sounding artificial. (See page 465 for more details on asking questions of the interviewer.) Even if you are not interviewing on campus, take advantage of any opportunities to visit schools or talk to students by telephone for precisely these reasons.

THE ADVANTAGES OF KNOWING A COLLEGE THOROUGHLY BEFORE INTERVIEWING

➤ Feeling prepared will enable you to relax somewhat during the interview and feel confident.

➤ You will be able to ask intelligent questions about the school, thereby impressing the interviewer and helping yourself to further determine the college's suitability for your needs.

➤ You will be able to convey your "fit" with the college to the interviewer.

➤ You will show yourself to be highly motivated, concerned about your future, and in possession of the right work ethic.

ANTICIPATING THE INTERVIEW QUESTIONS

You must also prepare for your interview by thinking about what questions you might be asked beforehand. The interviewer is likely to have two types of questions to ask you. One type includes the questions that are addressed to all applicants, such as "Why do you want to attend college X?" The other type includes responses to your file or to your comments during the interview. If you have claimed in your written application to have founded a new successful literary journal at your high school, for example, your interviewer might ask you about this endeavor to find out more or to ascertain that you have not exaggerated. She might ask you, for example, what your greatest barrier to starting the journal was, or what kinds of literature you personally enjoy most. Your interviewer might also want to probe to discuss your weaknesses or problems with your high school record. If, for example, you have one remarkably weak grade that stands out on your report card, she might want you to explain your troubles with the class.

Interview questions are often similar to essay questions. Therefore, before you interview, review the essay questions you had to answer for this school. Of course, you should also reread your answers—you do not want to repeat the same exact thing in the interview if your interviewer has just read over your application. In addition, review questions you answered for other schools and your responses.

If you are prepared to answer the types of questions listed here, you will be ready for just about anything else that can come up. Preparing for these questions, separated into four categories, will force you to think through all the main issues that are of interest to colleges. Note that the order in which the categories are listed is not meant to indicate their relative importance in any given interview. Some interviewers may spend more time asking you questions about your personal life than about your academic interests; likewise, some interviewers may not ever touch upon a certain subject matter, such as your future postcollegiate goals.

Academic Life and Interests

- Why do you want to attend college?
- Why do you want to attend this particular college?
- What is your favorite subject in high school? Why?
- What is your least favorite subject in high school? Why?
- What do you like most about your high school?
- What do you like least about your high school?
- How have you grown academically during high school?
- What have you found most challenging about high school?
- Who is your favorite teacher? Why?
- Who is your least favorite teacher? Why?
- What is your greatest academic accomplishment?
- What is your greatest academic failure?
- How do you compare with others in your high school class in terms of academic performance and academic effort?
- Are your high school grades mostly a reflection of hard work or of natural ability?
- Are you more concerned with getting good grades, or do you ever enjoy learning for learning's sake?
- Is your record an accurate reflection of your abilities?
- If you had to start high school over again, what would you do differently in terms of the classes you have followed and the way you have studied?

College and Future Goals

- Why do you want to go to college?
- What are you most looking forward to when you reach college?
- What are your most important criteria in looking at colleges?
- If you were prevented from going to college, what would you do instead?
- What do you think your major will be in college?
- What are your future career goals?
- How will attending our college help you to reach your goals?
- Where would you like to live in your adult life? Why?
- What is most important to you in your life?
- What do you think will be more important to you in later life, salary or job satisfaction?

Personal Life

- Tell me about yourself, including your family background and where you grew up.
- How would your friends and family describe you in terms of your personality?
- How would you describe your best and most valuable friendships?
- What is your favorite book? Why?
- What book has affected you most? How?
- Who is your favorite author? Why?
- What magazines or newspapers do you read regularly?
- What is your favorite movie? Why?
- What is your favorite TV show? Why?
- How do you feel about [certain current events, whatever has been dominating the headlines]?
- If you were the President of the United States, what one issue would you address before any others?
- How do you spend your free time?
- What person has most influenced you in your life to date?
- If you could meet one person, past or present, who would it be? Why?
- Who are your heroes? Why?
- Who in your mind has been the best U.S. president? Why?
- If a genie were to grant you three wishes, what would you ask for?
- What is your greatest personal accomplishment?

- What is your greatest personal failure?
- Why should we accept you?

Extracurricular Activities

- What extracurricular activity are you most committed to? Why?
- What has been your greatest contribution to an extracurricular activity or group?
- Please give an example of an activity in which you have demonstrated leadership.
- Please give an example of an activity in which you have displayed good teamwork and cooperation skills.
- Are you a better leader or follower? How has this changed (if at all) in the past few years?
- Please give an example of a time when you were accorded a large responsibility. How did you handle it?
- What is your greatest extracurricular success?
- What is your greatest extracurricular failure?
- If given a choice, would you choose to join an activity in which you would work alone, with friends, with strangers, or with your family?
- In hindsight, is there any high school activity you wish you had participated in but did not?

THE MOST COMMON INTERVIEW QUESTIONS

- ➤ Tell me about yourself.
- ➤ What do you envision yourself doing professionally after college?
- ➤ Why do you want to attend college?
- ➤ Why do you want to attend this particular college?
- ➤ Why should we accept you?
- ➤ What would you add to our campus and our student body?
- ➤ What is your favorite subject in high school? Why?
- ➤ Tell me about your extracurricular activities.
- ➤ What is your favorite book? Why?
- ➤ What do you like most about your high school? What do you like least about your high school?
- ➤ How have you grown both personally and academically during high school?
- ➤ Who is your favorite teacher? Why?
- ➤ What questions do you have?

THE TEN MOST IMPORTANT TIPS FOR ANSWERING THE QUESTIONS

1. Maintain a positive attitude. Avoid complaining, whining, or blaming failures or problems on someone or something else.

2. Use correct grammar (see "Get Your Grammar Straight" below).

3. Show that you are committed to learning.

4. If there are glitches in your academic record, show that you have since compensated for those failures and mistakes.

5. If you have changed your academic or extracurricular focus several times (or have no focus), show that you have become serious about one of your recent endeavors to the extent that you plan to continue with it.

6. Discuss any leadership experiences.

7. You are certainly not expected to have set your career goals in stone while in high school, but show that you are aware of some professional possibilities, given your current interests and strengths.

8. Remember that it does not much matter what your personal interests are (i.e., whether you like to play field hockey, read science fiction, or play the trombone)—what matters is that you show passion and commitment to your interests.

9. Be sure that you can have a sophisticated discussion about any heroes or historical figures you mention, as well as about any books or authors that you bring up. You should know "the facts," but also have developed your own viewpoint regarding these topics.

10. It is always a good idea to be up on current events when going on college interviews. If you do not already do so, read a good newspaper such as the *New York Times* regularly. Another fantastic way of becoming well-versed in current affairs is to read *The Economist* every week, particularly the lead articles in the first few pages of each issue. *The New Republic,* the *Atlantic Monthly,* and the *New Yorker* are some of the other sophisticated and well-written magazines that will help you to become more informed and give you provocative material to learn from and reflect upon.

GET YOUR GRAMMAR STRAIGHT!

There is nothing more annoying to an adult than a teenager who fails to use basic proper English grammar in speech. Many adults are exasperated by the fact that even the most educated high schoolers these days cannot seem to put a sentence together without making some glaring mistake. Make sure you refine your speech habits before embarking upon your college interviews, especially regarding these common (yet not at all excusable) mistakes:

> ➤ Know the difference between "good" (an adjective) and "well" (an adverb). If you are describing a noun, use "good": "My grades last year were very good." If you are describing a verb or an adjective, use "well": "This year is going really well." Your senior year cannot ever "go good."

> ➤ Do not use objective pronouns (as in "me," "her," or "him") as subjects of a sentence. In other words, "Me and my parents went to Italy" is entirely incorrect. Would you ever say "Me went to Italy"?

> ➤ Do not use words or phrases if you are not 100% certain how to use them correctly. Know the difference between "imply" and "infer." Remember that "irregardless" is not a word. Never use the phrase "I could care less" (unless you actually mean that you care a great deal).

PREPARING TO DESCRIBE KEY EVENTS

You should be ready to discuss major and minor events and milestones in your academic, personal, and extracurricular life. Some interviewers prefer to ask very general, open-ended questions; part of the test here is to see how well you can develop an organized, intelligent response. In other words, a general, open-ended question should not be answered with the same; your answers should, for the most part, always be detailed and specific. You must color your discussions with detailed incidents and situations, paying special attention to "inflection points," or points of change in your life. These locators along your personal timeline will help you to develop narratives about your life that make sense and offer reasonable explanations for success, failure, strengths, weaknesses, preferences, values, attachment to ideas, the development of passions, etc. Your inflection points might include, for example, the semester in which your grades began to improve; the period during which your parents' divorce began to burden you less; the fencing tournament at which you lost your first match; your move to a new neighborhood, which allowed you to attend a smaller and better school; or the year in which your dad lost his job, forcing you to get part-time work and take on more family responsibility. The ability to identify inflection points, explain their causes, and analyze their effects will help to create sensible discussions of your life events.

In preparation, it is useful to write down the half dozen or more important incidents you expect to discuss on index cards. Carry these cards with you for reading when you are waiting for the bus or have a spare moment. Learn them well enough that you can produce a well-organized, apparently spontaneous summary of each of them at the drop of a hat, but do not memorize stories by rote. You need to be prepared to be interrupted by the interviewer, and thus ready to carry on smoothly with a story if you are stopped in the middle of it.

DOING PRACTICE INTERVIEWS

There are two ways that you can practice your interviewing skills and responses. The first is by doing mock interviews with others who are applying to college or someone else who appreciates what is involved. This is a good first step to understanding what an interview will be like. The quality of the experience will depend in large part upon how prepared your interviewing partner is. If you can find someone who is willing to read your application carefully, and perhaps even read this chapter, then you will most likely have a good practice interview. The ideal person to team up with is someone who understands the college admissions process and is willing to be tough with you. A parent is generally not ideal. A parent knows you too intimately to be able to ask useful questions and look at you from an outsider's perspective; furthermore, most parents tend to be either too soft or too demanding on their children in mock interviews. A teacher or adult whom you trust (and whom you feel comfortable asking to help you) is ideal. It can be difficult to find the right person to help you practice your interviewing skills. This is why we at Degree of Difference routinely perform mock interviews with our clients as a major step in the process of preparing for college.

Set up a room so that it looks like a potential interview setting. There should be a chair for your interviewer and yourself, and perhaps a desk between the two of you. Practice interviewing in several different settings or positions: facing your interviewer with a desk separating the two of you; in a comfortable armchair (which is not always so comfortable when attempting to sit up straight and maintain a serious conversation) angled beside your interviewer's chair; at a table in a restaurant. This way you will be able to practice maintaining eye contact in a variety of different positions as well as catch any annoying habits that might not be noticeable from all angles, such as nervously swinging your foot back and forth. Wear your interview outfit (including jewelry and any "extras" that need to pass inspection for their suitability in an interview setting). Practice your entrance into the room, your handshake, your initial greeting, and the chatty conversation that precedes the serious questions. Practice your final questions, your thank-you, and your exit from the room as well.

Your interview partner can evaluate all aspects of your presentation, from the firmness of your handshake to the impact of your answers. She can tell you which responses were convincing and which were not (and why). Be persistent and force your interview partner to be specific in noting what worked and what did not. After all, it is not what you say but what your interviewer hears that determines the success of your interview. In fact, simply saying things out loud will often cause *you* to hear what is not right. Speaking out loud often makes it clear that you are wandering instead of staying focused, trying too hard to excuse some prior mistake, or pleading rather than convincing.

Tape recording, or better yet, videotaping, your practice sessions will help make your interviewing strengths and weaknesses apparent to you as well. If you can videotape your practice sessions, by all means do so. Many high schools give special permission to seniors to use videotaping equipment for this purpose if the students do not have access to such equipment at home. Seeing yourself in action will help you to eliminate extreme gestures and repetitive phrasings. Particularly annoying (and particularly prevalent among high schoolers) is the awful-sounding and inappropriate use of phrases such as "like," "you know," and "whatever." Although admissions officers and students may be somewhat used to teenage habits, your use of these speech patterns will certainly not help your case. Alum interviewers may become altogether turned off by your "teen speak," seeing it as a sign of immaturity, imprecision, or lack of intelligence. Wear your interview outfit on the video to be sure that it passes muster, too.

The second means of practicing is to be sure that you interview first with your safety schools. If you are applying to three "likely" choices, make sure your first interviews are with these colleges rather than the "possibles" or "reaches." This allows you to develop and refine your pitch and get rid of your first interview nerves without having too much at stake.

PHYSICAL PREPARATIONS

PHYSICAL ENERGY

Be sure to get plenty of sleep the two nights before the day of the interview. It is standard practice for marathon runners and other athletes to get plenty of sleep both the night before a big event and the night before that, in order to maximize the amount of energy and concentration available to them. This same practice can be applied to test taking, interviewing, and other events requiring peak mental performance. It is, for obvious reasons, not a good idea to schedule an interview immediately after an exam or paper for which you know you will be pulling an all-nighter.

Follow whatever your "normal" and comfortable meal routine is. Most books and college counselors will recommend that you "eat a good breakfast" before an interview, but if you never eat breakfast, do not like eating breakfast, and are perfectly comfortable without food in your stomach in the morning, then there is no reason you have to do anything different the morning of your nine o'clock interview! Remember, though, that interview schedules often run overtime, so be prepared to be unable to eat your next meal until an hour or more after your interview is scheduled to finish, just in case. In other words, if you normally do not eat breakfast but know that your stomach starts growling ferociously at noon if you do not eat by that time, you should eat something before your 10:30 interview.

APPEARANCE

It is no longer absolutely necessary to wear your fanciest clothes or your most conservative outfit to a college interview. In most cases, you should feel "yourself" at an interview, not as if you are pretending to be someone you are not. College administrators are by now quite used to the diverse appearances of college-age students and should not penalize you for your dress or personal presentation if it does not meet their taste. As long as you appear respectful and make it clear that you put an effort into looking neat and presentable, you should be fine. You can leave body piercings intact and should not have to worry about covering up tattoos and the like. There is likewise no reason to get rid of the red and orange streaks in your otherwise black hair for your college interview. As long as your dress conveys the idea that you have respect for the admissions process and take it seriously, you should have no problem. If anything, your unique hairdo might make you memorable.

Appearing respectful of the admissions staff and showing that you take the college admissions process seriously basically involve appearing neat and clean and not wearing anything that would be considered inappropriate for obvious reasons. Be sure you have bathed and that your clothes show no stains or rips. Avoid jeans. Do not wear wildly strong cologne or perfume. (It is a good idea not to wear any at all.) Clothes should be pressed, not wrinkled, although a few wrinkles from a car or plane ride are certainly acceptable. You should not wear cut-offs (shorts in general should be avoided), tank tops, clothing bearing foul or inappropriate language, or sloppy beach-type shoes (thongs, etc.). If wearing a tie, men should make sure it is centered and the knot is pulled up high and tight at the collar rather than hanging loosely. By no means should women ever wear a skirt that is very short (slightly above the knee is probably the shortest length you should consider) or blouses that are too tight or revealing. Makeup should be tame, not out of control; for example, do not wear so much lipstick that you are in danger of getting it on your teeth. Boys should always consider bringing an extra tie (in case you get a stain) and girls an extra pair of stockings (in case you get a run) if these are part of your outfit.

LOGISTICAL PREPARATION

Be sure that you have exact directions to the interview site and know where to park. Parking can be a big problem on college campuses (and many urban off-campus locations), so you should inquire ahead of time so you do not waste time (or get a parking ticket) when you get there. Arrive at the site slightly before the scheduled interview time so that you can find the restroom to check your appearance, go to the bathroom, and generally gather your thoughts and compose yourself.

You should take with you a copy of the college's brochure as well as copies of your application (to review or give to the interviewer) and a resume. You might also want to bring along index cards with interview notes on them to review before going in to the discussion. Also be sure to bring the name and telephone number of the admissions office or of your off-campus interviewer so that you can call if you have a travel emergency.

STAY RELAXED!

A modest degree of nervousness is good because it gives you the energy to perform at your best. If you tend to be too nervous, try one of these techniques to keep yourself calm.

➤ Remind yourself that you have prepared thoroughly (assuming you have followed the directions in this chapter) and that this preparation will see you through.

➤ Remind yourself that college admissions interviewers are aware that for many high schoolers, the college interview is the first interview they have ever experienced, and that they will excuse your jitters.

➤ Acting positive, by using the appropriate body language, will help you to feel the way you are acting. Keep your head up, your shoulders square, your back straight, and your eyes forward. Do not wring your hands or make nervous repetitive gestures. Your body should be still (avoid swinging a leg or drumming your fingers on the table) but not stiff.

➤ While in the restroom before the interview, take a deep breath and close your eyes for a minute to compose yourself.

DURING THE INTERVIEW

Your goal is to answer the questions thoroughly, support your profile, and appear interesting as well as interested in the college. It is best if you can also appear confident and at ease, although these seem to be emphasized more than they need to be for the purposes of a college interview. College admissions officers (and most alums and students who partake in the interview process) are aware that nervousness is common. They know that getting into the right college means the world to you and that you may not be practiced in interviewing techniques. So remember that you do not have to appear to have the confidence of Humphrey Bogart when you walk in the door. Still, you should try your best to remain poised and thoughtful throughout the interview. Even though the standards are not particularly high, you will certainly get good marks for being a pro. Follow this good advice, no matter what kind of interview you are preparing for:

General Appearance and Demeanor

- Greet the interviewer with a smile, an extended hand, and a firm handshake (match the interviewer's pressure, but do not use a death grip).

- Look the interviewer in the eye upon greeting him.

- Do not sit down until you are invited to do so and told where to do so.

- Do not put anything on the interviewer's desk.

- Do not smoke, drink, or eat anything even if invited to do so—and even if the interviewer himself does. This can distract either you or the interviewer.

- Remain physically at ease, without fidgeting. Do not fiddle with jewelry or belongings. Refrain from twirling your hair, drumming your fingers, bouncing your leg up and down, or picking at a part of your body or clothing. Many people have a tic of which they are completely unaware. Use your mock interview partner or videotape to determine if you have one, and then work on putting an end to it in the weeks before your interview.

- Do not chew gum or play with orthodonture.

- Maintain a moderate amount of eye contact throughout the interview, but do not stare.

- Gesticulate moderately to make points, but do not go overboard.

- Maintain good rapport with the interviewer by being warm and smiling often. Do not, however, smile without stopping throughout the entire interview!

- Sit up straight, but not too rigidly, and lean forward slightly, rather than slouching. This shows that you are serious, are interested in what the interviewer has to say, and are excited about conveying your own thoughts.

- Avoid crossing your arms in front of you or folding them up above your head.

- Keep your voice well-modulated and lively. Speak at a normal speed. Do not rush—this generally indicates nervousness or a lack of confidence.

Attitude and Presentation of Ideas

- Be upbeat and positive. Be sure to emphasize your strengths.

- Do not complain or whine about anything.

- Do not criticize others. You may be viewed as a chronic malcontent or worse.

- Assume that any interviewer who is not an admissions officer has not had access to your entire file of information.

- Be truthful. Do not lie in answering questions. Being honest, however, does not mean the same thing as being blunt, so do not volunteer negative information if it can be avoided.

■ Be yourself. Do not pretend to be someone other than yourself to impress the interviewer. Very few people are able to act well enough to carry this off successfully. Focus instead on presenting the best aspects of your own personality.

■ Do not try to take over the interview, but take advantage of opportunities to make your points. Interviewers want to feel that they are in charge of an interview, since they are likely to make decisions based upon the information they get about you. They need to feel confident that they will be able to get information relevant to their decision making, which may happen only if they are able to direct the interview. Taking over the interview may allow you to make the points you want to make, but the risk is far too great that your interviewer will react negatively to this and resent your aggressiveness. Use of polite phrases in a confident tone of voice can keep your interviewer from fearing that you are trying to take over the discussion: "Perhaps you wouldn't mind my sharing ..." or "Would it be helpful if I were to expand on that last point?"

■ Flatter the interviewer, but only subtly. Although a good interviewer will have you speaking 75% of the time, that does not mean that you will be excused for not having listened to him. Appear interested in what he has to say.

■ Adopt an attitude similar to the interviewer's. If your interviewer is deadly serious, avoid joking. If your interviewer is lighthearted and jocular, do not sit deadpan. In the first instance, jocularity will make you seem unsophisticated and unserious, whereas in the latter instance, seriousness will make you seem unintelligent and lacking spark.

■ Treat the interviewer respectfully, but do not overdo it. Give the interviewer due respect, especially if he is an adult, but do not be overly submissive. Do not use the interviewer's first name unless instructed to do so.

■ Relax and try to enjoy yourself. The relatively few people who enjoy interviews are those who view them as a chance to discuss important matters with someone with similar values and interests. If you are nervous, it may help to say so to your interviewer. It is perfectly acceptable for a college applicant to do so, and it will probably make both of you feel better if you get it out in the open lightheartedly.

■ Have a conversation. The best interview is an intelligent back-and-forth conversation. If there is a pause in the conversation, consider whether you have answered the question fully enough. If you suspect not, ask whether the interviewer would like you to add more, or consider whether you should follow up with a question of your own related to the same subject. You might, if neither of these applies, just want to sit quietly, without tension, with a pleasant smile. Try to make the interview a conversation with plenty of trading back and forth.

■ Avoid sounding like a robot. If you follow this book's advice and prepare thoroughly for your interviews, you do run the risk of sounding like an automaton, preprogrammed rather than spontaneous. It is good to sound prepared and confident about your answers, but not as though you have memorized answers to expected questions. There are several keys to avoiding this problem: (1) Avoid a robotic monotone voice. (2) Do not "fake" reaching into your memory, only to then pull out something that is obviously rehearsed or overly processed. (3) Focus upon your interviewer and the questions he asks. Make sure you are not moving questions completely away from what he wants to know and continuously gauge his reactions to what you say. (4) Occasionally pause before you speak, to get organized (or at least appear to be doing so) before starting.

■ Look interested. Do not look at your watch or appear bored, no matter how long the interviewer has gone on speaking.

■ Do not ramble. If your answer has gone on too long, cut your losses by briefly restating your main points. You can tell if your interviewer believes you are rambling if he hurries you through an answer or interrupts you with comments such as, "Let's move ahead quickly—we're running out of time."

Other Rules of Thumb

■ Do not ask your interviewer how you did at the end of the interview. This will put him on the spot and make you seem immature, lacking tact, or unable to wait for a decision to be made in due course. It will not do anything to improve your chances of success.

■ Assume that anyone at the office may be an informal "interviewer." Therefore, never be less than highly courteous and friendly to the staff. The staff is generally in charge of all logistical elements of your candidacy, so do not alienate them. Furthermore, though not part of the formal decision-making apparatus, the staff are certainly free to share their opinions of you informally with their coworkers. The admissions officers may even ask them to give their impression of you, so make sure it is a positive one.

THE END OF THE INTERVIEW

You will almost always be asked if you have any questions at the end of an interview. A failure to ask questions if invited to do so risks leaving the impression that you either did not do your homework or do not particularly care whether the school admits you. Asking questions gives you the opportunity to show how knowledgeable you are about the college as well as that you are taking a proactive approach to your educational future. Furthermore, the question, "Do you have any questions?" is generally the easiest question to prepare for! You should be ready with three to five questions that reflect your concerns about the school. Keep these in your head rather than on paper. Having to look at your notes will interrupt the pace of the interview and make it look as though you cannot remember a few questions (or, worse yet, that you are using the same "canned" questions at every college interview).

Do not ask questions that can be answered with a simple glance at the college's publications or brochures. In addition, try to avoid questions that require a simple "yes" or "no" response. Your questions should, for the most part, require an analysis or opinion from your responder. To understand an area in depth, plan to ask several related questions. See page 465 for the kinds of questions you should ask.

Do not try to baffle your interviewer by asking questions you know he will not be able to answer. If he is an alum of the college, for example, he probably will not be privy to the school's rationale for its recent decision to deny tenure to a certain professor. Being asked if you have questions is a genuine offer but also signals that the interview is coming to an end—so do not take too long.

If you have not yet had the opportunity to present all of your key points when the interviewer asks if you have any questions, do not rush into asking them. Ask instead if it would be acceptable for you to go back to an earlier question or add to a previous discussion. Even if these points are unrelated to any prior question, feel free to say, "I am glad to have the opportunity to ask you some questions, but I hope you will forgive my wanting to mention two things that I haven't yet addressed in our discussion." Briefly make your points, and then go on to your questions.

If you think the interviewer harbors major objections to you, try to get a sense of what his concern is so that you can address it if you have not had the opportunity to do so. This requires tact, of course, so as not to offend your interviewer or sound crass. You might, for example, say, "Are there any major issues concerning my candidacy that you think I could usefully address before leaving?"

At the end of the session, be sure to smile at the interviewer, shake hands, and thank him for seeing you. Be careful not to be taken in by an old trick, more often used in graduate school or job interviews, but also occasionally seen in college admissions offices. Once the official closing remarks have been made, sometimes the interviewer asks a potentially revealing question as you exit or as the two of you walk outside together, on the assumption that you have let down your guard. Assume that the interview is over only after you have left the premises!

INTELLIGENT QUESTIONS TO ASK YOUR INTERVIEWER

➤ In your opinion, what makes this college unique?

➤ Can you tell me a little bit about the relationship between the college campus and [the city or town in which it is located]? Is the town dominated by the college or is it the other way around? Are relations between "town and gown" generally friendly?

➤ In terms of improvement to or changes at the college, what are the administration's top priorities at the moment?

➤ If you had the chance to make one improvement to the school, what would it be?

➤ Do you think the character or personality of the college campus has changed at all in recent years? How?

➤ What is your opinion on [a recent campus debate or issue, such as the elimination of alcohol on campus or the administration's treatment of a racial incident]?

INTERVIEW WRECKERS

➤ Criticizing your teachers, school, or parents

➤ Being too nervous to answer questions confidently

➤ Appearing blasé about attending the school or about life in general

➤ Appearing too cynical or negative about life in general

➤ Asking no questions

➤ Whining or complaining, especially about grades or standardized test scores

➤ Blaming others for a weakness in your profile

SPECIAL INTERVIEW SETTINGS

RESTAURANTS

➤ If you arrive first, wait patiently in the entryway for your interviewer rather than taking a seat at a table.

➤ Do not sit until the interviewer invites you to be seated.

➤ Do not consider the menu until the interviewer invites you to. Do not order too much and do pick something midpriced. Do so without lengthy deliberations—

the point of the meeting is for you to stay focused on your presentation, not to have a gourmet feast. Make sure that you choose something familiar and easy to eat. Avoid things that splatter or require eating with your fingers (unless it is a sandwich or something else benign).

➤ Do not take any alcohol, even if the interviewer tries to buy it for you.

➤ Do not criticize the food, the decor, or the service.

➤ Treat all wait staff very politely.

➤ Wait for the interviewer to begin the interview. She may prefer to wait until after drinks arrive or the first course has been consumed.

YOUR INTERVIEWER'S HOME OR OFFICE

➤ Do not wander around or snoop if you are left alone before the interview begins.

➤ Do not sit until the interviewer invites you to be seated.

➤ If you are offered a drink or a snack, be modest in your consumption.

➤ Since this is your interviewer's private space, an honest (not convoluted) compliment or observation about the surroundings might be appropriate. ("I see from your photos that you visited the Great Wall with your family—what year were you there?" or "I love this area of town—my uncle's building is just down the block.")

➤ Treat anyone who helps to escort you or serve you very politely.

HOW TO DEAL WITH AN INCOMPETENT INTERVIEWER

What marks an incompetent interviewer? Talking too much, going off on tangents, failing to maintain control of the discussion, dwelling on inconsequential matters, or failing to pay attention. Here are some tips for dealing with the most common problems:

■ *If he talks too much:* The more an interviewer talks, the less information he can get about you. Build rapport with him by providing nonverbal encouragement. You do not want to offend him or be rude, but you want to get your points across before your time is up. Do so by appearing to agree with him, following up on one of his comments by immediately saying something like, "In fact, one of the things that first got me interested in your school was ..." And, of course, take advantage of his offer at the end of the interview for you to ask your own questions. Frame the statements you want to make as questions, but make sure they are really advertisements about yourself. For example, "Can you tell me a little bit about how I can incorporate my commitment to the study of modern dance into my curriculum here, since you have a Dance department but not a Dance major?"

■   *If he goes off on tangents, dwells on inconsequential matters, or constantly interrupts:* If you want to get the discussion back on track, use such phrases such as, "Let me be sure that I listed all my points to you earlier" (and then repeat your main points briefly); or "Could we go back to your previous question, so that I can tell you a little bit about my cultural background?"; or "In our remaining time, I hope that we will have the chance to touch on some points that I feel are particularly relevant to my application ...." Be very friendly and nonconfrontational, showing that you are not trying to take over the interview but are instead trying to take advantage of the opportunity to learn more about the school and sell your own abilities. He will be impressed that you have kept your focus while he was losing his.

■   *If he fails to pay attention:* Try to bring him back in, but do not be rude. For example, say something like, "It looks like I've lost you—maybe I am not being clear. Let me try to explain it differently ...."

AFTER THE INTERVIEW

There are several brief steps you should take after the interview is finished. First, debrief yourself regarding what went well and what went poorly and why. This will help you with later interviews for other schools; you will be able to anticipate what you might be asked concerning an apparent weakness.

Second, send a brief thank-you note to your interviewer. This can be handwritten (still a nice gesture) or typed (if your handwriting is particularly sloppy). Many interviewers, whether they are admissions officials, alums, or students, now communicate with interviewees by E-mail. If this is the case with your interviewer, you can send an E-mail thank-you, but an old-fashioned mailed note still conveys deeper appreciation and greater effort on your part. Note something that occurred during the interview or something specific she said that enlightened you to make it clear that this is not a form note. You can mention, for example, that you were glad to learn more about the administration's current debate regarding the campus alcohol policy. The one absolute requirement is that you spell your interviewer's name correctly. Be sure to get a business card from your interviewer or ask a staff member (you can always call the office later if you need to) for the correct spelling of his name.

SPECIAL CONCERNS FOR INTERNATIONAL APPLICANTS

Interviewing in a nonnative language is not easy, especially when you are under substantial performance pressure. This is precisely when your worst verbal tics are likely to show up. Similarly, normal manners of speaking in your own language can be bothersome to others. Highly educated French speakers are accustomed to using a large number of "uh"s and, if anything, seem to gain respect for doing so in their own culture. To English speakers, this same trait when expressed in English can be highly annoying. You certainly want to retain your unique cultural identity in your interview—and will generally be excused any foreign mannerisms—yet you do not want to inadvertently annoy or distract your interviewer. Check your performance under realistic conditions and go the extra step of asking a native speaker to help you eradicate any verbal mannerisms that seem strange when placed in an English-speaking setting.

Cultural differences manifest themselves at many points in interviews. The physical distance people maintain between themselves, the amount of eye contact that is considered polite, and many other similar behaviors are culturally defined. Give some consideration, and some practice time, to incorporating some American norms into your interview performance. Again, the point is not to rob you of your own cultural identity but to avoid distracting or alienating your interviewer. The best way to prepare for a cross-cultural interview is, of course, to speak the appropriate language frequently and spend time in the appropriate setting for as long as possible immediately prior to the interview.

SAMPLE INTERVIEW EVALUATION FORM

Figure 14-1 presents the interview report form that the University of Pennsylvania alumni use to rate candidates for admission after interviewing them.

Note that there is a box indicating in large letters (signaling its importance) whether the interviewee was interviewed or declined to be interviewed. Although not all colleges say that students must interview if offered the opportunity, the University of Pennsylvania reports that declining an interview can show the admissions committee you are not particularly interested in the school.

UNIVERSITY OF PENNSYLVANIA UNDERGRADUATE ADMISSIONS OFFICE

ALUMNI SECONDARY SCHOOL COMMITTEES
STUDENT CONTACT FORM

DATE

COMMITTEE

REGION

SSN	LAST NAME	FIRST NAME		
DOB:	E-MAIL ADDRESS		SEX	TELEPHONE NUMBER

HOME ADDRESS (STREET•CITY•STATE•ZIP)	TEMPORARY ADDRESS (STREET•CITY•STATE•ZIP)	SECONDARY SCHOOL AND ADDRESS

SCHOOL	INTENDED MAJOR	APPL STATUS	CHILD OF ALUMNUS/A	CHILD OF FAC/STAFF	OTHER	☐ INTERVIEWED ☐ INTERVIEW DECLINED

The interview serves equally to inform the applicant about Penn and to inform the Admissions Office about the applicant. Please be sure to address fully the interests and questions of the student. For our part, we are interested particularly in those personal and intellectual qualities of the applicant that might not be fully expressed in the application, for example, the student's enthusiasm, commitment, sensitivity, articulateness, depth of insight and thought, and social and cultural awareness. Since the student's academic profile is extensively examined elsewhere in the application, we do not feel it is necessary to discuss it here or in the interview. MY OVERALL IMPRESSION OF THE CANDIDATE IN COMPARISON TO OTHER APPLICANTS I HAVE MET:

INTERVIEWER'S SIGNATURE, SCHOOL/YEAR, INTERVIEW DATE

PLEASE PRINT IN THIS SPACE: INTERVIEWER'S NAME, ADDRESS, TELEPHONE NUMBER

COMMITTEE CHAIRPERSON, ADDRESS, TELEPHONE NUMBER

MAIL WHITE & BLUE COPIES TO:	U OF PA UNDERGRADUATE ADMISSIONS 1 COLLEGE HALL, PHILA., PA 19104	SEND PINK COPY TO CHAIRPERSON	KEEP YELLOW COPY

Figure 14-1.

Part III

ON THE ROAD TO COLLEGE

15

RESPONDING TO ACCEPTANCES, DEFERRALS, WAITLIST PLACEMENTS, AND DENIALS

— KEY POINTS —

Take the necessary steps to secure your place at your chosen school

∎

Do not panic if the first college you hear from denies you admission
—*Assuming that you have chosen your schools appropriately (balancing "stretches," "possibles," and "safeties"), you can expect better news in the future*
—*Remember that you will attend only one of your target schools, so you do not need to get into all of them*

∎

Recognize that no more than a small percentage of those waitlisted are likely to make it off the waitlist at the top schools
—*To optimize your chances of being accepted from a waitlist (or after being deferred), bring relevant new material to the attention of the admissions office*

∎

Note that if you do not get into your very top choice school, several options remain open to you:
—*Reapplying after a year or two off*
—*Transferring after one or two years at another school*
—*Attending the school as an exchange student*
—*Attending the school as a graduate student*

INTRODUCTION

There will be one of four basic possible responses lying within the envelope that each target college's admissions committee sends you after making its decisions: (1) A college can accept you, in which case it will also provide details regarding how to respond to the decision and the deadline for your decision. (2) If you have applied Early Decision, Early Action, or to a school with a rolling admissions process, a college can defer you. This means that the college neither accepts nor rejects you but will wait to make its final decision in a later round of application evaluations. (3) A college can place you on the waitlist, in which case there is a small to moderate chance that you may still be admitted to the school at a later date if there is space in the class after all accepted students decide whether or not to attend. (4) Finally, a college can deny you admission. If denied admission, you can always reapply for admission to the freshman class (if you decide to take a year or two off) or as a transfer student in a future year. This chapter tells you how to deal with each of these possibilities.

If you have followed this book's suggestions, you have applied to approximately eight colleges, two of which are almost certain to admit you and at least two more that are fairly likely to admit you. Likewise, if you have followed our approach (introduced in Chapter 3), you have also maintained enthusiasm for your safety and likely schools rather than setting all your hopes on attending one particular reach school. If you have consistently tried to picture yourself enjoying your college career on one of your safety or likely schools' campuses, then you should not suffer overwhelming bouts of disappointment if you are deferred, waitlisted, or denied admission by one or several of your reaches.

Do try to prepare yourself for rejection by some of your first choices. It is difficult not to take a denial of admission personally. You must try to remember that the school is not rejecting you as a person but merely denying your profile a place in its upcoming class. For example, you may have been denied a place simply because the school needed a soccer goalie or wanted to include another student from Arizona rather than because you are unfit for the college. Just as you should not take any nonacceptance personally, you also should not panic if you receive notices of rejection before you receive any acceptance letters in the mail. As you should realize by now, the vagaries of the admissions process and the differences between schools mean that one school's decision does not have much predictive value in terms of what another school might do. Try to remain calm until your mailbox brings more news.

RESPONDING TO AN ACCEPTANCE

Do not assume, as many candidates do, that a "thin" letter means rejection while only a "fat" letter carries good news. On the contrary, many offers of admission are made on one or two sheets of paper, just as negative messages are. Do not immediately panic upon the arrival of a thin rather than a fat letter or throw it away before opening it, assuming the worst.

If you are accepted by your top-choice college, congratulations. You should be sure to send in your confirmation of acceptance (telling the college that you will attend) as well as your deposit, which reserves your place, in a timely manner. The response and deposit deadline (the Candidates' Common Reply Date, followed by all of the top colleges, is May 1) is actually important, contrary to the beliefs of many college-bound students and their parents. In recent years, many colleges that have been oversubscribed have used a student's tardy deposit as an excuse to bar her from coming to the college—a convenient way to trim class size if necessary. You must get your deposit in to the college by May 1 (not postmarked May 1) or you risk losing your place at the school. Your acceptance letter or other materials will give you instructions on how to do so.

Likewise, as soon as you respond positively to one school, you should notify all other colleges to which you are accepted of your decision to decline their offer. Your acceptance letter will tell you how to go about notifying the college of your response. Do not begin to decline offers, however, until you have received an offer that is preferable to you—even if you feel certain that you will be admitted to a college whose response you have not yet received. Furthermore, if there is any doubt in your mind about which college to attend, you should do some more research (see Chapter 3, "Deciding Where to Apply"), most importantly by visiting the colleges. Many colleges now have special weekends for admitted students. One of the purposes of these events is to allow you to better assess a college before firmly deciding to attend.

If you are accepted by one of your secondary schools before you have heard from top choices, sit quietly while you wait for your other decisions. Most colleges now get their responses out by April 1 and abide by the Candidates' Common Reply Date of May 1. You should not have to respond to any particular college before hearing from all the schools to which you applied. Do not send in any sort of deposit to "hold" your place at a school tentatively, because deposits are nonrefundable.

The scenario becomes complex when you are accepted by a second-choice school and waitlisted at a preferred institution. It is important that you recognize that being on the waitlist is nowhere near certain future acceptance. Most of the top colleges, in fact, put hundreds of kids on their waitlists each year and take only a tiny fraction (if any) of those students in the end. (See page 477 for more detailed information on waitlist offers.)

Since you may never be admitted to a school at which you are waitlisted, you must choose another institution to attend, thus sending in a nonrefundable deposit. You will forfeit this amount of money if, in the end, you get into the first-choice school from the waitlist and decide to attend it instead. You and your parents must decide if this is a feasible and reasonable option for you. Most colleges require initial deposits of about $500; it is usually worthwhile to forfeit this small amount of money (in relation to the total amount you will spend over the next four years) in order to attend a college that is an obviously better fit or of decidedly superior quality.

FOR INTERNATIONAL STUDENTS ONLY

As soon as you have heard from all of your schools and made a decision to attend a college in the United States, you should begin the student visa application process. This means getting a Certificate of Eligibility (I-20) form from the school you will attend, which verifies that you have the appropriate credentials, language skills, and financial resources to attend the program. This form, along with the accompanying financial documents, must be submitted to the U.S. consular office to request the actual visa. The visa you will receive for full-time study in the United States is referred to as an F-1 student visa. The visa application process is often delayed by one party or another, so it is important to begin as soon as possible.

RESPONDING TO DEFERRALS

A deferral means that a college neither admits nor denies you but rather postpones its decision until a later round of admissions. When Early Decision and Early Action applicants are deferred, it means that the committee will wait to make its decision until the regular admissions process gets under way. The candidate is not being denied a place in the class (at least not yet), but he or she is not being admitted early either. (Note that for Early Decision applicants, a deferral means that you are no longer under an obligation to attend the college if admitted in the spring.)

Being deferred is not the end of the world, nor should it be the death of your hope of attending the college that is postponing its decision. What you should realize, however, is that the great majority of deferrals are actually prolonged rejections. In some cases, however, the college defers an applicant because it wants to wait for another piece of evidence before making a positive decision. In other words, you are under the gun. If a decision is deferred, it tends to mean that the college is waiting to see your next set of grades or a certain outcome in another area of involvement (such as athletics) before saying yes to you. It may also be waiting to see what the entire admissions pool looks like (i.e., how you compare to others in the pool) before making a decision.

So if you are serious about attending a college that defers you, you should be prepared to give your very best performances in the near future. For most Early Decision, Early Action, and rolling admissions candidates, this means performing well on the upcoming set of exams so that your senior fall record further solidifies your academic potential to the college. Or, if a particular extracurricular activity is a significant part of your profile, a deferral might indicate that you have to perform particularly well in a certain upcoming event. If you have evidenced some kind of discipline problem, the college may be waiting to confirm that no other similar situations occur during your senior year. Either way, know that you should be on your best behavior in all senses until the college makes its final decision, because chances are that it will be watching you closely.

If you are deferred, you should not wait quietly to see what happens. You should follow the general guidelines for waitlisted students by letting the school know of your continued interest in it as well as notifying the admissions committee of further evidence to support your candidacy. Read the next section, "Responding to Placement on a Waitlist," for more details on how to improve your chances of being admitted after being deferred. (A deferral and a waitlist placement are essentially the same thing. Both responses notify you that you are neither admitted nor denied and that a final decision will be made in the future regarding your candidacy. The difference between the two is that a deferral ends in some sort of final decision—although that "final" decision itself could be placement on the waitlist, which is essentially like being deferred once again!—whereas a waitlist placement can live on indefinitely.)

RESPONDING TO PLACEMENT ON A WAITLIST

HOW COLLEGES USE WAITLISTS

Being placed on the waitlist means that you might be admitted to the program only if enough accepted candidates decide to go elsewhere, thus freeing up space in the freshman class. Colleges know that a certain percentage of their admitted students will choose other schools, so they routinely admit more candidates than they can realistically take in the freshman class. The excess number admitted, however, is often not sufficient to make up for all those who decline the offer of admission. The waitlist is used to manage this situation.

Many of the students placed on the waitlist are legitimately put there because a college would like to be able to reevaluate its applications, should it need to accept more students for its freshman class in the future months. A student, however, can also be granted waitlist status out of courtesy rather than because of the college's sincere desire to reconsider his application (for example, a legacy applicant).

Sometimes a college finds itself with a number of empty spots for the freshman class after many admitted students decide to go elsewhere. This is when the admissions committee goes to the waitlist to offer places to additional candidates. In other years, colleges find themselves in trouble because more candidates than expected accept the offer of admission—thus causing freshman housing and course availability problems. During these years, colleges do not accept anyone at all from the waitlist because the incoming class is already too full. Some schools intentionally leave room to go to their waitlists each year. The University of Pennsylvania purposefully goes to its waitlist every year, taking about 25 to 50 applicants from it. The school uses the waitlist to make the final changes that shape the freshman class.

Unlike the University of Pennsylvania, however, most colleges go to their waitlists only on an as-needed basis, so the number of students accepted off waitlists at most institutions varies tremendously from year to year. In the past ten years at Harvard, there have been years in which the admissions committee has not even gone to the waitlist and other years when it has taken over 100 candidates. The chances of being accepted from the waitlist line-up are slim when you consider how many students sit on the list. Most of the top schools place anywhere from 400 to 900 candidates on the waitlist each year. Generally speaking, half of the waitlisted students choose to remain "active," meaning that they notify the school that they would like to remain on the list for consideration, should any spots in the freshman class become available. All other students are considered "inactive" once they either fail to respond to a college's waitlist offer or notify the college that they have made a decision to attend another school. The maximum number of students accepted from the waitlist in recent years is about 100 at the top schools. At best, you might have a one in four chance of being admitted this way, but chances are usually much slimmer than that.

Brown, for example, usually places about 700 applicants on the waitlist each year, with about half of those 700 students choosing to remain active on the list. In 1998, Brown took only one student off of the waitlist; the year before it accepted nearly 100 from the waitlist. Stanford puts about 700 on the waitlist each year, half of whom remain active. In 1998 Stanford ended up accepting 44 applicants from the waitlist, but in other years has taken no one from it.

As you can see, being placed on the waitlist is a bit like being put in purgatory indefinitely. The real trouble with being waitlisted is that even if you are eventually admitted, it might not be until very late in the game. (Note also that those accepted off the waitlist are not generally allowed to defer their acceptance until a later year. You must agree to come to the college right away, rather than a year or two later.) It is not uncommon for a college to notify a waitlisted student only days before classes begin in the fall—or, sometimes, even after the start of school!—that she is accepted. Many candidates like to save themselves the anxiety that can come with remaining on a waitlist by deciding to attend a college that is a notch lower on their preference list. You will have to decide for yourself how keeping yourself on a waitlist will affect you. Imagine that after arriving at one school and settling down there, you are finally admitted off the waitlist to Stanford, your top choice. You thus need to decide whether to pack up your belongings, head across the country, and start all over again, or remain where you are. If you do not think that you would want to be put in the position of having to make such a decision, you might not want to stay waitlisted.

WHAT THE ADMISSIONS OFFICERS SAY ABOUT THE WAITLIST

How Does the Waitlist Work?

"When we choose candidates from the waitlist, we're basically looking to balance the class. If the yield from California applicants is a bit low, we take more Californians. The purpose of the waitlist is to shape the class at the final hour."
—*Barbara-Jan Wilson, Dean of Admissions and Financial Aid, Wesleyan University*

"We try not to rank the waitlist if we can help it. If we know we'll have to use it, we might make a line-up of sorts."
—*Delsie Phillips, Director of Admissions, Haverford College*

"We don't always use our waitlist, although we like to use it a little if we can. We don't rank the candidates on the list. We basically sit down again in committee to review the applicants on the list, usually relying heavily upon senior spring grades and scores to make our decisions."
—*John Blackburn, Dean of Admissions, University of Virginia*

"The number we take off the waitlist for regular freshman September entrance varies—some years it's one student, in rare years close to 100. Each year we also take around twenty to twenty-five kids from the waitlist for January admission as well."
—*Michael Goldberger, Director of Admissions, Brown University*

"If we use our waitlist, we go back to committee all over again and look at everyone on the list."

—*Karl Furstenberg, Dean of Admissions and Financial Aid, Dartmouth College*

FOR WHAT REASONS MIGHT YOU WAITLIST A CANDIDATE? HOW IS THE WAITLIST USED BY THE ADMISSIONS OFFICERS?

"We certainly use the waitlist for a variety of purposes. We know that the vast
majority of kids won't get off it. Some we put there because they are sensitive
cases—perhaps someone at a high school where someone else applied and got in."

—*Marilee Jones, Dean of Admissions, Massachusetts Institute of Technology*

"We have a finite number of spots in our class. When we waitlist candidates, we
are saying 'We see you as a good candidate who could contribute to our campus,
but we just don't have room for everyone.' We are a bit conservative on the number we admit in April, and then we return to the waitlist a few months later. Our
yield has been increasing over the past few years, though—this year we didn't
even use the waitlist."

—*Eric J. Furda, Director of Undergraduate Admissions, Columbia University*

"There are all sorts of reasons to waitlist a student. Athletic waitlists are candidates
we put on the waitlist in case the coach's first choice recruit for a particular position
decides not to attend. We only need one quarterback for the football team, but we
have to make sure we *do* have that one—otherwise there's no football team at all. So
we'd put the second choice on the waitlist."

—*Barbara-Jan Wilson, Dean of Admissions and Financial Aid, Wesleyan University*

"We don't use our waitlist like some schools do. We don't put people on there as a
polite way of letting them down. We really would love for every one of them to be
able to come here."

—*Richard Avitabile, Director of Admissions, New York University*

WHAT TO DO IF YOU DECIDE TO REMAIN "ACTIVE" ON THE WAITLIST

If you decide to remain "active" on a waitlist, you should not wait in silence.
There are two tasks you must complete if you want to improve your shot of getting into a college off the waitlist:

1. Write the college a letter to convey your interest in the school (along with
   sending in a confirmation card, if the college has provided one, declaring
   that you wish to remain "active" on the waitlist). It is best if you convey to
   the school that you will definitely accept if admitted.

2. Augment your profile with updated information that will reflect positively on your candidacy.

The first task, writing the admissions committee a letter stating your continued interest in the school, is extremely important. Although many college admissions officers say that a candidate's interest in the college is not that relevant in the original admissions process, virtually all of them report that proof of interest in the school is practically mandatory for those who want to be admitted off the waitlist.

The colleges all confirm that whether or not interest in the school plays a part in regular admissions, it always makes a difference in the decision-making process when officers are choosing candidates from the waitlist. Waitlisted applicants should not just confirm their place by sending in a form, but should write a letter of real enthusiasm.

There are two reasons why you must show your commitment to attending a college to be admitted off the waitlist. First, the admissions committee has some difficult choices to make in admitting just a small fraction of the waitlisted students. The admissions people know how anxiety-ridden it can be for students to remain on a waitlist and feel badly that they cannot offer admission to every candidate. Committee members naturally feel better about accepting those who seem particularly enthusiastic about the college and leaving those who do not seem as excited about their school to go somewhere else.

Second, and much more important, there is a practical reason for the committee's need to see some real interest from waitlisted candidates. By the time a college goes to its waitlist, it needs desperately to finalize the list of incoming freshmen. Every college needs to meet its minimum size for each class, and a college's administration starts to get nervous if things are not settled and firm as the summer rolls by. In other words, the admissions officers want to admit students whom they know will accept admission, so that they can be done with the admissions process as quickly as possible.

The second task—updating the admissions committee on your successes and positive record—is as important as letting them know that the school is your first choice. You need to give the committee as much ammunition as possible to decide to admit you over other students on the waitlist. Providing them with updates about your accomplishments and other happenings throughout your senior year of high school reminds them not only of your interest in being accepted to the college but also that you are a candidate worth admitting. You should communicate to the admissions office any positive new information when it becomes available.

It is best if you can write a letter placing the qualification in a particular context that best highlights it and its relevance to your candidacy. For example, if you have made your commitment to writing a significant piece of your profile, you might want to say something like, "Winning the senior Composition Award has further cemented my desire to push toward a career in journalism. I am putting the $400 I received in prize money toward my tuition for a three-week writing seminar I am attending this summer at Hawthorne Community College. I hope to enroll in Professor Keene's creative writing class for freshmen—to become more experienced in another genre of writing—if accepted to your school." The more attention and emphasis you can give your accomplishments and qualifications, the better.

The information you will want to impart to the admissions officers might become available at different times. Thus, it is all right to send them more than one update for your file, but it is wise to limit your contact to two (at the most three) instances, unless you know for certain that they welcome your constant attention. Find out from the school at which you are waitlisted how it suggests that you carry out your contact—whether it wants to receive one or two notices from you or whether it enjoys continuous updates and inquiries from its waitlisted students.

Some admissions officers actually say that they like waitlisted students to bug them. MIT, for example, loves candidates who call all the time and prove to the committee that they are dying to attend. At most other schools, however, there is a limit to how often a waitlisted student can make contact before becoming a nuisance. If you contact the admissions committee more than two or three times without their solicitation, you risk annoying the department. You should remember not to overstep boundaries of propriety when communicating with the admissions office; find out what its feelings are on this matter before risking your candidacy.

What new information will be relevant to the admissions committee? Colleges generally require that you send them your updated transcript if you are to remain on the waitlist. You should also notify them of any academic awards or honors you receive, as well as any enrichment classes you enroll in for the summer. You should tell them about athletic achievements if they are significant, as well as any nominations to leadership positions that occur after your original application, such as an elected position as captain of the spring lacrosse team. Notify the committee of any positive changes in status or role regarding your job, community service work, or other extracurricular commitments. You can let them know about a summer job if it is especially impressive or significantly adds to your particular marketing efforts. (Do not write a letter to tell them that you will be mowing lawns again this summer. Save your updates for really special information.)

ADMISSIONS OFFICERS TALK ABOUT WHAT WAITLISTED APPLICANTS SHOULD DO TO IMPROVE THEIR CHANCES OF ADMISSION

"Waitlisted students absolutely should let us know that they're interested in coming here—they should not just confirm their place with a 'Yes, keep me on the waitlist,' but write us a real letter of enthusiasm."

—Eric Kaplan, Director of Admissions, University of Pennsylvania

"When we go to the waitlist, we will pick the kids who most want to come. Waitlisted candidates should write and call as much as they want to! Send us everything possible! Call a lot! We want to know they are dying to come to MIT."

—Marilee Jones, Dean of Admissions, Massachusetts Institute of Technology

"You should make yourself known if you are waitlisted, but going overboard can be shooting yourself in the foot."

—James Bock, Director of Admissions, Swarthmore College

"Applicants on the waitlist should send us updates, but be reasonable. Send us the important information, and do not overload us with letters and E-mails every day!"

—Richard Shaw, Dean of Undergraduate Admissions and Financial Aid, Yale University

"Don't nag us. That's not how we would expect you to handle things in school so don't do it at waitlist time."

—Nanci Tessier, Director of Admissions, Smith College

"Anyone wanting to get in off a waitlist should send us updates on performance. Any supplements to the original application are good as long as they add to the profile. They should also show that they *really* want to come here."

—Karl Furstenberg, Dean of Admissions and Financial Aid, Dartmouth College

RESPONDING TO DENIALS OF ADMISSION

Most denials of admission require and necessitate no official response. For most college-bound students, there is no benefit to analyzing your rejection too closely. As you know by now, the top colleges have to make very difficult decisions about whom to admit and deny, and many qualified candidates are denied admission. Unless you are seriously thinking about putting off college for another year in order to reapply, or have real reason to think that an error has been made, you should simply try as best you can to shrug off the rejection as one of many more to come in your life, and start putting all your energy into preparing for the college you will attend.

If, after receiving responses from all schools, you decide that your best option is to take a year or two off and reapply to college, then it may be beneficial to attempt to understand a college's decision. (Note that you should not jump quickly to the conclusion that reapplying is a good idea—especially if your aim is to be accepted at one particular school. Many applicants cannot significantly improve their candidacy during a "year off.") The first step to take in this case is to analyze why you were rejected. You may already know the reason, of course, if you were aware of one or two specific aspects of your application that were likely to keep you from being admitted. If you are not sure, you can try to contact the school's admissions office to get the committee's view on the matter. Some colleges are willing to tell you why they rejected you. The schools most likely to do so are the smaller ones that have relatively fewer applications. Colleges are most receptive to such inquiries during their slow periods, especially during the summer. They will generally refuse to discuss the matter during their busy periods.

Beware, however, of what even the responsive schools will tell you. They can address only substantive matters and will not tell you exactly what was said about you during their reviews and meetings. They will not say, for example, "Your essays were sloppy and you revealed yourself to be arrogant and insensitive in them." They might, however, let you know if your academic record was not as strong as those of other applicants or that they wish you had shown more extracurricular involvement during your high school career.

Remember that any school that takes the time to discuss your denial is doing you a real favor, so be ultrapolite in dealing with the admissions representatives. If you are defensive or hostile, natural reactions to being told that you are less than perfect, you will elicit less useful information and even less sympathy.

SHOULD YOU EVER APPEAL A REJECTION?

Only if you think that a true error has been made should you consider appealing a rejection. A college will listen to your appeal of its decisions, but all admissions officers at the top colleges say that rejections are very rarely appealed successfully, except in cases where there has been a computer or other serious error made in evaluating the student's file.

If you have no extremely strong conviction that the committee somehow made its decision based upon erroneous information, do not raise your blood pressure and that of the committee members by appealing a rejection.

Admissions committees go to great lengths to give all applicants' files a sympathetic and fair reading, so you can count on the school's having considered your application material fairly, as long as the information presented to them was correct.

If you have reason to believe an error was made and you present your case firmly and calmly, you will at the very least get the attention of your audience. If your high school registrar notifies you, for example, that he accidentally sent the transcript for your classmate Emilia Power rather than for you, Emily Power, to your target colleges (and Emilia's record is inferior to yours), then you have reason to call this error to the attention of an admissions committee. Contact the admissions office by telephone or by letter, politely explaining your situation as best as possible to inquire if it will review the case. Never, ever accuse the admissions office of wrongdoing. If the committee believes it has reason to entertain your appeal, bring all evidence or new information to them and reiterate your desire to attend the school.

Recognize that appeals are not generally welcomed by admissions committees. No college will change its decision if you (or your parents) appeal because you were not accepted while your neighbor with a lower GPA was given a place in the class. You must trust that the admissions committee has its reasons for admitting other students over you.

WHAT ADMISSIONS OFFICERS SAY ABOUT APPEALING DENIALS

"There are lots of students these days who call to appeal a denial—this has probably been precipitated by the movement toward making appeals for financial aid. Once in all my years we changed a decision—but it was only because we had actually misread a transcript. It was an international student whose record was difficult to understand."

—*Nancy Hargrave Meislahn, Director of Undergraduate Admissions, Cornell University*

"Sure, denied students can appeal. It's not a very smart use of time, though. We've never revised an offer yet."

—*Katie Fretwell, Director of Admissions, Amherst College*

"No appeal on an admissions decision has ever been successful. Every once in a while there's been an erroneous piece of information submitted as part of someone's file. If this is called to our attention after we have denied a candidate admission, we'll return to committee to look at it again, but in my memory never have we actually changed our decision."

—*Marlyn McGrath Lewis, Director of Admissions, Harvard University*

"There have been two cases in my entire memory in which we changed admissions decisions, and they were both a result of concrete errors in the information we used to evaluate the candidates. In one, we hadn't received the high school transcript. In the other, there was some sort of computer glitch that indicated scores that were lower than the student's actual scores. No one has ever appealed a case in a way that actually made us change our mind on an applicant for whom we had all the correct information."

—*Jonathan Reider, Senior Associate Director of Admissions, Stanford University*

"The only situation in which I might recommend a student ask a college to check its records is if the student has a very common name—'David Kim,' for example. Then there's always the possibility that there were two applicants with the same name, and misfiling might have occurred. Otherwise, there's really no reason for anyone to appeal a denial or double-guess a college's decision."

—*Sheppard Shanley, Senior Associate Director of Admissions, Northwestern University*

SHOULD YOU REAPPLY IN THE FUTURE?

REAPPLYING AFTER TAKING A YEAR OR TWO OFF

The question of whether or not to reapply is, of course, a complicated one. If you were accepted at one of your top-choice colleges, it would be foolish to decide to wait a year to reapply to your very favorite school, hoping that you would be successful the second time around. If you have followed the advice in this book and applied to approximately eight schools that are good fits for you, chances are that you will be accepted somewhere that will make you very happy. A year or two off can be beneficial, but in many cases does not radically change a student's profile, at least not enough to justify waiting an entire year in the hope that you can get into one particular college.

The situation is more difficult if you have gotten into your eighth-choice college and not into any of the seven colleges about which you are more enthusiastic. If you realistically think that you will be a better candidate after another year, in which you will have to do something extremely valuable in order to convince an admissions committee that your "year off" has made you a better candidate for college, then it might be a good idea to wait and reapply.

The important thing here is to do some serious research on your "year off" options and then decide whether or not you will or could be a stronger candidate with this experience under your belt.

Cast a critical eye over your file and talk to some guidance counselors. If you have a real weakness, can you improve it within the next year or two? For example, if you come from an obviously privileged background and have never performed any community service, you might consider that this was a significant detracting factor on your college applications. Spending a year volunteering in India at a free health service could really change the way that admissions officers view you in the future. Something like this could be doubly valuable if you are trying to market yourself as a premed candidate with a commitment to medical and health issues or as someone who is interested in studying the developing world. Or maybe you are one of those students whose freshman and sophomore grades really detracted from your overall high school record. Spending a postgraduate year at a tough prep school (and doing extremely well there) will give admissions officers more confidence that you have truly overcome your earlier difficulties. They will thus be more inclined to admit you than they were when looking at two rather than three years of solid work. Similarly, if you have just come to grips with a learning disability or have finally overcome a family tragedy that affected your school performance, another year or so of stellar academic performance can change how colleges view your potential.

If, on the other hand, you know that your academic profile is simply not as strong as that of the average admitted student at the school (if your standardized test scores and GPA are well below the college's published averages, for example), then there is little reason to think that you will be admitted next year. Ask yourself whether you are being realistic in thinking that you can change your profile significantly before next year.

REAPPLYING AS A TRANSFER STUDENT

Remember that there are a lot of very good colleges out there. The ones you were admitted to can probably give you an education that is just as good as (maybe even better than) the one you think you want to attend so badly. Still, if your heart is set on one school or you think it is the best fit for you, there is always the possibility of reapplying as a transfer student to your target college after one or two years attending another school. Many of the top colleges report that some of their successful transfer students each year are students who applied unsuccessfully for admission to the freshman class. Of course, you may ultimately decide not to try to transfer because you like the college in which you initially enrolled so much.

If you do go ahead to college with the plan that you will reapply as a transfer student to another particular school in one or two years, check that your future target school actually takes transfer students and investigate its transfer program thoroughly before setting your sights on it. You will want to know exactly what that college will expect of you as a transfer applicant before putting together your first- and second-year academic schedules. You will also want to begin preparing to market yourself as a transfer student early on. (See Chapter

7's section on "Transfer Applicants" for more information on how to prepare to market yourself as a transfer student.) In addition, be careful not to waste your time at the first school you attend by going in with the feeling that it is only a halfway house. Do not "check out" of collegiate life just because you plan to leave within a year or two. Be sure to get everything you can out of a college—its academics, its resources, and its social atmosphere—no matter how long you plan to stay there.

REAPPLYING AS AN EXCHANGE STUDENT

Most colleges have flexible exchange programs that allow you to spend a semester or two at another school. If you failed to get into a school you desperately want to attend, you can check into the possibility of studying there as a visiting student in the future. This will give you much of the social and intellectual experience of attending the school, as well as letting you tap into its network and list it on your resume. If you plan to follow this route, examine the various exchange possibilities at your potential colleges of attendance before deciding where to go. Restrictions and regulations governing exchange terms may become a factor in choosing which college you will attend, since schools are not equally flexible about these matters.

REAPPLYING FOR GRADUATE SCHOOL

Finally, remember that there is always graduate school. Some of the colleges with the most prestigious names generally provide much better educations to their graduate students than they do to their undergraduates. You never know—you just might end up going to your favorite school after all.

16

PREPARING FOR COLLEGE LIFE AND ACADEMICS

— KEY POINTS —

Maintain a strong academic performance during your senior year
—*Colleges can and will revoke an offer of admission for dismal grades or bad behavior*

■

Performing your best through the end of high school offers you the best chance of:
—*Beginning college courses as ready as possible for rigorous academics*
—*Fulfilling college requirements via Advanced Placement (AP) exam results or SAT II subject tests*
—*Impressing future employers with honors and awards, as well as a strong final GPA*

■

Upgrade your skills (especially in writing and research) in order to be able to compete effectively in your new college environment

■

Make the proper logistical, social, emotional, and health preparations for college

INTRODUCTION

Once you have finished the college application process, you will probably feel that you deserve to celebrate and take a break from the strains of your senior year. You should indeed congratulate yourself on a tough job out of the way, but you also need to remember that it is not yet time to "check out" of your high school existence. You need to maintain your focus in school as well as begin to prepare to leave home and enter your adult life at college.

In addition to reading this chapter, you may want to consult other people about how best to prepare for entering college in the fall. Contact friends who are already in college and ask their advice about what to bring and how to prepare for the changes ahead. Friends who are already attending your particular college are especially good resources. It never hurts to contact an admissions officer to get his or her advice regarding preparation for college.

MAINTAINING YOUR FOCUS
DURING THE SENIOR YEAR OF HIGH SCHOOL

It is very important that you maintain focus and avoid "senioritis" during your final months of high school. This is true at all points during the senior year, whether you have been accepted to your college of choice Early Decision, accepted to a school during the regular admissions round, or are waitlisted at any of your top-choice schools. There are several reasons you will want to keep on top of your academics and overall performance during the latter portion of your senior year:

■ Colleges request final high school transcripts of all accepted applicants. Colleges retain the right to withdraw an offer of admission to a previously accepted applicant if academic performance or general behavior during the senior year is unacceptable. Most schools report that they indeed exercise this right, usually in one or two cases per year.

■ If you are waitlisted by one of your top-choice colleges, admissions officers will want to see last-semester grades before finalizing their decision. An impressive senior year record will make all the difference between staying waitlisted and getting in.

■ If you decide to transfer to another college after your freshman or sophomore year, your total high school record will be evaluated in addition to your collegiate record.

■ Falling out of good study habits during your final high school semester might lead to greater difficulty coping with the heavy workload in college.

■ Much of the information learned during the senior year, especially in math and science courses, is bound to be of direct use in college. You should make sure to digest as much of the material as possible before moving on.

■ Maintaining a strong performance during the latter half of your senior year will ensure that any awards or honors for which you are under consideration will still be available to you. You should aim to finish the year well so that your permanent academic record remains as impressive as possible. This will be important for resume purposes, especially when applying for job opportunities during or immediately after college. Major awards received at the end of high school can be relevant far into the future, even mentioned on graduate school applications.

WHAT ADMISSIONS OFFICERS SAY ABOUT REVOKING OFFERS OF ADMISSION

"We have withdrawn offers of admission after getting final spring term transcripts. We review all the final transcripts of our incoming freshmen in June. If one of our incoming student's grades are truly deplorable, we do one of two things: We either ask the student to write us a letter explaining what's up, or we withdraw our offer of admission, encouraging the student to reapply after he gets his act together again. For disciplinary problems, we do not automatically withdraw our admission offer, but we do ask for a written explanation from the student and sometimes require an interview to discuss the circumstances."

—*Barbara-Jan Wilson, Dean of Admissions and Financial Aid, Wesleyan University*

"We have revoked offers of admission after the spring grades come in, as well as for significant behavior problems that occur after our offer of admission was made."

—*Marlyn McGrath Lewis, Director of Admissions, Harvard University*

"We do occasionally revoke an offer of admission—if the spring grades are truly deplorable."

—*Katie Fretwell, Director of Admissions, Amherst College*

ACADEMIC PREPARATIONS FOR COLLEGE

We certainly do not advocate that seniors headed for college in the fall cram their summers full of rigorous academic work! This is your time to relax a bit before heading off on your own. There are, however, several tasks you should take care of in order to ensure that you arrive on campus ready for a strong start. If you are ambitious enough to seek a degree at one of the top schools, then you are probably also eager to do well in the program.

The easiest way to accomplish this is by starting college well prepared. The student who is poorly prepared will find it difficult to succeed. The poorly prepared student is highly likely to struggle in the first term and barely get through the first set of courses. As a result, he will be perceived by his professors and fellow students as someone who has little to offer. As you may have witnessed of poor performers during high school, reputations have a way of following people around. The students who perform well initially pile up points with professors from the very beginning, demonstrating that they are committed scholars and learners.

Furthermore, a common complaint shared by graduating college seniors is that they did not have enough time to explore all of the things (academically and extracurricularly) in which they were interested. Because many spend the first one to two years in college coping with academic weaknesses or problems and trying to figure out where their interests lie, they are left with less time to pursue these interests. To the extent that you can remedy any academic sore spots as well as determine your interests and possible pathways before entering college, you should do so. The sooner you become involved in those things about which you are passionate, the more rewarding your college experience will be.

Here are our recommendations for ensuring that you arrive on campus as academically prepared as possible:

Before Arriving on Campus

- Take final AP tests and SAT II subject exams at the end of your senior year if your college will give you credit for AP scores or allow you to place out of requirements on the basis of certain standardized test scores. Your college's course offerings catalog will tell you about its policies regarding incoming credit for classes and placing out of requirements. If you have questions, call the admissions office to find out more.

- Ensure that your writing, research, and note-taking skills are up to par. Take a writing course if you are not entirely confident of your writing and/or research skills. Be sure that you know how to state, develop, and support a thesis and that you command a firm understanding of the mechanics of various forms of writing: the analytical essay, a lab report, a research paper using primary and secondary sources. You will have little time and energy once you start classes to hone these crucial skills for succeeding at the most competitive colleges.

- Hone your word processing or typing skills. You will write constantly during college and cannot afford to waste time with the hunt-and-peck typing style that got you through high school. Typing speed can be a huge advantage when taking exams (often written on laptops rather than in "blue books" these days), especially if you can type double the speed of others in the class.

■ If you have extra time over the summer to take a class at a community college or nearby university, contact the admissions department at the college you will attend in the fall to determine if there are any core curriculum requirements you can get out of the way before entering school.

■ Determine whether you are interested in any freshman seminars or honors programs offered by your college. Such programs usually require separate applications during the summer before college entry. Particularly at larger schools, these programs give students a rare opportunity for student–professor interaction in an intimate classroom setting.

■ Get your hands on the past year's course catalog (or the current one, if it is available) and start considering your curriculum. Even though you will probably be assigned an academic advisor, such advisors can only be as helpful as you allow them to be, given your own ideas and input. It is better that you have a sense of what you want to do and how you can do it before arriving on campus. Also give thought to possible research or independent study you could do in college. If you have no idea what academic path you want to take in college, go through the catalog and highlight all courses that sound remotely interesting to you, then analyze them for any recurring themes or interests. Check to see if any of the classes you are interested in require special registration or application prior to the first day of class. Other courses may require that you have met certain prerequisites before taking them.

Before or After Arriving on Campus

■ Get acquainted with the various services (tutoring, career advising, writing resources, etc.) offered at your college to help with academic problems as well as academic and career planning. Doing this early on will ensure that you will be ready when a problem arises to tackle it as efficiently as possible.

■ Make an appointment with your college advisor. Your school will most likely require that you meet with your advisor at the beginning of the year, but even if it does not, be certain to acquaint yourself with this person and solicit his or her advice. At most schools, professors, administration faculty, and other members of the campus community serve as advisors. Their job is to support and guide advisees to the right resources; they do not usually have all the answers themselves. In other words, do not assume that your chemistry professor advisor will know exactly what freshman writing seminar you should take in order to ensure entry into an upper-level creative writing class. He should, however, be able to direct you to the right places to find the answers you are looking for. If, over time, you do not feel comfortable with your advisor or find other faculty members who can better serve your needs, you can either change advisors officially or simply use other people for advice as needed.

LOGISTICAL PREPARATIONS FOR COLLEGE

When your senior year is over and the summer sets in, you should start thinking about the many logistical preparations you will need to make during the next five months or so. Some logistical preparations are best taken care of ahead of time, whereas some are best left until you arrive at your new location. This is apt to be a period of growth for you because you will be performing tasks that have probably not been within your jurisdiction during your life as a child and teenager so far. But growth is often accompanied by frustrations, so you should expect to feel both exhilarated and exhausted by completing the necessary tasks. Here are some of the preparations you must make upon leaving for college:

Before Arriving on Campus

- Take care of all housing details to ensure yourself a place in a dormitory or other housing option. Most colleges send out freshman housing information and registration materials soon after they receive your notice of acceptance at the college. Check to see whether your college's housing lottery operates on a first-come, first-served basis; if so, be sure to get your materials and deposit in as soon as possible to ensure the best treatment.

- Ensure that you have selected and registered for a proper meal plan, especially if you have special vegetarian, kosher, or other dietary restrictions.

- Purchase the clothing and other goods you will need at college. See page 495 for a list of necessities.

- Learn to do your own laundry and ironing. Take a mini home economics course from one of your parents if you are unsure how to do daily chores such as washing your clothes or cooking basic foods.

- Be sure that you know the basics about managing money. You should know how to write checks, withdraw and deposit funds, and balance an account.

- Compare long-distance phone services and sign up for one.

- Research airlines and transportation services to your college location to determine which offers the best student rates. Purchase initial fall and winter break tickets far in advance for the best availability and prices.

- Find out about and purchase parking permits if you are bringing a car to campus.

■ Talk to your parents about their expectations of you while you are away at college. Having a somewhat formal discussion about their ideas as well as your own guarantees that everyone in the family is in agreement on certain issues of mutual concern before you leave. Discuss finances: What are you responsible for financing yourself? What expenses will they pay? How will money be transferred to you? How often will money be transferred to you? Are there any conditions they expect to be met in order for them to continue financial support throughout college? Discuss vacation time: How often will they expect you to come home? Who will pay for trips home? Will they visit you on campus? Discuss academic issues: Do they expect you to share your grades with them? Are they comfortable with the idea of your switching fields? Are they open to the idea of your transferring if you are unhappy? What are their feelings about programs abroad?

Before or After Arriving on Campus

■ Set up a bank account (preferably in the state where you are attending college).

■ Get a credit card with a low monthly interest rate and no annual fee. There are plenty of available credit card options specifically for college students. If you do not receive offers in the mail at home, wait until you get to campus, where you are sure to be flooded with good credit card offers. Even if you do not plan to use a credit card on a regular basis, it is imperative that you have one for emergency purposes, such as car breakdowns. If you are on financial aid, you should have a credit card in case you need to cover regular living expenses when you are between funding disbursement periods.

■ Determine whether there are any easily accessible shopping venues that offer discounts and special deals. Join any shopping clubs or food coops that will make your everyday purchases less expensive.

LIST OF COLLEGE NECESSITIES

You should be sure to bring the following materials with you to college:

➤ An appropriate wardrobe for the weather in the college's location—raincoats, umbrellas, bathing suits, heavy parkas, boots, wool sweaters and socks, clothes that are good for "layering" (in climates where weather temperatures often vary considerably on any given day), etc.

➤ One formal outfit. Every student should have one dress outfit for formal occasions. For men, this means a coat and tie. For women, this means a nice suit or dress; women might find that they need one outfit appropriate for conservative dress occasions, such as awards ceremonies, and one appropriate for stylish evening occasions, such as dances or cocktail parties.

➤ A bathrobe. Most college dormitories require that students walk down the hallway to shower.

➤ An answering machine (unless you plan to use a voice mail service).

➤ An alarm clock. There will be no parental wake-up service at college!

➤ Appropriate bed linens (usually for a twin or extra-long twin size bed) and towels.

➤ At least one good reading lamp.

➤ Decorations and accessories for one's room.

➤ A dictionary, foreign language dictionary, and thesaurus.

➤ A writing guide or style manual that includes footnote and bibliography formatting information.

➤ A calculator. If you will be taking math, science, and engineering classes, you will need a calculator for academic purposes, but all students will need calculators for balancing their checkbooks and other daily calculations, so it is always a good idea to have one.

➤ (Optional) A computer and printer. Find out about the computing situation on your campus. Do most students bring or purchase their own computers or do they use on-campus computing centers? Does the school offer computers to students at discount prices? What is the availability of computers on campus (both during regular periods and during finals periods)? Is the campus PC or Mac compatible? Do you have Internet access from your room? For what purposes is E-mail used on campus? Is it used for formal communication between students and professors? Is it used for transmitting assignments to professors for grading?)

➤ (Optional): A means of transportation. At most schools, a bike or rollerblades are your best bet for commuting from dorm to class. If you bring a bike, be sure to bring a reliable lock—U-shaped locks are a good choice. Check on the availability of public transportation for traveling off-campus. If you have a car and want to bring it, first check to see that cars are allowed in general, and then if they are allowed for freshmen. (Many campuses have different car policies for freshmen and upperclassmen.) Inquire about prices for parking permits (sometimes these prices alone make bringing a car prohibitive). If you do bring a car, be sure to have it tuned up before leaving for college.

SOCIAL PREPARATIONS

Before leaving for college, try your best both to keep up old ties with the people who have been important in your life thus far and to begin forging relationships with the people who will surround you at school.

Before Arriving on Campus

■ Maintain correspondence with teachers, classmates, school administrators, coaches, and employers. You should do so out of respect and also in order to ensure the best treatment from these people down the road. (You never know when you might need their help for recommendations or career purposes.) Send an initial note and vouch that you will do the same at least once a year in the years to come. Put a reminder note in your agenda so that you will remember to do so.

■ Contact your future roommate or roommates. Your college will most likely send you information about your housing assignment and roommates at some point over the summer. You should contact your future living companions to introduce yourself as well as to discuss what you will need for your room and other logistical details.

■ Contact any professors or special instructors with whom you would like to speak before arriving on campus. An early call or E-mail to inquire about a course's curriculum or discuss your interests and needs over the summer can make a good impression on a professor. In addition, contacting a professor over the summer ensures you will receive adequate attention, whereas if you wait until the school year begins, you risk losing faculty attention to other pressing matters.

HEALTH PREPARATIONS

Whether you are perfectly healthy or have significant health problems, do some research on health care policies and take care of any necessary doctor visits before arriving on campus.

Before Arriving on Campus

■ It is unlikely that you will have the time or the inclination to make a doctor's appointment while in school, so it is best to visit your physician and get a check-up before heading to college. Some schools require a record of this visit (proof that you have had various immunizations—e.g., for measles, mumps, rubella, hepatitis B) before registering for classes freshman year.

■ Compare health care coverage plans and sign up for one. Most colleges offer decent, affordable student health insurance, but you should also investigate the possibility of remaining on your parents' plan as a dependent or taking out a different form of coverage. This is especially true for those with considerable health risks or preexisting conditions, because certain forms of health insurance might offer better services and more coverage for those services than what you would receive under a campus plan. Learn as much as you can about your health care policy, even if you plan to remain on a parental plan—you will need to understand its policies and limitations yourself since your parents will not always be with you when you visit doctors.

- If you decide to use an insurance plan other than your college's, you will need to bring a card demonstrating proof of insurance with you to college and carry it with you at all times.

- If you decide to use your college's health care plan and its prescription policy is especially affordable, buy only enough medication to get you through the first few weeks of school, and plan to purchase what you need later on campus. If, however, you will be using an outside health care plan, purchase a sufficient supply of any medications you take to last until your first vacation from college.

Before or After Arriving on Campus

- It is usually a good idea to select a primary care physician upon arriving on campus, whether you are utilizing the college's health care plan or an alternative one. You will probably need assistance or advice from a primary care physician at least once during your four-year stay, if not quite a bit more. Most special health needs also require an initial referral from a primary care doctor, so it is often best if you select one person to oversee your care—someone who will know your history and make the best recommendations for you over the years.

- Familiarize yourself with the college's emergency health procedures. Post emergency numbers on or near your dorm room phone, and memorize them as well. Know where the nearest emergency room is (often at a campus-based hospital).

FITNESS PREPARATIONS (FOR STUDENT ATHLETES)

Student athletes, whether recruited by the college to play a sport or not, will want to arrive on campus ready to perform their best. If you play a fall sport, it is likely you will need to arrive on campus early for practice. Find out from your coach ahead of time so that you can plan your summer and make travel arrangements accordingly.

Before Arriving on Campus

- Contact your new coach to determine what sort of training and conditioning you should be doing to prepare for your season.

■ Inquire about the fitness and ability tests you will be required to pass during pre-season and prepare accordingly.

FITNESS PREPARATIONS (FOR NONATHLETES)

The figure-wrecking habits of college life are well known to most students. The abundance of unhealthy food options, the prevalence of beer and alcohol, and the stresses of a rigorous academic schedule can mean that freshman students find themselves unfit for the first time in their lives. Taking care of yourself before you get to campus is one way to ensure that you do not fall prey to an unfit lifestyle.

Before Arriving on Campus

■ Begin a fitness regimen well before leaving for college so that you can arrive on campus with good habits already formed.

HELPING OTHERS TO PREPARE FOR YOUR LEAVING HOME

For many people, entering college is the first definitive step toward adulthood and independence. While monumentally significant in *your* life, this transition is also significant in the lives of your family and friends. Parents fear losing you to your new independent lifestyle while friends fear that you will begin new relationships and forget about them. This is especially true in the case of many students who are preparing to attend top colleges, because many of their friends may not be headed toward an institution of the same caliber—or may not be heading to college at all. People often fear that friends who are about to take bigger and better steps in the world will not want to retain ties to their ordinary childhood or high school buddies later in life. Being sensitive to these concerns can help those around you make the transition with you.

Spend a lot of quality time with both family and friends (even though you will probably be more inclined to spend time with friends) over the summer. Do not forget grandparents and other relatives who might be anxious about your move away from home and into adulthood. Having meaningful interactions with family and friends over the summer will reassure them that they are important to you.

17

STARTING COLLEGE ON THE RIGHT FOOT

— KEY POINTS —

Set appropriate goals in areas that are critical to you and reevaluate them throughout your college career

■

Keep your future (especially your future career) in mind when structuring your academic, extracurricular, work, and social activities
Capitalize upon your academic opportunities:
—*Decide whether you will be best off focusing on one field or sampling many different ones during your first year*
—*Choose the right major*
—*Take advantage of academic enrichment opportunities, such as research internships and exchange programs*
—*Keep plans for future employment or graduate school in mind when selecting classes*

■

Take advantage of campus resources, such as writing and career centers

■

Extracurricular activities allow you to explore interests, meet new people, practice leadership and other key skills, and maintain a balanced lifestyle

■

The social experience is a big part of what going to college is all about:
—*Enjoy it, but maintain sensible limits*

■

Develop or maintain positive physical and mental health habits

INTRODUCTION

To extract the most value out of your college experience, be ready to hit the ground running when you first step on campus. Four years of college may sound like a large chunk of time right now, but you will find that these years pass quickly, especially considering how busy you will be. This chapter will provide you with information and advice about starting your college career right.

SET GOALS NOW AND REEVALUATE THEM ALONG THE WAY

When you first arrive at college, if not before, you should try to determine some of your goals for the upcoming years. Your goals might reflect continued attention to interests and strengths developed in high school, a turnaround effort toward something at which you failed in high school, or an investigation into new territories. Contemplate what you want to achieve (academically and extracurricularly) in college and prioritize your goals.

- Set short- and long-term goals that are both measurable and achievable. These goals can be academic, extracurricular, social, personal, or career-oriented in nature. Some examples of long-term goals and possible short-term counterparts:

Academic goals:	*long term:* "I will get an A in Economics."
	short term: "I will attend every class, do every problem set, and attend every weekly section."
Extracurricular goals:	*long term:* "I will become the Sports Editor at the school newspaper."
	short term: "I will take the paper's training course and compete to become a staff writer this year."
Personal goals:	*long term:* "I will stay in shape."
	short term: "I will run three miles at least four times a week."

- Keep a record of goals met as your life progresses and interests change. Periodically (at the end of each term or so) reevaluate your goals to determine what you have achieved, as well as which goals have become obsolete because of changes in your life.

MAKE THE MOST OF YOUR ACADEMIC PURSUITS

Many students simply go through the motions when it comes to academics in college, taking just enough classes to fulfill graduation requirements or limiting themselves to a particular area of study in preparation for postgraduate careers or graduate work. This is unfortunate, because college presents you with an amazing and rare opportunity to explore a variety of disciplines as well as become engrossed in your academic pursuits. Furthermore, education becomes a far more rewarding experience when you immerse yourself in it. And in the long run, employers and graduate programs look for students who have taken advantage of the academic opportunities available to them. Try to get the most from your academic pursuits right off the bat.

- Learn what kinds of academic plans and goals you should be making based upon your presumed future intentions. For example, find out whether there is a minimum GPA required for students who want to study abroad.

- Explore interests before selecting a major.

- Balance your schedule each semester with requirements and courses you take for practical reasons (e.g., premed requirements or economics courses for those planning careers in medicine or finance) as well as those you take purely for personal enjoyment and interest (e.g., ceramics or sociology for those planning careers in medicine or finance).

WHO SHOULD FULFILL CURRICULUM REQUIREMENTS EARLY?

Most students should plan to fulfill distribution requirements by the end of sophomore or junior year. By completing these requirements early on, you avoid being stuck with limited options as you near the end of your college career. Those wishing to pursue part-time employment, summer employment, or an internship in a given field during the college years, though, should aim to complete requirements for that field even earlier. A student planning to pursue a career in biotechnology and wanting to do research in a biotech lab between her freshman and sophomore years, for example, should be sure that she has frontloaded her schedule with plenty of biology lab classes during her freshman year so that she will have the best chance of securing an ideal job.

- Develop relationships with professors right away. Few students develop long-lasting relationships with professors, yet this can make all the difference between having a good college experience and having a good college experience that is followed by a wealth of opportunities later in life. Professors can help you to find internships and jobs, write recommendations for job placement and graduate school, contact other adult colleagues to serve as resources, and allow you to network with others in the field.

■ Take advantage of special opportunities to enrich your education. See the next four boxes for specific ideas concerning how to make your education as special, unique, and personalized as possible.

OPPORTUNITIES FOR ACADEMIC ENRICHMENT AT COLLEGE

All colleges have a variety of programs aimed at enriching the education of their students. Utilize your advisor, school newspaper, professors, upperclass students, bulletin boards around campus, and your school's Web page in order to explore academic opportunities available to you. The following programs are among the various opportunities for educational enrichment that colleges offer:

➤ Honors programs

➤ Seminar programs

➤ Independent study

➤ Research internships

➤ An honors thesis

➤ Individually designed major

➤ Interdisciplinary major

➤ Double major

➤ Major and minor

➤ Study abroad programs

➤ Exchange programs

➤ Accelerated double-degree programs

➤ Early admission to professional schools

Generally speaking, grabbing onto academic enrichment opportunities can have enormous advantages:

➤ As part of a special recognized group of students, you will immediately command more clout and attention from professors.

➤ You can use such special opportunities to provide an even stronger foundation in a particular area, such as your major or knowledge of a foreign language.

➤ You can use such special opportunities essentially to "create" another foundation or area of recognized expertise, in addition to your major.

➤ Taking advantage of special opportunities shows graduate programs and future employers that you possess certain necessary ingredients for success: a love of challenges, persistence, insatiable curiosity, intellectual vitality, etc.

WHAT IS MOST IMPORTANT TO EMPLOYERS AND GRADUATE PROGRAMS?

Remember that employers tend to look for different strengths than do graduate programs when evaluating prospective candidates. Insofar as you know when you get to college where you will be headed after graduation (many of you will eventually be headed toward both graduate school and employment), you should keep the following in mind:

➤ Employers tend to look at majors, minors, and awards (items that should be mentioned on your resume), but not your GPA (which does not have to be featured on your resume unless it is especially impressive).

➤ Graduate programs—especially the professional programs in medicine, business, engineering, and law—focus more on the specific coursework that a candidate has completed as well as overall GPA, major GPA, and performance on standardized tests (i.e., MCAT, GMAT, LSAT, GRE, etc.).

SHOULD I EXPLORE OR FOCUS WHEN I GET TO COLLEGE?

Whether or not you know the academic path you want to follow, it is a good idea to explore multiple disciplines while at college. For those of you who enter college thinking you know what you want to do (e.g., major in political science in preparation for law school), exploring some other disciplines during your first year or two might lead you to find you have an equal or greater interest in another area. A student can simultaneously fulfill graduate school or career requirements while exploring a passion in another discipline. In fact, many graduate schools and professional disciplines today are looking for students with broad interests—even backgrounds unrelated to the profession—who have combined their fulfillment of required courses with involvement in other areas of study. For example, some of the most attractive medical school candidates are, contrary to common assumptions, not those with a major in biology or chemistry, but those who have pursued majors in the humanities while still fulfilling premed requirements. These candidates are considered academically balanced and better equipped to be physicians because they have a greater sense and appreciation of the human condition than people who have been wholly engrossed in science their entire lives.

TIPS FOR CHOOSING CLASSES AND MAJORS

➤ Solicit the advice of upperclass students regarding good classes, professors, and majors.

➤ Speak with professors about pertinent major and career possibilities.

➤ Speak to graduate students and professionals in areas of interest to find out about how their educational paths and careers have progressed.

➤ Attend senior or graduate student thesis presentations to meet professors and students and learn about new aspects of a discipline.

➤ Consult "unofficial" student-written and published guides to classes and majors at your college.

➤ Take advantage of departmental orientations and events for students interested in particular careers.

➤ Visit the career resources center.

➤ Sit in on classes during the first few weeks of each semester's "shopping period."

➤ Try to balance your schedule each semester by discipline (e.g., balance a math class with a humanities course) and by workload (e.g., match a class that requires many long papers throughout the quarter with one that demands only a midterm and a final exam).

TAKE ADVANTAGE OF VARIOUS RESOURCE AND ADVISING CENTERS

This might be the only time in your life that you have at your disposal free or relatively inexpensive services to help you perfect skills and find guidance. Be sure to use your college's resources wisely.

- The career guidance center
- The office for overseas study
- The community service center
- The writing center
- The library system

- The student union
- The student health center
- The peer counseling hotline or center
- The disability resource center
- The computing center

UTILIZE EXTRACURRICULAR OPPORTUNITIES

Much of the learning at a top college takes place outside of the classroom, while involved in activities with a diverse mixture of fascinating and intelligent peers. Involve yourself in extracurricular activities right away to take advantage of the benefits they provide:

1. Allow you to explore old and new interests.
2. Allow you to meet new people.
3. Provide balance to and diversion from academics.
4. Offer you leadership opportunities.
5. Allow you to give back to the campus and its surrounding community.

DO NOT FORGET THE SOCIAL EXPERIENCE

One of the most rewarding and memorable aspects of your college experience will be the relationships you develop while there. On the top college campuses, you will inevitably meet and have the opportunity to get to know people with vastly different racial, ethnic, socioeconomic, religious, geographical, personal, family, sexual preference, and educational backgrounds. In some cases, though, new college students struggle to appreciate the rare opportunities presented to them because of homesickness, loneliness, or ties to home relationships. It is best if you recognize these latter issues early on in order to remedy them.

COPING WITH LONELINESS OR HOMESICKNESS

Although you will not want to cut ties with your hometown, family, and high school friends, it is helpful to view your college community as your new home and to involve yourself in your community just as you did in your original one. The best way to avoid homesickness early on is to take advantage of dorm activities meant to ease the transition to college, socialize with dormmates, and get involved in extracurricular activities. Although you might be tempted to ease your homesickness by returning home regularly (in the event that your hometown is in close proximity to your school), this only makes the transition to college more difficult because it prohibits you from making ties and connections to your new community. If you are finding living in your new environment too difficult, take advantage of on-campus counseling services that can help ease your transition.

HOW TO COPE WITH HOMETOWN GIRLFRIENDS OR BOYFRIENDS

A common dilemma faced by incoming college freshmen is whether or not to stay in relationships with high school sweethearts. It is entirely up to you whether or not you choose to continue such a relationship. After all, there are certainly plenty of high school relationships that turn into rewarding marriages down the line, so you should not discard a former sweetheart just because you are separating geographically to attend college. But you should consider a few things when thinking about maintaining a relationship with someone who is now far away, probably engaging in his or her own new experience:

- Initially, the prospect of being in a new environment, away from your family and friends, can be an intimidating one. Many students attempt to alleviate this discomfort by maintaining a tie to a home environment through a boy- or girlfriend—in a sense, using that person as a security blanket. Using someone in this manner, however, is unfair and misleading, so be aware of your motivation in maintaining a former relationship.

- One of the most exciting aspects of college is the opportunity to meet new people. If you have a special someone at home, you may be less inclined to meet others (either due to complacency or for fear of being tempted to pursue a relationship with someone new), or you may become resentful that you feel "tied down" by being in the relationship.

- Another exciting aspect of the college experience is that it provides you an opportunity to think independently and develop your own opinions, passions, motivations, and dreams. Because a special friend has certain expectations of how you should behave (i.e., to remain the person she fell in love with), she might resent any change and consciously or subconsciously try to stunt your transformation. Beware that letting go of old ties often helps people in formative phases of their lives to mature and develop in positive ways.

- Maintaining a relationship with a hometown sweetheart who has not yet decided where to attend college can be detrimental to that person's future decisions. If your sweetheart is younger than you are (or is taking a year or two off before attending college), your relationship may influence him to attend your school or one nearby, which may not necessarily be the best option for that person.

STAY PHYSICALLY, MENTALLY, AND EMOTIONALLY HEALTHY

Your ability to get the most out of academic, extracurricular, social, and other opportunities in college is predicated upon maintaining good health. Start off on the right foot in your freshman year so that you do not slide into bad habits during your college career:

- Eat healthily.
- Partake in physical activity.
- Do not forego sleep.
- Treat common physical illnesses quickly and sensibly.
- Avoid excessive alcohol and drug use.
- Use proper precautions when engaging in sex.
- Be aware of the signs of mental stress and seek professional help when you need it.
- Practice positive coping skills by taking advantage of the on-campus counseling and advising resources available to you, balancing your academic workload with plenty of social and extracurricular involvement, and making solid new friendships.

Part IV

FINANCING COLLEGE

18

MAXIMIZING YOUR FINANCIAL AID PACKAGES FROM THE COLLEGES

— KEY POINTS —

We are currently shifting between two different worlds of college financial aid:
—In the old world, colleges generally shared uniform aid policies, granted aid based on financial need alone, and used standardized, quantitative analyses to create financial aid packages
—In the new world, colleges abide by a variety of different aid policies, grant aid based on merit as well as need, and use subjective, case-by-case analyses to create financial aid packages

∎

Understand the basics of financial aid:
—Cost of attendance
—Methodologies used for determining financial need
—How need is fulfilled

∎

Move beyond the basics to understand the range of policies in place at the top colleges:
—Similar schools do not necessarily have similar financial aid policies

∎

Exploit institution-by-institution differences in financial aid policies

∎

Improve your treatment at all colleges by increasing your demonstrated need, among other strategies

∎

Learn how to evaluate, compare, and appeal financial aid decisions

∎

There is ample opportunity to receive desirable financial aid packages from the top colleges if you apply the right strategies

INTRODUCTION

A four-year college education at the most exclusive institutions now costs $130,000–150,000, making the expense a burden for nearly everyone. What most college applicants and their families do not realize, though, is that there is actually ample opportunity to receive desirable financial aid packages from the colleges. Many colleges now apply carefully honed strategies to attract the students they want. It is time that college students and their families do the same, applying their own tactics in order to secure the most favorable outcomes. A positive aid package can result in, among other things:

- A family's financial solvency despite incoming tuition bills from an expensive college,

- A student's ability to attend the college of his or her choice regardless of its expense,

- A student's freedom from overwhelming financial debt, and

- A student's freedom to choose the career he or she wants upon college graduation rather than accepting a position primarily to support loan payments.

THE SHIFT BETWEEN THE OLD AND NEW WORLDS OF COLLEGE FINANCIAL AID

We are currently in the process of shifting between two different worlds of financial aid administration.

THE OLD WORLD OF COLLEGE FINANCIAL AID

The old world of college financial aid was governed by a fairly uniform and inflexible tableau of financial aid policies. The former policies generally awarded regular financial aid (as opposed to special scholarships offered at colleges with merit programs) to those with financial need while students without need received nothing. All schools generally adhered to one of two basic methodologies for determining financial need and awarding aid. As a result, all offers to one particular student were more or less identical. (The Ivy League institutions in fact once collaborated when putting together offers for common applicants.) Colleges did not apply strategies to get their most desired outcomes—they merely awarded aid where it was due on the basis of a straightforward calculation—and there was thus no room for negotiation on financial aid packages.

THE NEW WORLD OF COLLEGE FINANCIAL AID

The new world of financial aid administration has tossed out many of the old rules and assumptions in exchange for more flexibility and strategy on the part of the colleges. A wide assortment of financial aid policies and procedures are responsible for the fact that financial aid packages are no longer designed solely to cover student need. Many schools (including a number of the top colleges, such as Duke and Cal Tech) give merit scholarships to desirable students without need or go beyond students' need requirements in order to entice them away from the competition. At schools that oppose non-need aid, variable packaging policies (often called "differential" or "preferential" packaging) nonetheless grant better deals to some applicants than others. Even at the most selective colleges, packages from different institutions to one student can vary tremendously. Just as colleges now strategize to reach their desired outcomes, it is increasingly common for college applicants and their families to appeal aid decisions and negotiate for better packages.

OTHER NEW CHANGES IN COLLEGE FINANCIAL AID

The top colleges—even those that do not award any aid based on merit as opposed to need—are responding to changes in the financial aid marketplace with moves to improve need-based aid as well. A group of the some of the most selective schools followed Princeton's lead when it decided to substantially increase aid awards to lower- and middle-income families in 1998. Princeton, Yale, Dartmouth, MIT, Harvard, and others down the line also decided to pump more money into the international student aid budget and usher in other positive financial aid changes as well.

Similarly, many of the top colleges have recently decided to allow students to benefit from 100% of any outside scholarships they bring in. Previously, most of the top schools used a portion of the scholarship money that students won from organizations outside the school to replace their own institutional grant money, thereby leaving the student's financial situation virtually unchanged. Now outside aid at many top colleges entirely replaces self-help aid, so that students' efforts to obtain outside scholarships are better rewarded.

THE OLD AND NEW WORLDS OF COLLEGE FINANCIAL AID

The Old World	*The New World*
➤ Financial aid awards based on a standardized, quantitative analysis	➤ Financial aid awards based on a subjective, case-by-case analysis
➤ Colleges shared uniform financial aid policies	➤ A wide assortment of financial aid policies exists
➤ Most aid awarded on the basis of need	➤ More and more aid awarded on the basis of merit
➤ All offers (especially from the top colleges) to one student similar	➤ All offers (even among the top colleges) to one student different
➤ Little strategizing on the part of colleges	➤ Much strategizing on the part of colleges
➤ No room for negotiation by families	➤ Room for negotiation by families

THE CURRENT STATE OF AFFAIRS

Somewhere between the Old and the New Worlds of College Financial Aid

As it stands now, students have not yet risen to the occasion by applying their own strategies to gain the best possible financial aid treatment. We are thus operating in an atmosphere located somewhere between the old and the new worlds. Colleges have demonstrated that they are ready and willing to do what they have to do in order to achieve their desired outcomes. College applicants, on the other hand, are still lingering behind, trapped within the confines of the old world of financial aid. Our entry into the new world of financial aid administration will be complete when students and their families catch up to the colleges by employing their own strategies for improving their financial aid treatment.

FINANCIAL AID OFFICERS DISCUSS TRENDS AND AREAS OF CONCERN IN THE NEW WORLD OF COLLEGE FINANCIAL AID

"The marketplace is now driven more by the consumer. We're trying to listen a lot more to what families are saying."

—*Michael Bartini, Director of Financial Aid, Brown University*

"Certainly there is a lot more complexity to financial aid these days than there was years ago."

—*Joe Paul Case, Dean of Financial Aid, Amherst College*

"Many schools are moving to the 'enrollment management' model and using financial aid as a recruiting tool—rather than using it to fill in what needy families cannot afford to pay."
—*Patricia Coye, Director of Financial Aid, Pomona College*

"A lot of institutions have muddied the waters between need- and merit-based aid. And need is no longer consistently measured by schools."
—*Walter Moulton, Director of Financial Aid, Bowdoin College*

"I think as we move ahead there's going to be an increasing fractionalization of policies among schools. Understandings, principles, and the like will continue to erode."
—*James Miller, Director of Undergraduate Financial Aid, Harvard University*

"Parents are becoming more savvy and prepping more to market their kids and do the best they can in financial aid. The problem is that the parents who need aid most are least astute in this realm—the ones who know how to wheel and deal are the ones who need it least."
—*Leonard Wenc, Director of Student Financial Services, Carleton College*

"There is an entitlement mentality in the students and families we work with today. They make the assumption that being admitted is a tacit guarantee of financial assistance, either merit or need-based."
—*Julia Perreault, Director of Financial Aid, Emory University*

"One of the troubling things is that the federal government has not kept pace with rising costs. So more institutional aid must be used to cover student aid—and then costs go up again. It's a never-ending cycle."
—*Howard Thomas, Director of Financial Aid, Oberlin College*

"There seems to be more and more borrowing every year, which concerns us."
—*Myra Smith, Director of Financial Aid, Smith College*

A NOTE TO APPLICANTS AND THEIR PARENTS

Chapters 18 and 19 are addressed more to parents than to students, because parental figures are likely to take college financial matters most seriously. We hope that college applicants will read along, too, even if only to gain a better understanding of financial aid. Although most parents and guardians need to be central players in the financial aid application process, students should also take responsibility (and appreciate how much their parents are sacrificing for them!) by learning how financial aid works and what their own Work-Study and loan commitments will be.

SAMPLE COSTS FOR THE 1999–2000 ACADEMIC YEAR

	Stanford University	Princeton University	University of California, Berkeley
Tuition	$23,058	$24,630	$ 3,766 (in-state)
			$14,088 (out-of-state)
Other Fees	$ 275	—	$ 418
Room/Board	$ 7,881	$ 6,969	$ 8,122
Books/Personal	$ 2,658	$ 2,581	$ 2,738
Total Cost of Attendance	$33,842	$34,180	$15,044 (in-state)
			$25,366 (out-of-state)

FUTURE FINANCIAL AID REFORMS

As mentioned earlier, financial aid policies and procedures are changing all the time. College applicants and their families have to be on their toes, remembering to keep abreast of future changes. Perhaps the most controversial and radical of all the reforms currently discussed is a new federal eligibility formula that would determine a family's need by considering its income rather than its income *and* assets, and then assign it to a general bracket with other families of similar resources. The new formula would stop penalizing families who have saved money for college and stop rewarding those whose money has been spent to purchase valuable homes or has been funneled into retirement savings accounts rather than other savings plans. Yet another proposal in the works would require families applying for financial aid to report their financial information for the calendar year *two* years prior to a child's enrollment in college, rather than one year before.

UNDERSTANDING THE BASICS OF COLLEGE FINANCIAL AID

Learning how to get the best financial treatment possible from all colleges requires a thorough understanding of financial aid basics. The following pages will focus on the fundamentals of financial aid before moving on to our prescriptions for seeking financial aid from the colleges.

THE COST OF ATTENDANCE

The cost of attendance (COA), as you probably already know, surpasses the mere price of a college's tuition. The components that make up a college's COA are:

- **Tuition**

- **Fees and Other Institutional Expenses** include any college charges above and beyond general tuition. A college might, for example, charge a "registration fee" or "activity fees."

- **Room and Board** at a single institution can vary tremendously depending upon whether a student lives in campus housing or off-campus, and what kind of meal plan he or she chooses.

- **Health Insurance** costs vary depending on the health of the student and the program option that you choose.

- **Books and Supplies** costs vary depending upon what kinds of classes a student takes and whether she purchases new or used books.

- **Transportation** costs include fares for travel by airplane, bus, or train, as well as car expenses, including the costs of insurance, parking permits, gas, and tolls.

- **Personal Expenses and Entertainment** are highly variable depending on the student's habits and interests.

- **Miscellaneous Costs** associated with college include special lab or studio fees for science or art students, registrar fees (required for dropping and adding courses, changing to a different grading option, etc.), participation fees for club sports and other activities, and membership fees for a fraternity or sorority.

METHODOLOGIES USED TO CALCULATE NEED-BASED FINANCIAL AID

A school can award financial aid on the basis of financial need, academic or other merit, or some combination of both. When aid is based fully or partially upon financial need, the school calculates aid using one of many methodologies, which fall into one of two categories: the Federal Methodology (FM) or the Institutional Methodology (IM).

Most public institutions use the **Federal Methodology (FM),** which calculates need based upon information you supply on the Free Application for Federal Student Aid (FAFSA). Most private colleges use an **Institutional Methodology (IM),** which is not one formula but a variety of non-federal formulas. An IM calculates need based upon information you supply on the Financial Aid PROFILE (PROFILE) created by the College Scholarship Service or on an institution's own financial aid form. A school uses one of the FM or IM equations to determine how much a family can afford to pay for college, or the "Estimated Family Contribution" (EFC). The EFC is the amount that a student and his family will have to supply to pay for college costs. If one subtracts the EFC from a school's total cost of attendance (which includes not only tuition but also room and board, books, travel costs, etc.), the resulting figure is called "demonstrated need," or the amount of funding that a student requires from other sources in order to attend college.

A student's EFC and demonstrated need can be calculated in a variety of ways. Both the FM and the IM base their calculations on family income and assets from the calendar year prior to a student's entry into college, which is called the "base year." If a student is applying to enter college in September of 2001, financial aid calculations will be made according to the family's income and assets during the period beginning in January of 2000 and ending in December of that same year. (This usually means the calendar year that includes the student's spring semester of junior year and fall semester of senior year in high school). The box below shows how the two general methodologies differ in their aid calculations.

FEDERAL METHODOLOGY (FM) VERSUS INSTITUTIONAL METHODOLOGY (IM)

Federal Methodology	*Institutional Methodology**
➤ Considers total income of both parents, including child support, payments to retirement plans, and social security benefits.	➤ Considers total income of both parents, including child support, payments to retirement plans, and social security benefits.
➤ Considers all assets (value of business, savings, stocks, bonds, trusts, etc.), *excluding* home and farm equity, usually requiring a 3–6% contribution	➤ Considers all assets (value of business savings, stocks, bonds, trusts, etc.), *including* home and farm equity, usually requiring a 3–6% contribution
➤ Considers student's income at about 50%, with those earning up to a certain amount exempt from any contributions	➤ Considers student's income at about 50%, with all students required to make a minimum contribution no matter what their income
➤ Considers student's assets at about 35%	➤ Considers student's assets at about 35%

> Does not consider siblings' assets

> Accounts for multiple siblings in college

> Does not account for parents in college

> Does not grant allowances for private school tuition for siblings

> Does not grant allowances for business losses

> Does not grant allowances for unreimbursed medical expenses

> In cases of divorce or separation: Considers only the situation of the custodial parent and that parent's spouse, if remarried

> Considers siblings' assets

> Accounts for multiple siblings in college

> Does not account for parents in college

> Grants allowances for private school tuition for siblings

> Grants allowances for business losses

> Grants allowances for unreimbursed medical expenses that surpass 4% of Adjusted Gross Income

> In cases of divorce or separation: Considers only the situation of the custodial parent, and that parent's spouse, if remarried (Note that many private colleges use their own versions of IM to assess non-custodial parents as well.)

*Note that the Institutional Methodology referred to here is that calculated by the Financial Aid PROFILE. Colleges' own institutional methodologies may differ. PROFILE also offers colleges that use it several optional lines of inquiry, including information about additional real estate holdings; owned or leased motor vehicles; consumer debt; tax-deferred annuities, pensions, or savings; and the cost of supporting additional family members, such as grand-parents.

QUALIFYING FOR INDEPENDENT STATUS

To be considered financially independent as an undergraduate student (in which case no parental or family financial information will be assessed in calculating your need-based aid) you must be (at least one of the following):

> Age 24 or older (as of December 31 of the year you will receive aid)

> Married

> Able to claim a dependent (or dependents) other than a spouse

> An orphan or ward of the court

> A military veteran

HOW DEMONSTRATED NEED IS FULFILLED

Demonstrated need can be fulfilled through gift or self-help funding. **Gift funding** includes grants and scholarships—anything that is essentially "free money" and does not need to be paid back in any way. **Self-help funding** includes loans and earned contributions to college costs attained from working, often through the federal Work-Study program. Gift money and self-help can be combined in an endless variety of ways to make up a student's entire financial aid package.

TYPES AND SOURCES OF NEED-BASED FINANCIAL AID

GIFT FUNDING

GRANTS AND SCHOLARSHIPS

FEDERAL

Pell Grants make up the largest of the federal gift programs. Pell Grants represent the basic building block of student financial aid, the bottom layer to which all other aid is then added.

Student Educational Opportunity Grants (SEOGs), awarded in amounts of $100 to $4,000 per year, are intended to help low-income students with high demonstrated need pay for their educational opportunities.

STATE

State financial aid programs provide support to residents who attend public or private colleges within their state to help fill in the gaps after federal funds have been distributed.

COLLEGE

Collegiate institutional aid includes all monies given out by colleges from their own coffers.

PRIVATE ORGANIZATIONS

Private organizations award need-based grants to students who apply for special awards. (These sources of private aid are discussed further in Chapter 19.)

SELF-HELP FUNDING

LOANS

FEDERAL

The **Family Education Loan Program** and the **Federal Direct Student Loan Program** run in parallel. The Family Education Loans include Subsidized

Stafford Loans, Unsubsidized Stafford Loans, and PLUS Loans. These are all made by commercial lenders who design their own loan terms. Federal Direct Student Loans include Direct Subsidized Stafford Loans, Direct Unsubsidized Stafford Loans, and Direct PLUS Loans. The Federal Direct loan programs are simply variations of the usual loan programs that are distributed through the Treasury via colleges, requiring no intermediary to manage the loan process.

Stafford Loans are loans granted to those enrolled at least half-time. They are available to all families regardless of need. Students with demonstrated need receive subsidized loans, in which the government pays the interest while the student is still in school, for six months after graduation, and during deferment periods. Students with no need receive unsubsidized Staffords, in which they must pay the interest that accrues while they are in school. Staffords are granted by private lenders such as banks, credit unions, and insurance companies. Direct Staffords are granted by the government.

Perkins Loans are awarded to those with "exceptional need," as determined by the college.

PLUS Loans are not based on financial need and are granted to creditworthy parents of any financial background from private lenders or, in the case of Direct PLUS Loans, from the U.S. government.

STATE

State loans can be secured in addition to (or in place of) federal or college-based loans.

COLLEGE

The **college loan programs** are often used in place of grant money as a regular component of aid packages.

PRIVATE LENDING INSTITUTIONS

To obtain **loans from private lending institutions,** you apply directly to the lending institution after you have received your aid package and know how much money you will have to uncover in order to make up the difference between what the school expects you to fork over (the EFC) and what you can realistically afford to spend.

WORK-STUDY
FEDERAL

Work-Study is a program offering federal assistance in the form of earned wages to students with need. Work-study can include both on- and off-campus employment, and the salary must equal at least minimum wage.

GETTING BEYOND THE BASICS OF COLLEGE FINANCIAL AID: UNDERSTANDING THE RANGE OF FINANCIAL AID POLICIES

There is a lot more to financial aid administration than a simple determination and fulfillment of need. Financial aid administration is governed by policies, often backed by particular philosophies and values, that actually *supersede* the determination and fulfillment of demonstrated need. It is these policies, which vary substantially from institution to institution, especially in the new world of financial aid administration, that shape the true nature of aid awards. Determination of need is merely a tool that allows financial aid officers to create concrete offers of aid once institutional policy has been applied.

These policies can govern how your demonstrated need will be evaluated once it is determined, or whether or not your demonstrated need will be determined at all. For example, if you are an international student with financial need, and a school's policy does not grant financial aid (even need-based) to international students, then it does not matter what your demonstrated need is; you are ineligible for funds regardless of your need level.

The importance of policy over calculation of demonstrated need can mean that two students with the same financial need will not necessarily be treated equally by a particular school. Furthermore, all colleges maintain very different financial aid policies, so one student may be treated very differently by each of his target colleges. Even the most similar of schools do not necessarily share the same financial aid policies.

The following subsections highlight some of the most important policy areas in which colleges maintain a wide range of stances. Remember that we are in the midst of a wave of change in financial aid policy; institutions are constantly implementing changes, some of which may apply to these areas.

NEED CONSCIOUSNESS IN ADMISSIONS

"Need consciousness in admissions" refers to a school's policy concerning the relationship between a school's admissions decisions and the financial need of its candidates. When a school's admissions committee selects its admitted students without any knowledge whatsoever of their financial situation or degree of financial need, we call this "need-blind" admissions. Most of the top schools, including all of the Ivies (with the exception of Brown) and "little Ivies" (Amherst, Wesleyan, and Williams) still maintain need-blind admissions. "Need-aware," "need-conscious," or "need-sensitive" admissions all refer to an admissions process whereby some or all students are evaluated for admission with one eye on their financial situations as well. For most schools, need awareness applies only to some portion of the bottom tier of admitted students. Top students are admitted no matter what their financial need; it is the less-qualified students who are scrutinized carefully so that officers can ensure that remaining aid dollars are spent wisely. Other than Brown, Mount Holyoke, Carleton, Smith, Johns Hopkins, Bryn Mawr, Sarah Lawrence, and Oberlin are other examples of top colleges that have become need-sensitive in their decisions for (the bottom) 5 to 10% of their admitted students.

MEETING DEMONSTRATED NEED

"Meeting demonstrated need" refers to a school's agreement or lack thereof to cover the full financial need of all admitted students. Some colleges meet the full need of every student admitted. This is true of all the Ivy League schools, as well as places like Stanford, Duke, Cal Tech, and MIT, and most of the selective small liberal arts colleges. Most state universities meet the full need of their residents but do not meet the full need of all out-of-state students. At colleges that do not necessarily guarantee to meet the full need of their students, a student may be "gapped" or given an "admit/deny" decision. "Gapping" essentially means underfunding a student, not providing enough aid to cover his or her full demonstrated need. An "admit/deny" decision is one in which a student is admitted to the college but denied financial aid. Vanderbilt, for example, does not necessarily meet the full need of all students, with a handful of students lacking adequate aid packages each year. The University of Virginia also does not meet the full need of its students; rather than underawarding a few students by a substantial amount, though, UVA chooses to package everyone with slightly less aid than dictated by the school's need formulas.

FINANCIAL AID OFFICERS DISCUSS MEETING FULL NEED

"With our current funding level, we don't have enough to meet the needs of every student. We're currently doing a pretty good job of funding nearly all residents. And our very poorest nonresidents are getting full need filled because we target our dollars toward them. But the middle-income nonresident is the one who might not get enough aid from us."

—*Steve Van Ess, Director of the Office of Student Financial Services, University of Wisconsin (Madison)*

"We don't even use the phrase 'meet need' anymore. We use 'eligibility' instead, because we realized that many families like to interpret 'need' as their own perception of their need."

—*Lucia Whittelsey, Director of Financial Aid, Colby College*

"Our packages to low-income out-of-state students are actually not strong. We are not usually able to meet their full need."

—*Richard Black, Director of Financial Aid, University of California (Berkeley)*

AID FOR WAITLISTED STUDENTS

"Aid for waitlisted students" refers to a school's policy or procedure for granting financial aid to students who are accepted off the waitlist, often long after other financial aid decisions have been administered. Some schools treat waitlisted students exactly as they treat everyone else. At some schools, this means admitting students off the waitlist need-blind and giving them full need packages. Other colleges change their policies when it comes to admitting waitlisted students. For example, Northwestern, which normally meets the full need of all students, does not necessarily do so for waitlisted admits.

FINANCIAL AID OFFICERS DISCUSS WAITLISTED STUDENT AID

"If we even go to our waitlist, those students are evaluated need-blind and receive full packages just like everyone else."

—*Virginia Hazen, Director of Financial Aid, Dartmouth College*

"According to policy, it's possible for waitlisted students to receive aid. We don't deny it to them by design. But usually we don't have enough money left by the time we go to the waitlist."

—*Robert Massa, Dean of Enrollment, Johns Hopkins University*

"We can't promise waitlisted students aid in advance, but we've had such little use of the waitlist over the past five to seven years that we've been able to fully fund all of those offered admission from the waitlist."

—*Rebecca Dixon, Associate Provost, Northwestern University*

"As long as the applicant had applied for financial aid by our regular March first deadline, a person pulled from the waitlist gets packaged just like everyone else."

—*Yvone Hubbard, Director of Financial Aid, University of Virginia*

"We evaluate waitlisted students one by one. Their offers vary depending on how much money we have left at the time they are admitted."

—*Joseph A. Russo, Director of Financial Aid, University of Notre Dame*

AID FOR TRANSFER STUDENTS

"Aid for transfer students" refers to a school's policy on granting financial aid to students who transfer from other colleges. Some colleges treat transfer students the same way they treat incoming freshmen. Cornell, Davidson, Duke, Yale, the University of Chicago, and Pomona, for example, all admit transfers using need-blind admissions and offer them complete packages upon arrival. Other schools, though, consider transfer students as a separate admissions category. Amherst, Dartmouth, Northwestern, and Bowdoin, for example, technically do not guarantee transfer students full aid packages (although in practice transfers at these schools usually do not get treated any differently than other students). Sarah Lawrence caps transfer aid packages each year.

AID FOR INTERNATIONAL STUDENTS

"Aid for international students" refers to a school's policy on granting financial aid to students from overseas. (Note that most schools do not consider Canadians or legal residents international students.) Middlebury and Harvard treat overseas students exactly as they treat American citizens; both schools are need-blind *and* meet the full need of international students. Other schools with substantial international aid include Princeton, Mount Holyoke, Cal Tech, and Dartmouth, which meet the full need of all foreign students admitted but use need-sensitive admissions when deciding which international students to take. Other colleges with healthy international aid programs include Amherst, Colby, Wesleyan, Williams, and Yale. Some colleges, such as Georgetown, provide some international aid packages, but cap the awards for overseas students. Other top schools, such as Duke, Northwestern, Sarah Lawrence, Notre Dame, Vanderbilt, and Johns Hopkins, give no aid whatsoever to international students. The flagship public institutions also generally have no aid for overseas students.

FINANCIAL AID OFFICERS TALK
ABOUT INTERNATIONAL STUDENT AID

"We don't call ourselves need-blind with regard to international admissions, but usually we can admit all the needy foreign students that Admissions would like to have. So in reality, we are very very close to being need-blind
for international students."

—*Don Betterton, Director of Financial Aid, Princeton University*

"Generally, international students are expected to provide their own support while here. No aid is extended to them for their first year. After that, Services for International Students and Scholars department will provide some limited funding based on need, but it's not a significant source of aid."

—*Richard Black, Director of Financial Aid, University of California (Berkeley)*

"Our international students get the same self-help packages as everyone else—the difference is that the loans come through us, rather than through federal programs."

—*Philip Wick, Director of Financial Aid, Williams College*

"International aid? We essentially have none—the amount we give out is small enough that we simply say we don't have any. But we're looking into possibilities to fund international students in the future."

—*James Belvin, Director of Financial Aid, Duke University*

MERIT-BASED (NON-NEED) AID

"Merit-based (non-need) aid" refers to a school's policy on giving out non-need scholarship money. Some merit scholarships are called by name, and may even require a separate application at the time of admission to be considered for them. Other aid that is based on merit rather than need comes in the form of what is known in admissions circles as "discounting," in which tuition is knocked down in order to attract desirable students. Many of the top colleges do not currently grant aid on the basis of merit alone. The entire Ivy League, for example, opposes the idea of merit-based aid on principle. Note that some colleges—such as Bowdoin and Northwestern—that do not give regular academic merit aid do recognize National Merit Scholars with small to medium sized financial awards. Cal Tech, Duke, Davidson, Emory, Johns Hopkins, Rice, Swarthmore, Vanderbilt, and the University of Chicago, on the other hand, are examples of top colleges with substantial scholarship programs. In addition, all of the state universities have healthy scholarship programs, some of which can benefit out-of-state students as well. Note that some schools that do not give academic merit scholarships—such as Stanford, Notre Dame, and Georgetown—do give athletic merit scholarships.

FINANCIAL AID OFFICERS DISCUSS MERIT-BASED AID

"There is no separate application for our merit scholarships. We select students for these awards during the admissions process."

—*David Levy, Director of Financial Aid, California Institute of Technology*

"We're sticking to the 'tried-and-true' formula of need-based aid. We're trying to weather this storm and offer aid based only on financial need."

—*Patricia McWade, Director of Financial Aid, Georgetown University*

"Our stance on merit aid has changed. Our policy fifteen or twenty years ago was identical to that of the Ivies—we did not give out non-need aid. Now about 10% of our students receive merit aid."

—*Kathleen Stevenson-McNeely, Senior Associate Dean of Admissions and Financial Aid, Davidson College*

"Stanford does give athletic scholarships, but no academic merit awards."

—*Cynthia Hartley, Director of Student Awards, Stanford University*

"Our sense of merit is addressed in the admissions process rather than through financial aid. If we admit you, you have merit. But you won't receive any more financial aid because of it!"

—*Nancy Monnich, Director of Admissions and Financial Aid, Bryn Mawr College*

TREATMENT OF OUTSIDE AID

"Treatment of outside aid" refers to a college's policy on incorporating scholarships won from outside organizations into a student's aid package. Note that many colleges' policies on outside sources of aid are currently in flux. Some schools have generous policies that allow students to "keep" all of the outside scholarships they have worked hard to obtain, using it to replace the student's self-help aid, usually loans. In other words, the student benefits from the entire scholarship because it replaces money that he or she would have to pay back in loan payments after graduation. At schools such as Stanford, Harvard, Williams, Oberlin, Vanderbilt, Bryn Mawr, and the University of Virginia, all outside scholarships are used to replace self-help until there is no more self-help left to replace. Other schools use any outside scholarships won by a student to replace both self-help and grant. For most colleges operating on these terms, a designated sum of money—usually somewhere between $500 and $1,500—replaces self-help completely, and the remainder of the outside award is split evenly to replace self-help and grant funds. At Carleton, Bowdoin, and Amherst, for example, the first $1000 of outside aid replaces self-help; the remainder above $1000 is split evenly to replace self-help and grant funds.

TREATMENT OF TUITION FOR OFF-CAMPUS PROGRAMS

"Treatment of tuition for off-campus programs" refers to a school's policy on what kind of tuition is paid (and to whom) when a student does a semester abroad or fulfills a semester of study at another institution. Some colleges allow their students to receive substantial financial benefits (in addition to the obvious academic, cultural, and social pluses) by paying the host institution tuition when they attend off-campus programs, often cheaper than study at the top colleges. In recent years, though, many colleges have instituted policies that require students to pay the regular tuition of their home institution regardless of the price of the institution where the study will occur. Carleton and the University of Pennsylvania, for example, charge their own tuition rates for the off-campus programs that they administer.

CHANGES IN AID AFTER FRESHMAN YEAR (ASSUMING FINANCIAL CIRCUMSTANCES REMAIN THE SAME)

"Changes in aid after freshman year" refers to policies concerning aid package composition after a student's first year of school (assuming his or her financial situation is unchanged). Almost all schools, for example, give slightly greater amounts of self-help, either in the form of loans or Work-Study or both, as students get older. At Harvard, for example, the self-help component increases gradually from freshman packages to senior packages, with seniors receiving $1000 more in loans than do freshmen. At Williams, loans increase incrementally from $3000 in the freshman year to $5500 in the senior year, a fairly dramatic rise; furthermore, the expected summer contribution is $1250 for freshmen, while all other classes are expected to contribute $1900. Cal Tech's philosophy, however, is that freshman students need time and energy to adjust to the demands of a rigorous college environment. Thus, freshmen are not permitted to participate in Work-Study jobs during their first semester on campus. For this reason, the loan component of self-help at Cal Tech is actually *higher* for freshmen, and then drops after freshman year. The University of Virginia maintains a similar philosophy, disqualifying all but nonresident students from contributing to aid packages through their own earnings during the freshman year.

APPLICATIONS FOR AID AFTER FRESHMAN YEAR FOR STUDENTS WHO DO NOT RECEIVE AID FOR THEIR FIRST YEAR OF SCHOOL

"Applications for aid after freshman year" refers to a school's policy on how long students must wait before seeking financial aid if they did not apply for or receive it during their first year on campus. At some schools, anyone can apply for aid (and is eligible to receive it) at any time, be it in the middle of the freshman year or even as late as the middle of the senior year. At other colleges, there are strict policies governing applications for aid. Many schools using need-sensitive admissions have enacted these policies to prevent students from hiding financial issues in the admissions process in order to receive a better chance of being admitted. Thus at Brown and Colby, for example, if you do not apply for aid for your freshman year, you must wait until junior year to do so.

PACKAGING POLICIES

"Packaging policies" refers to the way in which a school combines grant, loan, and work-study funds to create aid packages for its students. Although two schools might tell you that they both fulfill 100% of all students' need, one might do so by giving you mostly grant money and low self-help expectations while the other "fulfills need" by shoving too many work hours and a large debt level at you.

Most schools package students with loans and work-study first. In other words, the first tier of need in students' packages at most schools is filled with self-help. At some places, like Johns Hopkins, you will receive almost $7000 of self-help each year before you see a dime of gift aid. At other schools, such as Princeton, the threshold is set much lower, with students receiving gift money after only $4000 of self-help has been applied. There are a few schools, however, that actually dispense their own grant money first, before adding self-help into anyone's package. At one of these schools, such as Pomona or Vanderbilt, you can get away without any loan component whatsoever in your packages if your need level is moderate. Everyone at Pomona is packaged the same way, with the first $6200 of every needy student's package covered by grant. If you have $6200 or less of financial need as a student at Pomona, you do not take on any loan or

Work-Study obligations at all. Vanderbilt packages each student a bit differently, but all students have their first $5000 covered by grant.

Aside from the issue of how colleges generally allocate money for the grant, loan, and work-study components of aid packages is the issue of how they treat various aid recipients in relation to one another. Some schools use **"equity" packaging,** whereby a set of policies holds across the entire spectrum of aid-worthy students. Yale, for example, designs its packages equitably, granting a uniform self-help amount (composed of both loans and work-study) to all freshmen and sophomores, as well as a slightly higher uniform self-help amount to all juniors and seniors. After the maximum self-help has been applied, then grant money fills in the rest of all students' financial aid packages to complete them.

Some schools, on the other hand, use what are called **"differential" packaging** guidelines, in which certain *categories* of aid-worthy students are given special treatment. These certain categories of students who receive beneficial treatment, usually in the form of reduced Work-Study or loan expectations (in exchange for greater amounts of grant aid), are sometimes chosen on the basis of financial need. Princeton, for example, has eliminated all loans for students from families earning less than $40,000 per year, replacing those loans with grants; students from families earning between $40,000 and $57,000 get reduced loan packages; and the value of home equity is not considered at all by Princeton when calculating EFC for those with incomes of $90,000 or less. One variety of differential packaging is the granting of special packages to certain minority or otherwise designated underprivileged students. The University of Chicago, for example, dispenses differential packages with lower self-help expectations to "students of color," meaning African Americans, Hispanics, and Native Americans.

FINANCIAL AID OFFICERS DISCUSS PACKAGING POLICIES

"We do some differential packaging based on need levels."

—*Cynthia Hartley, Director of Student Awards, Stanford University*

"We're talking about doing some preferential packaging in the future, giving better packages to 'merit' students. We've been losing a few students to other places who are doing this, so it's something we are considering."

—*Barbara-Jan Wilson, Dean of Admissions and Financial Aid, Wesleyan University*

"The first $5000 for every student's need is covered with grant money. Always. Even if he or she is one of our last students to be admitted. If there's any need at all, the first portion is covered in gift aid."

—*David Mohning, Director of Student Financial Aid, Vanderbilt University*

"We graduate our self-help levels depending on the family income. Very low-income students are not expected to take on as much debt as others."

—*Virginia Hazen, Director of Financial Aid, Dartmouth College*

"Our packaging system is computerized, untouched by human hands. We run a financial aid factory here. You can ask for anything you want, but we build it according to an assembly-line system. Sometimes we'll take the product off of the assembly line to take a good look at it—look at individual needs, if necessary— but mostly, it's a straightforward packaging system."

—Larry Burt, Director of the Office of Student Financial Services, University of Texas (Austin)

At some schools, *individuals* (rather than general categories of students) are chosen on the basis of merit to receive better financial aid packages than other admitted students. When individual students are chosen on the basis of merit (or some combination of merit and need), the policy is generally referred to as **"merit-within-need"** or **"preferential" packaging**. (Note that the terms "differential" and "preferential" are often treated synonymously. We use "differential" to denote non-equity packaging based on need or lack of privilege only and "preferential" to denote non-equity packaging based on academic or other merit.) This is not exactly the same thing as non-need merit aid, because the recipients have need; they are being rewarded on the basis of merit and need combined. At Bates, for example, some preferential packaging occurs based on academic merit. Everyone at Bates receives loan and Work-Study to fill the first $3000 of need. The most promising students receive grants after that point; others receive an additional $1500 in self-help, for a total of $4500 in self-help funding, before grant money is applied to fill in the rest of their need.

DETERMINATION OF TRAVEL ALLOWANCES

Although not a major policy area, the way in which colleges determine travel allowances can affect the value of your financial aid package. Some schools attempt to cover a certain number of trips back home, calculating the cost by region or state or zip code. Duke, for example, attempts to provide the equivalent of two "supersaver" fares for each student per year. Students from California thus are allotted about $1000 for their travel to and from Durham each year. Other schools admit that their figure represents only an "allowance," and is not meant to cover the whole cost of yearly travel to and from home. This is an area in which an appeal is often necessary, and frequently successful, because schools are well aware that their travel budgets do not always cover full need.

OTHER SPECIAL POLICY FEATURES

Many of the top colleges maintain unique financial aid policy features that benefit particular students. Watch out for special deals such as the following:

Amherst will help with special "one-time" financial needs. For example, it often helps needy seniors to buy a suit for job or graduate school interviewing. A student whose parent or sibling is severely ill can apply for special funds for frequent travel home.

Dartmouth caps home equity at three times the family's income. It also looks at nonliquid assets, making an adjustment if much of a family's finances are trapped in nonliquid assets. Dartmouth also sometimes makes allowances for a family's debts and business losses.

Oberlin caps the value of home equity at three times the family's income.

Princeton makes allowances for the full cost of sending parents to school in certain cases. A student can also file to be relieved of full summer earnings expectation if she does not make enough money to cover the entire amount. Princeton reduces the value of home equity one-quarter to one-half for all families and entirely eliminates home equity for those with incomes under $90,000.

Yale grants families allowances for money paid to fund a sibling's graduate school expenses. Yale also replaces a student's summer earnings expectation with grant money for one summer in his four years at Yale if he is participating in a public service internship, Yale traveling fellowship, or formal study abroad. The school also allows all families to exempt $150,000 of their assets.

GENERAL STRATEGIES TO IMPROVE COLLEGE FINANCIAL AID PACKAGES

By now you should realize how important it is that you find out what the financial aid policies are at your target schools. Similar schools do not have similar policies, and there is no point wasting your time seeking admission and financial aid at a school whose policies are not supportive of your individual needs. Keeping a school's policies in mind, you should also apply some general strategies for obtaining the best financial aid treatment from the colleges overall.

REALIZE THAT YOUR ADMISSIONS PROFILE AND YOUR FINANCIAL PROFILE OFTEN WORK HAND IN HAND

Even at the need-blind colleges, all applicants are now viewed within their socioeconomic contexts. One glance at a student's application for admission generally reveals the nature of his or her financial situation. A student's address and his parents' educational and professional backgrounds give meaningful clues as to where a student stands financially. Information about a student's socioeconomic background is usually divulged contextually within an essay or a teacher's recommendation as well.

In most cases, if you are a minority from a low-income family, the committee will be more impressed with your achievements than with those of someone who has lived a fairly easy life with plenty of opportunity. The selective schools tend to favor kids from humble backgrounds who show that they have applied great effort in order to succeed. Affluent students, on the other hand, are often examined more carefully than others for flaws and are not given as much leeway in terms of weaknesses in their profiles. With their abundance of opportunity, affluent students have little excuse for a shallow roster of extracurriculars or the inability to get academic help where needed. In addition, there is always the possibility that a privileged background might provoke feelings of injustice or disgust in an admissions officer. Furthermore, in their mission to diversify, the selective schools now try to take fewer students from the typically desirable communities and instead round out their classes using students representing as many different backgrounds and niches as possible. If you are privileged, taking certain measures to show that you are highly aware of your good fortune, that you have taken great advantage of the opportunities given to you, and (best of all) that you have contributed to the improvement of your community by helping others less fortunate than yourself, will stand you a better chance of earning the committee's respect.

PLAY SMART IN TIMING YOUR APPLICATION

You need to consider your financial background when thinking about when to apply to a particular college.

REGARDING EARLY DECISION

As noted in Chapter 5, your financial background matters when considering whether or not to apply under a school's binding Early Decision program. If you have substantial financial need, you should not apply Early Decision to schools that give merit-based aid, design preferential packaging policies based on merit, or do not guarantee to meet the full financial need of all students. These colleges might be tempted to design less-desirable packages for students who apply Early Decision because they know they are bound to attend their institutions no matter what. (Remember that many of the top colleges do not fall under these categories, though.) Do not apply Early Decision if you plan to decide where to attend college based on the aid you receive.

If a school conducts rolling admissions, in which candidates are evaluated on a first-come first-served basis, you need to apply (as well as apply for financial aid) as early as possible. Colleges have a limited financial aid budget each year. When the first admissions decisions are made under rolling admissions, there is plenty of money available for dispersing among students. As the process continues into the late winter and early spring months, the school's funds start to dwindle and there is more likelihood that you will be "gapped," not receiving enough aid to attend.

APPLY TO SEVERAL SCHOOLS THAT USE PREFERENTIAL PACKAGING POLICIES OR GIVE MERIT-BASED AID AND IN WHICH YOU FALL INTO THE UPPER 25% OF THE APPLICANT POOL

Because your application profile and financial need are so intertwined in the new world of financial aid, be careful to set yourself up to receive the best aid package possible and still negotiate for more later on, if need be. You will be wise to apply to at least two schools that grant better financial aid to preferred candidates and where your academic standing places you in the upper 25% of the applicant pool (even better if you fall in the upper 10%). (This is increasingly true even at schools that do not openly give merit scholarships, instead rewarding their top picks with disguised scholarships called tuition "discounts" or "rebates.")

APPLY TO SCHOOLS THAT ARE KNOWN FOR BEING GENEROUS WITH FINANCIAL AID

Some schools are known to be particularly generous with their financial aid. Some of these colleges launch short-lived aid campaigns as strategies for improving yield, while other schools are committed to granting good aid packages for the long haul. Princeton is the best example of a school that has initiated long-term generosity strategies. The school sent waves rippling through college admissions offices nationwide when in February of 1998 it announced a major change in its financial aid policy to reward students from middle- and lower-income families.

APPLY TO SCHOOLS THAT HAVE (OR ARE TRYING TO CULTIVATE) GOOD REPUTATIONS IN YOUR FIELD OF INTEREST

You can also find exceptional aid packages at colleges with a strong reputation in your selected field of study or activity (usually one in which you have demonstrated potential) or—often overlooked—colleges *without* a known reputation in your selected field of study or activity but *with* a recently initiated intention to beef up that area by recruiting new talent. Schools with reputations in certain areas not only give out their own money to promising incoming students in the field, but also receive endowment and gift money from corporations and outside sponsors to fund new students. (The money is administered by the school although provided by outside sponsors. You are not required to fill out separate aid applications for the sponsor.)

APPLY TO SIMILAR SCHOOLS

If you are savvy, you will also apply to groups of similar schools (of comparable academic caliber) for maximum leverage in the financial aid process. The traditional wisdom has always been to *avoid* applying to many similar and/or rival schools because the likelihood of obtaining admission as well as financial aid will generally be the same within each category or group of schools. But in the new world, where similar schools no longer subscribe to similar policies regarding financial aid, you could be treated very differently by each of three seemingly similar schools. Each of the several similar schools will have more incentive to provide you with a good financial aid package if it believes that a rival college might win you over with better financial aid. If you are a particularly desirable candidate applying to Amherst, Wesleyan, and Williams, for example, you have a better chance of receiving very good aid packages from them because each will want to entice you away from the other two schools.

CONSIDER WITHHOLDING A MINOR PIECE OF FINANCIAL INFORMATION TO PROVIDE YOU WITH A REASON TO APPEAL A FINANCIAL AID DECISION

It is sometimes a good idea to withhold a piece of minor financial information when first applying for financial aid. By doing so, you insure that you have a legitimate "in" to an appeals hearing if and when you need to negotiate your financial aid package in the end. (See page 539 for more information on appealing financial aid packages.) The withheld information might include childcare expenses, payments made to help support a grandparent or other relative, or health insurance fees for a child no longer on the family insurance tab.

INCREASE THE AMOUNT OF NEED-BASED FINANCIAL AID YOU ARE ENTITLED TO RECEIVE

By now you realize that financial need is not necessarily the single most important factor in acquiring aid. Still, the more financial assistance a college thinks you require, the more it will sense an obligation to give you aid. There are many measures you can take to increase your financial need, as it will be assessed by both the Federal Methodology (FM) and the various Institutional Methodologies (IM). (Note that you need to make all necessary adjustments to your finances before the "base year" begins. For this reason, you are encouraged to start thinking about college finances early, at the very least before the student begins junior year of high school.)

■ *Using Assets to Pay Off Debt:* Your financial aid is based upon your income and assets during the base year. Debts are never calculated into the equation. Thus, if you have $60,000 in a savings account but owe a total of $25,000 in credit card or car payment debt, the $60,000 is counted against you in aid formulas but the $25,000 does nothing to help you qualify for more aid. You will be better off if you simply pay off your debt.

■ *Moving Assets from Student Accounts to Parental Accounts:* Money held by parents and students is not considered equally in order to determine how much your family can afford to pay for college. Parents are expected to pay out 5.6% of their assets while students are expected to pay a whopping 35% of their savings on their college costs. $50,000 in a student's bank account will become $17,500 paid to the college, whereas the same amount of money in parental hands will only result in a $2,800 contribution to college costs. If your child holds a trust fund, bonds, or other financial assets in his name, you need to move them into your own name (or another relative's) to help him from losing out.

■ *Getting Rid of Assets through Gift Donations:* You are allowed to give away up to $10,000 per year in untaxed gift money to each recipient. Giving "gifts" to relatives or godparents is a good idea in the years before college so that you can shed extra assets before financial aid calculations get under way.

■ *Making Necessary Large Purchases:* If you know the family needs a new car, refrigerator, or roof, make your move before the beginning of the base year. This way, you will gain the object or service you will need down the line anyway, while at the same time reducing your reportable assets considerably.

■ *Reducing Base Pay:* If your income fluctuates considerably because of bonuses or commissions, see what you can do to time it so that extra earnings for the base year are deferred until after December 31 of that year. (Consult your financial or tax planner to make sure you are abiding by the proper codes and laws when making changes.)

■ *Taking Leave of a Career (and Salary):* If one of two wage-earning parents leaves a job to prepare for a future career change, you can maintain a portion of the family income while increasing your eligibility for aid. This is an especially good idea if a good fraction of the second wage-earner's salary is spent on day care for a child, a cost that is not taken into account by many colleges' aid calculations. Furthermore, if returning to school is something one parent has been needing to do, this would be a good move now, in order to benefit from a continued lack of second salary.

■ *Avoiding Capital Gains from Selling Stocks or Securities:* If you plan to sell appreciated stocks or securities, do so either before the base year begins or after your child has entered college. Capital gains and year-end dividends count as income and as such are taxed heavily by the colleges' analysis systems.

■ *Starting a Home Business:* If you have been planning to start your own home business, this would be the right time to do so. You can cut your current pay and reduce your personal assets by making capital investments in a self-owned business.

■ *Paying Off a Mortgage:* Home equity is not taken into consideration in the Federal Methodology. For schools using only FM, then, you will qualify for much more aid if you get rid of your savings to pay off your home mortgage. Schools using the IM, however, do consider home equity. If you own a pricey home, you will be expected to borrow against it in order to pay for a child's college education.

EVALUATING AND COMPARING AWARD PACKAGES

Most students and their families will have to do quite a bit of evaluating, comparing, and sometimes even negotiating before deciding where to attend college. When evaluating an aid package or comparing various aid packages you have received from schools to determine which is best, there are many factors to consider:

■ *The degree of unmet need:* If you are "gapped," or left with a big discrepancy between the amount of aid you need to attend a school and the amount you are given, get ready to negotiate if you want to enroll at that school.

■ *The portions of gift versus self-help funding:* Two schools can offer to fill 100% of your need in radically different ways. One college might grant you 80% of your $25,000 total need in gift aid while another gives you only 20% of the total in grant money, requiring you to take out 80% of the yearly total in loans. Attending the former college makes much more sense from a strictly financial point of view.

■ *The terms of the loan repayments:* Not all loans are created equal. Subsidized loans, for which the government or institutional lender will pay interest while you are still in school and not earning money, are better than unsubsidized ones. Low interest rates as well as terms will affect how much a loan will hamper you after graduation.

■ *How outside grants or scholarships are treated:* Compare how each school handles outside grants or scholarships, whether you have gained an outside grant for the freshman year or are planning to apply for one down the road.

BIDDING FOR STUDENTS

You have probably heard that if you are a talented student, some schools will offer you a lot of money—more money than is warranted by need—in order to convince you to enroll. This can be true even at schools that do not explicitly offer academic or merit-based scholarships. These discounts usually come in small amounts of a few thousand dollars or so. Only those colleges that can rely on their prestige and selectivity alone to maintain quality enrollment refrain from using money to entice the best candidates. Thus it is true that some of the very top colleges genuinely stay out of the bidding wars for candidates. This does not mean, however, that you cannot appeal a financial aid decision at a top college. You can and should appeal an award if you think you can bring something to the attention of a top college's financial aid department that will make it change your package.

APPEALING A FINANCIAL AID DECISION

MAKING AN APPEAL IS WORTH YOUR TIME AND EFFORT

Most schools claim that they do not "negotiate," but will hear out student appeals when they are based on new pieces of information or information that was originally overlooked. Although nearly all financial aid officers emphasize that they do not give out better offers of aid simply to "top" the offers of a competitor school, schools will generally take a good second look at information that they originally ignored if it is evident that other schools relied on it to award better aid packages.

HOW TO MAKE AN APPEAL

Follow the school's own procedure in order to start the process off on the right foot. If the school does not publish a formal appeals procedure outline in its application materials or its award letter, then write or call to obtain the policy. It is usually best to initiate the negotiation process (no matter what the format) with a letter outlining your case and documenting new information (supported by tax forms, receipts, medical bills, unemployment forms, or other documents). That way, the financial aid officer can see for himself the evidence you have to support your case. In addition, you can plan a letter more carefully than a phone call, to ascertain that your initial entry will be polite and tactful.

It is always best to hinge your negotiation on *facts* rather than *feelings*. Even if you do not have any new facts at your disposal, there are plenty of ways of turning old facts into new ones by placing them into a different context or presenting them in another fashion. For example, perhaps a college declined to grant you an allowance for the private school tuition of your children, but would reconsider granting you an allowance for these expenditures if it were reminded that you have a set of twins who will be added to the private school roster come next fall. (As mentioned on page 536, it is sometimes wise to keep a minor financial issue to yourself when applying for aid so that you can use it later if you need a legitimate "in" to the negotiation table. Whatever fact you decide to hold back, however, should be a small financial consideration, not a major one.)

Legitimate negotiating points include children's educational expenses; child-care expenses; payments made to help support a grandparent or other relative; health insurance fees; recent or upcoming income cuts; a parental separation or divorce; illness or death of a family wage earner; a parent's job loss or unemployment for other reasons (such as pregnancy or child care); family size increase (or anticipated family size increase); and transportation costs to and from the college.

If there is a major discrepancy between aid packages at two different schools resulting from the calculation of your Expected Family Contribution, analyze each school's methodology to determine what factor or factors accounted for the difference. Highlighting these factors might help to improve your situation at the school that has awarded the least beneficial package.

Enhancing your bargaining skills can help in financial aid negotiations, because the financial aid officer to whom you speak probably has the authority to use his or her professional and personal judgment to decide what to do with your case. If the information or data you present is legitimate and your negotiating skills are sharp, your chances of bargaining your way to success will be much improved. You may want to practice your plea in a mock interview format with a college financial aid counselor or consultant before presenting the real thing.

RULES FOR APPEALING FINANCIAL AID DECISIONS

1. Be polite and tactful. Avoid using threats and anger as weapons.

2. Begin the inquiry as a mutual discussion rather than as a debate.

3. Provide new financial information up front rather than starting with a complaint about the current assessment.

4. Use better packages from other colleges of the same (or higher) academic quality to extract a better offer.

5. Thank the officer for his or her time at the end of the conversation. If the officer helped to alter your package, you should write a brief follow-up thank-you note.

CHOOSING A FINANCIAL AID ADVISOR

The best financial aid counselors are those who are admissions experts as well. As you have seen from reading this book, the various pieces of the admissions process are interdependent. It would be unwise to trust your collegiate financial aid matters to someone with less than a full understanding of your admission profile and how college admissions work. When looking for a financial aid advisor, keep these points in mind:

➤ Start early. The best advisors will be able to do a lot more for you if you come to them several years before your child will apply to college.

➤ Avoid anyone who gives you any kind of guarantee.

➤ Look for those with established consulting practices and/or years of expertise working in an institutional setting.

➤ Ensure that the counselor emphasizes four-year planning (as well as postcollegiate implications) rather than planning for only the freshman year of college.

AVOID BUYING INTO POPULAR FINANCIAL AID MYTHS

Myth: The first plan of attack in finding financial aid is to investigate private scholarship sources.

Truth: You should not equate your search for financial help with a search for magical private scholarships. First of all, there are few to be found. The eligibility rules and guidelines for most scholarships exclude all but a handful of students. In addition, while many foundations and institutions give generous student scholarships and grants, the majority of them are administered through the colleges themselves.

Even if you win a nice merit scholarship, this "free money" will not necessarily reduce your portion of the college bill. Many schools use outside scholarships to substitute their own gift aid, thus leaving you in the same position that you would be in without a scholarship. Quite simply, your time and energy are often better spent understanding how to win aid through other channels. Hunting down private scholarships should be your last priority rather than your first.

Myth: Millions of dollars in scholarship money are unused every year.

Truth: While there may be a hint of truth to this statement, because there are plenty of established scholarships out there that remain unclaimed year after year, the reason is that there is simply no one eligible to claim them!

Myth: To find the best scholarships, you should pay a fee to a scholarship search service.

Truth: Most scholarship search services are money-making scams. Never buy into a company that claims a "guarantee" in finding you a scholarship. You can easily find the same information yourself, through either colleges, books, or the many helpful Web sites offering this kind of information. (For a list of Web sites offering free scholarship search services, see page 552.)

Myth: If a family's income is over $100,000 a student will not qualify for any financial aid.

Truth: Even a fairly wealthy family can be eligible for financial aid under the right circumstances. For example, using PROFILE or a college's own financial aid calculation form, a relatively high-income family with multiple children in college and/or private schools requiring tuition, or a high-income family with significant special medical expenditures, might qualify for aid. In addition, any family, no matter how wealthy, can borrow money (up to the total cost of college) from federal or private lending sources.

Myth: The cost of attending an inexpensive college will always be less than the cost of attending a high-priced institution.

Truth: Although it might seem illogical, a less-expensive college does not always cost less than an expensive one! The amount you will have to pay at any college depends on its needs analysis or what kind of methodology it employs when calculating your family's share of the burden. A good number of the most expensive colleges in fact have the most generous needs analysis tests, and therefore will cost you less!

IMPORTANT QUESTIONS TO ASK THE FINANCIAL AID OFFICER (FAO)

➤ What methodology does your school use in determining aid packages? Does your school rely on the information provided by FAFSA, PROFILE, the state's evaluation form, or your own aid evaluation form (or a combination of several of the above) in making award decisions?

➤ If your college relies upon its own institutional methodology, what specific adjustments does it make to the federal formula?

➤ What special circumstances will change my financial aid package?

➤ Will you assess the financial situation of my noncustodial parent as well as that of my custodial parent?

➤ What is your minimum student contribution?

➤ If I have my own savings, how much of it will you expect me to pay?

➤ If I earn significant wages instead of maintaining a work study job during college, how will that change my aid package?

➤ Do you consider special medical or dental expenses when determining how much a family can pay?

➤ Do you meet the full need of every student? If so, do you meet need for all four years of college?

➤ What percentage of last year's freshman class paid full tuition?

➤ What percentage of last year's freshman class received full need?

➤ What percentage of last year's freshman class received grant or scholarship funding (i.e., gift funding rather than self-help) from the college?

➤ How will my aid package change after freshman year? Is the continuation of my aid package dependent upon any particular circumstances, such as a minimum grade point average?

➤ How do I go about renewing my aid package each year?

➤ What if something unfortunate happens to change my family's financial situation, thus increasing my need later on?

➤ Can aid packages be adjusted midyear in the case of emergency situations?

➤ Is there a maximum grant that your institution offers?

➤ Do I have to meet a minimum need level in order to receive aid?

➤ How does your school treat outside scholarships or grants? Does an outside grant replace self-help (loan or work-study) or the school's own grant money, leaving me in no better position than without it?

➤ Does your school create financial aid waitlists?

➤ Does your school accept students on an "admit/deny" basis?

➤ If I don't qualify for or apply for aid in my freshman year, can I apply later on? When?

➤ Do you practice need-blind admissions? How will my request for financial aid impact the admissions decision?

➤ Does your school have an official policy on financial aid appeals?

➤ What is the best way to raise any concerns I might have after receiving my offer?

➤ What is your school's policy on tuition for outside programs? If I take a semester abroad or as a transfer student elsewhere, do I pay that school's tuition for the semester or the tuition of my home institution? Is your school's financial aid portable if I decide to go elsewhere for a semester?

FINANCIAL AID OFFICERS TALK ABOUT MISCELLANEOUS ISSUES

WHAT ATTEMPTS HAVE YOU MADE TO ENACT POSITIVE CHANGE IN THE FINANCIAL AID PROCESSES AT YOUR COLLEGE?

"We've been doing special case-by-case needs analysis for some time because we feel the current methodology is not fair or equitable. The financial aid community has been working to ameliorate many of the problems with the current needs analysis formula, one of which is its disincentive to save."

—Virginia Hazen, Director of Financial Aid, Dartmouth College

"We've recently seen a collision between what we expect kids to do with their education and the reality of the choices available to them. Students on financial aid were beginning to change their extracurricular activities and career choices in order to accommodate large amounts of self-help in the forms of work-study and borrowing. We had essentially created an 'upstairs/downstairs' mentality, which we felt was wrong. This is why we've enacted our recent policy to improve all students' aid packages with $2000 less in self-help."

—James Miller, Director of Undergraduate Financial Aid, Harvard University

"We focus our effort on personalized attention toward both prospective/incoming and continuing students—this includes counseling and providing help for families to make informed financial decisions. I believe schools need to focus on this kind of service."

—David Mohning, Director of Student Financial Aid, Vanderbilt University

WHAT COLLEGES ARE MOST AGGRESSIVE IN "BIDDING" FOR STUDENTS WITH FINANCIAL AID?

"The schools that use aid as a competitive weapon, to essentially bid against other schools for students, include Tulane, Johns Hopkins, Carnegie Mellon, and Washington University. Those are the ones I hear about all the time."

—A director of financial aid at one of the top colleges

"My sense is that it's usually places such as Georgetown, Emory, Johns Hopkins, Duke, and Carnegie Mellon that are getting into these bidding wars."

—A director of financial aid at one of the top colleges

HOW MUCH FLEXIBILITY IS THERE AT YOUR COLLEGE WITH REGARD TO FINANCIAL AID POLICIES AND PACKAGING?

"Our students have a lot of flexibility between work-study and loans in their packages. They can choose what proportion of their total self-help comes from each."

—David Levy, Director of Financial Aid, California Institute of Technology

"In terms of determining need, our officers have a lot of freedom to make individual decisions."

—*James Belvin, Director of Financial Aid, Duke University*

"We're pretty generous toward students with absentee parents. We have a policy that allows certain families with special situations to request a waiver for a missing or noncustodial parent—it doesn't even require third-party documentation."

—*Alicia Reyes, Director of Financial Aid, University of Chicago*

"I use my good judgment to change things all the time after our formulas have figured an estimated family contribution or need. I've been in this business thirty-six years, I've seen it all. I often see that there's more need (and sometimes less need) than what the formula dictates."

—*Walter Moulton, Director of Financial Aid, Bowdoin College*

"We really look at everyone on a case-by-case basis, so there is a lot of flexibility in terms of how we determine a family's expected contribution. We take special circumstances into account as much as possible."

—*Don Betterton, Director of Financial Aid, Princeton University*

"Assessing the income of students who take high-paying jobs to earn serious money—now this presents a tough issue. On the one hand, we don't want to penalize students for working hard and earning serious wages, so we want to look at this liberally. On the other hand, the purpose of earning money—either over the summer or during the term—is presumably to help pay for college. We try to be as flexible and generous as possible."

—*Leigh Campbell, Director of Financial Aid, Bates College*

"Our travel budgets cover very carefully thought out needs for students from every area of the country. If someone can show us they live in an area that is hard to access, we will certainly enhance the budget. Similarly, if a parent is ill and more trips home are required, we'll do the same."

—*Catherine Thomas, Associate Dean of Admissions and Financial Aid, University of Southern California*

"The Fathers are very understanding of personal and family circumstances, as you might expect. As an example: we don't normally give student aid to international students. But recently we had a bunch of foreign students who really got hit hard by the Asian financial crisis. They were already part of our student body, they got stuck in this situation, and we decided to help out—by giving them grant money in many cases, loans or on-campus work in other cases."

—*Bernard Pekala, Director of Financial Strategies, Boston College*

"We do have a financial aid application deadline each year, but in reality our students can come to us at any time. If drastic changes occur, we'll talk to them and do what we can at any point during the school year."

—*James Miller, Director of Undergraduate Financial Aid, Harvard University*

What Segment of the Population Has Felt the Impact of Rising College Costs the Most?

"Schools have found that it's middle-, not lower-, income students who are swayed most by financial concerns. We call this the 'middle-income melt.' At Amherst, $80,000 was the average family income of those who declined Amherst, citing financial reasons. That's well above the average family income."

—Joe Paul Case, Dean of Financial Aid, Amherst College

"We very consciously made this year's policy adjustments to benefit middle- and upper middle-income families. There had been a real decline in our enrollment of students from these backgrounds, even though we were doing fine maintaining enrollment of lower-income students."

—Donald Routh, University Director of Financial Aid, Yale University

To What Extent Are Your Financial Aid Policies Driven by the College's Philosophy?

"As costs go up each year, we like to make sure that the proportions of need and family contribution stay pretty much the same as what they are during the freshman year. We don't like to overload students with greater proportions of self-help during their later years in school."

—Tom Keane, Director of Financial Aid and Student Employment, Cornell University

"We believe that parents are responsible for educating their kids. It is not a parent's *willingness* to pay for college but his or her *ability* to pay for college that we are assessing."

—Leonard Wenc, Director of Student Financial Services, Carleton College

"We don't believe that divorce exonerates a noncustodial parent from paying his or her fair share of a child's educational expenses."

—James Belvin, Director of Financial Aid, Duke University

"We don't believe a student's ability to take full advantage of our education and meet financial expectations depends on the family financial situation. We believe it depends on his own situation, character, and work ethic. As a result, we treat all students equitably."

—Donald Routh, University Director of Financial Aid, Yale University

"Outside aid replaces the loan component of self-help but not work-study. Work-study stays intact. We want all our students to work—that's a policy based on philosophy."

—Kathleen Stevenson-McNeely, Senior Associate Dean of Admissions and Financial Aid, Davidson College

"We believe in equality and consistency. We don't believe in treating certain groups of students differently in financial aid awarding, so we use equity packaging."
— *David Hoy, Director of Financial Aid, Haverford College*

"Enrolling at a private college or university is a choice, not an entitlement. There is an excellent, state-funded educational system readily available. Those private colleges that are committed to providing access to disadvantaged students through need-based financial aid expect families to assume responsibility for paying for their child's education to the level of their maximum capability; this may involve considerable sacrifice. We view financial aid as a partnership, not a free lunch."
—*Jane B. Brown, Dean of Enrollment, Mount Holyoke College*

"Providing financial aid is a four-year commitment, not a one-year relationship."
—*Heather McDonnell, Director of Financial Aid, Sarah Lawrence College*

IS THE VALUE OF A TOP COLLEGE EDUCATION WORTH THE FINANCIAL INVESTMENT?

"Looking at things from a positive perspective, at least in most cases, American students' college debt levels support a good investment."
—*Michael Bartini, Director of Financial Aid, Brown University*

"Despite high levels of indebtedness, students are far better off with a good education. Education's value appreciates over time, it doesn't depreciate like normal consumer products do. I wish we could all start focusing more on the value in higher education."
—*Joseph A. Russo, Director of Financial Aid, University of Notre Dame*

"Investment in a first-class education is the best kind you can make. Still, we don't want our students taking on too much debt to come here, which is why we have lowered our loan expectations for all students."
—*James Miller, Director of Undergraduate Financial Aid, Harvard University*

"I wish colleges would stop talking so much about competing on price and start worrying more about competing on value."
—*Robert Massa, Dean of Enrollment, Johns Hopkins University*

19

USING OTHER STRATEGIES TO HELP FINANCE COLLEGE

— KEY POINTS —

Besides seeking the best financial aid treatment possible from the colleges, there are other ways that the financially needy and non-needy can cut down on the burden of paying for college:

—Applying for outside merit scholarships
—Attending a college with a lower "sticker price"
—Cutting the costs of college
—Earning serious money while in college
—Pursuing other strategies for making college financing less onerous

INTRODUCTION

The most important aspect to planning college finances is understanding college financial aid and applying the right strategies to receive the best treatment possible from your target colleges, as discussed in Chapter 18. Beyond that, however, there are other things you can do to help pay for college. This is true for those with financial need as well as for those who are not needy but simply want to make the college burden as light as possible. This chapter addresses the following ways of lightening the college burden:

- Applying for outside merit scholarships
- Choosing a college with a lower "sticker price"
- Cutting the costs of college
- Earning substantial income while in college
- Pursuing other strategies for making college financing less tedious

APPLYING FOR OUTSIDE MERIT SCHOLARSHIPS

Outside institutional aid includes all financial help that comes from organizational sources other than the government or the college itself. You apply for institutional awards—such as a scholarship from your local Rotary foundation—on your own rather than as part of the aid application process at a particular school. These outside scholarships come in many forms and are offered for a variety of reasons: academic merit, ethnicity, leadership, musical talent, athletic ability, gender, pursuit of a particular field or career, geographical location, membership in a particular community, or a parent's membership in a particular club or employment at a particular company.

If you expect to receive collegiate financial aid, though, find out what your targeted colleges will do in response to your winning an outside grant before embarking on an extensive hunt for scholarships. At many colleges, as discussed in Chapter 18, only a small part of your outside award will eliminate your self-help funding if you are receiving financial assistance from the college; most of the extra money you win will be subtracted from the grant portion of your financial assistance package. In other words, the outside award will not help you out substantially because it will merely replace what would have been covered by need-based government or collegiate grants. The only students who benefit substantially from outside scholarships at colleges with this type of policy are those who are receiving no financial assistance from the colleges in the first place.

Some colleges—with more changing their policies in this direction all the time—let students use all outside awards to replace self-help rather than grant funding. If your target colleges uphold a policy that allows students to benefit from the full amount of an outside award in this way, then there is every reason to search for outside scholarships, whether you are expecting college financial aid or not.

This matrix indicates whether it is worth your while to seek outside scholarships, based upon your own financial situation and the policies of your target colleges:

Your Financial Posture

College Policy		Expect to Receive Financial Aid from Colleges	Do Not Expect to Receive Financial Aid from Colleges
	Outside Scholarship Primarily Reduces Grant Funding	Do Not Seek Outside Scholarships	Seek Outside Scholarships
	Outside Scholarship Reduces Self-Help Funding	Seek Outside Scholarships	Seek Outside Scholarships

THE NONMONETARY VALUE OF OUTSIDE SCHOLARSHIPS

Many outside scholarships (although certainly not all) are small awards that do not realistically help with college expenses at all (especially if you have need and they merely replace grant money that would have come from the college anyway). You might naturally wonder if these scholarships are worth applying for.

Some of these minuscule scholarships are worth your effort *not* because of their immediate monetary value but because of their resume-building potential. An award of $300 for being a talented international policy debater, for example, is not going to provide substantial help with your college expenses. After all, you could earn the same amount of money in an afternoon of house painting (with the added benefit of enhancing your tan rather than contributing to your developing case of carpal tunnel syndrome!). But if you aspire to keep developing and utilizing your debate skills in the future and the award will contribute greatly to your profile as a public speaker and expert on international affairs, then you should apply for it. The long-term benefit of earning that award and being able to place it on your resume will certainly accrue additional benefits down the road.

On the other hand, if the award is not going to mean anything to you apart from its monetary value—as might be the case with, say, the Stanton County Male Yo-Yo Champion Scholarship Award of $50, then you are much better off using the time you would have to spend on the award application making money otherwise. If the award is small and carries no future career or resume-enhancing potential, then you will be wise to divide the total amount of the award by the number of projected hours it will take you to complete the application process (subtracting any application fees from the total award before dividing). If the amount you will "earn" per hour upon winning is worth your time, then go ahead and pursue it. If it is less than you would earn doing something else, then forget the scholarship and move on.

To find out about the many scholarships offered by various organizations, start by consulting a scholarship book or looking on the Web. You should also visit your local Chamber of Commerce and read smaller local newspapers carefully to spot the possibilities available from civic associations, social clubs, and other organizations within your community. Look for information at your church, temple, or other religious organization too.

FREE SCHOLARSHIP SEARCHES ON THE WEB

The following Web sites offer scholarship search services:

ExPAN (http://www.collegeboard.org/fundfinder/bin/fundfind01.pl)

FastWeb (http://www.fastWeb.com)

MACH25 (http://www.collegenet.com/mach25)

Minority On-Line Information System (http://www.fie.com/molis/scholar.htm)

RSP Funding Focus (access by using the keyword "RSP" on America Online)

SRN Express (http://www.rams.com/srn)

Additional resources for locating special scholarships for which you might qualify include:

College Aid Resources for Education, published by the National College Scholarship Foundation. NCSF, Box 8207, Gaithersburg, MD 20898.

Need a Lift?, published annually by the American Legion. American Legion, National Emblem Sales, PO Box 1050, Indianapolis, IN 46204. Or call 317-630-1251.

The Scholarship Book by Daniel J. Cassidy. Prentice Hall. Call 800-432-3782.

CHOOSING A COLLEGE WITH A LOWER "STICKER PRICE"

There are several ways that you can receive a top-notch education without attending a school whose sticker price will hurt your finances.

ATTENDING A "PUBLIC IVY"

First, you have the option of attending what are often called the "public Ivies" or "flagship public universities." This is an especially good deal if you happen to be a resident of one of the states in which these universities is located. The premier public institutions include the University of Michigan (Ann Arbor), the University of Virginia (Charlottesville), the University of North Carolina (Chapel Hill), the University of California (Berkeley and Los Angeles are considered the top campuses), and the University of Wisconsin (Madison). There are also some smaller high-quality state schools like Miami University of Ohio and the College of William and Mary in Virginia.

If you are a state resident and are admitted to one of these flagship universities, you are fortunate to have a very low-cost option at your disposal. The in-state tuition at UVA, for example, at $4,930 for the 1999–2000 school year (compared to about $25,000 at top private institutions) is a real bargain. If your state's premier public institution happens to be in your parents' hometown, you can take the extra benefit of living at home for a portion of your college career for further savings. Even out-of-state residents generally fare better at public universities than they do at private ones. The out-of-state tuition at UVA, though at $15,665 three times higher than the in-state cost, is still a good deal in comparison to the cost of attending a private school.

PUBLIC INSTITUTIONS REPRESENT A BARGAIN FOR IN- AND OUT-OF-STATE STUDENTS

1999–2000 ACADEMIC YEAR COSTS*

	University of Virginia	University of California (Berkeley)	Yale University
In-State Tuition	$ 4,930	$ 3,609	$23,780
Out-of-State Tuition	$15,665	$13,183	$23,780
Required Fees	—	$ 567	—
Room/Board	$ 4,415	$ 7,788	$ 7,050
Total In-State	$ 9,345	$11,964	$30,830
Total Out-of-State	$20,080	$21,538	$30,830

*Note that total amounts do not include the cost of books and personal expenses, estimated to be about $2,400.

States vary in their requirements for becoming residents. Some states, like California, will allow students to become residents within only one year of arrival as long as they follow a rigorous application program, so out-of-staters who go to Berkeley may only have to pay the out-of-state tuition for the freshman year. Other states such as Michigan, however, make it much tougher for students to become residents after the fact.

Furthermore, some of the public universities now have prestigious "honors programs," which can make attending a cheaper state school more attractive. The honors programs are reserved for the top freshman applicants, and many schools use them to lure quality students away from prestigious private schools. The honors programs are much more than just a marketing tool or a fancy label for your resume. They can be true enhancements to one's college experience and future career. Having an honors student status will get you into special programs and classes, often much smaller and more intimate than regular state university lectures, and possibly give you special entry into research programs, relationships with prominent faculty, or internships in your field. An honors student status will make you stand out when it comes time to transfer into a selective private school, look for a job, or apply to graduate school. It may also bring with it an additional merit stipend or scholarship to improve your financial situation.

ATTENDING A PUBLIC OR COMMUNITY COLLEGE AND THEN TRANSFERRING INTO A BETTER ONE

Another option for bringing down the four-year sticker price of college is to attend a public university (or even a community college) for two years, and then transfer into a more prestigious (and expensive) school for the junior and senior years. This strategy, which is used both as a means to boost one's record in order to qualify for acceptance at more selective schools and as a means of saving on two years of tuition, has become quite common in recent years. Beware, though, that many of the most prestigious and selective of the four-year schools accept few transfer students (and some do not accept transfers at all). This is not, therefore, a foolproof method for achieving your ideal education at a manageable cost.

GOING TO COLLEGE OVERSEAS

Going to college overseas (as a regular student rather than as part of a special student-abroad program) can also be a smart financial move, assuming that the overseas education meets your life and career goals. As discussed at length in Chapter 4, attending one of England's top universities as an alternative to attending a top American college can save a family some $50–60,000.

CUTTING THE COSTS OF COLLEGE

There are many ways to cut down on the usual college costs by making some often overlooked choices. As discussed in the previous Chapter 18, the cost of attendance (COA) consists of the following components:

- Tuition
- Fees and Other Institutional Expenses
- Room and Board
- Health Insurance
- Books and Academic Supplies
- Transportation
- Personal Expenses
- Entertainment
- Miscellaneous Costs

CUTTING THE COST OF TUITION

There are several ways you can cut down on the cost of tuition (not including receiving financial aid).

BY ACCELERATING THE COMPLETION OF THE COLLEGE PROGRAM

Take as many AP and other college-level courses as possible to achieve the best possible high school academic record for college admittance in the first place—but also to gain college credit for these courses, thus cutting down on the number of credits needed to graduate. About 1200 colleges give credit for passing scores on AP exams. Schools vary in what they consider a "passing" score; most require a score of 4 or 5 on AP exams.

By passing some AP exams before arriving on campus, perhaps along with taking a summer class or two at a community (or other inexpensive) college, you may be able to shave off an entire semester or even year of school. Taking summer classes at a less expensive school can be an especially wise strategy for those who need to get premed, engineering, or other tough requirements out of the way. Taking these classes at a community college or a less selective school can allow a student to learn the material at a sometimes slower pace, with less competition and pressure from other students, and without the distractions of normal campus life.

Another way to speed up the rate at which you finish your college require-ments—sometimes used in conjunction with using AP scores for college credit—is to take extra classes once or twice during your college career. This should be done with careful planning and foresight so that academic performance is not sacrificed. It is obviously not wise to increase your class load during a varsity sport season, when practice saps time and energy and you are required to travel two days every week, or during the same term as your tenure as editor-in-chief of the daily newspaper. Likewise, a student having trouble in her upper mathematics classes will not want to take more than one at a time. Beefing up a schedule should be done during a semester that will be quiet for the student in terms of extracurricular commitments and when one or more of the classes on the roster will require only limited devotion.

Doubling up on classes, especially if paired with the other tactics, might allow a student to graduate in three or three and a half years, thus saving you a term or two of tuition, up to about $25,000. (Note that it is much easier to race through certain schools, such as those with fewer course requirements, than oth-ers.) If you are worried about missing out on the college social scene or the other nonacademic benefits of college by graduating early, you can always remain on or near campus to finish out college career with your friends despite having no classes to attend. There are plenty of valuable work opportunities, service com-mitments, and internships available on or near all campuses, even those with the most remote locations.

There is also the option of attending a less expensive summer school (per-haps a community college) to take care of necessary credits as a way of speeding up college and graduating early. Some students need to use their summers to find valuable job experience and take a necessary break from studies to rev up for the next year, thus ruling out the inexpensive summer school option. Others, especially if they are attending highly competitive schools, need as much time as possible to master the normal load of coursework each semester and would only suffer academically from trying to do too much at once. Cheating yourself out of the most beneficial education is probably not worth saving on tuition.

Some colleges are now sponsoring their own "accelerated degree" pro-grams, in which students finish in three years instead of the normal four. At some schools the three-year tuition does not beat the regular four-year price (in this case, tuition is based upon coursework rather than time spent in school), but the economic advantages still accrue in other ways. You will save on an extra year of living expenses, in the first place. The bigger bonus, however, is the additional year of income for the student.

Although there are plenty of proponents of formal and informal accelerat-ed degree programs for those who can handle increased academic loads, some educators have their doubts. For some students, a college education is gained more from the collegiate experience as a whole than from classroom learning. Sacrificing a year of this important growth and self-discovery period may not be a good idea for all students, especially those who have found new outlets in college for their talents, leadership, and creativity through college-sponsored activities. A long-running stint as a literary magazine editor, leadership of an environmental group, or becoming a student government representative might be more helpful to your inner growth *and* future career than an early year out in the real world. Whereas some employers are impressed by students who race through college, others are actually turned off by this. Many employers today want candidates with plenty of interactive skills, extracurricular passions, and a fully developed personality. Some employers looking for college grads just starting their careers are hesitant to hire those who appear to be overly academic or anxious to escape college. If one year of college savings will make a big difference, though, the economic advantage should override these considerations in your case.

BY JOINING ROTC

You can also cut back on your tuition by joining the U.S. military at campuses with Reserve Officer Training Corps (ROTC) programs. Each branch of the military operates a ROTC program. ROTC gives out one-, two-, or four-year scholarships at three levels of tuition payment—from a few thousand dollars to $12,500 per year—in return for a service obligation after college. The service obligation can be met in a variety of ways, so that you do not necessarily have to go into a permanent military career after graduation. At some schools, ROTC scholarships cover all or nearly all of yearly tuition. Winners also get yearly stipends for books and other expenses. You can apply for a ROTC scholarship during your senior year of high school or once you are at college.

BY PARTICIPATING IN LESS EXPENSIVE STUDY-ABROAD OR EXCHANGE PROGRAMS

Looking into study-abroad programs may also help you pare down tuition while also giving you an exciting and valuable educational opportunity. Especially if offered by a public institution, study abroad programs can be less expensive than a regular semester at college, even after the travel expenses are figured in. Some schools even allow their regular students to attend multiple programs abroad. Thus, you might be able to save over several terms of reduced tuition and expenses.

Not all colleges will let their students get away with this tactic, though. In recent years, as colleges have suffered from the lost tuition resulting from the popularity of study-abroad programs, many have changed their policies on study-abroad tuition payments. The University of Pennsylvania, for example, now charges students going abroad the same amount as if they were staying on campus, regardless of the cost of the program. And although all federal student aid is portable, meaning a student can use it even if he is attending a program abroad, when it comes to institutional funds, schools have their own portability policies. Some schools do not let students use nongovernment funds to go overseas.

CUTTING THE COST OF ROOM AND BOARD

Room and board at a single institution can vary tremendously depending upon whether a student lives in campus housing or off-campus, and what kind of meal plan she chooses. Some schools have a set billable cost for room and board for all campus boarders, while others graduate the expenses depending upon the quality of the housing and/or meal plan. At some schools, single dormitory rooms, for example, cost more than shared rooms. Rooms within desirably located dormitories or with special features such as balconies or fireplaces may also cost more. If you are given several meal plans to choose from, be realistic and choose carefully. Meal plans offering more meals per week or more choice regarding eating facilities will cost you more. You may think that it is best that you eat three healthy meals a day, when in reality you always choose a few extra minutes of sleep over breakfast in the morning. Do not pay for it if you know you will never eat it! Likewise, be realistic if you are a finicky eater who shuns most of what is put in front of you. Some colleges offer meal plans with far more flexibility in choosing where to eat, thus allowing students the benefit of dining at sites with better quality food than that offered at the usual "full fare" mess hall. These will cost you more up front, but probably save you in the long run because you will not be shelling out extra money off-campus to fill your empty stomach after meals.

Depending on where the college is located, off-campus housing can be less expensive than what the college offers, especially if it is shared with others. For example, if you attend Cornell in Ithaca, New York, you will be able to find housing at a price that is much more affordable than what it costs to live in the dorms. On the other hand, if you attend Columbia or NYU, you will almost surely be better off going the campus dormitory route because housing in New York City is so expensive. Be careful when calculating off-campus rent—remember to add utility expenses (telephone service, electricity, etc.) to the monthly tab. Utilities will be far more expensive if you will be living alone rather than with others, in which case the costs are spread out among members of the household.

Likewise, cooking at home or in the dorm kitchen is often far less expensive than the meal plans that colleges offer. As an added incentive, you may learn to cook as part of your college education and your food might be more edible than those rubber things the college passes off as hamburgers. Home-cooked food might well contribute less to the "Freshman Fifteen" than much of the fattening fare on campus as well. If you are a particularly picky eater, your cooking on your own can be a smart money-saving idea—you probably will not get enough out of the campus meal plan to make it worth the expense.

Another way to save money on housing requires quite a bit of effort and commitment, but can be a real saver over four years of college—and perhaps a money-maker even farther into the future. Some parents buy a piece of property in a student's college town, thus investing in the building while also giving their child a place to live. There is often the opportunity to make extra money by renting out additional bedrooms or units to other students. After the student graduates from college, the parents have the option of selling the place for profit if the market is good, or keeping the property as an investment and finding someone else to manage it.

CUTTING THE COST OF HEALTH INSURANCE

Compare the college's health insurance with other policies to make sure you are getting the most for your money. Most colleges have very affordable health care policies, but they also usually allow a student to stay on a parent's plan or obtain other outside health insurance. If an outside option is less expensive, be sure to opt for that.

CUTTING THE COST OF BOOKS AND SUPPLIES

Most college towns now feature at least one handy used book agency that offers texts for all kinds of classes at bargain resale prices. Furthermore, these used text centers will buy your books back at the end of the semester, giving you a partial "rebate" after their use. Be sure to ask about each store's policies. Some buyback stores, such as Ned's in Berkeley (just across from the University of California at Berkeley campus), offer quite a bit more (sometimes up to three times as much) for books that will be used in classes during the next upcoming semester than they will for books that will not be used immediately. Thus, spending a few minutes with the bookbuyer to find out when your used books will be most valuable can earn you even more cash (as long as you have space to store them until sellback time!).

When used books are unavailable, you can always borrow from the library rather than shelling out dollars for new texts. If you plan to do this, check that the school library has several copies of the texts you plan to borrow so that you are not caught mid-semester without a book. This is especially important since most campus bookstores and text services return their overstock at mid-semester and may not have an extra copy of the needed book down the line. Some professors put copies of the texts they use "on reserve" at the university library so that they are available to those who choose not to buy them. These "reserve" books are not allowed to be checked out permanently, but are loaned for several hours or one night at a time so that all students have access to them.

CUTTING THE COST OF TRANSPORTATION

Most colleges have "ride boards," wall or Web-based bulletin boards with free-for-all information about student transportation, posted in their community centers, dining halls, and other public places. Students post information about where they need to go or where they are driving in order to join up with others and share the expenses. This is a smart move if you live close enough to home to make it back and forth by car, whether you own one or not. A student may find that he hooks up with someone who frequently travels to the same area, thus giving him a permanent ride share. Many colleges also charter inexpensive buses and/or vans that can save money on cabfare to the airport or train station if that is your mode of travel.

If you have not done so already, you should definitely join frequent flyer programs if you will be flying back and forth to college. Most programs allow people to donate their frequent flyer tickets to friends and family, so everyone in the family should be signed up in order to gain free tickets faster. Furthermore, tie your credit cards and long-distance telephone service into the frequent flyer programs to earn additional free miles to replace travel expenditures. Then talking on the phone to your faraway family will help you rack up extra miles. Some schools now accept credit cards as payment for tuition, so that miles accumulate faster than you imagined. One year of tuition at most expensive private colleges will get you a free round-trip ticket anywhere in the United States.

Be sure also to get hooked up with the Web sites now offering cheap airfares and other travel bonuses once you go to college.

EARNING SUBSTANTIAL INCOME WHILE IN COLLEGE

You can help with financial matters while in college by avoiding the typical low-wage student jobs and instead launching a meaningful and lucrative part-time career. Many students make the mistake of thinking that to earn money in college while avoiding ruining their academic records or social lives, they have to take jobs as pizza kitchen waiters, delivery persons, or campus administrative assistants. Not enough students take advantage of natural skills, learned talents, and easy-to-access student consumers to set themselves up in constructive jobs that also bring in substantial cash. Being able to earn a decent living while also preparing for the postcollegiate future is especially important today, in the new era of financial aid, because "gapping" and the prevalence of loans require that students fend for themselves a bit more than they had to in the old days.

It makes little sense that so many college students spend so much time and effort studying in preparation for their future careers, yet waste other valuable development efforts on meaningless and boring jobs that barely rake in enough cash to make them worthwhile. College students would be better off if they were to think about their lives within the context of "the bigger picture," meaning life after college and into mature adulthood. From a career management perspective, a student's collegiate years can be especially fruitful because you are given the luxury of developing interests and skills within the informal atmosphere of the campus environment, before crucial career decisions and evaluations come into play.

The ways in which a college student can make a good living while in school depend, naturally, on your interests and talents, but also upon the campus itself: its location, the makeup of its greater community, the kinds of students it attracts, and its regulations regarding campus employment. A student at Bowdoin, for example, may not be able to find any opportunities to work as a management consultant's assistant in rural Maine, but he will be able to take advantage of his outdoor leadership skills by leading backpacking and camping trips, either for the school's program or through his own business for students and nonstudents alike. A student at Columbia might not be able to take advantage of outdoor skills, but he would do well becoming a city dog-walker, charging $10 to $15 per dog per hour.

There are a number of student employment options that can either bring in more than the minimum wage, offer preparation for a future career, or accomplish both at once. Those with computer knowledge can use their skills to join an off-campus teaching and support facility or set up their own independent shop— whether it be for programming, general technical support and troubleshooting, or teaching classes and workshops. Other computer wizards with knowledge of html or another design language can become free-lance Web page designers. If you have a particular skill in a sport (swimming, sailing, tennis, yoga, aerobics) or craft (jewelry making, pottery, woodworking) you can offer independent lessons or even run mini-camps (for children or adults) on weekends or over holidays.

Every location—even small rural college towns—has at least one or two expensive, premier dining institutions. Rather than taking a job at the local pub, where the cost of food and student frequenters are not going to result in very big tips, why not look into a more serious job with much better financial benefits? Serving at a four-star operation will probably not lead directly to your future career, but it can certainly give you handy food and wine knowledge as well as serious spending cash.

Some of the more sophisticated student careers might require advance thought and planning, because their execution may depend upon completing particular classes or certification programs. A computer expert who would benefit from a certain skill or knowledge area will want to take a class to fill in the gaps of expertise in the beginning of the freshman year in order to get started as soon as possible. A student planning for an eventual career in architecture and wanting to earn extra cash by building models for local firms might have to complete certain basic design or architecture requirements in order to get her foot in the door.

Although letting a student job usurp the importance of academics is not a good idea, there is no reason why the average college student should not work. Studies show that wage-earning jobs do not generally result in lower academic performance. On the contrary, many students feel that they are better managers of time because of the extra commitment a job provides, and thus perform as well as if not better than they would without one. An outside job can also give a hardworking student a welcome relief from academics, a new social outlet, and an additional perspective on life.

OTHER STRATEGIES FOR MAKING COLLEGE FINANCING LESS TEDIOUS

In addition to the strategies we have outlined, there are a lot of new programs that have been designed to make the college experience less financially painful. Not all of these plans are for everyone, but you should be aware of the types of programs and options that are now available.

PREPAID TUITION PROGRAMS AND STATE SAVINGS PLANS

Although savvy financial investors may be able to get better rates of return than any investment in a prepaid tuition plan will earn, many families are uncomfortable with the idea of "gambling" with the money they need for their children's education. To encourage early and responsible planning for college, many states now sponsor prepaid tuition plans in which parents (or grandparents) can guarantee tuition and fees for a student at some specified time in the future by putting up money early on.

By throwing in a lump sum or periodic payments, parents can "lock in" four years at the current tuition at public (some states allow plans to be used for private schools as well) colleges years down the road. If four-year tuition in Florida, for example, was $40,000 for the 1999–2000 school year, then $40,000 invested at that time in Florida's prepaid tuition plan will pay for four years of college for a newborn baby who will attend school in 18 years—no matter what the price of tuition at that time. (If a family prepays only a portion of the current tuition, then it will have to pay a pro rata amount at the future price.)

No two state plans are identical, but most operate similarly. The state takes money in the name of an individual child, invests it, and then pays the bill when the student enters college, thus taking on the risk that the investment will not cover the rate of tuition inflation. Investment amounts for prepaid plans generally depend upon when the student will enter college, the percentage of costs the parents want to cover, and the degree of flexibility parents require in withdrawing funds. Most state plans are exempt from state and local taxes, but families pay federal tax (at the student's rate rather than the donors' rate) on the appreciation value when the money is redeemed. Most states require that the money from a prepaid tuition plan be used at their own universities, but some, like Florida, are more flexible and allow their residents to use the money at any college anywhere in the country. Other states, like Massachusetts, allow residents of any of the 50 states to be beneficiaries of their programs. All plans allow donations from residents of any state, regardless of whether or not the beneficiary student must be in-state or not.

Since 1997, with the adoption of that year's Taxpayer's Relief Act, the prepaid tuition plans have been expanded to cover not only tuition and mandatory fees, but also room, board, and books. If the money is withdrawn for anything other than higher education costs it is subject to a penalty in most states. Most states offer a degree of flexibility in allowing the prepaid plans to fund undergraduate or graduate education, and to be transferred into accounts for siblings and other relatives, thus providing options for those who have overinvested.

In addition to the prepaid tuition plans, some states have college savings plans that allow families to invest money in a state-sponsored fund whose earnings are sheltered from federal taxes until used for college (at which time the money is taxed at the student rate) and exempt from state taxes altogether. Each state has its own regulations regarding investment limits, penalties for using the money for purposes other than higher education, account management fees, who can contribute to a beneficiary's fund, and where the money can be used.

The advantages of both the prepaid tuition plans and the college savings plans generally go to higher-income families. People in higher tax brackets will benefit most from the deferral of federal taxes and the deferral of or exemption from state taxes. Those in lower tax brackets will not only benefit less from the tax deferrals, but also find it difficult to put money away where it is out of reach.

Families considering either plan should discuss with an investment advisor whether or not the plan is best for their particular situation. Many will determine that there are better ways to invest one's money for future educational purposes.

Additionally, families should carefully consider a state's flexibility when deciding whether or not to buy into its plan. Any plan that will significantly hamper a student's choice of colleges is questionable. If a plan is even slightly inflexible in its regulations regarding portability of funds, avoid it. By doing so, you will ensure that your investment does not put conscious or subconscious pressure on your child to make a choice that may not be ideal for him.

EDUCATION IRAS

A new class of educational savings accounts modeled on Individual Retirement Accounts (IRAs) was born in 1997. The accounts allow contributions of $500 per child per year until the child turns 18. Although the contributions are not tax-deductible as they are in regular IRAs, the earnings accumulate interest tax-free. Furthermore, withdrawals are tax-free as well (in retirement IRAs they are only tax-deferred) as long as they are made before the student's age of 30 and to finance undergraduate or graduate tuition and associated educational expenses. If all the money is not used for educational purposes, the excess money would be taxed at the normal income tax rate and be subject to an additional 10% penalty tax. The IRAs are available only to joint filers with adjusted gross incomes of $150,000 or less, or single filers with incomes of $95,000 or less. The education IRAs cannot be used in conjunction with either of the federal education tax credits (see the next section). Families in reasonably high tax brackets (but not those with joint incomes over $150,000 or $95,000 for single filers) will generally find the IRAs more valuable.

EDUCATION TAX CREDITS

In 1997, legislation was passed to grant a tax credit to tuition-paying parents of college students. (The credit can actually be used to pay for higher education for yourself, a spouse, or a child.) The Hope Scholarship Tax Credit amounts to 100% of the first $1,000 paid in tuition, plus 50% of the next $1,000 for a maximum credit of $1,500 each year for the first two years of college education, for students attending at least half-time. Remaining years of education are worth a $1,000 maximum ($2,000 maximum after the year 2002) credit per year. The credit is designed to help low- and middle-income families with the college burden, and is phased out for single taxpayers with adjusted gross incomes of $40,000 to $50,000 and joint filers with incomes of $80,000 to $100,000.

In conjunction, the Taxpayer Relief Act of 1997 allows taxpayers to claim a Lifetime Learning Credit, available for an unlimited number of years and amounting to 20% of the first $5,000 in annual education expenses. The Lifetime Learning Credit is different from the Hope Credit in that it is figured per tax return, not per student. The two credits cannot be used simultaneously for the same student, but a filer with more than one dependent student in college can claim more than one of the credits on a single tax return, as long as there is only one Lifetime Learning credit per return. Neither tax credit option can be used in conjunction with an Education IRA.

EXTENDED TUITION PAYMENT PLANS AND TUITION FREEZES

Some schools offer novel payment plans in which families can pay tuition in ten or twelve annual installments, with an initial fee of $50 or so to join the plan.

Other schools have begun to offer tuition "freeze" programs. Parents who can afford to prepay four years of tuition can pay the freshman year price for all four years rather than losing out because of tuition hikes later on. Depending upon what tuition hikes at your school are likely and what kind of loans you can access, it is sometimes wise to take out a loan in order to prepay four years of college. If, for example, the tuition at your school is rising at a rate of 7% annually and you can access a loan program with an interest rate of 5%, then it would be to your benefit to owe the lender rather than the college.

COMMERCIAL TUITION PAYMENT PLANS

Even if your college does not have an innovative payment plan in place, you can access a commercial plan yourself. You determine how much you need for a year of college and the organization forwards it to you so that you can make your tuition payments. Then the lender collects periodic (usually monthly) installments from you over the year. You must begin making payments before the academic year begins, and most plans charge a small flat fee ($50 or so) for participation. Contact one of the following organizations for more information about programs:

- Academic Management Services at 50 Vision Blvd., East Providence, RI 02914. 800-635-0120. http://www.amsweb.com
- Key Education Resources at 735 Atlantic Avenue, Boston, MA 02111. 800-540-1855.
- Tuition Management Systems at 4 John Clarke Road, Newport, RI 02842. 800-722-4867 or 401-849-1550. http://www.afford.com
- USA Group Tuition Payment Plan. 800-849-6510. http://www.usagroup.com

BORROWING FROM COMMERCIAL LENDERS

Before signing on the dotted line of a commercial lender's contract, be sure to talk with college and independent financial advisors about lending operations. There are nearly 100 options available for families who need to borrow money for college, and you need to fully understand which programs are best for you. Some schools have even worked out deals with certain lending operations, but may not have mentioned this to you if loan money was not part of your official financial aid package.

Loan terms vary considerably. Most require a good credit history plus a minimum annual income, will allow you to borrow up to the total cost of an education, and have maximum payment terms of 15 to 25 years. Most carry fees of 3 to 7% and have interest rates somewhere near the prime rate. Some of the better loans for educational purposes include: ExtraCredit and ExtraTime, offered by The College Board (800-874-9390); Achiever Loan, offered by Knight College

Resource Group (800-225-6783); TERI loans offered by The Education Resources Institute (800-255-8374); PLATO offered by University Support Services (800-467-5286); EXCEL offered by Nellie Mae (800-634-9308); and EducaidEXTRA Premier Loan, offered by Educaid (916-554-8517).

STATE COLLEGE SAVINGS BONDS

More than 20 states now sponsor bond programs to help their residents fund higher education. These bonds work the same way other zero-coupon bonds do: They are basically nearly risk-free IOUs in which the state promises to pay out a bond's worth with interest upon maturity but no sooner. Parents buy state-sponsored bonds (sometimes called "baccalaureate bonds") at a large discount. These zero-coupon bonds have high interest rates, and interest is tax exempt, but they do not start collecting interest until the bond reaches maturity (instead of gradually collecting at a much lower interest rate). They generally cost $1,000 to $1,500 and mature within five to twenty years. Ideally, a bond should mature the same year your student would enroll in college. Although marketed as a savings vehicle to fund college education, no state yet requires that these be used for higher education.

USING MONEY IN TRADITIONAL IRAS OR ROTH IRAS FOR EDUCATION PURPOSES

Since 1997, with the adoption of the new tax laws pertaining to education, penalty-free withdrawals from both traditional IRAs and Roth IRAs can be made to pay for the higher education expenses of the account owner, a spouse, a child, or a grandchild. Taking money away from funds originally planned to fund retirement or the purchase of a home is not a wise idea for all families, but the law gives families more options in paying for their children's education. This is a better option for parents who are relatively young and far away from retirement age, with increased earning potential in the years to come, or for those who have saved particularly well under their lifelong IRAs.

BORROWING THROUGH HOME EQUITY LOANS OR LINES OF CREDIT

If you own a home and need extra money to pay for college, you may be able to avoid commercial lenders altogether by borrowing through a home equity loan or line of credit. All interest (up to $100,000) paid on both options is tax deductible on your federal tax return, so these are very attractive loan alternatives for middle- and upper-middle-income families.

An equity loan is like a second mortgage. It will require that you pay interest on the full amount borrowed within a fixed period of time and most often at a fixed rate. It can be the less favorable of the two options despite the low fixed interest rate; you may end up paying extra interest because you use only a quarter of the total amount borrowed during the first loan year. With a home equity line of credit, you can receive a certain maximum line of credit based on the value of your home. You make payments only on those funds you withdraw, so you have no extra interest to pay, but the rate is usually variable.

USING CREDIT CARDS TO PAY FOR TUITION

Some colleges allow tuition to be paid on credit cards, giving families convenience and also a way to ring up frequent flyer miles on tie-in airline mileage programs. Clearly the benefits of this payment option are for the relatively wealthy who simply want to earn miles and are committed to paying off their monthly balances in full.

REFUSING THE TEMPTATION OF STUDENT CREDIT CARDS

In recent years, credit card companies have fed remorselessly upon students on college campuses by offering them an easy way out of their strapped-for-cash existence. Credit companies lure students into contracts with easy sign-up-on-the-spot offers, often accompanied by freebies and promotionals, and by not requiring students to demonstrate previous credit histories. Often unable to pay for extras (sometimes even necessities) with cash, college students are easily enticed by credit card offerings, only to regret the consequences of their use (and abuse) later on. High interest rates and histories of missed payments can ruin a student's finances and creditworthiness long into the future. If you think you might be one of those tempted to subsidize your lifestyle while in school by amassing a huge debt, you should probably stop yourself from getting into trouble by refusing the cards in the first place. If you cannot control your buying habits, you will be better off spending only when you have the cash up front; you can always get a credit card through your parents if you think you need one for emergency purposes.

LOAN FORGIVENESS AND CONSOLIDATION PROGRAMS

Once you are out of college and swimming in a little or a lot of debt, there are still ways to make your financial life less of a burden on you. There are several volunteer and community service programs, for example, that offer loan forgiveness in return for work. If you are the recipient of a Perkins loan, you can erase your loans by becoming a teacher of math, science, or foreign languages. The Perkins loan may forgive all of your debt if you teach full-time in an elementary or high school that serves students from underprivileged populations. It forgives 15% of your loan for each of your first two years of teaching, 20% for the third and fourth years, and the last 30% for the fifth. As another example, volunteering in the Peace Corps can erase up to 70% of your student loans while also deferring payments until you are out of service. The Peace Corps can teach you excellent career and language skills and give you a valuable and educational experience abroad, in addition to taking care of your debt.

Loan consolidation is often a money and headache saver for those who graduate from college with multiple loans. It is bad enough that managing multiple payment plans and writing multiple checks each month create organizational havoc—but having many loans rather than one consolidated loan often requires an unbearably large total payment each month, which can be a nightmare, especially for those just entering the workforce or going to graduate school. Your aim in consolidation should not be, however, to lower your payments as much as possible; doing so would only require you to pay more in interest rates over the long haul. Many of the federal loans (Perkins, Stafford, PLUS) qualify for consolidation, but you should think twice before doing so. You should avoid consolidating any subsidized loans with unsubsidized ones. Doing so will disqualify you from returning to a subsidized status should you return to graduate school or need to seek a deferment. Avoid consolidating Perkins loans as well, and instead keep the low 5% interest rate, unless it will help to draw the consolidation interest rate down considerably. (Even if you consolidate Perkins loans with other subsidized loans, you automatically lose all future subsidy benefits.)

Contact the following lenders to find out about the best bets in consolidation packages:

- Citibank at 800-967-2400. (Citibank will consolidate loans if it is the initial lender on one or more of them.)
- Federal Direct Consolidation Loan Information Center at 800-557-7293 (for consolidation of federal direct loans with others).
- Sallie Mae at 800-524-9100.
- USA Group, Inc. at 800-382-4506. (USA Group will consolidate loans if its affiliate, USA Funds, is the lender on one or more of them.)

Remember also that under certain trying circumstances, you may be eligible for deferment or forbearance of your loans. Most loan programs grant deferment or forbearance for temporary disabilities, unemployment, parenting young children, teaching or servicing underprivileged populations, membership in a uniformed service, working in certain areas of health care or law enforcement, and various forms of proven economic hardship.

Part V

APPLICATION ESSAY EXAMPLES

This section of the book contains 50 successful essays written by 23 recent applicants to top colleges. All of the applicants featured are currently attending one of the top colleges to which they applied. We chose our applicants and essays with a number of different criteria in mind. We wanted to include students who represented a wide variety of:

- locations in the United States and the world,
- races, ethnicities, and cultural backgrounds,
- high school types,
- academic and nonacademic interests,
- writing styles and approaches, and
- applicants to top schools and specialized programs.

These essays address many different topics from many different perspectives and have been selected in order to give you a wide range of materials from which to profit. We have not included every essay to every college for featured applicants, and in most cases have chosen only one or two pieces to reprint from each person. Following each applicant's essays are brief comments that will help you to understand what went right in the essays. The examples printed here are largely successful, although we have noted what an applicant might have done differently to improve a piece, where appropriate. Of course, you should never copy what these applicants have done. These examples will, however, give you an idea of the kinds of approaches top applicants have taken and what generally works.

Note that actual names have been used, as desired by all of the featured writers. Essay numbers do not correspond with the colleges' own numerals and are used only so that the essays can be easily referred to in the comments that follow each set. (Note that some colleges change their essay questions or alter them slightly from year to year.) All essays have been reprinted exactly as they appeared to admissions officers; no spelling, grammatical, or other changes of any kind have been made to them here.

Many applicants use the Common Application question when composing their main personal statements. That question is as follows:

Please write an essay on a topic of your choice or on one of the options listed below.

1. Evaluate a significant experience or achievement that has special meaning to you.
2. Discuss some issue of personal, local, national, or international concern and its importance to you.
3. Indicate a person who has had a significant influence on you, and describe that influence.

OVERVIEW OF THE APPLICANTS AND THEIR ESSAYS

APPLICANT	HIGH SCHOOL TYPE	COLLEGE ESSAYS INCLUDED HERE	ESSAY QUESTIONS	NOTES ON CANDIDACY AND PRINTED ESSAYS
Annie Palone (page 576)	Private	Stanford Columbia	Something important to you Most meaningful activity Intellectually stimulating project/idea Why interested in the college Supplemental writing piece	Avid photographer and coxswain interested in the Classics
Aileen Rodriguez (page 578)	Public	Dartmouth University of Pennsylvania (Georgetown)	Common Application question (option 1) Why interested in the college/your role on campus	Latino student originally from the Dominican Republic who attended high school in Miami, Florida
Eric Citron (page 580)	Private	Princeton Harvard	Opportunity to develop a skill Meaningful book you have read What you want in a roommate How to evaluate candidates for admission Common Application question (option 1) Summer activities	Jewish student from the Boston area interested in a law career
Liza Behles (page 583)	Public	Cornell University of Michigan	Person who has had important influence Why college is important to you	Applicant from Winnetka, Illinois who attended the highly regarded New Trier High School

APPLICANT	HIGH SCHOOL TYPE	COLLEGE ESSAYS INCLUDED HERE	ESSAY QUESTIONS	NOTES ON CANDIDACY AND PRINTED ESSAYS
Anne Lee (page 586)	Public	University of Pennsylvania	Why interested in the college/your role on campus	Korean American applicant from Maryland
Susan Roy (page 587)	Private	Dartmouth Colby (Amherst) (Bates) (Bowdoin) (Middlebury) (Mount Holyoke) (Swarthmore)	Common Application question (option 1) Describe your hometown	Applicant of working class background interested in pursuing a career in science
Nicole Peterson (page 589)	Public	Stanford	Something important to you	Applicant raised in Elkhorn, Nebraska, who took a real risk in this essay
Atul Joshi (page 590)	Public	Yale University of Pennsylvania Duke	Most meaningful activity Why interested in program/future goals Why interested in the college/your role on campus Page 217 of autobiography Why interested in the college/your role on campus Meaningful book you have read	Accomplished musician and Indian American applicant accepted to Penn's Huntsman program in international studies and business
April Levin (page 594)	Private	MIT Brown	Ask your own question and answer it Why career in medicine Area of academic interest	Applicant accepted to Brown's PLME program in medicine

APPLICANT	HIGH SCHOOL TYPE	COLLEGE ESSAYS INCLUDED HERE	ESSAY QUESTIONS	NOTES ON CANDIDACY AND PRINTED ESSAYS
Sharlene Wu (page 596)	Public/ magnet	UC Berkeley	Greatest learning experience	Immigrant applicant from mainland China who attended high school in San Francisco and won Berkeley's Incentive scholarship
Lauren Foley (page 597)	Public	Dartmouth	Ask your own question and answer it	Applicant from Ann Arbor, Michigan who asked a particularly creative question
Ambrose Faturoti (page 599)	Private	UVA (Georgetown) (Tufts) (Wesleyan) (Williams)	Most meaningful work of art/music/lit Describe community to which you belong	African American applicant from Massachusetts
Ainsley Seago (page 600)	Public	Cornell	Person who has had important influence Area of academic interest/what you will study in college	Naturalist from Tacoma, Washington who was accepted to Cornell's College of Agriculture and Life Sciences

APPLICANT	HIGH SCHOOL TYPE	COLLEGE ESSAYS INCLUDED HERE	ESSAY QUESTIONS	NOTES ON CANDIDACY AND PRINTED ESSAYS
Kristina Velez (page 602)	Parochial	Swarthmore (Amherst) (Dartmouth) (Haverford) (University of Pennsylvania) (Reed) (Tufts)	Common Application question (option 1) Most meaningful activity	Latino applicant from Miami, Florida with particularly creative writing style
Stephenie Park (page 605)	Public	Yale (Harvard)	Something about yourself	Korean American actress and musician from Illinois
Anand Kinkhabwala (page 606)	Public	University of Pennsylvania	Why interested in the college/your role on campus	Indian American applicant accepted to Penn's Wharton School of Business
Jaime Singley (page 606)	Private	Dartmouth (Harvard)	Area of academic interest Ask your own question and answer it	Applicant from a single-parent household who wrote a particularly personal essay about her absent father
Rachel Perschetz (page 608)	Private	Cornell	Area of academic interest/what you will study in college Optional supplemental essay	Applicant accepted at Cornell's College of Hotel Administration
Sarah Kwon (page 609)	Public	Brown	Something about yourself	Applicant from New Jersey who wrote successful "slice-of-life" essay

APPLICANT	HIGH SCHOOL TYPE	COLLEGE ESSAYS INCLUDED HERE	ESSAY QUESTIONS	NOTES ON CANDIDACY AND PRINTED ESSAYS
Tyler Thornton (page 610)	Private	Stanford Amherst Bowdoin	Something important to you Common Application question (option 1) Influential teacher	Applicant from a private girls' school in Ohio with leadership in community service projects
Amanda Sadacca (page 613)	Public/ magnet	UVA	Most meaningful work of art/music/lit	Applicant attended one of the country's premier public magnet schools for science but wrote on a literary topic
Nicholas Horbaczewski (page 614)	Private	Harvard Yale (Princeton)	Common Application question (option 1) Something about yourself	Applicant from the Boston area who is interested in a career in film
Laura Hosny (page 616)	Private	NYU	What diversity means to you	Applicant of mixed Middle Eastern, Indian, European background

ANNIE PALONE

Notes on her candidacy: An avid photographer and coxswain, Annie's greatest intellectual passion is for the study of the Classics. She now attends Stanford University.

STANFORD UNIVERSITY

1. Attach a small photograph of something important to you and explain its significance.

[The attached photograph is of a young woman, presumably the applicant herself.]

I am Annie, a child of the future and one of the past, small-bodied, but strong and determined. In Hebrew, I am the "graceful one." "Maverick," my father calls me, or "Diamond Head," diamonds being stronger than even rock. I am five-three, one fifteen, soft-voiced and a strong believer in equality and experience. I am the older child; I can my strong, slender, almost sixteen-year-old brother, "Little Mickey;" we laugh as he towers over me. I have been a coxswain for three years, the first two filled with laughter and losing, the third with confident joking and a New England Championship we dared not expect. I am a Pisces; I am a fish, a sea nymph and a lover of oceans, lakes, streams, and rivers, even brightly chlorinated swimming pools. I am a photographer and and experienced subject. For two years, I appeared in dozens of my roommate's prints, now I create my own images. I am strong-spirited and open-minded. I have lived in ten houses and known six cities. I am as much American as Canadian. Born in the northern Rocky Mountains and raised in Dallas, San Francisco, and Boston, I spent weeks of each summer on the, "blue lakes and rocky shore," of Ontario's northland. There, the blue sky stretches wider than anywhere and the loons cry eerily in the dark.

In my grandparents coursed the blood of Scotland, Italy, Ireland. I have heard the whispers of my past in the dark rock passages of Edinburgh Castle, seen glimmers of the places my ancestors loved, in the lush greens of Scottish hills and in the brilliant blues of sky and sea. I have read the *Aeneid,* about the brave Trojans who founded the Roman race, and wondered if the genes and spirit of some Trojan hero might not live in me. I cherish the idea that so many people, so many experiences, cultures, and languages come together I me. I am filled with fascination and pride by the diversity of my history.

I have kissed the cheeks of seven-year-old boys, sticky with the juice of mangoes, not yet ripe. I winced as they pulled and braided my hair, wondering at its lightness,

"!Mira, pelo amarillo!" I knew then, at Atenea, a Venezuelan home for poor, orphaned street children, as I know now, the sadness of their future, the hopelessness of their place in the social strata of their homeland. I feel privileged to be here, to be making a difference. I see the world through the eyes of an artist, notice beautiful light, the sudden permanence of a moment that is captured on film. I revel in the beauty of each instant.

I believe in myself, believe in the words of the lined, turbaned Indian physician-astrologer who examined my palm through his eyepiece when I was five years old. "This little girl will be very rich." I am already rich, blessed by travel, friendships, happy memories of a childhood and growing up, rich because I believe that I will live a life replete with friendships, experiences, travel, and knowledge, rich because the things I value most are not tangible, because it is memories and experiences that I treasure.

2. Of the activities, interests, and experiences listed above (on the extracurricular and personal activities list), which is the most meaningful to you and why?

Last fall, I discovered another world behind the lens of a camera. Photography quickly became my passion. I love the process: I love the product. I love the portraits of my friends and family, the people I cherish. Shooting is mysterious; until a roll has been processed, it is impossible to know what treasures will appear. I enjoy poring over contact sheets, choosing the images that I think best represent the subject and the art form. Finally, printing, choosing an exposure time, exposing paper, and waiting over the cool chemicals until the images appears and darkens is wonderful. I spend hours in the darkroom, never running out of things to do. It is enthralling to preserve a moment of laughter or loneliness, of a smile or tear that only film can capture. The sudden permanence that a photograph lends to an instant has made the darkroom my favorite place.

3. Sharing intellectual interests is an important aspect of university life. Describe an experience, book, class, project, or idea that you find intellectually exciting and explain why.

A story my Latin teacher told two years ago, about the remarkable trust and persistence of a German banker, who did the impossible by finding the ancient city of Troy, struck a chord with me. Heinrich Schliemann was a businessman who read Homer's *Odyssey* and fell in love. Schliemann believed, contrary to the assertion that it was a fairy tale, that *The Odyssey* was a true story, albeit one filled with romantic exaggeration. He believed that the high citadels of Troy once stood and he used Homer's rich description to find their ancient location no the coast of Turkey. There, he established a dig and found the ruins of the "imagined" city. Schliemann's discovery stimulated a great deal of intellectual discussion. Many scholars who previously believed that the mysterious Homer had imagined every detail of the epic adventure were now uncertain; it led many to believe that at least some of *The Odyssey* was true. The reality of Troy and the fact that archaeological evidence suggested that the city had been sacked and burned contributed further to the wave of questions about the Trojan War. Was *The Odyssey* in fact a history, exaggerated, which was based on fact?

Schliemann was not an expert in the classics. He read *The Odyssey* and intuitively felt that the Trojan War was more than a myth. It is amazing to me that one man, believing in a "fairy tale," encouraged so many analytical questions, and opened a previously unknown door on the ancient world.

COLUMBIA UNIVERSITY

1. Please tell us how you first became interested in Columbia and what you find most appealing about the school.

Columbia was etched indelibly in my mind in 1994 through an introduction to *The Dharma Bums* by Jack Kerouac; it was here that he met Cassady, Ginsberg, and Burroughs. In 1998, I stood in icy white sunshine, struck by the magnificent Butler Library, carved with Homer, Sophocles, and Vergil, masters whose wisdom has inspired for centuries. The myriad cultures, languages, tastes, and smells of the great city lapped at the wrought iron gates, splashing up, alluring, offering a thousand years more of wisdom and insight.

Supplemental writing piece included in all applications:
New England Interscholastic Rowing Championships, Lake Quinsigamond, Worcester May 1998

I am lying low in the white Vespoli, wired for sound, stomach tight with anticipation. Coach Gilmore's last minute advice echoes, "Make your boys laugh; it will unnerve the competition." We vow to one another that we will win today for him. Above the line, we are consumed by our laughter and then fight for composure. A falsestart jangles our nerves, awakens the need to pee—the oarsmen relieve themselves. We focus. Our heartbeats are thudding in our ears. I fade into a calm, going over every inch of the course in my mind.

"Sit ready," calls the starter; I feel the four bodies behind me tense. "Attention." Their legs, necks, backs lengthen, ready for the first short stroke. "ROW." We jump off the line, shooting ahead of the competition. We are dumbfounded by the power in our start. I call a power ten and we open our lead to a half-length that discourages other rowers, unable to see my boat. A taut excitement grips my stomach; this is more perfect that [sic] any of us had dared imagine.

At the half-way mark, I call the "gold medal ten" and suddenly the shell, the oars, the oarsmen and I, the coxswain, are one. There is no weight in my body, none in theirs, none in the narrow fiberglass. We seem to rise above the water and fly. Behind me, I hear the other voices, desperate, screaming at their crews to pull harder. We are walking away from them.

From the beach, the screams grow louder. I see the finish line. Groton is powering forward. I am afraid. I want this too badly to lose now. "Want this," I scream, "Want this more than they do." We do.

We cross the line with half a length on Groton. The air rushes out of me as I scream. We are five people again, the synchrony shattered. We are overjoyed. Our joy mixes with the despair in the boats around us, with the tumult on the shore. We are New England Champions. We have proven what we have known all along, that we are the fastest, the best.

Comments

- Stanford essay 1 is a wonderful piece that expresses exactly what Stanford is looking for in its applicants: intellectual vitality. The essay is cerebral, shows her passionate side, and works on many different levels at once (describing both the tangible and the intangible facets of Annie's existence). It also helps to introduce Annie's values, such as her appreciation of her fortunate position in life and her strong friendships.

- Stanford essay 2 builds on the first by again showing Annie's passion for her endeavors, the value she places on personal relationships, and the way in which she is able to cherish a single moment.

- In Stanford essay 3, Annie has wisely taken advantage of her background and interest in the Classics (a rarity among applicants these days). She also benefits from developing a unique topic from which a reader is likely to learn something new. The essay would not have been as compelling if she had focused upon *The Odyssey* itself, an example used by far too many college applicants when discussing favorite or most influential readings.

- Columbia 1 starts off with a fresh perspective. Again, Annie has realized how much she benefits from doing something different, rather than starting this type of essay with the usual "I want to attend Columbia because …" Ideally, however, she should have included some more realistic reasons for wanting to attend the school. This essay makes it seem as if she is not really sure why she should attend Columbia, or how its education and programs suit her needs. Note that the Roman poet usually referred to as "Virgil" can also be referred to as "Vergil"—the name is not misspelled. (It would have been a huge mistake for someone claiming a strength in Classics to misspell this name!)

AILEEN RODRIGUEZ

Notes on her candidacy: Originally from the Dominican Republic, Aileen attended high school in Miami, Florida, where she played varsity badminton and founded the Drug-Free Youth-in-Town organization.

DARTMOUTH COLLEGE

1. See Common Application question (option 1).

My bony knees and chubby fingers lured me into the room. The crawling adventure was cut short when two feet placed themselves before me. I looked up and contemplated the loose folds of skin that melted into the warm smile of the woman blocking my path. I was six months old and my mother had taken me to my grandparents' house in the Dominican Republic. I was not to see her again for half a decade. Mama Chela, my grandmother, took care of me, her other grandchildren, and her two youngest daughters. Obviously, this was not a household in which attention was easy to get. I knew from the first smile that Mama loved me and so I gathered enough confidence to venture into my own imaginative endeavors.

Mama would often tell me, with tears of laughter in her eyes, the little girl stories of my childhood. When I was three, I persuaded her to buy me a stool so that I could call Mommy or Daddy whenever I wanted to tell them about my wonderful world of plastic ice castles and intriguing unicorns. I was a very talkative child and the phone was my means of letting the world know who Aileen Rodriguez was.

I also liked to sell things so that I could help out my grandmother around the house. I was such an entrepreneurial little girl. I gathered up all my cousins, which were roughly between five and seven, and made them employees of my first business.

Daily, as if it were a religious ritual, I held a garage sale. I owned a little table filled with mended toys and false tonics that my services guaranteed. The elixirs, I professed, could cure everything from scrapes in your elbows to nightmares. They consisted of alcohol and food dye. I sold an average of about RD$2.50 pesos a day, approximately half a dollar, to whichever merciful soul took pity on me and my armless dolls and wheel barren cars. These funny games were vital steps in my steady and unusual yellow brick road of evolution.

The severance from my biological mother, at such an early age, and the natural depersonalization of being "lost in the crowd," prompted my desire to standout. Although never a rebel without a purpose or green hair, I carefully laid out steps to keep me on task of my responsibilities, as a four-year-old. With the road's gravel and rocks in my sandals and my grandma's bookkeeping notebook, I became (in my own little world) the queen of the neighborhood kids. Yes, the old wise one in the herd of children that settled disputes between toys, games to be played, and chicken to chase after. Although my trifling mandates were rarely executed, I found pleasure in the thought that they looked up to me to find encouragement and reliance.

My independence has gradually increased and when I was fifteen, I got my first legal and minimum wage paying job. I had a stingy boss; the clothes were moth eaten and smelled of wet puppies, but I miraculously stayed there for almost two years. I didn't have to rely on my parents to buy me clothes or pay for my school supplies. Devotedly and with open hands, I bequeathed half of my pay to my mother.

Today I have matured to a level of self-reliance that has been beneficial to me in situations where leaders are needed or where I have to make a choice for a group. I have shed the tediousness of managing a job and school, yet my unsatisfied nature compelled me to an even greater task. Once again, the nostalgia of helping out set into my stomach and sent spanks through my body, I saw a news report about teen drug problems and drug abuse. I talked a counselor into sponsoring me and I began a drug prevention club in school. Not only do we promote a drug-free environment, but we volunteer in our community to show this commitment. Some people call it masochism, but the overpowering drive to help someone whether its my grandma, the neighborhood kids of my childhood, or my community, even if it means putting my own pleasures aside, is a pleasure in itself. My world of unicorns and rainbow slides where magic and smiles were just beneath a rock or furry creature, has turned into a world in which my own hand becomes a magician. Now with it I can make an orphan child's face light up at the site of the horse or rainbow that I painted in his face.

THE UNIVERSITY OF PENNSYLVANIA (THE SCHOOL OF ARTS AND SCIENCES)

1. What characteristics of Penn, and yourself, make the University a particularly good match for you? Briefly describe how you envision your first year in college. How will your presence be known on campus?
(Essay also used in application to Georgetown.)

Last night I was in Denny's. I looked around and the waitress' hairnet was in disarray. Her expression held a blank stare and she gave off a feeling of detachment from this world. The AC was humming a depressing lullaby and the stillness of the place emitted a feeling of utter sadness from every crevice in the wall. I realized that I wanted to be a happy individual. I do not want to be stuck, like that poor waitress, in a job that I neither want nor like. Whatever the profession may be, I want to feel comfortable in it. Whether it means being an editor of a small town newspaper, an archaeologist in another part of the world, or a veterinarian, I want the opportunity to find a career that will make me happy and that is, in itself, a learning experience.

When I was a child, I changed careers like babies soil diapers. I glowed with happiness every time that I was asked what I wanted to be. Maybe I'll grow vineyards in the Mediterranean, perhaps I would build skyscrapers in Chicago, or teach orphans in Russia. Usually these ideas rose from movies, trips, or my own imagination. While others might consider my indecision a fault or maybe lack of personality, I think that it is the greatest decision that I have yet taken. This school's continual effort to grow and to provide its students with an infinite pool of majors and courses will definitely serve my purpose. One hour I might be studying the molecular formation of a certain bacteria and the next, I could be taking an introductory course in anthropology. Maybe I can become an anthropologist that studies the evolvement of bacteria in the development of the human species. The possibilities are endless.

Although I have yet to take on the gut-wrenching task of deciding my future, I do know that the academically strong and internationally known University of Pennsylvania should back my unplanned future. The known theory of the Masonic community to value every dimension of human experience is one that I would like to get on a first name basis with.

Furthermore, my one goal, that of a happy and fulfilling career is one that is very hard to achieve. My interest in studying at Penn has purely risen from the knowledge that this school will let me explore and submerge myself into things that I have never dreamed of. Talking to someone from Singapore, sitting in at a lecture from a renown professor, or enjoying a cup of coffee while I tread the busy streets of Philadelphia might not make me epiphanize on the meaning of life, but it might just make me enjoy it more.

Someone once said that a liberal arts education prepares you for nothing and for everything. I like to think of myself as an optimist. The opportunity of studying in another country and immersing myself in another culture from trying their foods, sipping their wines, laughing at their jokes, or enjoying their music, lures me to the gates of Penn. This wonderful opportunity as well as that of an internship that might push me toward an unadvertised field, are things that I would like to carry with me into the future. Is not the future a product of what we do in the present?

Around campus I will probably be the curly-haired girl that accepts everything and enjoys conversations that pertain to anything from the Rugrats to oncology. The president of the student government and maybe I will have my own suggestion column in the newspaper. Students could write cheesy questions to me and I will respond with corny jokes and cliche suggestions. Perhaps I could start another student organization like I did in high school. Hopefully it is a fun one and not one that deals with such serious issues such as drugs. How about Students Against Repeat Barfing or Anonymous with Names? Those are nice names for clubs and given some time I could probably come up with activities that each one of these potential clubs could do while helping out the community. By the way, do you guys have a Badminton team? I really like playing that and it will probably be the activity that I spend the most time enjoying too.

Comments

- Dartmouth essay 1 is a wonderful window into Aileen's personality and soul. We learn what moves her and the detailed stories tell us a lot about what she is like—independent, entrepreneurial, determined, caring—and how she came to be that way. At times the essay feels a bit unfocused, but the only instance in which this gets in the way is at the very end, with the mention of the "orphan"—it is not clear to what she is referring here.

- Penn essay 1 is a well-written and uniquely crafted answer to a question that all too often results in the same dull responses. The introduction to the essay—through the story of the Denny's waitress—is especially original. Aileen pulls off a successful discussion of her lack of a certain future, all the while mentioning some career possibilities so that it is clear that she has given thought to the question (just not come up with a final answer yet).

ERIC CITRON

Notes on his candidacy: Editor-in-chief of his high school newspaper and an extremely accomplished student with high grades and test scores, Eric plans to pursue a career in law after he finishes his undergraduate work at Harvard University.

PRINCETON UNIVERSITY

1. If you were given the time and resources to develop one particular skill, or talent, or area of expertise, what would you choose to pursue and why?

Guitar is neither my greatest talent, nor my most likely career choice, but if I were given unlimited time and opportunity, I would want to spend it honing my musical skills. I play constantly, I sing incessantly, and I love music for the way it makes me feel and the way I can be used to make others feel. I do not delude myself into thinking that I am an absolutely unbelievable player, nor do I consider myself capable of easily becoming a famous musician someday. I am not even sure I would want to play for a living: although rock stardom does sound like fun, I feel I have greater talents which would be better suited as career choices. My fear, however, is that someday, in the face of deadlines, workloads, family, and responsibility, my guitar will have to be put away with my old varsity letters and high school yearbook, and this I could not stand. I need guitar to always remain a prominent and "instrumental" part of my life, and it is for this reason that, given the chance, I would want to develop my musical skills over anything else.

2. What book that you've read in the past couple of years left the greatest impression on you? Explain why.

The book that has left the greatest impression on me is the one I listed earlier as my favorite, Ralph Ellison's *Invisible Man*. There is great debate over whether the novel is a personal story about Ellison's life or whether it is purely fiction, whether it is a protest novel about the treatment of blacks in America, or whether it is just a story about one man's life who happens to be black. In any event, the great impact of the book on me was that I finished it knowing more about myself, and understanding, in a way, my own unintentional racism. The protagonist in the novel, whose name we never know, is "invisible" because he is prejudged unendingly in such a way that, arguably, no one ever *truly* sees him. This element of the book led me to wonder: do I ever make people feel invisible? The answer I found was yes. There are those times when, subconsciously perhaps, we all might say or do things which are subtly and unintentionally hurtful. We may assume, for instance, that someone's character connects to their race, even if we make no judgement about their color. Even asking someone a question such as "what's it like to be a black student at Nobles?" however good our intentions may be, is often painful for that person who then feels they must be representative of their race. Invisible Man led me to understand that you do not have to be hateful to be racist, and that I may have hurt people through racism, not by defaming them, but simply by not actively ignoring color when it was appropriate to do so.

3. What do you want in a roommate?

I am sure that I am going to learn many fascinating things in class. Professors will lecture me on all sorts of interesting topics, books will inform me on a variety of subjects, and guest speakers will come to entertain and enlighten me on a broad range of subject-matter. Yet there is only so much that can be learned in a classroom, and I suspect that much of what I learn at college might actually be taught in the dorm. Sure, I want a roommate who is funny, into sports and music, who appreciates me and with whom I have a lot in common. Yet, at the same time, I want a roommate who is different enough to be constantly teaching me new things, and who is always willing to clue in a friend about a new idea they learned in Quantum Physics or Art History. Also, true friends respect each other's opinions, and I would love to find a roommate with whom I could agree to disagree. There is much potential for education and enjoyment in heated discussions about prevalent issues, or in philosophical conversation about unanswerable questions. I want a roommate who, though light and funny at times, can make my life at college richer by pursuing deep thoughts with me into the wee hours of the night. This type of sharing, respect, and intellectual experience builds the kind of friendship that lasts a lifetime, and I hope that I will be able to find such friends at Princeton and beyond.

4. If you were an admissions officer at Princeton, how would you evaluate candidates for admission?

College admissions is an extremely competitive process, where, supposedly, people who have studied long and hard are ultimately rewarded for their efforts. Yet, if I were in your shoes, I would not only give weight to academics and SAT scores, extracurricular activities and AP classes. I would give some weight to kindness as well. The world is full of ruthless corporate types and people for whom natural selection, where only the strong survive, is the modus operandi. In that context, I would want to find candidates who are "good people" in that they are compassionate, empathetic, and cheerful. Sure, one needs to look at those things which establish academic excellence, but some weight should be given to excellence of character. As I said in the answer above, part of what makes a place like Princeton so wonderful is the potential to learn from and interact with amazing peers. I would want to accept applicants who I feel can help to form an atmosphere of respect and admiration on campus and in the student body. So, if after an academic inspection, teachers and interviewers can say that they truly like a candidate as a person, that would be a wonderful reason to admit them. Thus, in your shoes, I would give extra weight to teacher recommendations or face-to-face interviews which can give some clue as to the person's character and not just his or her credentials.

HARVARD UNIVERSITY

1. See Common Application question (option 1).

I blew out a tire today. I was driving home from a football team dinner, perhaps a bit too fast, and a small black cat with shining yellow eyes darted out in front of the car. I swerved. I hit the curb. I heard a pop. I knew I was in trouble. I turned carefully onto the first side street, an unlit, unmarked roadway deep in a town I had never previously visited, and went to size up the damage after seeing those brilliant yellow eyes run safely off the other side of the road. Three gaping holes large enough to fit my fist through were visible—though only as jagged edged shapes even darker than the black wall of the tire—in the dim light cast by the bulb of the open car door. I was walking quite briskly towards the gas station I had passed, now about a hundred feet away, when I stopped myself to collect my thoughts.

As I saw it, the easy answer was only a few feet away. I could simply have walked to the gas station, bestowed my mother's credit card and my problem upon someone else, and have gotten my tired changed. I imagined doing this, however, and found the picture in my mind to be quite distasteful. I saw myself as the quintessential child of privilege, talented and independent in the classroom, perhaps, but helpless as far as completing one of those random and menial challenges that life finds it necessary to confer upon us. So I stopped and stood for a moment, feeling strangely empty in the bare light of a street lamp on Main Street in Dover, before deciding that I would change the tire myself.

Though there is no differential calculus involved in changing a tire, I still found the task to be quite difficult and quite humbling; it requires persistence, along with elbow grease of the most literal sense. After I managed to find the spare tire buried in the Volvo's trunk, I started the dirty task of finding the oil-slicked, sooty place in the undercarriage where the jack attaches to the car. Eventually, I managed to jack the car up, and I removed the busted tire with relative ease. I hit my first "roadblock" when I tried to install the spare. There was a small metal piece on the wheel base which apparently must be lined up with a pea-sized hole in the tire hub, but it took me almost ten minutes to see this metal guide and take appropriate action. So I tried, without success, to simply put the tire on the axle; I was trying to put it on backwards numerous times, dropping it on my own feet often, and becoming more and more frustrated all the while. Suddenly the irony of the situation hit me. Here I am, with grease on my hands and slacks, still wearing my prep-school uniform of shirt and tie, trying to do something which all the classroom time in the world could never possibly teach me.

I have long known that education is not confined to the classroom. So as I sat waiting for a replacement tire at National Tire and Battery—pondering my situation and watching Jeopardy—I realized that part of what makes me a good student is that I do not only learn in class. My private school education may have directly helped me to know that the correct response to the 600 dollar answer in category "B" was "What is Bora-Bora?", but less than a little of what I truly know has come from academic lectures. I read voraciously on a wide range of topics, I do crossword puzzles everyday, and I am often late for upcoming classes because I spend ten minutes after the previous one engaging the teacher in a more in-depth conversation. Even beyond academic pursuits, though, I have learned physical and mental toughness from football and wrestling, I have learned about leadership and journalism from my position on the newspaper, and I have learned much about expression and emotion from music and guitar. I even dropped Homer Simpson in favor of District Attorney Jack McCoy once I figured out how much I could learn from watching "Law and Order" on NBC. In fact, every dimension of my character and each even of my life is an invisible classroom, and so whether I am changing a tire or organizing Holocaust readings at school, I am learning and growing. Accepting the challenges of school and difficult courses is still extremely important to me, but accepting the challenges that life presents can be just as educational and equally important.

2. How have you spent the last two summers?

I have worked the last two summers at a Jewish, overnight camp called Bauercrest in Amesbury, Massachusetts. Two years ago I was a CI (counselor intern) largely still involved in camp as a camper, but my role in camp was to do manual labor cleaning up and maintaining the camp. This past year I was a camp counselor, caring for a bunk of small children among other daily duties. On top of this, I worked as a Bar-mitzvah tutor for the camp helping those children who were having their Bar-mitzvahs the next year to learn their portions and to study the torah and prophets. This was very rewarding not only as a well paying job, but also because I had the privilege of teaching children and knowing that I had helped them to reach their goals. I cared very deeply about my students' successes, and was often stricter than their tutors at home as far as the precision and practice I demanded from them. Being a teacher and a counselor was a maturing experience for me, and it is likely that I learned as much from it as some of my students did.

Comments

■   Eric's essays run the gamut from the good-but-ordinary to the extraordinary. While Princeton essays 1, 3, and 4 are solid but not especially creative or unique, Princeton essay 2 and Harvard essay 1 are excellent college essays.

- In his Princeton essay 2, Eric took a real risk and was successful in doing so. In discussing Ellison's *The Invisible Man*, Eric (who is white) explains that the book forced him to question his own unintentional acts of racism. Eric provides an intelligent discussion and offers an insightful example of the kind of racism he is referring to. The essay is effective because it demonstrates a solid command of the basic "issues" surrounding the text, but also delves into an analysis that is clearly Eric's own. He shows himself to be honest and sensitive to others as well.

- Harvard essay 1 is a fantastic "slice-of-life" essay that does a great job of telling readers who the applicant is and what he stands for. The story is very well written, even funny at times. Notice how effective the details are—the details about watching "Jeopardy" and the play-by-play on jacking up the car and trying to replace the flat tire make the writing sparkle. The essay, most importantly, shows through a very realistic story that the author values his privileged existence but does not wish to rely upon his fortunes to get through life the easy way.

- Harvard essay 2 is helpful in showing several important aspects of the applicant's personality. By discussing the extra role he took on as a bar mitzvah tutor at his camp, Eric makes it clear that he takes advantage of opportunities (rather than doing only what is expected of him), is a "people" person, and enjoys helping and sharing his gifts with others.

LIZA BEHLES

Notes on her candidacy: A graduate of one of the nation's strongest public schools, New Trier Township High School in Winnetka, Illinois, Liza played and coached field hockey as well as excelled in art classes.

CORNELL UNIVERSITY (THE COLLEGE OF ARTS AND SCIENCES)

1. Tell us about a person who has had an important influence on you. What qualities in that person do you most admire, and how have you grown from knowing that person?

"Let me tell you something about the hot dog business … It's no picnic." A booming, self assured voice assaults my eardrums, and I feel the familiar spray of saliva cascade across my face. I stare into the leathery face of my grandfather and note the bacon remnants that innocently loiter at the corner of his mouth. A gnarled finger targets me as he begins to elaborate on the perils of the mysterious industry. His eyes are electric and I see the vein in his forehead start to bulge as he launches into an eloquent sermon regarding the varying grades of meat. He mercilessly condemns the franks that abound in supermarket aisles and stresses that the only reputable hot dog is the Vienna Beef Fiver. Unlike the inadequate supermarket dogs, packaged at an appalling eight-per-pound rate, the majestic Fiver upholds its title by weighing in at a respectable (and self-explanatory) five-per-pound. All this, my Grandpa declares with unparalleled levels of vigor and intensity, while at the same time taking for granted my genuine interest in the topic. Once again the subject of my college education has spiraled into a career choice seminar, ultimately reaching yet another chapter in my Grandpa's vocational saga.

Never have I met a man as passionate as my Grandfather. I cannot recall a time in my life when that precipitating voice was not instilling in me some form of worldly knowledge. At eighty, Leonard, the silver-haired brute, is more alive than anyone I know. He runs three miles a day, trains for a phantom fight on the punching bag in his basement, and threatens to bestow a "knuckle sandwich" upon anyone who crosses him. He is forever arranging and cataloguing his extensive book collection on a computer that he continually breaks. Sitting at the head of the table, his bellowing conversation overpowers the "inside voices" of the rest of my family, and he is once again propelled back into the vicissitudes of one of his former careers. "When I owned the Grocery by Cabrini Green," or "When I was the paper boy," is the usual portal into one of life's lessons. His usual course of conversation flows like a flooded river channel from one account to another. His rich tales always rest on one of four pillars; the already mentioned career repertoire, books and their authors (and his relationship to the authors), Old Chicago, and Jewish History. Often the topics intertwine, weaving a tapestry that is the backdrop of my Grandpa's life.

Journeying through my Grandpa's study is like stepping inside this tapestry. I am surrounded by the artifacts from his tales. The lighting is dim and yellow, bathing the room in an eerie, old-world glow. The canvas wall hanging of a bearded rabbi confronts me as I enter. To the right sits the confounded computer and a stack of *The New Yorker* with a selected cartoon cutout lying on top. I see the crammed bookshelves adorned by a haphazardly placed "I Love Old Books" bumper sticker. On the wall is the watermarked autograph collection. A constant reminder of loss, this display contains many boyhood idols, but lacks the cherished Albert Einstein and Amelia Earhart signatures, both victims of a basement flood. Next to his exhibit is his ultimate seal of pride. It is a yellowed newspaper page, with "Little Samson" bold across the page. There are two pictures, one of a man ripping a phone book in half, and the other of the man holding two horses each pulling in opposite directions. This figure, "The world's smallest strong man," is my great grandfather, a touring Vaudeville headliner. His image governs the entire study, and becomes a perpetual inspiration for my Grandpa's powerful presence.

I am well-informed of Samson's infamy; Leonard, who has been known to repeat himself when it comes to matters of grave importance (as well as matters of little importance) has given his Samson spiel on more than one occasion. Like a knowledgeable tour guide plugging a favorite exhibit, my Grandpa stands proudly next to the clipping and proclaims with a sparkling haughty beam: "Now you know who this is, don't you? This is my father—strong as an ox—*an ox*! He would rip phone books in half—*Chicago phone books*—that's no piece of cake—and cards—I seen 'him rip a deck of Bicycles in two!" I never doubted the beloved family mascot's strength, but it held a new, more literal meaning on one of my recent visits. My parents were out of town, and I was in need of comfort. I had just suffered a deep personal misfortune (a whole different essay) and my parents desired that I remain in the safe custody of my grandparents. As I sat in their retro kitchen, submerged in my own low spirits, not particularly in the mood for a hot dog oration, I heard my Grandpa creak down the stairs. I peered up at the sturdy man in a gray jogging suit, and he had that constant wildly thoughtful look. He assessed my slumped posture and patted me on the back. "Hey, funny face, see this—Do you know who *this* is?" "Yeah," I said, as he handed me Samson, Xeroxed, and protected by a transparent plastic sheet. "Strongest man in Vaudeville-strong as Hell—why I seen 'im. . ." He continued with the familiar recital, and although my eyes were still teary, they now crinkled in a loving smile.

My Grandpa has that ability, the power to make me smile with the smallest gestures. I guess that is because when his ferocious vitality is directed towards me, I feel intelligent and important. When he is not delving into the depths of one of his four areas of expertise, he is striving to help me perfect any endeavor I undertake. If I am at his house for Sunday brunch, and I happen to excuse myself to go do homework, he is right behind me, on a quest for any book that will aid me in my studies. To his credit, most of my bibliographies have entertained a host of citations from his personal library.

In addition to providing me with endless sources of information, he has been a driving force behind my interest in art. Since the age of eight, I can recall sitting at this white laminate table, furiously scribbling on a Herbert B. Zak DDS dental scratch pad. These miniature canvases, each in the shape of a tooth, contain some of my earliest masterpieces; a frog, a camel (inspired by my Grandparents' Israel photographs), an elephant, three ladies shaded by parasols, Charlie Chaplin (my Grandpa's favorite comedian), and Jessica Rabbit. Out of the hundreds of tooth pads I defaced, my Grandpa painstakingly selected these sketches, and mounted them together on a wall. This dental collage has since been accompanied by many of my other works, creating a miniature gallery which he proudly shows off to guests. He is forever pressing me to produce works of art, and his willingness to display my work continues to give me confidence in my own abilities. With almost every visit, he has proceeded to enhance my awareness in this field. Constantly sitting me down to show me the styles of his favorite artists, giving me instructional art books, and introducing me to innovative art forms, he has become my own aesthetic booster club.

Whether he is bombarding my mind with knowledge, flooding it with stories from the past, brightening my spirits, or encouraging my own talents, Leonard, the gruff, old-world intellectual is truly part of my life. His character is so rich it seems to overflow his own body; he is a small planet, with a gravity all his own, magnetically engulfing anyone who stumbles into his orbit. I have vowed that if I ever do write a novel, that his persona will be intertwined with the plot in some way. My friends all know him from my stories, and usually assume my accounts of Leonard to be a bit exaggerated. It is almost impossible to describe him with words; instead, it would be more effective to simply hear his cacophonous voice, wailing about hot dogs or Samson, bathing all within close proximity in a shower of saliva and wisdom.

THE UNIVERSITY OF MICHIGAN

1. Why is college important to you?

I clawed at the vertical sheet of rock; my fingers passing over its face rapidly, trying to find even the smallest indentation. My whole body was shaking, but I took no notice. All I cared about was securing my grip. I could feel gravity tempting my frame as my feet mashed awkwardly into the foot holes. With my cheek pressed against the rock I saw the lake, eight thousand feet below. It looked like a canvas, or a movie; everything looked unreal. I knew that if I didn't keep climbing I would go nowhere, and I had to get to the top. Finally I located a grip for my hand, and I was able to proceed somewhat, a little bit at a time. Never mind that this was only the second of seven sixty-foot climbs I had to do, I had to concentrate on this portion. My breathing was shallow, and I was dehydrated. I could hear the guide at the top, but she wasn't talking to me. She was busy coaching one of the other thirteen group members who no doubt was having as much difficulty as myself. The rock was so unforgiving, and it seemed like there was nothing to grab onto. I felt so little: hanging off the side of this massive mountain, baking in the sun, and petrified beyond tears. I had never thought of myself as a brave person, and I could think of very few times when my courage had been truly tested. However, I don't think it was courage that willed me up that mountain, it was something else, something more reasonable. Hoisting myself up "The Cube," nine thousand feet in the Grand Tetons, I learned something about myself, or perhaps I had always known it. I had the ability to tell myself, quite consciously, to be strong. It might mean repeating this phrase over and over in my mind, or more bluntly telling myself, "come on Lize, you're good, you're OK."

Well, I finally did make it to the top of the mountain, and I will never forget how the vast Wyoming landscape seemed to spread itself out of me in a sublime act of congratulations. I was still shaking in my harness as my group members were patting each other on the back, and taking deep gulps of that thin energized air. This was the first mountain I had ever climbed, and at nine thousand feet, it was certainly the closest I had ever stood to the sky. I felt like I was standing in the clouds. Those clouds. They were obese down comforters looming lazily in an aquamarine seas. It seemed that if we could only get to the top of the next peak that I might be able to grab a fistful of that white cotton candy and stuff it into my pack. I remember standing on the edge of "The Cube" and staring down at the valley. My eyes followed the tree line until it gave way to the road, a thin ribbon that trailed off behind a butte and spilled over their horizon. Sky and horizon met in my vision, and I unconsciously recalled the cliched phrases "on top of the world" and "the sky is the limit." This was the top of the world. It had to be—and if I could get there, then certainly I could get anywhere.

I don't know when I will ever get the opportunity to climb in the Grand Tetons again, but I am sure that I will have other kinds of challenges to overcome. I know that in my life, mountains will take on many different forms, and it is my job to hold tight and make sure not to fall off. I know the feeling of being on top, the feeling that nothing can get to you, when the lightness of your heart is enough to let you float away. Climbing a mountain takes work though, and there is no way to get to the peak without a struggle for the footholds. In my life, I know that I want to succeed, and I know I want happiness. I see these goals high on top of the mountain; easily attainable through hard work and dedication. I want to get to the top, and I know that I can. With a solid college education, much life experience, and a positive attitude, I am equipped with the tools I need to get to the peak.

Comments

■ Cornell essay 1 is a fabulous tribute to the candidate's grandfather and how he has shaped her life. The details—everything from the traits of the Vienna hot dog to the details about Grandpa's tooth-shaped drawing pads—help bring this portrait to life and keep the reader entertained and drawn in, wanting to know more and more. Through this essay, we learn about the context in which Liza has developed, and the family myths under which she has been raised. Although the essay focuses on Grandpa, Liza also does a good job of showing how his unique character traits have influenced her and made her into the person she is today.

■ Michigan essay 1 uses an interesting approach to get at the answer to a question for which the university likely receives far too many of the same stale responses. Ultimately, the essay should have offered some more explicit connections with the importance of a college education, but it is generally a solid and compelling piece, which happens to also offer glimpses of Liza's courage, strength, and sense of adventurousness.

ANNE LEE

Notes on her candidacy: While attending a public high school in Maryland, Anne was an avid member of the Bethel Korean Presbyterian Church Youth Group and the varsity field hockey team.

THE UNIVERSITY OF PENNSYLVANIA (THE SCHOOL OF ARTS AND SCIENCES)

1. What characteristics of Penn, and yourself, make the University a particularly good match for you? Briefly describe how you envision your first year in college. How will your presence be known on campus?

" … and folks, it's gonna be another beautiful day here in the City of Brotherly Love—mostly sunny with a high of 74 deg—"

Fumbling for the "snooze" button, my hand reaches blindly towards the clock radio, pushing it closer and closer to the desk's edge until the its falls and crashes to the hard floor with a resounding thud. Stupid gravity. Yawning, I pull my pillow over my head, against my ears.

The sound of approaching footsteps … a muffled voice calls out … "Anne? Anne? What you are you doing still in bed?!?"

"Lemme alone, Zoe," I slur, lazily at the roommate from beneath the pillow. "You know I was up late finishing my paper."

"But Anne, it's almost ten—you're going to be late for your physics class—"

"TEN?!?!?!" OH MY GOSH!!! ZOE, WHY DIDN'T YOU WAKE ME?!?"

"YES!!!! WOOOHOOO—GO QUAKERS!"

Cheers erupt from the stands as the ball slams into the corner of the cage just as the clock runs down to zero. On the field, players raise their hockey sticks jubilantly, and hugs and high-fives abound in celebration over the hard-earned victory. Carrying my notebook and a small tape recorder, I make my way through the crowd, dodging fans and players, until I finally reach the scorer.

"Hi! I'm Anne Lee and I'm here from the Daily Pennsylvanian to cover the game. Congrats on the goal—that was some shot! Do you have any thoughts on today's win?"

"Thanks. I think the team played really well today. Our passing was—hey, are you the Anne Lee who wrote that article about Shakespeare in Highball? That thing was hilarious—I could not stop laughing. The line about Prospero was classic …"

"Anne! Over here! I'm open!"

Pivoting to the right, I quickly release the Frisbee and cringe as my pass is intercepted by an opposing player who flings it into the endzone for a goal

"Billy, I thought you said you were open," I ask my teammate.

Billy shrugs, "Sorry, I didn't see that guy coming."

"Yeah, well, you never 'see that guy coming.' … hey, find me a substitute—I've got to get to the museum before it closes."

"The Rodin?"

"No, the Philadelphia Museum of Art. There's this new exhibit on Surrealism that I want to see."

"Have fun then. Will you be back in time for the Bible study tonight?"

"Hey, what happened to your clock radio? Is it supposed to have all these cracks in it?"

"Um, it's a long story, Noah, happened months ago … I'm starving—let's eat." I open the paper bag and a smell unlike any other pervades the air: the delicious scent of hot, greasy, genuine Philly cheesesteaks. A collective "ooh" escapes from the hungry lips of my friends as the sandwiches are passed around. We sit scattered about the room, a diverse group of different individuals brought together by a love for unhealthy midnight snacks.

"Stop dripping stuff all over the floor!"

"I wish we had cheesesteaks like these back home in China."

"I think I've gained twenty pounds so far."

"You all are so weird … where did the admissions people find you guys?"

"Hola, me llamo Ana. Estoy estudiante de primer ano …"

I sit at the computer, typing away in virtual conversation at PennMoo. *Professor Hernandez was right; this is a cool way to practice Spanish.*

I glance at my watch. *Fifteen minutes until my freshman seminar starts—I'd better check my e-mail now.* Logging on to my account, I come across a message from my little brother:

"Hey, this is Matt … just wanted to say 'hi' … school's fine, got an A on my math test. . . thanks for sending me that Upenn sweatshirt … Mom and Dad want to know how you're doing … write back."

Quickly, I type up a reply: "Hi Matt, I got your e-mail … nice job on the test … so glad you like the shirt. I'll send you some shorts, too … tell everyone I'm doing great and that I miss them … and tell Mom and Dad not to worry too much about me—I LOVE IT HERE …"

Comments

■ Anne's Penn essay 1 was a favorite among the admissions staff for obvious reasons. She showed not only that she had done her research on the school, but also that she is a real "do-er" who will contribute actively to campus life. The essay is imaginative and demonstrates that Anne has spent time thinking about the realities of college life and picturing what her future will bring. She clearly put a lot of time and effort into this essay (which cannot be used for any other school) and evidenced a high level of enthusiasm for Penn in the essay as well.

SUSAN ROY

Notes on her candidacy: From a Massachusetts working-class background, Susan is most interested in pursuing a career in the sciences through Dartmouth's "Women in Science" program.

DARTMOUTH COLLEGE

1. See Common Application question (option 1).
(Essay also used in applications to Amherst, Bates, Bowdoin, Middlebury, Mount Holyoke, and Swarthmore.)

This past summer I went on a school trip to Ecuador. My trip to Ecuador included some of the most wonderful experiences in my life: my first visa, my first time being surrounded by another language, my first time trying different foods, and my first time being immersed in another culture. All of these new experiences were exciting, but the most worthwhile part of the trip was an unexpected lesson in gratitude.

For the first five days of the trip we stayed at Siempre Verde, a scientific research center in the cloud forest. Our days at Siempre Verde were filled with lectures on all aspects of the Cloud forest ecology, hikes through machete cut paths, and vegetation identification projects. In between our daily activities, we would relax at the research center with Edwin and Junior who were two young boys whose mother, Maria, worked in the kitchen. Everyone enjoyed their company. I especially loved talking to the boys, since they were always the most forgiving of my slightly awkward pronunciations. Therefore, on our final day at Siempre Verde we put together a gift for the boys. We had some leftover school supplies from the supplies we raised to donate to a nearby school, so we took the remaining two beginner's reading books, a coloring book, and a pack of markers to give to Maria.

Three of us crowded into the doorway of the kitchen where Maria stood preparing empanadas for that night's dinner. When Maria came over to ask if we needed her help. We handed over the small gift and explained in Spanish that it was a gift for her sons. As Maria took the present into her hands, her eyes filled with tears and the other two women who also worked in the kitchen ushered Maria out the back door giving the three of us friendly smiles.

At first I was shocked by Maria's unusual expression of gratitude. Then I began to think about what had caused me to be so surprised. I realized that I was shocked, because I was not accustomed to seeing a person react so appreciatively for a small gift. Maria's reaction made me think of all the small gifts I have taken for granted over the years. The fact that Maria was so shocked to receive a present for her children was as tragic as the fact that I was shocked to receive such gratitude.

Maria forced me to remember all those half-filled-in coloring books sitting in my attic at home. Since my grandmother always bought me a new 99 cent jumbo coloring book as a reward for behaving while we were grocery shopping, I had never thought about not finishing every page. I always appreciated being able to go to a bookstore and splurge on a new book to add to my bookshelves at home, but tended to forget about the library card that lies buried in the depths of my wallet, allowing me to borrow any book imaginable. Maria made me realize all of the privileges and opportunities I have taken for granted in the past. Since my trip, I have become more appreciative for the smaller gifts in life. One way I do this is by keeping a gratitude journal. Each night before bed I write five reasons I have for being thankful. In an effort to not be redundant, I have forced myself to think about everything I had never appreciated before. Now I don't need a person like Maria to remind me to be appreciative for the gifts my grandmother gives me or even for the public library system. I no longer take for granted even the most basic parts of my life and for this I can thank Maria, who helped me open my eyes.

COLBY COLLEGE

1. Describe your hometown.

Plainville, Massachusetts. Unheard of to even the people of the surrounding towns, yet it is the place where my parents were raised and the place where they choose to bring me up. It is not the most exciting town, but maybe that is exactly what makes Plainville so special. The speed limit for most streets remains at a residential 25 miles-per-hour. Plainville House of Pizza ranks as one of the finer restaurant facilities. The local newspaper is filled with eye-opening articles about the daily activities of local elementary school children. Every child in the town has learned to play either baseball or softball on the fields of Plainville Athletic League, affectionately referred to as the P.A.L. by the locals. Although Plainville has made some changes over the years (including the arrival of our very own post office and library), it has remained consistent enough to keep the same small-town feeling my parents grew up with thirty years ago.

Through growing up in Plainville, I have learned the community values of friendliness, honesty, and helpfulness. Where I live when you see people walking their dogs down the street or when you see a neighbor outside mowing their lawn, it is almost a requirement to greet them with a short hello or at least a smile and wave. When visiting my friends in other towns it seems that only people over fifty will return your greeting without a disturbed expression. I have also learned to expect honesty from people. In Plainville, it is custom to use the honor system when selling items from your front yard, as my brother did last summer with his night-crawler business. I have heard, however, that in other towns people would be more likely to take the can of money and leave the worms, rather than taking a container of worms and leaving some money. People in my neighborhood are not only honest, but also helpful. A few weeks ago, our neighbors, Jack and Chris, were sick with the flu so we brought them some bottled water to drink, brought in their mail, and offered to run to the pharmacy if they needed any sort of medications. For my family this was no trouble, yet once they were feeling better Chris came over and gave us this beautiful painting she painted as a thank you gift for being so neighborly. From my experiences of growing up here, I have learned to live by the community principles that make Plainville such a wonderful town.

Comments

■ Dartmouth essay 1 is very effective for many reasons. Although Susan is from a working-class family and thus has no need to defend a privileged existence, she shows that she is still grateful for all that she has. The story does double duty because it talks about one of the applicant's personal traits, but also lets the committee know the valuable way in which she spent her summer, incorporating the scientific component that relates to her expressed career interests. The conclusion of the essay is effective in that Susan provides evidence—through the discussion of the gratitude journal she writes in each evening—that the experience described here indeed has had a lasting impact on her. This ending makes the story that much more meaningful and Susan's claim of the Ecuador experience's impact on her that much more believable.

■ Colby essay 1 is saturated with detail (the House of Pizza, her brother's night crawler business), which makes it a wonderful read. Readers cannot help but feel as if they know who the applicant is and what her values are from learning about her hometown of Plainville. Susan was wise to realize that by praising the lifestyles and ways of her small town, she was forging a "fit" between herself and Colby, located in the small town of Waterville, Maine. If she had declared frustration over her community's ways of life, she would have caused the admissions committee to believe that their school was not an appropriate match for her.

NICOLE PETERSON

Notes on her candidacy: Raised in Elkhorn, Nebraska, Nicole was especially involved in dance activities and instruction, the National Honor Society, her student leadership team at church, and the Japanese Club; in addition, she worked about 25 hours a week.

STANFORD UNIVERSITY

1. Attach a small photograph of something important to you and explain its significance.
(The attached photograph is a silhouette of a woman's profile, presumably the applicant's own.)

Rhinoplasty. The word alone conjures up images of large prehistoric beasts and horned pachyderms, and for most people who know it by its common name—nose job—it produces pictures of spoiled prima-donnas and aging debutantes. Well, I'm proof enough that the images created by mere words have nothing to do with the real experience.

Since I was eight years old, I have harbored an intense hatred of as well as an enormous shame for my appearance for one reason: I had an imperfect nose. It was a bit too large and a lot too dramatic for my otherwise acceptable face. I didn't see it as slightly imperfect, however; I saw it as a reason I wasn't worthy to be just like everybody else. I begged my parents to fix it; every time Santa asked what I wanted for Christmas I answered with "rhinoplasty please." Santa never followed through, but my parents promised that one day they would.

My behavior was greatly affected by my distorted image of my face. When standing in a room, I could always be found in a corner, at the only place where I could see everyone, and no one could get a straight profile view of my nose. When walking past a window or room where people could catch a glimpse of my nose, I'd fake a cough or sneeze as an excuse to cover my hideous birthmark; or else I would turn my face the other way altogether, to spare onlookers from the monster I believed I was.

I was terrified to meet new people or enter a new situation because I always felt inferior to them and the way they looked. I was a bossy and self-centered child because I felt the need to demand any respect I could from my classmates, since my face couldn't win their instant admiration. I didn't understand then that my few friends didn't even notice my nose except when I pointed it out to them. It wasn't until early adolescence that people began noticing it on their own.

In middle school I found a set of pictures a classmate had drawn during study hall. One was of a tall, thin girl with a horrendously mal-proportioned nose. My name was scrawled across the top. I showed it to him and laughed to appear indifferent to his criticism, but then I went to the bathroom and cried out my pain to my friends. In the ninth grade a teacher told me my friends should call me Jimmy Durante. I just smiled because I didn't get it. When I went home and looked him up in the encyclopedia, I understood. The picture next to the small bio was that of a man with a big, ugly nose.

On June 8, 1994, at the age of fifteen, my greatest wish to date was finally granted. My large, hideous nose was replaced with a magnificent, flawless, new model.

I fully understand that the nose should have no effect on my personality, but it does. It gives me the confidence and self-acceptance I need to enjoy life. Society places so much emphasis on appearance and perfection that it is virtually impossible to grow up, even a little bit, without feeling a need to be flawless. My nose experience taught me compassion and sympathy for people with many problems, physical or otherwise.

In a dance class I teach, one little girl has a defect in her shoulder that makes a bone stick out and form a bump on the front of her upper arm. Because of this bump she will never remove her T-shirt during class. When forced to, she points out the flaw to everyone, so they won't first notice it themselves. She appears indifferent to their "eewws" and "yucks," but I understand how much it truly hurts her. I identify with her because I can still feel the pain of rejection for not being pretty.

I hear people talk about plastic surgery with superior scorn, saying they'd never resort to such superficial nonsense, but, ironically, these people are usually very attractive. I didn't do this so I could be prom queen or win a Miss American title. I did it so I could walk into a room and stand anywhere I want to, and people would notice me, not my nose.

Comments

▧ This Stanford essay is a real winner. Nicole went out on a limb and took a huge risk—one that most applicants could not have pulled off. The essay is extremely well-written, laugh-out-loud funny, and a bit cynical as well. The author shows that she knows as well as the next person that she should not be praised for having undergone plastic surgery and that she realizes all too well what this stigma suggests about her. Nicole's discussion of superficiality and her inability to cope with a lack of beauty is intelligent and honest—she takes some responsibility for her unhappiness rather than blaming it all on society, which is refreshing. She knows herself so well and delves into the topic with such insight that it is soon clear that she does not fit the "nose job" stereotype and that she in fact has gained life lessons from both her original state and the effects of her surgery. The details she provides about how she used to maneuver her body in order to avoid the gaze of others as well as the descriptions of others' taunts add depth and believability to her saga. This is a truly remarkable essay.

ATUL JOSHI

Notes on his candidacy: Having attended a competitive public high school in New Jersey, Atul played the trombone in the marching and jazz bands, was a co-captain of the debate team, played varsity tennis, and attended various programs such as the Governor's School of Public Issues and the National Young Leaders Conference. He now attends the University of Pennsylvania as a member of its Huntsman Program for the study of international relations and business.

YALE UNIVERSITY

1. Please write an essay about an activity or interest that has been particularly meaningful for you.

Not many people can see beyond my stern face as I gaze forward into the stands of my high school football field. I plan my next move on an image of the field that is etched in my brain. It is half time, but I am not in the locker room reviewing a football play. Rather, I remain on the field fulfilling one of my most important high school commitments: marching band. To many, the marching band is but an odd assemblage of out-of-shape "band geeks." However, in eighth grade, weighing this stereotype against my interest in the trombone, I signed up for marching band with some reservations. In retrospect, joining the band is one of the best decisions I have ever made.

Often, individuality is seen as the only way to express yourself. The marching band serves as a counterexample. Although we wear the same uniforms and must exercise utmost precision in each formation, our uniformity is essential to our function: entertaining the crowd. Likewise, the strict uniformity of marching band has taught me to recognize that I have a responsibility to a larger entity than myself. For instance, as Section Leader this year, I would gather my entire section in a circle before each rehearsal or performance in order to emphasize key areas of concern, including proper musical tone and balance. No matter how insignificant these team-building and review sessions may sound, in practice, they have tremendously boosted the quality of our performances.

One unique aspect of our marching band is that our director chooses not to compete at band events. Rather, we perform in the "exhibition" category. At first, I felt it was ridiculous to perform but not compete, especially because our band commands a great deal of respect in the region. By removing competition from our agenda, however, our director is able to create riskier and more appealing shows. Thus, my involvement in marching band challenges me to work for nobler causes than medals and prizes: in this case, it is for the sheer pleasure of knowing that the audience has enjoyed our performance and appreciated our effort.

In addition, marching band enriches my appreciation for music through the added dimension of precision choreography. With each position mapped out on an intricate grid of a football field, it seems unlikely that a fifty-page book of positions we must memorize can ever evolve into a beautiful art form. Yet, as we integrate the music with our movement, we express the emotions felt by those whose works we are performing. Our shows have complex structure that follow a story line. The challenge is to communicate this story to our audience with our music and movements. Thus, we are the vehicle that carries a set of instructions and calculated movements into a dynamic display for the spectators to enjoy.

The impact marching band has had on me is not confined to the playing field. Since most aspects of my high school career are somehow related to competition, it is refreshing to know that non-competitive activities are just as enjoyable and rewarding. Marching band has also taught me to respect those I work with, to recognize that leadership does not imply superiority, and to constantly strive for excellence. Finally, I have forged many strong friendships with members of the marching band. These friendships are based on not only a common interest but also a common experience—an experience that has contradicted all of the stereotypes that had originally daunted me.

THE UNIVERSITY OF PENNSYLVANIA
(THE SCHOOL OF ARTS AND SCIENCES AND THE WHARTON SCHOOL)

1. (For application to the Huntsman Program in International Studies and Business): Discuss your interest in international studies and business. How might this degree program in liberal arts, language, and business help you to meet your goals?

Friends sometimes ask me, "Atul, how can you possibly be so sure of doing this program? What if you don't like business or Spanish?" In other words, why limit oneself to such a focused program when the purpose of college is to obtain a broad education? However, my friends' opinions reflect a common misperception: I do not view the Huntsman Program as an obstruction to my pursuit of a balanced education; rather, this seemingly rigid structure actually provides the "best of both worlds." Not only will I have the opportunity to enroll in an undergraduate business program whose caliber is second to none, but I will also have, through Penn's manifold liberal arts offerings, the freedom to pursue other interests.

Granted, in spite of the options that are sure to exist, I cannot possibly enroll in the IS&B program without being committed to a career in business. As a boy of nine, I would reach for the Business section of the *New York Times* while my older brother reached for the Comics section of the *Sunday Record*. Since then, this initial interest has grown into a passion for me: I have been fascinated by the dynamics of the global economy and the intricacies of business. Consequently, I plan to seek formal education in this vast field.

While I read the *Economist* and other periodicals at leisure because of my interest in geopolitics and business, my most significant formal education in this topic came this past summer, perhaps my most defining summer to date. At New Jersey's Governor's School for Public Issues, I enrolled in a course entitled, "Global Village or Global Pillage? Globalization, Economic Development, and Democracy in the Changing World." With fundamental principles of economics in mind, we examined the effects of globalization on various areas of the world, studied economic development theories and growth models, and attempted to prescribe remedies for each situation. In doing so, I came to understand the complex difficulties of setting economic policy for different countries and realized the ramifications of poor economic planning.

What I found most interesting through the study of various development models is that, in the end, each one had to be tailored to the culture of the particular area. In realizing this, I understood why policy-makers must keep this in mind when they seek to improve a given economy. At Penn, as I continue my studies of the Spanish language, I will be securing what I consider to be the essential complement to my studies of economics. There are, indeed, many rewarding aspects of the program's interdisciplinary approach. The Huntsman Program's foreign language, study-abroad, and internship components will give me the tools to run a successful business abroad or plan viable economic policy for Spanish-speaking countries.

Nowhere else can I develop my interests in international studies and business so fully and completely as I can through the Huntsman Program. The joint-degree program will not only challenge me to continue to set high goals for myself and help me pursue my current interests, but also develop new interests along the way and make the most our of my college years.

2. What characteristics of Penn, and yourself, make the University a particularly good match for you? Briefly describe how you envision your first year in college. How will your presence be known on campus?

Living in a rather small town, I sometimes feel I am missing out on many valuable opportunities, and I long to get "closer to the action." Penn, with its broad range of opportunities and its urban setting, appeals to my interests. I expect myself to contribute to and gain tremendously from the fabric of Penn and its communities. As a student, I consider it imperative to gain experience in various disciplines, and the ability to enroll in courses at Penn's different schools, even outside my intended field, supports my philosophy. Yet, my efforts at Penn will certainly not be confined to academics. The abundance of resources at Penn will be of utmost benefit to me, as I am a person of many interests.

Though I have never seen Penn's musical ensembles perform, friends currently attending Penn have attested to their formidable quality. After downloading soundclips from Penn's website, I became particularly interested in the marching band. Aside from its obvious musical dimensions, high school marching band has instilled in me certain values and leadership qualities that I apply to other activities. By playing trombone in Penn's marching band, I will be pursuing not only my love of music, but also the leadership experiences that I know will help me face challenges and tackle problems.

Another rewarding aspect of Penn is its great diversity. I will be in a setting in which people of different origins have the chance to come together, learn from each other, and commit themselves to the rewards of multiculturalism. At the same time, I feel that in my high school years, I have not been able to develop stronger bonds between myself and others of Indian heritage. Through groups such as Rangoli (IAP) and the South Asia Society, I will be a part of a community that strives to learn and teach others about Indian cultures and works to keep them alive in the United States, an often daunting yet extremely worthwhile task.

Despite the vibrant atmosphere of Penn, I would be remiss if I did not mention a major concern of mine: the contrast between Penn's campus and Philadelphia's struggling underclass. Having recently worked with underprivileged children in the economically depressed Red Bank, New Jersey, I have a new-found devotion to working with and teaching the young. In addition, my experiences with the elderly at Sunrise Assisted Living heightened my awareness of the growing need to address the problems of this often neglected part of our population. The satisfaction of knowing I have touched and influenced the life of someone speaks more to me than medals and awards. Community involvement, in my high school years, has been a major source of my happiness and pride, and I look forward to continuing serving those in need through Penn's volunteer programs.

In my search for a broad range of experiences, I have learned that there is no substitute for dedication, focus, and teamwork. I will bring this understanding to Penn and get involved in areas which currently interest me, such as Penn's musical groups, cultural organizations, and community service programs. My goals, however, must not be limited in scope: I will not keep myself from finding new passions which are bound to arise in the coming years. My various encounters at Penn will continue to fuel my aspirations, shape my future, and define myself as an individual.

3. You have just completed your 300-page autobiography. Please submit page 217.

The cushion hissed as I sat on the bench in my living room. I placed my dry hands on the smooth, plastic keys of my piano, my fingers pressing down to produce a random sequence of notes. In these notes I heard the dissonance in my life. I touched my cold hands to my face and thought of the sorrow-filled wake I had just attended for my piano teacher, Mrs. Formoe. Why was I in the living room? Shouldn't I have simply gone to bed and hoped things would be better the following morning? Despite these thoughts, I instinctively opened a book to the last piece Mrs. Formoe had taught me: Frederic Chopin's "Prelude," Opus 28, Number 4.

Mrs. Formoe, my teacher for seven years, died October 13, 1994 of malignant melanoma. When I had first begun taking weekly piano lessons, I would practice right before she arrived, merely seeing piano lessons as a burden. Only after her passing would I thoroughly grasp the importance of the lessons, during which Mrs. Formoe was letting me discover my own self through music. I would continue to practice and refine my technique, but it took her death to make me understand why I loved playing piano so deeply.

Memories of Mrs. Formoe flooded my mind as I eyed the music for Chopin's "Prelude." I proceeded to take my standard posture, arching my fingers and keeping my elbows above the keyboard. As my right hand formed a perfect octave and played the first two solitary notes of the piece, I remembered Mrs. Formoe's story about how Chopin had composed his famous preludes in a state of depression; I could now understand the depression that went into the creation of this piece. The pulsating, rubato chords began the song and developed in to variations. With each driving beat the pain I felt increased until it reached its apex as the music rose to a powerful climax, the fury of the notes becoming one with the fury inside me. The pain then subsided as the song slowed to the softest, most tender ending I had ever played. For the first time in my life, I experienced the catharsis music can give.

After the night I played that piece, the night I realized the emotional releases music can bring, my passion for music has continued to grow. It has brought great rewards, rewards that go beyond trophies and good grades, rewards such as the magical smiles on the residents' faces as I played them Duke Ellington's "Mood Indigo" at a home for the elderly, or the memories a custodian at the Governor's School recalled as he heard me play Gershwin's "Rhapsody in Blue" on an out-of-tune piano in the grand hall of Woodrow Wilson's "Summer White House." Such is the true splendor of music—how it helps me communication with both myself and others.

Although I enjoy my school subjects, I have never fathomed the complexities of any subject so profoundly as I have with music. The very notion that a precise science of pitch, rhythm, and meter can mesh so beautifully with emotion and soul moves me each time I sit down to play. Through the piano, I find solace in deepening my joys and enduring my frustrations, knowing I can always find a piece that will help me express my emotions. There is no greater pleasure than to leaf through my collection of music and find a piece that "grabs" me because it reflects my mood. Though I sometimes regret that it took her death and the night of her wake for what Mrs. Formoe tried to instill in me to manifest itself, there exists this hope inside me, the hope that a day will come when she will hear me play and realize the impact she made on my life. I will always be grateful to her for showing me how to love and appreciate the piano and the language of music. Beyond the lasting beauty of music, she revealed to me the lasting beauty of reaching out to others and understanding myself.

DUKE UNIVERSITY

1. Why do you consider Duke a good match for you? Is there something in particular you anticipate contributing to the Duke Community?

In my search to find a college that will best complement my interests and expose me to new experiences, I find Duke to be a particularly good fit. After attending New Jersey's Governor's School for Public Issues last summer, I came to realize the manifold benefits that stem from teamwork and cooperation. I look to thrive socially and intellectually through Duke's FOCUS initiative and "small group learning experiences." Having worked with underprivileged children as well as the senior citizen community, I understand how such experiences are of mutual benefit to myself and the community I serve. For this reason, I intend to actively participate in Duke's volunteer programs. Academically, I am interested in Duke's certificate program in Markets and Management Studies, which will help me pursue my interests in business and law. Through Duke's extensive study abroad program, I will be able to continue my studies of Spanish at a school in Madrid and possibly take other courses related to my major at the London School of Economics and Political Science. At Duke I will also continue my contributions to areas which currently interest me, such as Duke's musical ensembles and cultural organizations. At the same time, I will not limit myself to these activities, because new interests are bound to arise in the coming years. Duke's study abroad, FOCUS, and community service components will serve as springboards for fueling my aspirations, shaping my future, and defining myself as an individual.

2. Consider the books you have read in the last year or two either for school or for leisure. Please discuss the way in which one of them has changed your understanding of the world, other people, or yourself.

Over the summer, amidst the plethora of assigned summer reading for my Advanced Placement English class, I decided to re-read Robert J. Serling's *Legend and Legacy: The Story of Boeing and Its People.* In 1991, I had the opportunity to tour Boeing's massive plant at Everett, Washington, and since then, my passion for airplanes has reached incredible proportions. The visit prompted me to write Boeing a letter thanking them for the tour of their facilities; I also expressed my interest in learning more about airplanes and asked them to assist me in this endeavor. To my surprise, they sent me a free copy of Serling's four hundred seventy-page book. After reading it the first time I gained a better understanding of the aviation business, including the dynamics of selling and marketing airplanes. In addition, I learned more about management, teamwork, the role of unions, and several other issues that interest me. Reading the book for the second time, however, I was able to better appreciate the stories of the people behind Boeing's seventy-five year history. The book showed me that it was more than "plane maker to the world." After my second reading, I was particularly touched by stories of how Boeing coped with hard times. For instance, Boeing's management decided to diversity into the dairy industry and also built trains for Boston's rapid transit system during the 1970's. The degree of dedication and personal sacrifice, ingenuity, and determination have taught me what it takes to succeed not only in business but also in life. In this way, despite the seemingly limited scope of *Legend and Legacy*, this chronicle has had a tremendous impact on me.

Comments

- Yale essay 1 is very successful. Not only does Atul show the valuable way in which he utilizes his talents and spends his time, but he also expresses intellectual and personal values. Atul provides a unique discussion of how the marching band encourages a certain positive brand of conformity rather than individuality and shows his sense of responsibility to a group or a team. He also demonstrates immense school spirit, always desirable to admissions committees.

- In Penn essays 1 and 2, as in Duke essay 1, Atul really demonstrates that he knows a lot about the programs to which he is applying and shows that he is a good fit with them. He does so through discussing both academic and nonacademic pursuits. He shows that he has clear goals, which is especially important for anyone applying for admission to a specific dual-degree and/or non–liberal arts program as an undergraduate, and expresses that his interests in international policy and business have been developed over a long period of time.

- Duke essay 2 is valuable in that it further supports Atul's positioning as a future business leader. In order to counteract any tendencies toward seeing him as a stereotypically "insensitive" business type, though, the applicant chose to incorporate a discussion of his interest in the *people* involved in the story and the social ramifications of Boeing's operations.

APRIL LEVIN

Notes on her candidacy: April, a graduate of a competitive private East Coast high school, is an extremely accomplished gymnast and science student who received 1600 on her SAT I exams. She now attends Brown's very selective Program in Liberal Medical Education (PLME), an eight-year undergraduate and medical school program.

MASSACHUSETTS INSTITUTE OF TECHNOLOGY

1. Make up a question that is personally relevant to you, state it clearly, and answer it.
Discuss an experience that has had a significant impact on your life. What did you learn from this experience?
(Essay also used in application to Brown.)

Flipping backwards is a dangerous feat. But I am a gymnast, and I learned how to do that trick with two twists added because every time I landed it I got a higher score from the judges and a tremendous sense of achievement. In gymnastics, landing on your feet instead of your head is a huge accomplishment.

Last year, I missed badly. One foot landed and the rest of me kept twisting. I heard a snap in my knew and collapsed onto the blue floormat. At the hospital, I was diagnosed with a completely torn anterior cruciate ligament. I would need reconstructive surgery. I was devastated that I would miss the rest of the season in gymnastics, but glad the doctors would be able to fix my knee for me. I took the soonest date available to have the surgery. The sooner I had it, the sooner I could start on the path to recovery, and I was willing to do anything necessary to recover quickly.

At the time of my injury, I was taking an independent class in sports medicine, a subject that had interested me even before my fall. After hurting my knee, I decided to become my own lab experiment. I studied the knee and the ACL in depth, and used my time at the doctor's office and at physical therapy to ask questions that my anatomy book could not answer. I read the posters on the wall at the doctor's office about bones and muscles and ligaments and how they worked. I studied my own x-rays and MRI. When the time came for my surgery, I asked the anesthesiologist if I could stay awake and watch, since hopefully I would only get to see surgery on my own knee once in my life. He agreed to give me an epidural and phenobarbital so that I would be numb and relaxed, but still awake.

The medicine made me tired, but I forced myself to keep my eyes open because I wanted to see what was going on. I could see the inside of my knee on the screen in front of me, and rather than becoming squeamish, I watched intently. I was proud o myself when could identify the ligaments and cartilage in my own knee that I had seen sketched in textbooks so many times before. I didn't care that there were IV needles in my arms or that I couldn't feel my legs or even that I would basically be attached to the couch for the next week, in too much pain even to sit up without the help of a devoted mom and a lot of Percocet. I was too curious to worry about all that. I spent the entire two hours of surgery asking questions. In this way, I managed to turn a bad situation into a learning opportunity.

My knee healed in four months instead of the six that doctors had predicted. I am now back in competition and preparing to participate in gymnastics at the college level. Although my recovery was physically painful and I would have loved to spend last year improving my gymnastics rather than rehabilitating my knee, what I learned from this injury was far more valuable than any new skill I could have mastered or any trophy I could have won. I learned that I love studying medicine and I want to be a doctor. I realized how much I want to help other people the way my doctors helped me. And I decided that landing safely on my feet is something I should never take for granted.

BROWN UNIVERSITY (Program in Liberal Medical Education)

1. Most high schoolers are unsure about eventual career choices. What factors led you to decide on a career in medicine?

I have always been extremely interested in science, especially that which relates to medicine. Most of the community service projects I have been involved in relate to people with medical problems in some way: I worked with a deaf child in my temple's kindergarten class, taught gymnastics to an autistic child, visited and corresponded with residents of the Boston Home who had multiple sclerosis, and am a board member of Campuses Against Cancer at school. When I tore my ACL, I became very interested in learning about my injury and even chose to watch my own knee surgery. Last spring I set up an independent course in sports medicine which piqued my interest even further.

2. PLME students are expected to pursue the liberal arts portion of their education in both breadth and depth. We know that your nonmedical interests may be unspecified at this point, but if you do have an area of academic interest outside of medicine, please describe this and how you might pursue it within the context of the PLME.

One area that I have a strong interest in is psychology. I have always enjoyed watching people's actions and trying to figure out what they are thinking, consciously or subconsciously. Recently, while I was visiting a friend who also is very interested in psychology, we found ourselves sitting on the floor of her bedroom reading old psychology textbooks. I found myself engrossed in reading as if I was looking at a novel rather than a textbook. Since our school does not offer a course in psychology, we chose to set up an independent psychology course which we will begin next term. I am eagerly looking forward to beginning this course.

Most premedical programs do not require extensive courses in psychology. In the context of the PLME, however, I hope to be able to pursue this subject alongside other medical and non-medical courses. At the very least, learning about psychology would help me relate to all different types of people that I meet every day. Beyond everyday relationships, however, studying psychology could lead me to a career relating to biopsychology, psychiatry, or eventually even brain surgery.

Comments

- ■ MIT essay 1 is wonderfully successful. April takes advantage of the opportunity to discuss two important aspects of her candidacy—medicine and gymnastics—at once. She shows that she's a go-getter, someone who takes advantage of all opportunities for improvement, even to the extent of turning bad situations into positive ones. She also shows that she is brave and adventuresome and "thinks outside of the box."

- ■ Brown essays 1 and 2 make admissions officers confident that the applicant knows Brown and the PLME program well, understands what she is getting into, and is planning for her future. She shows, most importantly, that she is not applying to the PLME program as a security measure—in order to have a plan to fall back on—but because she sincerely wants the opportunity to concentrate in liberal arts education while also acknowledging medicine as her future career goal.

SHARLENE WU

Notes on her candidacy: Sharlene, an immigrant from southern China, attended Thurgood Marshall, a public high school known for its rigorous academics in urban San Francisco. She won and has accepted one of the University of California, Berkeley's coveted Incentive scholarship awards.

THE UNIVERSITY OF CALIFORNIA, BERKELEY

1. What has been your greatest learning experience?

I have learned about myself from every hardship that I have encountered and overcome. I have been in the United States for twelve years. In my third year living in America, my family and I live in a San Francisco neighborhood called Hunter's Point where violence and gangs are virtually outside our door. I vividly remember my first week living in Hunter's Point. Our living room windows were broken and our house was robbed. But, it did not end there. My parents were attacked several times coming home from work. Our car windows were also smashed several times over the course of the year. Out of fear and desperation, my parents restricted my sister and I from going out of the house after 6:00 p.m. Rightfully so, they were afraid for our safety.

I was afraid of the community that I lived in. But, I decided to face my fears by talking and interacting with the people in my neighborhood. Gradually, I discovered that they were no different from other people. They were also victims of violence.

However, not only did I have to fact violence in my community, I also had to struggle with my parents to keep my dreams. They told me that my dream of becoming a doctor was not realistic for their immigrant daughter. "You're not smart enough and you don't have what it takes to become a doctor, so stop dreaming and be something realistic like an accountant or something ..."

It really hurt and confused me that my own parents were telling me to give up on my dreams. It seemed to me that they believed in the stereotypes that this society holds for immigrants. They still believe that their "poor immigrant child" is unlikely to gain entrance to a prestigious university because that is for those who have wealth and power.

At that point, giving up would have been very easy, but I asked myself if that was what I really wanted to do. I said, "No!" There was no way now that I would give up after all the hard work and the hard times.

I realized that to overcome the obstacles I had to motivate myself even more and work even harder than before in school or in the community. I continue to challenge myself to the fullest and seek out opportunities to fulfill my dream of becoming a doctor of medicine. One opportunity that became available to me was an internship at the University of California at San Francisco's Science Educational Partnership 1998 Summer Program. For eight weeks, (from mid June to mid August) I worked in a cancer research laboratory helping to test promising herbal remedies for Ovarian Cancer Cell Lines.

My work at the laboratory was, academically, very demanding and personally, very satisfying because the scientists were employing remedies that are part of the Chinese culture. Because of my dedication to the research the chief researcher, Dr. Karen Smith-McCure gave me the opportunity to develop and find ways of testing my own hypotheses. With her consent and under the supervision of her graduate research assistant, Jim Jackson, I went to Chinatown and interviewed several Chinese herbalists. They told me that, when preparing herbal remedies, time is very important. Some said that in order to obtain the strongest herbal extract, the herbs had to be soaked for one hour in water, others told me to soak the herbs overnight. I took both methods back to the lab and applied each to ovarian cancer cells such as SKOV-3 and HA8. The outcome was fascinating. I discovered that the shorter preparation time produced a better result.

Although research is a long and tedious process, I fell in love with my work. I am proud and fortunate to have contributed to ovarian cancer research. My internship opened new options for me and inspired me to go forward with my dreams. However, I realized that, if I had listened to the stereotypes, I would had never have had the courage to apply for such an intensive and competitive program and would have denied myself a great opportunity. Following my confidence-building summer internship, I got involved with the peer advising internship program in my school. As a peer adviser, I constantly advocate the importance of higher education and the value of early academic preparation; I share with my peers the story of my hardships and how I overcame them; and I encourage them not to give upon their dreams and to apply to wide variety of four-year institutions. I also assist them with their college/university applications and the essay writing process.

I have learned that my dreams can come true as long as I am willing to face the challenges and overcome the obstacles of life. I believe that my persistence in going forward with my education, despite my adversities, will definitely help me to succeed in college. Why? Because I have had to work patiently and deliberately to overcome my own fears and reject the stereotypes. I don't think that I need to be the smartest person in school in order to succeed academically. I am not. But, remembering what my family and I have been through and never forgetting what my main goal in life is (to be a doctor) has allowed me to consistently stay on task. Just like my teachers have at Thurgood Marshall, I think that my university professors will expect me to be mature in managing my own time and keeping up with my work. So, as I prepare to go to college/university, my success at that level will depend on the same values—patience, consistency, persistence, and deliberateness—that brought me through four challenging year sat Thurgood Marshall.

Comments

■ Berkeley essay 1 effectively shares the hardships the applicant has overcome. It does so with a simple and honest portrait of a tough existence; Sharlene does not try to tug at the heartstrings of admissions officers with unnecessary drama or exaggeration. She effectively shows that not only did she have to physically endure the realities of living in an impoverished neighborhood, but she also had to mentally endure the low expectations that her parents had for her. She shows that, though other applicants to Berkeley may have gotten where they are today because it was expected of them, she had to work especially hard for everything she has accomplished. Sharlene also astutely describes her cancer research, incorporating a tie to her Chinese ethnicity through the interesting bit about the trip to the herbalist, and demonstrating her potential through the fact that she has already made her mark in medical research.

LAUREN FOLEY

Notes on her candidacy: A twin from Ann Arbor, Michigan, Lauren is an accomplished trumpet player and was involved in many community service projects.

DARTMOUTH COLLEGE

1. If you yourself were in the position to ask a thought-provoking and revealing question of college applicants, what would that question be? Now that you have asked your ideal question, answer it.

If you had to choose three bumper stickers that express important aspects of who you are and what you believe in, which would you choose and why?

As the Foley family's 1989 Oldsmobile, I have experienced much in my day. Recently, when I became the twins' car, I have come to know Lauren a lot better. I have watched her mature physically, intellectually and emotionally. I have great pride in displaying the creative one-liners which she chooses to exhibit on my bumper. She seems to know these messages serve to formulate a first impression of her. Though some have changed, the following three have endured and currently adorn the rusted chrome above my muffler.

HATE IS NOT A FAMILY VALUE

This is certainly true of Lauren and her family. Often, one can see in a young adult evidence of her upbringing. Lauren respects the diversity of people and their different lifestyles. She passionately opposes those who evaluate situations with closed minds and pass judgments stemming from their own ignorance. Lauren knows how to disagree, how to reject, and how to oppose people and issues with fervor. She can dislike people but does not know how to hate them. Her parents simply left hate out when rearing her. An accidental oversight? Probably not. They preach tolerance, acceptance, respect, compassion, understanding, and freedom of expression. Not hate.

EXPECT MIRACLES

This may sound naive and arrogant to some, but to Lauren it expresses a simple truth. Her definition of a miracle is not found in some media hyped "act of God," but instead in the aspects of her life that are often taken for granted. To "expect," then, is to recognize their existence and not to overlook them. Lauren has been radically impacted by her life-long closeness with the person who once shared her egg. The need not to be perceived as a mirror image has caused her individuality to flourish and contributes to her proclivity for deep friendship and closeness. The gift of twinship has been Lauren's greatest miracle.

Another miracle to her is reflected in the "cosmic intelligence" of a flower growing from a seed that is scattered casually on the ground. She observes a child who becomes a teenager and wonders about the natural instinct that allows one to grow into the other. This is a "miracle." The ability to be sensitive in friendship is not taught by rules, but born from intuition and caring. This gift is a "miracle." If a person emerges from a sea of shallow materialism and expresses his or her opposition to drowning in that sea, then that is a "miracle."

Miracles, then, are the perceptions that anything can and does happen. To expect these phenomena is to respect, to acknowledge and to believe in "miracles."

The last sticker is a curiosity to me, yet it is the most important to her. It has been cemented down with glue as strong as the rivets which hold my own bumper. Its true purpose eludes me, but from my experience with Lauren I think I can penetrate its mystery and hypothesize about its true meaning.

The sticker is all white with a simple blue ribbon floating in the middle. Although the blue is bold, the message is subtle. I see motorists pondering this statement at red lights. They seem to be asking themselves, "How can I be for or against this person on this issue if I don't even know what she is saying?" I have concluded that this is Lauren's whole point. Since there are people who create and maintain their impressions of another based on his bumper stickers, the uncertainty about this final sticker keeps them engaged. Lauren has forced them to keep at least a partially open mind. They now have to meet her to solve this riddle and to establish a valid impression of her.

That is just like Lauren. She'll express herself in a brief introduction while deliberately preventing you from establishing a complete image until you know her. She exhibits a bumper sticker that stands for, "Not all I have to say and not all of what I am can be summarized on the rusted exterior of my '89 Olds."

2. What was the highlight of your summer?

I had always told myself that my goal in life was to help others; this was the chance to test my conviction. In February of my Junior year, I was accepted to join a mission trip to Reynosa, Mexico. Our goal: to build houses by hand for people in need.

Each day we worked side-by-side with Mexican families, building their cinder block houses. The immediate gratification I felt from watching the houses rise compelled me to the building site each day, forgetting the heat, forgetting the exhaustion. Everything I experienced, from the strength of our team work to my own enthusiasm, surprised me. Germans, Mexicans, and Anglos, we couldn't speak each other's words, but we shared a common goal as we worked, house by house, seeking better living conditions for these people. I was so heartened by what I was doing that I volunteered to stay late and continue working, even though the majority of the team had left for the day. Upon reflection I noticed that I was often the only woman volunteer.

I'd seen "Save the Children" commercials on TV, but I'd never been exposed to the poverty I saw in Reynosa. The teenagers with whom I mixed cement and laid cinder block will never be offered the opportunities I have. Many of them will remain illiterate and can, at best, anticipate earning a wage of four dollars a day at the local Magnavox or Zenith factories. I realized that my confident teenage self had been muted, my naiveté dissolved, my appreciation for all I have deepened. These were my sobering gifts of the trip.

Immediately after I returned home, I signed up for Habitat for Humanity to continue the experience I gained in Reynosa. As the summer activities fell into place, I relaxed with friends, worked a pleasurable job, and met new people as I volunteered locally. My physical appearance was the same, but inwardly the memories of what I saw and experienced in Mexico have changed me forever.

Comments

■ Dartmouth essay 1 takes advantage of the school's open-ended "make up your own question" question to show off a real sense of creativity. The question she poses is unique and Lauren does even more with it by narrating her piece from the point of view of her Oldsmobile. This gives her an opportunity to speak more thoroughly about herself without having to say, "I am x, I am y." The three bumper sticker slogans she chooses demonstrate important aspects of her persona, and she uses tangible details to make her case. She tells us that she is strong and opinionated but not cruel; that she appreciates the little things in life; and that she is interested in engaging others—whether they share her views of the world or not—in a dialogue. Her ending is clever: She is essentially stating that she is a complex, multifaceted character who cannot easily be understood on the basis of her bumper stickers, or, in effect, this one essay.

■ Dartmouth essay 2 addresses an ordinary topic—a summer community service project—but is effective in its expression of Lauren's personal skills and values. Lauren further demonstrates her humanity and sensitivity to others here.

AMBROSE FATUROTI

Notes on his candidacy: Ambrose, an African American student from a competitive private high school in the Boston area, played varsity football and basketball, won a nonfiction writing award, and was a counselor and leader at his camp for many years, among other pursuits.

THE UNIVERSITY OF VIRGINIA

1. What work of art, music, science, mathematics, or literature has influenced your thinking, and in what way?

Last fall, I took an African American literature course which led to explore areas of myself which were previously uncharted. I read The Souls of Black Folk by W.E.B. DuBois. In his book, DuBois states a theory he calls "double-consciousness." He proposes that blacks in American are indeed dually-conscious of themselves. He muses on how blacks in America are aware that they are both African and equally American as is implied by the politically correct nametag. Not only does this label imply that blacks are aware of themselves in this way, but it also begins to explain a feeling of confusion. This theory tells of an inner struggle African Americans go through between being grounded in their roots in Africa while still being a part of the mainstream United States. More so, while this classification of African Americans as both African and American exists, an "out of place" feeling will continue to exist among African Americans. The sentiment will be that we are still Africans in American which, though more true for me as I am the first generation born in America from my family, is something African Americans have been trying to move away from. This theory, however complex, has opened doors of understanding in my own life that have decisively shaped my outlook on society today and in years past.

2. Most people belong to many different communities—groups defined by (among other things) shared geography, religion, ethnicity, income, cuisine, interest, race, ideology, or intellectual heritage. Choose one of the communities to which you belong, and describe that community and your place within it.
(Essay also used in applications to Georgetown, Tufts, Wesleyan, and Williams.)

A special community I have been a part of for a significant amount of my life is a seven week overnight camp called Camp Pasquaney. The residents of this community strive, over the course of the summer, to create an atmosphere of trust and to sustain long-lasting friendships among campers and counselors alike. The camp setup is such that each boy lives in a dorm with other boys of his own age. This practice allows campers to grow with each other and foster strong bonds together through living and competing against one another. This competition is focused on pushing campers to be their best as opposed to emphasizing simply on winning. At camp, everyone is relieved of all the over-aggressiveness usually associated with sports and can have fun that is not marred by anyone yelling crudely in the stands. The youngest are 11 and the last year of camp eligibility is 16. The boy is then required to spend one year away from camp to consider how they have changed in their time there. Afterward, if he wishes to return as a counselor and is wished back, he may do so. This exercise creates continuity at camp and really develops a uniquely warm living environment. Being a part of this community for five summers out of my life instead of being home and working was probably one of the hardest decisions I have been faced with in my life. The part of camp that made this decision a bit easier, however, were the powerful bonds forged in five years with the people there. It was truly hard to confront that last summer might have been the last I would spend on that hill overlooking that lake. Though it was difficult to put aside my own personal interests for so many summers, when I look back on that investment of my time, I am thankful I made the decision I did. When I look at where I had come from and the position I am in now, it is clear to me the Pasquaney seeks to enable an environment where boys can go to become upstanding men in society. Because of all that Pasquaney has given me, it is difficult to say that I will not be back to visit some time next summer. Perhaps even being a counselor may be in my future.

Comments

- UVA essay 1 provides a convenient way for the applicant to explore his minority status without resorting to any discussions that suggest he is attempting to gain sympathy for his own experiences of oppression or discrimination. This essay is an intelligent discussion of a classic piece of literature.

- Ambrose wisely utilized UVA essay 2 to demonstrate his passion for and devotion to one of his activities. By discussing the way in which his five-year commitment has shaped him, he is also able to bring up values such as cooperation (as opposed to competition).

AINSLEY SEAGO

Notes on her candidacy: A native of Tacoma, Washington, Ainsley, the owner of a ferret and two black widow spiders, participated in a "Junior Naturalists" class for ten years, took courses in Russian History at the University of Puget Sound, and was an active member of her school's Pep Band. She now attends Cornell's College of Agriculture and Life Sciences.

CORNELL UNIVERSITY (College of Agriculture and Life Sciences)

1. Tell us about a person who has had an important influence on you. What qualities in that person do you most admire, and how have you grown from knowing that person?

As a small child, I was enthralled by insects, snails, and other wild things. I took to collecting bumble-bees, spiders, snakes, and earthworms and went thorough a succession of domestic animals as well, adopting mice, rats, hamsters, and a tarantula. When these failed to satisfy my interest, I was enrolled at the age of eight in "Junior Naturalists," a class at the nearby Snake Lake Nature Center, an urban nature preserve. For two Saturday mornings each month, I explored the natural world under the tutelage of a man who has become my most beloved and effective teacher. John Slipp, retired biology professor and award-winning aquarist, proved to be the ideal font of knowledge for the inquiring youngster, answering my questions for years to come.

In those years, I found that there was much more to nature than bug collections and caged rodents. John showed me how to identify bird calls and answer back. We analyzed the acidity of pond water and collected salamander eggs. We studied plankton from the lake, mounted insects, and became amateur taxidermists. After one full year of Junior Naturalists, a graduation ceremony was held; we were presented with diplomas and green "naturalist jackets." Most of the graduates, older than I, departed satisfied with their year of education and were ever seen again. I stayed, determined to keep coming back until I decided I had learned enough. I came back for another four years of nature study. Graduation was again suggested, with another recognition ceremony and certificates "for outstanding dedication ..." I ignored the hint, continuing to learn to track foxes and spot woodpecker nests. The small group of die-hard young naturalists I belonged to was now in middle school, and John began to drop Latin names.

"Hear that? Can you see the bird? Describe it."

"It's a brown bird, robin-sized, red eyes, orange chest ..."

"That's our native Rufus-Sided Towhee, *Pipillo maculatus.* Related to ..."

"I know this! Uh ... Robin! *Turdus migratoris!*"

We brought in recently collected specimens for show and tell, much to the relief of our mothers, whose freezers had contained dead birds for too many days. Numerous highly scientific experiments were conducted, including the great *How Many Other Fish Can We Put in With the Largemouth Bass Before It Stops Eating All of Them* project and the highly amusing *Aerodynamics of the Frozen Crow* test flights (it's all in the wrist). We ignited swamp gas. We dissected a yellow-bellied sapsucker. We hatched salmon eggs and released the fry into local streams. We counted birds around Snake Lake for the Audobon Society's Annual Bird Count. We cared for ill or orphaned animals brought to the Nature Center by worried homeowners, from a shivering baby opossum delivered in an ice chest to an injured weasel and a two-headed garter snake.

We learned to accept death as both an integral counterpart to life and a gift to the studious naturalist, welcoming every chance to inspect and handle a bird that would have been hopelessly elusive when alive. We treasured windshield-casualty butterflies that we never would have had the heart to euthanize, and many a raccoon that would have gnawed our fingers to bits had it not been frozen quite solid. As he pointed out the fantastic design of a specimen, John was frequently heard to quote Blake's famous poem: "What immortal hand or eye …" We'd chime in, "… could frame thy fearful symmetry."

Now into my tenth year of Junior Naturalism, I still wake up early on Saturdays, looking forward to another episode of nature education with John. I sometimes find myself the only student in attendance. I have begun to take notes, realizing that this class may not continue much longer as my college years approach and John climbs into his eighties. I've learned more from this class than from any other biology course; John has been both a great teacher and a sort of grandfather, combining the wisdom of age with the knowledge of a retired professor. As we've discussed anatomy, whale behavior patterns, bird calls, sea cows, and glaciation, John has not only taught me about natural history but has made a naturalist out of me as well. When I leave for college next fall, I will finally have graduated.

In learning the value of wild things and their habitats, I have become an advocate for conservation of wilderness. I firmly support the Endangered Species Act. I care about manatees and spotted owls. One may call me a tree-hugging, whale-saving nature nerd, but I prefer to answer to the title of Junior Naturalist.

2. Tell us what you would like to study at Cornell. What field(s) of study interest you, and why? How did your interest(s) evolve?

After ten years of examining specimens and spotting wildlife, I've seen most every species of bird and mammal indigenous to the area in which I live. The one taxon that consistently amazes and amuses me is the class Insecta.

I've lived in this city all my life, but it wasn't until last summer that I encountered my first Ten-lined Junebug. I was standing on my front porch looking for moths when I noticed on the doormat, by my foot, the largest beetle I'd ever seen. It was light brown, with white stripes down its back, and as I bent down for a better look, it hissed at me. Hissed! I was taken aback. I'd heard of hissing cockroaches, but this was certainly no cockroach; it had a chubby, fuzzy face, beady eyes, and weird shoehorn-shaped antennae. It hissed again, and I hurried into the house to find a jar.

That Saturday at my nature class, I pulled the jar out of my backpack and presented it to John, the teacher. He squinted at the trapped beetle and pronounced it a *Polyphillus decumlineatus*. Fetching a volume on entomology from the bookshelf, I looked it up and became better acquainted with this monster, the Ten-lined Junebug. According to this book, its hissing was produced by separating and rapidly vibrating the leaf-like layers of its strange, flat antennae. Simply put, this was much cooler than the Big Stupid Garden Beetles (*Caribus hortensis*) that I usually see around my house.

Since then, I've encountered the Pine Sawyer, which is larger by far but hasn't half the charisma of that junebug. I know how to spot ant lion lairs; I've kept water-boatman beetles in aquariums. I've learned a bit about the behavior and identifying characteristics of a number of local insect species, but I still have a great deal to learn about the finer workings of insects. It is for this reason that I would like to study entomology at Cornell's CALS [College of Agriculture and Life Sciences]. After a visit to Cornell and careful study of the Entomology Department's webpages, I am confident that Cornell has a superior entomology program: from Spider Biology to Advanced Coleopterology, CALS offers a better education in entomology than any other school I've looked at. The campus is also patched with and surrounded by green belts and wild places, wherein may be found many a species of insect unseen in the Pacific Northwest. Many of the courses that interest me promise field trips into the local wilderness areas and to collecting sites on and off campus; such opportunities would not exist on an urban campus. In order to eventually build a career in entomology, I see myself learning how insect pests might be deterred from destroying crops without the use of poisons, or which stretch of a forest must be preserved to ensure the continuation of a threatened species of beetle or moth.

Comments

■   Here is a formidable set of essays. They are both well-written and descriptive, and work well together to reinforce themes while also concentrating on different aspects of Ainsley's candidacy. While the first focuses on her interactions with a teacher—the human face of her development—the second focuses on her passion for insects and what she plans to do with that interest in the future.

■   Cornell essay 1 is a beautiful tribute to a teacher who has obviously had a tremendous influence on Ainley's intellectual and personal growth, even though she never says this in so many words. The essay is comical— especially in its descriptions of the experiments Ainsley has performed over the years—and establishes the roots of her long-term commitment to the study of nature. It shows great intellectual enthusiasm outside of the classroom. It illustrates how Ainsley has allowed herself to be shaped by someone else's knowledge, not only on the subject of biology, but also on the subject of life itself.

■   Cornell essay 2 further establishes Ainsley's fervent intellectual endeavors outside of the classroom. The opening of the essay in fact demonstrates that the author sees the entire world as her classroom or lab. Ainsley also shows that she is serious about Cornell and knows exactly what she is looking for in a college.

KRISTINA VELEZ

Notes on her candidacy: Having attended a Catholic girls' school in Miami, Florida, Kristina is accomplished in creative writing (in Spanish and English) and debate.

SWARTHMORE COLLEGE

1. See Common Application question (option 1).
(Essay also used in applications to Amherst, Dartmouth, Haverford, University of Pennsylvania, Reed, and Tufts.)

A plume of smoke emerged from the corner of his mouth, snaking its way across the visage. He took one sip of the black stimulant, casually leaned back, and asked:

"So what's going on in that little head of your, hmmm?

It was just another Friday at the usual franchised coffeehouse.

We sat in silence.

I watched him take a drag off his cigarette, sip his coffee, and hum a few bars from RENT. One year ago I met an individual whose life and words made me completely aware of myself. His name I will not write, so lets refer to him as J.

(When presented with an internal mirror, how many humans truly wish to see what is pooled in their reflection?)

But before I begin recounting my experiences, I would like to make it clear that I have found one thing to be true of those whose lives bend ours in a such a way: they are reflections of what has made them; they bring with them their beliefs, traditions, and ideas from the past, present and future.

It was during a break between postings at a debate tournament in 1997. A small group was meandering outside, wasting away between the cold cement walls and cigarette butts. The chatter consisted mostly of what had been occurring during the tournament and a little weekend gossip. I was introduced to J.

Postings went up in a matter of minutes. I was hitting J.'s team.

As time progressed, causal conversations through e-mail and over the phone established a bond between us. We began to go out during the weekends and I was quickly assimilated into his group of friends. (The cycle of apathy has no beginning nor end …)

T.S. Eliot, Camus, Sartre, Salinger, Heidegger, Andre Norton, Kierkegaard, Mercedes Lackey … These are some of the driving focus behind this tragic romantic. I soon noticed that both of us had indeed taken a large risk upon entering this compact—we were both isolationists, insecure in our manner.

He lived a bitter existence, full of introspection and self-inflicted torment. Neurotic apathy and misery ruled his days. He saw himself as King of Pain, a King of Nothing. Locked behind his facade of indifference, he believed himself to be untouchable.

Others saw J. as an unyielding pragmatist, spending his life with a perpetual cloud of negativity and realism hovering over him. Some described him as a self-centered basketcase on the verge of snapping. All of this King's infantry and horses could not hide the truth from my eyes.

I saw through his walls—partially because they were the same as mine.

(And so began the struggle for identity …)

Underneath the mortar was a need for understanding. Hypersensitive and overly compassionate, J. lived in anguish. He saw a society set on a downward spiral, to which he was utterly helpless in ending. His pain haunted his heart and racked his body.

The strength of the bond intensified as months passed. The level of empathy was clear—we were not afraid to break down in front of each other. Many nights were spent in silence, others were filled with words. We revealed all and were stripped completely naked of our protections.

(I quickly fell into the trap of dreams …)

Questions of no answers and cyclical dialogue became the subject of many late night chats. We worked off of each other and attempted to understand, to finalize, to conclude.

(Forget regret or life is yours to miss … no day but today …)

One day J. brought something to my attention. I exploded his idea, and told him it would be a good idea to follow through. My little optimist streak made this call without thought. J. did it, because his best friend had suggested it, and nothing else.

On that day in May I lost him.

I confess I felt part of me as dead. That aspect of me had been completely uprooted, leaving a bleak wasteland in its place. Ii was empty, and alone.

The few encounters after that spiraled around verbal accusations and anger, and always ended in acrimonious temperament.

I became his scapegoat. I was the excuse, the justification behind it all.

Communication was severed.

Two months later, he wrote me. He apologized indirectly.

He left to college and I would write now and then. The few responses told of manic depression, desperation, and melancholy. I felt completely helpless—I could do nothing to aid this tortured angel.

The misery was now mine.

Approximately one year after our initial meeting, I received a phone call. J. was back in town. We met at the usual place.

"Hey. What's up?"

My knees filled with water, and I felt as if I had been paralyzed. I didn't know how to react.

"Not much. Can I have a hug?"

He stood up.

"Sure."

I fell apart. I couldn't take it. Neither could he. The silence was long, but it was filled with emotion.

The reconciliatory phase has begun.

That is the story of J.

This twisted parallel of me forced me to think about what I had been doing with myself. I saw my obstinancy as a block towards improvement and growth. I would have to reach out to others and stop hiding in order to achieve maturity and realization of self.

His written words I keep in a binder. He was my muse. Through J., I was able to write out everything. his stories made me aware. I let out all my secrets, cast out my demons. I don't blame myself anymore. I don't paint myself as the victim. His music played in my heart and my head.

This was my catharsis.

Our bond is now distant … but alive. He told me to wake up and realize my potential.

I have surrendered to the truth. I have forged my true self.

2. Tell us about one of your extracurricular interests.

My entrance into the realm of debate as a sophomore completely changed my world view. I soon realized that I too could quickly create associations within my own arguments, and challenge anyone to a mental joust. ("Watch out! Here comes the line-by-line on the Topicality debate!") The forced lucidity made me organize my thoughts and prepare my words before they spilled out of my mouth.

Most people would probably accredit debate as the tool which "helped them speak in front of other people and get over their stage fright." While this is a natural side effect of the debate drug, it is the most basic need (without that power of speech, no debate would be able to occur … silence communicates little to strangers with unknown levels of empathy …) rendering that "ability to speak" as an essential tool, and nothing else. Elaborate language, polysyllabic words and persuasion can only go so far … Mind control, anyone? ("Give me hard evidence, then begin to theorize. Rack your brain for the answers. Start on a practical level, and then get esoteric. None of this metaphysical conceit that even you can't understand!"—My response to those who don't really think and just attempt to speak nicely in order to win that ballot.)

Although I have pursued types of debate that require teamwork (team debate and the Florida created Current Issues Debate) I have found that success can only come about as a result of the union of motivated individual efforts. My junior year I attempted to debate with someone who had little interest in the event, and found that I did rather poorly at most of my tournaments, doing progressively worse as the year went on. But I did not care. I was not in it to win, but rather to enjoy every single round of difficult argumentation. It was definitely a great way to get the adrenaline flowing.

Last year I began coaching incoming novices. While never having seen myself as the "teaching" type, I found my patience being tried as I realized that people cannot always follow my train of thought spontaneously. With time, I found different approaches to the instruction of my "kids" (as I soon began referring to all those I coached) and found that success would come, sooner or later. This year I have spent more time working behind the successes of others, and less on my own. I feel a great deal of satisfaction every time a novice runs up to me to tell me about what occurred during a round, or when our actual debate coach congratulates me on the "fruits of my labor." I can only foresee an actual improvement in my own technique as a result of critiquing and observing others' errors.

My next tournament will be my first policy tournament of the year, with a new partner who is also my best friend. I find myself saying, "Who me, worry?" every time someone reminds me that it is only one of the biggest national tournaments of the year. I guess I'll go armed with a smile and my numerous tubs to that little Ivy-wrapped institution in Cambridge and give it my all. ("Here's some prolif coming your way! And some Clinton! And some counter-plans!")

Three years later I have realized that I can let others into the systems of thought in my mind, and that they will listen and see the presentation of my ideas as a challenge. Tournaments allow me to speak to others from outside the intellectually brewed marketplace of ideas. Where else can you find teenagers actually interested in the state of Russian and Chinese relations? Or about biological warfare? Surely not on South Beach …

I will truly miss those rapid neuron and axon connections next year, but I have felt the powerful opiate of debate at its finest. Like an aged wine, debate and its ramifications have left behind casks of uncovered devices … Many years from now they shall be uncorked!

Comments

■ Swarthmore essay 1 is unusual and a bit risky. This is the kind of essay that is apt to be praised by some admissions officers while misunderstood or dismissed as teenage stream-of-consciousness angst by others. The piece is cerebral and shows some intellectual overtones, which help to boost its worth as something other than an excerpt from a high schooler's romance diary. The piece would not have worked but for the eventual parallels drawn between the main character, J., and the candidate herself. College essays are, after all, supposed to be about you, not someone else. Once it is clear that we are meant to see a picture of Kristina in her friend J., the essay takes on much more meaning.

■ Swarthmore essay 2 is a very successful description of a favorite activity. Here, Kristina digs into the heart and soul of debate, extracting everything about the endeavor that makes it attractive to her. Using jargon helps to establish her position as a knowledgeable "insider" to the world of debating. If she was concerned that her lackluster performance during her junior year may affect her shot at college admissions, she did a good job explaining her dip and showing that, despite some minor setbacks, she learned something from the experience. Kristina bolsters her case by demonstrating that she is not only a key participant on the debate team but also a valuable teacher and mentor to newcomers as well.

STEPHENIE PARK

Notes on her candidacy: Stephenie, a Korean American college applicant, is a multitalented musician (she plays the violin, viola, flute, and piano and sings, too) from Illinois.

YALE UNIVERSITY

1. Please use the space on this page to let us know something about you that we might not learn from the rest of your application.

(Essay also used in applications to Harvard and the University of Pennsylvania.)

The South Korea in which my parents were raised was one still deeply rooted in the old tradition. As a result, my parents and their generations grew up with a great pride in their heritage. My family always tried to teach me not only that Koreans were the hardest working and smartest people on the planet, but also that the language and customs were inherently superior. In the face of all these supposed facts, I did what any irrational child would do and rejected my culture.

At the age of five, I attended my first Korean school class. Although I have a bit of talent in picking up languages, I went faithfully for seven more years without ever learning the language. I started out well, listening in class and winning awards for my outstanding performance in class. I reached a time, though, when I no longer wanted to be unique, as my culture made me. I steeled myself against any further knowledge of the language I might have acquired and tried my hardest to forget that which I had already learned. It seems now that I succeeded all too well, because now that I wish I could speak fluently I have lost even the rudimentary comprehension I once possessed.

My rejection of the Asian culture extended far beyond language. I was ashamed of everything we did differently—eating rice instead of hot dogs and using vinegar instead of real bug repellent. My relatives dressed in the bright colors that used to be favored in Korea and I secretly though them senile bag ladies. I became determined to be an all-American girl. I did everything that Asian families disapprove of. Hearing the mothers brag of the wonders of Kuman math and seeing the articles about pre-adolescent Asian math wizards, I decided that I was a bad math and science student and that I hated both. They used to be my strongest areas but are now my weakest. When my family went to the acupuncturist/Oriental herbalist, I refused to let him examine me and poured the expensive medicine down the sink, preferring to rely on pills and men in white coats. If my parents spoke to me in Korean in public, I'd pretend not to understand until eventually, I truly didn't. I shunned all the Asian people I met, particularly Korean people, because I didn't want to be sucked into the odd, and, so I thought, primitive culture.

I am rootless now. I regret my detachment from the Korean culture because I can't go back without admitting defeat, but neither can I truly belong to the Caucasian world. My flat face and straight black hair will always be at odds with my American diphthongs and Celtic music. A part of my lack of definite identity is due to my youth and inexperience, but part of it is a lack of niche in the world. So many people have found that niche with their heritage, but I rejected mine and have nothing yet to fill the void. Perhaps one day I will rediscover the magic of being Korean and find it fits that football-shaped hole in my life perfectly.

Comments

- Yale number 1 is an honest and somewhat painful view into the applicant's feelings on an issue of great importance to her. The essay is especially effective because it admits a failure on the applicant's part and takes a tack that is the exact opposite of what most applicants these days do with their minority status: elevate it and make it a critical "card" in their favor. Rather than showing how she has benefited from embracing her differences, Stephenie lets readers in on the secret that she has in fact not learned all she can from her Korean heritage. In so doing, she lets us know other things about her instead, showing us what has made her "tick" since her childhood.

ANAND KINKHABWALA

Notes on his candidacy: A varsity tennis captain and member of Future Business Leaders of America, Anand now attends the Wharton School at the University of Pennsylvania.

THE UNIVERSITY OF PENNSYLVANIA (THE WHARTON SCHOOL)

1. What characteristics of Penn, and yourself, make the University a particularly good match for you? Briefly describe how you envision your first year in college. How will your presence be known on campus?

This should be pretty easy question for me considering my Cornell Big Red bleeding heart sister has often asked me the same thing. I guess it's okay with me if she wants to live in the middle of nowhere, but I definitely would like to see signs of civilization when I wake up each morning. It's great to know that Philadelphia gives me the option of going to see a show, watching the Mets take on the Phillies, or learning about the culture of one of the country's oldest cities.

Its location in a metropolis is not the only thing that attracts me to Penn, though I don't want to be someone who just goes to college: I want to be someone who does things at college. Heading up a Model United Nations conference is just one of the ways I hope to be involved in student life. Considering how much fun participating as a delegate has been, I would imagine being the Secretary General could only be better. Another thing I have always dreamed of doing is announcing athletic events on the television. I am one of those people who keeps a running commentary on life (if I ever wrote a book, it would be of the "Did You Ever Notice …" variety), so I figure being a color analyst would be the best way to mix this knack for highlighting the obscure with my passion for sports. In my estimation, with a number of squads that finish atop the Ivy League each year, Penn and its UTV 13 is the best place to start.

Above all, though, I realize extracurricular activities and my social life will play a secondary role to my academic life. Since the seventh grade I have religiously followed the market, checking up on my own portfolio as well as other active stocks. Thus, the obvious desire to attend business school, and with Wharton being the best, I naturally know that's where I want to study. The chance to be surrounded by people just like me, people for whom Monopoly was not just a board game but practice for the future, has excited me already. Some people wonder how I have known for so long that I ant to spend time at college taking classes like Personnel Management and Collective Bargaining, but with parents who are 5′7″ and 5′3″ I realize that my gene-pool is going to be prohibitive when it comes to becoming the missing link for the Knicks. In my mind, the next best thing would be having Ernie Grunfield's job. A business administration degree would surely prepare me to be general manager of a professional basketball team, but if the Knicks don't come calling, I'll still have a lot of options. With a Wharton education I can get a job with McKinsey, work for a global trade company in Hong Kong, or even start my own investment banking firm. Whatever I choose, I know that after four years at the Wharton School I will be ready to do anything I want to.

Comments

■ Penn essay 1 is ideal. It is full of personality and humor but also expresses the concrete reasons why Anand wants to and should attend Penn. The introduction about his sister at Cornell is appropriate, because it shows that he can distinguish between Penn and perhaps its most similar rival school. It also shows that the applicant has a mind of his own and has given a lot of thought to the issue of where he will attend college. The discussion of Wharton is intelligent. The candidate also does a good job of throwing out some possible career choices, again adding a pinch of humor to lighten the discussion.

JAIME SINGLEY

Notes on her candidacy: A dancer, soprano in the Chamber Singers, and writer on the school newspaper, Jaime also worked 16 hours a week during the school year while attending Deerfield Academy.

DARTMOUTH COLLEGE

1. Which academic subject is most meaningful to you? Why?

English is the academic subject that is most meaningful to me. I feel that the art of writing is the most powerful tool for personal expression and communication. This year I am enrolled in an Honors Literature course taught by Mr. Thomas-Adams. Mr. T-A pushes me to new creative and intellectual limits with every assignment. We are currently studying the shift form the traditional Victorian narrative to complex modernist texts such as Ford Madox Ford's *The Good Soldier* and Virginia Woolfe's *Jacob's Room*. In doing so, we have examined the impact of World War I on all literature in the twentieth century. It is fascinating to discuss the meaning of collective imagery, dualism, inversion, and satire with other students who show the same appreciation for the novels we read. While I am still contemplating a major in either history or English, I will continue writing in my free time and reading novels by my favorite author, Toni Morrison.

2. If you yourself were in the position to ask a thought-provoking and revealing question of college applicants, what would that question be? Now that you have asked your ideal question, answer it.

(Essay also used in application to Harvard.)

Are you still daddy's little girl?

A monotone buzzing echoed in the distance and my eyes scoured the restaurant to locate the culprit. The word "REMOVE" blinked rapidly above the vat of boiling fries. I began a mad dash towards the fry station, racing to extract the greasy mass and assemble the order on my drive-thru screen before the next car reached my window. As I gingerly placed a Big Mac in a brown paper bag, I narrowly escaped being crushed by two crew members furiously compiling their orders for the multitudes of customers forming lines in the lobby.

Another ringing, this time from the contraption that decorated my head. The clumsy headphones generated the sound of a rumbling car engine. I heard a gruff voice resonate in the drive-thru speaker. "I want two filet-o-fish, a small fry, and a medium coke; that's it." I rattled off the price and directed my latest customer to the second window. By my third year at McDonald's I had memorized the prices of a variety of items and meals, but this combination was new to me. I directed my focus to the bin, spotting the last two filet being eyed by a customer at the front counter. Knowing that it was only seconds before the sandwiches would disappear, I plowed through the masses of workers in front of me. "Out of filet," I shouted back to the grill team, emerging victorious from my quest.

The aroma of fried fish and tartar sauce penetrated my nostrils as I dodged the mop bucket, standing as an obstacle in my return path to the glass windows of the drive-thru station. A familiar face stared at me through the smudged glass shield. Despite a few wrinkles and the absence of hair on his head, I immediately recognized the man whose voice I had not placed. He looked on with an endless gaze that hollowed me from within and I felt slightly relieved when my father did not recognize me. I remembered when my dad used to take me to McDonald's as a young child. Although his order stayed the same, I reminded myself that this was not the same man I had once shared my fries with. Alcohol had transformed him.

My father had been absent for the majority of my life. He had not been there three years earlier when I first entered the shimmering glass doors of McDonald's clutching a job application in my hand in an effort to help my single mother support two children. He had not been there when I became the youngest manager on the staff at seventeen years old. He had not been there when I chose survival over accepting failure, when I learned from his mistakes, nor when I refused to submit to his example. My father had not been a witness to all those small successes that proved any dream attainable and prepared me for my current academic endeavors at Deerfield Academy and those beyond.

I opened the electronic window with a swift gesture of my hand. Trading the precisely creased brown bag for five crumpled dollar bills, I heard the words tumble from my lips, "Thank you and have a nice day." I closed my eyes for a moment until the rumbling of the car engine was nothing more than a dull whisper. A last glance through the foggy glass windows confirmed by suspicion that only a void remained on the other side. I took a step backward, into my world of congested paths and the constant buzzing of timers. With years of experience behind me, I navigated my way around the mop bucket that had previously hindered my course and directed my attention to the daunting lines of ravenous customers in the lobby.

Comments

- Dartmouth essay 1 does a good job of talking about the applicant's interest in English literature and writing in an intelligent fashion, incorporating some relevant details to focus the discussion and make her passion believable.

- Dartmouth essay 2 is fantastic. The question that Jaime poses (clearly written after she had composed the essay, and meant only for herself—not a question she would ask every applicant, boys included) immediately makes readers wonder what the essay will be about. The suspense builds as we read the story and see no sign of a discussion of family or father figures. Jaime makes her point—that her father has not been part of her life because of his alcohol problem—by stating it plainly and painting around the critical issue rather than dramatizing it or asking for our sympathy. While describing scenes of family violence or parental alcoholic stupors can be an effective way of telling this kind of story, Jaime's approach is equally if not more effective. The details about being a McDonald's shiftworker help us to feel what her position there is like and how hard she has worked at a job some would call "pointless" in order to help support her family. She deftly includes relevant details—becoming the youngest shift manager, breaking her back to hold down a job and attend Deerfield at the same time—that clarify her fortitude and goal-oriented nature. The ending of the essay is a nice metaphor and forces readers to think a bit more about what the candidate's father stands for in her life.

RACHEL PERSCHETZ

Notes on her candidacy: President of her school's chapter of Students Against Drunk Driving (SADD), secretary of her class, and an avid squash player, Rachel has always been interested in events planning and entertainment administration.

CORNELL UNIVERSITY (College of Hotel Administration)

1. Tell us what you'd like to study at Cornell. What field(s) of study interest you, and why? How did your interest(s) develop?

Like the proverbial "kid in a candy store," I was completely overwhelmed and excited by the Cornell undergraduate course catalogue. Before my visit, I had been positive (well, pretty sure) I wanted to study hotel administration, but once I actually visited the campus and got a better look at the course offered, my mind was made up. The instant my family and I got in our car after our admission session, I eagerly began poring over the piles of literature I had collected. By the edge of Collegetown, I had not only declared by desire to attend Cornell and the hotel school, but also my desire to concentrate in each and every of the nine specialization's. As I was beginning to wonder if I would be taking on a bit too much, I came across property-asset management , and my decision was finalized.

So, I'm it, and I don't like to admit it, but my mom first suggested the school to me. Everything about it screamed "Rachel!": the mix of creativity and business, the opportunity to work with people in a service-oriented field, the hands-on learning, and, of course, my obsession with food (cooking, and more specifically, eating).

This past summer I worked at PW Feats, the largest events-planning company in Baltimore. From NFL football games to black-tie galas, it was fascinating to see how much work goes into a finished product and how little of it the customer actually sees. I loved all the planning and creativity that went into making our customers and their guests happy. And I loved all my co-workers, from "the guy from Florida—the only one in America—who installs transparent pool-cover/dance-floors" to the purveyor of neon cocktail trays (New! With thumbholes!). There was even a man who blends banana daiquiris on his head. (It's true. I've even seen him.)

But what was most exciting was knowing that every day would bring new challenges and adventures. What more could a girl want?

2. Optional Essay: After you've finished filling out your application, you may feel something is missing. Feel free to write another short essay below telling us anything else about yourself that you want to know.

I've been planning my own themed birthday parties since I was 7. Since 9th grade I have been planning and organizing group bus trips to concerts. This summer I created Ravens trivia for the grand opening of Baltimore's new NFL stadium and escorted the team's marching band into the opening-night game. For the annual fundraising gala for the Maryland Science Center, I invented interactive science experiments and party favors for the guests. I even researched Arabian art for a casino opening in Las Vegas, and talked to scientists at MIT who could build a musical, talking tree. I also learned to file, use databases, and check budgets on spreadsheets. And if you're wondering why I have chosen to be secretary of my class for three years … who do you think plans the dances, handles the money, and organizes the fundraisers? I have traveled since I was 5, and what I remember most about the trips are the details about the hotels and restaurants. (Remind me to tell you about the midnight buffet on a cruise my family took when I was 6.) I am hoping to open a snowball (famous Baltimore treat) stand this summer at the Inner Harbor in conjunction with one of the city's biggest developers.

Comments:

- Cornell essay 1 is exactly what the college admissions committees are after. They love to see this kind of enthusiasm from their applicants, as long as it is founded on solid ideas (as Rachel's is) rather than empty clichés. The essay shows that she *feels* Cornell is right for her on the inside but also *knows* that Cornell is right for her, based on the evidence she has found. The discussion also makes it clear that she belongs at the hotel administration school and will benefit from such a focused undergraduate education.

- Rachel was smart to use Cornell essay 2 to her advantage. She clearly had more to say about her candidacy and was right to use the optional essay to further demonstrate her fit with the hotel school, her long-term experience with events planning, and her interest in the travel and entertainment industry.

SARAH KWON

Notes on her candidacy: Sarah, a Korean American student from a public New Jersey high school, was accepted Early Action at Brown.

BROWN UNIVERSITY

1. We ask that you use this opportunity to tell us something more about yourself that would help us toward a sense of who you are, how you think, and what issues and ideas interest you most.

Drop by drop, their eyes imbibe the world around them. Through their penetrating pools of innocence, they ravenously explore and discover, keenly absorb and express. Staring deeply into the infinite liquidity of my students' eyes, I feel as if I'm drowning amazed at the simple beauty. I am overwhelmed-exhilirated by the sight, sound, and touch that these tiny eyes afford me. I se the excitement, hear the yearnings, and feel the ebullience that each eye encapsulates. Smooth skin and rosy cheeks complement the eyes that turn to me and gaze. They look up at me, curious and admiring: believing me, trusting me, loving me. Stretching their attention spans to the fullest, they listen intently—wanting to learn, willing to try. I sense no pretensions, and I feel at ease. Sunday School has begun.

Standing before them, I see in their eyes the child I was, the part of me that I almost left behind. I reunite with the fresh inquisitiveness and wonder as I smile in nostalgic reverie, remembering myself as a carefree child. Feeling the bustle of the childhood days, I am reminded of the happiness found in the simplest aspects of life. I see my growth in every aspect: body, mind, and spirit. Welcoming maturity and embracing passions, the development of my character unfolds before me in my panoramic view of the past. Starting out as a lump of clay, my shaping begins: the church that nurtured me, that molded my values …the family that struggled to ensure my stability, that seflessly loved and tirelessly provided … countless displays of awesome faith, lives consumed to an unwavering purpose … fascinating people, young and old … respect and discipline, culture and heritage. At the end of the journey, the clay is firm-sculpted, defined, my eyes revealing that I cannot help but long for the bliss of childhood—to truly live.

I draw back from their eyes and return to my lesson. But the feeling does not leave me, the hope does not fade. As the lesson proceeds, the children participate, opening up and expressing opinions. Even their passing comments and nonchalant remarks often spark realizations in my own mind, putting the world into perspective. Other times, they express simple truths in a way that makes me see, understand, and believe. During a time when the disunity of our church resulted in an ugly separation, the children gave considerable insight: "God still loves all of us. Maybe he loves us even better now because the parents won't fight anymore." In the midst of my struggle with confusion and anxiety, those simple words cleared my blurry eyes and soothed my unrest. I saw the situation through a child's eyes, and it all made sense. Indeed, I benefit greatly from my students, perhaps learning more than I could ever teach.

My students display and understanding greater than their age and stronger than their bodies. The light in their eyes has opened my own, to a world I had forgotten, to things I should have seen. But my own light has carried me as well, leading the way on the many paths chosen, all in an effort to bring me here. Here I am.

Comments

■ Here is another example of an effective "slice-of-life" essay. While conveniently folding in several aspects of her candidacy—her Sunday school teaching, her religious faith, her insightful views into her own development, her "people" and communication skills—Sarah has written an evocative portrait of a weekly event in her life. The essay's spiritual overtones add to its effectiveness. Sarah shows that she is not only devoted to her pupils but also observant of the world around her.

TYLER THORNTON

Notes on her candidacy: A graduate of a girls' preparatory school in a suburb of Cleveland, Ohio, Tyler was a leader in various community service projects and an editor of a literary magazine. She now attends Amherst College.

STANFORD UNIVERSITY

1. Attach a small photograph of something important to you and explain its significance.
[The attached photograph is of a ring.]

I am not a big jewelry person. My friends walk around with fingers and wrists loaded with intricately designed rings and bracelets, but my small fingers and hands have always made such things look gaudy and overdone. I have a box at home where I keep the necklaces, earrings, and pins that I have been given by my mother and grandmother—the small diamond on a chain that my dad bought for my mom, the pearl pin that my grandfather gave my grandmother for their first anniversary, the gold earrings that I was given when I turned sixteen—and I treasure all of them for their sentimental and family value. Yet I wear them only on the rare occasions when I break out the heels and the short black dress. The rest of the time, I wear only two pieces of jewelry without fail: my watch and my Laurel School ring.

The day during my junior year that I received my Laurel School ring was one of the most memorable days of my high school career. I had spent hours the month before pondering what I wanted my ring to look like. Unlike at most schools, where a person has an unlimited supply of stones, metals, and insignias to choose from, I had a say only in what type of gold I got and whether or not my ring was antiqued. In the end, I chose the exact ring that my mother received when she was a junior at Laurel. That, I realized, was the beauty of the ring—knowing that I was being given a simple and elegant connection to my mother, to my grandmother, and great-grandmother, and to every other girl who had a Laurel ring. To me, the actual ring was worth nothing without the tradition and community that it represented.

My great-grandmother's Laurel ring is silver with a big, square green stone in the center. When she went there, the school was housed in a building in the middle of downtown Cleveland instead of in the suburbs, as it is now. My grandmother's Laurel ring is gold with a blue stone. She loves to tell me stories about how she used to live in my sixth grade homeroom when the school had boarders, how she actually showered in the bathroom that my middle school mind was convinced was haunted, and how she used to sneak out of school to go on a date with my grandfather. My mom, who is now a teacher at Laurel, had a few of the same teachers that I have now. There are pictures of her dancing with my dad in old yearbooks, and I love to hear her tell stories about the school pranks that she pulled as a teenager. When my sister is a junior, her ring will look like my mother's and mine—gold with a Laurel leaf insignia and the letters L and S on either side. She and I constitute the fourth generation of our family to attend Laurel, and she will be the sixth Thornton woman to graduate from the school. That is why Laurel is more than a school to me and why I care about Laurel traditions more than most other students. While at school, I feel a connection to my family and am more acutely aware of how traditions like choral concerts, class song contests, and uniforms link current students with those of the past and present. My ring is a symbol of those connections and of our shared values and goals. It is a constant reminder of those who came before me and their love of learning, empathy, tolerance, and discipline.

While Laurel has changed physically since my great-grandmother graduated, the philosophy behind it has remained the same. The school has taught generations of Thornton women to be independent, free-thinking, caring, honest, and responsible people. My teachers, family members, and friends have instilled in me a strong sense of who I am an what I can accomplish, and my ring is a constant reminder of what my classmates and I have learned during our first eighteen years. I have cherished the time that I have spent living at home and going to high school, but I am excited about the new possibilities and adventures that are before me. Luckily, I have been prepared to face new challenges and have been given the tools necessary to control what I do and who I am after I leave home. No matter what happens, I will continue to wear my watch so that I know what time it is. And I will continue to wear my Laurel School ring as both a tangible and intangible connection to the experiences and people who have helped to make me who I am.

AMHERST COLLEGE

1. See Common Application question (option 1).
(Essay also used in application to Bowdoin.)

Having spent my entire life at an independent girls' school, I have grown up surrounded by strong women role models. Feminism has always been a popular topic at school, and history teachers never miss an opportunity to explore the role of women throughout the centuries. In English, we have read the works of great women writers such as Jane Austen and the Bronte sisters. My junior AP English class was famous for its ability to find women's issues to discuss in every book that we read. This feminist training has prepared me well for the leadership roles that I have had the opportunity to assume through sports and extracurricular activities. In short, I have been raised to be an independent and free-thinking individual who was used to seeing no reason why every woman should not be the exact same way. As a result, I joined the many Americans who see their situation in life as superior to that of other cultures and who rush to impose their modern and Americanized views into situations where they simply do not fit.

This realization struck me this past summer while I was in the Dominican Republic helping to construct a church for the impoverished Haitian sugarcane workers who live in tenement slums called batays. This mission trip to the Dominican Republic with Fairmount Presbyterian Church was my third in as many years, yet I had previously worked in a city and had only visited a batay on a bus. One day, we helped the men of the batay to lay the foundation for the new building. One of the men taught me how to lay bricks, and I was lying on my stomach with a bucket of mortar when the women came to bring lunch for the men. I felt a tap on my shoulder and looked up to see one of the men pointing to a young woman and asking me to convince her to join the work. I couldn't understand all of his words, but the few I caught, in conjunction with his motions, conveyed the idea that he was trying to tease the woman into working. And his main argument was that the young woman from America was laying brick and enjoying herself. The young Dominican woman shook her head and shrank away. Without giving it much thought, I joined the man's attempt at persuasion because I could not come up with any reason why the woman would not want to help build the church.

Only later did it strike me how the women in the batay probably felt pressured by our presence. Maybe they even resented us. For not only were we bringing help to these people, we were also bringing our foreign culture and ideas. As a comparatively rich American volunteer who was only visiting the impoverished Dominican Republic, I was able to jump gender boundaries and to pretend to be a carpenter without threatening the identity of either the men or the women in the village. For the young Dominican woman, however, the situation had nothing to do with pretending. If she had joined in the work, her actions would have threatened the established roles of both the men and the women in her society, something that she could not psychologically or economically have afforded to do. The sugarcane workers are oppressed as a group, and the women have to worry about survival before they can worry about being female in a male dominated society. Our presence, therefore, made them uncomfortable, and not because it made them realize their inferior station in life, but because it tested a status quo that they could not risk messing with.

I'm not positive that the young woman in the batay resented my presence, or that she and the other women truly have no problem with their station in life. The experience, however, made me realize how different our culture is from theirs and how dangerous it can be for Americans to assume that our way of thinking should automatically prevail. The brief encounter with the young woman showed me the importance of exploring thoughts, not dictating them, and of realizing that our way is not the only way. Whether or not the women of the batays felt oppressed was not the issue at the time. What was the issue was that my initial reaction was to click into feminist mode and to pressure the young woman while I should have been attempting to understand what factors led her to act as she did. It was a simple lesson in empathy that will forever make me cautious about making patronizing and uninformed assumptions about other cultures.

BOWDOIN COLLEGE

1. Who is the secondary school teacher who has had the greatest positive impact on your development? Please describe the ways in which this teacher has influenced you.

It was the first day of BC Calculus class, and I was feeling a little anxious. Not only is calculus a notoriously nightmarish class, but I was about to face it as the only junior in a class of three students. In short, there was going to be nowhere to hide. No junior before me had ever taken on the challenge of the BC class, and the reasons why became apparent as Dr. Ellen Stenson entered the room and immediately handed us immense textbooks filled with incredibly tiny print. My anxiety quickly changed to fear as she announced that our lives were going to become calculus and that no one in her right mind took the class. She looked directly at me and expanded that statement—taking the class as a junior was a death sentence. I left that first class with three hours of homework and the feeling that I was never going to survive.

Dr. Stenson may have been the toughest and most intimidating teacher that I have ever encountered, and probably ever will, but she was also the most rewarding. She made it clear from the beginning that she would expect more from us than we would ever dream of expecting from ourselves, and that she would require us to work very hard to meet those expectations. Our lives did become calculus, but she submerged herself right along with us. She was willing to explain every aspect of a concept or problem until I understood exactly what I was dealing with and why, and she and I spent countless hours in her office integrating, differentiating, and finding the volume of the solid created by rotating a line segment around the x-axis. She took the time to go over every step of every problem that we did for homework and to correct our mistakes or congratulate us when we solved a problem differently than she had or finally figured out what we were supposed to be doing. It was apparent that she truly loved calculus and that she wanted nothing more than to share that love with us.

I have never worked harder in my life than I did to succeed in BC Calculus, but all of the work was worth it. Dr. Stenson pushed us hard, and I had to get accustomed to setting anywhere from two to four hours a night aside to find related rates and centroids, but I have never felt as proud as I did when I solved a difficult problem on my own or did well on an exam. I was often frustrated, and there were times when I wanted to give up, but Dr. Stenson was always there to support my efforts and to sit around occasionally and discuss life problems that had absolutely nothing to do with the math world. In my mind, she is a mathematical genius and an excellent teacher who taught me not only to do calculus, but also to stretch my imagination, to think in new ways, and to tackle problems head-on. She prepared me for the AP Calculus BC exam, but she also gave me the self-confidence and the work habits to excel in any math class that I take in the future. I owe a lot to Dr. Stenson, least of which is the five I earned on that AP.

Comments

▪ Stanford essay 1 is a winning response. Tyler successfully supports with solid evidence her assertion that the ring at the center of the essay is valuable to her because of the traditions and sense of community it symbolizes. She relies upon convincing anecdotes to show exactly why Laurel School means so much to her. She demonstrates a deep attachment to and appreciation for her family, recalling three previous generations of relatives who attended her school and connecting the Laurel School bond downward to her younger sister as well. No reader can resist feeling drawn toward an applicant who so believably shows she is pleasantly tickled rather than downright embarrassed to see pictures of her own parents dancing at the prom in old yearbooks! Tyler astutely conveys in the last portion of the essay that she understands that an education comprises more than just classroom learning, something that the top colleges want their students to acknowledge.

■ Amherst essay 1 positions Tyler as a unique candidate because of the foundation she has gained by attending an all-girls school her entire life. The piece is also valuable because it hammers home the applicant's commitment to community service (a crucial component of her candidacy), as shown through this description of a third annual mission visit to the Dominican Republic. Most important, though, is Tyler's main message here. The applicant demonstrates maturity and a willingness to take a risk in showing herself to have been at fault in assuming the superiority of her own cultural values. The lesson Tyler ultimately learned shows an open-mindedness that is particularly valuable to her, since she shows in other essays that she is confident, grounded, and shaped by a particularly fortunate and stable family background.

■ In Bowdoin essay 1, the applicant takes advantage of an opportunity to highlight that she was the first person in her school to take BC Calculus as a junior. Unlike most candidates who attempt to answer this question, though, Tyler gets past the emphasis on herself to produce a successful piece about her interaction with a teacher and how that teacher affected her development. The bulk of the essay indeed focuses on Dr. Stenson and why her instructional methods were particularly impressive, as is appropriate for this essay. The calculus-oriented phrases and details personalize the essay and bring it to life.

AMANDA SADACCA

Notes on her candidacy: A graduate of Thomas Jefferson High School for Science and Technology, a public "magnet" school in Fairfax County, Virginia, Amanda played field hockey and lacrosse, tutored elementary school children, and worked at the Capital Children's Museum to explore a possible career in social science research.

THE UNIVERSITY OF VIRGINIA

1. What work of art, music, science, mathematics, or literature has influenced your thinking, and in what way?

It was a cloudy Sunday morning, and I was in my room sorting laundry. Suddenly, there was a break in the clouds, and a ray of sunlight shone through the window. It caught a prism sitting on my bookshelf, and the light splintered into the visible spectrum. My eye stopped; I stood in awe of this simple phenomenon, even though I knew intellectually the physics lecture we had on prisms and light. I glanced at the laundry pile around me and, shoving it aside, reached for my copy of *Walden.*

"What should we think of the shepherd's life if his flocks always wandered to higher pastures than his thoughts?" asks Thoreau. Since that Saturday morning, this call for reflection, for stretching the mind beyond the everyday has become imbedded into my consciousness. With the whirlwind that is my life, finding time to contemplate the mysteries of the universe at times seems virtually impossible, yet it is something that I find essential. Without thought, we are mere substance; our life is not life at all, but simply existence. As Socrates said, "The unexamined life is not worth living." Stretching the mind does not require quiet reflection; mental exercise can come in all forms. Maybe instead of spending the lunch hour debating the latest movies, I debate the finer points of religion or philosophy. I take to heart Thoreau's message to simplify by using time more effectively. He tells us to rid ourselves of anything that takes up time unnecessarily, and thereby inhibits us form leading a full life, constantly stretching our minds and testing our limits.

Whether it's waking up a few minutes early to write and reflect in my journal or reading a work of literature instead of the latest Danielle Steele, I try to make time to think, to have the leisure to contemplate things, like the wonder of nature or the ends of the universe, that inhabit those "higher pastures" that Thoreau speaks of.

Walden underlined for me the necessity of reaching a higher level, of stretching my fingertips out to touch the bonds of human understanding.

Comments

■   UVA essay 1 shows Amanda's intellectual and spiritual side. Although *Walden* is a classic piece of literature that is frequently used in this type of essay, Amanda does something successful with the piece, showing with concrete examples how she has taken Thoreau's advice to heart.

NICHOLAS HORBACZEWSKI

Notes on his candidacy: Nicholas, who was involved in the theater and writing for a literary magazine at his private high school, is interested in a career in film production after he completes his undergraduate degree at Harvard.

HARVARD UNIVERSITY

1. See Common Application question (his own option).

The characteristic that most defines me is my readiness to throw myself completely into those aspects of my life that matter to me. I do not let life pass me by.

When I was ten years old, I went to art camp and was introduced to claymation. I was fascinated by the power which the process gave me to bring inanimate objects to life. When camp ended, I managed to find an ancient 8 millimeter camera at a yard sale and set up my own basement studio, in which I spend countless hours making short animation films. Working under the hot lights, manipulating little bits of clay in tiny incremental movements, I learned that it took patience and persistence as well as inspiration to make the animation seem realistic. I eventually became frustrated with the limitations of the equipment and the difficulty of finding film. Meanwhile, I was teaching myself about computers, and I discovered that 3-D animation software gave me the freedom to continue with animation without the limitation of using a camera. As my ambitions outstripped the capabilities of my home computer, I learned to upgrade it, replacing the processor and hard drive, adding memory and many other enhancements.

Two years ago, I decided that my interest in creating visual images had evolved beyond animation to telling more complete stories on film, using effects that only the computer made possible. I needed an opportunity to work with better equipment and to acquire more experience than I could get on my own. I wrote to many special effects studios, asking them about summer internships. A studio in Los Angeles responded favorably, and I have spent the last two summers with them, working on visual effects for real movies, like Independence Day and Godzilla, that were subsequently shown in theaters, and on television, learning from professionals, using state of the art equipment, and being totally fulfilled.

Keeping a network of vastly different platforms (like Macintoshes and DEC Alphas) running in a state of chronic overload resulted in many crises requiring immediate diagnosis and correction. There was no time to pore over manuals—the response had to be spontaneous and instinctual. I was fascinated by this process, and I spent my free time learning how to keep the machines up and running. When I got home, I discovered that the skills I had acquired enabled me to deal with a broad range of problems that afflict normal home and office computers. I started a computer repair and consulting business advising individuals and small businesses on maintaining and upgrading their systems.

However, the most important part of my experience was the creative work. Expressing myself in visual images is an intoxicating mixture of spontaneity and rigorous planning. A great deal of preparation and patience is required just to create one frame that is displayed for only a fraction of a second, and it is easy to lose sight of the final concept in the myriad of intermediate stages. Yet, it is the intermediate stages themselves that make this process so wonderful. The hours spent on minute details that flash by faster than human eye can register them are full of moments of enlightenment, making the process of creation itself even more rewarding than the final result. I have no doubt that working on the production of films will be part of my future.

YALE UNIVERSITY

1. Please use the space on this page to let us know something about you that we might not learn from the rest of your application.

(Essay also used in application to Princeton.)

I carry a little shard of metal in the coin holder of my wallet. It's maybe two inches long and, as far as I can tell, was once torn from the edge of a some circular metal plate. It falls out every time I dump out my change and people invariably ask me what it is. I tell them part of the story. "It popped my tire on a bike trip from Seattle to San Francisco I took the summer after ninth grade. I only got one flat in twelve hundred miles, and this thing caused it, so I carry it around as a talisman against future accidents." I smile. The subject changes. It really did pop my tire, but the real reason I carry it with me is too intimate to explain in a casual conversation, so I don't go into it.

I have gone to considerable lengths for that shard. I once left my wallet on an airplane and then forced my way back to the gate through the airport security—not for the cash or for my ID's, but because the shard was in it. Once, I reached into a spider infested hole (my personal hell) because I had dropped the shard into it. I don't know why I started to carry it around with me—I just did. I was cycling down the Pacific Coast Highway, it popped my tire and I put it in my wallet. I did not know when I pried it from the rubber somewhere in northern California that it would be my only tangible connection to an experience that changed my life. I had no real reason for keeping it. Only as the trip drew to a close did I begin to see how important it was to me, because it evoked so many memories and emotions. Then I started to hang on to it for dear life.

My rusty sliver of metal seems a humble monument to the experience that was an epiphany in my life. Reveling in my first flush of independence, enjoying the company of unforgettable people and accomplishing a demanding bike ride through the most glorious scenery I had ever seen would have been enough to alter my perspective on life, but the trip means even more than that. Only weeks before I stepped on the airplane for Seattle, I had been an invalid, both biceps ruptured, their blood vessels ripped in two from a catastrophic rowing injury. I had been away from school, my friends, in incredible pain and struggling with the knowledge that I would never regain total use of or strength in my arms. I had returned to school at the very end of the year only to feel isolated from my friends, whom I had been too ashamed to call when I could not even feed myself or straighten my arms. Going back only depressed me more, as I saw that I had lost my place in the highly structured world of high school society.

It seems like a simple story. Boy gets hurt, boy goes on trip, boy feels better. But the trip lifted me out of my daily existence and gave me a broader view of the world and a more positive way to approach life. The adventure, the companionship and the sense of personal accomplishment as we pedaled the final miles across the Golden Gate Bridge would probably have been enough to give me a more positive outlook anyway. It is merely a lucky coincidence that the experience also helped me recover physically and psychologically from my injury. It wasn't so much that the trip gave me back what the injury had taken away, but rather it gave me the perspective to see how much I had not lost: friendships, the joy of the moment, the ability to set physically and emotionally challenging goals and to achieve them. It was this change in attitude about my injury that allowed me to recover. Returning to school after that trip, I tried out, the for the first time, for a part in a play. I began to lift weights so strengthen my body, including my arms in order to minimize the effect of the injury. I found that sports had been pushed aside by these other aspects of my life that mattered more. Perspective is so essential that it can change your whole life. I think, you need to know what's important, like a little metal shard.

Comments

- Harvard essay 1 is effective in expressing Nicholas's long-term commitment to his intellectual areas of interest. In discussing the evolution of his work in film, animation, and computers, which all began at the young age of ten, as well as how he turned his passions into a serious and fruitful summer job, he shows the admissions committee that he is going somewhere. It is clear that he is a man with a mission, and that he will accomplish much in his life.

- Yale essay 1 demonstrates the effect a candidate can have when he orients an ordinary or unoriginal theme around something tangible. The way that Nicholas has pitched his story around the metal shard makes it much more compelling than if he had simply stated, "This summer I learned a lot about myself and learned to appreciate life more" and then told a little bit about the trip. The metal shard draws readers into the story immediately, making them wonder what it stands for, as well as feeling fully confident that the summer trip did indeed make a lasting impression on the applicant. Furthermore, the essay is successful because, as the author himself admits, he is revealing something intimate, something that he is not willing to discuss with many people.

LAURA HOSNY

Notes on her candidacy: Because of her cultural background—part Middle Eastern, part Indian, and part European—and her experience of living all over the world, Laura applied only to urban schools with substantial international populations.

NEW YORK UNIVERSITY

1. Please write an essay on what diversity means to you.

"I grew up to be 20-years old and I was always told that I was undesirable for one reason or another. I got to the United States and I expected there would be some of the same because I was an immigrant. And there wasn't."
—Andrew Grove, CEO, Intel Corp. and *Time Magazine*'s Man of the Year, 1997, who arrived here as a 20-year-old Hungarian Jew, fleeing the Nazis and the Soviets.

An issue of great personal and national concern to me is diversity. Being of mixed ethnic heritage, I have always been interested in the issue of diversity because my diversity is such a huge part of my life. My paternal grandparents were Egyptian and Indian, and my maternal grandparents were British. This multicultural existence has been compounded by my family's transient life, due to my father's job, that has taken me from Paris to New Zealand, Belgium and New Jersey. Since being exposed to so many cultures, people and lifestyles, I have always been interested in the issue of diversity in my own country, the United States.

Diversity in the United States is a consequence of our heritage. Even though we often feel lack of acceptance and understanding of our differences, Mr.Grove's comment shows us that we do enjoy a high degree of acceptance of diversity in relation to many other countries. We are a nation of immigrants lured on to American soil by the promise of freedom, equality and opportunity—"The American Dream." By definition, diversity means essentially different, distinct and capable of various forms. The question is how to best handle this diversity so that it works for the common good, enriches our American culture and does not lead to division and discrimination. Left alone, we risk the formation of many sub-groups, who know only themselves, their cultures, their beliefs and their ways. This could create opportunities for discrimination and result in lack of enrichment of our society and friction between the various groups. Remembering that we live in the United States of America, not the Diverse States of America, we must first be Americans, and then preserve our various ethnic heritages. How do we best achieve this end? We need the strength that comes from common agreement and common accord. Language is the key that can ensure us harmony and communication. My close friend is from a very diverse family—Danish father, Thai mother, raised in Belgium and educated in the International School system, which is predominantly American. Neither offspring speaks their parents' native tongue, and neither parent speaks the other's native tongue. So they had to choose a language of communication—in this case American English. Both children speak it fluently, but since it is not their native tongue, the parents have strong accents and somewhat limited vocabularies. This can mean that family communication is difficult. So, in our country, our family, we need one primary language of education, in which we learn to think in depth, to understand nuance and to express ourselves freely and accurately. Other languages as a secondary language are important as enrichment to our culture but should not become primary.

However, diversity and discrimination will still exist, as they are inherent to mankind. As Americans, do we react to diversity passively by allowing people to develop their potential naturally? By doing this, some will succeed and some fail, some will seize opportunity and some let it pass them by, unrecognized. Often the success of one group can be at the expense of another, and this leads to resentment and discrimination. The alternative is to "manage" diversity by governmental regulation. To have the federal government mandate our handling of diverse situations could be seen as a threat to our basic liberty. Is it truly equality of opportunity when students are rejected from a school because the school is looking for a gender balance, and the student doesn't fit? As in all things, the government and we must strive for balance. The regulation of diversity within society may lead to less discrimination, but the danger is that it leads to division. If the objective of diversity as a policy is to distinguish and elevate the differences between people, this could undermine our strength as a nation. Division in a nation is a dangerous idea, as we can see throughout history—our own and that of other countries. I have lived for a number of years in Belgium, a country with a very divided society, and have witnessed the negative effects of this very situation. Previously, the Walloon (French-speaking) Belgians held economic, political and social power. With the economic decline of the mining industry in the south, this has changed and the Flemish Belgians now have the upper hand. The resultant bad feeling causes friction on the streets, denigration of one group by the other, and allows for a certain corrupt behavior to exist. Similarly, in New Zealand, a country where I lived when I was young, the coexistence of the native Maoris and the European immigrants, the Pakehas, while originally peaceful and accepting, is now causing social unrest. The Maoris were treated in much the same way as the Native Americans, and it is only during the past decades that they have started demanding that their land be returned to them, and that they be accepted in professional and social milieus in an equal manner. Needless to say, the attitude of the Pakehas has changed toward them as a result.

Though our many different heritages in the United States can lead to division and unbalance, they can also give us incredible enrichment. Festivals of African Americans such as Kwanzaa, and of Irish-Americans such as St. Patrick's Day involve the whole of the nation in teaching traditional cultural values. Diversity in education creates a positive learning environment where students with special needs are not regarded as backward, or unable to learn. The classification of learning differences enables such students to understand that difference is okay, and therefore their view of themselves is not demolished. This opportunity to preserve a good self-image can lessen the tendency towards eating disorders and substance abuse and ultimately make for stronger citizens and a more secure society.

It is unlikely that the benefits of diversity will be achieved purely on the strength of goodwill and laissez-faire. Governmental regulation of diversity may infringe on liberty to a degree, but will hopefully achieve the desired result in the long run—a nation secure in its heritage and enriched by its diversity, without division and discrimination.

Comments

- Laura provides an intelligent discussion of diversity that expresses opinions while also rooting itself in her own experiences. In this way, she gives an issue of societal importance a personal touch. She debates critical issues such as the government regulation of diversity and illustrates her points with cogent examples, such as the situation with Belgium's conflicting populations.

INDEX